THIRD EDITION

CLASSICS OF CRIMINOLOGY

THIRD EDITION

CLASSICS OF CRIMINOLOGY

EDITED BY JOSEPH E. JACOBY
Bowling Green State University

WAVELAND
PRESS, INC.
Long Grove, Illinois

For information about this book, contact:
    Waveland Press, Inc.
    4180 IL Route 83, Suite 101
    Long Grove, IL 60047-9580
    (847) 634-0081
    info@waveland.com
    www.waveland.com

10-digit ISBN 1-57766-309-8
13-digit ISBN 978-1-57766-309-6

Printed in the United States of America

10   9   8   7   6   5   4

This work is dedicated to the following people,
who continue to shape my life:

To Martha Jacoby, my mother;
in memory of James M. Jacoby, my father;
in memory of Thorsten Sellin, my mentor's mentor and
Marvin E. Wolfgang, my mentor, who taught me to
enjoy and value the study of intellectual history;
to my fellow graduate students at the University of Pennsylvania;
to my own students;
and to my sons, David and Daniel Jacoby, and
my wife, Elayne Jacoby,
whose love challenges, inspires and sustains me.

Topical Contents

vii

Section II   Theories of Causation of Crime   99

Section III   The Social Response to Crime   347

Chronological Contents

Preface

Whether history is the product of great social forces or great people, the history of an academic discipline is embodied in the works of identifiable individuals. The history of criminology could be related as a progression of schools of thought; most texts in the field present it this way. Students who receive their education solely through these texts do get a sense of the grand sweep of criminological history and ideas. If students do not read the original works of the various schools, however—if they read only *about* and not *in* criminology—their experience is but secondhand, and their conclusions are determined by textbook authors.

By reading Bentham's writings we are forced to deal with the complexity, as well as the content, of his thoughts. By reading Lombroso's works, we share vicariously in the excitement of his discovery: "At the sight of that skull I seemed to see all at once, standing out clearly illuminated as in a vast plain under a flaming sky, the problem of the nature of the criminal." By reading Beccaria's work we can appreciate not only the power of his ideas, but also the persuasiveness of his simple, eloquent style. There is no adequate substitute for reading scholarly works in their original form.

Included in this volume are both authors whose work is widely recognized as significant in itself, and authors whose work substantially influenced the thinking of subsequent scholars, although their conclusions may have been repudiated. Many of the selections are representative writings of some authors whose important, voluminous contributions could not all be presented here.

The selections arguably are all classics of criminology. They are not *the* classics; they do not comprise a comprehensive collection. Graduate and upper-level undergraduate students, for whom this volume is intended, are invited to develop their own competing lists of classics.

The volume is organized into three sections. Section I, The Classic Descriptions of Crime, contains writings whose primary contribution is descriptive, although they also offer important theoretical insights. These works illuminate with great clarity certain aspects of the phenomenon of crime. Section II, Theories of Causation of Crime, covers over two centuries of theorizing about the causes of crime. Most of these writings are specifically about crime, although some emphasize larger social issues that have direct implications for criminology. Section III, The Social Response to Crime, includes writings that variously describe, theorize about, or advocate specific social responses to crime. Some of the best works on the criminal justice process as it operates internally and as it functions in its social setting are included here. An editorial statement indicating the significance of the included works and their historical or intellectual context introduces each of the sections.

To be eligible for inclusion in this collection, a work had to be published at least ten years ago and have demonstrated substantial impact on criminological theory, research, or practice. The selection of classics is a subjective process, however, potentially influenced by academic provincialism and personal whim. In selecting works for inclusion, I have been fortunate in having colleagues who have kept me from overlooking some works and overvaluing others.

Recommendations for changes to the list of included works were solicited from instructors who used the Second Edition with their students. The following people responded with suggestions: Mark Austin (University of Louisville), Thomas Babcock (California State University), Allen R. Barnes (University of Alaska), Julia Beeman (University of North Carolina), Victoria Brewer Titterington (Sam Houston State University), Ray Calluori (Montclair State University), Mitchell Chamlin (University of Cincinnati), Steven M. Cox (Western Illinois University), Mark L. Dantzker (University of Texas–Pan American), Lee Derr (University of Pennsylvania), R. Thomas Dull (California State University–Fresno), John P. Esser (Wagner College), Lynette Feder (Portland State University), Cecil E. Greek (Florida State University), Thomas McAninch (Scott Community College), Elizabeth H. McConnell (Charleston Southern University), Anne Nurse (College of Wooster), Xin Ren (California State University–Sacramento), Robert J. Sampson (Harvard University), Amie Scheidegger (Charleston Southern University), Matthew Silberman (Bucknell University), Ted Skotnicki (Niagara County Community College), Robert E. Stanfield (University of Vermont), and John F. Wozniak (Western Illinois University). Several of my colleagues at Bowling Green State University also offered suggestions: Jefferson Holcomb, Steven P. Lab, Stephen DeMuth, and Stephen Cernkovich.

My publisher, Neil Rowe, saw the value of this work and encouraged me to produce this Third Edition. Bonnie Highsmith and Gayle Zawilla of Waveland Press worked hard to obtain reprint permissions, correct my mistakes, and shepherd the project to completion. Finally, Elayne Jacoby (Nurse Practitioner to hundreds of Bowling Green students, Therapist to the World, and my wife) shared with me the pleasures and burdens of professional and domestic life in the many years between the three editions.

I thank all these good people for their encouragement and assistance.

Joseph E. Jacoby
Bowling Green, Ohio

Section I

The Classic Descriptions of Crime

Two thousand years ago, Greek physicians were exceptionally astute observers of the human body, its anatomy, and its diseases. Ailments of the body have been subjected to increasingly refined systematic observation for the past two hundred years. The Italian physicians of the late nineteenth century studied the body of the criminal in detail. Aberrant behavior, however, did not receive such attention until U.S. positivists of the second quarter of the twentieth century began to look upon crime and deviance as a form of behavior that could be studied in the same manner as other less disvalued behavior.

From the 1920s through the 1940s U.S. sociology and criminology were overwhelmingly dominated by the contributions and methods of the sociologists at the University of Chicago: Ernest Burgess, Clifford Shaw, Henry McKay, Edwin Sutherland, and their colleagues. The influence of these scholars was so pervasive that scholarship performed either by them or in their style has become known as work of the "Chicago School." This style is characterized by participant observation methodology and a nonjudgmental analysis of the perspective of the deviant. Its greatest contribution has been to reveal previously unimagined normative structures among deviant groups.

One of the earliest works in the tradition of the Chicago School was Frederick Thrasher's *The Gang*, appearing in 1927. The definition of the gang and the origins

1

of the gang—a group given cohesion by conflict with its environment—that he postulated are still valid.

Edwin Sutherland recorded the career of a professional criminal in greater detail and with greater theoretical insight than any previous scholar. His *The Professional Thief* revealed the complex recruitment, training and normative mechanisms that distinguish the true professional from the amateur crook. With *Juvenile Delinquency in Urban Areas*, Clifford Shaw and Henry McKay introduced another thread to the fabric of U.S. sociological and criminological methodology—human ecology. In Chicago, they found that crime rates naturally formed a pattern of concentric rings around the center of the city. Within each ring, the crime rate remained stable over long periods, even with changes in the ethnicity of the residents. Shaw and McKay attributed the stability of high crime rates in the zone in transition to the disorganized social structure of the population residing in that area.

In his presidential address to the American Sociological Association in 1939, Edwin Sutherland—whose impact on criminology is suggested by the fact that three of his works are included in this volume—introduced the term "white-collar crime." The attention he brought to the criminal offenses committed by ostensibly law-abiding upper- and middle-class citizens in the course of their occupations was a dramatic shift from the traditional focus on the street crimes of the lower class.

In 1948, Hans von Hentig contributed the theoretical underpinnings of a recently formed sub-field within criminology known as victimology—the study of the victims of crime and the relationship of the characteristics and behavior of the victims to their victimization. Marvin Wolfgang conducted the first significant empirical study of the victim-offender relationship in homicide, concluding that homicide victims are likely to be killed by close relatives and friends and that they frequently act in ways that precipitate their own demise.

The largest-scale effort to study the incidence, causes, and response to violent crime in the United States was the work of the National Commission on the Causes and Prevention of Violence. From the 13 volumes published by the commission, a brief selection presented here summarizes the incidence of serious violent crime.

The Philadelphia birth-cohort study is the first attempt to document the criminal experience of an entire birth cohort (i.e., a group of people born during the same year) in a large city. By studying the patterns of offenses after intervention by the juvenile justice system, Wolfgang, Sellin, and Figlio were able to describe patterns in offense careers. Their study was among the first to provide persuasive evidence that a small proportion of juveniles are responsible for the majority of offenses, particularly serious, violent offenses. Their analysis also suggested the optimum time in a young offender's career when intervention was most likely to be beneficial.

The themes of human ecology and victimization introduced by earlier studies were brought together by Lawrence Cohen and Marcus Felson, who focus on changes in the ordinary "routine activities" of daily living. They report that widespread, life-enhancing changes in employment patterns, educational opportunities, recreational pursuits, and the proliferation of consumer goods have increased our vulnerability to crime.

"Environmental criminology" focuses on the locations in time and space where offenders encounter victims and commit crimes. Paul and Patricia Brantingham describe how the arrangement of buildings and transportation facilities shape the movement of offenders and victims in specific urban areas, so that crimes are likely to be concentrated in those areas.

Alfred Blumstein and Jacqueline Cohen introduced the concept of "career" to the study of criminal offenders. They describe the frequency and diversity of offenders' crimes over their lifetime and draw implications from the pattern of offenses for a strategy of incapacitating offenders.

Robert Sampson and John Laub challenge a long-held assumption—that the environmental factors that influence criminal behavior throughout life occur only during childhood and adolescence. They reanalyzed longitudinal data gathered decades earlier by Sheldon and Eleanor Glueck and found that factors associated with delinquency during adolescence, leading to crime in adulthood, could be offset by a good job and a stable marriage.

Jack Katz takes an entirely different direction and perspective in describing crime and deviance. Katz provides detailed accounts of the thinking of offenders before, during, and after they commit offenses. These accounts emphasize the emotional benefits derived by criminal offenders from committing their crimes—sensuality, excitement, and empowerment.

These descriptions of crime were major historical landmarks for the field of criminology. Each was an important brush stroke in what was a rough sketch and is still becoming a detailed picture. Therefore, each had great impact on our understanding of the nature of crime.

1

What Is a Gang?

Frederick M. Thrasher

What is a gang? What characteristics does it possess which distinguish it from other forms of collective behavior such as a play-group, a crowd, a club, a ring, or a secret society? This a question which is not answered either by the dictionary or by the scanty literature on gangs. The answer must come from a careful examination of actual cases and a comparison of them with related social groups.

The Individuality of Gangs

No two gangs are just alike. The cases investigated present an endless variety of forms, and every one is in some sense unique. In this respect the gang exhibits the principle, universal throughout the natural world, that, although like begets like, the single instance is variable.

Wide divergency in the character of its personnel combined with differences of physical and social environment, of experience and tradition, give to every gang its own peculiar character. It may vary as to membership, type of leaders, mode of organization, interests and activities, and finally as to its status in the community. This fact of individuality must be recognized both by the student who attempts to classify it as a form of collective behavior and by the social worker who deals with it as a practical problem.

A Descriptive Definition of the Gang

Yet science proposes to discover what is typical rather than what is unique and does so, first of all, by making classifications. Interest centers, therefore, not so much in the individual gang for itself as in the characteristics which set it off from other types of collective behavior, discoverable through its *natural* history. . . .

The first fact to be observed about the Dirty Dozen, a characteristic which may be regarded as typical of all gangs, as distinguished from more formal groups, is its spontaneous and unplanned origin. Unlike a college club or labor union, its beginnings were unreflective—the natural outgrowth of a crowd of boys meeting on a street corner.

Source: Frederick M. Thrasher, *The Gang*, pp. 56–46, 50, 52–57. Copyright © 1927, The University of Chicago Press. Notes renumbered.

Another significant mark of the gang is its intimate face-to-face relations. Sometimes its members actually live together in a place of common abode. Although many of its enterprises may be carried on by small groups, the majority of the bona fide members of a real gang must get *together* periodically if it is to continue its corporate existence.

Orgiastic (Expressive) Behavior

The most rudimentary form of collective behavior in the gang is interstimulation and response among its own members—motor activity of the playful sort, a "talkfest," the rehearsal of adventure, or a "smut session." It may be mere loafing together. It may assume the character of a common festivity such as gambling, drinking, smoking, or sex. It is in this type of behavior that the gang displays and develops at the outset its enthusiasms, its spirit, its *esprit de corps.* If it behaved only in this way, however, it would remain a merely orgiastic or festive group. . . .

Although this group developed spontaneously, was unconventional in its behavior, and possessed tradition and a natural structure, its chief activity was exploiting the senses rather than linear action and conflict. It was primarily a feeling, rather than an action, group. It sought to avoid hostile forces, whereas the gang ordinarily welcomes a fight. This is quite a common type of social group, of which many examples have come to the attention of the investigator.[1]

The Gang and the Mob

When the gang becomes inflamed it may behave like a mob. Moreover, it may become the actual nucleus for a mob, as is shown by the Dirty Dozen's invasion of the Black Belt. The superior organization, solidarity, and morale of the gang give the mob an unwonted stability and direct its excited activities to greater destruction. The less active elements in the mob, on the other hand, and even the mere spectators, give moral support to or provide an appreciative audience for the more active nucleus— the gang. . . .

Action and Conflict in the Gang

To become a true gang the group as a whole must move through space (linear action) and eventually, as has been shown in the preceding chapter, must meet some hostile element which precipitates conflict.[2] Movement through space in a concerted and co-operative way may include play, the commission of crime,—such as robbing or rum-running—and migration from one place to another with change of hang-out or resort—for example, the migration of the Dirty Dozen to Detroit or of the "Ratters" from Toledo to Chicago.

Conflict, as already indicated, comes in clashes with other gangs or with common enemies such as the police, park officials, and so on. It takes place under a multiplicity of circumstances and assumes a variety of forms, of which, perhaps, open attack and defense are the most common. Whether the gang always fights openly as a unit or not, it usually seems to carry on warfare against its enemies co-operatively. It is as the result of collective action and particularly of conflict that the gang, especially in its solidified form, develops morale.[3]

Fig. 1
TYPES OF COLLECTIVE BEHAVIOR IN THE GANG

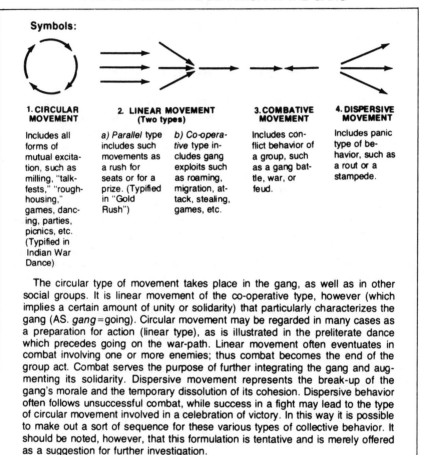

Symbols:

1. CIRCULAR MOVEMENT	2. LINEAR MOVEMENT (Two types)		3. COMBATIVE MOVEMENT	4. DISPERSIVE MOVEMENT
Includes all forms of mutual excitation, such as milling, "talk-fests," "rough-housing," games, dancing, parties, picnics, etc. (Typified in Indian War Dance)	a) *Parallel* type includes such movements as a rush for seats or for a prize. (Typified in "Gold Rush")	b) *Co-opera-tive* type includes gang exploits such as roaming, migration, attack, stealing, games, etc.	Includes conflict behavior of a group, such as a gang battle, war, or feud.	Includes panic type of behavior, such as a rout or a stampede.

The circular type of movement takes place in the gang, as well as in other social groups. It is linear movement of the co-operative type, however (which implies a certain amount of unity or solidarity) that particularly characterizes the gang (AS. *gang*=going). Circular movement may be regarded in many cases as a preparation for action (linear type), as is illustrated in the preliterate dance which precedes going on the war-path. Linear movement often eventuates in combat involving one or more enemies; thus combat becomes the end of the group act. Combat serves the purpose of further integrating the gang and augmenting its solidarity. Dispersive movement represents the break-up of the gang's morale and the temporary dissolution of its cohesion. Dispersive behavior often follows unsuccessful combat, while success in a fight may lead to the type of circular movement involved in a celebration of victory. In this way it is possible to make out a sort of sequence for these various types of collective behavior. It should be noted, however, that this formulation is tentative and is merely offered as a suggestion for further investigation.

Many gangs seem capable of reflective behavior—discussion and planning, leading to co-operative action. As in the case of the individual, this collective thinking on the part of the gang seems to arise as a response to a crisis situation, and has for its purpose an attempted adjustment of the group.

Development of Tradition and Group-Awareness

If the gang has had any degree of continuity of experience, the collective behavior and common purposes lead to the development of a common tradition—a heritage of memories which belongs more or less to all its members and distinguishes the gang from more ephemeral types of group such as the crowd and the mob.

Reactions of the gang's members which indicate a feeling of distinctness from other groups arise in part through the possession of this common tradition, but they are even more the result of the integrating effects of conflict.[4] In the case of the Dirty Dozen the hostile forces were "out-groups," such as competing athletic teams, rival gangs, the despised "niggers," and the police whose meddlesome interference represented the moral and legal standards of the larger community.

Other Characteristics

Like its beginning, the organization of the gang is nonconventional and unreflective. The rôles and status of the members are determined, not by formal standards, reasoned choices, or voting in the ordinary sense, but through the mechanisms of interaction in social situations. So the gang represents a social order which is natural and crescive rather than enacted.

The Dirty Dozen, like other gangs, is an interstitial group, detached and free from the social anchorages or moorings which hold the more conventional types of group within the bounds of social control.

A final characteristic which the Dirty Dozen possesses in common with most other gangs is its attachment to a local territory, within which is its accustomed hangout. Gangs like to roam about, and sometimes their exploits carry them far afield—in this case the excursions into the Black Belt and the trip to Detroit—but they usually have their home territory, with every nook and corner of which they are thoroughly acquainted, which they regard as particularly their own, and which they are ready to defend against the encroachments of outsiders.

A definition of the gang, then, based upon this study of 1,313 cases, may be formulated as follows:

> The gang is an interstitial group originally formed spontaneously, and then integrated through conflict. It is characterized by the following types of behavior: meeting face to face, milling, movement through space as a unit, conflict, and planning. The result of this collective behavior is the development of tradition, unreflective internal structure, *esprit de corps*, solidarity, morale, group awareness, and attachment to a local territory.

Notes

1. The origin of the sect has been attributed to a certain type of orgiastic group. "Just as the gang may be regarded as the perpetuation and permanent form of the 'crowd that acts,' so the sect, religious and political, may be regarded as a perpetuation and permanent form of the orgiastic (ecstatic) or expressive crowd." (R. E. Park and E. W. Burgess, *Introduction to the Science of Sociology*, p. 872.)
2. See chap. xi. William McCormick regards the gang as a conflict group; he says, in *The Boy and His Clubs*, "This is the day of gangs in boy's work. A gang can never thrive without another gang to fight with." J. Adams Puffer also defines a gang as a number of boys who go together and "will stand by each other," implying the conflict test. See Puffer, "Boys' Gangs," *Pedagogical Seminary*. XII (1905), 175.
3. Morale refers to that quality—of an individual or of a group—of unwavering pursuance of an aim in the face of both victory and defeat. Gangs vary widely in the possession of morale. For those of the more unstable type, it may be easily shattered. For those with a long history, however, which has included the vanquishing of common enemies and the acquiring of more effective organization and solidarity, morale may become very strong. As a tactical maneuver the gang may scatter before its enemies, but that does not mean necessarily that it has lost its morale; it may mean simply that it is achieving its purpose by some other method than overt fighting.

4. See R. E. Park and E. W. Burgess, *op. cit.*, p. 51. ''Group self-consciousness,'' which is produced in the process of conflict, may be described behavioristically as the positive responses of a group or its members to symbols standing for the group (collective representations) such as the group name, flag, slogan, password, and grip, or some tradition representing past common experience.

2

The Professional Thief

Edwin H. Sutherland

The Profession of Theft as a Complex of Techniques

The professional thief has a complex of abilities and skills, just as do physicians, lawyers, or bricklayers. The abilities and skills of the professional thief are directed to the planning and execution of crimes, the disposal of stolen goods, the fixing of cases in which arrests occur, and the control of other situations which may arise in the course of the occupation. Manual dexterity and physical force are a minor element in these techniques. The principal elements in these techniques are wits, "front," and talking ability. The thieves who lack these general abilities or the specific skills which are based on the general abilities are regarded as amateurs, even though they may steal habitually.[1] Also, burglars, robbers, kidnappers, and others who engage in the "heavy rackets" are generally not regarded as professional thieves, for they depend primarily on manual dexterity or force. A few criminals in the "heavy rackets" use their wits, "front," and talking ability, and these are regarded by the professional thieves as belonging to the profession.

The division between professional and nonprofessional thieves in regard to this complex of techniques is relatively sharp. This is because these techniques are developed to a high point only by education, and the education can be secured only in association with professional thieves; thieves do not have formal educational institutions for the training of recruits.[2] Also, these techniques generally call for co-operation which can be secured only in association with professional thieves. Finally, this complex of techniques represents a unified preparation for all professional problems in the life of the thief. . . .

The Profession of Theft as Status

The professional thief, like any other professional man, has status. The status is based upon his technical skill, financial standing, connections, power, dress, manners, and wide knowledge acquired in his migratory life. His status is seen in the attitudes of other criminals, the police, the court officials, newspapers, and others. The term

Source: Reprinted with permission from Edwin H. Sutherland, *The Professional* Thief, pp. 197–198, 200–204, 206–207, 209–212. Copyright © 1937 The University of Chicago Press. Introductory paragraph omitted, notes renumbered.

"thief" is regarded as honorific and is used regularly without qualifying adjectives to refer to the professional thief. It is so defined in a recent dictionary of criminal slang:

> **Thief**, *n*. A member of the underworld who steals often and successfully. This term is applied with reserve and only to habitual criminals. It is considered a high compliment.[3]

Professional thieves are contemptuous of amateur thieves and have many epithets which they apply to the amateurs. These epithets include "snatch-and-grab thief," "boot-and-shoe thief," and "best-hold cannon." Professional thieves may use "raw-jaw" methods when operating under excellent protection, but they are ashamed of these methods and console themselves with the knowledge that they could do their work in more artistic manner if necessary. They will have no dealings with thieves who are unable to use the correct methods of stealing. . . .

The Profession of Theft as Consensus

The profession of theft is a complex of common and shared feelings, sentiments, and overt acts. Pickpockets have similar reactions to prospective victims and to the particular situations in which victims are found. This similarity of reactions is due to the common background of experiences and the similarity of points of attention. These reactions are like the "clinical intuitions" which different physicians form of a patient or different lawyers form of a juryman on quick inspection. Thieves can work together without serious disagreements because they have these common and similar attitudes. This consensus extends throughout the activities and lives of the thieves, culminating in similar and common reactions to the law, which is regarded as the common enemy. Out of this consensus, moreover, develop the codes, the attitudes of helpfulness, and the loyalties of the underworld. . . .

One of the most heinous offenses that a thief can commit against another thief is to inform, "squeal," or "squawk." This principle is generally respected even when it is occasionally violated. Professional thieves probably violate the principle less frequently than other criminals for the reason that they are more completely immune from punishment, which is the pressure that compels an offender to inform on others. Many thieves will submit to severe punishment rather than inform. Two factors enter into this behavior. One is the injury which would result to himself in the form of loss of prestige, inability to find companions among thieves in the future, and reprisals if he should inform. The other is loyalty and identification of self with other thieves. The spontaneous reactions of offenders who are in no way affected by the behavior of the squealer, as by putting him in coventry, are expressions of genuine disgust, fear, and hatred.[4] Consensus is the basis of both of these reactions, and the two together explain how the rule against informing grows out of the common experiences of the thieves.

Consensus means, also, that thieves have a system of values and an *esprit de corps* which support the individual thief in his criminal career. . . .

The Profession of Theft as Differential Association

Differential association is characteristic of the professional thieves, as of all other groups. The thief is a part of the underworld and in certain respects is segregated from the rest of society. His place of residence is frequently in the slums or in the "white-light" districts where commercial recreations flourish. Even when he lives in a residential hotel or in a suburban home, he must remain aloof from his neighbors more than is customary for city dwellers who need not keep their occupations secret.

The differential element in the association of thieves is primarily functional rather than geographical. Their personal association is limited by barriers which are maintained principally by the thieves themselves. These barriers are based on their community of interests, including security or safety. These barriers may easily be penetrated from within; since other groups also set up barriers in their personal association, especially against known thieves, the thieves are, in fact, kept in confinement within the barriers of their own groups to a somewhat greater extent than is true of other groups. On the other hand, these barriers can be penetrated from the outside only with great difficulty. A stranger who enters a thieves' hangout is called a "weed in the garden." When he enters, conversation either ceases completely or is diverted to innocuous topics. . . .

The final definition of the professional thief is found within this differential association. The group defines its own membership. A person who is received in the group and recognized as a professional thief is a professional thief. One who is not so received and recognized is not a professional thief, regardless of his methods of making a living. . . .

The Profession of Theft as Organization

Professional theft is organized crime. It is not organized in the journalistic sense, for no dictator or central office directs the work of the members of the profession. Rather it is organized in the sense that it is a system in which informal unity and reciprocity may be found. This is expressed in the *Report of the* [Chicago] *City Council Committee on Crime* as follows:

> While this criminal group is not by any means completely organized, it has many of the characteristics of a system. It has its own language; it has its own laws; its own history; its traditions and customs; its own methods and techniques; its highly specialized machinery for attack upon persons and particularly upon property; its own highly specialized modes of defense. These professional criminals have interurban, interstate and sometimes international connections.[5]

The complex of techniques, status, consensus, and differential association which have been described previously may be regarded as organization. More specifically, the organization of professional thieves consists in part of the knowledge which becomes the common property of the profession. . . .

The preceding description of the characteristics of the profession of theft suggests that a person can be a professional thief only if he is recognized and received as such by other professional thieves. Professional theft is a group-way of life. One can get into the group and remain in it only by the consent of those previously in the group. Recognition as a professional thief by other professional thieves is the absolutely necessary, universal, and definitive characteristic of the professional thief. This recognition is a combination of two of the characteristics previously described, namely, status and differential association. A professional thief is a person who has the status of a professional thief in the differential association of professional thieves.

Selection and tutelage are the two necessary elements in the process of acquiring recognition as a professional thief. These are the universal factors in an explanation of the genesis of the professional thief. A person cannot acquire recognition as a professional thief until he has had tutelage in professional theft, and tutelage is given only to a few persons selected from the total population.

Selection and tutelage are continuous processes. The person who is not a professional thief becomes a professional thief as a result of contact with professional thieves, reciprocal confidence and appreciation, a crisis situation, and tutelage. In the course of this process a person who is not a professional thief may become first a neophyte and then a recognized professional thief. A very small percentage of those who start on this process ever reach the stage of professional theft, and the process may be interrupted at any point by action of either party. . . .

Notes

1. Several statistical studies of habitual thieves, defined in terms of repeated arrests, have been published. Some of these are excellent from the point of view of the problems with which they deal, but they throw little light on professional thieves because they do not differentiate professional thieves from other habitual thieves. See Roland Grassberger, *Gewerbs-und Berufsverbrechertum in den Vereinigten Staaten von Amerika* (Vienna, 1933); Fritz Beger, *Die rückfälligen Betrüger* (Leipzig, 1929); Alfred John, *Die Rückfallsdiebe* (Leipzig, 1929).
2. Stories circulate at intervals regarding schools for pickpockets, confidence men, and other professional thieves. If formal schools of this nature have ever existed, they have probably been ephemeral.
3. Noel Ersine, *Underworld and Prison Slang* (Upland, Indiana, 1935).
4. Philip S. Van Cise, *Fighting the Underworld* (Boston, 1936), p. 321; Josiah Flynt Willard, *Tramping with Tramps* (New York, 1899), pp. 23–24, and *My Life* (New York, 1908). pp. 331–40.
5. P. 164.

3

White-Collar Criminality

Edwin H. Sutherland

. . . The thesis of this paper is that the conception and explanations of crime which have just been described are misleading and incorrect, that crime is in fact not closely correlated with poverty or with the psychopathic and sociopathic conditions associated with poverty, and that an adequate explanation of criminal behavior must proceed along quite different lines. The conventional explanations are invalid principally because they are derived from biased samples. The samples are biased in that they have not included vast areas of criminal behavior of persons not in the lower class. One of these neglected areas is the criminal behavior of business and professional men, which will be analyzed in this paper.

The "robber barons" of the last half of the nineteenth century were white-collar criminals, as practically everyone now agrees. Their attitudes are illustrated by these statements: Colonel Vanderbilt asked, "You don't suppose you can run a railroad in accordance with the statutes, do you?" A. B. Stickney, a railroad president, said to sixteen other railroad presidents in the home of J. P. Morgan in 1890, "I have the utmost respect for you gentlemen, individually, but as railroad presidents I wouldn't trust you with my watch out of my sight." Charles Francis Adams said, "The difficulty in railroad management . . . lies in the covetousness, want of good faith, and low moral tone of railway managers, in the complete absence of any high standard of commercial honesty."

The present-day white-collar criminals, who are more suave and deceptive than the "robber barons," are represented by Krueger, Stavisky, Whitney, Mitchell, Foshay, Insull, the Van Sweringens, Musica-Coster, Fall, Sinclair, and many other merchant princes and captains of finance and industry, and by a host of lesser followers. Their criminality has been demonstrated again and again in the investigations of land offices, railways, insurance, munitions, banking, public utilities, stock exchanges, the oil industry, real estate, reorganization committees, receiverships, bankruptcies, and politics. Individual cases of such criminality are reported frequently, and in many periods more important crime news may be found on the financial pages of newspapers than on the front pages. White-collar criminality is found in every occupation, as can be discovered readily in casual conversation with a representative of an occupation by asking him, "What crooked practices are found in your occupation?"

Source: American Sociological Review, Vol. 5, No. 1 (February 1940), pp. 2–10, Copyright © 1940, American Sociological Association. Note renumbered.

White-collar criminality in business is expressed most frequently in the form of misrepresentation in financial statements of corporations, manipulation in the stock exchange, commercial bribery, bribery of public officials directly or indirectly in order to secure favorable contracts and legislation, misrepresentation in advertising and salesmanship, embezzlement and misapplication of funds, short weights and measures and misgrading of commodities, tax frauds, misapplication of funds in receiverships and bankruptcies. These are what Al Capone called "the legitimate rackets." These and many others are found in abundance in the business world.

In the medical profession, which is here used as an example because it is probably less criminalistic than some other professions, are found illegal sale of alcohol and narcotics, abortion, illegal services to underworld criminals, fraudulent reports and testimony in accident cases, extreme cases of unnecessary treatment, fake specialists, restriction of competition, and fee-splitting. Fee-splitting is a violation of a specific law in many states and a violation of the conditions of admission to the practice of medicine in all. The physician who participates in fee-splitting tends to send his patients to the surgeon who will give him the largest fee rather than to the surgeon who will do the best work. It has been reported that two thirds of the surgeons in New York City split fees, and that more than one half of the physicians in a central western city who answered a questionnaire on this point favored fee-splitting.

These varied types of white-collar crimes in business and the professions consist principally of violation of delegated or implied trust, and many of them can be reduced to two categories: misrepresentation of asset values and duplicity in the manipulation of power. The first is approximately the same as fraud or swindling; the second is similar to the double-cross. The latter is illustrated by the corporation director who, acting on inside information, purchases land which the corporation will need and sells it at a fantastic profit to his corporation. The principle of this duplicity is that the offender holds two antagonistic positions, one of which is a position of trust, which is violated, generally by misapplication of funds, in the interest of the other position. A football coach, permitted to referee a game in which his own team was playing, would illustrate this antagonism of positions. Such situations cannot be completely avoided in a complicated business structure, but many concerns make a practice of assuming such antagonistic functions and regularly violating the trust thus delegated to them. When compelled by law to make a separation of their functions, they make a nominal separation and continue by subterfuge to maintain the two positions.

An accurate statistical comparison of the crimes of the two classes is not available. The most extensive evidence regarding the nature and prevalence of white-collar criminality is found in the reports of the larger investigations to which reference was made. . . .

White-collar criminality in politics, which is generally recognized as fairly prevalent, has been used by some as a rough gauge by which to measure white-collar criminality in business. James A. Farley said, "The standards of conduct are as high among officeholders and politicians as they are in commercial life," and Cermak, while mayor of Chicago, said, "There is less graft in politics than in business." John Flynn wrote, "The average politician is the merest amateur in the gentle art of graft, compared with his brother in the field of business." And Walter Lippmann wrote, "Poor as they are, the standards of public life are so much more social than those of business that financiers who enter politics regard themselves as philanthropists."

These statements obviously do not give a precise measurement of the relative criminality of the white-collar class, but they are adequate evidence that crime is not so highly concentrated in the lower class as the usual statistics indicate. Also, these statements obviously do not mean that every business and professional man is a criminal, just as the usual theories do not mean that every man in the lower class is a criminal. On the other hand, the preceding statements refer in many cases to the leading corporations in America and are not restricted to the disreputable business and professional men who are called quacks, ambulance chasers, bucket-shop operators, dead-beats, and fly-by-night swindlers.[1]

The financial cost of white-collar crime is probably several times as great as the financial cost of all the crimes which are customarily regarded as the "crime problem.". . .

The financial loss from white-collar crime, great as it is, is less important than the damage to social relations. White-collar crimes violate trust and therefore create distrust, which lowers social morale and produces social disorganization on a large scale. Other crimes produce relatively little effect on social institutions or social organization.

White-collar crime is real crime. It is not ordinarily called crime, and calling it by this name does not make it worse, just as refraining from calling it crime does not make it better than it otherwise would be. It is called crime here in order to bring it within the scope of criminology, which is justified because it is in violation of the criminal law. The crucial question in this analysis is the criterion of violation of the criminal law. Conviction in the criminal court, which is sometimes suggested as the criterion, is not adequate because a large proportion of those who commit crimes are not convicted in criminal courts. This criterion, therefore, needs to be supplemented. When it is supplemented, the criterion of the crimes of one class must be kept consistent in general terms with the criterion of the crimes of the other class. The definition should not be the spirit of the law for white-collar crimes and the letter of the law for other crimes, or in other respects be more liberal for one class than for the other. Since this discussion is concerned with the conventional theories of the criminologists, the criterion of white-collar crime must be justified in terms of the procedures of those criminologists in dealing with other crimes. The criterion of white-collar crimes, as here proposed, supplements convictions in the criminal courts in four respects, in each of which the extension is justified because the criminologists who present the conventional theories of criminal behavior make the same extension in principle.

First, other agencies than the criminal court must be included, for the criminal court is not the only agency which makes official decisions regarding violations of the criminal law. The juvenile court, dealing largely with offenses of the children of the poor, in many states is not under the criminal jurisdiction. The criminologists have made much use of case histories and statistics of juvenile delinquents in constructing their theories of criminal behavior. This justifies the inclusion of agencies other than the criminal court which deal with white-collar offenses. The most important of these agencies are the administrative boards, bureaus, or commissions, and much of their work, although certainly not all, consists of cases which are in violation of the criminal law. The Federal Trade Commission recently ordered several automobile companies to stop advertising their interest rate on installment purchases as 6 percent, since it was actually 11½ percent. Also it filed complaint against *Good Housekeeping*, one of the Hearst publications, charging that its seals led the public to believe that all products bearing those seals had been tested in their laboratories, which was contrary to fact. Each of these involves a charge of dishonesty, which might have been tried in a criminal court as fraud. A large proportion of the cases before these boards should be included in the data of the criminologists. Failure to do so is a principal reason for the bias in their samples and the errors in their generalizations.

Second, for both classes, behavior which would have a reasonable expectancy of conviction if tried in a criminal court or substitute agency should be defined as criminal. In this respect, convictability rather than actual conviction should be the criterion of criminality. The criminologists would not hesitate to accept as data a verified case history of a person who was a criminal but had never been convicted. Similarly, it is justifiable to include white-collar criminals who have not been convicted, provided reliable evidence is available. Evidence regarding such cases appears in many civil suits, such as stockholders' suits and patent-infringement suits. These cases might have been referred to the criminal court but they were referred to the civil court because the injured party was more interested in securing damages than in seeing punishment inflicted. This also happens in embezzlement cases, regarding which surety companies have much evidence. In a short consecutive series of embezzlements known to a surety company, 90 percent were not prosecuted because prosecution would interfere with restitution or salvage. The evidence in cases of embezzlement is generally conclusive, and would probably have been sufficient to justify conviction in all of the cases in this series.

Third, behavior should be defined as criminal if conviction is avoided merely because of pressure which is brought to bear on the court or substitute agency. Gangsters and racketeers have been relatively immune in many cities because of their pressure on prospective witnesses and public officials, and professional thieves, such as pickpockets and confidence men who do not use strong-arm methods, are even more frequently immune. The conventional criminologists do not hesitate to include the life histories of such criminals as data, because they understand the generic relation of the pressures to the failure to convict. Similarly, white-collar criminals are relatively immune because of the class bias of the courts and the power of their class to influence the implementation and administration of the law. This class bias affects not merely present-day courts but to a much greater degree affected the earlier courts which established the precedents and rules of procedure of the present-day courts. Consequently, it is justifiable to interpret the actual or potential failures of conviction in the light of known facts regarding the pressures brought to bear on the agencies which deal with offenders.

Fourth, persons who are accessory to a crime should be included among white-collar criminals as they are among other criminals. When the Federal Bureau of Investigation deals with a case of kidnapping, it is not content with catching the offenders who carried away the victim; they may catch and the court may convict twenty-five other persons who assisted by secreting the victim, negotiating the ransom, or putting the ransom money into circulation. On the other hand, the prosecution of white-collar criminals frequently stops with one offender. Political graft almost always involves collusion between politicians and business men but prosecutions are generally limited to the politicians. Judge Manton was found guilty of accepting $664,000 in bribes, but the six or eight important commercial concerns that paid the bribes have not been prosecuted. Pendergast, the late boss of Kansas City, was convicted for failure to report as a part of his income $315,000 received in bribes from insurance companies but the insurance companies which paid the bribes have not been prosecuted. In an investigation of an embezzlement by the president of a bank, at least a dozen other violations of law which were related to this embezzlement and involved most of the other officers of the bank and the officers of the clearing house, were discovered but none of the others was prosecuted.

This analysis of the criterion of white-collar criminality results in the conclusion that a description of white-collar criminality in general terms will be also a description of the criminality of the lower class. The respects in which the crimes of the two classes differ are the incidentals rather than the essentials of criminality. They differ principally in the implementation of the criminal laws which apply to them. The crimes of the lower class are handled by policemen, prosecutors, and judges, with penal sanctions in the form of fines, imprisonment, and death. The crimes of the upper class either result in no official action at all, or result in suits for damages in civil courts, or are handled by inspectors, and by administrative boards or commissions, with penal sanctions in the form of warnings, orders to cease and desist, occasionally the loss of a license, and only in extreme cases by fines or prison sentences. Thus, the white-collar criminals are segregated administratively from other criminals, and largely as a consequence of this are not regarded as real criminals by themselves, the general public, or the criminologists.

This difference in the implementation of the criminal law is due principally to the difference in the social position of the two types of offenders. . . . The statement of Daniel Drew, a pious old fraud, describes the criminal law with some accuracy:

> Law is like a cobweb; it's made for flies and the smaller kinds of insects, so to speak, but lets the big bumblebees break through. When technicalities of the law stood in my way, I have always been able to brush them aside easy as anything.

The preceding analysis should be regarded neither as an assertion that all efforts to influence legislation and its administration are reprehensible nor as a particularistic interpretation of the criminal law. It means only that the upper class has greater influence in moulding the criminal law and its administration to its own interests than does the lower class. The privileged position of white-collar criminals before the law results to a slight extent from bribery and political pressures, principally from the respect in which they are held and without special effort on their part. The most powerful group in medieval society secured relative immunity by "benefit of clergy," and now our most powerful groups secure relative immunity by "benefit of business or profession.". . .

The theory that criminal behavior in general is due either to poverty or to the psychopathic and sociopathic conditions associated with poverty can now be shown to be invalid for three reasons. First, the generalization is based on a biased sample which omits almost entirely the behavior of white-collar criminals. The criminologists have restricted their data, for reasons of convenience and ignorance rather than of principle, largely to cases dealt with in criminal courts and juvenile courts, and these agencies are used principally for criminals from the lower economic strata. Consequently, their data are grossly biased from the point of view of the economic status of criminals and their generalization that criminality is closely associated with poverty is not justified.

Second, the generalization that criminality is closely associated with poverty obviously does not apply to white-collar criminals. With a small number of exceptions, they are not in poverty, were not reared in slums or badly deteriorated families, and are not feebleminded or psychopathic. They were seldom problem children in their earlier years and did not appear in juvenile courts or child guidance clinics. The proposition, derived from the data used by the conventional criminologists, that "the criminal of today was the problem child of yesterday" is seldom true of white-collar criminals. The idea that the causes of criminality are to be found almost exclusively in childhood similarly is fallacious. Even if poverty is extended to include the economic stresses which afflict business in a period of depression, it is not closely correlated with white-collar criminality. Probably at no time within fifty years have white-collar crimes in the field of investments and of corporate management been so extensive as during the boom period of the twenties.

Third, the conventional theories do not even explain lower class criminality. The sociopathic and psychopathic factors which have been emphasized doubtless have something to do with crime causation, but these factors have not been related to a general process which is found both in white-collar criminality and lower class criminality and therefore they do not explain the criminality of either class. They may explain the manner or method of crime—why lower class criminals commit burglary or robbery rather than false pretenses. . . .

Note

1. Perhaps it should be repeated that "white-collar" (upper) and "lower" classes merely designate persons of high and low socioeconomic status. Income and amount of money involved in the crime are not the sole criteria. Many persons of "low" socioeconomic status are "white-collar" criminals in the sense that they are well-dressed, well-educated, and have high incomes, but "white-collar" as used in this paper means "respected," "socially accepted and approved," "looked up to." Some people in this class may not be well-dressed or well-educated, nor have high incomes, although the "upper" usually exceed the "lower" classes in these respects as well as in social status.

4

Juvenile Delinquency and Urban Areas

Clifford R. Shaw   Henry D. McKay

The 1900–1906 Juvenile Court Series

Series Studied and Types of Defenses

Third in this sequence is the series of 8,056 male delinquents brought into the juvenile court of Cook county from Chicago during 1900–1906 (the first 7 years of the juvenile court's existence). By comparing this series with that for 1927–33 it will be possible to determine the extent to which variations in the rates correspond and the extent to which changes in rates can be related to changes in the physical or social characteristics of the local areas.

The age distribution of the boys in the 1900–1906 series indicates that, on the whole, they were a little younger than those in the more recent series. At that time the upper age limit in the juvenile Court was 15 instead of 16, and a somewhat larger number of boys were under 10 years of age (6.1 percent). The highest frequencies were in ages 13, 14, and 15. With regard to offenses, it seems probable that some boys were taken to court in these earlier years on charges for which no petitions would be filed by the police probation officers at the present time. This is indicated both by the fact that the number of cases in court was greater in proportion to the population than at present and by the fact that the classification of offenses indicated a somewhat higher proportion of less serious charges.

Distribution of Delinquents

Map 12 [not reproduced here] shows the distribution by home address of the 8,056 boys brought to court in the 7-year period 1900–1906. In this series, as in those previously discussed, it will be noted that a preponderance of the delinquent boys lived either in areas adjacent to the central business and industrial district or along the two forks of the Chicago River, Back of the Yards, or in South Chicago, with relatively few in other outlying areas.

While this series exhibits the same general configuration found in the others, there are two noticeable variations. First, the concentrations are somewhat more restricted and closer to the central business district and to the industrial centers than

Source: Reprinted with permission from Clifford R. Shaw and Henry D. McKay, *Juvenile Delinquency in Urban Areas*, pp. 60–61, 63–68. Copyright © 1942 The University of Chicago Press.

in the later series. This is to be expected, since many of the areas used for residential purposes in this early period have since been depopulated by expanding industry and commerce. Second, on this map there are relatively few delinquents in the areas east of State Street, south from the Loop. These areas, it will be remembered, contain many delinquents in the 1917–23 map and were also areas of heavy concentration in 1927–33.

Rates of Delinquents

Map 13 shows the rates of delinquents in the 106 square-mile areas used for this 1900-1906 series. The population upon which these rates were calculated was secured by combining into 106 comparable areas the 1,200 enumeration districts of 1900 and the 431 census tracts of 1910 and computing the yearly increase or decrease of population in each. The population for the midyear of this series was then estimated from the aged 10–15 male population in 1910. The areas for which rates are presented are practically the same as those used in the 1917–23 juvenile court series, except that in 7 instances it was necessary to construct combinations of the 113 areas in order to secure a larger population in districts which were sparsely settled at that time.

The rates in this series range from 0.6 to 29.8. The median is 4.9 and the rate for the city as a whole 8.4. Four areas have rates of 20.0 and over; 7 have rates of 15.0 or over; and 12 have rates of 12.0 or over. At the other extreme, 3 areas have rates of less than 1.0, and 12 of less than 2.0.

Map 13 indicates that the variation in rates of delinquents is quite similar to the variations presented previously. The four areas with highest rates are all immediately adjacent to the Loop, and other high-rate areas are in the Stock Yards district and in South Chicago. The areas with low rates, on the other hand, are located, for the most part, near the city's periphery. As compared to rate maps for subsequent series, it can be seen that the areas with very high rates are somewhat more closely concentrated around the central business district. This is especially noticeable south from the Loop and east of State Street, where, after the first two miles, the rates of delinquents are below the average for the city as a whole.

Comparisons Among Juvenile Court Series
(1927–33, 1917–23, and 1900–1906)

Three methods will be employed to determine the extent to which the variations in rates of delinquents in the several time series correspond: (1) comparisons by zones, (2) area comparisons and correlations, and (3) extent of concentration.

Rates by Zones

Rates of delinquents were calculated for each of 5 zones drawn at 2-mile intervals, with a focal point in the heart of the central business district. These rates were computed on the basis of the number of delinquents and the total aged 10–16 male population in each zone.[1]

It should be borne in mind that zone rates of delinquents are presented chiefly because of their theoretical value. They show the variations in rates more conceptually

Map 13
RATES OF MALE JUVENILE DELINQUENTS
(CHICAGO, 1900–1906)

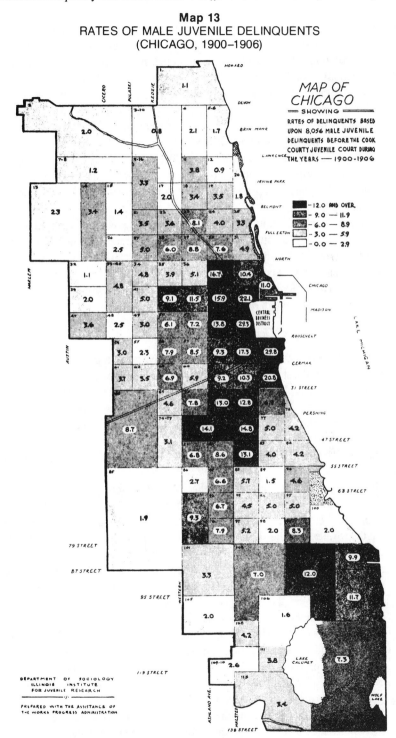

and idealistically than do the rates for smaller units. The number of zones used for this purpose is not important, as it is not assumed that there are actual zones in the city or sharp dividing lines between those presented. It is assumed, rather, that a more or less continuous variation exists between the rates of delinquents in the areas close to the center of the city and those outlying and that any arbitrary number of zones will exhibit this difference satisfactorily.

Inspection of the rate maps indicates that there are wide differentials among the rates for the same square miles within each zone, just as there are among rates for census tracts within each square-mile area. These fluctuations do not greatly affect the general trend, however; in fact, it is because the zone rates eliminate the fluctuations evident for smaller areas and present the general tendencies that they are interesting and important.

Maps A, B, and C, Figure 1, show rates of delinquents by 5 complete zones, and also by the north and south halves of the city separately, for the three juvenile court series that have been presented. On the same figure are given the critical ratios between the rates in outer and inner zones, which are so great that clearly they could not be due to chance alone. The critical ratios for adjacent zones (not shown) are also statistically significant in every instance.

Area Comparisons and Correlations

Of the 24 areas with the highest rates of delinquents in the 1927–33 series, 20 are among the 24 highest also in 1917–23. On the other hand, a few areas where significant changes took place in community characteristics show also marked changes in rates of delinquents. When the 1917–23 and 1927–33 rates are correlated by the 113 areas used for the earlier series the coefficient is found to be .70 ± .02. This coefficient is greatly reduced by the fact that the rates in 6 areas have changed so much that the points representing them fell entirely outside the line of scatter on the correlation sheet.

Most of the areas of high rates in the 1900–1906 series also correspond with those ranking highest in the two later series. Of the 12 highest in 1900–1906, 9 were among the 12 highest in 1927–33. Three of the 5 highest-rate areas in the latter series, but not in the former, are the same 3 found among the high-rate areas as of 1917–23. Although some new areas appear among those with high rates in the more recent series, it is significant to note that all 12 of the areas of highest rates in the 1900–1906 series are among the areas of high rates in 1927–33. Because of these areas, the correspondence between the series is even more clearly seen when comparisons involving a larger number of areas are made. Of the 25 areas with the highest rates of delinquents in the 1900–1906 series, 19 are included among the 25 highest in the 1917–23 series, and 18 among the 25 highest in 1927–33, even though these series are separated by approximately 2 and 3 decades, respectively. This is especially significant in view of the fact that the nationality composition of the population has changed completely in some of these neighborhoods.

A more general statement of the relationship is found when the rates in the 1900–1906 series are correlated with those for each of the other juvenile court series.

Fig. 1
ZONE MAPS FOR THREE JUVENILE COURT SERIES

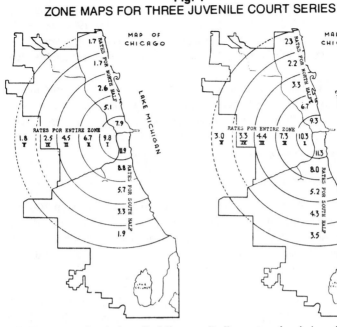

A. Zone rates of male juvenile delinquents, 1927–33 series

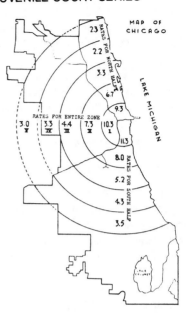

B. Zone rates of male juvenile delinquents, 1917–23 series

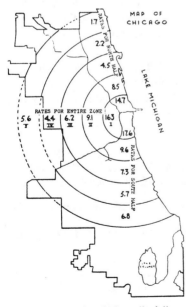

C. Zone rates of male juvenile delinquents, 1900–1906 series

CRITICAL RATIOS OF SELECTED ZONE RATES

Juvenile Court Series (Individuals)

Zones	Difference	Standard Error of the Difference	Critical Ratio
A. 1927–33			
1 and 4	7.3	.301	24.2
1 and 5	8.0	.302	26.5
2 and 4	4.2	.142	29.6
2 and 5	4.9	.142	34.5
B. 1917–23			
1 and 4	7.0	.293	23.9
1 and 5	7.3	.314	23.2
2 and 4	4.0	.162	24.7
2 and 5	4.3	.196	21.9
C. 1900–1906			
1 and 4	11.9	.371	32.1
1 and 5	10.7	.467	22.9
2 and 4	4.7	.241	19.5
2 and 5	3.5	.371	9.4

To accomplish this, it was necessary to calculate rates in the two later juvenile court series for the same 106 areas used in the early series. The coefficient secured for 1900–1906 and 1917–23 was .85 ± .04, and that for 1900–1906 and 1927–33 was .61 ± .04. In the latter case the coefficient was reduced by the few values which fell far out of the line of scatter, indicating areas where considerable change had occurred.

These coefficients are remarkably high when it is recalled that the series are separated by about 20 and 30 years, respectively. They reveal that, in general, the areas of high rates of delinquents around 1900 were the high-rate areas also several decades later. This consistency reflects once more the operation of general processes of distribution and segregation in the life of the city.

Extent of Concentration

The distribution of delinquents in relation to male population 10–16 years of age for each of the three juvenile court series has been further analyzed by dividing the population into four equal parts on the basis of the magnitude of rates of delinquents, then calculating the percentage of the total number of delinquents and total city area for each population quartile, as shown in Table 6. [Tables 1–5 in sections of book not reprinted here.]

It is apparent that the quarter of the population living in the areas of highest rates occupied only 19.2 percent of the geographic area of the city in the 1927–33 series 17.8 percent in 1917–23, and 13.1 percent in 1900–1906. Yet, in each instance this quarter of the population produced about one-half of the delinquents.

When the delinquents in each series, in turn, are divided into four equal parts according to magnitude of rate of delinquents and the corresponding distribution of population and city area is analyzed, the concentration of delinquents is again clearly evident (see Table 7).

Table 7 shows that the upper quarter of the delinquents, living in high-rate areas, represented only 7.7 percent of the population in the 1927-33 series, 10.9 percent as of 1917–23, and 10.6 percent in 1900–1906; and occupied respectively only 5.5,

Table 6

PERCENTAGE OF DELINQUENTS AND OF CITY AREA FOR QUARTILES
OF MALE POPULATION AGED 10-16, WHEN AREAS ARE RANKED
BY RATE OF DELINQUENTS: THREE JUVENILE COURT SERIES

Quartiles of Population	Percentage of Delinquents			Percentage of City Area		
	1927-33	1917-23	1900-1906	1927-33	1917-23	1900-1906
Upper one-fourth, in high-rate areas	54.3	46.1	47.3	19.2	17.8	13.1
Second one-fourth	23.9	27.3	26.6	19.4	24.8	12.1
Third one-fourth	14.6	17.7	17.4	32.3	27.1	21.7
Lower one-fourth, in low-rate areas	7.2	8.9	8 7	29.1	30.3	53.1

Table 7

PERCENTAGE OF MALE POPULATION AGED 10-16 AND OF CITY AREA
FOR QUARTILES OF DELINQUENTS WHEN AREAS ARE RANKED BY
RATE OF DELINQUENTS: THREE JUVENILE COURT SERIES

Quartiles of Delinquents	Percentage of Population			Percentage of City Area		
	1927-33	1917-23	1900-1906	1927-33	1917-23	1900-1906
Upper one-fourth, from high-rate areas	7.7	10.9	10.6	5.5	6.0	3.7
Second one-fourth	13.8	12.1	16.6	8.6	11.1	10.1
Third one-fourth	24.3	29.0	24.1	22.0	27.4	17.8
Lower one-fourth, from low-rate areas	54.2	48.0	48.7	63.9	55.5	68.4

6.0, and 3.7 percent of the total city area. At the opposite extreme, the one-fourth of the delinquents in the areas of lowest rates came from 54.2 percent of the population and 63.9 percent of the area in 1927–33, 48 percent of the population and 55.5 percent of the area a decade earlier, and 48.7 percent of the population and 68.4 percent of the area in 1900–1906. . . .

Note

1. When a square-mile area was divided by one of the concentric circles, the aged 10-16 population and the number of delinquents allocated to each zone corresponded to the proportion of the area which fell in each.

5

The Criminal and His Victim

Hans von Hentig

The Duet Frame of Crime

Crime, for the most part, is injury inflicted on another person. Setting aside felonies directed against fictitious victims, the state, order, health, and so forth, there are always two partners: the perpetrator and the victim.

This doer-sufferer relation is put by our codes in mechanical terms. A purse is snatched, bodily harm is done. The sexual self-determination of a woman is violated. Mental factors are, of course, taken into account. So is felonious intent or malice aforethought. The "consent" of an adult woman changes the otherwise criminal act of rape into a lawful occurrence, or at least a happening in which the law is not very much interested. *Volenti non fit iniuria.* No one can complain of injury to which he has submitted willingly. In many other instances consent changes the legal aspect while the factual situation remains unaltered. By his or her decision the victim can, in spite of loss and pain endured, turn factual crime into a situation devoid of legal significance.[1] Non-complaint after the event practically stands on a par with consent.

Yet experience tells us that this is not all, that the relationships between perpetrator and victim are much more intricate than the rough distinctions of criminal law.[2] Here are two human beings. As soon as they draw near to one another male or female, young or old, rich or poor, ugly or attractive—a wide range of interactions, repulsions as well as attractions, is set in motion. What the law does is to watch the one who acts and the one who is acted upon. By this external criterion a subject and object, a perpetrator and a victim are distinguished. In sociological and psychological quality the situation may be completely different. It may happen that the two distinct categories merge. There are cases in which they are reversed and in the long chain of causative forces the victim assumes the role of a determinant.[3]

We are wont to say and to think that the criminal act is symptomatic for the lawbreaker, as a suicide would be, or a red rash on the skin. We have gone to great lengths, in studying our society, to classify and reclassify groups. Among common situations usually enumerated, however, we do not find the evildoer—evil-sufferer

Source: Reprinted by permission from Hans von Hentig, *The Criminal and His Victim* (New Haven, CT: Yale University Press, 1948). Copyright © 1948 Yale University Press. All rights reserved.

group. It is not always true that common interests give rise to a group; the problem presents many more depths. I maintain that many criminal deeds are more indicative of a subject-object relation than of the perpetrator alone. There is a definite mutuality of some sort. The mechanical outcome may be profit to one party, harm to another, yet the psychological interaction, carefully observed, will not submit to this kindergarten label. In the long process leading gradually to the unlawful result, credit and debit are not infrequently indistinguishable.

In a sense the victim shapes and molds the criminal.[4] The poor and ignorant immigrant has bred a peculiar kind of fraud. Depressions and wars are responsible for new forms of crimes because new types of potential victims are brought into being.[5] It would not be correct nor complete to speak of a carnivorous animal, its habits and characteristics, without looking at the prey on which it lives. In a certain sense the animals which devour and those that are devoured complement each other. Although it looks one-sided as far as the final outcome goes, it is not a totally unilateral form of relationships. They work upon each other profoundly and continually, even before the moment of disaster. To know one we must be acquainted with the complementary partner. . . .

Notes

1. Although morally dubious and under censure of other social controls.
2. It is therefore rather naive to maintain, "All sight has been lost of the fact that for every criminal there must be an innocent sufferer . . ." C. R. Cooper, *Here's to Crime* (Boston, Little, Brown & Co., 1937), p. 434. Read in the "Notable British Trials" series the case of the lawyer H. R. Armstrong by Filson Young, *Trial of Herbert Rowse Armstrong* (Edinburgh, William Hodge & Co., 1927).
3. The title of a well-known novel by Werfel, *Der Ermordete ist schuld*, expresses the moral transposition. It is already met in the legal notion of self-defense and the concept of grave provocation. The idea of the responsible victim is belatedly conveyed by decisions of the pardoning power; it cannot easily be rendered vocal by laws and court sentences.
4. In others it determines the question of guilt or the degree of penalty. In explaining a sentence of first degree murder and the death penalty in a case of manslaughter, Warden Lawes writes, "the deceased had been well liked and there was a certain amount of prejudice against Chapeleau's foreign origin"—the perpetrator being a Canadian. *Meet the Murderer*, p. 4.
5. A wave of war bond rackets swept the United States in 1944. Utilizing and shrewdly increasing the fear of many bond-holders that the bonds might not be redeemed at full value after the war, and playing upon their patriotic reluctance to sell, these frauds proposed to lonely housewives to take orders for merchandise or other transactions, making payment in the bonds. See chapter on war and crime in Hentig, *Crime: Causes and Conditions*.

6

Victim-Precipitated Criminal Homicide

Marvin E. Wolfgang

In many crimes, especially in criminal homicide, the victim is often a major contributor to the criminal act. Except in cases in which the victim is an innocent bystander and is killed in lieu of an intended victim, or in cases in which a pure accident is involved, the victim may be one of the major precipitating causes of his own demise.

Various theories of social interaction, particularly in social psychology, have established the framework for the present discussion. In criminological literature, however, probably von Hentig in *The Criminal and His Victim* has provided the most useful theoretical basis for analysis of the victim-offender relationship. In Chapter XII, entitled "The Contribution of the Victim to the Genesis of Crime," the author discusses this "duet frame of crime" and suggests that homicide is particularly amenable to analysis.[1] In *Penal Philosophy*, Tarde[2] frequently attacks the "legislative mistake" of concentrating too much on premeditation and paying too little attention to motives, which indicate an important interrelationship between victim and offender. And in one of his satirical essays, "On Murder Considered as One of the Fine Arts," Thomas De Quincey[3] shows cognizance of the idea that sometimes the victim is a would-be murderer. Garofalo,[4] too, noted that the victim may provoke another individual into attack, and though the provocation be slight, if perceived by an egoistic attacker it may be sufficient to result in homicide.

Besides these theoretical concepts, the law of homicide has long recognized provocation by the victim as a possible reason for mitigation of the offense from murder to manslaughter, or from criminal to excusable homicide. In order that such reduction occur, there are four prerequisites.[5]

(1) There must have been adequate provocation.

(2) The killing must have been in the heat of passion.

(3) The killing must have followed the provocation before there had been a reasonable opportunity for the passion to cool.

(4) A causal connection must exist between provocation, the heat of passion, and the homicidal act. Such, for example, are: adultery, seduction of the offender's juvenile daughter, rape of the offender's wife or close relative,

Source: Reprinted by special permission of Northwestern University School of Law, *Journal of Criminal Law and Criminology.*

etc. . . . Perkins claims that "the adequate provocation must have engendered the heat of passion, and the heat of passion must have been the cause of the act which resulted in death."[6]

Definition and Illustration

The term *victim-precipitated* is applied to those criminal homicides in which the victim is a direct, positive precipitator in the crime. The role of the victim is characterized by his having been the first in the homicide drama to use physical force directed against his subsequent slayer. The victim-precipitated cases are those in which the victim was the first to show and use a deadly weapon, to strike a blow in an altercation—in short, the first to commence the interplay or resort to physical violence.

In seeking to identify the victim-precipitated cases recorded in police files it has not been possible always to determine whether the homicides strictly parallel legal interpretations. In general, there appears to be much similarity. In a few cases included under the present definition, the nature of the provocation is such that it would not legally serve to mitigate the offender's responsibility. In these cases the victim was threatened in a robbery, and either attempted to prevent the robbery, failed to take the robber seriously, or in some other fashion irritated, frightened, or alarmed the felon by physical force so that the robber, either by accident or compulsion, killed the victim. Infidelity of a mate or lover, failure to pay a debt, use of vile names by the victim, obviously means that he played an important role in inciting the offender to overt action in order to seek revenge, to win an argument, or to defend himself. However, mutual quarrels and wordy altercations do not constitute sufficient provocation under law, and they are not included in the meaning of victim-precipitated homicide.

Below are sketched several typical cases to illustrate the pattern of these homicides. Primary demonstration of physical force by the victim, supplemented by scurrilous language, characterizes the most common victim-precipitated homicides. All of these slayings were listed by the Philadelphia Police as criminal homicides, none of the offenders was exonerated by a coroner's inquest, and all the offenders were tried in criminal court.

- A husband accused his wife of giving money to another man, and while she was making breakfast, he attacked her with a milk bottle, then a brick, and finally a piece of concrete block. Having had a butcher knife in hand, she stabbed him during the fight.

- A husband threatened to kill his wife on several occasions. In this instance, he attacked her with a pair of scissors, dropped them, and grabbed a butcher knife from the kitchen. In the ensuing struggle that ended on their bed, he fell on the knife.

- In an argument over a business transaction, the victim first fired several shots at his adversary, who in turn fatally returned the fire.

- The victim was the aggressor in a fight, having struck his enemy several times. Friends tried to interfere, but the victim persisted. Finally, the offender retaliated with blows, causing the victim to fall and hit his head on the sidewalk, as a result of which he died.

- A husband had beaten his wife on several previous occasions. In the present instance, she insisted that he take her to the hospital. He refused, and a violent quarrel followed, during which he slapped her several times, and she concluded by stabbing him.

- During a lover's quarrel, the male (victim) hit his mistress and threw a can of kerosene at her. She retaliated by throwing the liquid on him, and then tossed a lighted match in his direction. He died from the burns.

- A drunken husband, beating his wife in their kitchen, gave her a butcher knife and dared her to use it on him. She claimed that if he should strike her once more, she would use the knife, whereupon he slapped her in the face and she fatally stabbed him.

- A victim became incensed when his eventual slayer asked for money which the victim owed him. The victim grabbed a hatchet and started in the direction of his creditor, who pulled out a knife and stabbed him.

- A victim attempted to commit sodomy with his girlfriend, who refused his overtures. He struck her several times on the side of her head with his fists before she grabbed a butcher knife and cut him fatally.

- A drunken victim with knife in hand approached his slayer during a quarrel. The slayer showed a gun, and the victim dared him to shoot. He did.

- During an argument in which a male called a female many vile names, she tried to telephone the police. But he grabbed the phone from her hands, knocked her down, kicked her, and hit her with a tire gauge. She ran to the kitchen, grabbed a butcher knife, and stabbed him in the stomach.

The Philadelphia Study

Empirical data for analysis of victim-precipitated homicides were collected from the files of the Homicide Squad of the Philadelphia Police Department, and include 588 consecutive cases of criminal homicide which occurred between January 1, 1948 and December 31, 1952. Because more than one person was sometimes involved in the slaying of a single victim, there was a total of 621 offenders responsible for the killing of 588 victims. The present study is part of a much larger work that analyzes criminal homicide in greater detail. Such material that is relevant to victim-precipitation is included in the present analysis. The 588 criminal homicides provide sufficient background information to establish much about the nature of the victim-offender relationship. Of these cases, 150, or 26 percent, have been designated, on the basis of the previously stated definition, as VP cases.[7] The remaining 438, therefore, have been designated as non-VP cases.

Thorough study of police files, theoretical discussions of the victim's contribution, and previous analysis of criminal homicide suggest that there may be important differences between VP and non-VP cases. The chi-square test has been used to test the significance in proportions between VP and non-VP homicides and a series of variables. Hence, any spurious association which is just due to chance has been reduced to a minimum by application of this test, and significant differences of distributions are revealed. Where any expected class frequency of less than five existed, the test was not applied; and in each tested association, a correction for continuity was used, although the difference resulting without it was only slight. In this study a value of P less than .05, or the 5 percent level of significance, is used as the minimal level of significant association. Throughout the subsequent discussion, the term *significant* in italics is used to indicate that a chi-square test of significance of association has been made and that the value of P less than .05 has been found. The discussion that follows (with respect to race, sex, age, etc.) reveals some interesting differences and similarities between the two. [Table omitted.]

Race

Because Negroes and males have been shown by their high rates of homicide, assaults against the person, etc., to be more criminally aggressive than whites and females, it may be inferred that there are more Negroes and males among VP victims than among non-VP victims. The data confirm this inference. Nearly 80 percent of VP cases compared to 70 percent of non-VP cases involve Negroes, a proportional difference that results in a *significant* association between race and VP homicide.

Sex

As victims, males comprise 94 percent of VP homicides, but only 72 percent of non-VP homicides, showing a *significant* association between sex of the victim and VP homicide.

Since females have been shown by their low rates of homicide, assaults against the person, etc., to be less criminally aggressive than males, and since females are less likely to precipitate their own victimization than males, we should expect more female *offenders* among VP homicides than among non-VP homicides. Such is the case, for the comparative data reveal that females are twice as frequently offenders in VP slayings (29 percent) as they are in non-VP slayings (14 percent)— a proportional difference which is also highly *significant*.

The number of white female offenders (16) in this study is too small to permit statistical analysis, but the tendency among both Negro and white females as separate groups is toward a much higher proportion among VP than among non-VP offenders. As noted above, analysis of Negro and white females as a combined group does result in the finding of a *significant* association between female offenders and VP homicide.

Age

The age distributions of victims and offenders in VP and non-VP homicides are strikingly similar; study of the data suggests that age has no apparent effect on VP homicide. The median age of VP victims is 33.3 years, while that of non-VP victims is 31.2 years.

Methods

In general, there is a *significant* association between method used to inflict death and VP homicide. Because Negroes and females comprise a larger proportion of offenders in VP cases, and because previous analysis has shown that stabbings occurred more often than any of the other methods of inflicting death,[8] it is implied that the frequency of homicides by stabbing is greater among VP than among non-VP cases. The data support such an implication and reveal that homicides by stabbing account for 54 percent of the VP cases but only 34 percent of non-VP cases, a difference which is *significant*. The distribution of shootings, beatings, and "other" methods of inflicting death among the VP and non-VP cases shows no significant differences. The high frequency of stabbings among VP homicides appears to result from an almost equal reduction in each of the remaining methods; yet the lower proportions in each of these three other categories among VP cases are not separately very different from the proportions among non-VP cases.

Place and Motive

There is no important difference between VP and non-VP homicides with respect to a home/not-home dichotomy, nor with respect to motives listed by the police. Slightly over half of both VP and non-VP slayings occurred in the home. General altercations (43 percent) and domestic quarrels (20 percent) rank highest among VP cases, as they do among non-VP cases (32 and 12 percent), although with lower frequency. Combined, these two motives account for a slightly larger share of the VP cases (3 out of 5) than of the non-VP cases (2 out of 5).

Victim-Offender Relationships[9]

Intra-racial slayings predominate in both groups, but inter-racial homicides comprise a larger share of VP cases (8 percent) than they do of non-VP cases (5 percent). Although VP cases make up one-fourth of all criminal homicides, they account for over one-third (35 percent) of all inter-racial slayings. Thus it appears that a homicide which crosses race lines is often likely to be one in which the slayer was provoked to assault by the victim. The association between inter-racial slayings and VP homicides, however, is not statistically significant.

Homicides involving victims and offenders of opposite sex (regardless of which sex is the victim or which is the offender) occur with about the same frequency among VP cases (34 percent) as among non-VP cases (37 percent). But a *significant* difference between VP and non-VP cases does emerge when determination of the sex of the victim, relative to the sex of his specific slayer, is taken into account. Of all criminal homicides for which the sex of both victim and offender is known, 88 involve a male victim and a female offender; and of these 88 cases, 43 are VP homicides. Thus, it may be said that 43, or 29 percent, of the 150 VP homicides, compared to 45, or only 11 percent, of the 400 non-VP homicides, are males slain by females.

It seems highly desirable, in view of these findings, that the police thoroughly investigate every possibility of strong provocation by the male victim when he is slain by a female—and particularly, as noted below, if the female is his wife, which is also a strong possibility. It is, of course, the further responsibility of defense counsel, prosecuting attorney, and subsequently the court, to determine whether such provocation was sufficient either to reduce or to eliminate culpability altogether.

The proportion that Negro male/Negro male[10] and white male/white male homicides constitute among VP cases (45 and 13 percent) is similar to the proportion these same relationships constitute among non-VP cases (41 and 14 percent). The important contribution of the Negro male as a victim-precipitator is indicated by the fact that Negro male/Negro female homicides are, proportionately, nearly three times as frequent among VP cases (25 percent) as they are among non-VP cases (9 percent). It is apparent, therefore, that Negroes and males not only are the groups most likely to make positive and direct contributions to the genesis of their own victimization, but that, in particular, Negro males more frequently provoke females of their own race to slay them than they do members of their own sex and race.

For both VP and non-VP groups, close friends, relatives, and acquaintances are the major types of specific relationships between victims and offenders. Combined, these three relationships constitute 69 percent of the VP homicides and 65 percent of the non-VP cases. Victims are relatives of their slayers in one-fourth of both types of homicide. But of 38 family slayings among VP cases, 33 are husband-wife killings; while of 98 family slayings among non-VP cases, only 67 are husband-wife killings. This proportional difference results in a *significant* association between mate slayings and VP homicide.

Finally, of VP mate slayings, 28 victims are husbands and only 5 are wives; but of non-VP mate slayings, only 19 victims are husbands while 48 are wives. Thus there is a *significant* association between husbands who are victims in mate slayings and VP homicide. This fact, namely, that *significantly* more husbands than wives are victims in VP mate slayings means that (1) husbands actually may provoke their wives more often than wives provoke their husbands to assault their respective mates; or (2) assuming that provocation by wives is as intense and equally as frequent, or even more frequent, than provocation by husbands, then husbands may not receive and define provocation stimuli with as great or as violent a reaction as do wives; or (3) husbands may have a greater felt sense of guilt in a marital conflict for one reason or another, and receive verbal insults and overt physical assaults without retaliation as a form of compensatory punishment; or (4) husbands may withdraw more often than wives from the scene of marital conflict, and thus eliminate, for the time being, a violent overt reaction to their wives' provocation. Clearly, this is only a suggestive, not an exhaustive, list of probable explanations. In any case, we are left with the undeniable fact that husbands more often than wives are major, precipitating factors in their own homicidal deaths.

Alcohol

In the larger work of which this study is a part, the previous discovery of an association between the presence of alcohol in the homicide situation and Negro male offenders, combined with knowledge of the important contribution Negro males make to their own victimization, suggests an association (by transitivity) between VP homicide and the presence of alcohol. Moreover, whether alcohol is present in the victim or offender, lowered inhibitions due to ingestion of alcohol may cause an individual to give vent more freely to pent up frustrations, tensions, and emotional conflicts that have either built up over a prolonged period of time or that arise within an immediate emotional crisis. The data do in fact confirm the suggested hypothesis above and reveal a *significant* association between VP homicide and alcohol in the homicide situation. Comparison of VP to non-VP cases with respect to the presence of alcohol in the homicide situation (alcohol present in either the victim, offender, or both), reveals that alcohol was present in 74 percent of the VP cases and in 60 percent of the non-VP cases. The proportional difference results in a *significant* association between alcohol and VP homicide. It should be noted that the association is not necessarily a causal one, or that a causal relationship is not proved by the association.

Because the present analysis is concerned primarily with the contribution of the victim to the homicide, it is necessary to determine whether an association exists between VP homicide and presence of alcohol in the victim. No association was found to exist between VP homicide and alcohol in the offender. But victims had been drinking immediately prior to their death in more VP cases (69 percent) than in non-VP cases (47 percent). A positive and *significant* relationship is, therefore, clearly established between victims who had been drinking and who precipitated their own death. In many of these cases the victim was intoxicated, or nearly so, and lost control of his own defensive powers. He frequently was a victim with no intent to harm anyone maliciously, but who, nonetheless, struck his friend, acquaintance, or wife, who later became his assailant. Impulsive, aggressive, and often danger-ously violent, the victim was the first to slap, punch, stab, or in some other manner commit an assault. Perhaps the presence of alcohol in this kind of homicide victim played no small part in his taking this first and major physical step toward victimiza-tion. Perhaps if he had not been drinking he would have been less violent, less ready to plunge into an assaultive stage of interaction. Or, if the presence of alcohol had no causal relation to his being the first to assault, perhaps it reduced his facility to com-bat successfully, to defend himself from retaliatory assault and, hence, contributed in this way to his death.

Previous Arrest Record

The victim-precipitator is the first actor in the homicide drama to display and to use a deadly weapon; and the description of him thus far infers that he is in some respects an offender in reverse. Because he is the first to assume an aggressive role, he probably has engaged previously in similar but less serious physical assaults. On the basis of these assumptions several meaningful hypotheses were established and tested. Each hypothesis is supported by empirical data, which in some cases reach the level of statistical significance accepted by this study; and in other cases indicate strong associations in directions suggested by the hypotheses. A summary of each hypothesis with its collated data follows:

1. In VP cases, the victim is more likely than the offender to have a previous arrest, or police, record. The data show that 62 percent of the victims and 54 percent of the offenders in VP cases have a previous record.

2. A higher proportion of VP victims than non-VP victims have a previous police record. Comparison reveals that 62 percent of the VP victims but only 42 percent of non-VP victims have a previous record. The association between VP victims and previous arrest record is a *significant* one.

3. With respect to the percentage having a previous arrest record, VP victims are more similar to non-VP offenders than to non-VP victims. Examina-tion of the data reveals no significant difference between VP victims and non-VP offenders with a previous record. This lack of a significant differ-ence is very meaningful and confirms the validity of the proposition above. While 62 percent of VP victims have a police record, 68 percent of non-VP offenders have such a record, and we have already noted in (2) above that only 42 percent of non-VP victims have a record. Thus, the existence of a statistically *significant* difference between VP victims and non-VP victims and the *lack* of a statistically significant difference between VP victims and non-VP offenders indicate that the victim of VP homicide is quite sim-ilar to the offender in non-VP homicide—and that the VP victim more closely resembles the non-VP offender than the non-VP victim.

4. A higher proportion of VP victims than of non-VP victims have a record of offenses against the person. The data show a *significant* association between VP victims and a previous record of offenses against the person, for 37 percent of VP victims and only 21 percent of non-VP victims have a record of such offenses.

5. Also with respect to the percentage having a previous arrest record of offenses against the person, VP victims are more similar to non-VP

offenders than non-VP victims. Analysis of the data indicates support for this assumption, for we have observed that the difference between VP victims (37 percent) and non-VP victims (21 percent) is *significant*; this difference is almost twice as great as the difference between VP victims (27 percent) and non-VP offenders (46 percent), and this latter difference is not significant. The general tendency again is for victims in VP homicides to resemble offenders in non-VP homicides.

6. A lower proportion of VP offenders have a previous arrest record than do non-VP offenders. The data also tend to support this hypothesis, for 54 percent of offenders in VP cases, compared to 68 percent of offenders in non-VP cases have a previous police record.

In general, the rank order of recidivism—defined in terms of having a previous arrest record and of having a previous record of assaults—or victims and offenders involved in the two types of homicide is as follows:

	Percent with Previous Arrest Record	Percent with Previous Record of Assault
1. Offenders in non-VP Homicide	68	46
2. Victims in VP Homicide	62	37
3. Offenders in VP Homicide	54	33
4. Victims in non-VP Homicide	42	21

Because he is the initial aggressor and has provoked his subsequent slayer into killing him, this particular type of victim (VP) is likely to have engaged previously in physical assaults which were either less provoking than the present situation, or which afforded him greater opportunity to defer attacks made upon him. It is known officially that over one-third of them assaulted others previously. It is not known how many formerly provoked others to assault them. In any case, the circumstances leading up to the present crime in which he plays the role of victim are probably not foreign to him since he has, in many cases, participated in similar encounters before this, his last episode.

Summary

Criminal homicide usually involves intense personal interaction in which the victim's behavior is often an important factor. As Porterfield has recently pointed out,

> the intensity of interaction between the murderer and his victim may vary from complete non-participation on the part of the victim to almost perfect cooperation with the killer in the process of getting killed. . . . It is amazing to note the large number of would-be murderers who become the victim.[11]

By defining a VP homicide in terms of the victim's direct, immediate, and positive contribution to his own death, manifested by his being the first to make a physical assault, it has been possible to identify 150 VP cases.

Comparison of this VP group with non-VP cases reveals *significantly* higher proportions of the following characteristics among VP homicide:

- Negro victims;
- Negro offenders;

- husbands who are victims in mate slayings;

- male victims;
- female offenders;
- stabbings;
- victim-offender relationship involving male victims of female offenders;
- mate slayings;

- alcohol in the homicide situation;
- alcohol in the victim;
- victims with a previous arrest record; and
- victims with a previous arrest record of assault.

In addition, VP homicides have slightly higher proportions than non-VP homicides of altercations and domestic quarrels; inter-racial slayings, victims who are close friends, relatives, or acquaintances of their slayers.

Empirical evidence analyzed in the present study lends support to, and measurement of, von Hentig's theoretical contention that "there are cases in which they (victim and offender) are reversed and in the long chain of causative forces the victim assumes the role of a determinant."[12]

In many cases the victim has most of the major characteristics of an offender; in some cases two potential offenders come together in a homicide situation and it is probably often only chance which results in one becoming a victim and the other an offender. At any rate, connotations of a victim as a weak and passive individual, seeking to withdraw from an assaultive situation, and of an offender as a brutal, strong, and overly aggressive person seeking out his victim, are not always correct. Societal attitudes are generally positive toward the victim and negative toward the offender, who is often feared as a violent and dangerous threat to others when not exonerated. However, data in the present study—especially that of previous arrest record—mitigate, destroy, or reverse these connotations of victim-offender roles in one out of every four criminal homicides.

Notes

[1] von Hentig, Hans, *The Criminal and His Victim*, New Haven: Yale University Press, 1948, pp. 383–385.

[2] Tarde, Gabriel, *Penal Philosophy*, Boston: Little, Brown, & Company, 1912, p. 466.

[3] De Quincey, Thomas, "On Murder Considered as One of the Fine Arts," *The Arts of Cheating, Swindling, and Murder*, Edward Bulwer-Lytton, and Douglas Jerrold, and Thomas De Quincey, New York: The Arnold Co., 1925, p. 153.

[4] Garofalo, Baron Raffaele, *Criminology*, Boston: Little, Brown, & Company, 1914, p. 373.

[5] For an excellent discussion of the rule of provocation, from which these four requirements are taken, see: Rollin M. Perkins, "The Law of Homicide," *Journal of Criminal Law and Criminology*, (March–April, 1946), 36: 412–427; and Herbert Wechsler and Jerome Michael, *A Rationale of the Law of Homicide*, pp. 1280–1282. A general review of the rule of provocation, both in this country and abroad, may be found in *The Royal Commission on Capital Punishment, 1949–1952 Report*, Appendix II, pp. 453–458.

[6] *Ibid.*, p. 425. The term "cause" is here used in a legal and not a psychological sense.

[7] In order to facilitate reading of the following sections, the *victim-precipitated* cases are referred to simply as VP cases or VP homicides. Those homicides in which the victim was not a direct precipitator are referred to as non-VP cases.

[8] Of 588 victims, 228, or 39 percent, were stabbed; 194, or 33 percent, were shot; 128, or 22 percent, were beaten; and 38, or 6 percent, were killed by other methods.

[9] Only 550 victim-offender relationships are identified since 38 of the 588 criminal homicides are classified as unsolved, or those in which the perpetrator is unknown.

[10] The diagonal line represents "killed by." Thus, Negro male/Negro male means a Negro male killed by a Negro male; the victim precedes the offender.

[11] Porterfield, Austin L. and Talbert, Robert H., *Mid-Century Crime in our Culture: Personality and Crime in the Cultural Patterns of American States*, Fort Worth: Leo Potishman Foundation, 1954, pp. 47–48.

[12] von Hentig, *op. cit.*, p. 383.

7

Violent Crime: Homicide, Assault, Rape, Robbery

National Commission on the Causes and Prevention of Violence

When citizens express concern about high levels of violence in the United States, they have in mind a number of different types of events: homicides and assaults, rioting and looting, clashes between demonstrators and police, student seizures of university buildings, violence in the entertainment media, assassinations of national leaders. Foremost in their minds, no doubt, is what appears to be a rising tide of individual acts of violent crime, especially "crime in the streets."

Only a fraction of all crime is violent, of course. Major crimes of violence—homicide, rape, robbery, and assault—represent only 13 percent (or 588,000) of the Federal Bureau of investigation's Index of reported serious crimes (about 4.5 million in 1968).[1] Moreover, deaths and personal injuries from violent crime cause only a small part of the pain and suffering which we experience: one is five times more likely to die in an auto accident than to be criminally slain, and one hundred times more likely to be injured in a home accident than in a serious assault.

But to suffer deliberate violence is different from experiencing an accident, illness or other misfortune. In violent crime man becomes a wolf to man, threatening or destroying the personal safety of his victim in a terrifying act. Violent crime (particularly street crime) engenders fear—the deep-seated fear of the hunted in the presence of the hunter. Today this fear is gnawing at the vitals of urban America.

In a recent national survey, half of the women and one-fifth of the men said they were afraid to walk outdoors at night, even near their homes. One-third of American householders keep guns in the hope that they will provide protection against intruders. In some urban neighborhoods, nearly one-third of the residents wish to move because of high rates of crime, and very large numbers have moved for that reason. In fear of crime, bus drivers in many cities do not carry change, cab drivers in some areas are in scarce supply, and some merchants are closing their businesses. Vigilante-like groups have sprung up in some areas.

Source: Reprinted from *To Establish Justice and to Ensure Domestic Tranquility*, Final Report of the National Commission on the Causes and Prevention of Violence (Washington, DC: Government Printing Office, 1969), pp. 17–27. An edited version of statement issued November 24, 1969.

Fear of crime is destroying some of the basic human freedoms which any society is supposed to safeguard—freedom of movement, freedom from harm, freedom from fear itself. Is there a basis for this fear? Is there an unprecedented increase in violent crime in this country? Who and where are most of the violent criminals and what makes them violent? What can we do to eliminate the causes of that violence?

Profile of Violent Crime

Between 1960 and 1968, the national rate of criminal homicide per 100,000 population increased 36 percent, the rate of forcible rape 65 percent, of aggravated assault 67 percent, and of robbery 119 percent. These figures are from the *Uniform Crime Reports* published by the Federal Bureau of Investigation. These Reports are the only national indicators we have of crime in America. But, as the FBI recognizes, they must be used with caution.

There is a large gap between the reported rates and the true rates. In 1967 the President's Commission on Law Enforcement and Administration of Justice stated that the true rate of total major violent crime was roughly twice as high as the reported rate.[2] This ratio has probably been a changing one. Decreasing public tolerance of crime is seemingly causing more crimes to be reported. Changes in police practices, such as better recording procedures and more intensive patrolling, are causing police statistics to dip deeper into the large well of unreported crime. Hence, some part of the increase in reported rates of violent crime is no doubt due to a fuller disclosure of the violent crimes actually committed.

Moreover, while current rates compare unfavorably, even alarmingly, with those of the 1950s, fragmentary information available indicates that at the beginning of this century there was an upsurge in violent crime which probably equaled today's levels. In 1916, the city of Memphis reported a homicide rate more than seven times its present rate. Studies in Boston, Chicago and New York during the years of the First World War and the 1920s showed violent crime rates considerably higher than those evident in the first published national crime statistics in 1933. Despite all these factors, it is still clear that *significant and disturbing increases in the true rates of homicide and, especially, of assault and robbery have occurred over the last decade.* While the reported incidence of forcible rape has also increased, reporting difficulties associated with this crime are too great to permit any firm conclusion on the true rate of increase.

Violent crimes are not evenly distributed throughout the nation. Using new data from a Victim-Offender Survey conducted by our staff Task Force on Individual Acts of Violence, standard data from the FBI, and facts from other recent studies, we can sketch a more accurate profile of violent crime in the United States than has hitherto been possible. We note, however, that our information about crime is still unsatisfactory and that many critical details in the profile of violent crime remain obscure. Moreover, we strongly urge all who study this profile to keep two facts constantly in mind. First, violent crime is to be found in all regions of the country, and among all groups of the population—not just in the areas and groups of greatest concentration to which we draw attention. Second, despite heavy concentrations of crime in certain groups, the overwhelming majority of individuals in these groups are law-abiding citizens.

1. **Violent crime in the United States is primarily a phenomenon of large cities. This is a fact of central importance.**

The 26 cities with 500,000 or more residents and containing about 17 percent of our total population contribute about 45 percent of the total reported major violent crimes. Six cities with one million or more residents and having ten percent of our total population contribute 30 percent of the total reported major violent crimes.

Large cities uniformly have the highest reported violent crime levels per unit of population.[3] Smaller cities, suburbs and rural areas have lower levels. The average rate of major violent offenses in cities of over 50,000 [sic] inhabitants is eleven times greater than in rural areas, eight times greater than in suburban areas, and five and one-half times greater than in cities with 50,000 to 100,000 inhabitants.

For cities of all sizes, as well as for suburbs and rural areas, there has been a recent upward trend in violent crime; the increase in the city rate has been much more dramatic than that for the other areas and subdivisions.

The result in our larger cities is a growing risk of victimization: in Baltimore, the nation's leader in violent crime, the risk of being the victim of a reported violent crime is one in 49 per year. Thus, in the context of major violent crimes, the popular phrase "urban crisis" is pregnant with meaning.

2. Violent crime in the city is overwhelmingly committed by males.

Judgments about overall trends and levels of violent crime, and about variations in violent crime according to city size, can be based upon reported offense data. But conclusions about the sex, age, race, and socioeconomic status of violent offenders can be based only on arrest data. Besides the gap previously mentioned between true offense rates and reported offense rates, we must now deal also with the even larger gap between *offenses reported* and *arrests made*. Accordingly, conclusions in these areas must be drawn with extreme care, especially since arrests, as distinguished from convictions, are made by policemen whose decisions in apprehending suspects thus determine the nature of arrest statistics.[4]

In spite of the possibly wide margins of error, however, one fact is clearly indisputable: violent crimes in urban areas are disproportionately caused by male offenders. To the extent that females are involved, they are more likely to commit the more "intimate" violent crimes like homicide than the "street crimes" like robbery. Thus, the 1968 reported male homicide rate was five times higher than the female rate; the robbery rate twenty times higher.

3. Violent crime in the city is concentrated especially among youths between the ages of fifteen and twenty-four.

Urban arrest rates for homicide are much higher among the 18-24 age group than among any other; for rape, robbery and aggravated assault, arrests in the 15-24 age group far outstrip those of any other group. Moreover, it is in these age groups that the greatest increases in all arrest rates have occurred. Surprisingly, however, there have also been dramatic and disturbing increases in arrest rates of the 10-14 age group for two categories—a 300 percent increase in assault between 1958 and 1967, and 200 percent in robbery in the same period.

4. Violent crime in the city is committed primarily by individuals at the lower end of the occupational scale.

Although there are no regularly collected national data on the socio-economic status of violent offenders, local studies indicate that poor and uneducated individuals with few employment skills are much more likely to commit serious violence than persons higher on the socioeconomic ladder. A forthcoming University of Pennsylvania study of youthful male offenders in Philadelphia, for example, will show that boys from lower income areas in the city have delinquency rates for assaultive crimes nearly five times the rates of boys from higher income areas; delinquency rates for robbery are six times higher.[5] Other studies have found higher involvement in violence by persons at the lower end of the occupational scale. A succession of studies at the University of Pennsylvania, using Philadelphia police data, show that persons ranging from skilled laborers to the unemployed constitute about 90-95 percent of the criminal homicide offenders, 90 percent of the rape offenders and 92-97 percent of the robbery offenders. A St. Louis study of aggravated assault found that blue collar workers predominate as offenders. The District of Columbia Crime Commission found more than 40 percent of the major violent crime offenders to be unemployed.

5. Violent crime in the cities stems disproportionately from the ghetto slum where most Negroes live.

Reported national urban arrest rates are much higher for Negroes than for whites in all four major violent crime categories, ranging from ten or eleven times higher for assault and rape to sixteen or seventeen times higher for robbery and homicide.[6] As we shall show, these differences in urban violent crime rates are not, in fact, racial; they are primarily a result of conditions of life in the ghetto slum. The gap between Negro and white crime rates can be expected to close as the opportunity gap between Negro and white also closes—a development which has not yet occurred.

The large national urban differentials between Negroes and whites are also found in the more intensive Philadelphia study previously cited. Of 10,000 boys born in 1945, some 50 percent of the three thousand non-whites had had at least one police contact by age 18, compared with 20 percent of the seven thousand whites. (A police contact means that the subject was taken into custody for an offense other than a traffic violation and a report recording his alleged offense was prepared and retained in police files.) The differences were most pronounced for the major violent offenses: of fourteen juveniles who had police contacts for homicide, all were non-whites; of 44 who had police contacts for rape, 86 percent were non-whites and fourteen percent whites; of 193 who had police contacts for robbery, 90 percent were non-whites and ten percent whites; and of 220 who had police contacts for aggravated assault, 82 percent were non-whites and eighteen percent whites. When the three sets of figures for rape, robbery and assault are related to the number of non-whites and whites, respectively, in the total group studied (3,000 vs. 7,000), the differences between the resulting ratios closely reflect the differentials in the national urban arrest rates of non-whites and whites in the 10-17 age group.

6. The victims of assaultive violence in the cities generally have the same characteristics as the offenders: victimization rates are generally highest for males, youths, poor persons, and blacks. Robbery victims, however, are very often older whites.

There is a widespread public misconception that most violent crime is committed by black offenders against white victims. This is not true. Our Task Force Victim-Offender Survey covering seventeen cities has confirmed other evidence that serious assaultive violence in the city—homicide, aggravated assault and rape—is predominantly between white offenders and white victims and black offenders and black victims. The majority of these crimes involves blacks attacking blacks, while most of the remainder involve whites victimizing whites. Indeed, our Survey found that 90 percent of urban homicide, aggravated assaults and rapes involve victims and offenders of the same race.

In two-thirds of homicides and aggravated assaults in the city, and in three-fifths of the rapes, the victim is a Negro. Rape victims tend strongly to be younger women; the victims of homicide and aggravated assault are usually young males but include a higher proportion of older persons. Nearly four-fifths of homicide victims and two-thirds of the assault victims are male. Generalizing from these data, we may say that the typical victim of a violent assaultive crime is a young Negro male, or in the case of rape, a young Negro woman.

Robbery, on the other hand, is the one major violent crime in the city with a high inter-racial component: although about 38 percent of robberies in the Survey involve Negro offenders and victims, 45 percent involve Negroes robbing whites— very often young black males robbing somewhat older white males. In three-fifths of all robberies the victim is white and nearly two-thirds of the time he or she is age 26 or over. Four-fifths of the time the victim is a man.

Data collected by the Crime Commission indicate that victimization rates for violent crimes are much higher in the lower-income groups. This is clearly true for robbery and rape, where persons with incomes under $6,000 were found to be victimized three to five times more often than persons with incomes over $6,000. The same relation held, but less strongly, for aggravated assault, while homicide victimization rates by income could not be computed under the investigative techniques used.

7. Unlike robbery, the other violent crimes of homicide, assault and rape tend to be acts of passion among intimates and acquaintances.

The Victim-Offender Survey shows that homicide and assault usually occur between relatives, friends or acquaintances (about two-thirds to three-fourths of the cases in which the relationship is known). They occur in the home or other indoor locations about 50-60 percent of the time. Rape is more likely to be perpetrated by a stranger (slightly over half of the cases), usually in the home or other indoor location (about two-thirds of the time). By contrast, robbery is usually committed outside (two-thirds of the cases) by a stranger (more than 80 percent of the cases).

The victim, the offender, or both are likely to have been drinking prior to homicide, assault, and rape, and the victim often provokes or otherwise helps precipitate the crime. The ostensible motives in homicide and assault are often relatively trivial, usually involving spontaneous altercations, family quarrels, jealous rages, and the like. The two crimes are similar; there is often no reason to believe that the person guilty of homicide sets out with any more intention to harm than the one who commits an aggravated assault. Except for the seriousness of the final outcomes, the major distinction is that homicides most often involve handguns while knives are most common in assault.[7]

8. By far the greatest proportion of all serious violence is committed by repeaters.

While the number of hard-core repeaters is small compared to the number of one-time offenders, the former group has a much higher rate of violence and inflicts considerably more serious injury. In the Philadelphia study, 627 of the 10,000 boys were chronic offenders, having five or more police contacts. Though they represented only six percent of the boys in the study, they accounted for 53 percent of the police contacts for personal attacks—homicide, rape and assault—and 71 percent of the contacts for robberies.

Offenders arrested for major criminal violence generally have long criminal histories, but these careers are mainly filled with offenses other than the final serious acts. Generally, though there are many exceptions, the more serious the crime committed, the less chance it will be repeated.

9. Americans generally are no strangers to violent crime.

Although it is impossible to determine accurately how many Americans commit violent crimes each year,[8] the data that are available suggest that the number is substantial, ranging from perhaps 600,000 to 1,000,000—or somewhere between one in every 300 and one in every 150 persons. Undoubtedly, a far greater number commit a serious violent crime at some time in their lives. The Philadelphia study found that of about 10,000 boys 35 percent (3,475) were taken into police custody for delinquency, and of the delinquents ten percent (363) were apprehended once or more for a major crime of violence before age eighteen.

A comparison of reported violent crime rates in this country with those in other modern, stable nations shows the United States to be the clear leader. Our homicide rate is more than twice that of our closest competitor, Finland, and from four to twelve times higher than the rates in a dozen other advanced countries including Japan, Canada, England and Norway. Similar patterns are found in the rates of other violent crimes: averages computed for the years 1963-1967 show the United States rape rate to be twelve times that of England and Wales and three times that of Canada; our robbery rate is nine times that of England and Wales and double that of Canada; our aggravated assault rate is double that of England and Wales and eighteen times that of Canada. . . .

Notes

1. The FBI Index of Reported Crime classifies seven offenses as "serious crimes"—homicide, forcible rape, robbery, aggravated assault, burglary, larceny of more than $50 and auto theft. It classifies the first four—homicide, rape, robbery and assault—as "violent crimes" because they involve the doing or threatening of bodily injury.

2. Reasons for the gap include failure of citizens to report crimes because they believe police cannot be effective in solving them; others do not want to take the time to report, some do not know how to report, and others fear reprisals.

3. The direct correlation between city size and violent crime rates may not be as uniform in the South as in other regions. Available data indicate higher suburban violent crime rates relative to city rates in the South, suggesting the possibility that smaller city rates may also be higher relative to larger city rates in the South (although direct evidence on this point is not presently available).

   Also, it should be kept in mind that the relationships noted in the text are for cities within certain population ranges (e.g., more than 250,000, 100,000-250,000, etc.), not for individual cities. Thus the five cities with the highest metropolitan violent crime rates in 1968—Baltimore, Newark, Washington, San Francisco and Detroit—had smaller populations than some very large cities with somewhat lower rates of violent crime.

4. According to the FBI *Uniform Crime Reports*, about half of all arrests for serious crimes result in pleas of guilty or convictions; in only 88 percent of all arrests does the prosecutor decide he has sufficient evidence to try the case, and of those cases that are prosecuted, only 62 percent result in a plea of guilty or a conviction, often for a lesser offense than the one originally charged. A wide margin of error thus exists between the making of an arrest and proof that the person arrested has committed an offense.

5. This is a study of 9,945 males born in 1945 and who lived in Philadelphia at least from age 10 to 18. Of this group, 3,475, or 35 percent, were taken into custody by the police for delinquent offenses other than traffic violations. Race, socio-economic status and many other variables are analyzed in this study, supported by NIMH, to be published shortly by Thorsten Sellin and Marvin E. Wolfgang under the title, *Delinquency in a Birth Cohort*.

6. Because some police commonly associate crime with Negroes more than with whites, Negroes may be disproportionately arrested on suspicion, thus producing a higher reported Negro involvement in crime than is the true situation.

7. In Chapter 6, "Violence and Law Enforcement," this Commission indicates that gun attacks are fatal in one out of five cases, on the average; knife attacks are fatal in one out of twenty.

8. The FBI has reported that, in 1968, 588,000 violent crimes occurred. This is about 300 crimes of major violence per each 100,000 Americans. It is generally estimated that only about half of all violent crimes are reported; if this is true, the total number of violent crimes per year is in the range of 1,200,000 or 600 per 100,000 people. These are *offenses*, not *offenders*. Since violent crimes often involve several offenders committing a single crime—particularly among the large number of juvenile offenders—a fair guess might be that twice as many offenders (2,400,000) were involved. But some offenders account for more than one crime per year. If we assume the commission of two crimes per year per offender, the total number of offenders drops back to 1,200,000; if we assume the commission of four crimes per year per offender, the total number of offenders is 600,000. Thus the number of Americans who commit violent crimes each year appears to be somewhere between these figures—between one in every 150 and one in every 300 Americans. Since children under twelve and adults over 45 commit relatively few crimes, the rate for persons between 12 and 45 is even higher.

8

Delinquency in a Birth Cohort

Marvin E. Wolfgang   Thorsten Sellin   Robert Figlio

. . . Most studies of recidivism have been retrospective, that is, based on selected groups of offenders—such as juveniles committed to correctional schools, or persons convicted of crimes or committed to penal institutions—whose prior history of delinquency or crime could be analyzed. Prospective studies have been much less common, that is, studies of the conduct of selected groups of offenders during a period of considerable length usually beginning at the adjudication of a person as delinquent, his conviction of crime, or his commitment to or release from a correctional institution.

Because neither of these two types of research can arrive at more than partial information about recidivism, we thought it would be worthwhile to approach the problem in a different manner: namely, by a study of the history of the delinquency of a birth cohort—a population born in a particular year, whose conflicts with the law could be examined during a segment of the cohort's lifetime, ending with entry into adulthood. Such an inquiry would permit us to note the age of onset and the progression or cessation of delinquency. It would allow us to relate these phenomena to certain personal or social characteristics of the delinquents and to make appropriate comparisons with that part of the cohort that did not have official contact with the law.

We therefore decided to study delinquency and its absence in a cohort consisting of all boys born in 1945 and residing in Philadelphia from a date no later than their tenth birthday until at least their eighteenth. Girls were excluded, partly because of their low delinquency rates and partly because the presence of the boys in the city at the terminal age mentioned could be established from the record of their registration for military service. The fact that no large-scale study of this particular kind had been done previously in the United States gave an additional stimulus to the project and aided us in securing financial support for it from the National Institute of Mental Health.

The Recognized Need for Cohort Studies

The desirability of investigating the offensivity of cohorts has been recognized for a long time. As early as 1890, H. von Scheel, director of Germany's National Bureau of Statistics, wrote:

Source: Reprinted with permission from Marvin E. Wolfgang, Thorsten Sellin and Robert Figlio, *Delinquency in a Birth Cohort*, pp. 4–5, 244–245. Copyright © 1972 The University of Chicago Press. Notes renumbered; some notes omitted.

Ideal criminal statistics that would follow carefully the evolution of criminal tendencies in a given population should work not with crude annual contingents but with generations. They should start with the first offenders of a given year and continue to observe these persons, showing their later convictions, instead of counting them as new individuals each time they are convicted.[1]

Later, Otto Köbner noted that "correct statistics of offenders can be developed only by a study of the total life history of individuals."[2]. .

In order to provide enough cases for assessing our probability model we decided to obtain information on *all* boys born in 1945 who lived in Philadelphia at least between their tenth and their eighteenth birthdays. This complete enumeration (within the limits of our knowledge and accuracy of the school and police records) yielded 9,945 boys, of whom 3,475 had at least one recorded police contact.

From the school records we obtained most of the background data such as: name, birth date, race, name of parents or guardians, addresses, country of origin for parents and subject, I.Q. scores, achievement level, number of unexcused absences, behavior (if incorrigible), highest grade completed, and termination date. From the records of the Juvenile Aid Division of the Philadelphia Police Department we obtained information on the number, type; and dates of offenses committed by members of the cohort, as well as the full descriptions of the events, including aspects of physical injury, property theft or damage, use of weapons, disposition of the case, and any other relevant information about the event, victim, or offender which was deemed important for this and future analysis. Finally, as an additional check on the whereabouts of the cohort members during the time period ending with the eighteenth birthday, we checked the selective service registration for Philadelphia residency at the terminal year.

Through a collation of these three data banks we were able to account for the physical location of the cohort members at least from the tenth birthday—and generally from birth—through the eighteenth birthday.

Of the 9,945 cohort subjects, 3,475 or some 35 percent of the boys were involved with the police at least once to the extent that an official recording of the act resulted, while 6,470 or 65 percent never had any such experience. Seven thousand and forty-three (71%) boys were white, and 2,902 (29%) were nonwhite. Of the whites, 2,071 or 28.6 percent were classified as offenders while 1,458 or 50.2 percent of the nonwhite boys were likewise designated. Slightly more than half (54%) of the cohort members were from the higher socioeconomic status (SES) group, of whom 26.5 percent were delinquent: 46 percent of the cohort were in the lower SES classification, of whom 44.8 percent were delinquent.

After examining the relationship between the various background variables of race, SES, types of schools attended, residential and school moves, highest grade completed, I.Q., achievement level, and the state of being delinquent or not, we concluded that the variables of race and SES (of somewhat lesser importance) were most strongly related to the offender-nonoffender classification. The remaining variables in the school records had little or no relationship to delinquency status. For example, the variable of achievement level is inversely related to delinquency, that is, high achievers are much less likely to be classified as offenders than are low achievers. However, the relationship between race and achievement is such that most of the variation between achievement and delinquency status is explained by race, for being a poor achiever is highly related to being nonwhite. This relationship also exists between race and the remaining background variables, with the exception of SES.

Thus we found a nexus of factors related to race and delinquency which we referred to as a "disadvantaged" position. The nonwhite delinquent boy is likely to belong to the lower socioeconomic group, experience a greater number of school and residential moves (that is, be subject to the disrupting forces of intracity mobility more than the nondelinquent) and have the lowest average grade completed, the lowest achievement level, and the lowest I.Q. score.

We were then led to divide the cohort further into groups of nonoffenders, one-time offenders, and recidivists. Of the delinquents in the cohort, 54 percent were recidivists and 46 percent one-timers.

In comparing the three groups on the various background variables, we found that the recidivists, one-time offenders, and nonoffenders lie on a continuum. Recidivists experience the greatest school and residential mobility, attain the lowest I.Q. scores and achievement levels, and complete the least number of school years. Nonoffenders lie on the other end of the continuum, and one-timers fall between the two.

Recidivists are more likely to be low SES nonwhites than are onetime offenders or nonoffenders. Low SES boys have a higher rate of multiple than of single offense commission, but the reverse is true among high SES boys. Nonwhites exhibit a higher multiple offender rate, 328.4 as against 173.3 for one-timers, while the white multiple rate is 129.1 as against 157.6 for one-timers. When race and SES are considered jointly, low SES white boys have a higher rate of recidivism than of one-time offense commission, and high SES white boys are more likely to be one-time offenders. Such was not the case with nonwhites. Both high and low SES nonwhite youths generated higher rates of recidivism than of one-time violative behavior. In terms of the offense rate, rather than the offender rates discussed above, the nonwhite rate is about three times as high as that of the whites (1,983.4 compared to 632.9), while the offense rate for the whole cohort is 1,027 offenses per 1,000 cohort members.

In addition to describing certain characteristics of offenders we may also outline some facets of the offenses, particularly those of the severe or "index" variety. Nonwhite rates for offenses against both body and property are higher than those of whites, especially for attacks of robbery. Although low SES boys exhibited higher rates for these kinds of offenses than did high SES boys, the differentials were not so great as those according to race.

Because recidivists are more than twice as likely to commit index offenses than are one-time offenders, the index crime rate of recidivists is higher than that of one-timers; such is the case regardless of race or SES. Nonetheless, the spread between the white one-time and recidivist index crime rates is about three times the nonwhite spread, indicating that a proportionately greater number of index crimes are being committed by one-time, nonwhite boys. On the basis of SES rather than race, the spread between one-time and recidivist rates is only about twice as great among high SES boys as among low SES boys.

In this study an additional dimension has been added for the assessment of offense severity, the S-W seriousness score. Thus, when we examined the relative seriousness of injury offenses, we observed that the more serious forms of bodily harm are committed by nonwhites. The highest injury mean seriousness score follows from attacks by low SES, recidivist, nonwhite offenders (241.9), while the lowest injury mean seriousness score results from attacks by high SES, one-time, nonwhite offenders (100.00). Within each SES level across racial groups, the differences in weighted rates of injury and mean seriousness scores are insignificant for one-time offenders, although the weighted rate based on seriousness score indicates that the 14 homicides committed by nonwhite recidivists represent more community harm than the total seriousness for all of the 465 acts of physical injury perpetrated by all white offenders during their juvenile years.

Most damage offenses are trivial (under $10 in value). The median amount of damage done by whites is $14.63 and is higher than that inflicted by nonwhites ($11.43). About two-fifths of the theft offenses involve amounts of less than $10. White boys commit fewer thefts but steal more per offense.

We undertook an additional subgrouping of the offenders by defining as chronic offenders those boys who committed more than four violations. This group of 627 chronic offenders (18% of the total number of offenders) was responsible for over one-half of all offenses. The nonchronic recidivists (more than one offense but less than five) accounted for 36 percent of the offenders but for only 33 percent of the offenses.

Because there were proportionately three times as many nonwhite recidivists as white recidivists, nonwhites were much more likely than whites to appear in both the chronic and nonchronic offender groups. In fact, nonwhites were most overrepresented in the chronic category, being found five times as frequently as were whites, and in the nonchronic group, twice as frequently.

When SES is controlled, the same pattern emerges. Within both SES levels, nonwhites are more likely than whites to be recidivists, and of the recidivists, nonwhites are more likely than whites to be chronic offenders. Within both races, low SES boys are more likely to be chronic offenders than are high SES boys, although the differences between SES groups, holding race constant, are not so great as the differences between whites and nonwhites.

Chronic offenders in the cohort had a greater number of residential moves, lower I.Q. scores, a greater percentage classified as retarded, and fewer grades completed than did either the nonchronic or the one-time offenders, even when race and SES are considered.

The relationship between the total number of offenses a boy commits and the mean seriousness score of those offenses is direct and positive. The mean seriousness score of one-time offenders is lower than that of the nonchronics, which in turn is lower than that of the chronic offenders. However, it does not follow that, as a delinquent commits more offenses, his seriousness score necessarily escalates. On the contrary, we found that the seriousness score for all offenses, excepting attacks against the person by nonwhites, remained practically constant and in a few instances (certain damage, combination, and injury offenses committed by whites) actually diminished as the number of offenses increased.

If, as we have suggested, the probabilities of offense commission when classified by type (nonindex (N), injury (I), theft (T), damage (D), and combination of I, T, or D) are relatively constant over offense number, then the average seriousness score per person must be greater for those boys who commit many offenses because they are likely to commit a greater number of more serious offenses. Thus we are not saying, in general, that offense careers escalate in seriousness as the number of offenses increases, but that the simple addition of serious offenses will force up the average score per person for recidivists—particularly for chronics.

The relationship between offense number and offense severity, however, is not so easily explained, for we know from the dynamic analysis of offense histories . . . that, once a boy has committed an index offense, the likelihood of a repeat sometime in his career is much greater than the initial probability of commission, be it injury, theft, or a combination of these offense types. This inference is based on the assumption that a constant probability matrix of offense transitions obtains for each offense number (the first, second, third offense, and so on). Thus the probability of a serious offense repeat sometime in a delinquent's career must be positively related to increasing offense number.

Nevertheless, with the exception of injury offenses committed by nonwhites, which are typified by a strong positive relationship between offense number and severity, it is not readily apparent from the plots of offense severity by types of offense that repeats of index offenses are likely to be more serious with each additional commission, for these plots refer to the severity of offenses regardless of the types or types of previous offenses. Under such conditions, escalation does appear in some offense types but it is of a very small magnitude.

If, on the other hand, the type of previous offense is considered, then the repeat of the same type of offense (if it occurs) is very likely to be more serious. The magnitude of that increase depends upon offense type and race (comparatively large for nonwhite injury and white theft repeats, rather small for nonindex repeats, and nonexistent for damage repeats).

Thus we see that the accumulation of seriousness scores by cohort members is a complex phenomenon, being a function of (a) the number of offenses under the assumption of a fixed transition matrix, (b) some increase in seriousness score of repeats of like offense types, and (c) a weak propensity toward offense type specialization.

We may discuss briefly here some of the findings introduced above concerning the offense transition matrices. First, it will be recalled, we discovered that the probability of offense commission when classified by type (nonindex, injury, theft, damage, and combination of I, T, D) varies very little from the initial probability vectors (probabilities associated with the commission of the first offense) over the first fifteen offenses when the type of previous offense is disregarded. This is a very significant finding, for it implies that the delinquents in this cohort are not shifting in any uniform way to the index offenses as offense number increases. If such shifts were to exist, the probabilities of offense commission for those types of offenses having such increased likelihoods of occurrence would become higher with each additional offense. Thus we would have evidence for a hypothesis of "channeling" along these index pathways. Although the slopes of the regression lines of offense probability on offense number are positive for most offense types and for all race and SES groups, the increment per offense number is quite small, offering us little support for the above hypothesis.

If we carry this mode of analysis further by including the type of prior offense through the medium of the offense transition matrix, we uncover an even more surprising result. The offense transition matrices appear to be independent of offense number and, in fact, the same process seems to operate at each step in the offense histories. There is no "break" after which the offenders specialize along some discernible pathways. Indeed, with the exception of a small tendency of like offense repetition (particularly for theft offenses), the choice of the next offense follows the first offense probability vectors as mentioned above. The same conclusion holds for all offenders taken together and for whites and nonwhites separately.

Thus we concluded that the probability of offense commission, when classified by type, is independent of offense number. Conversely, the probability of desisting from further delinquency is also unrelated to the number of offenses committed, especially after the first two offenses.

Substantively, white boys are less likely than nonwhites to follow an offense with an act of physical violence, and whites are about twice as likely as nonwhites to desist from further delinquency after each offense.

We may now turn to the relationship of age to offense commission. The proportion of offenses committed of the total, and the proportion of boys violating the law, increase steadily from age 10 to just under age 16. From that point to age 18 the proportions decrease. These findings obtain for all race-SES combinations.

Another way of looking at this likelihood of offense commission over age is to use the probability of remaining in a state of desistance, which declines from .955 between 10 and 10 1/2 years of age uniformly to .675 at age 17 and back up to .720 and .795 from 17 1/2 to 18 years of age. The likelihood of violent criminality increases with age, while the likelihood of property offense commission irregularly increases and decreases over age. Overall, the offense switch matrices based on age groups indicate that the likelihood of all types (nonindex and index) of delinquent events increases during the years 14 to 17, and that the trend toward index offensivity is not at all marked (as we would expect from our findings on the probability of offense commission over offense number).

In comparing across race and SES we find that both whites and nonwhites commit a greater number of violent crimes as they age, although the rate of increase is greater for nonwhites. On the other hand, the number of property offenses declines with age for nonwhites and remains unchanged for whites. For low SES boys, violence increases while property theft and damage decrease as age advances. For high SES boys only violence increases, though only to a small extent, while property, theft, and damage remain unchanged.

Although the likelihood of offense commission is directly related to age, it must be stressed that those boys who commit many offenses are doing so within rather short time spans. We found that the mean age at commission of the first offense on out to the fifteenth, for those boys who went that far, ranged from about age 15 at the first offense to a little over age 16 at the fifteenth for all offense types taken together. Although some boys who started their delinquent careers at an early age and continued to accumulate many offenses may be lost in the mean ages at commission of the early offenses due to the influx of large numbers of one-time offenders at age 15-16, such would not be the case for the higher offense numbers, where the age dispersion would seem to be much less.

In terms of a crude offender rate based on age at onset of delinquency, 72 percent of the delinquents experienced their first police contact between the ages of 12 and 16. The probability of *first* offense commission increases from age 7 to age 14, sharply peaks at age 16, and decreases to age 18. These probabilities obtain for all race-SES combinations.

We have briefly analyzed the disposition of offenders taken into custody by the police. Some were given a remedial disposition, which means that the police recorded the delinquent behavior but did not further process the case for consideration by the juvenile court. Others were arrested formally and had their cases "adjusted" at an intake interview; still others were formally dealt with by means of a court penalty, such as probation or incarceration. Variables associated with a greater likelihood of a court penalty included being nonwhite, being of low SES level, committing an index offense, being a recidivist, and committing an offense with a relatively high seriousness score. However, in an effort to determine the relative effect of each of these variables, we had to conclude that the most significant factor related to a boy's not being remedialed by the police, but being processed to the full extent of the juvenile justice system, is his being nonwhite. That differential treatment based on race occurs is once again documented from this cohort study.

Finally, we may briefly note that the effect of disposition on the offense histories of the cohort members is unclear. It appears that the juvenile justice system has been able to isolate the hard core offender fairly well. Unfortunately, the product of this encounter with sanctioning authorities is far from desirable. Not only do a greater number of those who receive punitive treatment (institutionalization, fine, or probation) continue to violate the law, but they also commit more serious crimes with greater rapidity than those who experience a less constraining contact with the judicial and correctional systems. Thus, we must conclude that the juvenile justice system, at its best, has no effect on the subsequent behavior of adolescent boys and, at its worst, has a deleterious effect on future behavior. For it is clear that, if a selection process is operating which routes hard core delinquents into the courts and correctional institutions, no benefit is derived from this encounter, for the subsequent offense rates and seriousness scores show no reduction in volume and intensity. If the other process is in operation—that of random entrance into the juvenile justice system from the delinquent population—then we would expect either (1) no difference in subsequent offense rate and seriousness scores between those who were treated and those who were not, under the hypothesis that the justice system has no effect, or (2) higher subsequent offense rates and more serious offenses committed by those who were treated when compared to those who were not, under the hypothesis that the juvenile justice system is in fact doing more harm than good.

The task of tying this array of data together is difficult indeed, for this study of interrelationships offers a myriad of investigative avenues, of which we have explored only a few. We have, however, isolated several detrimental conditions which indirectly accompany the delinquent state, such as withdrawal from school without graduating, poor school achievement, weak performance on I.Q. tests, repeated intracity migration, and membership in the lower socioeconomic groups. We say that these factors are indirectly related to delinquency because they are strongly correlated with race, specifically with being nonwhite, which in turn relates to the likelihood of (a) being an offender, (b) being a recidivist or chronic offender, and (c) being an offender who commits serious violent crimes.

Although we have no data which may accurately be called etiological, we may at least suggest that the strength of these interrelationships among the various background and delinquency variables is sufficient to permit our discussing some appropriate implications. We know that boys who commit many offenses, some of them very serious, are very likely to be nonwhite members of the low socioeconomic group. We also know that only 35 percent of these particular boys desist from further delinquency after their first contact with the law. With this knowledge in mind, as unsurprising as it may be, it seems appropriate to suggest that community action programs which have as their goals the alleviation or modification of the above-mentioned conditions may also influence the course of juvenile delinquency within the subject areas. It has not been within the scope of the present investigation to comment on the character or form of such a program. Our data are such that we may refer only to those aspects of officially recorded existence which seem to be related to delinquent behavior.

If, on the other hand, an intervention program were to be suggested, the target of which would be the individual child rather than the community, some insight into the timing of such a program might be gained from the offense transition matrices in chapter 11. For it was in this chapter that we discussed the probabilities associated with various crime types in our investigation of the Markovian properties of the cohort offense histories.

We found that the offense transition matrices did not vary significantly over offense number. We also discovered that the choice of the type of the next offense is only very slightly related to the type of the prior offense or offenses. This finding leads us to the conclusion that the type of the next offense—be it injury, theft, damage, combination, or nonindex—cannot well be predicted by examination of the prior offense history, at least when that history is represented by our typology. There is practically no evidence to support a hypothesis of the existence of offense specialization among juvenile delinquents.

We are able to assert, however, that once an offense has been committed, the probability of a repeat of the same type of violation is somewhat greater than the likelihood of the initial offense. But as we earlier pointed out, these increased probabilities of repeats of the same type of offense can be explained, under the assumption of a stationary transition process, as the product of the accumulation of a large number of offenses rather than as the product of any special proclivity toward offense specialization. Thus, in order to prevent the occurrence of serious crimes in a delinquent boy's future, efforts should be made to prevent all forms of recidivism.

The most relevant question, then, is at what point in a delinquent boy's career an intervention program should act. One answer would be that the best time is that point beyond which the natural loss rate, or probability of desistance, begins to level off. Because 46 percent of the delinquents stop after the first offense, a major and expensive treatment program at this point would appear to be wasteful. We could even suggest that intervention be held in abeyance until the commission of the third offense, for an additional 35 percent of the second-time offenders desist from then on. Thus we could reduce the number of boys requiring attention in this cohort from 3,475 after the first offense, to 1,862 after the second offense, to 1,212 after the third offense, rather than concentrating on all 9,945 or some other large subgroup (such as nonwhites or lower SES boys) under a blanket community action program. Beyond the third offense the desistance probabilities level off. . . .

This study of delinquency in a birth cohort was not originally designed to be etiological; it did not seek to predict, nor was it meant to evaluate the way in which society's agencies respond to or dispose of juvenile law violators. Yet in our descriptive statistics and through the use of a Markov model we have found broad sociological variables related to higher frequencies of certain kinds of delinquency, we have generated a model for prediction of future delinquency at specific points in time, and we have produced findings from which efficient timing of intervention schemes might logically be inferred. The posture of these inferences may still be in the form of new sets of hypotheses. But, most importantly, they are derived from probabilities based on a dynamic longitudinal analysis of a birth cohort traced through time.

Notes

1. H. von Scheel. "Zur Einführung in die Kriminalstatistik, insbesondere diejenige des Deutschen Reichs," *Allgemeines statistisches Archiv* 1 (1900):191.
2. O. Köbner, "Die Methode einer wissenschaftlichen Rückfallsstatistik als Grundlage einer Reform der Kriminlstatistik," *Zeitschrift gesamter Strafrechtswissenschaft* 13 (1893):670.

9

Social Change and Crime:
A Routine Activity Approach

Lawrence E. Cohen   *Marcus Felson*

. . . In the present paper we consider . . . trends in crime rates in terms of changes in the "routine activities" of everyday life. We believe the structure of such activities influences criminal opportunity and therefore affects trends in a class of crimes we refer to as *direct-contact predatory violations*. Predatory violations are defined here as illegal acts in which "someone definitely and intentionally takes or damages the person or property of another" (Glaser, 1971:4). Further, this analysis is confined to those predatory violations involving direct physical contact between at least one offender and at least one person or object which that offender attempts to take or damage.

We argue that structural changes in routine activity patterns can influence crime rates by affecting the convergence in space and time of the three minimal elements of direct-contact predatory violations: (1) motivated offenders, (2) suitable targets, and (3) the absence of capable guardians against a violation. We further argue that the lack of any one of these elements is sufficient to prevent the successful completion of a direct-contact predatory crime, and that the convergence in time and space of suitable targets and the absence of capable guardians may even lead to large increases in crime rates without necessarily requiring any increase in the structural conditions that motivate individuals to engage in crime. That is, if the proportion of motivated offenders or even suitable targets were to remain stable in a community, changes in routine activities could nonetheless alter the likelihood of their convergence in space and time, thereby creating more opportunities for crimes to occur. Control therefore becomes critical. If controls through routine activities were to decrease, illegal predatory activities could then be likely to increase. In the process of developing this explanation and evaluating its consistency with existing data, we relate our approach to classical human ecological concepts and to several earlier studies. . . .

The Ecological Nature of Illegal Acts

This ecological analysis of direct-contact predatory violations is intended to be more than metaphorical. In the context of such violations, people, gaining and losing

Source: American Sociological Review, Vol. 44 (August), pp. 588–608. Copyright © 1979 by the American Sociological Association. Reprinted with permission.

sustenance, struggle among themselves for property, safety, territorial hegemony, sexual outlet, physical control, and sometimes for survival itself. The interdependence between offenders and victims can be viewed as a predatory relationship between functionally dissimilar individuals or groups. Since predatory violations fail to yield any net gain in sustenance for the larger community, they can only be sustained by feeding upon other activities. As offenders cooperate to increase their efficiency at predatory violations and as potential victims organize their resistance to these violations, both groups apply the symbiotic principle to improve their sustenance position. On the other hand, potential victims of predatory crime may take evasive actions which encourage offenders to pursue targets other than their own. Since illegal activities must feed upon other activities, the spatial and temporal structure of routine legal activities should play an important role in determining the location, type and quantity of illegal acts occurring in a given community or society. Moreover, one can analyze how the structure of community organization as well as the level of technology in a society provide the circumstances under which crime can thrive. For example, technology and organization affect the capacity of persons with criminal inclinations to overcome their targets, as well as affecting the ability of guardians to contend with potential offenders by using whatever protective tools, weapons and skills they have at their disposal. Many technological advances designed for legitimate purposes— including the automobile, small power tools, hunting weapons, highways, telephones, etc.—may enable offenders to carry out their own work more effectively or may assist people in protecting their own or someone else's person or property.

Not only do routine legitimate activities often provide the wherewithal to commit offenses or to guard against others who do so, but they also provide offenders with suitable targets. Target suitability is likely to reflect such things as value (i.e., the material or symbolic desirability of a personal or property target for offenders), physical visibility, access, and the inertia of a target against illegal treatment by offenders (including the weight, size, and attached or locked features of property inhibiting its illegal removal and the physical capacity of personal victims to resist attackers with or without weapons). Routine production activities probably affect the suitability of consumer goods for illegal removal by determining their value and weight. Daily activities may affect the location of property and personal targets in visible and accessible places at particular times. These activities also may cause people to have on hand objects that can be used as weapons for criminal acts or self-protection or to be preoccupied with tasks which reduce their capacity to discourage or resist offenders.

While little is known about conditions that affect the convergence of potential offenders, targets and guardians, this is a potentially rich source of propositions about crime rates. For example, daily work activities separate many people from those they trust and the property they value. Routine activities also bring together at various times of day or night persons of different background, sometimes in the presence of facilities, tools or weapons which influence the commission or avoidance of illegal acts. Hence, the timing of work, schooling and leisure may be of central importance for explaining crime rates. . . .

Microlevel Assumptions of the Routine Activity Approach

If the routine activity approach is valid, then we should expect to find evidence for a number of empirical relationships regarding the nature and distribution of predatory violations. For example, we would expect routine activities performed within or near the home and among family or other primary groups to entail lower risk of criminal victimization because they enhance guardianship capabilities. We should also expect that routine daily activities affect the location of property and personal targets in visible and accessible places at particular times, thereby influencing their risk of victimization. Furthermore, by determining their size and weight and in some cases their value, routine production activities should affect the suitability of consumer goods for illegal removal. Finally, if the routine activity approach is useful for explaining the paradox presented earlier, we should find that the circulation of people and property, the size and weight of consumer items etc., will parallel changes in crime rate trends for the post-World War II United States.

The veracity of the routine activity approach can be assessed by analyses of both microlevel and macrolevel interdependencies of human activities. While consistency at the formal level may appear noncontroversial, or even obvious, one nonetheless needs to show that the approach does not contradict existing data before proceeding to investigate the latter level.

Empirical Assessment

Circumstances and Location of Offenses

The routine activity approach specifies that household and family activities entail lower risk of criminal victimization than nonhousehold-nonfamily activities, despite the problems in measuring the former.

National estimates from large-scale government victimization surveys in 1973 and 1974 support this generalization. . . . The rates are far lower at or near home than elsewhere and far lower among relatives than others. The data indicate that risk of victimization varies directly with social distance between offender and victim. Furthermore, risk of lone victimization far exceeds the risk of victimization for groups. These relationships are strengthened by considering time budget evidence that, on the average, Americans spend 16.26 hours per day at home, 1.38 hours on streets, in parks, etc., and 6.36 hours in other places [Hindelang, et al., 1977] (Szalai, 1972:795). . . . For example, personal larceny rates (with contact) are 350 times higher at the hands of strangers in streets than at the hands of nonstrangers at home. Separate computations from 1973 victimization data (USDJ, 1976) indicate that there were two motor vehicle thefts per million vehicle-hours parked at or near home, 55 per million vehicle-hours in streets, parks, playgrounds, school grounds or parking lots, and 12 per million vehicle-hours elsewhere. While the direction of these relationships is not surprising, their magnitudes should be noted. It appears that risk of criminal victimization varies dramatically among the circumstances and locations in which people place themselves and their property.

Target Suitability

Another assumption of the routine activity approach is that target suitability influences the occurrence of direct-contact predatory violations. Though we lack data to disaggregate all major components of target suitability (i.e., value, visibility, accessibility and inertia), together they imply that expensive and movable durables, such as vehicles and electronic appliances, have the highest risk of illegal removal.

As a specific case in point, we compared the 1975 composition of stolen property reported in the Uniform Crime Report (FBI, 1976) with national data on personal consumer expenditures for goods (CEA, 1976) and to appliance industry estimates of the value of shipments the same year (*Merchandising Week*, 1976). We calculated that $26.44 in motor vehicles and parts were stolen for each $100 of these goods consumed in 1975, while $6.82 worth of electronic appliances were stolen per $100 consumed. Though these estimates are subject to error in citizen and police estimation, what is important here is their size relative to other rates. For example, only 8¢ worth of nondurables and 12¢ worth of furniture and nonelectronic household durables were stolen per $100 of each category consumed, the motor vehicle risk being, respectively, 330 and 220 times as great. Though we lack data on the "stocks" of goods subject to risk, these "flow" data clearly support our assumption that vehicles and electronic appliances are greatly overrepresented in thefts.

The 1976 Buying Guide issue of *Consumer Reports* (1975) indicates why electronic appliances are an excellent retail value for a thief. For example, a Panasonic car tape player is worth $30 per lb., and a Phillips phonograph cartridge is valued at over $5,000 per lb., while large appliances such as refrigerators and washing machines are only worth $1 to $3 per lb. Not surprisingly, burglary data for the District of Columbia in 1969 (Scarr, 1972) indicate that home entertainment items alone constituted nearly four times as many stolen items as clothing, food, drugs, liquor, and tobacco combined and nearly eight times as many stolen items as office supplies and equipment. In addition, 69% of national thefts classified in 1975 (FBI, 1976) involve automobiles, their parts or accessories, and thefts from automobiles or thefts of bicycles. Yet radio and television sets plus electronic components and accessories totaled only 0.10% of the total truckload tonnage terminated in 1973 by intercity motor carriers, while passenger cars, motor vehicle parts and accessories, motorcycles, bicycles, and their parts, totaled only 5.5% of the 410 million truckload tons terminated (ICC, 1974). Clearly, portable and movable durables are reported stolen in great disproportion to their share of the value and weight of goods circulating in the United States.

Family Activities and Crime Rates

One would expect that persons living in single-adult households and those employed outside the home are less obligated to confine their time to family activities within households. From a routine activity perspective, these persons and their households should have higher rates of predatory criminal victimization. We also expect that adolescents and young adults who are perhaps more likely to engage in peer group activities rather than family activities will have higher rates of criminal victimization. Finally, married persons should have lower rates than others. . . . [V]ictimization rates appear to be related inversely to age and are lower for persons in "less active" statuses (e.g., keeping house, unable to work, retired) and persons in intact marriages. A notable exception is [that] persons unable to work appear more likely to be victimized by rape, robbery and personal larceny with contact than are other "inactive persons." Unemployed persons also have unusually high rates of victimization. However, these rates are consistent with the routine activity approach offered here: the high rates of victimization suffered by the unemployed may reflect their residential proximity to high concentrations of potential offenders as well as their age and racial composition, while handicapped persons have high risk of personal victimization because they are less able to resist motivated offenders. Nonetheless, persons who keep house have noticeably lower rates of victimization than those who are employed, unemployed, in school or in the armed forces.

Burglary and robbery victimization rates are about twice as high for persons living in single-adult households as for other persons in each age group examined. Other victimization data (USDJ, 1976) indicate that, while household victimization rates tend to vary directly with household size, larger households have lower rates per person. . . .

Changing Trends in Routine Activity Structure and Parallel Trends in Crime Rates

The main thesis presented here is that the dramatic increase in the reported crime rates in the U.S. since 1960 is linked to changes in the routine activity structure of American society and to a corresponding increase in target suitability and decrease in guardian presence. If such a thesis has validity, then we should be able to identify these social trends and show how they relate to predatory criminal victimization rates.

Trends in Human Activity Patterns

The decade 1960–1970 experienced noteworthy trends in the activities of the American population. For example, the percent of the population consisting of female college students increased 118%. Married female labor force participant rates increased 31%, while the percent of the population living as primary individuals increased by 34% (USBC, 1975). We gain some further insight into changing routine activity patterns by comparing hourly data for 1960 and 1971 on households *unattended* by persons ages 14 or over when U.S. census interviewers first called [USBC, 1973b]. These data suggest that the proportion of households unattended at 8 A.M. increased by almost half between 1960 and 1971. One also finds increases in rates of out-of-town travel, which provides greater opportunity for both daytime and nighttime burglary of residences. Between 1960 and 1970, there was a 72% increase in state and national park visits per capita (USBC, 1975), an 144% increase in the percent of plant workers eligible for three weeks vacation (BLS, 1975), and an 184% increase in overseas travellers per 100,000 population (USBC, 1975). The National Travel Survey, conducted as part of the U.S. Census Bureau's Census of Transportation, confirms the general trends, tallying an 81% increase in the number of vacations taken by Americans from 1967 to 1972, a five-year period (USBC, 1973a: Introduction).

The dispersion of activities away from households appears to be a major recent social change. Although this decade also experienced an important 31% increase in the percent of the population ages 15–24, age structure change was only one of many social trends occurring during the period, especially trends in the circulation of people and property in American society.

The importance of the changing activity structure is underscored by taking a brief look at demographic changes between the years 1970 and 1975, a period of continuing crime rate increments. Most of the recent changes in age structure relevant to crime rates already had occurred by 1970; indeed, the proportion of the population ages 15–24 increased by only 6% between 1970 and 1975, compared with a 15% increase during the five years 1965 to 1970. On the other hand, major changes in the structure of routine activities continued during these years. For example, in only five years, the estimated proportion of the population consisting of husband-present, married women in the labor force households increased by 11%, while the estimated number of non-husband-wife households per 100,000 population increased from 9,150 to 11,420, a 25% increase (USBC, 1976; USBC, 1970–1975). At the same time, the percent of population enrolled in higher education increased 16% between 1970 and 1975.

Related Property Trends and Their Relation to Human Activity Patterns

Many of the activity trends mentioned above normally involve significant investments in durable goods. For example, the dispersion of population across relatively more households (especially non-husband-wife households) enlarges the market for durable goods such as television sets and automobiles. Women participating in the labor force and both men and women enrolled in college provide a market for automobiles. Both work and travel often involve the purchase of major movable or portable durables and their use away from home.

Considerable data are available which indicate that sales of consumer goods changed dramatically between 1960 and 1970 (as did their size and weight), hence providing more suitable property available for theft. For example, during this decade, constant-dollar personal consumer expenditures in the United States for motor vehicles and parts increased by 71%, while constant-dollar expenditures for other durables increased by 105% (calculated from CEA, 1976). In addition, electronic household appliances and small houseware shipments increased from 56.2 to 119.7 million units (*Electrical Merchandising Week*, 1964; *Merchandising Week*, 1973). During the same decade, appliance imports increased in value by 681% (USBC, 1975).

This same period appears to have spawned a revolution in small durable product design which further feeds the opportunity for crime to occur. Relevant data from the 1960 and 1970 Sears catalogs on the weight of many consumer durable goods were examined. Sears is the nation's largest retailer and its policy of purchasing and relabeling standard manufactured goods makes its catalogs a good source of data on widely merchandised consumer goods. The lightest television listed for sale in 1960 weighed 38 lbs., compared with 15 lbs. for 1970. Thus, the lightest televisions were 2 1/2 times as heavy in 1960 as 1970. Similar trends are observed for dozens of other goods listed in the Sears catalog. Data from *Consumer Reports Buying Guide*, published in December of 1959 and 1969, show similar changes for radios, record players, slide projectors, tape recorders, televisions, toasters and many other goods. Hence, major declines in weight between 1960 and 1970 were quite significant for these and other goods, which suggests that the consumer goods market may be producing many more targets suitable for theft. In general, one finds rapid growth in property suitable for illegal removal and in household and individual exposure to attack during the years 1960–1975.

Related Trends in Business Establishments

Of course, as households and individuals increased their ownership of small durables, businesses also increased the value of the merchandise which they transport and sell as well as the money involved in these transactions. Yet the Census of Business conducted in 1958, 1963, 1967, and 1972 indicate that the number of wholesale, retail, service, and public warehouse establishments (including establishments owned by large organizations) was a nearly constant ratio of one for every 16 persons in the United States. Since more goods and money were distributed over a relatively fixed number of business establishments, the tempo of business activity per establishment apparently was increasing. At the same time, the percent of the population employed as sales clerks or salesmen in retail trade declined from 1.48% to 1.27%, between 1960 and 1970, a 14.7% decline (USBC, 1975).

Though both business and personal property increased, the changing pace of activities appears to have exposed the latter to greater relative risk of attack, whether at home or elsewhere, due to the dispersion of goods among many more households, while concentrating goods in business establishments. However, merchandise in retail establishments with heavy volume and few employees to guard it probably is exposed to major increments in risk of illegal removal than is most other business property.

Composition of Crime Trends

If these changes in the circulation of people and property are in fact related to crime trends, the *composition* of the latter should reflect this. We expect relatively greater increases in personal and household victimization as compared with most business victimizations, while shoplifting should increase more rapidly than other types of thefts from businesses. We expect personal offenses at the hands of strangers to manifest greater increases than such offenses at the hands of nonstrangers. Finally, residential burglary rates should increase more in daytime than nighttime.

The available time series on the composition of offenses confirm these expectations. For example, commercial burglaries declined from 60% to 36% of the total, while daytime residential burglaries increased from 16% to 33%. Unlike the other crimes against business, shoplifting increased its share. Though we lack trend data on the circumstances of other violent offenses, murder data confirm our expectations. Between 1963 and 1975, felon-type murders increased from 17% to 32% of the total. Compared with a 47% increase in the rate of relative killings in this period, we calculated a 294% increase in the murder rate at the hands of known or suspected felon types [FBI, 1976].

Thus the trends in the composition of recorded crime rates appear to be highly consistent with the activity structure trends noted earlier. In the next section we apply the routine activity approach in order to model crime rate trends and social change in the post-World War II United States.

The Relationship of the Household Activity Ratio to Five Annual Official Index Crime Rates in the United States, 1947–1974

In this section, we test the hypothesis that aggregate official crime rate trends in the United States vary directly over time with the dispersion of activities away from family and household. The limitations of annual time series data do not allow construction of direct measures of changes in hourly activity patterns, or quantities, qualities and movements of exact stocks of household durable goods, but the Current Population Survey does provide related time series on labor force and household structure. From these data, we calculate annually (beginning in 1947) a household activity ratio by adding the number of married, husband-present female labor force participants (source: BLS, 1975) to the number of non-husband-wife households (source: USBC, 1947–1976) dividing this sum by the total number of households in the U.S. (source: USBC, 1947–1976). This calculation provides an estimate of the proportion of American households in year t expected to be more highly exposed to risk of personal and property victimization due to the dispersion of their activities away from family and household and/or their likelihood of owning extra sets of durables subject to high risk of attack. Hence, the household activity ratio should vary directly with official index crime rates.

Our empirical goal in this section is to test this relationship, with controls for those variables which other researchers have linked empirically to crime rate trends in the United States. Since various researchers have found such trends to increase with the proportion of the population in teen and young adult years, we include the population ages 15–24 per 100,000 resident population in year t as our first control variable (source: USBC, various years). Others have found unemployment rates to vary directly with official crime rates over time, although this relationship elsewhere has been shown to be empirically questionable. Thus, as our second, control variable, we take the standard annual unemployment rate (per 100 persons ages 16 and over) as a measure of the business cycle (source: BLS, 1975). . . .

Findings

Our time-series analysis for the years 1947–1974 consistently revealed positive and statistically significant relationships between the household activity ratio and each official crime rate change. Whichever official crime rate is employed, this finding occurs—whether we take the first difference for each crime rate as exogenous or estimate the equation in autoregressive form (with the lagged dependent variable on the right-hand side of the equation); whether we include or exclude the unemployment variable; whether we take the current scales of variables or convert them to natural log values; whether we employ the age structure variable as described or alter the ages examined (e.g., 14–24, 15–19, etc.). In short, the relationship is positive and significant in each case. . . .

The positive and significant relationship between the household activity variable and the official crime rates is robust and appears to hold for both macro- and microlevel data; it explains five crime rate trends, as well as the changing composition of official crime rates. These results suggest that routine activities may indeed provide the opportunity for many illegal activities to occur. . . .

References

Bureau of Labor Statistics (BLS) (1975). *Handbook of Labor Statistics 1975—Reference Edition*. Washington, DC: U.S. Government Printing Office.

Consumer Reports Buying Guide (1959). *Consumer Reports* (December). Mt. Vernon: Consumers Union.

———. (1969). *Consumer Reports* (December). Mt. Vernon: Consumers Union.

———. (1975). *Consumer Reports* (December). Mt. Vernon: Consumers Union.

Council of Economic Advisors (CEA) (1976). *The Economic Report of the President*. Washington, DC: U.S. Government Printing Office.

Electrical Merchandising Week (1964). *Statistical and Marketing Report* (January). New York: Billboard Publications.

Federal Bureau of Investigation (FBI) (1976). *Crime in the U.S.: Uniform Crime Report*. Washington, DC: U.S. Government Printing Office.

Glaser, Daniel (1971). *Social Deviance*. Chicago: Markham.

Hindelang, Michael J., Christopher S. Dunn, Paul Sutton and Alison L. Aumick (1977). *Sourcebook of Criminal Justice Statistics—1976*. U.S. Dept. of Justice. Law Enforcement Assistance Administration. Washington, DC: U.S. Government Printing Office.

Interstate Commerce Commission (ICC) (1974). *Annual Report: Freight Commodity Statistics of Class I Motor Carriers of Property Operative in Intercity Service*. Washington, DC: U.S. Government Printing Office.

Merchandising Week (1973). *Statistical and Marketing Report* (February). New York: Billboard Publications.

_____. (1976). *Statistical and Marketing Report* (March). New York: Billboard Publications.

Scarr, Harry A. (1972). *Patterns of Burglary*. U.S. Dept. of Justice. Law Enforcement Assistance Administration. Washington, DC: U.S. Government Printing Office.

Szalai, Alexander (ed.), (1972). *The Use of Time: Daily Activities of Urban and Suburban Populations in Twelve Countries*. The Hague: Mouton.

U.S. Bureau of the Census (USBC) (1973a). *Census of Transportation, 1972. U.S. Summary*. Washington, DC: U.S. Government Printing Office.

_____. (1973b) *Who's Home When. Working Paper 37*. Washington, DC: U.S. Government Printing Office.

_____. (1975-1976). *Statistical Abstract of the U.S.* Washington, DC: U.S. Government Printing Office.

_____. (1947-1976). *Current Population Studies*. P-25 Ser. Washington, DC: U.S. Government Printing Office.

U.S. Department of Justice (USDJ) (1976). *Criminal Victimizations in the U.S., 1973*. Washington, DC: Law Enforcement Assistance Administration (NCJISS).

10

Environmental Criminology

Paul J. Brantingham   Patricia L. Brantingham

Introduction: The Dimensions of Crime

A crime is a complex event. A crime occurs when four things are in concurrence: a law, an offender, a target, and a place. Without a law there is no crime. Without an offender, someone who breaks the law, there is no crime. Without some object, target, or victim, there is no crime. Without a place in time and space where the other three come together, there is no crime. These four elements—law, the offender, the target, and the place—can be characterized as the four dimensions of crime. Environmental criminology is the study of the fourth dimension of crime. . . .

The fourth dimension of crime is place, a discrete location in time and space at which the other three dimensions intersect and a criminal event occurs. Environmental criminologists begin their study of crime by asking questions about where and when crimes occur. They ask about the physical and social characteristics of crime sites. They ask about the movements that bring the offender and target together at the crime site. They ask about the perceptual processes that lead to the selection of crime sites and the social processes of ecological labeling. Environmental criminologists also ask about the spatial patterning in laws and the ways in which legal rules create crime sites. They ask about the spatial distributions of targets and offenders in urban, suburban, and rural settings. Finally, environmental criminologists ask how the fourth dimension of crime interacts with the other three dimensions to produce criminal events. . . .

Environmental Criminology: Focus on the Fourth Dimension

. . . Environmental criminology is a dynamic and expanding field. The field largely developed out of the work of two men who worked independently of one another, but in the same university, during the late 1960s and early 1970s. C. R. Jeffery, in his book *Crime Prevention through Environmental Design* (1971), argued that the modification of specific features of urban design would reduce crime. Oscar Newman, in *Defensible Space: Crime Prevention through Urban Design* (1972), argued that the modification of specific features of urban architecture would reduce crime. The intellectual excitement triggered by these works attracted criminologists,

Source: Excerpted from Brantingham, Paul J., and Brantingham, Patricia L., *Environmental Criminology*, 1981, pp. 7–8, 18–22, 24–25, 28–29, and 48–54. Permission granted by the authors.

planners, geographers, environmental psychologists and architects to the study of the environment in which crimes occur.

Shifts in Perspective

At least three related and critical shifts in perspective separate contemporary environmental criminology from the nineteenth-century and early twentieth-century research: (1) the shift from a disciplinary to a criminological relationship, (2) the shift from concern with offender motives to concern with criminal events, and (3) the shift from the sociological to the geographic imagination.

Until recently, most scholars who conducted research into crime did so from a specific disciplinary bias. Crime was seen as an interesting special example of more general processes. As such, it was studied in order to illustrate general propositions. Sociologists, for instance, saw crime as a special case of the more general problem of social deviance—behavior differing from the commonplace and frequently observed patterns within a society. Crime could be viewed as a special, extreme example of deviant behavior, and general principles developed by studying it could also be used to explain other, less sinister forms of deviance such as rudeness, piety, or sainthood (Wilkins, 1964: 47). For psychologists, criminality was seen as illustrative of some general psychological process. Criminal behavior, for instance, might be one form of abnormal personality development (Abrahamsen, 1960); or criminal behavior might illustrate the problems caused by faulty social conditioning techniques, or by effective conditioning to the wrong social rules (Trasler, 1962).

Contemporary environmental criminologists study crimes as discrete events. Crimes are seen as separated from other, similar forms of behavior by their special legal status. They are illuminated by information about various forms of deviance or psychological abnormality, but for most environmental criminologists they are not merely part of a disciplinary continuum. Any particular environmental criminologist may borrow techniques and knowledge from many different disciplines in order to understand any particular crime.

Most criminological research conducted between about 1870 and 1970 focused on the origins of criminal motivation. . . .

Environmental criminologists tend to assume that some people are criminally motivated (Brantingham and Brantingham, 1978; Carter and Hill, 1980) and begin instead with an analysis of the location of crimes. The objective of this analysis is to sort out patterns in where, when, and how crimes occur. From a purely academic standpoint, this form of analysis is interesting because little, really, turns out to be known about the patterns inherent in the occurrence of most types of crime. From a policy perspective this approach is promising because, once understood, available technologies can be used to modify these patterns and abate some crimes without doing significant damage to basic human rights, while it is not so clear that we have ethically acceptable techniques for changing human motivation.

The third shift in perspective involves a change in the way we see the world. David Harvey (1974) characterized this as a shift from the sociological to the geographic imagination. He followed C. Wright Mills in concluding that the sociological imagination drives the social scientist to "grasp history and biography and the relations between the two within society." By contrast, Harvey held that the geographic imagination "asks the individual to recognize the role of space and place in his own biography, to relate the spaces he sees around him, and to recognize how transactions between individuals and between organizations are affected by the space that separates them."

The sociological imagination asks questions about the social backcloth, the social scenery around and through which social beings move; about the perceptual directions of time; the mechanics and direction of social change; and about people, as individuals and as aggregations. These are questions of social structures, of social changes, and of social stratifications. They are phrased and answered in what Harvey calls a logical substance language in which an individual event or thing or person is identified as having a specified set of properties $(p_1, p_2, p_3 \cdots p_n)$. The sociological imagination searches for patterns in groups of events or things or persons having similar sets of identifying properties.

The geographic imagination asks the questions "Where?" and "What is where?" in both absolute and relative space. Absolute space is measured by simple Euclidian metrics on the surface of the earth. Absolute space places distance relationships between Los Angeles, New York, Toronto, Paris, and London. Relative space is measured by more complex or less common metrics. One example is the relative space defined by travel time. In absolute space, midtown Manhattan, Philadelphia, and Atlanta are very different distances from JFK International Airport, but using different methods of travel, they are equidistant, about two hours' travel time away. Another is the relative space defined by personal knowledge: business executives who routinely travel between New York and San Francisco may treat the two cities as closely connected because they are well known, but view places such as Buffalo or Seattle as much further away because they are unknown. Relative spaces can be defined by economic metrics, by political metrics, by time metrics, by information or knowledge metrics, by belief metrics and many others. The geographic imagination sorts out a spatial metric and puts questions in what Harvey calls a logical space-time language in which individual events or things or people are identified by specification of a location within a space-time coordinate system (x, y, z, t). The geographic imagination seeks patterns in sets of similar individuals.

It follows that events or individuals that are treated as equal by the sociological imagination may be treated as totally unrelated by the geographic imagination, and vice versa. Two burglaries committed by two unemployed minority youths in the suburbs of Dallas and Calgary a month apart may be equal to the sociological imagination, having properties (same law violation, same age offenders, same minority status offenders, same employment status offenders) that are identical, but may be seen as different from one another by the geographic imagination because their space-time coordinates (1500 miles apart; one month apart) are different. At a different level of analysis, a robbery committed by a minority youth one block from his home in the ghetto and a burglary committed by a middle-class white youth one block from home in the suburbs might be treated as unrelated by the sociological imagination, but as identical (one block from home, at noon) by the geographic imagination.

Clearly, a full statement of a criminal event must use both geographic and sociological perspectives to describe it and make possible the search for full patterns. Such a description must take the form $(x, y, z, t, p_1, p_2, p_3 \cdots p_n)$. This third shift in perspective introduced the geographic imagination into the study of crime.

Environmental criminologists set out to use the geographic imagination in concert with the sociological imagination to describe, understand, and control criminal events. Locations of crimes, the characteristics of those locations, the movement paths that bring offenders and victims together at those locations, and people's perceptions of crime locations all become substantively important objects for research from this shifted perspective. Moreover, overt policy choices which create or maintain crime locations or areas of criminal residence also become important objects of research.

Levels of Analysis

Environmental criminology is currently studied at three separate levels of analysis. *Macro-analysis* involves studies at the highest levels of spatial aggregation. It involves studies of distribution of crime between countries, between the states or provinces or cities within a particular country, or between the counties or cities within a state. *Meso-analysis* involves studies at intermediate levels of spatial aggregation. Meso-analysis involves the study of crime within the subareas of a city or metropolis. The range of such studies includes very large subunits such as the constituent cities of a metropolitan area, or smaller subunits such as planning areas or police precincts or census tracts, or very small subunits such as the faces of individual city blocks. Research at this level of analysis examines the distribution of crimes in relation of the distribution of targets; of offender populations; of routine daily activities such as work, school, shopping, and recreation locations; of criminal justice system or security functionaries; of traffic channels; and of zoned land uses. *Micro-analysis* involves the study of specific crime sites. At this level of analysis the focus is on building type and its placement on a lot, landscaping and lighting, interior form, and security hardware.

Attention to level of analysis is important. Spatial patterns in crime differ depending on the level of analysis selected. Areal patterns at a high level of aggregation represent some statement of within-area variations at the next lower level of aggregation. Appearances of homogeneity mask criminologically important differences in the distribution of crimes, offenders, targets, facilitating social circumstances, and so on. Brantingham et al. (1976) demonstrate this point in a five-level cone of resolution for burglary in 1970: the national pattern based on state level data; the Florida pattern based on county level data; the pattern for the city of Tallahassee based on census tract level data; a census tract pattern based on block group data; and a block group's burglary pattern based on data for individual city blocks. In each case, an apparently homogeneous unit at one level of analysis can be resolved into subunits having very different crime rates.

This problem can be especially misleading when the areal units have been defined for administrative purposes. Census tract boundaries, for instance, typically run down the middle of major traffic arteries. Such roads tend to attract large numbers of crimes which would be assigned to two different tracts, making them both appear to have medium crime levels, when in fact, virtually all parts of both tracts have very low crime rates, while the small portion of each that runs along the common boundary road has a very high crime rate. Inattention to the level of analysis obscures the real underlying pattern and can lead the researcher into severe misinterpretation of the actual crime patterns being analyzed: a spatial variant on the ecological fallacy that plagued research in the Chicago School-dominated second wave.

Patterns of Crime

Research into the spatial patterning of crime has developed rapidly in the past decade. Long established regional patterns in American crime have been confirmed

(Kowalski et al., 1980). Intermetropolitan analyses have moved from simple description to powerful modeling of the ways in which differing socioeconomic situations and occupational and employment patterns affect the criminal opportunity structures in different cities (Brantingham and Brantingham, 1980). The most extensive progress, however, has been made in meso-analysis of urban crime patterns. The spatial patterning of several crimes has now been mapped, the sophisticated urban models developed by planners and geographers in the half-century since Burgess first articulated the zonal hypothesis have been used to order and understand these crime patterns, and initial steps have been taken toward the development of explicitly spatial theories of crime. . . .

Crime Sites and Criminal Areas

. . . Contemporary environmental criminologists are engaged in analyzing and modeling the "journey to crime" within the context of more general knowledge about urban movement and behavior patterns developed by environmental psychologists, social geographers, and urban planners, and uses a formal deductive modeling procedure to develop a set of general predictive statements about the distribution of crime sites within cities. . . .

Notes on the Geometry of Crime

Spatial patterning of crime has long been observed. . . .

Much current work on crime patterning assumes (explicitly or implicitly) an opportunity/motivation interaction rubric for explaining observed crime (see Jeffery, 1977; Baldwin and Bottoms, 1976; Brantingham and Brantingham, 1978; Carter and Hill, 1980, Mayhew et al., 1976). . . .

We have previously proposed a model for crime site selection which can be described by the following propositions (Brantingham and Brantingham, 1978):

(1) Individuals exist who are motivated to commit specific offenses.

    (a) The sources of motivation are diverse. Different etiological models or theories may appropriately be invoked to explain the motivation of different individuals or groups.

    (b) The strength of such motivation varies.

    (c) The character of such motivation varies from affective to instrumental.

(2) Given the motivation of an individual to commit an offense, the actual commission of an offense is the end result of a multistaged decision process which seeks out and identifies, within the general environment, a target or victim positioned in time and space.

    (a) In the case of high affect motivation, the decision process will probably involve a minimal number of stages.

    (b) In the case of high instrumental motivation, the decision process locating a target or victim may include many stages and much careful searching.

(3) The environment emits many signals, or cues, about its physical, spatial, cultural, legal, and psychological characteristics.

    (a) These cues can vary from generalized to detailed.

(4) An individual who is motivated to commit a crime uses cues (either learned through experience or learned through social transmission) from the environment to locate and identify targets or victims.

(5) As experiential knowledge grows, an individual who is motivated to commit a crime learns which individual cues, clusters of cues, and sequences of cues are associated with "good" victims or targets. These cues, cue clusters, and cue sequences can be considered a template which is used in victim or target selection. Potential victims or targets are compared to the template and either rejected or accepted depending on the congruence.

(a) The process of template construction and the search process may be consciously conducted, or these processes may occur in an unconscious, cybernetic fashion so that the individual cannot articulate how they are done.

(6) Once the template is established, it becomes relatively fixed and influences future search behavior, thereby becoming self-reinforcing.

(7) Because of the multiplicity of targets and victims, many potential crime selection templates could be constructed. But because the spatial and temporal distribution of offenders, targets, and victims is not regular, but clustered or patterned, and because human environmental perception has some universal properties, individual templates have similarities which can be identified.

These propositions are not spatially specific. They posit that criminals engage in a search behavior which may vary in intensity, and that criminals use previous knowledge to evaluate and select targets. The propositions do not describe the spatial characteristics of the search patterns or the selection patterns. . . .

Consequences

. . . [I]t is possible, deductively, to arrive at some general statements about crime patterns and to explain certain empirically reported patterns which previously had been unexplained.

(1) *Older cities with a generally concentric zonal form, and with a dense core, will have a crime pattern which clusters toward the core. There should be a relatively steep crime gradient.*

In a city with a concentric zone form there is a central business district surrounded by a zone-in-transition which is, in turn, surrounded by residential areas of increasing cost. In such a city, the socioeconomic groups with the highest incidence of criminal behavior are likely to live in or near the zone-in-transition. Entertainment and work opportunities are likely to be close to the homes of potential offenders. Commercial and industrial targets will be close to the residences of potential criminals. There is also likely to be foot traffic in the core areas. All of these conditions provide targets for crime. Employing concepts of "distance decay," crime should be highest toward the core and around the zone-in-transition, and decrease away from the zone-in-transition. This, of course, is the classic pattern reported by the Chicago School ecologists.

(2) *Newer cities with a mosaic urban form will have a more dispersed crime pattern, with less concentration of crime than in older, denser cities.* With a mosaic urban form, concentrations of potential criminals will be dispersed in clusters through-

out the urban area. Entertainment centers and work locations are likely to be separated from the residential areas where many potential criminals live. The potential offenders of a mosaic city are likely to have larger awareness spaces than potential offenders in a concentric zone city because they must move more extensively in order to reach work, shopping and entertainment locations. With larger awareness spaces, the potential offenders of a mosaic city will have a broader target search area and will be likely to find targets in more places, producing a dispersed crime pattern. This is the pattern reported in post-World War II studies in cities affected by dispersed public housing policies or by rapid development keyed to the transport potentials of the automobile.

(3) *New cities with dispersed shopping and much strip commercial development have a higher potential for property crime.*

. . . [D]ispersed shopping and strip development put retail and commercial business into the awareness spaces of more individuals and within close reach of more people. Such easier access, which is the obvious marketing rationale for dispersing commercial activity, should make property offenses more frequent. An individual who is weakly motivated to commit a commercial property offense might be deterred if he had to walk two miles to find a target, but might not be deterred if he only had to walk two blocks. . . .

(4) *Development of major transportation arteries leads to a concentration of criminal events close to the highways, particularly near major intersections.*

Major transportation arteries are likely to become part of the awareness space of many urban residents, including potential criminals. To use Kevin Lynch's terminology (1960), the transportation arteries become paths. Major intersections are likely to become nodal points. We have argued in this chapter that a criminal's search area begins within his awareness space. Paths and nodes become reasonable starting points in such a search.

Areas close to major paths and intersections have other attractions for instrumental type offenses such as robbery or burglary. Robbers and burglars look for targets within "safe" crime areas. Major transportation arteries, if the criminal has a car, offer easy escape.

Because of easy access and availability to customers, stores and services locate along the traffic arteries and at nodes. Such stores and services are potential targets.

The areas adjacent to major transportation arteries are likely to have a disproportionate number of potential targets, be perceived as relatively "safe" crime search areas, and be part of many offenders' awareness spaces. All this should lead to higher crime rates near major arteries, particularly near nodal points on arteries (see Fink, 1969; Wilcox, 1973; Luedtke and Associates, 1970).

(5) *Areas with grid networks, in general, have higher potential crime rates than areas with organic street layouts.*

In order for a crime to occur, the criminal has to locate a target or victim in his awareness space. A criminal's awareness space will change with new information and as the result of searching. The expansion of an awareness space will most probably occur in a connected fashion; the borders or edges of currently known areas will be explored first. In exploring new areas, the potential offender will find it easier to penetrate areas with predictable road networks. Areas with grid street layouts are more predictable than areas with winding roads, cul-de-sacs, or dead ends.

Criminal behavior in searching new areas is *spatially* similar to other urban residents. Since residential areas with more organic street layouts and cul-de-sacs and dead ends are more difficult to use as through paths, these residential areas are less likely to experience much through traffic. Nonresidents are less likely to be found in these areas, therefore they are more likely to be identified by residents when present. Because nonresidents are more easily identifiable, and because they may become lost or disoriented, offenders are less likely to expand their search areas very far into nongrid residential areas (see Bevis and Nutter, 1977).

(6) *Older cities with dispersed low-income housing and public transit are likely to have a concentration of crime around the core, and nodes of higher crime around the low income housing areas.*

This statement about crime patterns is really just a corollary to the first statement which described crime gradients in the "zonal" city. Because of public policy in many countries, particularly Britain, subsidized low-income housing has been dispersed in many older cities. Given that, historically, more criminals have been found in low-income groups (a point reaffirmed by Hindelang's 1978 cross-analysis of arrest, victimization, and self-report data), this dispersal will have an obvious impact on crime patterns. In older cities with a dominant core, the awareness spaces of criminals living in the low-income housing areas will include their home area and the core area. Their search for targets will be biased towards these areas. . . .

(7) *The shifting of work areas out of core areas into fringe areas of a city will tend to increase crime in suburban areas.*

In many growing urban areas industrial and wholesale trade operations are increasing in urban fringe areas, or in the outer ring of urban areas, and decreasing in the urban core. The shift away from the core is partly the result of the industrial move to one-floor plants, which obviously require the larger blocks of land, which are available at lower cost in fringe areas and partly the result of improved urban highway systems which decrease the accessibility advantage of central core locations.

Whatever the reasons for the shift, the movement of work locations to the urban fringe should influence crime patterns. Because journey-to-work patterns will change, awareness spaces will change for those criminals who work (regularly or occasionally). Those fringe and suburban work locations and suburban residential and commercial areas along the paths to and from work areas will become part of the awareness spaces of employed criminals and may even become part of the awareness spaces of nonworking criminals who communicate with workers.

In addition, the movement of industrial and wholesale trade changes the opportunity structure, putting more targets within the reach of those people who live in suburban areas and may be motivated to commit property offenses.

(8) *Major entertainment complexes such as sports arenas are likely to produce localized associated increases in crime. If these complexes are near residential areas with many potential offenders, the associated crime should increase disproportionately.*

Major entertainment complexes are likely to become part of the awareness space of most urban residents. These complexes also produce temporally concentrated clusters of victims and targets when activities are going on. Thus, a concentration of targets is likely to occur within the awareness space of many criminals.

If, in addition, the entertainment complexes are located near residential areas with many people who are motivated to commit crimes, the easy accessibility and the strength of the awareness space of residents should increase associated crime even more.

(9) *Cities with a core "red light district" are likely to have concentrations of crime in those areas. However, dispersing the activities which cluster in a "red light district" will not necessarily decrease the total amount of crime, though the spatial patterning of crime should change.*

Historically, cities have always had "red light districts," areas where prostitution, gambling, and bars concentrate. These areas attract potential victims and potential offenders. In fact, in these areas the offender and victim distinction can become blurred. In the case of murder and assault, the victim precipitation literature shows how easily the victim might have been the offender (Vetter and Silverman, 1978: 76). In street robbery, the victim may become an offender on another day.

City administrators try to control such areas through traditional means such as enforcing criminal code violations, passing municipal ordinances controlling businesses, and increasing police presence. In some cities the activities in the district are broken up, often to appear in a more dispersed pattern in other parts of the city. Reckless (1933) documented such a dispersal of the Chicago red light district in 1912 and noted the migration of the vice area from the urban core to the suburban fringe.

The dispersal of the red light activities may increase or decrease the amount of crime. Whether crime increases or decreases depends on the distribution of targets after the dispersal and how the awareness spaces of potential criminals change. If the breakup of a red light district results in a total decrease in red light activities and the remaining activities become part of the awareness spaces of fewer potential criminals (or patrons in general), then the total amount of crime may decrease. However, breaking up a red-light district may backfire on city administrators. New areas may pick up the red light businesses, the awareness spaces of the former patrons and criminals who "worked" the old red light district will change. For some, new areas with increased red light activities will be incorporated into their awareness spaces. Potential criminals will be attracted into previously unknown parts of the city. If these previously unknown parts of the city have many good targets or victims, then crime may increase. . . .

Conclusion

In conclusion, it has been argued . . . that crime occurrence is not the direct result of motivation, but is mediated by perceived opportunity. This, in turn, is influenced by the actual distribution of opportunities, urban form, and mobility. It has been argued that criminals are not random in their behavior and that by exploring urban structure and how people interact with the urban spatial structure, it should be possible to predict the spatial distribution of crime and explain some of the variation in volume of crime between urban areas and between cities.

References

Abrahamsen, D. (1960) *The Psychology of Crime.* (New York: Columbia University Press).

Baldwin, J. and Bottoms, A. E. (1976) *The Urban Criminal: A Study in Sheffield.* (London: Tavistock).

Bevis, C. and Nutter, J. B. (1977) "Changing Street Layouts to Reduce Residential Burglary." Paper presented at American Society of Criminology annual meeting, Atlanta, November.

Brantingham, P. J. (1978) "A Theoretical Model of Crime Site Selection," pp. 105–118 in M. Krohn and R. L. Akers (eds.) *Crime, Law and Sanction* (Beverly Hills: Sage Publications).

———. (1980) "Crime, Occupation and Economic Specialization: A Consideration of Inter-Metropolitan Patterns," pp. 93–108 in D. E. Georges-Abeyie and K. D. Harries (eds.) *Crime: A Spatial Perspective.* (New York: Columbia University Press).

Brantingham, P. J., Dyreson, D. A., and Brantingham, P. L. (1976) "Crime Scenes Through a Cone of Resolution." *American Behavioral Scientist* 20: 261–273.

Carter, R. and Hill, K. Q. (1980) "Area Images and Behavior: An Alternative Perspective for Understanding Crime," pp. 193–204 in D. E. Georges-Abeyie and K. D. Harries (eds.) *Crime: A Spatial Perspective*. (New York: Columbia University Press).

Fink, G. "Einsbruchstatorte vornehmlich an einfallstrassen?" *Kriminalistik* 4 23:358–360.

Forman, R. E. (1971) *Black Ghettos, White Ghettos, and Slums*. (Englewood Cliffs, NJ: Prentice-Hall).

Harvey, D. (1974) *Social Justice and the City*. (London: Edward Arnold).

Jeffery, C. R. (1971) *Crime Prevention Through Environmental Design*. (Beverly Hills: Sage Publications).

———. (1977) *Crime Prevention Through Environmental Design* (2nd ed.). (Beverly Hills: Sage Publications).

Kowalski, G. S., Dittmann, R L., Jr. and Bung, W. L. (1980) "Spatial Distribution of Criminal Offences by States, 1970–76." *Journal of Research in Crime and Delinquency* 17: 4–25.

Luedtke, G. and Associates (1970) *Crime and the Physical City: Neighborhood Design Techniques for Crime Reduction*. (Springfield, VA: National Technical Information Service).

Lynch, K. (1960) *The Image of the City*. (Cambridge, MA: MIT Press).

Mack, J. (1964) "Full-Time Miscreants: Delinquent Neighborhoods and Criminal Networks." *British Journal of Sociology* 15: 38–53.

Mayhew, P., Clarke, R. V. G., Sturman, A., and Hough, J. M. (1976) *Crime as Opportunity*. Home Office Research Study No. 34. (London. HMSO).

Newman, O. (1972) *Defensible Space*. (New York: Macmillan).

Reckless, W. C. (1933) *Vice in Chicago*. (Chicago: University of Chicago Press).

Trasler, G. (1962) *The Explanation of Criminality*. (London Routledge and Kegan Paul).

Vetter, H. J. and Silverman, I. J. (1978) *The Nature of Crime*. (Philadelphia: W. B. Saunders Company).

Wilcox, S. (1973) *The Geography of Robbery*. (The Prevention and Control of Robbery 3). (Davis, CA: The Center of Administration of Criminal Justice, University of California).

Wilkins, L. T. (1964) *Social Deviance*. (London: Tavistock).

11

Characterizing Criminal Careers

Alfred Blumstein   *Jacqueline Cohen*

The policy choice at the center of most public debate involves the use of imprisonment, primarily the choice of who should go to prison and for how long. . . .

Information on criminal careers—the longitudinal sequence of offenses committed by individual offenders—is potentially an important element for informing the choices made at the various decision points. Knowledge about criminal careers is most directly useful for assessing the effects on crime through incapacitation. The magnitude of the incapacitative effect of incarceration depends fundamentally on the nature of criminal careers: the more frequently an individual offender engages in crime, the more benefit that would accrue by removing him from the street and thereby eliminating his opportunity to commit crimes in the community. The dynamics of criminal careers, especially their potential for change, are also relevant for assessing likely rehabilitation or individual deterrent effects. An important question when assessing general deterrence is distinguishing between the impact of deterrent threats in curtailing the careers of already active offenders and in inhibiting initiation of criminal careers among nonoffenders. . . .

Research on criminal careers involves the characterization of the longitudinal pattern of crime events for offenders and assessment of the factors that affect that pattern. Use of the concept of a "career" is not meant to imply that crime need be the primary economic activity from which an offender derives a substantial part of his livelihood; it is merely a metaphor for the longitudinal process. It is also important to distinguish the concept of criminal careers from the policy-oriented reversal of that phrase, the "career criminal," which refers to offenders whose criminal careers are of such serious dimension that they represent prime targets for the criminal justice system.

Basic Structure of a Criminal Career

Examining the basic structure of criminal careers within any population involves first assessing the fraction that participates in crime and then, for that subset, developing information on the statistical properties of the parameters that characterize their criminal careers. "Participation" represents a primary filter between

Source: Reprinted with permission from Alfred Blumstein and Jacqueline Cohen, "Characterizing Criminal Careers," *Science*, Vol. 237, pp. 985–991. Copyright © 1987, American Association for the Advancement of Science. Notes renumbered.

the general population and the subset who are criminally active. If crime is defined very broadly to include many minor infractions, participation in crime is virtually universal. However, as interest is focused more narrowly on serious offenses, participation becomes an important filter in distinguishing active offenders from nonoffenders. The intensity of criminal activity may vary considerably across these participants. "Frequency" refers to these individual crime rates, or the number of crimes per year committed by those who are active.

The basic identity linking the aggregate population crime rate, C, to the fraction participating, P, and their individual crime frequency, λ is $C = P\lambda$ when crime types and offender subgroups are treated homogeneously.[1] In this identity, the crimes per year per capita (C) is partitioned between participation, P (in terms of active criminals per capita), and frequency, λ (in terms of crimes per year per active criminal). This basic partition provides the opportunity to distinguish those factors that affect participation, which in general may be quite different from those that influence frequency by active offenders.

Among active offenders, three fundamental parameters represent the simplest characterization of a career structure: (i) age of initiation, A_0; (ii) age at termination, A_N; and (iii) mean number of crimes committed per year while active, λ. An important parameter of the criminal career is thus the career length represented by the interval $T = A_N - A_0$. Also at any point in the career, A_t, we are interested in the residual career length, $T_R = A_N - A_t$.

A simple configuration of a criminal career that invokes these basic parameters is shown in figure 1. Here the career begins at age A_0 and the individual crime frequency rises immediately to λ, stays constant at that value for the duration of the career, and drops instantaneously to 0 at age A_N when the career is terminated. . . .

Figure 1
An Individual Criminal Career[2]

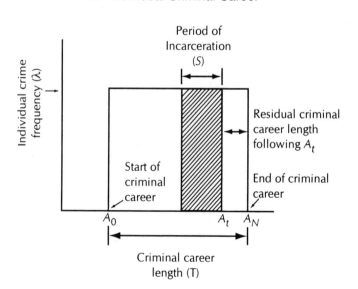

Criminal career
length (T)

Estimation of Criminal Career Parameters

Estimation of criminal career parameters is particularly difficult because of the general invisibility of most crimes to any observer. An ideal observation method would involve a random sample of the population who would maintain a regular log of their criminal activities. The obvious fancifulness of such an approach requires a diversity of indirect approaches, relying on multiple data sources to develop estimates of the parameters.

A long-standing data source, which has now been available for over 40 years in the United States, is the Uniform Crime Reports (UCR). . . .

The UCR arrest data are particularly valuable because they provide some basic descriptive information about the offenders, and thus serve as a basis for distinguishing among them. Arrest statistics, however, are also subject to biases. In addition to reporting errors like those found in crime counts, arrest counts may be distorted by differential vulnerability to arrest (for example, more careful or more experienced offenders may be less likely to be arrested), or from differences in police discretion in issuing a warning as opposed to recording an arrest. . . .

Participation Rates

. . . The probability that an American male would be arrested some time in his life for a nontraffic offense has been estimated as 50 to 60%,[3] a level of participation in crime that is probably an order of magnitude higher than most people would guess. In Great Britain, the lifetime conviction probability for males is estimated to be in the same range—44%.[4]

These surprisingly high estimates might be dismissed because they include arrests for any kind of offense (other than traffic), and many people may be vulnerable to arrest for minor offenses like disorderly conduct. Subsequent estimates have focused more narrowly on only the FBI "index" offenses (murder, forcible rape, aggravated assault, robbery, burglary, larceny, and auto theft) that comprise the usual reports on "serious" crime published periodically by the FBI. Examining these data for the 55 largest cities (with populations over 250,000), the lifetime chance of an index arrest for a male in these cities was estimated to be 25%, with important differences between the races in their participation rates—the chances were 14% for whites and 50% for blacks.[5] Further, excluding larceny arrests—relatively minor offenses (including shoplifting and theft of auto parts and bicycles) that account for 50% of all index arrests—does not significantly affect participation rates.[5] The adjustment eliminates those individuals who were arrested only for larceny, and these are only a small fraction of those ever arrested for index offenses.

In sharp contrast to the large race difference in participation rates, the recidivism rates for serious crimes were about the same for blacks and for whites, about an 85 to 90% chance of rearrest for both groups.[5] This highlighted an important substantive insight: whereas there appears to be an important difference in the degree to which individuals from the two groups became offenders, those who did become offenders in the two race groups appear much more similar in their offending patterns.

Of course, the policy implications of this are also very important: since the criminal justice system deals with people only after they have passed through the "participation filter," that system has no direct interest in the factors that affect participation. Rather, their primary professional concern is with the factors that distinguish among those who do penetrate the "filter"—namely, the factors associated with active criminal careers. If race is not one of those factors, then racial discrimination by the criminal justice system, aside from being ethically wrong, is also empirically incorrect. . . .

Crime Frequency by Active Offenders

Knowledge about the magnitude of λ in various populations is of particular interest in developing crime-control policies. The mean λ indicates the troublesomeness of any group of offenders, whereas the distribution over the group indicates the variation across individual offenders. For any fixed total crime rate, if the mean λ is high, then the total crime rate is attributable to a reasonably small number of offenders, and perhaps the crime problem might be significantly alleviated by isolating them. On the other hand, if the mean frequency is low with the same total crime rate, then the number of offenders is large and may well exceed the capacity of the criminal justice system, and it would be well to focus on other crime-control strategies, including strategies directed at reducing participation in offending.

Some rather surprising results have emerged in studies of λ. Considerable diversity was found in estimates of λ based on inmates' self-reports of the crimes they committed during the period just before the arrest leading to their current incarceration. . . .[6] For those who ever committed a robbery during the measurement period, half reported committing fewer than 4 robberies per year while they were free on the street, but 10% reported committing more than 70 robberies per year while free. Similarly for burglary, the median rate was 5 per year, but the 90th percentile claimed a rate of over 195 per year. . . .

With data drawn from computerized criminal history files maintained by the FBI, longitudinal arrest histories were obtained for all adults arrested for murder, rape, robbery, aggravated assault, burglary, or auto theft in Washington, D.C., during 1973, or in the Detroit Standard Metropolitan Statistical Area (SMSA) during the period 1974 to 1977.[7, 8] The arrest histories included information on any arrests as adults occurring before or during the sampling years for sampled individuals, as well as dispositions in court and dates of admission or release from correctional institutions.

Adult arrestees for serious offenses were almost exclusively male ($\geq 90\%$) in both sites. The two populations differed markedly with respect to race. The Washington, D.C., arrestees, who reflected the racial composition of that city in the early 1970s (71% black in the 1970 census), included 92% nonwhites. The arrestees from the Detroit SMSA, which included the suburban counties surrounding Detroit, included 43% nonwhites, a figure that much more closely resembles the racial composition found nationally (45% nonwhite) among urban arrestees for serious offenses.[9]

The arrestee populations in both study sites numbered several thousand—5,338 in Washington, D.C.; 10,588 whites and 8,022 blacks in the Detroit SMSA. The analyses of frequencies, λ, however, focused on selected cohorts of about 150 arrestees active in a crime type within these annual cross-sections. Cohort subsamples permit analysis of changes in A over time for the same arrestees. Examination of changes in λ with age in the histories of the full sampling cross section, for example, includes different subsets of arrestees at different ages. Estimates at age 20 are based on a broad cross section of offenders, some who were age 20 many years ago but most of whom were near age 20 at the time of sampling because most arrestees are young (see fig. 2). In contrast, λ estimates at older ages, say 35, are based on individuals who are 35 or older at the time of sampling; arrestees who were younger at the time of sampling cannot be observed at these older ages. Thus the estimates at older ages are dominated by individuals who grew up at an earlier time and also who persisted in their criminal careers for a long time. Analyses of age differences in cross-sectional data—even longitudinal data for the cross-section sample—thus result in different sample compositions at each age, thereby confounding changes over age with possible cohort effects and historical period changes.

Figure 2

U. S. age-specific arrest rates (arrests per 100,000 population of each age) for 1983. The curve for each offense type is displayed as a percentage of the peak arrest rate. The curves show the age at which the peak occurs (at 100%) and the age at which the peak falls to 50% of the peak rate.[2]

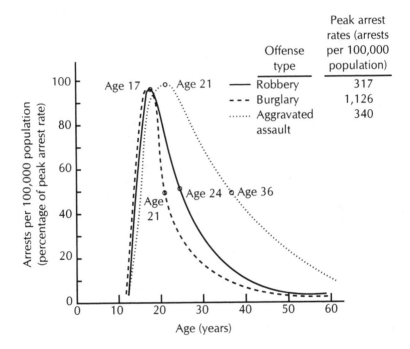

Cohorts included those arrestees who reached age 18 in the same year and whose first arrest as adults occurred at ages 18 to 20, thereby ensuring that they were active in criminal careers as adults before age 21. The resulting estimates were thus based on the arrest experiences of offenders who had at least two arrests, one in the sampling year and another earlier in their careers at age 18, 19, or 20. This restriction, combined with the further requirement that the arrest in the sampling year be for a serious offense, limits the analysis to frequency rates for reasonably serious adult arrestees who were presumably criminally active throughout the estimation interval.

Individual annual arrest frequencies, μ, were estimated for the cohorts in Washington, D.C., and in the Detroit SMSA. The required arrests at either end of the estimation period were excluded, and time spent incarcerated was excluded from the time at risk of arrest in the estimation period. The mean frequencies estimated for adult arrestees who were in their 20s between 1966 and 1973[10] are reported for the two jurisdictions in table 1.[7, 9] When not incarcerated, arrestees active in robbery, burglary, or larceny are arrested about once every 4 years for these crime types; mean interarrest intervals are longer for aggravated assault (5 years) and auto theft (7 years).

Table 1

Mean individual arrest frequencies (μ) from official arrest histories, probabilities of arrest per crime (q), and associated estimates of mean individual crime frequencies (λ), 1966–1973.

Offense type	Washington, D.C.			Detroit SMSA		
	μ	q	λ	μ	q	λ
Robbery	0.23	0.069	3.3	0.20	0.043	4.7
Aggravated assault	0.19	0.111	1.7	0.18	0.062	2.9
Burglary	0.26	0.049	5.3	0.20	0.038	5.3
Larceny	0.27	0.026	10.4	0.22	0.030	7.3
Auto theft	0.14	0.047	3.0	0.14	0.015	9.3

These μ estimates can be used to develop estimates of λ that include the many more crimes committed that do not result in arrest. If the q is independent of λ, then $\mu = \lambda q$. The ratio of police statistics on reported arrests, A, divided by reported crimes, R, represents a starting point for estimating the offense-specific probability of arrest per crime. This simple ratio is adjusted by the offense-specific rate at which victims report crimes to the police, r, to account for unreported crimes among total crimes committed. Another offense-specific adjustment is made to account for the average number of multiple offenders arrested for the same crime incident, O.[7]

From the relationship $q = (A/O)/(R/r)$, for each crime type, an average probability of arrest per crime for the different offenses is reported in table 1. These estimates are generally under 0.05.[7,9] The somewhat higher value for aggravated assault probably reflects the direct confrontation between offender and victim, and the high proportion of offenders who are known to victims, 36.5% in 1980.[11] These estimates of q based on aggregate published data are similar to other estimates of q based on self-reports of arrests and crimes by prison inmates. . . .[12, 13]

The relationship of μ with age is also surprising when the effects of μ are separated from those of P. The typical information suggesting very sharp age differences in involvement in crime is given by age-specific arrest rates in the general population (where the age effect on crime is inferred from the ages of arrestees), as shown in figure 2. Many presume that this pattern of a rapid rise to a peak in the late teens, followed by a steady decline at older ages, must also apply to the age-specific pattern of μ. Empirically, however, μ's for individual crime types are much less sensitive to age: when average μ's are compared, none of the expected large declines with age are observed for cohorts of arrestees during their 20s.[7]

Arrest frequencies for active offenders are thus found to be much more similar across different demographic groups than are aggregate arrest rates. This suggests, of course, that the considerable variability in population arrest rates with demographic variables is attributable predominantly to differences in P with these variables. This reflects higher participation in crime by males and by blacks, and a rapid buildup of participation in the early teen years, followed by steady termination of criminal careers in the later teen years and early 20s. For those offenders who remain active, however, the value of μ seems to be fairly constant over age and across race and sex.

It is striking how few variables have yet been identified as significantly influencing λ. One of the important ones is the frequency and intensity of drug use. During periods of heavy drug use offenders commit crimes at frequencies six times as high as nonusing offenders (pp. 74–75).[2]

Duration of Criminal Careers

Aside from the frequencies, the second most important parameter describing the criminal career is career length, and particularly the related residual career length. These are difficult to observe directly, partly because of the difficulty of determining just when the career is actually terminated. We have addressed this issue by using methods similar to those in life-table analysis.[16]

In this approach, if there are significantly fewer 30-year-olds than 25-year-olds among active offenders, then one explanation for that decline is career termination between ages 25 and 30. Obviously, other competing explanations include differences in the sizes of the age cohorts in the general population, different rates of recruitment into criminal activity across the different cohorts, differential imprisonment with age, and decreases in λ with age. Controlling for these alternative explanations, Blumstein and Cohen[17] develop estimates of termination rates and of their reciprocal, the mean residual career length, as a function of age. These estimates are shown in figure 3 for offenders whose adult careers began before age 21.

Conventional wisdom about criminal career termination is unduly influenced by examination of figure 2. In that figure, it is apparent that by age 30 there is a sharp decline in the number of active offenders. Thus, common belief suggests that offenders are about to terminate their criminal careers by age 30, so that long sentences for such offenders would be particularly wasteful of prison resources. From figure 3, however, it becomes clear that among those offenders who do remain active, mean residual career length actually rises until about age 30, is fairly flat though the 30s, and then begins to decline rapidly in the early 40s.

This process is similar to many other lifetime phenomena that are characterized by high failure early in life (infant mortality, break-in failures of machines), maximum expected lifetime in the middle, and high failure again at the end (aging, wear-out failures in machines). Because a large number of offenders do terminate their careers quickly during the early break-in period, adult careers are reasonably short, averaging under 6 years for serious offenses. Relatively few offenders survive these early high termination rates and remain active in criminal careers into their 30s, but they are the ones with the most enduring careers. Termination rates do begin to increase at older ages, but that does not occur until after age 40.

It is interesting to speculate on those factors that might be contributing to the high termination rates in the later years. They could be attributable to increased mortality, but the career termination rates, in the order of 15% per year, are a factor of more than 10 higher than ordinary mortality rates for males of under 1.5% at ages 45 to 54.[18] Of course, the population of individuals who are still active offenders in

Figure 3

Variation in mean residual career length (T_R) with time already in a career for 18- to 20-year-old starters.[17]

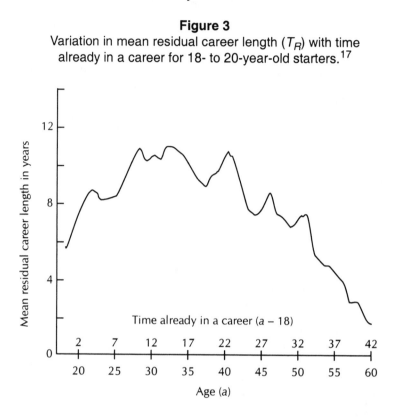

their 40s may be subject to higher death rates than those of the general population. Indeed, death rates among parolees are two to three times as high as general population rates.[17] This difference in mortality rates, however, is not sufficient to fully explain the higher termination rates that are observed. Another possible explanation could be associated with the kind of physiological effects one sees in many other facets of young male activity (for example, athletics) with peaking in the early ages followed by a gradual decline and then a rapid decline at later ages.

Policy Implications of Emerging Criminal-Career Knowledge

Although much of the research on criminal careers is still embryonic and not yet ready for significant policy application, some of the emerging insights represent important challenges to the prevailing conventional wisdom about crime and about means for dealing with crime. . . .

Incapacitation

The mechanism of crime control which is most directly related to criminal careers is incapacitation. Incapacitation refers to the crimes averted in the community by removing an offender who would otherwise be active in a criminal career. Those crimes are averted only if the crimes "leave the street" with the offender's removal. To the extent that crimes derive from an economic market—as is the case with drug sales, for example—then removing a single supplier is not likely to affect the market in any significant way because a replacement supplier is likely to appear to meet the continuing demand. Even burglaries that are carried out in the service of a fence, for example, could simply be continued by the fence finding new recruits to replace an imprisoned burglar. Continued offending by criminal groups after the incarceration of some group members also decreases incapacitation effects.[19]

Crimes that are carried out without such obvious structural sources, but which are linked more to the personal circumstances of individual offenders, and particularly acts of personal violence, are much more likely to be averted through incapacitation. For such crimes, in the context of the simple criminal-career structure indicated in figure 1, a sentence of S years served between A_0 and A_N should avert λS crimes.

It is possible, however, that the sentence is imposed later in the criminal career so that the time served extends after the career would have been terminated anyway at A_N. In that case the period between the end of the career (A_N) and the end of the sentence is "wasted" in terms of incapacitative effects. Obviously, if the judge could anticipate when the career would be terminated, he could take account of that in his sentence. The stochastic quality of the termination process, however, limits his ability to make that prediction.

Avi-Itzhak and Shinnar[20] developed a model to estimate the incapacitative effects of a sentence with mean length S for an individual who commits crime at a Poisson rate λ, with a probability of arrest q and a conditional probability of incarceration after arrest J. The mean time between crimes while active and free on the street is $1/\lambda$; the mean street time between arrests is $1/\lambda q$; the mean street time between incarcerations is $1/\lambda qJ$; and so in cycles between spells of imprisonment, the fraction of time spent in prison is $S/(S + 1/\lambda qJ)$. This is the fraction of the career that is spent in prison $I = (\lambda qJS)/(1 + \lambda qJS)$.

This model forms the basis for several recent estimates of incapacitative effects.[21–24] The model assumes a Poisson crime committing process, an exponential distribution of time in prison, infinite career length, and values of each of the parameters independent of each other. Although those assumptions are highly simplified, the results are reasonably robust to most minor violations. The failure to account for finite career length, however, and the resulting loss in incapacitative effect when time is served after careers have terminated can be considerable. That effect is accommodated by replacing S in the last equation with $ST/(T + S)$ when career length is exponentially distributed with finite mean T. If careers are long compared to sentence length, finite career length would not have much effect. For careers that average 5 to 10 years and time served averaging 2 to 3 years, however, that effect can be significant.[2,25] . . .

Some Summary Issues

The Issue of Race

One of the important insights on crime that results from the research on criminal careers is the isolation of the role of the race variable. General population arrest rates are very different between blacks and whites, and especially so for violent crimes. This difference is due primarily to large race differences in participation, with very little difference between the races in the crime frequency of active offenders. Since the cases seen by the criminal justice system have already penetrated the participation filter, where race differences are large, this argues strongly that racial discrimination in arrest, sentencing, or parole decisions, which is unambiguously prohibited on normative grounds, is also empirically wrong as a basis for decisions about active offenders.

The Role of Drug Use

The important influence of heavy drug use on λ is consistent with conventional wisdom, which suggests that drug users without other economic sources of support resort to other forms of crime to obtain the resources for their drug use. This has led some observers to argue that reduced enforcement, possibly even decriminalization, would lower the price and thereby diminish the need for crime to finance the purchase of drugs. Of course, this fails to account for any influence of higher price on inhibiting initiation or diminishing use by those who are current users.

Recognition of the relation between drug use and λ has also been used to argue for stricter enforcement against all drug offenses. Such a policy, however, fails to distinguish between drug users who engage primarily in drug offenses and those who engage in more threatening predatory crimes like robbery and burglary. To the extent that drug offenders are otherwise economically self-sufficient (for example, by earning considerable income from legitimate employment or by selling drugs to other users) a crackdown on their drug offenses will not affect predatory crimes directly. The strong association between drug use and λ for nondrug offenses, however, does suggest that, at least from the viewpoint of incapacitative effectiveness, the fact that a robber or other predatory offender uses drugs intensively should be viewed as an aggravating factor that would warrant a more certain sentence. Such a policy is contrary to the common practice of viewing drug involvement in the commission of a crime as a mitigating factor in establishing the sentence, largely because of concern over the diminished capacity—and the associated reduction in blameworthiness—of individuals under the influence of drugs.

Older Criminals

The results here also suggest reconsideration of the conventional views about offenders who remain active in criminal careers into their 30s. After the teenage years, age certainly appears to be monotonically negatively related to P, that is, there is reasonably high termination and relatively little recruitment after about age 20, and so participation levels continue to decline. However, the common belief that offenders who remain in their criminal careers into their 30s will imminently terminate their careers is not empirically justified. On the contrary, those offenders who are still actively involved in crime at age 30 have survived the more typical early termination of criminal careers, and so are more likely to be the more persistent offenders. After their early 40s, however, their termination rates are quite high.

It is clear from the existing research that the microperspective of examining individual criminal careers does indeed provide the opportunity for significant new insights that are not otherwise available from examination of aggregate data regarding crime rates. It is also clear that the issues are quite complex and the causal connections are often elusive. Prospective longitudinal research on a large sample of individuals from multiple cohorts relying on official-record data and repeated self-reports of criminal activity and individual life events, would provide more precise indications of causal sequences. More effectively disentangling the apparent drug-crime nexus is of particular concern. The greatly enriched data on changes in life circumstances would also provide an expanded basis for identifying some of the factors most strongly associated with high and low crime frequencies and with early and late career terminations—aspects of criminal careers that bear directly on the effectiveness of various crime-control strategies.

References and Notes

1. For the heterogeneous case, with crimes of type i and offenders of group j, the relation becomes C_i $\Sigma_j n_j P_{ij} \lambda_{ij} / \Sigma_j n_j$; $C = \Sigma_i C_i$.
2. A. Blumstein, J. Cohen, J. Roth, C. A. Visher, Eds., *Criminal Careers and "Career Criminals,"* National Research Council (National Academy Press, Washington, DC, 1986), vol. 1.
3. R. Christiansen, in *Task Force Report: Science and Technology* (Government Printing Office, Washington, DC, 1967), p. 216; J. Belkin, A. Blumstein, W. Glass, *J. Crim. Justice* 1, 7 (1973).
4. D. P. Farrington, *Br. J. Criminol.* 21, 173 (1981).
5. A. Blumstein and E. Graddy, *Law Soc. Rev.* 16, 265 (1982).
6. J. Chaiken and M. Chaiken, *Varieties of Criminal Behavior* (Rand Corporation, Santa Monica, CA, 1982).
7. A. Blumstein and J. Cohen, *J. Crim. Law Criminol.* 70, 561 (1979).
8. J. Cohen, in *Crime and Justice*, M. Tonry and N. Morris, Eds. (Univ. of Chicago Press, Chicago, 1983), vol. 5, p. 1.
9. J. Cohen, in (2), p. 292.
10. The populations sampled were arrested in the mid-1970s. This raises a question about the direct applicability of these results to samples that might be drawn today. Such replication is clearly desirable.
11. Bureau of Justice Statistics, *Criminal Victimization in the United States, 1980* (U.S. Department of Justice, Washington, DC, 182).
12. M. A. Peterson, H. B. Braiker, S. Pouch, *Who Commits Crimes* (Oelgeschlager, Gunn, Hain, Cambridge, MA, 1981).
13. J. Petersilia, *Racial Disparities in the Criminal Justice System* (Rand Corporation, Santa Monica, CA, 1983).
14. A. Blumstein, J. Cohen, C. A. Visher, in preparation.
15. R. F. Sparks, in *Indicators of Crime and Criminal Justice: Quantitative Studies*, S. E. Fienberg and A. J. Reiss, Jr., Eds. (U.S. Criminal Justice Department of Justice, Washington, DC, 1980), p. 18.
16. D. R. Cox, *Renewal Theory* (Methuen, London, 1962).
17. A. Blumstein and J. Cohen, in preparation.
18. U.S. Bureau of Census, *Statistical Abstract of the U.S. 1985* (U.S. Department of Commerce, Washington, DC, 1984), p. 71.
19. A. J. Reiss, Jr., in (2), vol. 2, p. 121.
20. B. Avi-Itzhak and R. Shinnar, *J. Crim. Justice* 1, 185 (1973).
21. R. Shinnar and S. Shinnar, *Law Soc. Rev.* 9, 581 (1975).
22. J. Cohen, in Blumstein, Cohen, and Nagin, Eds., *Deterrence and Incapacitation: Estimating the Effects of Criminal Sanctions on Crime Rates* (National Academy of Sciences, Washington, DC, 1978).
23. P. W. Greenwood, *Selective Incapacitation* (Rand Corporation, Santa Monica, CA, 1982).
24. M. Moore, S. R. Estrich, D. McGillis, W. Spelman, *Dangerous Offender: The Elusive Target of Justice* (Harvard Univ. Press, Cambridge, MA, 1984).
25. J. Cohen, in preparation.

12

Crime and Deviance over the Life Course: The Salience of Adult Social Bonds

Robert J. Sampson   *John H. Laub*

Sociological criminology has neglected early childhood characteristics, and consequently has not come to grips with the link between early childhood behaviors and later adult outcomes (Caspi, Bem, and Elder 1989; Farrington 1989; Gottfredson and Hirschi 1990). Although criminal behavior peaks in the teenage years, there is substantial evidence of early delinquency as well as continuation of criminal behavior over the life course. By concentrating on the teenage years, sociological perspectives on crime fail to address the life-span implications of childhood behavior (Wilson and Herrnstein 1985). At the same time, criminologists have not devoted much attention to what Rutter (1988, p. 3) calls "escape from the risk process," limiting our understanding of desistance from crime and the transitions from criminal to noncriminal behavior.

To address these limitations, we develop a theoretical model of age-graded informal social control to account for persistence and desistance in criminal behavior. Our basic thesis is that while continuity in deviant behavior exists, social ties in adulthood—to work, family, and community—explain changes in criminality over the life span. Our model acknowledges the importance of early childhood behaviors while rejecting the implication that later adult factors have little relevance (Wilson and Herrnstein 1985). We contend that social interaction with adult institutions of informal social control has important effects on crime and deviance. As such, ours is a "sociogenic" theoretical model of adult crime and deviance. This model is examined using a unique longitudinal data set that follows two samples of delinquent and nondelinquent boys from early adolescence into their thirties.

The Life Course Perspective

The life course has been defined as "pathways through the age differentiated life span," where age differentiation "is manifested in expectations and options that

Source: From Robert J. Sampson and John H. Laub, "Crime and Deviance Over the Life Course: The Salience of Adult Social Bonds," *American Sociological Review*, Vol. 55, pp. 609–627, 1990. Permission granted by the American Sociological Association. All rights reserved.

impinge on decision processes and the course of events that give shape to life stages, transitions, and turning points" (Elder 1985, p. 17). Two central concepts underlie the analysis of life course dynamics. A trajectory is a pathway or line of development over the life span such as worklife, marriage, parenthood, self-esteem, and criminal behavior. Trajectories refer to long-term patterns of behavior and are marked by a sequence of life events and transitions (Elder 1985, pp. 31–2). *Transitions* are specific life events that are embedded in trajectories and evolve over shorter time spans (e.g., first job or first marriage). Some of them are age-graded and some are not. What is often assumed to be important is the timing and the ordering of significant life events (Hogan 1980).

These two concepts are related: "the interlocking nature of trajectories and transitions, within and across life stages . . . may generate turning points or a change in course" (Elder 1985, p. 32). Adaptation to life events is crucial: "The same event or transition followed by different adaptations can lead to different trajectories" (Elder 1985, p. 35). This perspective implies both a strong connection between childhood events and experiences in young adulthood, and that transitions or turning points can modify life trajectories—they can "redirect paths."

Criminology and the Life Course

Criminology has been slow to recognize the importance of the life-course perspective (Hagan and Palloni 1988). Not only are the data needed to explore such relationships sparse (see Blumstein, Cohen, Roth, and Visher 1986), some researchers argue that ordinary life events (e.g., getting married, becoming a parent) have little effect on criminal behavior. Gottfredson and Hirschi argue that crime rates decline with age "whether or not these events occur" and note "that the longitudinal/developmental assumption that such events are important neglects its own evidence on the stability of personal characteristics" (1987, p. 604; see also Hirschi and Gottfredson 1983).

The extent of stability and change in behavior and personality attributes over time is one of the most complex and hotly debated issues in the social sciences (Brim and Kagan 1980; Dannefer 1984). The research literature in criminology contains evidence for both continuity and change over the life course. . . .

Childhood Behavior and
Informal Social Control over the Life Course

Recognizing the importance of both stability and change in the life course, our model focuses on two propositions. First, we contend that childhood antisocial behavior (e.g., juvenile delinquency, conduct disorder, violent temper tantrums) is linked to a wide variety of troublesome adult behaviors including criminality, general deviance, offenses in the military, economic dependency, educational failure, employment instability, and marital discord. These long-term relationships are posited to occur independent of traditional variables such as social class background and race/ethnicity. As Hagan and Palloni (1988) argue (see also Hagan 1989, p. 260), delinquent and criminal events "are linked into life trajectories of broader significance, whether those trajectories are criminal or noncriminal in form" (p. 190). Because most research by criminologists has focused either on the teenage years or adult behavior limited to crime, this hypothesis has not been definitively studied.

Second, we argue that social bonds to adult institutions of informal social control (e.g., family, education, neighborhood, work) influence criminal behavior over the life course despite an individual's delinquent and antisocial background. We seek to identify the transitions embedded in individual trajectories that relate to adult informal social control, and contend that childhood pathways to crime and deviance can be significantly modified over the life course by adult social bonds.

The important institutions of social control vary across the life span: in childhood and adolescence these are the family, school, and peer groups; in the phase of young adulthood they are higher education and/or vocational training, work, and marriage; and in later adulthood, the dominant institutions are work, marriage, parenthood, and investment in the community.

Within this framework, our organizing principle derives from social control theory (Durkheim 1951; Hirschi 1969; Kornhauser 1978): crime and deviance result when an individual's bond to society is weak or broken. We argue that changes that strengthen social bonds to society in adulthood will thus lead to less crime and deviance; changes that weaken social bonds will lead to more crime and deviance. Unlike most life-course research, we emphasize the *quality* or *strength* of social ties more than the occurrence or timing of specific life events. For example, while we agree with Gottfredson and Hirschi (1990, pp. 140–1) that marriage per se does not increase social control, a strong attachment to one's spouse and close emotional ties increase the social bond between individuals and, all else equal, should lead to a reduction in criminal behavior. Similarly, employment per se does not increase social control. It is employment coupled with job stability, job commitment, and ties to work that should increase social control and, all else equal, lead to a reduction in criminal behavior (see also Crutchfield 1989, p. 495). Therefore, we maintain that it is the *social investment* or social capital (Coleman 1988) in the institutional relationship, whether it be in a family, work, or community setting, that dictates the salience of informal social control at the individual level.

Our model assumes that life-event transitions and adult social bonds can modify quite different childhood trajectories. . . .

Data

We are currently engaged in a long-term project analyzing data from Sheldon and Eleanor Glueck's *Unraveling Juvenile Delinquency* (1950) and their subsequent follow-up studies (Glueck and Glueck 1968). These data are uniquely suited to our analytical goals due to the sampling design, the extensive measurement of key theoretical concepts, the long-term nature of the follow-up, and the historical context.

The Gluecks' research design began with samples of delinquent and nondelinquent boys born between 1924 and 1935. The *delinquent* sample comprised 500 10- to 17-year-old white males from Boston who, because of their persistent delinquency, were committed to one of two correctional schools in Massachusetts. The *nondelinquent* sample, or what they called a "control-group" (Glueck and Glueck 1950, p. 14), was made up of 500 10- to 17-year-old white males from the Boston public schools. Nondelinquent status was determined on the basis of official record checks and interviews with parents, teachers, local police, social workers and recreational leaders, as well as the boys themselves. The sampling procedure was designed to maximize differences in delinquency and by all accounts was successful. For example, the average number of convictions in the delinquent sample was

3.5. The nondelinquent boys were different from the Boston youth remanded to reform school, "but compared with national averages the men in this study did not represent a particularly law-abiding group" (Long and Vaillant 1984, p. 345). Although clearly not a random selection, the samples appear to be representative of their respective populations at that time.

Boys in the two samples were matched on a case-by-case basis according to age, race/ethnicity, general intelligence, and neighborhood socioeconomic status (for details see Glueck and Glueck 1950, pp. 33–9; Laub and Sampson 1988). These classic variables are widely thought to influence both delinquency and official reaction. Boys in each sample grew up in high-risk environments characterized by poverty, social disorganization, and exposure to delinquency and antisocial conduct (Glueck and Glueck 1950, pp. 30–2).

From 1940 to 1965, the Gluecks' research team collected data on these individuals. They were originally interviewed at an average age of 14, at age 25, and again at age 32. On average, then, the original subjects were followed for 18 years. Data were collected for all three time periods for 438 of the 500 delinquents and 442 of the 500 nondelinquent controls (88 percent). The follow-up success was 92 percent when adjusted for mortality—relatively high by current standards (see e.g., Wolfgang, Thornberry, and Figlio 1987).

During the first wave, a wide range of biological, psychological, and sociological information concerning each boy and his life from birth until adolescence was gathered. The second-wave field investigation and interview began as each subject approached his 25th birthday and concerned the period from age 17 to 25 (the juvenile court in Massachusetts had jurisdiction up to the 17th birthday). The third-wave interview covered the period from age 25 to 32. The second- and third-wave interviews concentrated on social factors, including criminal histories. Data are available on life transitions relating to living arrangements, schooling, employment, work habits, marital status, leisure-time activities, companionship, and participation in civic affairs. The data on criminal justice interventions (e.g., all arrests, convictions, and dispositions including actual time served) pertain to the period from first contact to age 32. . . .

Despite this rich body of longitudinal data, the Gluecks' main analyses were cross-sectional (Glueck and Glueck 1950). Their attention to the follow-up data was sparse and the resulting book (Glueck and Glueck 1968) was a simple descriptive overview of the samples. Fortunately, the Gluecks' coded data and raw interview records were stored in the Harvard Law School Library. A major effort of our project has been devoted to coding and computerizing the full longitudinal data set. The reconstruction and validation of these data involved numerous steps, reported in detail elsewhere (Laub, Sampson, and Kiger 1990; Sampson and Laub, forthcoming). . . .

Patterns of Stability and Change

The long-term effects of juvenile delinquency are not limited to adult criminal behavior. Seven adult behaviors spanning economic, educational, employment, and family domains are also strongly related to adolescent delinquency. Antisocial subjects were much less likely to finish high school by age 25. For both delinquency measures, delinquent boys were at least seven times more likely than nondelinquents to have a history of unstable employment as adults. A similar pattern emerges for economic dependence (e.g., welfare) and divorce among those ever married—delinquents were three to five times more likely to be divorced or receive welfare as adults.

In short, childhood delinquent behavior has a significant relationship with a wide range of adult criminal and deviant behaviors, including charges initiated by military personnel, reports of involvement in deviance and excessive drinking, and arrest by the police. The same childhood antisocial behaviors are also predictive of economic, family, educational, and employment problems up to eighteen years later. These results are robust as to measurement of delinquency. Because of the matched design, they cannot be explained in terms of original differences between delinquents and nondelinquents in age, intelligence, socioeconomic status, and race/ethnicity—variables often associated with stratification outcomes. Clearly, the boys in the Gluecks' delinquent and nondelinquent samples exhibited behavioral consistency well into adulthood (Glueck and Glueck 1968).

Adult Social Bonds

. . . Job stability in young adulthood has a large inverse relationship with each measure of adult crime and deviance for both the delinquent and nondelinquent samples. Moreover, young-adult job stability has substantial *predictive* power, exhibiting very large negative effects on alcohol use, general deviance, and arrest in the subsequent 25–32 age period. For both samples, subjects with low job stability at ages 17–25 were at least four times more likely to have severe alcohol problems in later adulthood and at least five times more likely to have engaged in deviant behavior compared to those with high job stability. It thus seems unlikely that adult crime itself can account for the patterns observed. Because these relationships obtain within both samples, the results cannot be dismissed on the basis of a "stability" or "self selection" argument that antisocial children simply replicate their antisocial behavior as adults—that delinquent kids invariably continue their interactional styles in adult spheres of life, and hence have incompatible relations with family, work, and other institutions of social control (Caspi 1987). Rather, it appears that job stability in adulthood significantly modifies trajectories of crime and deviance regardless of strong differences in childhood delinquent and antisocial conduct.

Adult commitment to conventional educational and occupational goals results in a similar pattern. Subjects with high aspirations and efforts to advance educationally and occupationally were much less likely to engage in deviant behavior, use alcohol excessively, or be arrested at ages 17–25 and 25–32.

The pattern is consistent for the relationship between attachment to spouse and adult crime among those ever married (approximately 50 percent of each sample). All relationships are in the expected direction, significant, and substantively large. As with job stability and commitment, the influence of attachment to wife at ages 17–25 is salient not only in the concurrent period but in the later 25–32 period as well.

The evidence strongly suggests that informal social controls in young adulthood are significantly and substantially related to adult antisocial behavior, regardless of childhood delinquency. The "ontogenetic" model's emphasis on stability . . . is clearly insufficient as an explanatory model for the life course. Social bonds to the adult institutions of work, education, and the family exert a powerful influence on adult crime and deviance.

Models of Adult Crime among Original Delinquents

A major question may be raised concerning these results—do individual differences in crime within the delinquent and control groups confound the results? The most delinquent subjects in the delinquent group may have self-selected themselves into later states of job instability, conflict-ridden marriages, and crime (Caspi 1987). Similarly, despite the absence of an official record, the nondelinquent subjects were not equally nondelinquent.

We address this question through a multivariate strategy that controls for prior delinquency and crime in four ways. . . . The results are rather clear—once other factors are controlled, income and marriage do not have significant effects on adult crime and deviance.

On the other hand, job stability shows consistent effects for all indicators of crime and deviance—all coefficients are at least two times their standard errors. Job stability has the largest effect on the most precise estimate of crime—the number of arrests per year free in the community at ages 17–25 (t-ratio = –4.85). This is particularly important given that two measures of delinquency are controlled and exhibit significant direct effects. . . .

The results suggest that it is cohesiveness that is central rather than marriage per se. Marital attachment has significant negative effects on all measures of crime and deviance, net of other factors. Among ever-married men, the influence of job stability declines in magnitude—it has a significant negative effect only on crime frequency. Similar results obtained when we examined arrests in the latter half of the first follow-up (i.e., at ages 22–25). Therefore, the data suggest the importance of both job stability and attachment to wife as factors promoting reductions in crime that are not explained by the original designation as delinquent.

It is possible that crime itself may have influenced observed levels of attachment and job stability. To address this issue, the predictive effects of social bonds were examined. . . . In fact, for crime frequency at ages 25–32, both job stability and attachment to spouse were significant net of prior crime and other factors. . . .

For all men in the delinquent group, the results indicate that controlling for prior levels, job stability in later adulthood has relatively large negative effects for each indicator of crime and deviance. For crime frequency at ages 25–32, both prior and current job stability have significant negative effects. It thus appears that prior levels *and* relative increases in job stability have negative effects on change in adult criminality. Commitment to conventional occupational goals also inhibits general deviance and drinking, but not arrest or crime frequency.

. . . [M]arital attachment at ages 25–32 is a significant and substantively important explanation of crime in later adulthood. Men with close ties to their spouses at ages 25–32 had much lower levels of crime and deviance than men with discordant relations, net of other factors including prior adult crime. The independent effect of marital attachment on crime frequency at ages 25–32 is especially large (t-ratio = –4.45, beta = –.31). The latter compares to a beta of .38 for prior arrest rate at ages 17–25. Moreover, the t-ratios for marital attachment are larger than those for the prior arrest rate in explaining general deviance and excessive drinking. Thus, marital attachment is an important factor in explaining later adult patterns of crime—at least as important as prior levels of crime. Job stability, as in previous models, is reduced in predictive power among ever-married men. The data again suggest a two-part explanation: for the majority of men, job stability is central in explaining adult desistance from crime; however, this effect is reduced among those who were ever married, for whom attachment to wife assumes greater relative importance. Once marital attachment and job stability are taken into account, the effect of commitment is relatively weak. . . .

Adult Crime and Deviance among Original Nondelinquents

We turn to an analysis of adult crime and deviance among the men in the control group—a sample that differs dramatically from the one just examined. . . . The results for all men in the control group indicate that variations in reported but unofficial childhood delinquency predict excessive drinking and arrest in young adulthood. Although some of the officially nondelinquent boys committed delinquencies, these unofficial acts were generally minor (e.g., truancy, smoking). Independent of these prior differences in juvenile delinquency, job stability has a significant negative effect on general deviance and excessive drinking but not on arrest. The pattern for commitment to conventional goals is more consistent: High commitment in young adulthood reduces involvement in all three antisocial behaviors. As in the delinquent sample, the effects of income and marriage are not significant.

[Considering only] . . . ever-married men, attachment to spouse has large independent effects on excessive drinking and arrest in young adulthood. The effects of commitment are eliminated in the married subsample, while job stability has a significant negative effect only on excessive drinking. The model for general deviance is rather weak in explanatory power—the only significant factor is the positive effect of income. Except for this one anomaly, the general pattern is similar to the delinquent group—job instability and weak marital attachment are directly related to adult crime and deviance. . . .

Comparative Models of Persistence in Adult Crime and Deviance

We now compare the effects of adult social bonds on an overall measure of adult antisocial behavior for the delinquent and control groups. We constructed a scale by summing the indicators of excessive drinking, general deviance, and arrest over the entire 17–32 age span. This scale ranges from 0 to 6, and better reflects an individual's breadth of involvement in crime and deviance during adulthood than previous measures, especially for the control group in which adult crime was relatively rare. The social control variables are determined from the interview at age 25 to reduce the possibility of reciprocal effects from deviancy itself. . . .

The results for all men are consistent across samples—independent of juvenile delinquency, the largest significant influence on overall adult crime is job stability. . . . Job stability has significant and essentially identical negative effects on adult crime (compare unstandardized coefficients). Furthermore, the largest effect on overall adult criminal and deviant behavior . . . is marital attachment—ever-married men with close ties to their spouses in young adulthood were much less likely to engage in adult crime and deviance than men with weak ties, net of other factors. . . .

Conclusion

. . . We have offered a life-course model that does not deny early childhood differences, but at the same time recognizes that adult life events matter. The basic organizing principle derived from linking the life-course perspective with social control theory is that both continuity and change are evident, and that trajectories of crime and deviance are systematically modified by social bonds to adult institutions of informal social control. . . .

Consistent with a model of adult development and informal social control, we have shown that job stability and marital attachment in adulthood are significantly related to changes in adult crime—the stronger the adult ties to work and family, the less crime and deviance among both delinquents and controls. The results were strong, consistent, and robust over a wide variety of measures and analytical techniques. The effects of job stability were independent of prior and concurrent levels of commitment (i.e., aspirations and ambitions), suggesting that labor-market instability rather than weak occupational commitment is a key factor in understanding adult crime and deviance.

Sociologists need not be hostile to research establishing early childhood differences in delinquency and antisocial behavior—influences that may persist well into adulthood. Indeed, the other side of continuity is change, and the latter appears to be systematically structured by adult bonds to social institutions. Our results raise serious questions about perspectives that focus exclusively on childhood and ignore the adult life course. . . .

References

Blumstein, A., J. Cohen, J. Roth, and C. Visher (Eds.). 1986. *Criminal Careers and "Career Criminals."* Washington, DC: National Academy Press.

Brim, Orville G. and Jerome Kagan. 1980. "Constancy and Change: A View of the Issues." Pp. 1–25 in *Constancy and Change in Human Development*, edited by Orville G. Brim and Jerome Kagan. Cambridge: Harvard University Press.

Caspi, Avshalom. 1987. "Personality in the Life Course." *Journal of Personality and Social Psychology* 53:1203–13.

Caspi, Avshalom, Darryl J. Bem, and Glen J. Elder, Jr. 1989. "Continuities and Consequences of Interactional Styles Across the Life Course." *Journal of Personality* 57:375–406.

Coleman, James S. 1988. "Social Capital in the Creation of Human Capital." *American Journal of Sociology* 94:S95–120.

Crutchfield, Robert D. 1989. "Labor Stratification and Violent Crime." *Social Forces* 68:489–512.

Dannefer, Dale. 1984. "Adult Development and Social Theory: A Paradigmatic Reappraisal." *American Sociological Review* 49:100–16.

Durkheim, E. 1951. *Suicide* (translated by J. Spaulding and G. Simpson). New York: Free Press.

Elder, Glen H., Jr. 1974. *Children of the Great Depression*. Chicago: University of Chicago Press.

———. 1985. "Perspectives on the Life Course." Pp. 23–49 in *Life Course Dynamics*, edited by Glen H. Elder, Jr. Ithaca NY: Cornell Univ. Press.

Farrington, David P. 1989. "Later Adult Life Outcomes of Offenders and Nonoffenders." Pp. 220–44 in *Children at Risk: Assessment, Longitudinal Research, and Intervention*, edited by M. Brambring, F. Losel, and H. Skowronek. New York: Walter de Gruyter.

Glueck, Sheldon and Eleanor Glueck. 1950. *Unraveling Juvenile Delinquency*. New York: Commonwealth Fund.

———. 1968. *Delinquents and Nondelinquents in Perspective*. Cambridge: Harvard University Press.

Gottfredson, Michael and Travis Hirschi. 1990. *A General Theory of Crime*. Stanford, CA: Stanford University Press.

Hagan, John. 1989. *Structural Criminology*. New Brunswick, NJ: Rutgers University Press.

Hagan, John and Alberto Palloni. 1988. "Crimes as Social Events in the Life Course: Reconceiving a Criminological Controversy." *Criminology* 26:87–100.

Hirschi, Travis. 1969. *Causes of Delinquency*. Berkeley: University of California Press.

Hirschi, Travis and Michael Gottfredson. 1983. "Age and the Explanation of Crime." *American Journal of Sociology* 89:552–84.

Hogan, Dennis P. 1980. "The Transition to Adulthood as a Career Contingency." *American Sociological Review* 45:261–76.

Kornhauser, Ruth. 1978. *Social Sources of Delinquency.* Chicago: University of Chicago Press.

Laub, John H. and Robert J. Sampson. 1988. "Unraveling Families and Delinquency: A Reanalysis of the Gluecks' Data." *Criminology* 26:355–80.

Laub, John H., Robert J. Sampson, and Kenna Kiger. 1990. "Assessing the Potential of Secondary Data Analysis: A New Look at the Gluecks' *Unraveling Juvenile Delinquency Data.*" Pp. 244–57 in *Measurement Issues in Criminology,* edited by Kimberly Kempf. New York: Springer-Verlag.

Rutter, Michael. 1988. "Longitudinal Data in the Study of Causal Processes: Some Uses and Some Pitfalls." Pp. 1–28 in *Studies of Psychosocial Risk: The Power of Longitudinal Data,* edited by Michael Rutter. Cambridge: Cambridge University Press.

Sampson, Robert J. and John H. Laub. Forthcoming. *Crime and Deviance Over the Life Course.* New York: Springer-Verlag.

Vaillant, George E. 1977. *Adaptation to Life.* Boston: Little, Brown, and Co.

Wilson, James Q. and Richard Herrnstein. 1985. *Crime and Human Nature.* New York: Simon and Schuster.

Wolfgang, Marvin, Terrence Thornberry, and Robert Figlio. 1987. *From Boy to Man: From Delinquency to Crime.* Chicago: University of Chicago Press.

13

Seductions of Crime: Moral and Sensual Attractions in Doing Evil

Jack Katz

Introduction

The study of crime has been preoccupied with a search for background forces, usually defects in the offenders' psychological backgrounds or social environments, to the neglect of the positive, often wonderful attractions within the lived experience of criminality. The novelty of [the] book [from which this reading is taken] is its focus on the seductive qualities of crimes: those aspects in the foreground of criminality that make its various forms sensible, even sensually compelling, ways of being.

The social science literature contains only scattered evidence of what it means, feels, sounds, tastes, or looks like to commit a particular crime. Readers of research on homicide and assault do not hear the slaps and curses, see the pushes and shoves, or feel the humiliation and rage that may build toward the attack, sometimes persisting after the victim's death. How adolescents manage to make the shoplifting or vandalism of cheap and commonplace things a thrilling experience has not been intriguing to many students of delinquency. Researchers of adolescent gangs have never grasped why their subjects so often stubbornly refuse to accept the outsider's insistence that they wear the "gang" label. The description of "cold-blooded, senseless murders" has been left to writers outside the social sciences. Neither academic methods nor academic theories seem to be able to grasp why such killers may have been courteous to their victims just moments before the killing, why they often wait until they have dominated victims in sealed-off environments before coldly executing them, or how it makes sense to them to kill when only petty cash is at stake. Sociological and psychological studies of robbery rarely focus on the *distinctive* attractions of robbery, even though research has now clearly documented that alternative forms of criminality are available and familiar to many career robbers. In sum, only rarely have sociologists taken up the challenge of explaining the qualities of deviant experience.[1] . . .

Source: Jack Katz, *Seductions of Crime: Moral and Sensual Attractions in Doing Evil.* Copyright © 1988 by Perseus Books Group. Reproduced with permission of Perseus Books Group in the format Textbook via Copyright Clearance Center. Notes renumbered.

The Magic in Motivation

Whatever the relevance of antecedent events and contemporaneous social conditions, something causally essential happens in the very moments in which a crime is committed. The assailant must sense, then and there, a distinctive constraint or seductive appeal that he did not sense a little while before in a substantially similar place. Although his economic status, peer group relations, Oedipal conflicts, genetic makeup, internalized machismo, history of child abuse, and the like remain the same, he must suddenly become propelled to commit the crime. Thus, the central problem is to understand the emergence of distinctive sensual dynamics.

To believe that a person can suddenly feel propelled to crime without any independently verifiable change in his background, it seems that we must almost believe in magic. And, indeed, this is precisely what we must do. When they are committing crimes, people feel drawn and propelled to their criminality, but in feeling determined by outside forces, they do nothing morally special. The particular seductions and compulsions they experience may be unique to crime, but the sense of being seduced and compelled is not. To grasp the magic in the criminal's sensuality, we must acknowledge our own.

A sense of being determined by the environment, of being pushed away from one line of action and pulled toward another, is natural to everyday, routine human experience. We are always moving away from and toward different objects of consciousness, taking account of this and ignoring that, and moving in one direction or the other between the extremes of involvement and boredom. In this constant movement of consciousness, we do not perceive that we are controlling the movement. Instead, to one degree or another, we are always being seduced and repelled by the world.[2] "This *is* fascinating (interesting, beautiful, sexy, dull, ugly, disgusting)," we know (without having to say), as if the thing itself possessed the designated quality independent of us and somehow controlled our understanding of it. Indeed, the very nature of mundane being is emotional; attention is feeling, and consciousness is sensual.

Only rarely do we actually experience ourselves as subjects directing our conduct. How often, when you speak, do you actually sense that you are choosing the words you utter? As the words come out, they reveal the thought behind them even to the speaker whose lips gave them shape. Similarly, we talk, walk, and write in a sense of natural competence governed by moods of determinism. We rest our subjectivity on rhythmic sensibilities, feelings for directions, and visions of unfolding patterns, allowing esthetics to guide us.[3] Self-reflexive postures in which one creates a distance between the self and the world and pointedly directs the self into the world, occur typically in an exceptional mood of recognizing a malapropism, after a misstep, or at the slip of the pen. With a slight shock, we recognize that it was not the things in themselves but our perspective that temporarily gave things outside of us the power to seduce or repel.

Among the forms of crime, the range of sensual dynamics runs from enticements that may draw a person into shoplifting to furies that can compel him to murder. . . .

The challenge for explanation is to specify the steps of the dialectic process through which a person empowers the world to seduce him to criminality. On the one hand, we must explain how the individual himself *conjures up* the spirit. On the other hand, we must accept the attraction or compulsion as *authentic*.

It is not a simple matter to raise these spirits. One cannot be blindly enraged, coolly sadistic, or secretly thrilled at will, simply by the conscious choice to be evil, no more than one can transport himself to erotic heights simply and instantly by opting for pleasure. For a person to experience being influenced or determined, he must lose a reflective awareness of the abiding, constructive workings of his subjectivity. Thus, part of the challenge is to recognize steps in raising a spirit of determinism that are sufficiently subtle that their contingencies go unnoticed.

Typically, the person will not be able to help us with the analysis because he is taken in by his efforts to construct the dynamic. If we ask, "Why did you do it?" he is likely to respond with self-justifying rhetoric. But he can help us with a detailed account of the processual development of his experience. If we ask, "How did you do that? And then what did you do?" we are likely to discover some poignant moments. And, because the person constructs his definition of the situation through bodily comprehension, we may catch the conditions of his involvement in exceptional circumstances when it is undermined by an incongruent sensuality. Thus, the interrogator's victim may defecate, triggering a life-saving perception by her torturer that *he* is the shit. Or, to offer an erotic example, the lovers' child may suddenly walk in and prove that what they had sensed as an abandoned involvement was not.

That emotions are contingent on definitions of the situation is a commonplace both in existentialist writing and in the sociological tradition of symbolic interaction. What has been more difficult to appreciate is the ontological validity of passion—the authentic efficacy of sensual magic. In sex, as well as in mock fighting on street corners, initially lighthearted thrusts and parries may turn into the real thing without warning. Such preliminaries to passion are playful in an existentially specific sense: the participants are playing with the line between the sense of themselves as subject and object, between being in and out of control, between directing and being directed by the dynamics of the situation. To complete successfully the transition from subject to object and achieve the emotional extremes of eros or thanatos, a person may have to arrange the environment to "pacify" his subjectivity.[4] He may then submit to forces that transcend his subjectivity even while he tacitly controls the transition.

What phenomenology uniquely has appreciated is not simply that a person's lived world is his artifact but that by experiencing himself as an object controlled by transcendent forces, an individual can genuinely experience a new or different world. By pacifying his subjectivity, a person can conjure up a magic so powerful that it can change his ontology. What begins as idle slapping or fondling may lead to the discovery of rare truths or the acquisition of a new incompetence.[5]

It is necessary to indulge a fiction or invoke a ritual to begin the process, but if one does not hedge on the commitment of faith, otherwise inaccessible phenomena may come into reach, bringing revelations or shutting off part of one's freedom and confirming that the initial commitment was authentic. In religious practice, we may find the results of this dialectical process inspiring; in sex, delightful. As unattractive morally as crime may be, we must appreciate that there is *genuine experiential creativity* in it as well. We should then be able to see what are, for the subject, the authentic attractions of crime and we should then be able to explain variations in criminality beyond what can be accounted for by background factors.

Criminal Projects

. . . By way of explanation, I will propose for each type of crime a different set of individually necessary and jointly sufficient conditions, each set containing (1) a path of action—distinctive practical requirements for successfully committing the crime, (2) a line of interpretation—unique ways of understanding how one is and will be seen by others, and (3) an emotional process—seductions and compulsions that have special dynamics. Raising the spirit of criminality requires practical attention to a mode of executing action, symbolic creativity in defining the situation, and esthetic finesse in recognizing and elaborating on the sensual possibilities.

Central to all these experiences in deviance is a member of the family of moral emotions: humiliation, righteousness, arrogance, ridicule, cynicism, defilement, and vengeance. In each, the attraction that proves to be most fundamentally compelling is that of overcoming a personal challenge to moral—not to material—existence. For the impassioned killer, the challenge is to escape a situation that has come to seem otherwise inexorably humiliating. Unable to sense how he or she can move with self-respect from the current situation, now, to any mundane-time relationship that might be reengaged, then, the would-be killer leaps at the possibility of embodying, through the practice of "righteous" slaughter, some eternal, universal form of the Good.

For many adolescents, shoplifting and vandalism offer the attractions of a thrilling melodrama about the self as seen from within and from without. Quite apart from what is taken, they may regard "getting away with it" as a thrilling demonstration of personal competence, especially if it is accomplished under the eyes of adults.

Specifically "bad" forms of criminality are essentially addressed to a moral challenge experienced in a spatial metaphor. Whether by intimidating others' efforts to take him into their worlds ("Who you lookin' at?") or by treating artificial geographic boundaries as sacred and defending local "turf" with relentless "heart," "badasses" and *barrio* warriors celebrate an indifference to modern society's expectation that a person should demonstrate a sensibility to reshape himself as he moves from here to there.

To make a habit of doing stickups, I will argue, one must become a "hardman." It is only smart to avoid injuring victims unnecessarily, but if one becomes too calculating about the application of violence, the inherent uncertainties of face-to-face interaction in robberies will be emotionally forbidding. Beneath the surface, there may be, to paraphrase Nietzsche, a ball of snakes in chaotic struggle. But the stickup man denies any uncertainty and any possibility of change with a personal style that ubiquitously negates social pressures toward a malleable self.

Perhaps the ultimate criminal project is mounted by men who culminate a social life organized around the symbolism of deviance with a cold-blooded, "senseless" murder. Mimicking the ways of primordial gods as they kill, they proudly appear to the world as astonishingly evil. Through a killing only superficially justified by the context of robbery, they emerge from a dizzying alternation between affiliation with the great symbolic powers of deviant identity and a nagging dis-ease that conformity means cowardice.

Overall, my objective is to demonstrate that a theory of moral self-transcendence can make comprehensible the minutia of experiential details in the phenomenal foreground, as well as explain the general conditions that are most commonly found in the social backgrounds of these forms of criminality. This inquiry will best serve those who wish to address evil—not as judged by moral philosophy or imputed by political ideology but as lived in the everyday realities of contemporary society. In the end, I suggest that the dominant political and sociological understanding that crime is motivated by materialism is poorly grounded empirically—indeed, that it is more a sentimentality than a creditable causal theory. Because of its insistence on attributing causation to material conditions in personal and social backgrounds, modern social thought has been unable either to acknowledge the embrace of evil by common or street criminals, or, and for the same reason, develop empirical bite and intellectual depth in the study of criminality by the wealthy and powerful. By opening up systematic, theoretical, and empirical inquiry into the experience of criminality, this study points toward a comparative sociology that is capable of examining the seductions of crime as they are experienced up and down the social and political order. Those who follow the argument to its end may not find encouragement for broad-based social welfare policies, but readers should discover that the domestic deceits and foreign atrocities of our elites are no longer tangential to social research on crime. . . .

The Sensual Metaphysics of Sneaky Thrills

Although they know they are breaking the law, nonprofessional shoplifters and vandals commonly feel, when they are arrested, an irresistible protest that "this can't be happening to me!" It is as if they lived the process of the crime like a character moving in a myth or a dream. And in the emotional meaning or sensual dimension of the event, they do.

Sometimes the mythical quality of the experience is highlighted. The 13-year-old housebreaker who would enter neighbors' homes not to take things but in search of she knew not what, and who would run the risk of being caught by surprise to rearrange items, is reminiscent of Goldilocks entering the home of the Three Bears.[6] More commonly, if less obviously, the mythical meaning of the event is experienced emotionally. To understand the experience of sneaky thrills, we must appreciate how the structure of everyday sensuality is continuous with the structure of fantasy worlds.

As Alfred Schutz specified, there are fundamental contrasts between experience in mundane activities and in various alternative "worlds," such as those of the theater, night and day dreams, and jokes or laughter.[7] Experience in the mundane world of practical reality is confined by time, space, and social boundaries. People conduct practical social action with the limiting awareness that they are acting in a specific "here," during a specific "now," and in a particular type of publicly recognizable social situation. Dreams, fantasies, and various meta-mundane worlds do not respect these limitations.

The dreamer (asleep, while daydreaming, in the theater, or caught up in listening to a fairy tale) suspends the focus of his consciousness on the historical time and the geopolitical space he is in and the socially bounded process of sleeping and dreaming that he is going through. As a member of the audience who becomes absorbed in the theatrical drama, he "suspends disbelief" on these three dimensions. He dulls his awareness of the clock time during which the drama transpires, the physical location of the theater, and the fact that he is watching a dramatization of life. The dreamer witnesses movements through time, over space, and across the boundaries that usually separate internal awareness and externally visible expression and that are inconsistent with what he rationally knows of the structures of everyday practical life.

The world of everyday practical life and dream worlds are not existentially inconsistent. (And indeed, they may always be co-present. Even in the deepest sleep, we maintain an awareness of time, space, and social situations; we are not lost to the noises around us or the pressures of our autonomous physical selves.) Thus pilferers do not move through department stores as sleepwalkers or daydreamers, but neither do they construct their sneaky crimes simply as exercises of self-reflective reason. Through their feelings and the evolving sensuality of the event, they walk through its mythical dimensions. . . .

For both the pilferer and the passion killer, a dash of reality is often an effective "cure," although in the latter case it comes much too late. Those who murder in a passionate effort to dramatize their defense of the Good, like shoplifters who are arrested, are surprisingly without emotional defenses. Many wait for the police to arrive or confess quickly; few make good on escapes. Brought to the fatal moment by a leap to a timeless, primordial version of the Good, the impassioned killer momentarily transcends the demand to relate his behavior "now" to the meaning it will have "then." When he returns to practical everyday concerns a few moments later, he realizes that he must innovate an escape if he is to have one.

Similarly, the essence of the sneaky thrill is an attempt to transcend an existential dilemma, but, in this case, the dilemma is to relate the inner to outer identity. The shoplifter goes about her sneaky efforts to see if she can get away with it—"it" being a freely drawn, playfully artificial projection of the self into the world. Must I appear to be who I know I am? Need I struggle to shape what I know about myself into an acceptable appearance to others, or can I play with it? Can I dispense, not with moral appearances but with the *struggle* to produce moral appearances? Thus, the thrill embodies an awareness that the experience is essentially a play about dilemmas of moral authenticity arranged on a public staging of the self.

Those who pursue sneaky thrills appreciate this perspective with emotional immediacy. They know it sensually, not self-reflectively. Ask, and they may cite one of the stock background explanations, such as peer pressure; find the causation mysterious; or simply state, because it's fun. . . .

Moral Emotions and Crime

The closer one looks at crime, at least at the varieties examined here, the more vividly relevant become the moral emotions. Follow vandals and amateur shoplifters as they duck into alleys and dressing rooms and you will be moved by their delight in deviance; observe them under arrest and you may be stunned by their shame. Watch their strutting street display and you will be struck by the awesome fascination that symbols of evil hold for the young men who are linked in the groups we often call gangs. If we specify the opening moves in muggings and stickups, we describe an array of "games" or tricks that turn victims into fools before their pockets are turned out. The careers of persistent robbers show us, not the increasingly precise calculations and hedged risks of "professionals," but men for whom gambling and other vices are a way of life, who are "wise" in the cynical sense of the term, and who take pride in a defiant reputation as "bad." And if we examine the lived sensuality behind events of cold-blooded "senseless" murder, we are compelled to acknowledge the power that may still be created in the modern world through the sensualities of defilement, spiritual chaos, and the apprehension of vengeance.

Running across these experiences of criminality is a process juxtaposed in one manner or another against humiliation. In committing a righteous slaughter, the impassioned assailant takes humiliation and turns it into rage; through laying claim to a moral status of transcendent significance, he tries to burn humiliation up. The badass, with searing purposiveness, tries to scare humiliation off; as one ex-punk explained to me, after years of adolescent anxiety about the ugliness of his complexion and the stupidity of his every word, he found a wonderful calm in making "them" anxious about *his* perceptions and understandings. Young vandals and shoplifters innovate games with the risks of humiliation, running along the edge of shame for its exciting reverberations. Fashioned as street elites, young men square off against the increasingly humiliating social restrictions of childhood by mythologizing differences with other groups of young men who might be their mirror image. Against the historical background of a collective insistence on the moral nonexistence of their people, "bad niggers" exploit ethnically unique possibilities for celebrating assertive conduct as "bad.". . .

Notes

1. The two prominent exceptions in the sociology of deviance are Howard S. Becker, "Becoming a Marihuana User," *American Journal of Sociology* 59 (November 1953): 235–42; and David Matza, *Becoming Deviant* (Englewood Cliffs, NJ: Prentice-Hall, 1969), built directly on Becker's interactionist perspective, turning it in a more phenomenological direction but making a cautiously narrow concrete application only to the marijuana "high." Although these works have been widely respected by a generation of academic researchers on deviance, fields of substantive study have not taken off from them. But a number of recent studies may indicate that this situation is finally changing. See, for example, Trevor Bennett and Richard Wright, *Burglars on Burglary* (Aldershot, Hampshire, England: Gower, 1984); and Malin Åkerström, *Crooks and Squares* (New Brunswick, NJ: Transaction Books, 1985).
2. M. Merleau-Ponty, *Phenomenology of Perception*, trans. Colin Smith (London: Routledge & Kegan Paul, 1962).
3. An exemplary study is David Sudnow, *Ways of the Hand* (Cambridge, MA: Harvard University Press, 1970.
4. Matza, *Becoming Deviant.*
5. William James treated religious ecstasy, even the "supernatural," as authentic. He would grant ontological authenticity to "multiple" worlds. See *The Varieties of Religious Experience* (Cambridge, MA: Harvard University Press, 1985); and *A Pluralistic Universe* (Cambridge, MA: Harvard University Press, 1977). Merleau-Ponty did not use existentialist understandings of inescapable human freedom to deny the authentic terror in a madman's haunted consciousness. See *Phenomenology of Perception*, p. 125.
6. Goldilocks tries, but she cannot take the place of the infant nor that of either parent. Her struggle is the child's dilemma between infancy and adulthood, a struggle that becomes extended and intensified in adolescence. See Bruno Bettelheim, *The Uses of Enchantment* (New York: Alfred A. Knopf, 1977). The fable is, in several respects, also an instructive metaphor for understanding adolescent sneak theft. The listener has an unusually ambivalent emotional relationship to the heroine in that Goldilocks is not morally pure; in effect, she vandalizes and burglarizes the bears' home. There is a related and equally unusual tension in the story. That is, Goldilocks does not worry; she eats and goes to sleep, while the listener remains apprehensive about the bears' return. The question that animates the listener's anxiety is not precisely the same as in Little Red Riding Hood or Hansel and Gretel—Will the good little ones get away?—but has to do with anxiety about the thief: Will she get away with it?
7. Alfred Schutz, *Collected Papers* (The Hague: Martinus Nijhoff, 1962), 1:207–59.

Section II

Theories of Causation of Crime

The fact that detailed observations of criminal behavior have been conducted only since the 1920s is not a historical anomaly. The methods used to study crime have been closely related to implicit assumptions about human nature and the causes of crime. Thus, if crime were a product of demoniac possession the state of a person's soul would be at issue, not whether delinquent peers influenced him or her.

Although our modern conception of the human condition in general is rooted in ancient Jewish, Greek, and Christian philosophy, expressly criminological theory appeared in the late eighteenth century, the beginning of the "Age of Reason." With the twilight of the omnipotent monarchy and a reduction in the hold of the church on human consciousness, a new conception of human nature was formulated. The rationalists—Rousseau, Voltaire, Montesquieu, Bentham, Beccaria—viewed human behavior not as a product of spiritual forces but as a matter of free choice by beings who had the capacity to use logic and reason to choose from among alternative courses of action.

In criminology, the rationalists comprised what has become known as the "classical school," taking its name from the characteristic mode of inquiry (i.e., armchair philosophy) practiced by the ancient Greek theorists. The most prominent figure of the classical school was the British philosopher, Jeremy Bentham, who, with his first essay appearing in 1789, described the "felicific calculus" by which people supposedly weigh the anticipated pleasures and pains of a contemplated action. Some people choose to commit crimes because they anticipate that the pleasures they will derive will be greater than the pains they might suffer.

Beginning in the late nineteenth century, rationalism was overlaid with many other explanations of criminal behavior. The late twentieth century, however, saw a reemergence of interest in rationalism, most recently called "rational choice theory," in the fields of economics, psychology, sociology, and criminology. Ronald Clarke and Derek Cornish applied rational choice theory to explain why individual prospective offenders decide to commit (or refrain from committing) specific crimes.

Aside from rationalism, all theories of human behavior are to some degree deterministic, either at the microscopic level, involving the unique forces that determine a single individual's behavior, or at the macroscopic level, involving the large-scale social forces that influence the behavior of large groups of people.

Émile Durkheim drastically reshaped thought about the place of crime in society by observing that crime is present in all societies and is therefore a normal phenomenon. Moreover, it may actually be beneficial to the social order.

The social theorist who has had the greatest impact on society in the last 150 years is Karl Marx. Although Marx did not write specifically about the causes of crime, his writings about the relationships between the law and the state contain the origins of the socialist school of criminology. This school originated in the mid-nineteenth century and forms the basis for all public expressions concerning crime in communist countries. Only since the mid-1960s, however, have Western criminologists begun articulating the relationship between economic organization and criminality. (The work of Dutch sociologist William Bonger, *Criminality and Economic Conditions*, published in 1916, is a notable exception to this generalization.)

The writings of Marxist criminologists are generally difficult to understand. With his more accessible writing style, Richard Quinney brought contemporary conflict theory within the reach of a broad, general audience. Quinney's work is represented here by selections from his *Class, State, and Crime*.

Scientific or positivist criminology is considered to have its origins in the late-nineteenth-century work of the Italian physician, Cesare Lombroso. In his writings are found the scientific bases of the concept of the "born criminal." Lombroso, strongly influenced by Charles Darwin's writings on evolution, theorized that the born criminal was an atavism, a throwback to an earlier stage of human development, who committed crimes because he lacked a sufficiently developed moral sense and could be identified by certain characteristic physical anomalies.

Lombroso's first and most influential work, *L'uomo delinquente* (Criminal Man), appeared in 1876 and was never published in an English translation. The selection appearing here is from a summary of that work, which was written by his daughter Gina Lombroso-Ferrero and first published in 1911. It reflects both Lombroso's earliest preoccupations with physiological correlates of criminality and the position he took in later editions of *Criminal Man*, in which he gave greater weight to environmental influences.

Several studies tracing the allegedly hereditary transmission of criminal propensities seemed to lend weight to theories asserting that crime is caused by (or at least associated with) specific physical characteristics of the offender. Richard Dugdale's *The Jukes* traces crime, pauperism, and mental illness in one family in an attempt to demonstrate the hereditary perpetuation of social pathological traits.

Among the positivists, Lombroso and his colleagues formed one of the typological schools, so named because they concentrated on a particular attribute, which they hypothesized characterized the "criminal type" of person. Another of these typological schools was the mental testers, who proposed that mental deficiency, then called "feeble-mindedness," was responsible for a large proportion of criminal behavior. The work of H. H. Goddard is given here as a prominent example of the theory and methods of the mental testers.

When knowledge of the workings of the human mind was advanced around the turn of the twentieth century, primarily through the contributions of Sigmund Freud, criminologists responded by applying psychoanalytic and psychological analysis to criminal offenders. Psychologist William Healy was a founder of the Child Guidance Clinic movement in the United States—an important contribution because it focused attention on the problems of each individual delinquent and away from the social bases of delinquency.

The work of Lombroso diminished in popularity after Charles Goring published his study, *The English Convict*, which many considered a complete repudiation of Lombroso's work. Nevertheless, the application of anthropometric techniques initiated by Lombroso was rejuvenated by several Americans from the 1930s through the 1950s. Ernest Hooton was prominent among those who studied the relationship between body shape ("somatotype") and delinquency.

From the 1950s to the 1970s criminology emphasized sociological theories of crime, largely ignoring insights about human behavior from the field of biology. C. Ray Jeffery, an influential criminologist who brought recent advances in behavioral biology to the attention to criminologists, urged criminologists to consider the important impact that biology has on criminality. James Q. Wilson and Richard Herrnstein combined knowledge of biological factors that influence behavior with the concept of rational choice to explain criminality.

Émile Durkheim's sociological writings (represented here by selections from his book *Suicide*) provided the origins of strain theory, which is rooted in Durkheim's concept of anomie or normlessness—a condition that prevails when upheavals in society or rapid social change cause a reduction in the allegiance of members of the society to traditional rules and sources of social order.

In 1938, Robert Merton further developed the concept of anomie to show how social disorganization—a disjunction between the socially expected goals and the availability of means to attain those goals—creates strain, which some individuals relieve by choosing a criminal adaptation. Although Merton's theory was about social structural pressures encouraging crime, it was often misinterpreted to be an explanation of criminal psychology. Robert Agnew applied psychological insights to Merton's theory to create a general strain theory of delinquency.

Beginning in the 1930s, a number of important authors emphasized various aspects of the concept of culture and its influence on crime. Thorsten Sellin, writing during a period when the United States was experiencing large-scale in-migration, explained how culture conflict produced criminal behavior whenever two groups with different cultures come into contact. Clifford Shaw and Henry McKay, again using an ecological approach, discovered that in certain high-delinquency areas the rates of particular types of offenses remained stable over long periods because successive generations of juveniles trained one another in the techniques of delinquency through an age-graded gang structure.

Albert Cohen, in studying the content of juvenile gang culture, found that much delinquency was nonutilitarian and negativistic—destructive without providing any benefit to the participants. He reasoned that lower-class juveniles, blocked from the advantages of the middle class, derived their ideology by turning middle-class values upside down.

Walter Miller, however, argued that lower-class culture is characterized by a widely held set of "focal concerns," distinctive issues that were not simply a response to inaccessibility of middle-class advantages. The behavior of lower-class juveniles is oriented by these focal concerns—trouble, toughness, autonomy, and others—so that they are highly likely to violate the law while complying with the behavior norms of their social class.

Most people are neither consistently law-abiding nor criminal; even the most active criminal offenders spend most of their time engaged in lawful behavior. The challenge taken up by Sykes and Matza was to determine why kids whose behavior is mostly conventional occasionally commit acts of delinquency. Sykes and Matza found that such kids commonly use "techniques of neutralization" to suspend, temporarily, the restraining influence of conventional norms.

Edwin Sutherland's theory of differential association is perhaps the best known theoretical statement in sociological criminology. After proposing a number of preliminary formulations, Sutherland presented the theory in its final version in the 1947 edition of his text, *Principles of Criminology*. The theory of differential association removes from the process of preparing to commit crimes any suggestion of moral, physical, or intellectual inferiority in the prospective offender. To the contrary, it asserts that criminal behavior is learned, just like all other forms of behavior, through interaction with significant others. Criminality, then, becomes a probabilistic event determined by the frequency and quality of interactions with people that have attitudes and behavior patterns that either encourage or discourage crime.

A well-justified criticism of Sutherland's formulation of differential association was the ambiguity of some of its central concepts. Robert Burgess and Ronald Akers translated and extended differential association through modern learning theory to make it clearer and more readily testable.

Richard Cloward and Lloyd Ohlin built on the works of both Robert Merton and Edwin Sutherland by postulating that a criminal career is not the simple consequence of the unavailability of legitimate opportunities, but that an illegitimate opportunity structure exists parallel to the legitimate opportunity structure. People pursue conventional or criminal careers depending in part on their position in both structures and their perception of the likelihood of success through each.

Among the most prolific researchers and authors in criminology are Sheldon and Eleanor Glueck. Their major contribution has been an exploration of the multi-factor approach to the study of delinquency. Observing that no single factor seemed to explain involvement in crime and that many social, psychological, and physical factors were associated with delinquency, the Gluecks designed large-scale studies to determine which among hundreds of measures are most closely related to delinquent behavior. Their work was a largely atheoretical precursor to the interdisciplinary criminology that developed in the late 1970s.

Travis Hirschi's control theory took an entirely different approach to explaining delinquency. Beginning with the simple observation that much delinquent behavior is fun and rewarding, Hirschi noted that participation in delinquency requires no explanation. The key question, then, becomes, why do most children *not* participate regularly in delinquency? Hirschi's control theory asserts that the source of children's restraint lies in their social bonds.

By the last quarter of the twentieth century a consensus had formed among criminologists that criminal behavior was too diverse—including activities as different as violence, theft, fraud, rape, and drug use—for any single factor to be the cause of all kinds of crime. Travis Hirschi and Michael Gottfredson, in their bold *A General Theory of Crime*, rejected this consensus, asserting that low self-control was the cause of all crime.

The labeling perspective on crime grew out of the social-psychological writings of George Herbert Meade and the social interactionist school that he started. The labeling perspective emphasizes the culturally bound definition of crime—certain behaviors are crimes because they are labeled crimes—and the parallel attachment of the label "criminal."

Frank Tannenbaum stresses the problematical nature of becoming a deviant based on his observation that, regardless of why an initial deviant act is performed, only people whose evil act is emphasized and tagged by others adopt the status of deviant. Edwin Lemert builds on the importance of labeling by others. He developed the concept of "secondary deviance," a pattern of deviant behavior that is adopted as an adjustment to the response of others to the initial deviance. Finally, Howard Becker gives the clearest statement of the importance of the response of others to behavior, which is deviant only if so labeled, and to the person, who is a deviant only if that label is successfully applied.

In the 1970s feminist theorists and advocates sensitized criminologists to the importance of gendered power relationships in relation to female delinquency and crime. Dorie Klein and Meda Chesney-Lind provided some of the earliest statements of feminist criminology. Klein criticizes the "sexist, racist, classist" conceptions of crime formulated by Lombroso, Freud, and others writing in the same tradition. Chesney-Lind argues that female delinquency is often a response to the abuse and oppression to which girls are subjected, both in the community and by the juvenile justice system.

This brief sketch of criminological theory illuminates a trend from the eighteenth-century free-will philosophy to a late-nineteenth and early-twentieth-century biological determinism based on a variety of supposed causes, back to a "soft determinism" couched in terms of the probability of a confluence of environmental factors, and then a return to free will.

Recent developments in criminological theory have advanced several themes. The rational choice perspective experienced renewed interest and support under conservative politics since the 1980s. Biological determinism is supported through findings of similar criminal behavior patterns in twins and between adopted children and their biological parents. New biochemical interventions into mental disorders may portend advances in physiological explanations for some types of criminal behavior.

In international politics, since the 1980s the reunification of Germany and the dissolution of the Soviet Union have resulted in deadly political, ethnic, and religious struggles throughout Europe, while battles based on ethnicity and religion have continued in Africa and the Middle East, and political oppression occurs within many countries throughout the world. Meanwhile, ironically, criminological conflict theories have received less attention since the 1970s. Feminist theories are the single exception to this generalization. By emphasizing how the existing sex-based hierarchy encourages and shapes crimes by girls and women, feminist theories remind us that law violation occurs within large-scale, enduring social, economic, and political structures in which the majority of citizens are disadvantaged.

As this brief overview indicates, the evolution of criminological theory has paralleled, sometimes closely and sometimes only loosely, developments in philosophy, politics, and the natural sciences.

14

An Introduction to the Principles of Morals and Legislation

Jeremy Bentham

Of the Principle of Utility

Nature has placed mankind under the governance of two sovereign masters, *pain* and *pleasure*. It is for them alone to point out what we ought to do, as well as to determine what we shall do. On the one hand the standard of right and wrong, on the other the chain of causes and effects, are fastened to their throne. They govern us in all we do, in all we say, in all we think: every effort we can make to throw off our subjection, will serve but to demonstrate and confirm it. In words a man may pretend to abjure their empire: but in reality he will remain subject to it all the while. The *principle of utility*[1] recognises this subjection, and assumes it for the foundation of that system, the object of which is to rear the fabric of felicity by the hands of reason and of law. Systems which attempt to question it, deal in sounds instead of sense, in caprice instead of reason, in darkness instead of light.

But enough of metaphor and declamation: it is not by such means that moral science is to be improved.

The principle of utility is the foundation of the present work: it will be proper therefore at the outset to give an explicit and determinate account of what is meant by it. By the principle[2] of utility is meant that principle which approves or disapproves of every action whatsoever, according to the tendency which it appears to have to augment or diminish the happiness of the party whose interest is in question: or, what is the same thing in other words, to promote or to oppose that happiness. I say of every action whatsoever; and therefore not only of every action of a private individual, but of every measure of government.

By utility is meant that property in any object, whereby it tends to produce benefit, advantage, pleasure, good, or happiness, (all this in the present case comes to the same thing) or (what comes again to the same thing) to prevent the happening of mischief, pain, evil, or unhappiness to the party whose interest is considered: if that party be the community in general, then the happiness of the community: if a particular individual, then the happiness of that individual. . . .

Source: Reprinted from An Introduction to the Principle of Morals and Legislation (1789), pp. 1-2, 29-32. Footnotes renumbered.

Value of a Lot of Pleasure or Pain, How to be Measured

Pleasures then, and the avoidance of pains, are the *ends* which the legislator has in view: it behoves him therefore to understand their *value*. Pleasures and pains are the *instruments* he has to work with: it behoves him therefore to understand their force, which is again, in other words, their value.

To a person considered *by himself*, the value of a pleasure or pain considered *by itself*, will be greater or less, according to the four following circumstances:[3]

1. Its *intensity*.
2. Its *duration*.
3. Its *certainty* or *uncertainty*.
4. Its *propinquity* or *remoteness*.

These are the circumstances which are to be considered in estimating a pleasure or a pain considered each of them by itself. But when the value of any pleasure or pain is considered for the purpose of estimating the tendency of any *act* by which it is produced, there are two other circumstances to be taken into the account; these are,

5. Its *fecundity*, or the chance it has of being followed by sensations of the *same* kind: that is, pleasures, if it be a pleasure: pains, if it be a pain.
6. Its *purity*, or the chance it has of *not* being followed by sensations of the *opposite* kind: that is, pains, if it be a pleasure: pleasures, if it be a pain.

These two last, however, are in strictness scarcely to be deemed properties of the pleasure or the pain itself; they are not, therefore, in strictness to be taken into the account of the value of that pleasure or that pain. They are in strictness to be deemed properties only of the act, or other event, by which such pleasure or pain has been produced; and accordingly are only to be taken into the account of the tendency of such act or such event.

To a *number* of persons, with reference to each of whom the value of a pleasure or a pain is considered, it will be greater or less, according to seven circumstances: to wit, the six preceding ones; *viz.*

1. Its *intensity*.
2. Its *duration*.
3. Its *certainty* or *uncertainty*.
4. Its *propinquity* or *remoteness*.
5. Its *fecundity*.
6. Its *purity*

And one other; to wit:

7. Its *extent*; that is, the number of persons to whom it *extends*; or (in other words) who are affected by it.

To take an exact account then of the general tendency of any act, by which the interests of a community are affected, proceed as follows. Begin with any one person of those whose interests seem most immediately to be affected by it: and take an account,

1. Of the value of each distinguishable *pleasure* which appears to be produced by it in the *first* instance.
2. Of the value of each *pain* which appears to be produced by it in the *first* instance.
3. Of the value of each pleasure which appears to be produced by it *after* the first. This constitutes the *fecundity* of the first *pleasure* and the *impurity* of the first *pain*.
4. Of the value of each *pain* which appears to be produced by it after the first. This constitutes the *fecundity* of the first *pain*, and the *impurity* of the first pleasure.
5. Sum up all the values of all the *pleasures* on the one side, and those of all the pains on the other. The balance, if it be on the side of pleasure, will give the *good* tendency of the act upon the whole, with respect to the interests of that *individual* person; if on the side of pain, the *bad* tendency of it upon the whole.
6. Take an account of the *number* of persons whose interests appear to be concerned; and repeat the above process with respect to each. *Sum up* the numbers expressive of the degrees of good tendency, which the act has, with respect to each individual, in regard to whom the tendency of it is *good* upon the whole: do this again with respect to each individual, in regard to whom the tendency of it is *bad* upon the whole. Take the *balance*; which, if on the side of *pleasure*, will give the general *good tendency* of the act, with respect to the total number or community of individuals concerned; if on the side of pain, the general *evil tendency*, with respect to the same community.

It is not to be expected that this process should be strictly pursued previously to every moral judgment, or to every legislative or judicial operation. It may, however, be always kept in view: and as near as the process actually pursued on these occasions approaches to it, so near will such process approach to the character of an exact one.

The same process is alike applicable to pleasure and pain, in whatever shape they appear: and by whatever denomination they are distinguished: to pleasure, whether it be called *good* (which is properly the cause or instrument of pleasure) or *profit* (which is distant pleasure, or the cause or instrument of distant pleasure,) or *convenience*, or *advantage*, *benefit*, *emolument*, *happiness*, and so forth: to pain, whether it be called *evil*, (which corresponds to good) or *mischief*, or *inconvenience*, or *disadvantage*, or *loss*, or *unhappiness*, and so forth.

Nor is this a novel and unwarranted, any more than it is a useless theory. In all this there is nothing but what the practice of mankind, wheresoever they have a clear view of their own interest, is perfectly conformable to. An article of property, an estate in land, for instance, is valuable, on what account? On account of the pleasures of all kinds which it enables a man to produce, and what comes to the same thing the pains of all kinds which it enables him to avert. But the value of such an article of property is universally understood to rise or fall according to the length or shortness of the time which a man has in it: the certainty or uncertainty of its coming into possession: and the nearness or remoteness of the time at which, if at all, it is to come into possession. As to the *intensity* of the pleasures which a man may derive from it, this is never thought of, because it depends upon the use which each particular person may come to make of it; which cannot be estimated till the particular pleasures he may come to derive from it, or the particular pains he may come to exclude by means of it, are brought to view. For the same reason, neither does he think of the *fecundity* or *purity* of those pleasures. . . .

Notes

1. Note by the Author, July 1822: To this denomination has of late been added, or substituted, the *greatest happiness* or *greatest felicity* principle: this for shortness, instead of saying at length *that principle* which states the greatest happiness of all those whose interest is in question, as being the right and proper, and only right and proper and universally desirable, end of human action: of human action in every situation, and in particular in that of a functionary or set of functionaries exercising the powers of Government. The word *utility* does not so clearly point to the ideas of *pleasure* and *pain* as the words *happiness* and *felicity* do: nor does it lead us to the consideration of the *number*, of the interests affected; to the *number*, as being the circumstance, which contributes, in the largest proportion, to the formation of the standard here in question; the *standard of right and wrong*, by which alone the propriety of human conduct, in every situation, can with propriety be tried. This want of a sufficiently manifest connexion between the ideas of *happiness* and *pleasure* on the one hand, and the idea of *utility* on the other, I have every now and then found operating, and with but too much efficiency, as a bar to the acceptance, that might otherwise have been given, to this principle.
2. The word principle is derived from the Latin principium: which seems to be compounded of the two words *primus*, first, or chief, and *cipium*, a termination which seems to be derived from *capio*, to take, as in *mancipium*, *municipium*; to which are analogous, *auceps*, *forceps*, and others. It is a term of very vague and very extensive signification: it is applied to anything which is conceived to serve as a foundation or beginning to any series of operations: in some cases, of physical operations; but of mental operations in the present case.

   The principle here in question may be taken for an act of the mind; a sentiment; a sentiment of approbation; a sentiment which, when applied to an action, approves of its utility, as that quality of it by which the measure of approbation or disapprobation bestowed upon it ought to be governed.
3. These circumstances have since been denominated *elements* or *dimensions* of *value* in a pleasure or a pain.

   Not long after the publication of the first edition, the following memoriter verses were framed, in the view of lodging more effectually, in the memory, these points, on which the whole fabric of morals and legislation may be seen to rest.

   Intense, long, certain, speedy, fruitful, pure—
   Such marks in *pleasures* and in *pains* endure.
   Such pleasures seek if private be thy end:
   If it be *public*, wide let them *extend*.
   Such *pains* avoid, whichever be thy view:
   If pains *must* come, let them *extend* to few.

15

Modeling Offenders' Decisions: A Framework for Research and Policy

Ronald V. Clarke   *Derek B. Cornish*

Most theories about criminal behavior have tended to ignore the offender's decision making—the conscious thought processes that give purpose to and justify conduct, and the underlying cognitive mechanisms by which information about the world is selected, attended to, and processed. The source of this neglect is the apparent conflict between decision-making concepts and the prevailing determinism of most criminological theories. Whether framed in terms of social or psychological factors, these theories have traditionally been concerned to explain the criminal dispositions of particular individuals or groups. More recently, faced with the need to explain not just the genesis of people's involvement in crime but also the occurrence of particular criminal acts, greater attention has been paid by theory to the immediate environmental context of offending. But the resulting accounts of criminal behavior have still tended to suggest deterministic models in which the criminal appears as a relatively passive figure; thus he or she is seen either as prey to internal or external forces outside personal control, or as the battlefield upon which these forces resolve their struggle for the control of behavioral outcomes.

A number of developments, however, have combined to question the adequacy of explanations or models of offending that do not take account of the offender's perceptions and thought processes. Interest in the criminal's view of his world—characteristic of the "Chicago School" of sociology—revived during the early 1960s within the sociology of deviance that was beginning to stress the importance of developing an understanding of the offender's perspective. In mainstream criminology a similar revival of interest was also fueled by the apparent failure of the rehabilitative ideal—and hence, many argued, of deterministic approaches to criminological explanation. Disenchantment with treatment also shifted attention and resources to other means of crime control, such as incapacitation, deterrence, and environmental approaches to crime prevention; and it became apparent that offenders' perceptions might be salient to the success of these alternatives. As a result, interest grew in the 1970s in ecological studies of criminal activity, in criminal life histories, in cohort studies of criminal careers, and in offenders' accounts of

Source: From Ronald V. Clarke & Derek B. Cornish, "Modeling Offenders' Decisions: A Framework for Research and Policy," *Crime and Justice: An Annual Review of Research, Vol. 6* (1985), pp. 147–185. Used by permission of The University of Chicago Press.

how they went about their activities. At the same time, other academic disciplines such as economics and psychology were exploring, and in some cases applying to criminological problems, concepts and models of information processing and decision making. . . .

It is with the enhancement and refinement of rational choice models of crime, made necessary by the recent growth of research interest documented below, that this essay is concerned.

. . . [T]here has been a notable confluence of interest in the rational choice, nondeterministic view of crime. This is a natural perspective for law and economics, but it has also achieved wide currency in criminology's other parent disciplines—sociology and psychology—as well as within the different schools of criminology itself. That the shift is part of a broader intellectual movement is suggested by the increasing popularity of economic and rational choice analyses of behaviors other than crime. Why there should be this movement at the present time and what social forces and events might be implicated is difficult to say, but cross-fertilization of ideas between different groups of people working on similar problems always occurs, and certain individuals have deliberately applied the same theoretical perspective to a variety of different problems. For instance, Gary Becker (1968) pioneered his economic analyses of crime when dealing with the economics of discrimination and has since extended his method to choice of marriage partner (Becker 1973, 1974).

Despite the shift of interest described above, there has been little attempt to construct a synthesis—within a rational choice framework—of the concepts and findings provided by the various approaches. . . .

The models, which need to be separately developed for each specific form of crime, are not theories in themselves but rather the blueprints for theory. They owe much to early attempts to model aspects of criminal decision making by Brantingham and Brantingham (1978), Brown and Altman (1981), and Walsh (1978, 1980). But these earlier models were largely confined to just one of the criminal decision processes—target selection—and they also depended upon a commonsense explication of the likely decision steps taken by the "rational" criminal. Our models are concerned not just with the decision to commit a particular crime, but also with decisions relating to criminal "readiness" or involvement in crime; and they also take some account of the recent psychological research on cognitive processing.

This research is still at a relatively early stage, and as yet there is only a comparatively small body of criminological data relevant to decision making upon which to draw. Any attempt to develop decision models of crime must at this stage be tentative. Thus our aim is only to provide models that are at present "good enough" to accommodate existing knowledge and to guide research and policy initiatives. Even such "good enough" models, however, have to meet the criticism that they assume too much rationality on the part of the offender . . . rationality must be conceived of in broad terms. For instance, even if the choices made or the decision processes themselves are not optimal ones, they may make sense to the offender and represent his best efforts at optimizing outcomes. Moreover, expressive as well as economic goals can, of course, be characterized as rational. And lastly, even where the motivation appears to have a pathological component, many of the subsequent planning and decision-making activities (such as choice of victims or targets) may be rational.

A. Modeling Criminal Involvement and Criminal Events

There is a fundamental distinction to be made between explaining the involvement of particular individuals in crime and explaining the occurrence of criminal events. Most criminological theorists have been preoccupied with the former problem and have neglected the latter. They have sought to elucidate the social and psychological variables underlying criminal dispositions, on the apparent assumption that this is all that is needed to explain the commission of crime itself. But the existence of a suitably motivated individual goes only part of the way to explaining the occurrence of a criminal event—a host of immediately precipitating, situational factors must also be taken into account. And a further distinction that must be recognized by theorists concerns the various stages of criminal involvement—initial involvement, continuance, and desistance. That these separate stages of involvement may require different explanatory theories, employing a range of different variables, has been made clear by the findings of recent research into criminal careers (see Farrington 1979; Petersilia 1980).

The distinctions between event and involvement have to be maintained when translating traditional perspectives into decision terms. It may be that the concepts of choice or decision are more readily translatable and more fruitful in relation to continuance and desistance than to initial involvement, but to some extent this may depend on the particular offense under consideration. For some offenses, such as shoplifting or certain acts of vandalism, it might be easier to regard the first offense as determined by the multiplicity of factors identified in existing criminological theory and as committed more or less unthinkingly, that is, without a close knowledge or consideration of the implications. But however much people may be propelled by predisposing factors to the point where crime becomes a realistic course of action, it may still be legitimate (or, at least, useful) to see them as having a choice about whether to become involved. Once the offense is committed, however, the individual acquires direct knowledge about the consequences and implications of that behavior; and this knowledge becomes much more salient to future decisions about continuance or desistance. It may also provide the background of experience to render initial involvement in another crime a considered choice (see Walsh's [1980] discussion of burglary as a training ground for other crimes).

B. The Need for Models to Be Crime Specific

The discussion above has anticipated another important requirement of decision models of crime: whether of involvement or of event, these must be specific to particular kinds of crime. Recent preoccupation with offender pathology and the desire to construct general statements about crime, deviancy, and rule breaking have consistently diverted attention from the important differences between types of crime—the people committing them, the nature of the motivations involved, and the behaviors required. Whatever the purposes and merits of academic generalization, it is essential for policy goals that these important distinctions be maintained. And, moreover, it will usually be necessary to make even finer distinctions between crimes than those provided by legal categories. For instance, it will not usually be sufficient to develop models for a broad legal category such as burglary (Reppetto 1976). Rather it will be necessary to differentiate at least between commercial and residential burglary (as has already been done in a number of studies) and perhaps even between different kinds of residential and commercial burglaries. For example, burglary in public housing projects will be a quite different problem from burglary in affluent commuter areas, or from burglary in multioccupancy inner-city dwellings. And the same is obviously true of many other crimes, such as vandalism, robbery, rape, and fraud. The degree of specificity required will usually demand close attention to situational factors, especially in event models. . . .

C. The Example of Residential Burglary

We have chosen below to illustrate the construction of decision models of crime through the example of residential burglary in a middle-class suburb. . . .

D. Initial Involvement

Figure 1 represents the process of initial involvement in residential burglary in a middle-class suburb. There are two important decision points: the first (box 7) is the individual's recognition of his "readiness" to commit this particular offense in order to satisfy certain of his needs for money, goods, or excitement. Readiness involves rather more than receptiveness: it implies that the individual has actually contemplated this form of crime as a solution to his needs and has decided that under the right circumstances he would commit the offense. In reaching this decision he will have evaluated other ways of satisfying his needs and this evaluation will naturally be heavily influenced by his previous learning and experience—his moral code, his view of the kind of person he is, his personal and vicarious experiences of crime, and the degree to which he can plan and exercise foresight. These variables in turn are related to various historical and contemporaneous background factors—psychological, familial, and sociodemographic (box 1). It is with the influence of these background factors that traditional criminology has been preoccupied; they have been seen to determine the values, attitudes, and personality traits that dispose the individual to crime. In a decision-making context, however, these background influences are less directly criminogenic; instead they have an orienting function—exposing people to particular problems and particular opportunities and leading them to perceive and evaluate these in particular (criminal) ways. Moreover, the contribution of background factors to the final decision to commit crime would be much moderated by situational and transitory influences; and for certain sorts of crime (e.g., computer fraud) the individual's background might be of much less relevance than his immediate situation.

The second decision (box 8), actually to commit a burglary, is precipitated by some chance event. The individual may suddenly need money, he may have been drinking with associates who suggest committing a burglary (for many offenses, especially those committed by juveniles, immediate pressure from the peer group is important), or he may perceive an easy opportunity for the offense during the course of his routine activities. In real life, of course, the two decision points may occur almost simultaneously and the chance event may not only precipitate the decision to burgle, but may also play a part in the perception and evaluation of solutions to generalized needs.

Figure 1
Initial involvement model (example: burglary in a middle-class suburb)

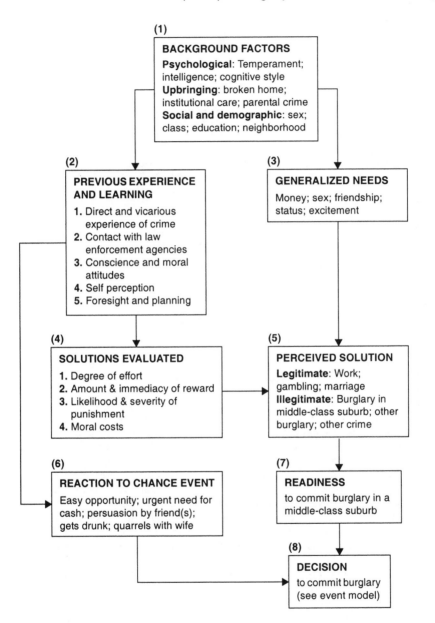

Figure 2
Event model (example: burglary in a middle-class suburb)

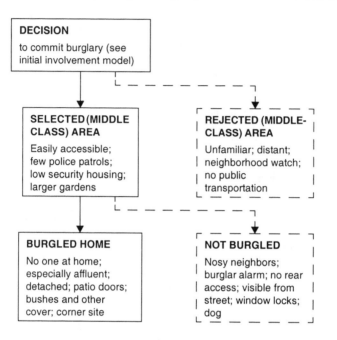

E. The Criminal Event

Figure 2 depicts the further sequence of decision making that leads to the burglar selecting a particular house. As mentioned above, for some other crimes the sequence will be much lengthier; and the less specific the offense being modeled, the more numerous the alternative choices. For example, should a more general model of burglary be required, a wider range of areas and housing types would have to be included (see Brantingham and Brantingham 1978). In the present case, however, there may be little choice of area in which to work, and in time this decision (and perhaps elements of later decisions) may become routine.

This is, of course, an idealized picture of the burglar's decision making. Where the formal complexity of the decision task is laid out in detail, as in Walsh's (1978, 1980) work, there may be a temptation to assume that it entails equally complex decision making. In real life, however, only patchy and inaccurate information will be available. Under these uncertain circumstances the offender's perceptions, his previous experience, his fund of criminal lore, and the characteristic features of his information processing become crucial to the decision reached. Moreover, the external situation itself may alter during the time span of the decision sequence. The result is that the decision process may be telescoped, planning may be rudimentary, and there may be last-minute (and perhaps ill-judged) changes of mind. Even this account may overemphasize the deliberative element, since alcohol may cloud judgment. Only research into these aspects of criminal decision making will provide event models sufficiently detailed and accurate to assist policy-making.

F. Continuance

Interviews with burglars have shown that in many cases they may commit hundreds of offenses (see, e.g., Maguire 1982); the process of continuing involvement in burglary is represented in figure 3. It is assumed here that, as a result of generally positive reinforcement, the frequency of offending increases until it reaches (or subsequently reduces to) some optimum level. But it is possible to conceive of more or less intermittent patterns of involvement for some individuals; and intermittent patterns may be more common for other types of offenses (e.g., those for which ready opportunities occur less frequently). It is unlikely that each time the offender sets out to commit an offense he will actively consider the alternatives, though this will sometimes be necessary as a result of a change in his circumstances or in the conditions under which his burglaries have to be committed. (These possibilities are discussed in more detail in regard to the "desistance" model of figure 4.)

More important to represent in the continuing involvement model are the gradually changing conditions and personal circumstances that confirm the offender in his readiness to commit burglary. The diagram summarizes three categories of relevant variables. The first concerns an increase in professionalism: pride in improved skills and knowledge; successive reductions of risk and an improvement in haul through planning and careful selection of targets; and the acquisition of reliable fencing contacts. The second reflects some concomitant changes in lifestyle: a recognition of increased financial dependence on burglary; a choice of legitimate work to facilitate burglary; enjoyment of "life in the fast lane"; the devaluation of ordinary work; and the development of excuses and justifications for criminal behavior. Third, there will be changes in the offender's network of peers and associates and his relationship to the "straight" world. These trends may be accelerated by criminal convictions as opportunities to obtain legitimate work decrease and as ties to family and relations are weakened.

This picture is premised upon a more open criminal self-identification. There will be, however, many other offenses (e.g., certain sexual crimes) that are more encapsulated and hidden by the offender from everyone he knows.

G. Desistance

It is in respect of the subject of figure 4 in particular—desistance from burglary—that paucity of relevant criminological information is especially evident. While the work of, for example, Parker (1974), Greenberg (1977), West (1978), Trasler (1979), Maguire (1982), and West (1982) provides some understanding of the process of desistance, empirical data, whether relating to groups or individuals and in respect of particular sorts of crime, are very scanty. Nevertheless, there is sufficient information to provide in figure 4 an illustration of the offender's decision processes as he begins a renewed evaluation of alternatives to burglary. This follows aversive experiences during the course of offending and changes in his personal circumstances (age, marital status, financial requirements) and the neighborhood and community context in which he operates (changes of policing, depletion of potential targets). These result in his abandoning burglary in favor of some alternative solution either legitimate or criminal. While desistance may imply the cessation of all criminal activity, in other cases it may simply represent displacement to some other target (commercial premises rather than houses) or to another

Figure 3

Continuing involvement model (example: burglary in a middle-class suburb)

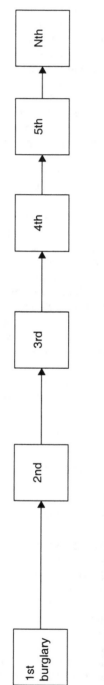

1st burglary → 2nd → 3rd → 4th → 5th → Nth

INCREASED PROFESSIONALISM

Pride in improved skills and knowledge; successively reduces risk and increases haul through planning and careful selection of targets; acquires fencing contacts; develops skills in dealing with police and courts.

CHANGES IN LIFE STYLE AND VALUES

Recognition of financial dependence on burglary; chooses work to facilitate burglary; enjoys life in fast lane; devalues legitimate work; justifies criminality.

CHANGES IN PEER GROUP

Becomes friendly with other criminals and receiver; labeled as criminal; loses contact with straight friends; quarrels with relations.

form of crime. Desistance is, in any case, not necessarily permanent and may simply be part of a continuing process of lulls in the offending of persistent criminals (West 1963) or even, perhaps, of a more casual drifting in and out of particular crimes. . . . The particular crime under consideration must be considered sufficient to justify the investment in research.

Figure 4
Desistance model (example: burglary in a middle-class suburb)

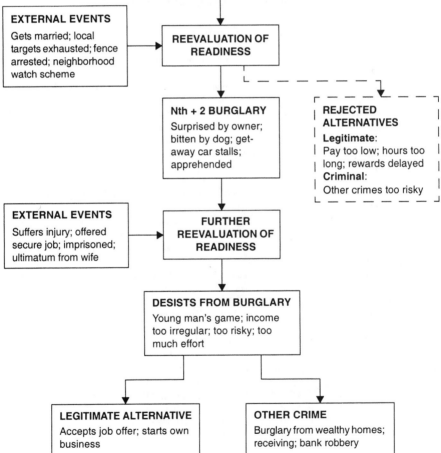

Conclusions

During the course of this discussion a number of deficiencies in current criminological theorizing have been identified. Many of these flow from two underlying assumptions: that offenders are different from other people and that crime is a unitary phenomenon. Hence, the preoccupation with the issue of initial involvement in crime and the failure to develop explanations for specific kinds of offending. Moreover, explanatory theories have characteristically been confined to a limited selection of variables derived from one or another of criminology's contributory disciplines; and none of the dominant theories has taken adequate account of situational variables. A decision-making approach, however, stresses the rational elements in criminal behavior and requires explanations to be specific to particular forms of crime. It also demands that attention be paid to the crucial distinction between criminal involvement (at its various stages) and criminal events. By doing so it provides a framework that can accommodate the full range of potentially relevant variables (including situational ones) and the various competing but partial theories. . . .

References

Becker, Gary S. 1968. "Crime and Punishment: An Economic Approach." *Journal of Political Economy* 76:169–217.

——— 1973. "A Theory of Marriage: Part One." *Journal of Political Economy* 81(4):813–46.

——— 1974. "A Theory of Marriage: Part Two." *Journal of Political Economy* 82(2):11–26.

Brantingham, Paul J., and Patricia L. Brantingham. 1978. "A Theoretical Model of Crime Site Selection." In *Crime, Law and Sanctions*, edited by Marvin D. Krohn and Ronald L. Akers. Beverly Hills, CA: Sage.

Brown, B. B., and I. Altman. 1981. "Territoriality and Residential Crime: A Conceptual Framework." In *Environmental Criminology*, edited by Paul J. Brantingham and Patricia L. Brantingham. Beverly Hills, CA: Sage.

Farrington, David P. 1979. "Longitudinal Research on Crime and Delinquency." In *Crime and Justice: An Annual Review of Research*, vol. 1, edited by Norval Morris and Michael Tonry. Chicago: University of Chicago Press.

Greenberg, D. F. 1977. "Delinquency and the Age Structure of Society." *Contemporary Crises* 1:189–223.

Maguire, Mike, in collaboration with Trevor Bennett. 1982. *Burglary in a Dwelling*. London: Heinemann.

Parker, Howard J. 1974. *View from the Boys: A Sociology of Down-Town Adolescents*. Newton Abbot, England: David & Charles.

Petersilia, Joan. 1980. "Criminal Career Research: A Review of Recent Evidence." In *Crime and Justice: An Annual Review of Research*, vol. 2, edited by Michael Tonry and Norval Morris. Chicago: University of Chicago Press.

Reppetto, Thomas A. 1976. "Crime Prevention and the Displacement Phenomenon." *Crime and Delinquency* 22:166–77.

Trasler, Gordon B. 1979. "Delinquency, Recidivism, and Desistance." *British Journal of Criminology* 19:314–22.

Walsh, Dermot P. 1978. *Shopping: Controlling a Major Crime*. London: Macmillan.

———1980. *Break-Ins: Burglary from Private Houses*. London: Constable.

Warr, P. B., and C. Knapper. 1968. *The Perception of People and Events*. Chichester: Wiley.

West, Donald J. 1963. *The Habitual Prisoner*. London: Macmillan.

——— 1982. *Delinquency: Its Roots, Careers and Prospects*. London: Heinemann.

West, W. Gordon. 1978. "The Short Term Careers of Serious Thieves." *Canadian Journal of Criminology* 20:169–90.

16

The Normal and the Pathological

Émile Durkheim

1. *A social fact is normal, in relation to a given social type at a given phase of its development, when it is present in the average society of that species at the corresponding phase of its evolution.*
2. *One can verify the results of the preceding method by showing that the generality of the phenomenon is bound up with the general conditions of collective life of the social type considered.*
3. *This verification is necessary when the fact in question occurs in a social species which has not yet reached the full course of its evolution.*

The custom of resolving these difficult questions with a pat phrase and of deciding hastily, from superficial observations supported by syllogisms, whether a social fact is normal or not prevails to such an extent that our procedure will perhaps be judged needlessly complicated. It seems unnecessary to go to such lengths in order to distinguish between morbidity and health. It is true that we make these distinctions every day, but it remains to be seen whether we make them correctly. The fact that the biologist solves these problems with relative ease obscures in our minds the difficulties they involve. We forget that it is much easier for him than for the sociologist to observe how the resistance of the organism is affected by each phenomenon and to determine thereby its normal or abnormal character with sufficient exactness for practical purposes. In sociology the greater complexity and inconstancy of the facts oblige us to take many more precautions, and this is all too evident in the contradictory judgments on the same phenomenon given by different scholars. In order to show clearly the great necessity for circumspection, we shall illustrate by a few examples the errors resulting from the opposite attitude and show in how different a light the most essential phenomena appear when treated methodically.

If there is any fact whose pathological character appears incontestable, that fact is crime. All criminologists are agreed on this point. Although they explain this pathology differently, they are unanimous in recognizing it. But let us see if this problem does not demand a more extended consideration.

We shall apply the foregoing rules. Crime is present not only in the majority of societies of one particular species but in all societies of all types. There is no

Source: Reprinted with the permission of The Free Press, a Division of Simon & Schuster Adult Publishing Group, from *The Rules of Sociological Method* by Émile Durkheim, translated by Sarah A. Solovay and John H. Mueller. Edited by George E. G. Catlin. Copyright © 1938 by George E.G. Catlin. Copyright © renewed 1966 by Sarah A. Solovay, John H. Mueller, George E.G. Catlin.

society that is not confronted with the problem of criminality. Its form changes; the acts thus characterized are not the same everywhere; but, everywhere and always, there have been men who have behaved in such a way as to draw upon themselves penal repression. If, in proportion as societies pass from the lower to the higher types, the rate of criminality, i.e., the relation between the yearly number of crimes and the population, tended to decline, it might be believed that crime, while still normal, is tending to lose this character of normality. But we have no reason to believe that such a regression is substantiated. Many facts would seem rather to indicate a movement in the opposite direction. From the beginning of the [nineteenth] century, statistics enable us to follow the course of criminality. It has everywhere increased. In France the increase is nearly 300 percent. There is, then, no phenomenon that presents more indisputably all the symptoms of normality, since it appears closely connected with the conditions of all collective life. To make of crime a form of social morbidity would be to admit that morbidity is not something accidental, but, on the contrary, that in certain cases it grows out of the fundamental constitution of the living organism; it would result in wiping out all distinction between the physiological and the pathological. No doubt it is possible that crime itself will have abnormal forms, as, for example, when its rate is unusually high. This excess is, indeed, undoubtedly morbid in nature. What is normal, simply, is the existence of criminality, provided that it attains and does not exceed, for each social type, a certain level, which it is perhaps not impossible to fix in conformity with the preceding rules.[1]

Here we are, then, in the presence of a conclusion in appearance quite paradoxical. Let us make no mistake. To classify crime among the phenomena of normal sociology is not to say merely that it is an inevitable, although regretable phenomenon, due to the incorrigible wickedness of men; it is to affirm that it is a factor in public health, an integral part of all healthy societies. This result is, at first glance, surprising enough to have puzzled even ourselves for a long time. Once this first surprise has been overcome, however, it is not difficult to find reasons explaining this normality and at the same time confirming it.

In the first place crime is normal because a society exempt from it is utterly impossible. Crime, we have shown elsewhere, consists of an act that offends certain very strong collective sentiments. In a society in which criminal acts are no longer committed, the sentiments they offend would have to be found without exception in all individual consciousnesses, and they must be found to exist with the same degree as sentiments contrary to them. Assuming that this condition could actually be realized, crime would not thereby disappear; it would only change its form, for the very cause which would thus dry up the sources of criminality would immediately open up new ones.

Indeed, for the collective sentiments which are protected by the penal law of a people at a specified moment of its history to take possession of the public conscience or for them to acquire a stronger hold where they have an insufficient grip, they must acquire an intensity greater than that which they had hitherto had. The community as a whole must experience them more vividly, for it can acquire from no other source the greater force necessary to control these individuals who formerly were the most refractory. For murderers to disappear, the horror of bloodshed must become greater in those social strata from which murderers are recruited; but, first it must become greater throughout the entire society. Moreover, the very absence of crime would directly contribute to produce this horror; because any sentiment seems much more respectable when it is always and uniformly respected.

One easily overlooks the consideration that these strong states of the common consciousness cannot be thus reinforced without reinforcing at the same time the more feeble states, whose violation previously gave birth to mere infraction of convention—since the weaker ones are only the prolongation, the attenuated form, of the stronger. Thus robbery and simple bad taste injure the same single altruistic sentiment, the respect for that which is another's. However, this same sentiment is less grievously offended by bad taste than by robbery; and since, in addition, the average consciousness has not sufficient intensity to react keenly to the bad taste, it is treated with greater tolerance. That is why the person guilty of bad taste is merely blamed, whereas the thief is punished. But, if this sentiment grows stronger, to the point of silencing in all consciousnesses the inclination which disposes man to steal, he will become more sensitive to the offenses which, until then, touched him but lightly. He will react against them, then, with more energy; they will be the object of greater opprobrium, which will transform certain of them from the simple moral faults that they were and give them the quality of crimes. For example, improper contracts, or contracts improperly executed, which only incur public blame or civil damages, will become offenses in law.

Imagine a society of saints, a perfect cloister of exemplary individuals. Crimes, properly so called, will there be unknown; but faults which appear venial to the layman will create there the same scandal that the ordinary offense does in ordinary consciousnesses. If, then, this society has the power to judge and punish, it will define these acts as criminal and will treat them as such. For the same reason, the perfect and upright man judges his smallest failings with a severity that the majority reserve for acts more truly in the nature of an offense. Formerly, acts of violence against persons were more frequent than they are today, because respect for individual dignity was less strong. As this has increased, these crimes have become more rare; and also, many acts violating this sentiment have been introduced into the penal law which were not included there in primitive times.[2]

In order to exhaust all the hypotheses logically possible, it will perhaps be asked why this unanimity does not extend to all collective sentiments without exception. Why should not even the most feeble sentiment gather enough energy to prevent all dissent? The moral consciousness of the society would be present in its entirety in all the individuals, with a vitality sufficient to prevent all acts offending it—the purely conventional faults as well as the crimes. But a uniformity so universal and absolute is utterly impossible; for the immediate physical milieu in which each one of us is placed, the hereditary antecedents, and the social influences vary from one individual to the next, and consequently diversify consciousnesses. It is impossible for all to be alike, if only because each one has his own organism and that these organisms occupy different areas in space. That is why, even among the lower peoples, where individual originality is very little developed, it nevertheless does exist.

Thus, since there cannot be a society in which the individuals do not differ more or less from the collective type, it is also inevitable that, among these divergences, there are some with a criminal character. What confers this character upon them is not the intrinsic quality of a given act but that definition which the collective conscience lends them. If the collective conscience is stronger, if it has enough authority practically to suppress these divergences, it will also be more sensitive, more exacting; and, reacting against the slightest deviations with the energy it otherwise displays only against more considerable infractions, it will attribute to them the same gravity as formerly to crimes. In other words, it will designate them as criminal.

Crime is, then, necessary; it is bound up with the fundamental conditions of all social life, and by that very fact it is useful, because these conditions of which it is a part are themselves indispensable to the normal evolution of morality and law.

Indeed, it is no longer possible today to dispute the fact that law and morality vary from one social type to the next, nor that they change within the same type if the conditions of life are modified. But, in order that these transformations may be possible, the collective sentiments at the basis of morality must not be hostile to change, and consequently must have but moderate energy. If they were too strong, they would no longer be plastic. Every pattern is an obstacle to new patterns, to the extent that the first pattern is inflexible. The better a structure is articulated, the more it offers a healthy resistance to all modification; and this is equally true of functional, as of anatomical, organization. If there were no crimes, this condition could not have been fulfilled; for such a hypothesis presupposes that collective sentiments have arrived at a degree of intensity unexampled in history. Nothing is good indefinitely and to an unlimited extent. The authority which the moral conscience enjoys must not be excessive; otherwise no one would dare criticize it, and it would too easily congeal into an immutable form. To make progress, individual originality must be able to express itself. In order that the originality of the idealist whose dreams transcend his century may find expression, it is necessary that the originality of the criminal, who is below the level of his time, shall also be possible. One does not occur without the other.

Nor is this all. Aside from this indirect utility, it happens that crime itself plays a useful role in this evolution. Crime implies not only that the way remains open to necessary changes but that in certain cases it directly prepares these changes. Where crime exists, collective sentiments are sufficiently flexible to take on a new form, and crime sometimes helps to determine the form they will take. How many times, indeed, it is only an anticipation of future morality—a step toward what will be! According to Athenian law, Socrates was a criminal, and his condemnation was no more than just. However, his crime, namely, the independence of his thought, rendered a service not only to humanity but to his country. It served to prepare a new morality and faith which the Athenians needed, since the traditions by which they had lived until then were no longer in harmony with the current conditions of life. Nor is the case of Socrates unique; it is reproduced periodically in history. It would never have been possible to establish the freedom of thought we now enjoy if the regulations prohibiting it had not been violated before being solemnly abrogated. At that time, however, the violation was a crime, since it was an offense against sentiments still very keen in the average conscience. And yet this crime was useful as a prelude to reforms which daily become more necessary. Liberal philosophy had as its precursors the heretics of all kinds who were justly punished by secular authorities during the entire course of the Middle Ages and until the eve of modern times.

From this point of view the fundamental facts of criminality present themselves to us in an entirely new light. Contrary to current ideas, the criminal no longer seems a totally unsociable being, a sort of parasitic element, a strange and unassimilable body, introduced into the midst of society.[3] On the contrary, he plays a definite role in social life. Crime, for its part, must no longer be conceived as an evil that cannot be too much suppressed. There is no occasion for self-congratulation when the crime rate drops noticeably below the average level, for we may be certain that this apparent progress is associated with some social disorder. Thus, the number of assault cases never falls so low as in times of want.[4] With the drop in the crime rate, and as a reaction to it, comes a revision, or the need of a revision in the theory of punishment. If, indeed, crime is a disease, its punishment is its remedy and cannot be otherwise conceived; thus, all the discussions it arouses bear on the point of determining what the punishment must be in order to fulfil this role of remedy. If crime is not pathological at all, the object of punishment cannot be to cure it, and its true function must be sought elsewhere. . . .

Notes

1. From the fact that crime is a phenomenon of normal sociology, it does not follow that the criminal is an individual normally constituted from the biological and psychological points of view. The two questions are independent of each other. This independence will be better understood when we have shown, later on, the difference between psychological and sociological facts.
2. Calumny, insults, slander, fraud, etc.
3. We have ourselves committed the error of speaking thus of the criminal, because of a failure to apply our rule (*Division du travail social*, pp. 395–96).
4. Although crime is a fact of normal sociology, it does not follow that we must not abhor it. Pain itself has nothing desirable about it; the individual dislikes it as society does crime, and yet it is a function of normal physiology. Not only is it necessarily derived from the very constitution of every living organism, but it plays a useful role in life, for which reason it cannot be replaced. It would, then, be a singular distortion of our thought to present it as an apology for crime. We would not even think of protesting against such an interpretation, did we not know to what strange accusations and misunderstandings one exposes oneself when one undertakes to study moral facts objectively and to speak of them in a different language from that of the layman.

17

Class Conflict and Law

Karl Marx

. . . The history of all hitherto existing society is the history of class struggles. Freeman and slave, patrician and plebeian, lord and serf, guild-master and journeyman, in a word, oppressor and oppressed, stood in constant opposition to one another, carried on an uninterrupted, now hidden, now open fight, a fight that each time ended either in a revolutionary reconstitution of society at large, or in the common ruin of the contending classes.

In the earlier epochs of history, we find almost everywhere a complicated arrangement of society into various orders, a manifold gradation of social rank. In ancient Rome we have patricians, knights, plebeians, slaves; in the Middle Ages, feudal lords, vassals, guild-masters, journeymen, apprentices, serfs; in almost all of these classes, again, subordinate gradations.

The modern bourgeois society that has sprouted from the ruins of feudal society has not done away with class antagonisms. It has but established new classes, new conditions of oppression, new forms of struggle in place of the old ones.

Our epoch, the epoch of the bourgeoisie, possesses, however, this distinctive feature; it has simplified the class antagonisms. Society as a whole is more and more splitting up into two great hostile camps, into two great classes directly facing each other—bourgeoisie and proletariat. . . .

Can the *State* act in any other way? The *State* will never look for the cause of *social imperfections "in the State and social institutions themselves,"* as "A Prussian" demands of his king. Where there are political parties, each party finds the source of *such* evils in the fact that the opposing party, instead of itself, is at the *helm of State.* Even the radical and revolutionary politicians look for the source of the evil, not in the *nature* of the State, but in a particular *form of the State,* which they want to replace by *another* form.

The *State* and the *structure of society* are not, from the standpoint of *politics, two* different things. The State is the structure of society. In so far as the State admits the existence of *social* evils, it attributes them to *natural laws* against which no human power can prevail, or to *private life* which is independent of the State, or to the *inadequacies of the administration* which is subordinate to it. Thus in England poverty is explained by the *natural law* according to which population always increases beyond

Source: Selected Writings in Sociology and Social Philosophy by Karl Marx, trans. by T. B. Bottomore, pp. 200–201, 215–220, 222–230. Copyright © 1956 McGraw-Hill Book Company. Used with permission of McGraw-Hill Book Company.

the means of subsistence. From another aspect, England explains *pauperism* as the consequence of the *evil dispositions of the poor*, just as the king of Prussia explains it by the *unchristian disposition of the rich*, and as the Convention explains it by the *sceptical, counter-revolutionary outlook of the property owners*. Accordingly, England inflicts penalties on the poor, the king of Prussia admonishes the rich, and the Convention beheads property owners.

In the last resort, *every* State seeks the cause in *adventitious or intentional defects in the administration*, and therefore looks to a *reform* of the administration for a redress of these evils. Why? Simply because the *administration* is the *organizing* activity of the State itself.

The *contradiction* between the aims and good intentions of the administration on the one hand, and its means and resources on the other, cannot be removed by the State without abolishing itself, for it rests upon this contradiction. The State is founded upon the contradiction between *public* and *private life*, between *general* and *particular interests*. The *administration* must, therefore, limit itself to a *formal and negative* sphere of activity, because its power ceases at the point where civil life and its work begin. In face of the consequences which spring from the unsocial character of the life of civil society, of private property, trade, industry, of the mutual plundering by the different groups in civil society, *impotence* is the *natural law* of the administration. These divisions, this debasement and *slavery of civil society*, are the natural foundations upon which the *modern* State rests, just as *civil society* was the natural foundation of *slavery* upon which the State of *antiquity* rested. The existence of the State and the existence of slavery are inseparable. The State and slavery in antiquity—frank *classical* antithesis—were not more intimately *linked* than are the modern State and the modern world of commerce—sanctimonious *Christian* antithesis. If the modern State wished to end the *impotence* of its administration it would be obliged to abolish the present conditions of *private life*. And if the State wished to abolish these conditions of private life it would have also to put an end to its own existence, for it exists *only* in relation to them. . . .

The more powerful the State, and therefore the more *political* a country is, the less likely it is to seek the basis of *social* evils and to grasp the *general* explanation of them, in the *principle of the State* itself, that is in the *structure of society*, of which the State is the active, conscious and official expression. *Political* thought is really *political* thought in the sense that the thinking takes place within the framework of politics. The clearer and more vigorous political thought is, the *less* it is able to grasp the nature of social evils. The *classical* period of political thought is the *French Revolution*. Far from recognizing the source of social defects in the principle of the State, the heroes of the French Revolution looked for the sources of political evils in the defective social organization. Thus, for example, Robespierre saw in the coexistence of great poverty and great wealth only an obstacle to *genuine democracy*. He wished, therefore, to establish a universal *Spartan* austerity. The principle of politics is the will. The more partial, and the more perfected, *political* thought becomes, the more it believes in the *omnipotence* of the will, the less able it is to see the *natural* and mental *limitations* on the will, the less capable it is of discovering the source of social evils. . . .

It has been shown that the *recognition of the rights of man* by the *modern State*, has only the same significance as the *recognition of slavery* by the *State in antiquity*. The basis of the State in antiquity was slavery; the basis of the *modern* State is civil society and the *individual* of civil society, that is, the independent individual, whose only link with other individuals is private interest and *unconscious*, natural necessity, the *slave* of wage labour, of the *selfish* needs of himself and others. The modern State has recognized this, its natural foundation, in the universal rights of man. But it did not create it. As the product of civil society which was impelled by its own development beyond the old political shackles, it only recognized its own origins and basis in *proclaiming the rights of man. . . .*

The basis of present-day *"public affairs,"* that is, of the developed modern State, is not, as the "Critical School" thinks, the society of feudal privileges, but a society in which *privileges* have been *abolished* and *dissolved*, a developed *civil society*, where the elements of existence which were politically fettered by privilege have been freed. *"No privileged exclusiveness"* is not levelled against anyone, nor against public affairs. Just as free industry and free trade abolish privileged enclaves, and replace them with the individual freed from all privileges (which separate the individual from the community as a whole, but also involve him in a smaller exclusive community), the individual who is no longer related to other men by even the *appearance* of a general bond, and create a general conflict between man and man, individual and individual, so the whole of *civil society* is only this mutual conflict of all individuals who are no longer distinguished by anything but their *individuality*. It is only the universal movement of the individual life forces freed from the shackles of privilege. The opposition between the *democratic, representative State* and *civil society* is the perfection of the classical opposition between *public social life* and *slavery*. In the modern world, every individual participates *at the same time* in slavery and in social life. But the *slavery of civil society* is, *in appearance*, the greatest *liberty*, because it appears to be the realized *independence* of the individual for whom the frantic movement, released from general shackles and from the limitations imposed by man, of the vital elements of which he has been stripped, for example property, industry and religion, is a manifestation of his *own* liberty, when in reality it is nothing but the expression of his absolute enslavement and of the loss of his human nature. Here, *privilege* has been replaced by *right. . . .*

To speak precisely and in ordinary language, the members of civil society are not *atoms*. The *characteristic quality* of an atom is to have *no* qualities, and consequently no relations determined by its own *nature* with other beings outside itself. The atom has *no needs* and is *self-sufficient*; the external world is a complete *void*, has neither content, nor sense, nor meaning, precisely because the atom possesses *everything* in itself. The egoistic individual of civil society may in abstract and lifeless conceptions, inflate himself into an *atom*, that is, into a being without relations, self-sufficient, without needs, *absolutely perfect* and contented. But profane, *sensuous reality* has no concern for his imagination. The individual finds himself forced by everyone of his senses to believe in the existence of the world and of other individuals; and everything, down to his *profane* stomach reminds him daily that the *external* world is not a void, that it is, on the contrary, that which *fills* (his stomach). Every one of his activities and qualities, every one of his aspirations, becomes a *need*, a *want*, which transforms his *egoism* into a desire for things and human beings outside himself. But since the need of one individual is not self-evident to another egoistic individual who possesses the means of satisfying it, every individual finds himself obliged to create this relation in making himself so to speak the middleman between the needs of others and the objects of these needs. It is, therefore, *natural necessity*, it is the *essential qualities of man*, however alienated the form in which they appear, it is *interest*, which hold together the members of civil society, whose *real* bond is constituted by *civil* and not by *political* life. Thus it is not the *State* which holds together the *atoms* of civil society; it is the fact that these *atoms* are only *atoms* in *idea*, in the *heaven* of the imagination, and that *in reality* they are beings very different from atoms. They are not *god-like egoists* but *egoistic men*. Only *political superstition* believes at the present time that civil life must be held together by the State, when in reality the State is upheld by civil life. . . .

Just because individuals seek *only* their particular interest, which for them does not coincide with their common interest (for the ''general good'' is an illusory form of community life), the common interest is imposed as an interest ''alien'' to them, and ''independent'' of them, as itself in turn a particular ''general'' interest; or else the individuals must encounter each other in this discord, as in democracy. On the other hand, the *practical* struggle of these particular interests, which are always *really* in conflict with the community and illusory community interests, makes *practical* intervention and control necessary through the illusory ''general'' interest in the form of the State. The social power, i.e. the multiplied productive force, which results from the co-operation of different individuals as it is determined by the division of labour, appears to these individuals, since their co-operation is not voluntary but natural, not as their own united power but as an alien force existing outside them, of whose origin and purpose they are ignorant, and which they therefore cannot control, but which, on the contrary, passes through its own proper series of phases and stages, independent of the will and the action of man, even appearing to govern this will and action. . . .

Since the State is the form in which the individuals of a ruling class assert their common interests, and in which the whole civil society of an epoch is epitomized, it follows that the State acts as an intermediary for all community institutions, and that these institutions receive a political form. Hence the illusion that law is based on will, and indeed on will divorced from its real basis—on *free* will. Similarly, law is in its turn reduced to the actual laws.

Civil law develops concurrently with private property out of the disintegration of the natural community. Among the Romans the development of private property and civil law had no further industrial and commercial consequences because their whole mode of production remained unchanged. Among modern peoples, where the feudal community was disintegrated by industry and trade, a new phase began with the rise of private property and civil law, which was capable of further development. The first town which carried on an extensive trade in the Middle Ages, Amalfi, also developed at the same time maritime law. As soon as industry and trade developed private property further, first in Italy and later in other countries, the perfected Roman civil law was at once taken up again and raised to authority. When, subsequently, the bourgeoisie had acquired so much power that the princes took up their interests in order to overthrow the feudal nobility by means of the bourgeoisie, there began in all countries—in France in the sixteenth century—the real development of law, which in all countries except England proceeded on the basis of the Roman Code. Even in England, Roman legal principles had to be introduced for the further development of civil law (especially in the case of personal movable property). It should not be forgotten that law has not, any more than religion, an independent history. . . .

Nothing could be more comical than Hegel's analysis of private property in land. According to him, man as an individual must give reality to his will as the soul of external Nature, and must therefore take possession of Nature as his private property. If this were the destiny of "the individual," of man as an individual, it would follow that every human being must be a landowner in order to realize himself as an individual. Free private property in land, a very recent product, is not, according to Hegel, a definite social relation, but a relation of man as an individual to Nature, "the absolute right of appropriation which man has over all things" (Hegel, *Philosophy of Right*, Berlin, 1840). So much is at once evident, that the individual cannot maintain himself as a landowner by his mere "will" against the will of another individual who likewise wants to incarnate himself in the same piece of land. It requires many other things besides the good will. Furthermore it is quite impossible to understand where "the individual" sets the limits for the realization of his will, whether his will should realize itself in a whole country, or whether it requires a whole collection of countries by whose appropriation I might "manifest the supremacy of my will over the thing." Here Hegel breaks down completely: "The appropriation is of a very individual kind; I do not take possession of more than I touch with my body, but the second point is at the same time that external things have a greater extension than I can grasp. While I thus have possession of a thing, something else is likewise in touch with it. I exercise my appropriation by my hand but its scope may be extended" (*ibid.*). But this other thing is again in contact with still another, and so the boundary disappears, within which my will as soul can flow into the soil. "If I own anything, my reason at once passes on to the idea that not only this property, but also the thing it touches, is mine. Here positive right must fix its boundaries, for nothing more can be deduced from the concept" (*ibid.*). This is an extraordinarily naïve confession of "the concept," and it proves that this conception, which from the outset makes the blunder of regarding as absolute a particular legal conception of landed property which belongs to bourgeois society, does not understand anything of the real forms of this property. This implies at the same time an avowal that "positive law" can and must, change its affirmations in accordance with the needs of social, i.e. economic, development. . . .

In historical fact the theorists who considered *force* as the basis of law were directly opposed to those who saw *will* as the basis of law. . . . If force is taken to be the basis of law, as by Hobbes, law and legislative enactments are only a symptom or expression of *other* conditions upon which the State power rests. The material life of individuals, which certainly does not depend on their mere "will," their mode of production and their form of intercourse, which reciprocally influence each other, are the real basis of the State. This material life is, at every stage in which the division of labour and private property are still necessary, quite independent of the *will* of individuals. These real conditions are not created by the State power; they are rather the power which creates it. The individuals who rule under these conditions, quite apart from the fact that their power has to constitute itself as a State, must give their will, as it is determined by these definite circumstances, a general expression as the will of the State, as law. The content of this expression is always determined by the situation of this class, as is most clearly revealed in the civil and criminal law. Just as the bodily weight of individuals does not depend upon their ideal will or caprice, so it does not depend on them whether they embody their own will in law, and at the same time, in accordance with individual caprice give everyone beneath them his independence. Their individual domination must at the same time form a general domination. Their individual power rests upon conditions of existence which develop as social conditions and whose continuance they must show to involve their own supremacy and yet be valid for all. Law is the expression of this will conditioned by their common interests. It is just the striving of independent individuals and their wills, which on this basis are necessarily egoistic in their behavior to each other, which makes self denial through law and regulation essential, or rather self denial in exceptional cases and maintenance of their interest in general. . . . The same holds good for the subject classes, on whose will the existence of law and the State is equally little dependent. For instance, as long as the productive forces are insufficiently developed to make competition superfluous, with the consequence that competition is always reappearing, the subject classes would be willing the impossible if they "willed" to abolish competition and with it the State and law. Moreover, until conditions have developed to a point where they can produce this "will" it exists only in the imagination of the ideologists. Once conditions are sufficiently developed to produce it, the ideologist can imagine it as purely capricious and therefore conceivable at any period and under any circumstances. Crime, i.e. the struggle of the single individual against the dominant conditions, is as little the product of simple caprice as law itself. It is rather conditioned in the same way as the latter. The same visionaries who see in law the rule of an independent and general will see in crime a simple breaking of the law. The State does not rest on a dominating will, but the State which arises out of the material mode of life of individuals has also the form of a dominating will. If this will loses its domination this means not only that the will has changed but also that the material existence and life of individuals has changed despite their will. It is possible that law and legislation have an autonomous evolution but in that case they are purely formal and no longer dominating, as many striking examples in Roman and English legal history show. We have already seen how, through the activity of philosophers, a history of pure thought could arise by the separation of thought from the individuals and their actual relations which are its basis. In the present case, also, law can be separated from its real basis, and thereby we can arrive at a "ruling will" which in different periods has a different expression and which, in its creations, the laws, has its own independent history. By this means political and civil history is ideologically transformed into a history of the dominance of self-developing laws. . . .

. . . it would be very difficult, if not altogether impossible, to establish any principle upon which the justice or expediency of capital punishment could be founded, in a Society, glorying in its civilization. Punishment in general had been defended as a means either of ameliorating or of intimidating. Now what right have you to punish me for the amelioration or intimidation of others? And besides, there is history—there is such a thing as statistics—which prove with the most complete evidence that since Cain the world has neither been intimidated nor ameliorated by punishment. Quite the contrary. From the point of view of abstract right, there is only one theory of punishment which recognizes human dignity in the abstract, and that is the theory of Kant, especially in the more rigid formula given to it by Hegel. Hegel says: "Punishment is the *right* of the criminal. It is an act of his own will. The violation of right has been proclaimed by the criminal as his own right. His crime is the negation of right. Punishment is the negation of this negation, and consequently an affirmation of right, solicited and forced upon the criminal by himself."

There is no doubt something specious in this formula, inasmuch as Hegel, instead of looking upon the criminal as the mere object, the slave of justice, elevates him to the position of a free and self-determined being. Looking, however, more closely into the matter, we discover that German idealism here, as in most other instances, has but given a transcendental sanction to the rules of existing society. Is it not a delusion to substitute for the individual with his real motives, with multifarious social circumstances pressing upon him, the abstraction of "free-will"— one among the many qualities of man for man himself? This theory, considering punishment as the result of the criminal's own will, is only a metaphysical expression for the old "jus talionis," eye against eye, tooth against tooth, blood against blood. Plainly speaking, and dispensing with all paraphrases, punishment is nothing but a means of society to defend itself against the infraction of its vital conditions, whatever may be their character. Now, what a state of society is that which knows of no better instrument for its own defence than the hangman, and which proclaims through the "leading journal of the world" its own brutality as eternal law?

Mr. A. Quételet, in his excellent and learned work, *l'Homme et ses Facultés*, says: "There is a budget which we pay with frightful regularity—it is that of prisons, dungeons and scaffolds. . . . We might even predict how many individuals will stain their hands with the blood of their fellow-men, how many will be forgers, how many will deal in poison, pretty nearly the same way as we may foretell the annual births and deaths."

And Mr. Quételet, in a calculation of the probabilities of crime published in 1829, actually predicted with astonishing certainty, not only the amount but all the different kinds of crimes committed in France in 1830. That it is not so much the particular political institutions of a country as the fundamental conditions of modern *bourgeois* society in general, which produce an average amount of crime in a given national fraction of society, may be seen from the following tables, communicated by Quételet, for the years 1822–24. We find in a number of one hundred condemned criminals in America and France:

Age	Philadelphia	France
Under twenty-one years	19	19
Twenty-one to thirty	44	35
Thirty to forty	23	23
Above forty	14	23
	100	100

Now, if crimes observed on a great scale thus show, in their amount and their classification, the regularity of physical phenomena—if, as Mr. Quételet remarks, "it would be difficult to decide in respect to which of the two (the physical world and the social system) the acting causes produce their effect with the utmost regularity"—is there not a necessity for deeply reflecting upon an alteration of the system that breeds these crimes, instead of glorifying the hangman who executes a lot of criminals to make room only for the supply of new ones?

18

Class, State, and Crime

Richard Quinney

Crime and the Development of Capitalism

The Understanding of Crime

. . . An understanding of crime in our society begins with the recognition that the crucial phenomenon to be considered is not crime per se, but the historical development and operation of capitalist society.[1] The study of crime involves an investigation of such natural products and contradictions of capitalism as alienation, inequality, poverty, unemployment, spiritual malaise, and the economic crisis of the capitalist state. To understand crime we have to understand the development of the political economy of capitalist society.

The necessary condition for any society is that its members produce their material means of subsistence. Social production is therefore the primary process of all social life. Furthermore, in the social production of our existence we enter into relations that are appropriate to the existing forces of production.[2] According to Marx, it is this "economic" structure that provides a grounding for social and political institutions, for everyday life, and for social consciousness. Our analysis thus begins with the *conditions* of social life.

The *dialectical method* allows us to comprehend the world as a complex of processes, in which all things go through a continuous process of coming into being and passing away. All things are studied in the context of their historical development. Dialectical analysis allows us to learn about things as they are in their actual interconnection, contradiction, and movement. We critically understand our past, informing our analysis with possibilities for our future.

A Marxist analysis shares in the larger *socialist struggle*. There is the commitment to eliminating exploitation and oppression. Being on the side of the oppressed, only those ideas are advanced that will aid in transforming the capitalist system. The objective of understanding is change—revolutionary change. The purpose of our intellectual labors is to assist in providing knowledge and consciousness for building a socialist society. Theories and strategies are developed to increase conscious class struggle; ideas for an alternative to capitalist society are formulated; and

Source: Richard Quinney, *Class, State, and Crime*, 2nd Edition, Copyright © 1980 by Longman Publishing Group. Reprinted with permission.

strategies for achieving the socialist alternative are proposed. In the course of intellectual-political work we engage in activities and actions that will advance the socialist struggle.

Finally, the questionable character of spiritual as well as material life under capitalism is understood in an analysis of crime. Marxism is a necessary method for unmasking the hidden levels of the material world. The far-reaching implications, however, are found in the *prophetic understanding* of reality. Recovered is the urgency of the human nature revealed in the contemporary condition and in its transformation. Socialism, Tillich observes, "acts in the direction of the messianic fulfillment; it is a messianic activity to which everybody is called."[3]

With these characteristics of understanding—encompassing a dialectical and historical analysis of the conditions of capitalist society in relation to socialist revolution—we begin to formulate significant substantive questions about crime. In recent years, as socialists have turned their attention to the study of crime, the outline for these questions has become evident. At this stage in our intellectual development the important questions revolve around *the meaning of crime in capitalist society*. Furthermore, there is the realization that the meaning of crime changes in the course of the development of capitalism.

The basic question in the analysis of crime is thus formulated: what is the meaning of crime in the development of capitalism? In approaching this question, we give attention to several interrelated processes: (1) the development of capitalist political economy, including the nature of the forces and relations of production, the formulation of the capitalist state, and the class struggle between those who do and those who do not own and control the means of production; (2) the systems of domination and repression established in the development of capitalism, operating for the benefit of the capitalist class and secured by the capitalist state; (3) the forms of accommodation and resistance to the conditions of capitalism by all people oppressed by capitalism, especially the working class; and (4) the relation of the dialectics of domination and accommodation to patterns of crime in capitalist society, producing the crimes of domination and the crimes of accommodation. These processes are dialectically related to the developing political economy. Crime is to be understood in terms of the development of capitalism.

The Development of a Capitalist Economy

As noted, crime is a manifestation of the conditions—material and spiritual— of society. The failure of conventional criminology is to ignore, by design, the conditions of capitalism. Since the phenomena of crime are products of material and spiritual conditions, any explanation of crime in terms of other elements is no explanation at all. Our need is to develop a general framework for understanding crime, beginning with the underlying historical processes of social and moral existence.

Production, as the necessary requirement of existence, produces its own forces and relations of social and economic life. The material factors (such as resources and technology) and personal factors (most importantly the workers) present at any given time form the productive *forces* of society. In the process of production, people form definite relations with one another. These *relations* of production, in reference to the forces of production, constitute the particular *mode* of production of any society at any given time.

Once the outlines of *political economy* (the productive forces, the relations of production, and the superstructure) have been indicated, the *class structure* and its dynamics can be recognized. A class society arises when the system of production is owned by one segment of the society to the exclusion of another. All production requires ownership of some kind; but in some systems of production ownership is private rather than social or collective. In these economies social relations are dependent on relations of domination and subjection. Marxist economists thus observe: "Relations of domination and subjection are based on private ownership of the means of production and express the exploitation of man by man under the slave-owning, feudal and capitalist systems. Relations of friendly co-operation and mutual assistance between working people free of exploitation are typical of socialist society. They are based on the public ownership of the means of production, which cut out the exploitation."[4]

Social life in capitalist society, which includes crime, therefore, is related to the economic conditions of production and the struggle between classes produced by these conditions. In other words, in capitalist society the behavior of any group or any individual is part of the conflict that characterizes class relations, a conflict produced by the capitalist system of production. The life of one class is seen in relation to that of the other. . . . Hence, class in capitalist society is analyzed in reference to the relationship to the process of production and according to the relationship to other classes in the society.

Moreover, the problematics of *labor* (as a foremost human activity) characterize the nature and specific relationship of the classes. For the capitalist system to operate and survive, the capitalist class must exploit the labor (appropriate the *surplus labor*) of the working class. . . . The capitalist class survives by appropriating the labor of the working class, and the working class as an exploited class exists as long as labor is required in the productive process: each class depends on the other for its character and existence.

The amount of labor appropriated, the techniques of labor exploitation, the conditions of working-class life, and the level of working-class consciousness have all been an integral part of the historical development of capitalism.[5] In like manner, the degree of antagonism and conflict between classes has varied at different stages in the development. Nevertheless, it is the basic contradiction between classes, generalized as class conflict, that typifies the development of capitalism. Class conflict permeates the whole of capitalist development, represented in the contradiction between those who own property and those who do not, and by those who oppress and those who are oppressed.[6] All past history that involves the development of capitalism is the history of class struggle.

Capitalism as a system of production based on the exploitation by the capitalist class that owns and controls the means of production is thus a dynamic system that goes through its own stages of development. In fact, capitalism is constantly transforming its forces and relations of production. As a result, the whole of capitalist society is constantly being altered—within the basic framework of capitalist political economy. . . .

Domination and Repression

The capitalist system must continuously reproduce itself. This is accomplished in a variety of ways ranging from the establishment of ideological hegemony to the further exploitation of labor, from the creation of public policy to the coercive repression of the population. Most explicitly, it is the *state* that secures the capitalist order. Through various schemes and mechanisms, then, the capitalist class is able to dominate. And in the course of this domination, crimes are carried out. These crimes, committed by the capitalist class, the state, and the agents of the capitalist class and state, are crimes of domination.

Historically, the capitalist state is a product of a political economy that depends on a division of classes. With the development of an economy based on the exploitation of one class by another, a political form was needed that would perpetuate that order. With the development of capitalism, with class divisions and class struggle, the state became necessary. . . .The state thus arose to protect and promote the interests of the dominant class, the class that owns and controls the means of production. The state exists as a device for controlling the exploited class, the class that labors, for the benefit of the ruling class. Modern civilization, as epitomized in capitalist societies, is founded on the exploitation of one class by another. Moreover, the capitalist state is oppressive not only because it supports the interests of the dominant class but also because it is responsible for the design of the whole system within which the capitalist ruling class dominates and the working class is dominated.[7] The capitalist system of production and exploitation is secured and reproduced by the capitalist state.

The coercive force of the state, embodied in law and legal repression, is the traditional means of maintaining the social and economic order. Contrary to conventional wisdom, law, instead of representing the community custom, is an instrument of the state that serves the interests of the developing capitalist class.[8] Law emerged with the rise of capitalism. As human labor became a commodity, human relations in general began to be the object of the commodity form. Human beings became subject to juridic regulation; the capitalist mode of production called forth its equivalent mode of regulation and control, the legal system.[9] And criminal law developed as the most appropriate form of control for capitalist society. Criminal law and legal repression continue to serve the interests of the capitalist class and the perpetuation of the capitalist system.

Through the legal system, then, the state forcefully protects its interests and those of the capitalist class. Crime control becomes the coercive means of checking threats to the existing social and economic order, threats that result from a system of oppression and exploitation. As a means of controlling the behavior of the exploited population, crime control is accomplished by a variety of methods, strategies, and institutions. The state, especially through its legislative bodies, establishes official policies of crime control. The administrative branch of the state formulates and enforces crime-control policies, usually setting the design for the whole nation. Specific agencies of law enforcement, such as the Federal Bureau of Investigation and the recent Law Enforcement Assistance Administration, determine the nature of crime control. And the state is able through its Department of Justice officially to repress the "dangerous" and "subversive" elements of the population. Together, these state institutions attempt to rationalize the legal system by employing the advanced methods of science and technology. And whenever any changes are to be attempted to reduce the incidence of crime, rehabilitation of the individual or reform within the existing institutions is suggested.[10] To drastically alter the society and the crime-control establishment would be to alter beyond recognition the capitalist system.

Yet the coercive force of the state is but one means of maintaining the social and economic order. A more subtle reproductive mechanism of capitalist society is the perpetuation of the capitalist concept of reality, a nonviolent but equally repressive means of domination. . . .

Those who rule in capitalist society—with the assistance of the state—not only accumulate capital at the expense of those who work but impose their ideology as well. Oppression and exploitation are legitimized by the expropriation of consciousness; since labor is expropriated, consciousness must also be expropriated.[11] In fact, *legitimacy* of the capitalist order is maintained by controlling the consciousness of the population. A capitalist hegemony is established. . . .

Although the capitalist state creates and manages the institutions of control (employing physical force *and* manipulation of consciousness), the basic contradictions of the capitalist order are such that this control is not absolute and, in the long run, is subject to defeat. Because of the contradictions of capitalism, the capitalist state is more weak than strong.[12] Eventually the capitalist state loses its legitimacy and no longer is able to perpetuate the ideology that capital accumulation for capitalists (at the expense of workers) is good for the nation or for human interests. The ability of the capitalist economic order to exist according to its own interests is eventually weakened. The problem becomes especially acute in periods of economic crisis, periods that are unavoidable under capitalism.

In the course of reproducing the capitalist system crimes are committed. One of the contradictions of capitalism is that some of its laws must be violated in order to secure the existing system. The contradictions of capitalism produce their own sources of crime. Not only are these contradictions heightened during times of crisis, making for an increase in crimes of domination, but the nature of these crimes changes with the further development of capitalism.

The crimes of domination most characteristic of capitalist domination are those crimes that occur in the course of securing the existing economic order. These *crimes of economic domination* include the crimes committed by corporations, ranging from price fixing to pollution of the environment in order to protect and further capital accumulation. Also included are the economic crimes of individual businessmen and professionals. In addition, the crimes of the capitalist class and the capitalist state are joined in organized crime. The more conventional criminal operations of organized crime are linked to the state in the present stage of capitalist development. The operations of organized crime and the criminal operations of the state are united in the attempt to assure the survival of the capitalist system.

Then there are the *crimes of government* committed by the elected and appointed officials of the capitalist state. The Watergate crimes, carried out to perpetuate a particular governmental administration, are the most publicized instances of these crimes. There are also those offenses committed by the government against persons and groups who would seemingly threaten national security. Included here are the crimes of warfare and the political assassination of foreign and domestic leaders.

Crimes of domination also occur in the course of state control. These are *crimes of control*. They include the felonies and misdemeanors that law-enforcement agents, especially the police, carry out in the name of the law, usually against persons accused of other violations. Violence and brutality have become a recognized part of police work. In addition to these crimes of control, there are crimes of a more subtle nature in which agents of the law violate the civil liberties of citizens, as in the various forms of surveillance, the use of provocateurs, and the illegal denial of due process.

Finally, many *social injuries* committed by the capitalist class and the capitalist state are not usually defined as criminal in the legal codes of the state.[13] These systematic actions, involving the denial of basic human rights (resulting in sexism, racism, and economic exploitation), are an integral part of capitalism and are important to its survival.

Underlying all capitalist crimes is the appropriation of the surplus value created by labor. The working class has the right to possess the whole of this value. The worker creates a value several times greater than the labor power purchased by the capitalist. The excess value created by the worker over and above the value of labor power is the surplus value appropriated by the capitalist, being the source of accumulation of capital and expansion of production.

Domination and repression are basic to class struggle in the development of capitalism. The capitalist class and the state protect and promote the capitalist order by controlling those who do not own the means of production. The labor supply and the conditions for labor must be secured. Crime control and crimes of domination are necessary features and natural products of a capitalist political economy. . . .

Crime in Capitalist Society

An understanding of crime, as developed here, begins with an analysis of the political economy of capitalism. The class struggle endemic to capitalism is characterized by a dialectic between domination and accommodation. Those who own and control the means of production, the capitalist class, attempt to secure the existing order through various forms of domination, especially crime control by the capitalist state. Those who do not own and control the means of production, especially the working class, accommodate to and resist the capitalist domination in various ways.

Crime is related to this process. Crime control and criminality (consisting of the crimes of domination and the crimes of accommodation) are understood in terms of the conditions resulting from the capitalist appropriation of labor. Variations in the nature and amount of crime occur in the course of developing capitalism. Each stage in the development of capitalism is characterized by a particular pattern of crime. The meaning and changing meanings of crime are found in the development of capitalism.

What can be expected in the further development of capitalism? The contradictions and related crises of a capitalist political economy are now a permanent feature of advanced capitalism. Further economic development along capitalist lines will solve none of the internal contradictions of the capitalist mode of production.[14] The capitalist state must therefore increasingly utilize its resources—its various control and repressive mechanisms—to maintain the capitalist order. The dialectic between oppression by the capitalist class and the daily struggle of survival by the oppressed will continue—and at a quickened pace.

The only lasting solution to the crisis of capitalism is socialism. Under late, advanced capitalism, socialism will be achieved in the struggle of all people who are oppressed by the capitalist mode of production, namely, the workers and all elements of the surplus population. An alliance of the oppressed must take place.[15] Given the objective conditions of a crisis in advanced capitalism, and the conditions for an alliance of the oppressed, a mass socialist movement can be formed, cutting across all divisions in the working class. . . .

Political Economy of Criminal Justice

. . . The repressive apparatus of the state becomes ever more important in the development of capitalism in the attempt to regulate the class struggle. Policies of control—especially crime control—are instituted to regulate problems and conflicts that otherwise can be solved only by social and economic changes that go beyond capitalist reforms. Criminal justice, as the euphemism for controlling class struggle and administering legal repression, becomes a major social policy in the advanced stages of capitalism.

Emerging within the political economy of late capitalism is a political economy of criminal justice. The political economy of criminal justice is one of the fundamental characteristics of advanced capitalism. To understand its various features is to understand a crucial part of the capitalist system. Criminal justice is a capitalist response to the contradictions of late capitalism.

State Expenditures on Criminal Justice

The capitalist state must increasingly expend its resources on programs that secure the capitalist order. These *social expenses* of the state, as defined by James O'Connor, consist of "projects and services which are required to maintain social harmony—to fulfill the state's 'legitimization' function."[16] Whereas *social capital* is expended in the promotion of profitable private accumulation, the social expenses of the state are not directly productive, for they produce no surplus value. They are designed to keep "social peace" among unemployed workers, or among the surplus population in general. Welfare and law enforcement are the primary forms of the state's social expenses, regulating class struggle, repressing action against the existing order, and giving legitimacy to the capitalist system. The creation and administration of the criminal justice system as a whole have become a principal social expense of the capitalist state.

The state in promoting capital accumulation in the monopoly sector stimulates overproduction and creates a surplus population and the resultant need for state expenses to cope with the surplus population. Such social services as education, family support, health services, and housing benefits give legitimacy to the capitalist system and satisfy some of the needs of the working class. These services compensate in part for the oppression and suffering caused by capitalism.

The criminal justice system, on the other hand, serves more explicitly to control that which cannot be remedied by available employment within the economy or by social services for the surplus population. The police, the courts, and the penal agencies—the entire criminal justice system—expand to cope as a last resort with the problems of surplus population. As the contradictions of capitalism increase, the criminal justice system becomes a preventive institution as well as a control and corrective agency. State expenditures on criminal justice occupy a larger share of the state's budgetary expenses. Criminal justice as a social expense of the state necessarily expands with the further development of capitalism. . . .

As the crisis of the state and the capitalist economy accelerates, forms of control will be devised to be more pervasive and more certain and, at the same time, less of an expense for the state. The state and monopoly capital will try to create crime-control programs that do not require a major outlay of capital, capital that does not promote further capital accumulation. For example, halfway-house programs may sometimes be substituted for large and costly institutions. Surveillance may replace some other forms of confinement and control. Yet the contradiction is only furthered: criminal justice is inevitably a losing battle under late capitalism.

In other words, spending on criminal justice is only a partial, temporary, and self-defeating resolution to capitalist economic contradictions. It is like military spending. Although expenditures on warfare and the military may have some immediate functions for the state and the economy, an economy based on such expenditures is subject to more contradictions than ultimate resolutions.[17] A substantial criminal justice budget, like a military budget, cannot successfully solve the economic and political problems of the capitalist system. And in the long run, criminal justice as a social expenditure can only further the contradictions of capitalism. . . .

Control of the Surplus Population

Social expenditures on criminal justice necessarily increase with the development of advanced capitalism. In the late stages of capitalism the mode of production and the forms of capital accumulation accelerate the growth of the relative surplus population. The state must then provide social-expense programs, including criminal justice, both to legitimate advanced capitalism and to control the surplus population. Instead of being able to absorb the surplus population into the political economy, advanced capitalism can only supervise and control a population that is now superfluous to the capitalist system. The problem is especially acute when the surplus population threatens to disturb the system, either by overburdening the system or by political action. Criminal justice is the modern means of controlling the surplus population produced by late capitalist development.

The state attempts to offset the social expense of criminal justice by supporting the growth of the criminal justice-industrial complex. The fiscal crisis of the capitalist state is temporarily alleviated by forming an alliance between monopoly capital and state-financed social programs. The social programs of the state are thereby transformed into social capital, providing subsidized investment opportunities for monopoly capital and ameliorating some of the material impoverishment of the surplus population.[18] The new complex thus ties the surplus population to the state and to the political economy of advanced capitalism. While a growing segment of the population is absorbed into the system as *indirectly productive workers*—the army of government and office workers, paraprofessionals, and those who work in one way or another in the social-expense programs—there is also a large surplus population controlled by these programs. These unemployed, underemployed, reserve army workers now find themselves dependent on the state. They are linked to the state (and to monopoly capital) for much of their economic welfare, and they are linked by being the object of the social-control programs of the state. The criminal justice system is the most explicit of these programs in controlling the surplus population. Criminal justice and the surplus population are thus symbiotically interdependent.

As the surplus population grows with the development of capitalism, the criminal justice system or some equivalent must also grow. By expanding the system, late capitalism attempts to "integrate" the surplus population into the economic and political system. The notion that the social problems generated by capitalism can be solved becomes obsolete. Instead, problems such as crime are dealt with as *control* problems. When the underlying conditions of capitalism cannot be changed—without changing the capitalist system—controlling the population oppressed by existing conditions is the only "solution." Thus, as one theorist-strategist of the capitalist state puts it, we must "learn to live with crime"; and the important question then becomes "what constitutes an effective law-enforcement and order-maintenance system?"[19]

On all levels of the criminal justice system, new techniques of control are being developed and instituted. Not only has there been increased implementation of a military-hardware approach to criminal justice but, developing more recently along with it, there are more subtle approaches. A dual system is developing whereby some of the surplus population's actions defined as criminal are dealt with harshly by strong-arm techniques and punitive measures. Other actions by other portions of the surplus population are handled by such software techniques as diversion from the courts and community-based corrections. In general, however, whatever the current techniques, the new model is one of *pacification*.[20] The surplus population is not only to be controlled but is to accept this control. The capitalist state, in alliance with monopoly capital, must continually innovate in expanding the criminal justice system.

Whatever the technique of control, the fact remains that the surplus population in need of control is being controlled by the criminal justice system. Control is especially acute in those periods when the economic crisis is most obvious—during periods of depression and recession. It is then that the surplus population, expanding because of unemployment, is affected most.

As usual during these periods, the hardest-hit groups are women, blacks, the young, and unskilled workers. . . .

A way of controlling this unemployed surplus population is simply and directly by confinement in prisons. The rhetoric of criminal justice—and that of conventional criminology—is that prisons are for incarcerating criminals. In spite of this mystification, prisons are used to control the part of the surplus population subject to the discretion of criminal law and the criminal justice system. The figures and the conclusion that prisons are differently utilized according to the extent of economic crisis are not usually presented. The finding is clear: the prison population increases as the rate of unemployment increases.[21] Unemployment simultaneously makes necessary various actions of survival by the unemployed surplus population and requires the state to control that population in some way. Containing the unemployed in prison is a certain way of controlling a threatening surplus population. Until other solutions of control are found, the capitalist state will need the prison's certainty for controlling portions of the surplus population. . . .

Notes

1. Paul Q. Hirst, "Marx and Engels on Law, Crime and Morality," *Economy and Society* 1 (February 1972): 28–56.
2. Karl Marx, *A Contribution to the Critique of Political Economy*, ed. M. Dobb (New York: International Publishers, 1970), pp. 20–21.
3. Paul Tillich, *Theology of Culture*, ed. Robert C. Kimball (New York: Oxford University Press, 1959), p. 198.

4. L. Afanasyev et al., *The Political Economy of Capitalism* (Moscow: Progress Publishers, 1974), p. 12.
5. Jurgen Kuczynski, *The Rise of the Working Class* (New York: McGraw-Hill, 1967).
6. Robert Heiss, *Engels, Kierkegaard, and Marx* (New York: Dell, 1957), p. 390.
7. David A. Gold, Clarence Y. H. Lo, and Erik Olin Wright, "Recent Developments in Marxist Theories of the State," *Monthly Review* 27 (November 1975): 36–51.
8. Stanley Diamond, "The Rule of Law Versus the Order of Custom," *Social Research* 38 (Spring 1971): 42–72; and Michael Tigar, with the assistance of Madeleine Levy, *Law and the Rise of Capitalism* (New York: Monthly Review Press, 1977).
9. E. B. Pashukanis, "The General Theory of Law and Marxism," in *Soviet Legal Philosophy*, trans. and ed. Hugh W. Babb (Cambridge, MA.: Harvard University Press, 1951), pp. 111–225; and Isaac D. Balbus, "Commodity Form and Legal Form: An Essay on the 'Relative Autonomy' of the Law," *Law and Society Review* 11 (Winter 1977): 571–88.
10. Alexander Liazos, "Class Oppression: The Functions of Juvenile Justice," *Insurgent Sociologist* 5 (Fall 1974), pp. 2–24.
11. Alan Wolfe, "New Directions in the Marxist Theory of Politics," *Politics and Society* 4 (Winter 1974): 155–57.
12. Wolfe, "New Directions in the Marxist Theory of Politics," p. 155.
13. Tony Platt, "Prospects for a Radical Criminology in the United States," *Crime and Social Justice* 1 (Spring-Summer 1974): 2–10; and Herman and Julia Schwendinger, "Defenders of Order or Guardians of Human Rights?" *Issues in Criminology* 5 (Summer 1970): 123–57.
14. Ernest Mandel, "The Industrial Cycle in Late Capitalism," *New Left Review* 90 (March-April 1975): 3–25.
15. O'Connor, *Fiscal Crisis of the State*, pp. 221–56.
16. James O'Connor, *The Fiscal Crisis of the State* (New York: St. Martin's, 1973), p. 7.
17. Clarence Y. H. Lo, "The Conflicting Functions of U.S. Military Spending after World War II," *Kapitalistate*, no. 3 (Spring 1975): 26–44.
18. O'Connor, *The Fiscal Crisis of the State*, p. 221.
19. James Q. Wilson, "Crime and Law Enforcement," in *Agenda for the Nation*, ed. Kermit Gordon (Washington, D.C.: U.S. Government Printing Office), pp. 199, 204.
20. Center for Research on Criminal Justice, *The Iron Fist and the Velvet Glove*, pp. 126–31.
21. Ivan Jankovic, "Labor Market and Imprisonment," *Crime and Social Justice* 8 (Fall-Winter 1977): 17–31. Also see report in *NEPA News* (Northeast Prisoner's Association), February 1976, p. 16. Theoretical background is found in Georg Rusche and Otto Kirchheimer, *Punishment and Social Structure* (New York: Columbia University Press, 1939).

19

Criminal Man

Gina Lombroso-Ferrero

. . . The Classical School of Penal Jurisprudence, of which Beccaria was the founder and Francesco Carrara the greatest and most glorious disciple, aimed only at establishing sound judgments and fixed laws to guide capricious and often undiscerning judges in the application of penalties. In writing his great work, the founder of this School was inspired by the highest of all human sentiments—pity; but although the criminal incidentally receives notice, the writings of this School treat only of the application of the law, not of offenders themselves.

This is the difference between the Classical and the Modern School of Penal Jurisprudence. The Classical School based its doctrines on the assumption that all criminals, except in a few extreme cases, are endowed with intelligence and feelings like normal individuals, and that they commit misdeeds consciously, being prompted thereto by their unrestrained desire for evil. The offence alone was considered, and on it the whole existing penal system has been founded, the severity of the sentence meted out to the offender being regulated by the gravity of his misdeed.

The Modern, or Positive, School of Penal Jurisprudence, on the contrary, maintains that the antisocial tendencies of criminals are the result of their physical and psychic organization, which differs essentially from that of normal individuals; and it aims at studying the morphology and various functional phenomena of the criminal with the object of curing, instead of punishing him. The Modern School is therefore founded on a new science, Criminal Anthropology, which may be defined as the Natural History of the Criminal, because it embraces his organic and psychic constitution and social life, just as anthropology does in the case of normal human beings and the different races.

If we examine a number of criminals, we shall find that they exhibit numerous anomalies in the face, skeleton, and various psychic and sensitive functions, so that they strongly resemble primitive races. It was these anomalies that first drew my father's attention to the close relationship between the criminal and the savage and made him suspect that criminal tendencies are of atavistic origin.

When a young doctor at the Asylum in Pavia, he was requested to make a post-mortem examination on a criminal named Vilella, an Italian Jack the Ripper, who by atrocious crimes had spread terror in the Province of Lombardy. Scarcely

Source: Reprinted from Gina Lombroso-Ferrero, *Criminal Man, According to the Classification of Cesare Lombroso* (New York: G. P. Putnam's Sons, 1911), pp. 4–13, 24–29, 48–49, 130–152. Some illustrations omitted.

141

had he laid open the skull, when he perceived at the base, on the spot where the internal occipital crest or ridge is found in normal individuals, a small hollow, which he called *median occipital fossa*. . . . This abnormal character was correlated to a still greater anomaly in the cerebellum, the hypertrophy of the vermis, *i.e.*, the spinal cord which separates the cerebellar lobes lying underneath the cerebral hemispheres. This vermis was so enlarged in the case of Vilella, that it almost formed a small, intermediate cerebellum like that found in the lower types of apes, rodents, and birds. This anomaly is very rare among inferior races, with the exception of the South American Indian tribe of the Aymaras of Bolivia and Peru, in whom it is not infrequently found (40%). It is seldom met within the insane or other degenerates, but later investigations have shown it to be prevalent in criminals.

This discovery was like a flash of light. "At the sight of that skull," says my father, "I seemed to see all at once, standing out clearly illumined as in a vast plain under a flaming sky, the problem of the nature of the criminal, who reproduces in civilized times characteristics, not only of primitive savages, but of still lower types as far back as the carnivora."

Thus was explained the origin of the enormous jaws, strong canines, prominent zygomae, and strongly developed orbital arches which he had so frequently remarked in criminals, for these peculiarities are common to carnivores and savages, who tear and devour raw flesh. Thus also it was easy to understand why the span of the arms in criminals so often exceeds the height, for this is a characteristic of apes, whose fore-limbs are used in walking and climbing. The other anomalies exhibited by criminals—the scanty beard as opposed to the general hairiness of the body, prehensile foot, diminished number of lines in the palm of the hand, cheek-pouches, enormous development of the middle incisors and frequent absence of the lateral ones, flattened nose and angular or sugar-loaf form of the skull, common to criminals and apes; the excessive size of the orbits, which, combined with the hooked nose, so often imparts to criminals the aspect of birds of prey, the projection of the lower part of the face and jaws (prognathism) found in negroes and animals, and supernumerary teeth (amounting in some cases to a double row as in snakes) and cranial bones (epactal bone as in the Peruvian Indians): all these characteristics pointed to one conclusion, the atavistic origin of the criminal, who reproduces physical, psychic, and functional qualities of remote ancestors.

Subsequent research on the part of my father and his disciples showed that other factors besides atavism come into play in determining the criminal type. These are: disease and environment. Later on, the study of innumerable offenders led them to the conclusion that all law-breakers cannot be classed in a single species, for their ranks include very diversified types, who differ not only in their bent towards a particular form of crime, but also in the degree of tenacity and intensity displayed by them in their perverse propensities, so that, in reality, they form a graduated scale leading from the born criminal to the normal individual.

Born criminals form about one third of the mass of offenders, but, though inferior in numbers, they constitute the most important part of the whole criminal army, partly because they are constantly appearing before the public and also because the crimes committed by them are of a peculiarly monstrous character; the other two thirds are composed of criminaloids (minor offenders), occasional and habitual criminals, etc., who do not show such a marked degree of diversity from normal persons.

Let us commence with the born criminal, who as the principal nucleus of the wretched army of law-breakers, naturally manifests the most numerous and salient anomalies.

The median occipital fossa and other abnormal features just enumerated are not the only peculiarities exhibited by this aggravated type of offender. By careful research, my father and others of his School have brought to light many anomalies in bodily organs, and functions both physical and mental, all of which serve to indicate the atavistic and pathological origin of the instinctive criminal.

It would be incompatible with the scope of this summary, were I to give a minute description of the innumerable anomalies discovered in criminals by the Modern School, to attempt to trace such abnormal traits back to their source, or to demonstrate their effect on the organism. This has been done in a very minute fashion in the three volumes of my father's work *Criminal Man* and his subsequent writings on the same subject, *Modern Forms of Crime, Recent Research in Criminal Anthropology, Prison Palimpsests*, etc., etc., to which readers desirous of obtaining a more thorough knowledge of the subject should refer.

The present volume will only touch briefly on the principal characteristics of criminals, with the object of presenting a general outline of the studies of criminologists.

Physical Anomalies of the Born Criminal

The Head

As the seat of all the greatest disturbances, this part naturally manifests the greatest number of anomalies, which extend from the external conformation of the brain-case to the composition of its contents.

The criminal skull does not exhibit any marked characteristics of size and shape. Generally speaking, it tends to be larger or smaller than the average skull common to the region or country from which the criminal hails. It varies between 1,200 and 1,600 c.c.; *i.e.*, between 73 and 100 cubic inches, the normal average being 92. This applies also to the cephalic index; that is, the ratio of the maximum width to the maximum length of the skull multiplied by 100, which serves to give a concrete idea of the form of the skull, because the higher the index, the nearer the skull approaches a spherical form, and the lower the index, the more elongated it becomes. The skulls of criminals have no characteristic cephalic index, but tend to an exaggeration of the ethnical type prevalent in their native countries. In regions where dolichocephaly (index less than 80) abounds, the skulls of criminals show a very low index; if, on the contrary, they are natives of districts where brachycephaly (index 80 or more) prevails, they exhibit a very high index.

In 15.5% we find trochocephalous or abnormally round heads (index 91). A very high percentage (nearly double that of normal individuals) have submicrocephalous or small skulls. In other cases the skull is excessively large (macrocephaly) or abnormally small and ill-shaped with a narrow, receding forehead (microcephaly, 0.2%). More rarely the skull is of normal size, but shaped like the keel of a boat (scaphocephaly, 0.1 % and subscaphocephaly 6%, see Fig. 2). Sometimes the anomalies are still more serious and we find wholly asymmetrical skulls with protuberances on either side (plagiocephaly 10.9%, see Fig. 3), or terminating in a peak on the bregma or anterior fontanel (acrocephaly, . . .), or depressed in the middle (cymbocephaly, sphenocephaly). At times, there are crests or grooves along the sutures (11.9%) or the cranial bones are abnormally thick,

SKULL FORMATION

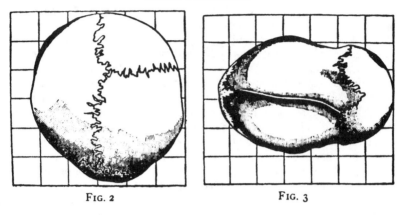

Fig. 2   Fig. 3

a characteristic of savage peoples (36.6%) or abnormally thin (8.10%). Other anomalies of importance are the presence of Wormian bones in the sutures of the skull (21.22%), the bone of the Incas already alluded to (4%), and above all, the median occipital fossa. Of great importance also are the prominent frontal sinuses found in 25% (double that of normal individuals), the semicircular line of the temples, which is sometimes so exaggerated that it forms a ridge and is correlated to an excessive development of the temporal muscles, a common characteristic of primates and carnivores. Sometimes the forehead is receding, as in apes (19%), or low and narrow (10%).

The Face

In striking contrast to the narrow forehead and low vault of the skull, the face of the criminal, like those of most animals, is of disproportionate size, a phenomenon intimately connected with the greater development of the senses as compared with that of the nervous centres. Prognathism, the projection of the lower portion of the face beyond the forehead, is found in 45.7% of criminals. Progeneismus, the projection of the lower teeth and jaw beyond the upper, is found in 38%, whereas among normal persons the proportion is barely 28%. As a natural consequence of this predominance of the lower portion of the face, the orbital arches and zygomae show a corresponding development (35%) and the size of the jaws is naturally increased, the mean diameter being 103.9 mm. (4.09 inches) as against 93 mm. (3.66 inches) in normal persons. Among criminals 29% have voluminous jaws.

The excessive dimensions of the jaws and cheek-bones admit of other explanations besides the atavistic one of a greater development of the masticatory system. They may have been influenced by the habit of certain gestures, the setting of the teeth or tension of the muscles of the mouth, which accompany violent muscular efforts and are natural to men who form energetic or violent resolves and meditate plans of revenge.

Asymmetry is a common characteristic of the criminal physiognomy. The eyes and ears are frequently situated at different levels and are of unequal size, the nose slants towards one side, etc. This asymmetry, as we shall see later, is connected with marked irregularities in the senses and functions. . . .

Sensory and Functional Peculiarities of the Born Criminal

The above-mentioned physiognomical and skeletal anomalies are further supplemented by functional peculiarities, and all these abnormal characteristics converge, as mountain streams to the hollow in the plain, towards a central idea—the atavistic nature of the born criminal.

An examination of the senses and sensibility of criminals gives the following results:

General Sensibility

Tested simply by touching with the finger, a certain degree of obtuseness is noted. By using an apparatus invented by DuBois-Reymond and adopted by my father, the degree of sensibility obtained was 49.6 mm. in criminals as against 64.2 mm. in normal individuals. Criminals are more sensitive on the left side, contrary to normal persons, in whom greater sensibility prevails on the right.

Sensibility to Pain

Compared with ordinary individuals, the criminal shows greater insensibility to pain as well as to touch. This obtuseness sometimes reaches complete analgesia or total absence of feeling (16%), a phenomenon never encountered in normal persons. The mean degree of dolorific sensibility in criminals is 34.1 mm. whereas it is rarely lower than 40 mm. in normal individuals. Here again the left-handedness of criminals becomes apparent, 39% showing greater sensibility on the left.

Tactile Sensibility

The distance at which two points applied to the finger-tips are felt separately is more than 4 mm. in 30% of criminals, a degree of obtuseness only found in 4% of normal individuals. Criminals exhibit greater tactile sensibility on the left. Tactile obtuseness varies with the class of crime practised by the individual. While in burglars, swindlers, and assaulters, it is double that of normal persons, in murderers, violators, and incendiaries it is often four or five times as great.

Sensibility to the Magnet, which scarcely exists in normal persons, is common to a marked degree in criminals (48%).

Meteoric Sensibility

This is far more apparent in criminals and the insane than in normal individuals. With variations of temperature and atmospheric pressure, both criminals and lunatics become agitated and manifest changes of disposition and sensations of various kinds, which are rarely experienced by normal persons.

Sight is generally acute, perhaps more so than in ordinary individuals, and in this the criminal resembles the savage. Chromatic sensibility, on the contrary, is decidedly defective, the percentage of colour-blindness being twice that of normal persons. The field of vision is frequently limited by the white and exhibits much stranger anomalies, a special irregularity of outline with deep peripheral scotoma, which we shall see is a special characteristic of the epileptic.

Hearing, Smell, Taste are generally of less than average acuteness in criminals. Cases of complete anosmia and qualitative obtuseness are not uncommon.

Agility

Criminals are generally agile and preserve this quality even at an advanced age. When over seventy, Vilella sprang like a goat up the steep rocks of his native Calabria, and the celebrated thief "La Vecchia," when quite an old man, escaped from his captors by leaping from a high rampart at Pavia.

Strength

Contrary to what might be expected, tests by means of the dynamometer show that criminals do not usually possess an extraordinary degree of strength. There is frequently a slight difference between the strength of the right and left limbs, but more often ambidexterity, as in children, and a greater degree of strength in the left limbs.

Psychology of the Born Criminal

The physical type of the criminal is completed and intensified by his moral and intellectual physiognomy, which furnishes a further proof of his relationship to the savage and epileptic.

Natural Affections

These play an important part in the life of a normally constituted individual and are in fact the *raison d'être* of his existence, but the criminal rarely, if ever, experiences emotions of this kind and least of all regarding his own kin. On the other hand, he shows exaggerated and abnormal fondness for animals and strangers. La Sola, a female criminal, manifested about as much affection for her children as if they had been kittens and induced her accomplice to murder a former paramour, who was deeply attached to her; yet she tended the sick and dying with the utmost devotion.

In the place of domestic and social affections, the criminal is dominated by a few absorbing passions: vanity, impulsiveness, desire for revenge, licentiousness.

Moral Sense

The ability to discriminate between right and wrong, which is the highest attribute of civilised humanity, is notably lacking in physically and psychically stunted organisms. Many criminals do not realize the immorality of their actions. In French criminal jargon conscience is called "la muette," the thief "l'ami," and "travailler" and "servir" signify to steal. A Milanese thief once remarked to my father: "I don't steal. I only relieve the rich of their superfluous wealth." Lacenaire, speaking of his accomplice Avril, remarked, "I realized at once that we should be able to work together." A thief asked by Ferri what he did when he found the purse stolen by him contained no money, replied, "I call them rogues." The notions of right and wrong appear to be completely inverted in such minds. They seem to think they have a right to rob and murder and that those who hinder them are acting unfairly. Murderers, especially when actuated by motives of revenge, consider their actions righteous in the extreme.

Repentance and Remorse

We hear a great deal about the remorse of criminals, but those who come into contact with these degenerates realize that they are rarely, if ever, tormented by such feelings. Very few confess their crimes: the greater number deny all guilt in a most strenuous manner and are fond of protesting that they are victims of injustice, calumny, and jealousy. As Despine once remarked with much insight, nothing resembles the sleep of the just more closely than the slumbers of an assassin.

Many criminals, indeed, allege repentance, but generally from hypocritical motives; either because they hope to gain some advantage by working on the feelings of philanthropists, or with a view to escaping, or, at any rate, improving their condition while in prison. . . .

The Criminal Type

All the physical and psychic peculiarities of which we have spoken are found singly in many normal individuals. Moreover, crime is not always the result of degeneration and atavism; and, on the other hand, many persons who are considered perfectly normal are not so in reality. However, in normal individuals, we never find that accumulation of physical, psychic, functional, and skeletal anomalies in one and the same person, that we do in the case of criminals, among whom also entire freedom from abnormal characteristics is more rare than among ordinary individuals.

Just as a musical theme is the result of a sum of notes, and not of any single note, the criminal type results from the aggregate of these anomalies, which render him strange and terrible, not only to the scientific observer, but to ordinary persons who are capable of an impartial judgment.

Painters and poets, unhampered by false doctrines, divined this type long before it became the subject of a special branch of study. The assassins, executioners, and devils painted by Mantegna, Titian, and Ribera the Spagnoletto embody with marvellous exactitude the characteristics of the born criminal; and the descriptions of great writers, Dante, Shakespeare, Dostoyevsky, and Ibsen, are equally faithful representations, physically and psychically, of this morbid type. . . .

Criminality in Children

The criminal instincts common to primitive savages would be found proportionally in nearly all children, if they were not influenced by moral training and example. This does not mean that without educative restraints, all children would develop into criminals. According to the observations made by Prof. Mario Carrara at Cagliari, the bands of neglected children who run wild in the streets of the Sardinian capital and are addicted to thievish practices and more serious vices, spontaneously correct themselves of these habits as soon as they have arrived at puberty.

This fact, that the germs of moral insanity and criminality are found normally in mankind in the first stages of his existence, in the same way as forms considered monstrous when exhibited by adults, frequently exist in the fœtus, is such a simple and common phenomenon that it eluded notice until it was demonstrated clearly by observers like Moreau, Perez, and Bain. The child, like certain adults, whose abnormality consists in a lack of moral sense, represents what is known to alienists as a morally insane being and to criminologists as a born criminal, and it certainly resembles these types in its impetuous violence.

Perez (*Psychologie de l'enfant*, 2d ed., 1882) remarks on the frequency and precocity of anger in children:

> During the first two months, it manifests by movements of the eyebrows and hands undoubted fits of temper when undergoing any distasteful process, such as washing or when deprived of any object it takes a fancy to. At the age of one, it goes to the length of striking those who incur its displeasure, of breaking plates or throwing them at persons it dislikes, exactly like savages.

Moreau (*De l'Homicide chez les enfants*, 1882) cites numerous cases of children who fly into a passion if their wishes are not complied with immediately. In one instance observed by him a very intelligent child of eight, when reproved, even in the mildest manner by his parents or strangers, would give way to violent anger, snatching up the nearest weapon, or if he found himself unable to take revenge, would break anything he could lay his hands on.

A baby girl showed an extremely violent temper, but became of gentle disposition after she had reached the age of two (Perez). Another, observed by the same author, when only eleven months old, flew into a towering rage, because she was unable to pull off her grandfather's nose. Yet another, at the age of two, tried to bite another child who had a doll like her own, and she was so much affected by her anger that she was ill for three days afterwards.

Nino Bixio, when a boy of seven (*Vita*, Guerzoni, 1880) on seeing his teacher laugh because he had written his exercise on office letter-paper, threw the inkstand at the man's face. This boy was literally the terror of the school, on account of the violence he displayed at the slightest offence.

Infants of seven or eight months have been known to scratch at any attempt to withdraw the breast from them, and to retaliate when slapped.

A backward and slightly hydrocephalous boy whom my father had under observation, began at the age of six to show violent irritation at the slightest reproof or correction. If he was able to strike the person who had annoyed him, his rage cooled immediately; if not, he would scream incessantly and bite his hands with gestures similar to those often witnessed in caged bears who have been teased and cannot retaliate.

The above cases show that the desire for revenge is extremely common and precocious in children. Anger is an elementary instinct innate in human beings. It should be guided and restrained, but can never be extirpated.

Children are quite devoid of moral sense during the first months or first years of their existence. Good and evil in their estimation are what is allowed and what is forbidden by their elders, but they are incapable of judging independently of the moral value of an action.

"Lying and disobedience are very wrong," said a boy to Perez, "because they displease mother." Everything he was accustomed to was right and necessary.

A child does not grasp abstract ideas of justice, or the rights of property, until he has been deprived of some possession. He is prone to detest injustice, especially when he is the victim. Injustice, in his estimation, is the discord between a habitual mode of treatment and an accidental one. When subjected to altered conditions, he shows complete uncertainty. A child placed under Perez's care modified his ways according to each new arrival. He began ordering his companions about and refused to obey any one but Perez.

Affection is very slightly developed in children. Their fancy is easily caught by a pleasing exterior or by anything that contributes to their amusement; like domestic animals that they enjoy teasing and pulling about, and they exhibit great antipathy to unfamiliar objects that inspire them with fear. Up to the age of seven or even after, they show very little real attachment to anybody. Even their mothers, whom they appear to love, are speedily forgotten after a short separation.

In conclusion, children manifest a great many of the impulses we have observed in criminals; anger, a spirit of revenge, idleness, volubility and lack of affection.

We have also pointed out that many actions considered criminal in civilised communities, are normal and legitimate practices among primitive races. It is evident, therefore, that such actions are natural to the early stages, both of social evolution and individual psychic development.

In view of these facts, it is not strange that civilised communities should produce a certain percentage of adults who commit actions reputed injurious to society and punishable by law. It is only an atavistic phenomenon, the return to a former state. In the criminal, moreover, the phenomenon is accompanied by others also natural to a primitive stage of evolution. These have already been referred to in the first chapter, which contains a description of many strange practices common to delinquents, and evidently of primitive origin—tattooing, cruel games, love of orgies, a peculiar slang resembling in certain features the languages of primitive peoples, and the use of hieroglyphics and pictography.

The artistic manifestations of the criminal show the same characteristics. In spite of the thousands of years which separate him from prehistoric savages, his art is a faithful reproduction of the first, crude artistic attempts of primitive races. The museum of criminal anthropology created by my father contains numerous specimens of criminal art, stones shaped to resemble human figures, like those found in Australia, rude pottery covered with designs that recall Egyptian decorations or scenes fashioned in terra-cotta that resemble the grotesque creations of children or savages.

The criminal is an atavistic being, a relic of a vanished race. This is by no means an uncommon occurrence in nature. Atavism, the reversion to a former state, is the first feeble indication of the reaction opposed by nature to the perturbing causes which seek to alter her delicate mechanism. Under certain unfavourable conditions, cold or poor soil, the common oak will develop characteristics of the oak of the Quaternary period. The dog left to run wild in the forest will in a few generations revert to the type of his original wolf-like progenitor, and the cultivated garden roses when neglected show a tendency to reassume the form of the original dog rose. Under special conditions produced by alcohol, chloroform, heat, or injuries, ants, dogs, and pigeons become irritable and savage like their wild ancestors.

This tendency to alter under special conditions is common to human beings, in whom hunger, syphilis, trauma, and, still more frequently, morbid conditions inherited from insane, criminal, or diseased progenitors, or the abuse of nerve poisons, such as alcohol, tobacco, or morphine, cause various alterations, of which criminality—that is, a return to the characteristics peculiar to primitive savages—is in reality the least serious, because it represents a less advanced stage than other forms of cerebral alteration.

The ætiology of crime, therefore, mingles with that of all kinds of degeneration: rickets, deafness, monstrosity, hairiness, and cretinism, of which crime is only a variation. It has, however, always been regarded as a thing apart, owing to a general instinctive repugnance to admit that a phenomenon, whose extrinsications are so extensive and penetrate every fibre of social life, derives, in fact, from the same causes as socially insignificant forms like rickets, sterility, etc. But this repugnance is really only a sensory illusion, like many others of widely diverse nature.

Pathological Origin of Crime

The atavistic origin of crime is certainly one of the most important discoveries of criminal anthropology, but it is important only theoretically, since it merely explains the phenomenon. Anthropologists soon realized how necessary it was to supplement this discovery by that of the origin, or causes which call forth in certain individuals these atavistic or criminal instincts, for it is the immediate causes that constitute the practical nucleus of the problem and it is their removal that renders possible the cure of the disease.

These causes are divided into organic and external factors of crime: the former remote and deeply rooted, the latter momentary but frequently determining the criminal act, and both closely related and fused together.

Heredity is the principal organic cause of criminal tendencies. It may be divided into two classes: indirect heredity from a generically degenerate family with frequent cases of insanity, deafness, syphilis, epilepsy, and alcoholism among its members; direct heredity from criminal parentage.

Indirect Heredity

Almost all forms of chronic, constitutional diseases, especially those of a nervous character: chorea, sciatica, hysteria, insanity, and above all, epilepsy, may give rise to criminality in the descendants.

Of 559 soldiers convicted of offences, examined by Brancaleone Ribaudo, 10% had epileptic parents. According to Dejerine, this figure reaches 74.6% among criminal epileptics. Arthritis and gout have been known to generate criminality in the descendants. But the most serious, and at the same time most common, form of indirect heredity is alcoholism, which, contrary to general belief, wreaks destruction in all classes of society, amongst the rich and poor without distinction of sex, for alcohol may insinuate itself everywhere under the most refined and pleasant disguises, in liqueurs, sweets, and coffee.

According to calculations made by my father, 20% of Italian criminals descend from inebriate families; according to Penta the percentage is 27 and in dangerous criminals, 33%. The Jukes family, of whom we shall speak later, descended from a drunkard.

The first salient characteristic in hereditary alcoholism is the precocious taste for intoxicants; secondly, the susceptibility to alcohol, which is infinitely more injurious to the offspring of inebriates than to normal individuals; and thirdly, the growth of the craving for strong drinks, which inevitably undermine the constitution.

Direct Heredity

The effects of direct heredity are still more serious, for they are aggravated by environment and education. Official statistics show that 20% of juvenile offenders belong to families of doubtful reputation and 26% to those whose reputation is thoroughly bad. The criminal Galletto, a native of Marseilles, was the nephew of the equally ferocious anthropophagous violator of women, Orsolano. Dumollar was the son of a murderer; Patetot's grandfather and great-grandfather were in prison, as were the grandfathers and fathers of Papa, Crocco, Serravalle and Cavallante, Comptois and Lempave; the parents of the celebrated female thief Sans Refus, were both thieves.

The genealogical study of certain families has shown that there are whole generations, almost all the members of which belong to the ranks of crime, insanity, and prostitution (this last being amongst women the equivalent of criminality amongst men). A striking example is furnished by the notorious Jukes family, with 77 criminal descendants.

Ancestor, Max Jukes: 77 criminals; 142 vagabonds; 120 prostitutes; 18 keepers of houses of ill-fame; 91 illegitimates; 141 idiots or afflicted with impotency or syphilis; 46 sterile females.

A like criminal contingent may be found in the pedigrees of Chrêtien, the Lemaires, the Fieschi family, etc.

Race

This is of great importance in view of the atavistic origin of crime. There exist whole tribes and races more or less given to crime, such as the tribe Zakka Khel in India. In all regions of Italy, whole villages constitute hot-beds of crime, owing, no doubt, to ethnical causes: Artena in the province of Rome, Carde and San Giorgio Canavese in Piedmont, Pergola in Tuscany, San Severo in Apulia, San Mauro and Nicosia in Sicily. The frequency of homicide in Calabria, Sicily, and Sardinia is fundamentally due to African and Oriental elements.

In the gipsies we have an entire race of criminals with all the passions and vices common to delinquent types: idleness, ignorance, impetuous fury, vanity, love of orgies, and ferocity. Murder is often committed for some trifling gain. The women are skilled thieves and train their children in dishonest practices. On the contrary, the percentage of crimes among Jews is always lower than that of the surrounding population; although there is a prevalence of certain specific forms of offences, often hereditary, such as fraud, forgery, libel, and chief of all, traffic in prostitution; murder is extremely rare.

Illnesses, Intoxications, Traumatism

These causes, although apparently as important as heredity, are in fact, decidedly less so. Both disease and trauma may intensify or call forth latent perversity, but they are less frequently the cause of it. There are, however, certain cases in which traumatism meningitis, typhus, or other diseases that affect the brain have undoubtedly evoked criminal tendencies in individuals hitherto normal. Twenty out of 290 criminals studied by my father with minute care had suffered from injury to the head in childhood; and recently a case came under his notice in which a youth of good family and excellent character received an injury to his head at the age of fourteen and became epileptic, developing subsequently into a gambler, thief, and murderer. Such cases, however, are not very common.

There is one disease that without other causes—either inherited degeneracy or vices resulting from a bad education and environment—is capable of transforming a healthy individual into a vicious, hopelessly evil being. That disease is alcoholism, which has been discussed in a previous chapter, but to which I must refer briefly again, because it is such an important factor of criminality.

Temporary drunkenness alone will give rise to crime, since it inflames the passions, obscures the mental and moral faculties, and destroys all sense of decency, causing men to commit offences in a state of automatism or a species of somnambulism. Sometimes drunkenness produces kleptomania. A slight excess in drinking will cause men of absolute honesty to appropriate any objects they can lay their hands upon. When the effects of drink have worn off, they feel shame and remorse and hasten to restore the stolen goods. Alcohol, however, more often causes violence. An officer known to my father, when drunk, twice attempted to run his sword through his friends and his own attendant.

Among Oriental sects of murderers, as is well known, homicidal fury was excited and maintained by a drink brewed for the purpose from hempseed.

Büchner shows that dishonest instincts can be developed in bees by a special food consisting of honey mixed with brandy. The insects acquire a taste for this drink in the same way as human beings do, and under its influence cease to work. Ants show similar symptoms after narcosis by means of chloroform. Their bodies remain motionless, with the exception of their heads, with which they snap at all who approach them.

The above cited cases show that there exists a species of alcoholic psychic epilepsy, similar to congenital epilepsy, in which after alcoholic poisoning, the individual is incited to raise his hand against himself or others without any due cause. But besides the crimes of violence committed during a drunken fit, the prolonged abuse of alcohol, opium, morphia, coca, and other nervines may give rise to chronic perturbation of the mind, and without other causes, congenital or educative, will transform an honest, well-bred, and industrious man into an idle, violent, and apathetic fellow,—into an ignoble being, capable of any depraved action, even when he is not directly under the influence of the drug.

When we were children, a frequent visitor at our house was a certain Belm . . ., a very intelligent man and an accomplished linguist. He was a military officer, but later took to journalism, and his writing's were distinguished by vivacious style and elevation of thought. He married and had several children, but at the age of thirty some trouble caused him to take to drink. His character soon underwent a complete change. Although formerly a proud man, he was not ashamed to pester all his friends for money and to let his family sink into the direst poverty.

Social Causes of Crime

Education

We now come to the second series of criminal factors, those which depend, not on the organism, but on external conditions. We have already stated that the best and most careful education, moral and intellectual, is powerless to effect an improvement in the morally insane, but that in other cases, education, environment, and example are extremely important, for which reason neglected and destitute children are easily initiated into evil practices.

At Naples, ''Esposito'' (foundling) is a common name amongst prisoners, as is at Bologna and in Lombardy the name ''Colombo,'' which signifies the same thing. In Prussia, illegitimate males form 6% of offenders, illegitimate females 1.8%; in Austria, 10 and 2% respectively. The percentage is considerably larger amongst juvenile criminals, prostitutes, and recidivists. In France, in 1864, 65% of the minors arrested were bastards or orphans, and at Hamburg 30% of the prostitutes are illegitimate. In Italy, 30% of recidivists are natural children and foundlings.

This depends largely on hereditary influences, which are generally bad, but still more on the difficulty of finding a means of subsistence, owing to the state of neglect in which these wretched beings exist, even when herded together in charity schools and orphanages—both of which are even more antihygienic morally, than they are physically.

A depraved environment, which counsels or even insists on wrongdoing, and the bad example of parents or relatives, exercise a still more sinister influence on children than desertion. The criminal family Cornu, finding one of their children, a little girl, strongly averse to their evil ways, forced her to carry the head of one of their victims in her pinafore for a couple of miles, after which she became one of the most ferocious of the band.

Meteoric Causes are frequently the determining factor of the ultimate impulsive act, which converts the latent criminal into an effective one. Excessively high temperature and rapid barometric changes, while predisposing epileptics to convulsive seizures and the insane to uneasiness, restlessness, and noisy outbreaks, encourage quarrels, brawls, and stabbing affrays. To the same reason may be ascribed the prevalence during the hot months, of rape, homicide, insurrections, and revolts. In comparing statistics of criminality in France with those of the variations in temperature, Ferri noted an increase in crimes of violence during the warmer years. An examination of European and American statistics shows that the number of homicides decreases as we pass from hot to cooler climates. Holzendorf calculates that the number of murders committed in the Southern States of North America is fifteen times greater than those committed in the Northern States. A low temperature, on the contrary, has the effect of increasing the number of crimes against property, due to increased need, and both in Italy and America the proportion of thefts increases the farther north we go.

Density of Population

The agglomeration of persons in a large town is a certain incentive to crimes against property. Robbery, frauds, and criminal associations increase, while there is a decrease in crimes against the person, due to the restraints imposed by mutual supervision.

He who has studied mankind, or, better still, himself [writes my father], must have remarked how often an individual, who is respectable and self-controlled in the bosom of his family, becomes indecent and even immoral when he finds himself in the company of a number of his fellows, to whatever class they may belong. The primitive instincts of theft, homicide, and lust, the germs of which lie dormant in each individual as long as he is alone, particularly if kept in check by sound moral training, awaken and develop suddenly into gigantic proportions when he comes into contact with others, the increase being greater in those who already possess such criminal tendencies in a marked degree.

In all large cities, low lodging-houses form the favourite haunts of crime.

Imitation

The detailed accounts of crimes circulated in large towns by newspapers, have an extremely pernicious influence, because example is a powerful agent for evil as well as for good.

At Marseilles in 1868 and 1872, the newspaper reports of a case of child desertion provoked a perfect epidemic of such cases, amounting in one instance to eight in one day.

Before Corridori murdered the Headmaster of his boarding-school, he is said to have declared: "There will be a petition of what happened to to the Headmaster at Catanzaro" (who had been murdered in the same way).

The anarchist Lucchesi killed Banti at Leghorn shortly after the murder of Carnot by Caserio, and in a similar manner. Certain forms of crime which become common at given periods, the throwing of bombs, the cutting up of the bodies of murdered persons, particularly those of women, and frauds of a peculiar type may certainly be attributed to imitation, as may also the violence committed by mobs, in whom cruelty takes the form of an epidemic affecting even individuals of mild disposition.

Immigration

The agglomeration of population produced by immigration is a strong incentive to crime, especially that of an associated nature,—due to increased want, lessened supervision and the consequent ease with which offenders avoid detection. In New York the largest contingent of criminality is furnished by the immigrant population.

The fact of agglomeration explains the greater frequency of homicide in France in thickly populated districts.

The criminality of immigrant populations increases in direct ratio to its instability. This applies to the migratory population in the interior of a country, specially that which has no fixed destination, as peddlers, etc. Even those immigrants whom we should naturally assume to be of good disposition—religious pilgrims—commit a remarkable number of associated crimes. The Italian word *mariuolo* which signifies "rogue" owes its origin to the behaviour of certain pilgrims to the shrines of Loreto and Assisi, who, while crying *Viva Maria!* ("Hail to the Virgin Mary!") committed the most atrocious crimes, confident that the pilgrimage itself would serve as a means of expiation. In his *Reminiscences* Massimo d'Azeglio notes that places boasting of celebrated shrines always enjoy a bad reputation.

Prison Life

The density of population in the most criminal of cities has not such a bad influence as has detention in prisons, which may well be called "Criminal Universities."

Nearly all the leaders of malefactors: Maino, Lombardo, La Gala, Lacenaire, Soufflard, and Hardouin were escaped convicts, who chose their accomplices among those of their fellow-prisoners who had shown audacity and ferocity. In fact, in prison, criminals have an opportunity of becoming acquainted with each other, of instructing those less skilled in infamy, and of banding together for evil purposes. Even the expensive cellular system, from which so many advantages were expected, has not attained its object and does not prevent communication between prisoners. Moreover, in prison, mere children of seven or eight, imprisoned for stealing a bunch of grapes or a fowl, come into close contact with adults and become initiated into evil practices, of which these poor little victims of stupid laws were previously quite ignorant.

Education

Contrary to general belief, the influence of education on crime is very slight.

The number of illiterates arrested in Europe is less, proportionally, than that of educated individuals. Nevertheless, although a certain degree of instruction is often an aid to crime, its extension acts as a corrective, or at least tends to mitigate the nature of crimes committed, rendering them less ferocious, and to decrease crimes of violence, while increasing fraudulent and sexual offences.

Professions

The trades and professions which encourage inebriety in those who follow them (cooks, confectioners, and innkeepers), those which bring the poor (servants of all kinds, especially footmen, coachmen, and chauffeurs) into contact with wealth, or which provide means for committing crimes (bricklayers, blacksmiths, etc.) furnish a remarkable share of criminality. Still more so is this the case with the professions of notary, usher of the courts, attorneys, and military men.

It should be observed, however, that the characteristic idleness of criminals makes them disinclined to adopt any profession, and when they do, their extreme fickleness prompts them to change continually.

Economic Conditions

Poverty is often a direct incentive to theft, when the miserable victims of economic conditions find themselves and their families face to face with starvation, and it acts further indirectly through certain diseases: pellagra, alcoholism, scrofula, and scurvy, which are the outcome of misery and produce criminal degeneration; its influence has nevertheless often been exaggerated. If thieves are generally penniless, it is because of their extreme idleness and astonishing extravagance, which makes them run through huge sums with the greatest ease, not because poverty has driven them to theft. On the other hand the possession of wealth is frequently an incentive to crime, because it creates an ever-increasing appetite for riches, besides furnishing those occupying high public offices or important positions in the banking and commercial world with numerous opportunities for dishonesty and persuading them that money will cover any evil deed.

Sex

Statistics of every country show that women contribute a very small share of criminality compared with that furnished by the opposite sex. This share becomes still smaller when we eliminate infanticide, in view of the fact that the guilty parties in nearly all such cases should be classed as criminals from passion. In Austria, crimes committed by females barely constitute 15% of the total criminality; in Spain 11%; and in Italy 8.2%.

However, this applies only to serious crimes. For those of lesser gravity, statistics are at variance with the results obtained by the Modern School, which classes prostitutes as criminals. According to this mode of calculation, the difference between the criminality of the two sexes shows a considerable diminution, resulting perhaps in a slight prevalence of crime in women. In any case, female criminality tends to increase proportionally with the increase of civilization and to equal that of men.

Age

The greater number of crimes are committed between the ages of 15 and 30, whereas, outbreaks of insanity between these ages are extremely rare, the maximum number occurring between 40 and 50. On the whole, criminality is far more precocious than mental alienation, and its precocity, which is greater among thieves than among murderers, swindlers, and those guilty of violence and assault is another proof of the congenital nature of crime and its atavistic origin, since precocity is a characteristic of savage races.

Seldom do we find among born criminals any indication of that so-called criminal scale, leading by degrees from petty offences to crimes of the most serious nature. As a general rule, they commence their career with just those crimes which distinguish it throughout, even when these are of the gravest kind, like robbery and murder. Rather may it be said that every age has its specific criminality, and this is the case especially with criminaloids. On the borderland between childhood and adolescence, there seems to be a kind of instinctive tendency to law-breaking, which by immature minds is often held to be a sign of virility. The Italian novelist and poet Manzoni describes this idea very well in his *Promessi Sposi*, when speaking of the half-witted lad Gervaso, who "because he had taken part in a plot savouring of crime, felt that he had suddenly become a man."

This idea lurks in the slang word *omerta* used by Italian criminals, which signifies not only to be a man but a man daring enough to break the law.

20

The Jukes: A Study in Crime, Pauperism, and Heredity

Richard Dugdale

In July, 1874, the New York Prison Association having deputed me to visit thirteen of the county jails of this State and report thereupon, I made a tour of inspection in pursuance of that appointment. No specially striking cases of criminal careers, traceable through several generations, presented themselves till _____ county was reached. Here, however, were found six persons, under four family names, who turned out to be blood relations in some degree. The oldest, a man of fifty-five, was waiting trial for receiving stolen goods; his daughter, aged eighteen, held as witness against him; her uncle, aged forty-two, burglary in the first degree; the illegitimate daughter of the latter's wife, aged twelve years, upon which child the latter had attempted rape, to be sent to the reformatory for vagrancy; and two brothers in another branch of the family, aged respectively nineteen and fourteen, accused of an assault with intent to kill, they having maliciously pushed a child over a high cliff and nearly killed him. Upon trial the oldest was acquitted, though the goods stolen were found in his house, his previous good character saving him; the guilt belonged to his brother-in-law, the man aged forty-two, above mentioned, who was living in the house. This brother-in-law is an illegitimate child, an habitual criminal and the son of an unpunished and cautious thief. He had two brothers and one sister, all of whom are thieves, the sister being the contriver of crime, they its executors. The daughter of this woman, the girl aged eighteen above mentioned, testified at the trial which resulted in convicting her uncle and procuring his sentence for twenty years to State prison, that she was forced to join him in his last foray; that he had loaded her with the booty, and beat her on the journey home, over two miles, because she lagged under the load. When this girl was released, her family in jail and thus left without a home, she was forced to make her lodging in a brothel on the outskirts of the city. Next morning she applied to the judge to be recommitted to prison "for protection" against specified carnal outrages required of her and submitted to. She has since been sent to the house of refuge. Of the two boys, one was discharged by the Grand Jury; the other was tried and received five years' imprisonment in Sing Sing.

Source: From Richard Dugdale, *The Jukes: A Study in Crime, Pauperism, and Heredity.* (New York: Putnam, 1877), pp. 7–8, 11–15, 41, 43, 47, 66–69. Tables renumbered.

These six persons belonged to a long lineage, reaching back to the early colonists, and had intermarried so slightly with the emigrant population of the old world that they may be called a strictly American family. They had lived in the same locality for generations, and were so despised by the reputable community that their family name *had come to be used generically as a term of reproach.*

That this was deserved became manifest on slight inquiry. It was found that out of twenty-nine males, in ages ranging from fifteen to seventy-five, the immediate blood relations of these six persons, seventeen of them were criminals, or fifty-eight percent; while fifteen were convicted of some degree of offense, and received seventy-one years of sentence. . . .

Observation discloses that any given series of social phenomena—as honest childhood, criminal maturity and pauper old age, which sometimes occur in the life of a single individual—may be stretched over several generations, each step being removed from the other by a generation, and in some cases, by two. Consequently, the nature of the investigation necessitated the study of families through successive generations, to master the full sequence of phenomena and include the entire facts embraced in the two main branches of inquiry into which the subject necessarily divides itself: THE HEREDITY that fixes the organic characteristics of the individual, and THE ENVIRONMENT which affects modifications in that heredity. It reduces the method of study, then, to one of historico-biographical synthesis united to statistical analysis, enabling us to estimate the cumulative effects of any condition which has operated through successive generations: heredity giving us those elements of character which are derived from the parent as a birthright, environment all the events and conditions occurring after birth which have contributed to shape the individual career or deflect its primitive tendency.

Heredity and environment, then, are the parallels between which the questions of crime and public dependence and their judicious treatment extend: the objective point is to determine how much of each results from heredity, how much from environment. The answer to these determines the limits of possibility in amending vicious lives, and the scrutiny will reveal some of the methods which the present organization of society automatically sets in motion, which, without conscious design nevertheless convert harmful careers into useful ones. The discovery of such spontaneous social activities will furnish models to be followed in dealing with the unbalanced.

Now heredity takes two leading forms that need to be contrasted; consanguinity and crossing, each presenting modified results. Environment may judiciously be divided into two main branches: the surroundings which throw men into criminal careers and keep them in such; the surroundings which rescue them from criminal careers and keep them out. These two natural divisions, with their subdivisions, form the keynote to the present inquiry. A reference to the four charts contained in this *essay* will show how the events in the life of the parent are reproduced in the career of the child, and allows a strict comparison to be made between the life of the latter and that of his generation or his posterity, so that any characteristic which is hereditary will thus be revealed. On the other hand, the environment of each generation can be studied, the changes in that environment can be noted, and the results of the same can be ascertained.

Taking a general survey of the characteristics of the "Jukes" and for the purpose of convenient illustration, the leading facts are grouped in the following diagram which, however, is not offered as a generalization.

	Consanguinity	
Prostitution		Illegitimacy
Exhaustion	Fornication	Intemperance
Disease		Extinction
Crime	**Not Consanguineous**	Pauperism

In other words, *fornication*, either consanguineous or not, is the backbone of their habits, flanked on one side by *pauperism*, on the other by *crime*. The secondary features are *prostitution*, with its complement of *bastardy*, and its resultant neglected and miseducated childhood; *exhaustion*, with its complement *intemperance* and its resultant unbalanced minds; and *disease* with its complement *extinction*.

The Habitat of the "Jukes"

The ancestral breeding-spot of this family nestles along the forest-covered margin of five lakes, so rocky as to be at some parts inaccessible. It may be called one of the crime cradles of the State of New York; for in subsequent examinations of convicts in the different State prisons, a number of them were found to be the descendants of families equivalent to the "Jukes," and emerging from this nest. Most of the ancestors were squatters upon the soil, and in some instances have become owners by tax-title or by occupancy. They lived in log or stone houses similar to slave-hovels, all ages, sexes, relations and strangers "bunking" indiscriminately. One form of this bunking has been described to me. During the winter the inmates lie on the floor strewn with straw or rushes like so many radii to the hearth, the embers of the fire forming a centre towards which their feet focus for warmth. This proximity, where not producing illicit relations, must often have evolved an atmosphere of suggestiveness fatal to habits of chastity. To this day some of the "Jukes" occupy the self-same shanties built nearly a century ago. The essential features of the habitat have remained stationary, and the social habits seem to survive in conformity to the persistence of the domiciliary environment. I have seen rude shelters made of boughs covered with sod, or the refuse slabs of saw mills set slanting against ledges of rock and used in the summer as abodes, the occupants bivouacking much as gypsies. Others of the habitations have two rooms, but so firmly has habit established modes of living, that, nevertheless, they often use but one congregate dormitory. Sometimes I found an overcrowding so close it suggested that these dwellings were the country equivalents of city tenement houses. Domesticity is impossible. The older girls, finding no privacy within a home overrun with younger brothers and sisters, purchase privacy at the risk of prudence, and the night rambles through woods and tangles end, too often, in illegitimate offspring. During the last thirty years, however, the establishment of factories has brought about the building of houses better suited to secure domesticity, and with this change alone, an accompanying change in personal habits is being introduced, which would otherwise be impossible.

The Origin of the Stock of the "Jukes"

Between the years 1720 and 1740 was born a man who shall herein be called Max. He was a descendant of the early Dutch settlers, and lived much as the backwoodsmen upon our frontiers now do. He is described as ''a hunter and fisher, a hard drinker, jolly and companionable, averse to steady toil,'' working hard by spurts and idling by turns, becoming blind in his old age, and entailing his blindness upon his children and grandchildren. He had a numerous progeny, some of them almost certainly illegitimate. Two of his sons married two out of six sisters (called ''Jukes'' in these pages) who were born between the year 1740 and 1770, but whose parentage has not been absolutely ascertained. The probability is they were not full sisters, that some, if not all of them, were illegitimate. The family name, in two cases, is obscure, which accords with the supposition that at least two of the women were half-sisters to the other four, the legitimate daughters bearing the family name, the illegitimate keeping either the mother's name or adopting that of the reputed father. Five of these women in the first generation were married; the sixth one it has been impossible to trace, for she moved out of the county. Of the five that are known, three have had illegitimate children before marriage. One who is called in these pages Ada Juke, but who is better known to the public as ''Margaret, the mother of criminals,'' had one bastard son, who is the progenitor of the distinctively criminal line. Another sister had two illegitimate sons, who appear to have had no children. A third sister had four, three boys and one girl, the three oldest children being mulattoes, and the youngest—a boy—white. The fourth sister is reputed chaste, while no information could be gathered respecting the fifth in this respect, but she was the mother of one of the distinctively pauperized lines and married one of the sons of Max. The progeny of these five has been traced with more or less exactness through five generations, thus making the total heredity which has been enrolled stretch over seven generations, if we count Max as the first. The number of descendants registered includes 540 individuals who are related by blood to the Jukes, and 169 by marriage or cohabitation; in all, 709 persons of all ages, alive and dead. The aggregate of this lineage reaches probably 1,200 persons, but the dispersions that have occurred at different times have prevented the following up and enumeration of many of the lateral branches. . . .

Crime

In the table here appended [Table 1], as only official records of crimes are entered, two principal causes for the smallness of the number of offenses need explaining. As respects crimes, the records of only one county were examined, and these reached back only to 1830; the earlier records, your committee was told, are down in the cellar of the county clerk's office, under the coal. To get a full record of the crimes of the ''Juke'' family the criminal records of three other counties need to be examined. As respects misdemeanors, these are to be found in the books of justices of the peace and the books of the sheriffs, both of which are either destroyed or laid away in private hands, packed in barrels or stowed in garrets, and are inaccessible. In addition we must note that in the latter part of the last century and the beginning of this, many acts which now subject a man to imprisonment then went unpunished, even cases of murder, arson and highway robbery, so that the absence of a man's name from the criminal calendar is no criterion of his honesty.

Table 1

CRIMES AGAINST PROPERTY.

| | | NUMBER OF OFFENSES. | | | | | | | | | | | | |
| | | 2d Gen. | | 3d Gen. | | 4th Gen. | | 5th Gen. | | 6th Gen. | | Total. | | Total |
		M.	F.	M.	F.	M.	F.	M.	F.	M.	F.	M.	F.	
Misdemeanor	Juke..	..	..	1	..	7	6	14	14	1	2	24	22	
	X	..	..	1	..	1	1	8	1	..	..	9	3	..
Petit larceny	Juke..	..	..	..	..	1	..	6	..	..	..	7	..	
	X	..	..	..	..	3	..	2	..	..	..	5	.	
Grand larceny	Juke	..	..	..	..	..	..	..	..	..	..	..	..	
	X	..	..	..	..	1	..	2	..	..	..	3	..	
Burglary	Juke..	..	..	..	..	2	..	11	..	..	..	..	..	
	X	..	..	..	..	2	1	..	..	..	..	..	..	
Forgery	Juke..	..	..	..	..	..	..	..	..	..	..	..	..	
	X	..	..	..	..	1	..	..	..	..	..	1	..	
False pretenses	Juke..	..	..	..	..	..	..	..	..	..	..	1	..	
	X	..	..	1	..	..	..	..	..	..	..	1	..	
Robbery	Juke..	..	..	..	..	..	..	1	..	..	..	1	..	
	X	..	..	..	..	..	..	..	..	..	..	..	..	
Total	Juke..	..	..	1	..	10	6	32	14	1	2	44	22	66
	X	..	..	2	..	8	2	12	1	.		22	3	25
Grand total, offenses		..	..	3		18	8	44	15	1	2	66	25	91
Number of offenders.	Juke..	..	..	1	..	8	4	12	9	1	2	22	15	37
	X	2	..	2	..	6	2	8	1	..	..	16	3	19
Total		2	..	3	..	14	6	20	10	1	2	38	18	56

CRIMES AGAINST THE PERSON.

| | | 2d Gen. | | 3d Gen. | | 4th Gen. | | 5th Gen. | | 6th Gen. | | Total. | | Total |
		M.	F.	M.	F.	M.	F.	M.	F.	M.	F.	M.	F.	
Assault and battery	Juke..	..	..	..	..	3	..	3	..	..	..	6	..	..
	X	..	..	..	..	1	..	3	..	..	..	4	..	..
Assault, intent to kill	Juke..	..	..	..	..	1	1	..	..	1	..	2	1	..
	X	..	..	..	..	..	..	..	..	..	..	..	..	..
Murder	Juke..	..	..	..	..	1	..	1	..	..	..	2	..	..
	X	1	..	..	..	2	..	1	..	..	..	4	..	..
Rape, and attempt at rape.	Juke..	..	..	..	..	..	..	5	..	..	..	5	..	..
	X	..	..	..	..	..	..	..	..	..	..	..	..	..
Total offenses	Juke..	..	..	..	..	5	1	9	..	1	..	15	1	16
	X	1	..	..	..	3	..	4	..	..	..	8	..	8
Grand total, offenses		1	..	..	..	8	1	13	..	1	..	23	1	24
Number of offenders.	Juke..	..	..	..	..	4	1	6	..	1	..	11	1	12
	X	1	..	..	..	4	..	4	..	..	..	9	..	9
Total number of offenders		1	..	..	..	8	1	10	..	1	..	20	1	21

In the first place, the illegitimates who have become parent stocks are the oldest children of their respective mothers, Ada, Bell and Delia; but as the bastards of the latter had no children, this leaves only those of her other sisters to be considered. In the study of crime we take the males as the leading sex, skipping the women just as in studying harlotry we skipped the men, but at the same time it will be well to notice how harlotry prevails among those families where the boys are criminals. . . .

Tentative Inductions respecting Crime

1. The burden of crime is found in the illegitimate lines.
2. The legitimate lines marry into crime.
3. Those streaks of crime found in the legitimate lines are found chiefly where there have been crosses into X.
4. The eldest child has a tendency to be the criminal of the family.
5. Crime chiefly follows the male lines.
6. The longest lines of crime are along the line of the eldest son. . . .

Extension of the Field of Genealogical Study

The "Jukes" take in only a fraction of the domain of investigation into crime, its cause and cure. The essential characteristics of the group are great vitality, ignorance and poverty. They have never had a training which would bring into activity the æsthetic tastes, the habits of reasoning, or indeed a desire for the ordinary comforts of a well-ordered home. They are not an exceptional class of people: their like may be found in every county in this State. For this reason an exhaustive analysis of this family is valuable, because the inductions drawn from their careers are applicable to a numerous and widely disseminated class who need to be reached by similar agencies.

The study here presented is largely tentative, and care should be taken that the conclusions drawn be not applied indiscriminately to the general questions of crime and pauperism, for we are here dealing mainly with blood relations living in a similar environment, physical, social and governmental, in whom the order of events noted may be hereditary characteristics special to themselves, and not of unvarying recurrence.

Nevertheless, it opens the way and supplies the method for a study of other cases, supplementing and complementing this one, and presenting a different point of departure, whether it be the progeny of influential landed proprietors who lapse into pauperism, or the children of people of culture and refinement who become felons; or again, of the converse of these, of children whose parents were criminals, and yet have re-entered the ranks of the reputable.

Different kinds of crime need special study. Thus crimes of contrivance in their various forms, as burglary, embezzlement; crimes of education, as forgery; crimes of brutality, as malicious mischief and murder; crimes of cunning, as pocket picking, false pretenses; crimes of weakness, crimes of debauchery, crimes of ambition, crimes of riches, crimes of disease. Pauperism also needs a series, and this and crime need to be compared to each other, and, respectively, to a third series, investigating the growth and permanence of generations morally developed. The study of human nature thus pursued would give us a classified variety of characters, conditions and tendencies covering gradations so perfectly distributive that we could take any typical case, follow from this as a central point in any direction and note the shades of change which lead to other typical cases and so get a right conception of the continuity and essential unity of sociological phenomena, and perhaps discover a law of social equivalents. Such a series would form a body of evidence which would furnish data enabling us to pronounce judgment upon any scheme put forth to counteract the increase of crime, and supplant the empirical method now in vogue,

Table 2

STATISTICAL SUMMARY OF THE "JUKES"

	Total number in generation.	Total each sex.	Legitimate.	Illegitimate.	Marriageable age.	Unmarried adults.	Married.	Had bastards before marriage.	Had bastards after marriage.	Prostitutes.	Unascertained.	Barren persons.	Kept brothels.	Syphilis.	Acquired.	Lost.	Out-door relief, No. persons.	No. of years.	Alms-house, No. persons.	No. of years.	No. of persons.	No. of years.	No. of offenses.
			PARENTAGE BY SEX.		MARRIAGE RELATIONS.										PROPERTY.		PAUPERISM.				CRIME.		
2d Gen. Juke women	5	5			5		5	3			1	5			1	1	8	20	3	2	1	3	1
X men	5	5	2		5	2	5	1			5	4			4	1	6	14	3	6	2		9
3d Gen. Juke women	34	16	15		16		13			3				1			18	122	7	7	5	1	7
X women		7	3	6	7	6	4	1		3	6	3	1	12		1	8	63	8	3	2	½	
Juke men	16	18	3	2	18		11		8	4	23	4	1	7	2		19	129	8	12	12	11¼	15
X men		9	12	1	9	5	5	3		15		1	3	2	5		11	50	3	3	10	13	11
4th Gen. Juke women	117	46	88	17	80	10	37	6	3	36	7	5	5	25		1	24	100	12	18	9	7	13
X women		23	6	2	33	1	15	2	1	14	4	4	1	2	5		11	49	2	4	1	2	1
Juke men		57	46	20	69		21			14	9	7		7	2		25	87	11	9	18	7	41
X men		34	5	3	51	14	28			14	11	6		4	3	1	14	33	7	1	12		16
5th Gen. Juke women	59	119	94	13	90	10					7		5										
X women		33	4		33																		
Juke men		102	70		69																		2
X men		51	12		51																		8
6th Gen. Juke women	224	63																					
X women		9																					
Juke men	84	48																					
X men		5																					
7th Gen. Juke women	152																						
Juke men	5																						
	8																						
Tot. Gen. Juke blood	540	477	337	82	305		138	18	12	73	58	31	12	51	15	5	95	612	53	81	49	91¼	67
X blood	169	169	31	9	169		82	6	1	55	23	15	6	16	7	3	47	122	11	15	27	24½	38
Grand total	709	645	368	91	474	46	220	24	13	128	81	46	18	67	22	8	142	734	64	98	78	11C	115

by one of exact and well-founded laws, derived from a patient and extensive study of the phenomena involved.

Having discussed the elements of the subject, the various parts are presented (Table 2) in a statistical aggregate. The line headed ''Marriageable Age'' will give, very nearly, the number of adults in each generation: girls of 14 and boys of 18 are included under that heading.

The Social Damage of the "Jukes" Estimated

Passing from the actual record, I submit an estimate of the damage of the family, based on what is known of those whose lives have been learned. The total number of persons included in the foregoing statement reach 709; besides these, 125 additional names have been gathered since the text of this *essay* was prepared, whose general character is similar. If all the collateral lines which have not been traced could be added to the 709 here tabulated, the aggregate would reach at least 1,200 persons, living and dead. Now, out of 700 persons we have 180 who have either been to the poor-house or received out-door relief to the extent of 800 years. Allowing that the best members of the family have emigrated, it would be a low estimate to say that 80 of the additional 500 are, or have been, dependents, adding 350 years to the relief, making an aggregate of 280 persons under pauper training, receiving 1,150 years of public charity. Great as this is, it is not all. In a former portion of this report, it was stated the pauper records cover 255 years, of which only 64 could be consulted, the difficulties of getting the remaining 191 years being, in most cases, insuperable. Allowing that these 191 years would yield as many years of relief as the 64 which have actually been searched, we should have an aggregate of 2,300 years of out-door relief. . . .

21

Feeble-mindedness

H. H. Goddard

. . . Society's attitude toward the criminal has gone through a decided evolution, but that evolution has been in the line of its treatment rather than of its understanding of him and of his responsibility. Almost up to the present time there has been a practically universal assumption of the responsibility of all except the very youngest children and those recognized as idiots, imbeciles or insane. The oldest method of treatment was in accordance with the idea of vengeance, an eye for an eye. The god Justice was satisfied if the offender suffered an equal amount with those whom he had made suffer. Later came the idea of punishing an offender for the sake of deterring others from similar crimes. This is the basis of much of our present penal legislation. But students of humanity have gone farther and now realize that the great function of punishment is to reform the offender.

We have had careful studies of the offender from this standpoint. Studies have been made of his environment and of those things which have led him into crime. Attempts have been made to remove these conditions, so that criminals shall not be made, or having reformed, they shall not again be led into a criminal life. A great deal has been accomplished along these lines. But we shall soon realize, if we have not already, that on this track there is a barrier which we cannot cross. Environment will not, of itself, enable all people to escape criminality. The problem goes much deeper than environment. It is the question of responsibility. Those who are born without sufficient intelligence either to know right from wrong, or those, who if they know it, have not sufficient will-power and judgment to make themselves do the right and flee the wrong, will ever be a fertile source of criminality. This is being recognized more and more by those who have to do with criminals. We have no thought of maintaining that all criminals are irresponsible. Although we cannot determine at present just what the proportion is, probably from 25 percent to 50 percent of the people in our prisons are mentally defective and incapable of managing their affairs with ordinary prudence. A great deal has been written about the criminal type and its various characteristics. It is interesting to see in the light of modern knowledge of the defective that these descriptions are almost without exception accurate descriptions of the feeble-minded.

The hereditary criminal passes out with the advent of feeble-mindedness into

Source: Reprinted from H. H. Goddard, *Feeble-mindedness* (New York: Macmillan, 1914), pp. 6–10, 26–29, 47–49, 514–518. Footnote renumbered.

the problem. The criminal is not born; he is made. The so-called criminal type is merely a type of feeble-mindedness, a type misunderstood and mistreated, driven into criminality for which he is well fitted by nature. It is hereditary feeble-mindedness not hereditary criminality that accounts for the conditions. We have seen only the end product and failed to recognize the character of the raw material.

Perhaps the best data on this problem come from the prisons and the reformatories. It is quite surprising to see how many persons who have to do with criminals are coming forward with the statement that a greater or less percentage of the persons under their care are feeble-minded. They had always known that a certain proportion were thus affected, but since the recognition of the moron and of his characteristics, the percentage is found ever higher and higher. The highest of all come from the institutions for juveniles, partly because it is difficult to believe that an adult man or woman who makes a fair appearance but who lacks in certain lines, is not simply ignorant. We are more willing to admit the defect of children. The discrepancy is also due to the fact that the mental defectives are more apt to die young leaving among the older prisoners those who are really intelligent.

The following list of reformatories and institutions for delinquents with the estimated number of defectives undoubtedly gives a fair idea of the amount of feeble-mindedness. The differences in the percentages are probably due more to the standards used in estimating the defective than to actual differences in numbers. It is the most discouraging to discover that the more expert is the examiner of these groups, the higher is the percentage of feeble-minded found. For example, Dr. Olga Bridgman, who has made one of the most careful studies on record, finds that 89 percent of the girls at Geneva, Illinois, are defective.

The percentages above given are not in all cases the official figures given out by the examiners, but are the author's interpretation based on the facts given in the reports.

Unfortunately we cannot average the percentages because the reports from which these figures were taken do not always state the number of persons upon whom the estimate is made.

A glance will show that an estimate of 50 percent is well within the limit. From these studies we might conclude that at least 50 percent of all criminals are mentally defective. Even if a much smaller percentage is defective it is sufficient for our argument that without question one point of attack for the solution of the problem of crime is the problem of feeble-mindedness.

It is easier for us to realize this if we remember how many of the crimes that are committed seem foolish and silly. One steals something that he cannot use and cannot dispose of without getting caught. A boy is offended because the teacher will not let him choose what he will study, and therefore he sets fire to the school building. Another kills a man in cold blood in order to get two dollars. Somebody else allows himself to be persuaded to enter a house and pass out stolen goods under circumstances where even slight intelligence would have told him he was sure to be caught. Sometimes the crime itself is not so stupid but the perpetrator acts stupidly afterwards and is caught, where an intelligent person would have escaped. Many of the "unaccountable" crimes, both large and small, are accounted for once it is recognized that the criminal may be mentally defective. Judge and jury are frequently amazed at the *folly* of the defendant—the lack of common sense that he displayed in his act. It has not occurred to us that the folly, the crudity, the dullness, was an indication of an intellectual trait that rendered the victim to a large extent irresponsible. . . .

Institution	Percent Defective
St. Cloud Minnesota Reformatory	54
Rahway Reformatory, New Jersey (Binet)*	46
Bedford Reformatory, New York—under 11 years	80
Lancaster, Massachusetts (girl's reformatory)	60
Lancaster, Massachusetts, 50 paroled girls	82
Lyman School for Boys, Westboro, Massachusetts	28
Pentonville, Illinois, Juveniles	40
Massachusetts Reformatory, Concord	52
Newark, New Jersey, Juvenile Court	66
Elmira Reformatory	70
Geneva, Illinois (Binet)	89
Ohio Boys School (Binet)	70
Ohio Girls School (Binet)	70
Virginia, 3 Reformatories (Binet)	79
New Jersey State Home for Girls	75
Glen Mills Schools, Pennsylvania, Girl's Department, about	72

*Tested by the Binet Scale.

The field worker went armed with a card of introduction from the superintendent of the institution. This means much. The admissions to this institution are all voluntary. Parents ask for the privilege of sending their children here. When at last they are admitted, the parents are happy. They receive answers to all the letters they write inquiring about their children. They receive periodical reports on progress. They are allowed to come to see the child at any time desired, and although they are urged to come on a particular day of the week, they are not refused on other days. Whenever they come they receive a friendly greeting and cheerful word from the superintendent. Their attitude toward the superintendent, the institution and its work is one characterized by a feeling of happiness and confidence. In consequence of this, when the field worker approaches the family, saying, ''I have come from Vineland, from Superintendent Johnstone, I bring you a message from your Willie or your Katie,'' she is received with the most cordial welcome. And when she sits down with them and gradually discloses the fact that we are studying Willie's case and that we want information along such and such lines, they gladly give every aid in their power. It may well be remembered in this connection, that the majority of these people are of the type that like to talk about their own affairs.

The results have proved eminently satisfactory. Not that we have obtained all that we desired; not that we have scientifically accurate information on all the phases of the problem that would be valuable to us; but we have secured, in a large number of cases, thoroughly corroborated facts which show us many conditions little understood previously.

As a rule, our workers have easily been able to decide the mentality of the persons they saw. In some cases, indeed, this was not so easy and only after much observation and questioning of neighbors and friends as to the conduct and life of these persons was it possible to come to a reasonably satisfactory conclusion. In many cases it has been impossible to decide even after all our care; and these cases are therefore left undetermined.

In regard to the persons not seen, and especially those of earlier generations who are no longer living, the task at first sight seems more difficult. Some even assume that it is impossible to determine the mentality of such cases unless they were commonly recognized idiots or imbeciles. That such is not the fact however will become evident from a little thoughtful consideration. It must be remembered that the field worker goes out with a background of knowledge of four hundred feeble-minded boys and girls, men and women, of all grades of intelligence, and a great variety of temperaments and hereditary influences. With this background it is possible to project any individual into a known group and decide that he is or is not like someone in the group. This of course must not be done, and is not done, by any superficial resemblance but on the basis of many fundamental characteristics.

The idea that it is impossible to determine the mentality of a person who is three or four generations back of the present is partly an ill-considered one and partly the result of erroneous logic. One says—"I don't know my own grandparents, and as for my great-grandparents I do not even know their names." And the implied argument is "If a person as intelligent as I am, does not know his grandparents how can these ignorant defectives know theirs." The argument is fallacious throughout. To begin with, family ties are often much closer with these defectives than with more intelligent people who are often too busy to keep up these relationships; the defectives are more apt to remain for generations in the same community, while the intelligent migrate and so leave their ancestors. This was well shown in *The Kallikak Family* where the members of the bad side are practically all to be found within a narrow area around the ancestral home, while the good side are scattered over the United States and Canada.

Again, the fact that I do not know my grandparents does not prove that no one now living knew them. As a matter of fact, there are numerous people now living who knew them well.

Further, three generations back is easy and six is not impossible. We labor under a fallacy in regard to this point. We are apt to conclude that because a man rarely remembers *his* great-grandparent, no one can have known a person four generations back. It is a surprise to us to be told that there are persons now living who remember heroes of the American Revolution! John Doe enlisted in the Continental army in 1775 at the age of twenty. He died in 1845 at the age of ninety. Richard Roe was twelve years old at that time and vividly remembers hearing the old man Doe tell of the exciting experiences of '76. Richard Roe is eighty-one years old now. That is a rare occurrence? Certainly. And we have been able to determine that a person in the sixth generation back was feeble-minded in only one family out of 327—the Kallikak family. For the fifth generation we have made determinations in only four cases and even these are not involved in our conclusions.

The ease with which it is sometimes possible to get satisfactory evidence on the fifth generation is illustrated in *The Kallikak Family*.

The field worker accosts an old farmer—"Do you remember an old man, Martin Kallikak (Jr.), who lived on the mountainedge yonder?" "Do I? Well, I guess! Nobody'd forget him. Simple, not quite right here (tapping his head) but inoffensive and kind. All the family was that. Old Moll, simple as she was, would do anything for a neighbor. She finally died—burned to death in the chimney corner. She had come in drunk and sat down there. Whether she fell over in a fit or her clothes caught fire, nobody knows. She was burned to a crisp when they found her. That was the worst of them, they would drink. Poverty was their best friend in this respect, or they would have been drunk all the time. Old Martin could never stop as long as he had a drop. Many's the time he's rolled off of Billy Parson's porch. Billy always had a barrel of cider handy. He'd just chuckle to see old Martin drink and drink until finally he'd lose his balance and over he'd go!''[1]

Is there any doubt that Martin was feeble-minded?

Physicians conclude upon evidence infinitely weaker than ours that Napoleon, Julius Caesar and St. Paul were epileptic. Historians reconstruct out of a few charred posts, straw, grain, etc., the habits, mode of life and almost the mental level of the Swiss Lake Dwellers. Surely the person who rejects our data on the basis that such things cannot be determined, would discard a large part of the world's history as now written.

It is not difficult for one versed in the subject to tell whether or not a man was feeble-minded even though he lived a hundred years ago, providing he made enough impression upon his time for traditions of him to have come down. As a matter of fact it is this latter proviso which cuts out most of the people back of the third generation. It is very rare that we find feeble-minded persons in the fourth generation unless they were so markedly feeble-minded that it has been a tradition in the family or among the neighbors all these years. This has sometimes happened, as will be seen from the charts. In such cases of tradition there is no doubt about the accuracy of the determination. Any person living or dead, who was so abnormal that neighbors or friends or descendants always spoke of him as ''not quite right'' is certain to have been decidedly defective. . . .

Classification

Our 327 families naturally fall into six fundamental groups as follows:

1. Where feeble-mindedness is *certainly* hereditary—designated hereafter for brevity's sake as the Hereditary Group or Hereditary (H). *164 families.*

2. A group which, while not so *certainly* hereditary, yet shows high degrees of probability that the feeble-mindedness is hereditary—designated as Probably Hereditary (P.H.). *34 families.*

3. A group in which there is no evidence of hereditary feeble-mindedness, but in which the families show marked neuropathic conditions—designated as the Neuropathic Group or Neuropathic (Neu). *37 families.*

4. A group where it is clear that some accident either to mother or child, including disease, injury at birth, etc., is the cause of the feeble-mindedness—designated the Accident Group. *57 families.*

5. A small group where it has been impossible to assign a cause. The family history is known and is good; there are no accidents. We have designated this No Cause Discovered, or briefly, No Cause (N.C.). *8 families.*

6. A group where so little of a definite character could be learned that it was impossible to classify them—designated as Unclassifiable (Uncl.). *27 families.* This group is not counted at all in making up the percentages. One case in this group was thrown out because it proud to be a case of insanity and not of feeble-mindedness. . . .

Each of these *fundamental groups* of charts is subdivided and arranged according to mental age as determined by the Binet-Simon Measuring Scale of

Intelligence. This gives the child's mentality in terms of a normal child, *e.g.* mentality 7 means like a normal or average child of 7 years in intelligence. We may speak of a man 40 years old as having a mentality of any age from 1 to 12. We say he tests 7, or his mental age is 7.

Each chart is accompanied by a condensed description of the child. The information comes from parents, physicians and the Institution records, including the school department and the department of research. The latter are incomplete on the physical and the physiological (bio-chemical) side because we have not yet completed systematic studies of these cases. That must wait for a later report. . . .

Criminality and Feeble-mindedness

Every feeble-minded person is a potential criminal. This is necessarily true since the feeble-minded lacks one or the other of the factors essential to a moral life—an understanding of right and wrong, and the power of control. If he does not know right and wrong, does not really appreciate this question, then of course he is as likely to do the wrong thing as the right. Even if he is of sufficient intelligence and has had the necessary training so that he does know, since he lacks the power of control he is unable to resist his natural impulses.

Whether the feeble-minded person actually becomes a criminal depends upon two factors, his temperament and his environment. If he is of a quiet, phlegmatic temperament with thoroughly weakened impulses he may never be impelled to do anything seriously wrong. In this case when he cannot earn a living he will starve to death unless philanthropic people provide for him. On the other hand, if he is a nervous, excitable, impulsive person he is almost sure to turn in the direction of criminality. Fortunately for the welfare of society the feeble-minded person as a rule lacks energy. But whatever his temperament, in a bad environment he may still become a criminal, the phlegmatic temperament becoming simply the dupe of more intelligent criminals, while the excitable, nervous, impulsive feeble-minded person may escape criminality if his necessities are provided for, and his impulses and energies are turned in a wholesome direction.

It is not easy to decide beforehand which of these conditions is fulfilled in any particular group. In the data that we are studying, criminality seems at first sight to be surprisingly small. This is partly explained by the fact that our cases include only those who have been under arrest. Thirty-two charts with a total of forty-five individuals show criminality. That is, criminality appears on 10 percent of the charts, but only one-third of 1 percent of the individuals are criminalistic. It is perhaps significant that the greater proportion of these are in the Hereditary Group. Thirty of the charts in the Hereditary Groups, or 15.1 percent, have criminals on them; in the Neuropathic Group two charts or 5.4 percent; in the Accidents none. The criminal individuals are 0.52 percent of the persons in the Hereditary Groups; 0.24 percent of those in the Neuropathic Group and none of the accidents. Of the 45 criminals 41 are men, 4 are women, while 24 are known to be feeble-minded, 1 is normal and 20 unknown.

It is probable that in these cases two factors account for the small proportion of criminals. These people are very largely from rural districts, and their temptations perhaps have not been so great. But more significant is the fact that in such communities minor kinds of crime are not taken account of, so that they do not get

Total Men, 41. Total Women, 4. Total Criminal, 45.
In direct line with our cases, 27—in collateral lines, 18.
Nine criminals (not included in above) have married into these families—7 men, 2 women. Eight of these are in the Hereditary Group, one in the Neuropathic.

Of	6,868 Persons in Hereditary Group	37 or 0.53% are Criminalistic
Of	1,115 Persons in Probably H. Group	5 or 0.44% are Criminalistic
Of	1,212 Persons in Neuropathic Group	3 or 0.24% are Criminalistic
Of	1,913 Persons in Accident Group	0 are Criminalistic
Of	281 Persons in No Cause Group	0 are Criminalistic

Of 11,389 Persons in all Groups   45 or 0.39% are Criminalistic

The following table shows what would be expected compared with what we actually find.

Group	Expectation	Actual	Too Many	Too Few
Hereditary	27	37	10	
Probably H	4	5	1	
Neuropathic	5	3		2
Accident	8	0		8
No Cause	1	0		1

The strong preponderance in the Hereditary Group is significant.

marked "criminal" because they were never arrested. In the city cases our data are always much less complete. There are individuals of whom we have learned enough to determine their mentality while not being able to follow their careers. They have left home or have been lost sight of and may be today in prison without their friends and relatives knowing anything about it. Undoubtedly there are cases that escape in this way, but on the whole it seems probable that the fact of a criminal life would be one that we would be likely to discover if it existed. Such facts are hard to conceal.

There are nine criminalistic individuals on the charts that do not belong to the family, that is to say, they have married in, and they are only significant as showing the kind of company these people keep. . . .

Note

1. See *Kallikak Family* (New York: Macmillan, 1912), p. 83.

22

The Individual Delinquent

William Healy

THE INDIVIDUAL

Dynamic Center of the Problem

The dynamic center of the whole problem of delinquency and crime[1] will ever be the individual offender.

Definite and Practical Knowledge of the Individual is Necessary

It is impossible to get away from the fact that no general theories of crime, sociological, psychological or biological, however well founded, are of much service when the concrete issue, namely the particular offense and the individual delinquent, is before those who have practically to deal with it. The understanding needed is just that craved by Solomon—the understanding of the one who has actually to deal with people, the one who formally is the therapeutist. It does not require prolonged observation of any treatment of the offender to realize what knowledge will prove of most worth in the procedure; one quickly perceives that it must be information concerning characteristic variations of physical and psychical equipment, concerning laws of mental mechanics, and the influence of the various forms of experience on various types of mankind. From this arises scientific and common-sense appreciation of the relation of antecedent to consequent in the life history of the individual offender whose actions and person are to be dealt with.

Collected statistics and groups of facts concerning criminality are offered from time to time as the bases upon which measures of public policy may be erected. So far, however, there has been astonishingly little written into social ordinances as the result of much labor expended in the effort to determine the general facts of crime. There may be several reasons for this. Sometimes the criminologist, even of wide renown, has allowed himself to become almost obsessed by theories and doctrines which have led for the most part only to controversy. But perhaps the

Source: Reprinted from William Healy, *The Individual Delinquent* (Boston: Little, Brown, 1915), pp. 22-34. References deleted; footnotes renumbered.

greatest cause for slight effect upon legislation and other practical procedure may be found in the fact that when face to face with the complications of the actual case many of the generalizations of criminology are seen to crumble away.

Weakness of General Causation Theories

Nothing is shown by our data more convincingly than the predictable inadequacy of social measures built upon statistics and theories which neglect the fundamental fact of the complexity of causation, determinable through study of the individual case. Many of the works on social misconduct deal with what is often denominated "general causation," and attempt to establish geographical, climatological, economic and many other correlations. Much of this is interesting and even seductive, intellectually, and it is true that there are some relationships, such as that between alcoholism and crime, well enough verified to justify social alteration. But that many of these suggested correlations contain only half-truths, one is constrained to believe after prolonged attempt to gather in all available facts in many individual cases. To illustrate a couple of these "general causation" inferences, we might take the failure of the treatment of drunkards during the last decade under the English Inebriate Acts. It was soon found that the projected curative measures, proposed without any adequate estimation of the personal equipment of those who would come under treatment, could not combat, for example, innate mental deficiencies. In other words, many of the great army of topers are such because of their feeblemindedness, and it is that, and not the ingestion of alcohol, which must be fundamentally reckoned with. For another illustration, we may take the findings, often alluded to, that several forms of crime are more prevalent in certain seasons of the year. Sex assault and violence are notably more frequent during hot weather; is it then safe to assert summer temperature as the main cause? One might well ask, is there not rather a lowering of moral inhibitions during that season through the excess of alcoholic beverages then ingested? The above are two of the very simplest instances of the neglect to ascertain the complexities in the causation of crime.[2] Studies of individual cases, and final summary analysis of these cases, such as we present in the latter part of this work, form the only way of arriving at the truth. Results of such work make the investigator exceedingly chary of theories built upon the consideration of single causes.

Thorough Study Means Balancing of Factors

Thorough study of individual cases does not imply that we shall always find the main cause of the offender's tendency in his own make-up—it merely implies the logical balancing of causative factors. One has seen an extensive family chart exhibited as proof that criminalism is inherited, because of its springing up in several side lines. But in addition to the chart the investigator possessed information that the various persons showing delinquent tendencies all lived in an atrocious environment. The facts not plotted on the chart could be used to show, if we took them also by themselves, that in this family criminalism was uniformly the result of bad social circumstances. On the other hand, it may be conditions in the home, or other environmental agents, which at first sight loom large. But then one finds other individuals in the same family turning out well, . . . others on the same street or with the same associates who do not become criminals. Complicating the argument again, we may discover grave delinquent tendencies appearing in some one member of the most upright families, while, contrariwise, we have occasionally found all the numerous immediate descendants of a terrible drunkard successfully arising in full strength of character from the squalor in which he placed them. So it goes; to single out and blame this or that specific condition, without proceeding by the scientific process of elimination and attempting to rule out other possible causes, will not lead far towards real solutions. Indeed, without well-rounded studies of the pivotal facts in the particular case it ensues that "experience is fallacious and judgment difficult."

Growth of Idea of Studying the Offender

The idea that the individual must be carefully studied in order that crime may be ameliorated has been steadily growing since the day of Lombroso. The humanitarian efforts of John Howard were evidence of the appreciation of the needs of offenders as individual human beings; the view of Lombroso was that of the scientific man who sees in this field the inexorable laws which govern man's nature and environment. It makes little difference which theoretical view of penology is held; the problem of society ever is to handle a given offender satisfactorily. Recently the Japanese authority, Oba, a strong believer in the necessity of meeting evil by evil, maintains that at the beginning of the handling of the offender there must be the most exact research into the characteristics and conditions of both him and his family. In his plans for effectively dealing with recidivism this writer insists that only through such a method could the punishment be made proportionate to the guilty—and that is a prime necessity in his scheme.

The Problem of Personality

Clear comprehension of the make-up of human personality will prove a gain to the student of our subject. A person is not fairly to be regarded merely as the soul and body of the moment. It is only our own temporal limitations which prevent us from seeing people as they really are—as products of the loom of time. Every individual is partly his ancestors, and partly the result of his developmental conditions, and partly the effects of many reactions to environment, and to bodily experiences, and even of reactions to his own mental activities. An ideal description of a human person would refer each trait or condition to its proper source. Most serviceable to us is the conception of the individual as the product of conditions and forces which have been actively forming him from the earliest moment of unicellular life. To know him completely would be to know accurately these conditions and forces; to know him as well as is possible, all of his genetic background that is ascertainable should be known. The interpretations that may be derived from acquaintance with the facts of ancestry, ante-natal life, childhood development, illnesses and injuries, social experiences, and the vast field of mental life, lead to invaluable understandings of the individual and to some idea of that wonderful complex of results which we term personality.

THE MENTAL BASES OF DELINQUENCY

Conduct an Expression of Mental Life

All conduct is directly an expression of mental life. Immediately back of the action is the idea, or the wish, or the impulse, existing as mental content. Of course many actions have no representation in consciousness, either before or after performance, but nevertheless they are just as truly controlled by mental processes. One starts to walk down the street, thereby engaging in public conduct, and continues to walk, and finally stops; all without the slightest thought about this succession of acts. Yet every part of the performance has been impelled by operations of the mind, that part of the mind which, fortunately for our ability to pay attention to other things, is subconscious. Proof of all this is found in the normal power to produce similar action as consciously controlled behavior; to see, as it were, how it was done. More evidence on the same point is derived from our ready recollection that actions arose from mental activity which at the moment of action was not above the threshold of consciousness. We remember how we walked down the street and that the walking was carried out at the bidding of our desires, although we did not at the time formulate this sequence. Altogether, a great deal of mental life at any given moment is subconscious, and a great deal of conduct which appears for the moment uncontrolled, nevertheless is directly dependent on subconscious mental activity.

Even conduct in the pathological mental states which supervene during the varied conditions of epilepsy or insanity is just as truly the direct outcome of mental activity, although not controlled by the conscious will, and frequently not in the least representable at any time in consciousness. The anti-social actions of such periods are the fault of the disordered mental mechanism which at the time precludes normal conscious mental life. Disordered though the higher mentality may then be, some parts of the mind are actively at work creating conduct.[3] We can be sure of this through the easy determination of hallucinations and morbid ideations and impulses which are often discernible in such cases.

In its physiological aspect conduct may be traced back to origins which, reasoning from the well-established correlation of brain-cell activity with mental life, show also the mental processes back of the deed. Conduct may be readily stated in terms of muscular action; the latter activity, in turn, is propagated by currents of nervous force which, for all such complicated processes, are known to arise from the coordinated energy of cerebral cells. The parts of the brain involved are the higher levels, those which we know are correlated with mental phenomena rising on occasion above the threshold of consciousness. So it seems that all analysis of the dynamics back of conduct leads directly to contemplation of mental activity.

Practical Bearings of the Psychological Viewpoint

However, for the pragmatic ends of this work, one would not be satisfied with any *a priori* considerations alone, however logically fundamental, in the study of the causative factors of delinquency. To be suited for our purposes, such a line of approach as the above must present tangible evidences of practical worth. It must appear that by deliberately turning our studies towards the phenomena of mental life, paths will be discovered to amendment of the moral situation. The psychological point of view, if it fail in this, must be discarded as not inherently essential.

In taking up the actual problem of the sources of delinquency it was apparent that just this method of approach afforded the quickest and clearest understanding, the surest interpretation, and by far the greatest promise of success; and altogether was a much less difficult path to follow than might be expected. Our own case studies have gradually led us to the overwhelming conclusion that, for practical purposes, what we particularly want to know about the offender are the immediate mental antecedents of his conduct.

Misconduct is only a branch of conduct in general; and nowhere can the relationships between conduct and mental life be perceived better than in studying the immediate causations of social misdoing. The robbery was preceded by the mental presentation, the plan; the assault followed upon the mental reaction of anger to the displeasing pictures which the spoken word brought up; the temptation was followed because the idea of immediate satisfaction was not counterbalanced just then by conscious representation of consequences. Thus illustrations might be indefinitely multiplied of how a mental process immediately precedes conduct.

Hence it is clear that *whatever* influences the individual towards offense must influence first the mind of the individual. It is only because the bad companion puts dynamically significant pictures into the mind, or because the physical activity becomes a sensation with representation in psychic life, or the environmental conditions produce low mental perceptions of one's duty towards others, that there is any inclination at all towards delinquency.

So true is this that, through application of the methods of individual study, it soon becomes apparent that really the only safe way to ascertain the driving forces which make for social offense is to get at the mental mechanisms antecedent to the behavior in question.

Not reckoning with the mental factor leads to many errors in the drawing of conclusions. The force of the actual findings is the strongest argument against the student of delinquency becoming an externalist, an investigator merely of outward and overt circumstances. If the facts are taken all together the following sorts of complications are to be found: The family life may have been faulty, but it was actually the influence of certain pernicious experiences which made recurrent imagery that has consciously or subconsciously driven to offense. Study of heredity may show wanderers in a family line, but in this member of the family it was a hidden mental conflict about a terrible secret that led to the running away from home. We came to know this because we brought the conflict to light, and the light cured both it and the running away. In another case frightful crowding of the home could not be blamed except that it induced ideas and mental pictures which led straight to bad conduct.

Such facts, and what is brought out by differential psychology, give some suggestion as to why other persons in the same family, or house, or street, or gang, have not turned to delinquency. These comparisons should be ever a barrier to the acceptance of general social or biological theories of crime. Realization of the mental factors must prevent our giving credit to mouthfilling declarations that crime is an atavistic phenomenon, or a disease, or that "the criminal" belongs to this or that human sub-species—declarations in which definition is bought for too cheap an intellectual outlay.

Importance of Mental Abnormality

Turning now to abnormal mental traits and conditions correlated with delinquency, we have further corroboration of mental life standing to conduct as antecedent to consequent. The part insanity plays in the production of social disturbance is too obvious to need illustration. Border-line individuals with their morbid, overwhelming impulsions and compulsions are also well recognized as having a mental equipment prone to develop delinquency. Showing mostly negative aspects we have the mental defectives. In them it is not so much that their actual concepts give rise to delinquency, as that through their lack of judgment and counterbalancing power, influences and suggestions coming either from their own physical selves or from the external world, lead to impulses and pictures which determine the misdeed.

Therefore, even in these abnormal individuals it is clearly improbable that peculiar palates, or insensitive finger tips, or queerly-shaped heads will ever be found in any such close relationship to delinquency as are the mental phenomena we discuss. With full respect for those who earliest apprehended the problem of the delinquent as an individual, we nevertheless see the utter inadequacy of work which did not, first and foremost, determine the offender's mental content, his mental traits, peculiarities and abilities. Vastly important though social and biological backgrounds are, yet they must take at least second place to these more immediate causative factors of delinquency.

We have previously insisted on the impossibility of applying in all cases the criterion of responsibility as definable in the law. We believe this matters little because cases can be satisfactorily handled from other standpoints. But as students of mental life we are forced to unequivocally commit ourselves to the opinion that many individuals who commit misdeeds have abnormal impulsions, or are temporarily or chronically weak in the powers of self-control. This is the basis for the idea of lessened moral responsibility which accords truly with the facts. We may call the attention of the reader to our studies of types primarily defective in self-control, types of those affected by adolescent impulsions, of those assailed by the curious phenomena of the epilepsies, of menstrual mental disorders, of senile failures of inhibition, and so on. When one has surveyed such groups as these, two practical conclusions must be drawn; one, that there often is prodigious difficulty in defining legal responsibility, and, next, that these cases, for their own welfare and for the protection of society, need appropriate physical, educational, or even disciplinary treatment under highly individualized surveillance.

Psychological Standpoint Taken Alone is Unsafe

We will not attempt to review the opinions of the several criminologists who upon *a priori* grounds have already declared themselves for the psychological point of view.[4] We can do better by presenting the facts gleaned from life studies which lead us directly to the same position. The concrete argument is to be read in almost every page of our case histories. Mental and moral problems may there be seen to merge.

Notwithstanding all this I fully recognize that there are many cases in which sole dependence on the psychological standpoint would be a grave mistake. Repeatedly I have asserted the opinion, still held, that it is very difficult to decide which is in general the most important investigatory vantage ground—social, medical, or psychological. The point is clear, however, that one can most surely and safely arrive at remedial measures through investigation of the mental factors.

There is no doubt that certain groups of physicians and educators will best understand the importance of the above truths—physicians who have been especially engaged with psychiatric and neurological problems, and educators who are interested in applied psychology. Sociologists and psychologists have nowadays rapidly growing conceptions of the value of individual study.[5] Those who under the law have to deal with offenders are, however, foremost in needing to understand fundamentals. And if it be intimated that these issues are too abstruse, we should feel justified in asserting that those who have not the capacity to appreciate these things are certainly not fitted to pass judgments on delinquents or hold authority over them.

Specific Features of Mental Life Underlying Delinquency

This chapter, dealing with the general survey of the mental bases of delinquency, is hardly the proper place in which to offer specific details. Not that the fundamentals are too technical, but that they are best presented in connection with concrete findings. The study of actual cases is imperative for understanding the part which mental life plays in the production of misconduct. It may be useful here, however, to itemize some of those features of mental life which study shows directly underlie delinquency. Perusal of concrete instances in the second part of this volume will lead to completer understanding of what is now merely enumerated. The proof of the validity of the psychological data will often be found in the actual outcome of the case as predicted in accordance with them.

We may find existing as bases of delinquency any of the following:

- Mental dissatisfactions; those developed from cravings of no special moral significance in themselves, or even from unfulfilled creditable ambitions.
- Criminalistic imagery, sometimes fairly obsessional, which persists, and is strong enough to impel misconduct.
- Irritative mental reactions to environmental conditions, seeking expression or relief in misdoing.
- The development of habits of thought involving persistent criminalistic ideas and reactions.
- Adolescent mental instabilities and impulsions.
- Mental conflicts, worries or repressions concerning various experiences or matters of mental content. These sometimes interfere with that smooth working of the inner life which fosters socially normal conduct. The misdeed here, too, may be a relief phenomenon.
- The chronic attitude of the offender representing himself to himself as one, like Ishmael, whose hand shall be against every man and every man's hand against him. The remarkable phenomenon of anti-social grudge may be included here.
- Mental peculiarities or twists which are agents in the production of anti-social conduct, but which do not overwhelm the personality enough to warrant us in grading the subject as aberrational.
- Aberrational mental states:—all the way from fully-developed psychoses to temporary or border-line psychotic conditions.

• Mental defect in any of the several forms described in our special chapter on the subject.

Notes

1. The terms "delinquency" and "crime," or "criminality," will be used throughout our work as synonymous. There is no logical line of demarcation of meaning, in European terminology the words are interchangeable. In our country "delinquency" and "delinquent," because of their seemingly less harsh connotation, are applied to youthful offenders. For the vital reasons given above we have concerned ourselves most largely with the study of youthful offenders and have chosen for our title the less offensive term.

2. As an example of the bare collection of minute data concerning the social and biological background of a group of offenders, which omits many of the psychological possibilities, and fails to analyze the relative bearings of the total facts in the respective cases, we might cite Gruhle's recent book. Here even an extreme application of the statistical method fails to demonstrate its value when applied to only 105 cases.

3. On several occasions I have had the opportunity of attempting with intelligent subjects, analysis of criminalistic behavior enacted during a previous aberrational period. A woman of fine character, who in her attacks of insanity, for which she had to be confined, was very prone to commit violence, said she always knew at the time it was wrong, but something stronger than her reason impelled her. Another particularly high-minded woman, who in ephemeral outbreaks of her psychoses made attempts at murder which she finally accomplished, said the voice which she heard at the time was so commanding that it seemed to be the word of God. An epileptic young man who during one of his whim-controlled, almost automatic states nearly perpetrated a most heinous crime—wrecking a passenger train—has since frequently discussed it. His consciousness, judging by his memory of the event and by witnesses to his actions at almost the same time, seems to have been narrowed to the one impulse and the cunning scheming for its satisfaction. Clear though it is that the fellow was not right mentally at the time, he has always felt that, since his action followed an idea, the deed was mentally controlled, and from the evidence of his memory, he never has been inclined to assert his own actual irresponsibility. This is another example of the great difficulty of adjudication according to criteria of responsibility.

4. The psychological point of view in the study of individual delinquents is well stated by Bechterew. His program is based upon the distinction between general and individual factors in the development of delinquency, and involves an actual study of the criminal's personality. It is strange that in the literature of criminology there are so many works designated "psychology of the criminal," which nevertheless deal with psychology in only the most indirect way, without development of a methodology, and which really set us onward very little towards a better understanding of the mental mechanisms standing as immediate precursors of delinquent conduct. For a general statement of "such a pragmatic applied psychology as will deal with all states of mind that might possibly be involved in the determination and judgment of crime" no one can afford to neglect the work of Gross. He gives a long list of authors who have written from the standpoint of psychology, and includes in his text many of their best ideas.

23

The American Criminal

Ernest A. Hooton

. . . The present investigation is an effort to ascertain whether or not the physical characteristics of criminals are in any sense relevant to their crimes. Criminals are a sociological category of men. For purposes of this study they are individuals undergoing imprisonment as a result of conviction for some offense punishable by commitment to a penal institution. They are merely persons who have committed offenses against society which are considered (at least for the time being) of a sufficiently grave character as to justify the temporary or permanent incarceration of the offender. Since criminals are of all groups sociologically the most clearly stigmatized, they ought to present a favorable opportunity for an inquiry into the association of physical characteristics with patterns of behavior.

If there are any differences in the behavioristic tendencies of different human races, they ought to manifest themselves in criminal acts. If there are any physical differences between criminals, classified according to the nature of their offenses, the possibly complicating influence of race can be eliminated only by studies of criminals in racial groups. It should be emphasized that a possible discovery that some class of offender possesses distinguishing group characteristics of a physical nature, implies little or nothing as to the nature of the relationship between the bodily features and the type of behavior manifested. . . .

History and Material of the Survey

The present survey was initiated in the summer of 1926 as an anthropological study of Massachusetts County Jail prisoners, supplementary to a sociological and psychiatric investigation carried on by the Massachusetts State Department of Mental Diseases. The anthropological survey was subsequently extended to include the prison and reformatory inmates of ten states chosen to represent as adequately as possible the different racial and ethnic elements in the population of the entire country. These states were Massachusetts, Tennessee, Kentucky, Texas, North Carolina, Wisconsin, Arizona, Colorado, New Mexico, and Missouri. The total of anthropometric records analyzed by the survey is 17,077. This number includes some 3,203 civilians

Source: Reprinted by permission of the publisher from *The American Criminal: An Anthropological Study* by Earnest Albert Hooton, pp. 252–254, 298–309, Cambridge, MA: Harvard University Press. Copyright © 1939 by the President and Fellows of Harvard College. Copyright © renewed 1967 by Mary C. Hooton.

measured for comparative purposes in Massachusetts, Tennessee, North Carolina, and Colorado. The total excludes 604 individuals who were measured and observed but concerning whom parentage data were lacking, or who belonged to ethnic groups too poorly represented for use in statistical analysis. The present volume analyzes only native White criminals of native parentage in prisons and reformatories and the civilian check samples of similar origin. . . .

Metric and Indicial Differentiation Between Criminals and Civilians of Similar Parentage

Are criminals physically different from law-abiding citizens of the same ethnic origin? This is a more important question than that of the offense group differentiation of criminals. For comparison with the criminals a check sample of civilians of native birth and native parentage was gathered in Massachusetts and in Tennessee. The combined civilian series from the two states was compared with the total criminal series. When, however, it become apparent that criminals are physically differentiated according to the state of their birth, the validity of this comparison with the restricted check sample became exceedingly dubious. Since it was impossible to reopen the field work and secure civilian samples from the remaining seven states, the following expedient was adopted. Massachusetts criminals were compared with Massachusetts civilians and Tennessee criminals with Tennessee civilians. Then the values of differences between the total criminal series and the total check sample were appraised in terms of their agreements or disagreements with the two intrastate comparisons. There can scarcely be a doubt of the general criminological validity of a difference between criminals and civilians when it occurs both in Massachusetts and in Tennessee and in the comparison of the total criminal series with the combined check sample from the two states.

In the total series comparisons 19 of 33 measurements and indices (57.58 percent) showed a significant differentiation between criminals and civilians. Of these 7, or 21.21 percent were fully substantiated in the two state comparisons and a considerable number of the other differences were shown to be, in all probability, valid for criminals in general of this nativity, as compared with civilians of the same origin.

In appraising the comparisons of the two intra-state series—Massachusetts and Tennessee—with the total series comparison of criminals from nine states with a civilian check sample derived from Massachusetts and Tennessee only, there arose very puzzling problem. When both intra-state comparisons agree with the total comparison, one can conclude immediately that the general and common result is valid. When one state comparison agrees with the total series and the other differs, it is necessary to decide which state comparison is the more reliable. Initially it seemed that the Tennessee comparison of civilians with criminals was less dependable than the Massachusetts comparison, because the former state civilian sample was entirely composed of Nashville firemen, a physically and occupationally selected group. Ultimately this decision was reversed because of the fact that the Massachusetts series comparison gave evidence of a certain ethnic and perhaps racial disparity, owing to the presence in the criminal series of a considerable element of French Canadian extraction. Consequently, in cases of doubt the evidence of the Tennessee comparison was leaned upon more heavily. Since the civilian sample considerably exceeds the criminal series in mean age, it was necessary to re-seriate the criminals by age groups, and to compare them with civilians of the same age whenever a difference might be considered as a possible effect of disparate age.

Criminals average 3.80 years younger than the civilian check sample. This difference seems to lie the expression of a tendency for antisocial conduct to reach its maximum in late adolescence and early adult years.

Criminals are inferior to civilians in nearly all of their bodily measurements. These differences attain statistical significance and general criminological validity in body weight, in stature, in biacromial breadth, chest depth, chest breadth, cranial circumference, nose height, ear length, head height, and upper facial height. Criminals also diverge from civilians in having higher fronto-parietal indices, lower facial indices, higher nasal indices, higher zygo-frontal indices, and greater relative sitting height. These differences appear to be independent of age and of state sampling.

Every individual offense group is anthropometrically differentiated from the total check sample of civilians. Most of the offense groups differ from the civilians in the same direction as does the total criminal series. A few individual offense group peculiarities may be recapitulated here.

First degree murderers are, on the average, older than civilians, are not inferior in stature, but have broader jaws, relatively narrower, longer, and lower heads. In addition they display most of the general inferiorities and excesses which characterize the total criminal comparison with civilians, although these are of lesser magnitude than in the series as a whole. Second degree murderers do not fall significantly below the check sample in age but are markedly inferior in most measurements. They are also relatively longer-headed and lower-headed than civilians and have higher nasal indices.

Assault offenders are less differentiated from civilians, probably because of the small size of this offense group. In addition to several metric inferiorities they are distinguished by relatively broader shoulders than are found in the civilians.

Robbers are 7.75 years younger than civilians and are much slighter in body build. Most of their divergences from the check sample are of the same nature as those manifested by total criminals. Burglars and thieves are 8 years younger, on the average, than civilians, and are inferior to them in every measurement except forehead breadth. They also show many indicial divergences.

The forgery and fraud group is younger and lighter than the civilian check sample and shows similar divergences from the latter to those displayed by the entire criminal series. However these fraudulent offenders exhibit deviations from civilians which are, in general, smaller than those of most other offense groups.

Rapists are the shortest of offenders and are greatly inferior to civilians in every dimension except in minimum frontal diameter. Other sex offenders show very similar differences.

Versus public welfare offenders are especially characterized by excessive breadth dimensions of the forehead and of the face, and high index values derived from these measurements. Otherwise they show ordinary criminal divergences from the civilians, except in their excess of age, their parity of stature and of ear measurements and indices.

The residual offense group (arson and all others) shows ordinary minus deviations in dimensions, except in notably small stature and relatively great shoulder breadth.

Metrically these criminals are vastly inferior to the civilians. The offense groups differ from each other less markedly than total criminals diverge from law-abiding citizens. In other words, irrespective of nature of offense, criminals present an united front of biological inferiority.

Sociological and morphological differences between criminals and civilians have been tabulated and subjected to a detailed analysis and summary in the body of this work. Nevertheless these differences most be recapitulated, albeit briefly, because it is a sheer impossibility for the reader to retain the mass of minutiae upon which our final argument must rest.

It has been necessary in each sociological and morphological category firstly to appraise the significance of crude differences between total criminals and the total civilian check sample; secondly to go hack to the Massachusetts and Tennessee intra-state comparisons of criminals and civilians; finally to return to the total series comparisons and to judge their validity on the basis of state agreements.

These sociological facts seem to represent our yield, after the chaff has been winnowed away:

1. Apart from age considerations, these criminals are less often married, more often widowed, and more frequently divorced than comparable civilians.
2. After due allowance is made for the partially rural character of our criminal series and for the almost exclusively urban provenience of our check sample, there remain in the criminals probable excesses of extractive, laborer, and personal service occupations, and deficiencies of trade, professional, and clerical occupations.
3. Criminals are greatly inferior to civilians of the same ethnic origin in educational attainments.

The outstanding morphological differences between criminals and civilians are as follows:

1. Tattooing is commoner among criminals than among civilians.
2. Criminals probably have thinner beard and body hair and thicker head hair.
3. Criminals have more straight hair and less curved hair.
4. Criminals have more red-brown hair and less gray and white hair.
5. Dark eyes and blue eyes are deficient in criminals, and blue-gray and mixed eyes are in excess. Homogeneous irides are rare in criminals, and zoned and speckled irides are excessively present. Eye folds are commoner in criminals and thin eyebrows occur more frequently.
6. Low and sloping foreheads are excessively present among criminals.
7. High narrow nasal roots, high nasal bridges, undulating nasal profiles. nasal septa inclined upward and deflected laterally, extreme variations in thickness of the nasal tip, are more frequent in criminals than in civilians.
8. Thin lips and compressed jaw angles are commoner in criminals.
9. Marked overbites are rarer in criminals than in civilians.
10. The ear of the criminal is more likely to have a slightly rolled helix and a perceptible Darwin's point than is that of the civilian. More extreme variations of ear protrusion are found in criminals than in civilians. The criminal ear tends to be small.
11. Long, thin necks and sloping shoulders are in excess among criminals.

Many other significant morphological differences between the criminals and the civilians have been discounted or disregarded because of contradictions or inconsistencies in the state series, because of age complications, or because of the probable effect of observational equations.

The various offense groups tend to present, for the most part, similar or identical deviations from the civilian check sample in both sociological and morphological features. Apart from the great bulk of these differences from civilians common to the total series and to the individual offense groups, the latter are distinguished by some particular sociological and morphological deviations from the combined civilian check sample, a few of which may be mentioned here:

1. First degree murderers are outstanding in their especially large excess of divorced men and widowers, of extractives, of laborers, of illiterates and poorly educated persons. They are also notable in their extremely high proportions of straight hair. In general this class of offender exaggerates the common morphological deviations of the total criminal series.

2. Second degree murderers parallel the sociological deviations of first degree murderers, but are somewhat less extreme. They are deficient in golden hair, have broad nasal roots and nasal bridges, thick nasal tips, excess of slight alveolar prognathism.

3. Assault offenders are sociologically distinguished by high percentage of divorced men, of persons in skilled trades and in personal service. They have an excess of olive skin color, and include a disproportionately high number of persons with broad noses, which are high rather than medium or low.

4. Robbers are notable for their deficiency of married men and for their excess of factory workers. They show excesses of olive skin, and median eye folds.

5. Burglars and thieves display no important sociological deviations from the check sample which are not shared by the total criminal series. Again there is an excess of olive skin color. Concave noses are common in this group.

6. The forgery and fraud group exhibits only the general criminological differences from the check sample of civilians.

7. Rapists are notable for large excesses of divorced men and widowers. Their morphological deviations from civilians are those of the entire criminal group.

8. Other sex offenders have no sociological peculiarities which distinguish their deviations from the check sample from those of total criminals. Excesses of ruddy skin, of olive skin, and a deficiency of golden hair are perhaps worthy of mention.

9. Versus public welfare criminals are outstanding in their high percentage of married men. They have excessively thick head hair and thin beard hair in spite of an advanced mean age; they also show excess of red-white skin, of external eye folds, of pronounced malars, of full cheeks.

10. Arson and all other offenders have a deficiency of single men, excesses of ruddy skin, black hair, ash-blond hair, epicanthic folds, protruding ears.

Table XIII-5 presents a summary and comparison of the totals of differences between all criminals and all civilians and between the two state comparisons in metric, sociological, and morphological features (the two latter by subcategories of observations). These are significant but crude differences, with no allowances made for age variations and other complicating factors. In the total series comparison it may be noticed that significant differences between criminals and civilians in categories of sociological features (80.77 percent) are considerably in excess of the metric differences (57.58 percent) and of the morphological subcategory differences (61.73 percent). In the Tennessee comparison the sociological differences (61.54 percent) are sharply reduced, and in the Massachusetts comparison they sink to 50 percent. The total series sociological comparison involves the checking of sociological data of criminals from nine states, principally rural in their populations except Massachusetts, with an almost exclusively urban civilian sample derived from two states only. In the Tennessee comparison both series are equalized as to state of origin and residence, but the criminals are mixed urban and rural, while the check sample consists of Nashville firemen only. In the Massachusetts comparison both series are urban. It therefore appears that the Massachusetts comparison is most valid in sociological features. Its difference of 50 percent of characters represents most closely the normal amount of difference between criminals and civilians.

In metric data both state comparisons show the same number and percentages of significant deviations (63.64 percent), which slightly exceeds the proportion found in the total series comparison (57.58 percent). Here again, and for the same reasons, the state figures should be more valid than those of the combined series.

In the morphological comparisons the Tennessee data should be the best, since both series were recorded by the same observer and at the same time. On the whole, the safest appraisal of the percentages of the various categories of significant differences which may be taken to apply to all native White criminals of native parentage, as contrasted with sociologically and ethnically comparable civilians would be:

Table XIII-7
I.Q. IN CONCORD REFORMATORY

	Number	Percent
Estimated low normal or borderline intelligence	3	1.95
45 or under	2	1.30
46-55	3	1.95
56-65	7	4.54
66-75	29	18.83
76-85	40	25.97
86-95	40	25.97
96-105	29	18.83
106-and over	1	.65
Total	154	

	Percent
Measurements and indices	57.58
Sociological observations	50.00
Morphological observations	43.83

This would imply that criminals and civilians are differentiated to about the same extent in physical features as in sociological characters.

Let us now consider the absolutely minimum differences between criminals and civilians, which are significant and in the same direction in both states and in the total series, and are, so far as can be determined, independent of age and other complicating factors.

The left side of Table XIII-6 provides these data which comprise 21.21 percent of metric and indicial differences, 12.00 percent of sociological differences and 7.14 percent of differences in morphological observations. These percentages are, of course, sufficient in each case to differentiate the criminal series from the check sample of civilians. However, this array of differences by no means represents the complete assemblage of valid criminal deviations. For example it disregards the vast educational inferiority in the criminals, merely because of certain eccentricities in the state check samples, whereby one or other state comparisons fails to agree with the total series comparison in exhibiting a significant criminal deficiency in each of the several educational grades. Yet there can be no doubt that criminals differ from civilians in educational attainments more strongly than in any other sociological character.

The right side of Table XIII-6 lists also the deviations in which the total series and one state agree in exhibiting significant deviations in the same direction, but in which the other state comparison does not attain statistical significance in its deviation, although the latter agrees in direction. These are almost certainly valid and may be so accepted. The list has been purged of differences which are either seriously affected by age or by some observational equation which raises a doubt as to their correctness. This second list of acceptable general criminological deviations includes 15.15 percent of metric features, 24.00 of sociological subcategories, 14.93 percent of subcategories of morphological observations. Thus we have as a total of dependable differences between criminals and civilians 36.36 percent of measurements and indices, 36 percent of subcategories of sociological features, 22.07 percent of subcategories of morphological observations. This may be contrasted with the rough estimate of 57.58 percent of metric features, 50 percent of sociological features, and 45.51 percent of morphological features derived from the optimum choice of the state comparisons and without elimination of age-affected features and certain dubious observations.

Actually there seems little doubt that the larger figures represent the real deviations of criminals from civilians more justly than the diminished percentages. Inadequacies of the civilian check samples and recurrent doubts of the comparability of various observations in which the standards of the field workers appear to have fluctuated have necessitated drastic reductions in the differences. An ideal check sample and a complete elimination of observational equations might well increase the differences rather than diminish them.

Causes of Criminal Differentiation From Civilians

The outstanding feature of differentiation between criminals and law-abiding citizens of the same ethnic origin is the unanimity of criminal deviation irrespective of offense. Although most of the offense groups are distinct physically and

Table XIII-6

NUMBERS AND PERCENTAGES OF SIGNIFICANT CRIMINAL
DEVIATIONS FROM CIVILIANS INDEPENDENT OF AGE

Total Comparisons and State Comparisons Significant and in Same Direction			Total and One State Comparison Significant, All Agreeing in Direction		
Category	Number	Percent	Category	Number	Percent
Measurements and indices Deficiencies of age, weight, chest breadth, head circumference, upper face height, nose height, ear length	7	21.21	Measurements and indices Deficiencies of height, biacromial, chest depth; excesses of nasal and zygo-frontal indices	5	15.15
Sociological observations Excess of divorced men, laborers and personal servants	3	12.00	Sociological observations Deficiencies of married men, of public servants, of students, excesses of extractives and factory operatives, deficiencies of 3rd-4th high	6	24.00
Morphological observations Excess of straight hair, deficiency of low waves, deficiencies of blue eyes and homogeneous irides, excesses of submedium cheek fullness and of submedium gonial angles, deficiency of marked overbite, excess of submedium roll of helix, deficiency of medium and pronounced, deficiency of medium necks and excess of long, thin necks	11	7.14	Morphological observations Deficiency of dark brown eyes, excesses of zoned and speckled irides, excess of submedium forehead height, deficiency of medium nasal root height and excess of pronounced, deficiencies of medium nasal root breadth and nasal bridge breadth, deficiencies of convex and straight noses and excess of concavoconvex, deficiency of medium nasal tip thickness, excess of right nasal septum deflections, excess of slight overbite, deficiency of Darwin's point absent and excess of submedium or medium, deficiency of medium antihelix prominence and excess of pronounced, excess of submedium ear protrusion and deficiency of medium, deficiency of short thick necks, deficiency of medium shoulder slope and excess of pronounced	23	14.93

sociologically from the criminal series as a whole, nevertheless the entire body of delinquents presents a uniformity of differences from the civilians which seems to be capable of but one interpretation. Criminals as a group represent an aggregate of sociologically and biologically inferior individuals. The distinctions between civilians and murderers, thieves, rapists, and other categories of offenders are, for the most part, the same indications of criminal inferiority which stigmatize the entire criminal series, irrespective of nature of crime.

Excesses of single men and of divorced men indicate an inability or unwillingness to undertake successfully the normal family responsibilities of the adult male. Deficient educations and low occupational status are bound up with mental inferiority, lack of industry and stability, and general weakness of character. The fact that criminals as a whole are younger than random samples of the adult male population suggests clearly enough that antisocial tendencies manifest themselves with greatest intensity in the no-man's-land between childhood and maturity, and in that post-adolescent stage when physical powers are fully developed, but when judgment and responsibility lag. Marked deficiencies in gross bodily dimensions and in head and face diameters are unequivocal assertions of undergrowth and poor physical development, since there are in this material no serious racial differences which might confuse the issue. The general lack of important racial criteria among the differentiating metric characters reinforces the conclusion that the great gap between native White criminals of native parentage and civilians of the same origin is not a matter of the selection of certain ethnic blends for antisocial careers. Deficiencies of dark brown eyes and of blue eyes suggest that these criminals include fewer of the relatively pure racial types and more of the mixed types than occur among civilians. Noses broader relative to their height than are characteristic of the civil check sample are an evidence of infantilism or of primitiveness. Poor development of other facial dimensions favors the former interpretation.

Low foreheads, high pinched nasal roots, nasal bridges and tips varying to both extremes of breadth and narrowness, excesses of nasal deflections, compressed faces and narrow jaws, fit well into the picture of general constitutional inferiority. The very small ears with submedium roll of helix, prominent antihelix, and frequent presence of Darwin's point, hint at degeneracy. At the same time it should be noted that the Lombrosian stigmata of auricular deformity are not characteristic of this series.

Our data, of course, provide a complete physical description of the native White American criminal of native parentage. Here we have concerned ourselves principally with those deviations from the presumed law-abiding citizens which set apart the incarcerated offender. But even these differences are sufficiently descriptive to enable us to envisage a sort of general average of criminals of this nativity and parentage. They sketch rather vaguely and with a good many gaps the outline of an Old American type which is smaller, more weedy, and possibly with more degenerative features than would be found in the composite of respectable citizens of the same ethnic origin. This nebular criminal composite can be resolved into offense groups slightly more definite in their physical characterizations. Doubtless it could be broken up into physical combinations which would be real individual types, but these diverse types would be found in each offense group. There would be no type exclusive to a group and embracing the majority of its members. Each individual type would find its counterpart in the civilian population and would doubtless differ from the law-abiding type only in its smaller size and featural inferiority.

Just as there is no single uniform type of the native born American citizen of

American parentage, but a diversity of physical types, so there is no unity of type in the American born criminal of American parentage. Individual variation, familial inheritance, inbreeding of certain strains, and diverse blends of various racial and ethnic factors create a wide variety of physical types. In the molding of these types physical environment may well operate with varying intensity. From each of the physical types thus cooperatively produced, the poorer and weaker specimens tend to be selected for antisocial careers and for ultimate incarceration. The dregs of every population draught, pure or mixed, are poured into the prison sinks.

There can be no doubt of the inferior status of the criminal, both in physical and in sociological characters. Can this inferiority be attributed to an unfavorable environment? It is completely obvious that poor housing, lack of nourishing food, absence of medical care, and an unhealthy habitat may deteriorate individuals sprung from healthy stocks, or may even depress the physical status of the entire stock. I am not aware that moral degeneration and the increase of antisocial proclivities are a necessary consequence of such physical depression. Many of our immigrant stocks have been shown to produce offspring of superior size and better constitution in this country than in the homelands where they presumably abode under less favorable environmental conditions. Possibly and probably bodily size and health were there lessened by those depressing factors. The resiliency of the immigrant stock manifests itself in this country by the increments of size in offspring born here. But this increase in the bodily size of children of immigrants is notoriously accompanied by an increase of criminality, rather than a diminution. Criminality in immigrant stocks will be considered in detail in the next volume of this work. I merely cite this instance as an indication of the dubious value of an inference that physiques deteriorated by a poor environment are in themselves necessarily conducive to antisocial behavior. There are innumerable undernourished and under-sized individuals in every population who are not in the least criminalistic.

If we add to the physical depression of an adverse environment such factors as broken homes, criminalistic parents, and vicious associates, together with the corrupting influences of automobiles, the radio, moving pictures, and the tabloid press, we have nearly filled the complement of mainly environmental influences which may be claimed to produce the criminal. Here, however, we are mingling hereditary influences with those which are purely environmental, since at least the character of the home and the social attitudes of the parents are partially the resultants of the quality of gem plasm found in the latter. In other words, family inheritance may to a great extent determine family environment in so far as respect for law and morality are concerned. The criminal who is brought up in a criminalistic home can scarcely be claimed to be an exclusively environmental product.

In this work we have completely neglected the mental status of the criminal, except in so far as it may be indicated by his educational and occupational attainments. Our data upon the intelligence of the native White criminal of native parentage in prisons and reformatories are entirely inadequate for scientific analysis and deduction. Such usable information as we possess pertains to other groups of delinquents and will be discussed in subsequent volumes of this work.

There is, of course, no reason to doubt that this criminal series includes a considerable excess of dull and mentally deficient individuals as compared with the check sample of the normal population. We have, indeed, the intelligence quotients or ratings of 154 men, inmates of the Concord Reformatory in Massachusetts. These were copied from the prison records and are seriated in Table XIII-7. If we assume

Table XIII-5

NUMBER AND SIGNIFICANCE OF DEVIATIONS OF TOTAL SERIES
AND OF STATE SERIES IN MEASUREMENTS AND INDICES,
AND IN SUBCATEGORIES OF SOCIOLOGICAL OBSERVATIONS,
AND MORPHOLOGICAL OBSERVATIONS

| | Significant | | Insignificant | | Total |
	Number	Percent	Number	Percent	**Number**
Total Series					
Measurements and indices	19	57.58	14	42.42	33
Sociological observations	21	80.77	5	19.23	26
Morphological observations	100	61.73	62	38.27	162
Massachusetts					
Measurements and indices	21	63.64	12	36.36	33
Sociological observations	13	50.00	13	50.00	26
Morphological observations	96	59.26	66	40.74	162
Tennessee					
Measurements and indices	21	63.64	12	36.36	33
Sociological observations	16	61.54	10	38.46	26
Morphological observations	71	43.83	91	56.17	162

that an I.Q. of 96 or above indicates normal intelligence, we have only 19.48 percent of such persons in our tiny sample.

Sheldon and Eleanor T. Glueck secured intelligence ratings upon 466 persons who had been inmates of the Concord Reformatory, and found the following distribution: normal (I.Q. 90–110) 33 percent, dull (I.Q. 80–90) 24.1 percent, borderline (I.Q. 70–80) 22.3 percent, feeble-minded (I.Q. 50–70) 20.6 percent.[1] That stupidity and mental defect are more potent factors in crime causation than inferior physique and impoverished environment seems undeniable. Actually physical inferiority is so highly correlated with mental defect that there is little doubt that our findings in regard to the former are principally significant in their implicit association with the latter. There is no inevitable or usual causal relationship between physical defect and mental defect; both are expressions of organic inferiority, whether environmentally induced or inherited.

In every population there are hereditary inferiors in mind and in body, as well as physical and mental deficients whose condition may perhaps be attributed to an unfortunate concatenation of environmental circumstances. Our information definitely proves that it is from the physically inferior element of the population that native born criminals of native parentage are mainly derived. My present hypothesis is that physical inferiority is of principally hereditary origin; that these hereditary inferiors naturally gravitate into unfavorable environmental conditions; and that the worst or weakest of them yield to social stresses which force them into criminal behavior.

Certainly not every individual criminal of our series is mentally deficient or physically inferior. Force of circumstances, evil tradition, and sheer "cussedness" undoubtedly turn the scale in favor of delinquency in many cases. Nevertheless, by and large, within every occupational and educational category, it seems clear that the criminal is inferior to the civilian of corresponding status, either physically or mentally, or both.

Differences in constitutional type, whether of racial origin or due to familial or individual factors of endocrine or other causation, undoubtedly are agents in determining the choice of offense, especially in conjunction with the opportunities afforded by the specific social environment. But in any case these constitutional and environmental factors operate upon the physical and (putatively) mental inferiors, in whatever walk of life.

In this portion of our anthropological survey of criminals we have not investigated racial and ethnic factors in their relation to delinquency, because we have been dealing with a series which is comparatively homogenous. Only here and there minor indications of possible racial differences in offense types have cropped out. In the next volume devoted to native Whites of foreign parentage by nationality and to foreign Whites of various countries of origin, we shall attack this problem.

Up to this point the results of our investigation cannot be said to have any great practical utility. That is, there are few if any findings which can be put to the use of the police in the detection of criminals. An accurate description of an average gangster will not help to catch a Dillinger. Certain theoretical conclusions are, however, of no little importance. Criminals are organically inferior. Crime is the resultant of the impact of environment upon low grade human organisms. It follows that the elimination of crime can be effected only by the extirpation of the physically, mentally, and morally unfit, or by their complete segregation in a socially aseptic environment.

Note

1. Sheldon Glueck and Eleanor T. Glueck, *500 Criminal Careers*, p. 156.

24

Criminology as an
Interdisciplinary Behavioral Science
C. R. Jeffery

. . . Two major problems emerge immediately if we are to regard criminology as a behavioral science. (1) Criminology does not have a theory of behavior, and, in fact, does not even focus its attention on either criminal behavior or behavior. (2) Criminology is confused with criminal justice and the eighteenth-century legal view of man, deterrence, retribution, and justice. Criminal justice means the police, courts, and prisons. It is assumed that this is the correct and only way in which the crime problem can be conceived. We in criminology are so dominated by the legal and political issues involved in law enforcement, court administration, and prison administration that we have a difficult time defining criminology. Politicians say we need more police, not more professors, and we encourage our professors to become police.

Criminology is dominated by the nineteenth-century view of the psychosocial nature of man. Criminal justice is dominated by the eighteenth-century view of political man. The assumptions we make about human nature must be challenged.

Basic Assumptions of Classical Criminology

The following statements represent the classical approach to crime control.

1. Crime is a legal process. This is a *justice* model of crime control, involving both a *crime control* model of the police and a *due process* model of the lawyer (Packer, 1968).

2. The major weapon against crime is *punishment*. Punishment acts as a deterrent to those who commit crimes and to those who are about to commit crimes, and it acts as a source of retribution and revenge for those who do the punishing (Newman, 1978).

3. If we put people in institutions (Rothman, 1971), we will handle the crime problem. We can make better citizens out of criminals (most of whom come from brutal and neglecting environments) by subjecting them to the brutalization of our prisons.

Source: C. R. Jeffery, "Criminology as an Interdisciplinary Behavioral Science," *Criminology*, Vol. 16, pp. 149–169, 1978. Copyright © 1978 by the American Society of Criminology. Reprinted with permission.

4. We can control crime by waiting until the crime occurs and then taking action. In this way we can insure a large "crimes unknown to police" figure, a small "arrest by police" figure, a large "plea bargaining" figure, and a small "sent to prison" figure. We can also insure a large "number of victims" figure and a high "cost of crime" figure.

5. We can control crime by leaving the environment in which crimes occur untouched.

6. We can control crime by leaving the personality structure of the criminal untouched.

7. Criminals are not to be treated. Criminal law is for those who voluntarily and immorally violate the law. They deserve punishment. We can only treat those whose behavior has been caused by a mental disease. If a man is insane he is treated; if he is guilty he is punished (Jeffery, 1967).

8. We have no legal guarantees for the treatment of those who are accused of crimes. All we have is due process for the punishment of those found guilty of crime (Kittrie, 1971).

9. We know all we need to know about human behavior to operate the criminal justice system. The criminal justice system and crime control policy must be in the hands of politicians, police, lawyers, and prison guards. Biologists, psychologists, and sociologists are not allowed to testify as to the causes of criminal behavior, nor does federal policy encourage basic research on criminal behavior.

Basic Assumptions of Positivistic Criminology

1. Crime can be cured by treatment. Punishment of the offense must be replaced with treatment of the offender. Individual differences must be taken into account in sentencing and disposition of criminals.

2. We need not be concerned about the legal and ethical aspects of a treatment model.

3. We need not be concerned about the lack of a basic theory of behavior in psychology or sociology which will allow us to treat criminal behavior successfully.

4. We need not change the environment in which crimes occur in order to reduce the crime rate.

5. We need not change criminal behavior in order to change the criminal. We can change his mind with its internal conflicts (psychoanalysis), or we change his education, job training, opportunity structure, or socioeconomic status (sociology).

6. We can develop biological, psychological, and sociological theories of behavior in total isolation from one another and still have a sound basis for criminological theory.

7. The proper time to treat the criminal is after he is mature and vicious. We need not worry about prevention techniques which would start at the prenatal period.

The Failures of Criminology and Criminal Justice

As Radzinowicz (1977) reminds us, the failures of criminology and criminal justice are found in such facts as (a) we have more people in custody in the United States than any other country reporting, (b) we have more people in custody than at any time in history, (c) we are experiencing a 60%–70% recidivism rate, (d) we have no evidence that punishment and deterrence are solutions to the crime problem, and (e) we have no theory of behavior in criminology that stands close scrutiny. . . .

The failure of psychiatry and psychology during the 1920–1950 era is matched by the failure of the sociological model as found in the war against poverty program in the 1960 era. The notion that the opportunity structure could be altered through education and job training, thus altering poverty and delinquency, was also a total disaster (Jeffery, 1977; Radzinowicz, 1977). The failure of criminology as a science of the individual offender was matched by its failure as a science of the social offender. . . .

We have given up the treatment model at a time when the behavioral sciences are about to make a major contribution to our knowledge of human behavior. It is ironic that in the 1970s, when we are returning to an eighteenth-century punishment model of crime control, twenty-first-century breakthroughs are occurring in our understanding of human behavior. . . .

A New Model: Biosocial Criminology

Elements of the New Model

The new model must contain several basic elements now absent in criminology: (1) It must move from deterrence, punishment, and treatment to *prevention*. (2) It must move from a social to a *physical environment*. (3) It must move from a social to a *biosocial* model of learning.

Crime Prevention.   By crime prevention we mean those actions taken before a crime is committed to reduce or eliminate the crime rate. The public health model of medical care is a prevention model. Today medicine is more concerned with the prevention of heart disease and cancer than with the treatment and institutionalization of those already afflicted.

The present criminal justice model waits for the crime to occur before responding. The LEAA [Law Enforcement Assistance Administration] and federal government response has been to increase the capacity of the criminal justice system. The more police we have, the more arrests; the more arrests, the more courts and lawyers; the more courts, the more prisons; the more prisons, the more people who will return to prisons.

Behavior is the product of two sets of variables: a *physical environment* and a *physical organism* in interaction. Crime prevention must be based on a social ecology which recognizes the interaction of man and environment as complementary physical systems in interactions. . . .

The Physical Environment.   Criminology must move from Sutherland, Shaw, and McKay, from the cultural conflict perspective, to a physical environment perspective (Jeffery, 1976). Crime rates are highly correlated with the physical features of the environment, such as buildings, streets, parks, automobiles, and highways. Most areas of the urban environment are crime-free; crime is very selective in where it occurs. Some blocks have many murders and robberies; others have none. Crime prevention involves the design of physical space. This is a joining of urban design, environmental psychology, and social ecology into a meaningful relationship. . . .

Biosocial Criminology.   The new criminology must represent a merging of biology, psychology, and sociology. It must reflect the hierarchies of sciences as found in systems analysis.

Behavior reflects both genetic and environmental variables. The equipotentiality environmentalism of the past must be replaced with a model which clearly recognizes that each and every individual is different genetically (except perhaps for MZ twins). Williams (1967), a biochemist and past president of the American Chemical Society, argues that only 15% of the population has what is termed normal anatomical features. If our noses varied as much as our hearts and kidneys and hormonal systems, some of us would have noses the size of beans, others would have noses the size of watermelons.

The sociologist/criminologist often assumes that if behavior is learned, then learning in no way involves biology or psychology. This argument ignores the fact that learning is a psychobiological process involving changes in the biochemistry and cell structure of the brain. Learning can only occur if there are physical changes in the brain. The process is best summarized as a system of information flow from environment to organism:

$$\text{Genetic code} \times \text{Environment} = \text{Brain code} \times \text{Environment} = \text{BEHAVIOR}$$

Genetic codes and brain codes are of a biochemical nature, involving the biochemical structure of genes and of neutral transmission in the brain. The type of behavior (response) exhibited by an organism depends on the nature of the environment (stimulus) and the way in which the stimulus is coded, transmitted, and decoded by the brain and nervous system. This is what is meant by the biological limitations on learning (Jeffery, 1977).

We do not inherit behavior any more than we inherit height or intelligence. We do inherit a capacity for interaction with the environment. Sociopathy and alcoholism are not inherited, but a biochemical preparedness for such behaviors is present in the brain which, if given a certain type of environment, will produce sociopathy or alcoholism.

The brain contains a center for emotion and motivation, based on pleasure and pain, a center for reason and thought, and a center for the processing of information from the environment. This is almost a Freudian model put within the context of modern psychobiology, as suggested by Pribram and Gill (1976) in their work on the new Freud. The concept of social control is a neglected theory in criminology, although it is to be found in Reckless, Nye, Hirschi, and others. Certainly biosocial learning theory, as I have presented it, is control theory. In summary, what biosocial control theory holds is that behavior is controlled by the brain. Behavior involves biochemical changes in the neurons which then activate muscles and glands. An incoming impulse or experience from the social environment must be encoded, stored, acted upon, and decoded by the brain before it comes out as social behavior. Social behavior, be it conforming or deviant, must go into a brain and come out of a brain. G. H. Mead made this a basic part of his social behaviorism, but this has been totally neglected by the symbolic interactionists.

Emerging Issues in Criminology

If one regards behavior as a product of the interaction of a physical organism with a physical environment, then one must be prepared to find different sorts of things in criminology in the near future, assuming the courage to look for them. Gordon (1976) and Hirschi and Hindelang (1977) have in recent articles suggested a link between low intelligence and delinquency. Mednick and his associates found that 41.7% of the XYY cases identified in Denmark had a history of criminal careers, compared to 9% of the XY population. They also found that the link between XYY and criminality was not aggression and high testosterone levels but rather low intelligence. They also found that criminals from the XY population had low intelligence. Since genes interact with one another, this suggests the possibility that the Y chromosome is involved in those biochemical processes labeled intelligence (Mednick and Christiansen, 1977).

Intelligence is related to both genetics and environment (Oliverio, 1977; Halsey, 1977; Stine, 1977). This means the impact of poverty and social class on crime rates must be reinterpreted in terms of intelligence. Education and social class are influenced by intelligence, as well as influencing intelligence. To take one example, protein intake is a crucial variable in brain development and thus intelligence. Protein intake is also very dependent on the educational and socioeconomic background of the parents. The link between poverty and crime is intelligence and protein intake, at least as one of several interacting variables.

Criminal and delinquent behaviors have also been related to learning disabilities, hypoglycemia, epilepsy, perceptual difficulties, and sociopathy (Hippchen, 1978; Lewis and Balla, 1976; Williams and Kalita, 1977).

The new model of treatment emerging in biological psychiatry is one involving the biochemistry of the brain (Rosenthal and Kety, 1968; Brady et al., 1977; Maser and Seligman, 1977; Van Praag and Bruinvels, 1977; Hamburg and Brodie, 1975). The genetic factor in mental disorders in now well recognized. Dopamine and norepinephrine levels in the brain are related to behavioral disorders; the more norepinephrine, the greater the level of excitation, as in schizophrenia; the lower the norepinephrine level, the lower the level of excitation, as in sociopathy and depression.

The use of drugs in the treatment of behavioral disorders has resulted in a dramatic decrease in institutionalization for schizophrenics. Chlorpromazine (Thorazine) is the major drug used in the United States (Julien, 1975). . . . Lithium and Thorazine act to block the norepinephrine postsynaptic sites, thus reducing the amount of norepinephrine available for the neurochemical transmission of information. As noted, behavior depends on the encoding and decoding of information by the brain.

A Private Criminal Justice System

The future of crime control must depend on the development of a crime prevention program involving both the physical organism and the physical environment. The environmental design aspects of crime control must be addressed within the structure of federal policy concerning housing and urban design. The more crucial issue, as far as implementation of policy is concerned, is at the level of the individual offender.

In order to implement a biosocial approach to crime prevention, we must have early diagnosis and treatment of neurological disorders. This will mean experimentation and research. It will mean brain scans and blood tests. It will mean tests for learning disabilities and hypoglycemia. All of this involves medical examinations, intrusions into the privacy of the individual, and controversial and experimental surgeries and/or drug therapies. Under such circumstances, and with as much opposition as exists today to the control of human behavior by the state system, it will be difficult if not impossible to turn biomedical research over to a federal agency.

Because of the major failures of the federal government with health, education, and welfare problems, including crime, and because of the great dangers attendant upon the use of behavioral control systems by the state, it is recommended that a private treatment system be set up to parallel or to replace the present criminal justice system. The treatment of behavioral disorders, including those labeled as crime, must be removed *from the political arena*. The lawyer and politician are so committed to a given view of human nature and justice that an impossible gap has been created between the behavioral sciences and the criminal justice system. . . .

We worry about not providing counsel for a defendant before we send him to the electric chair or to prison, but we do not show the same amount of concern for placing neurologically disordered people in prison. We worry about the insanity defense and all the nonsense it has produced about behavioral disorders, but we do not ask why the definitions of insanity do not include those found today in biological psychiatry. We would rather put Charles Manson in prison or put Gary Gilmore before a firing squad than spend the time and money needed to find out why they became what they became. . . .

It goes without saying that a major research effort is needed to join biology, medicine, psychology, criminology, and criminal law into a new crime prevention model. We must approach the crime problem as a behavioral problem and not as a political problem. We must recognize that the police, courts, and corrections cannot handle a genetic defect, hypoglycemia, or learning disabilities any more than they can handle cancer or heart disease. . . .

References

Brady, J. P. (1977). *Psychiatry*. New York: Spectrum.

Gordon, R. (1976). "Prevalence: the rare datum in delinquency," in M. Klein (ed.) *The Juvenile Justice System*. Beverly Hills, CA: Sage.

Halsey, A. H. (1977). *Heredity and Environment*. New York: Free Press.

Hamburg, D. and H. Brodie (1975). *American Handbook of Psychiatry, Vol. 6: New Psychiatric Frontiers*. New York: Basic Books.

Hippchen, L. (1978). *The Ecologic-Biochemical Approaches to Treatment of Delinquents and Criminals*. New York: Van Nostrand Reinhold.

Hirschi, T. (1969). *The Causes of Delinquency*. Berkeley: Univ. of California Press.

———— and M. Hindelang (1977). "Intelligence and delinquency." *Amer. Soc. Rev.* 42: 571–586.

Jeffery, C. R. (1977). *Crime Prevention through Environmental Design*. Beverly Hills, CA: Sage.

————. (1976). "Criminal behavior and the physical environment." *Amer. Behav. Scientist* 20: 149–174.

————. (1967). *Criminal Responsibility and Mental Disease*. Springfield, IL: Thomas.

Lewis, D. and D. Balla (1976). *Delinquency and Psychopathology*. New York: Grune & Stratton.

Maser, J. and M. Seligman (1977). *Psychopathology: Experimental Models*. San Francisco: Freeman.

Mednick, S. and K. O. Christiansen (1977). *Biosocial Bases of Criminal Behavior*. New York: Gardner.

Nettler, G. (1978). *Explaining Crime*. New York: McGraw-Hill.

Newman, G. (1978). *The Punishment Response*. Philadelphia: Lippincott.

Oliverio, A. (1977). *Genetics, Environment, and Intelligence*. New York: Elsevier.

Packer, H. L. (1968). *The Limits of the Criminal Sanction*. Stanford, CA: Stanford Univ. Press.

Pribram, K. and M. Gill (1976). *Freud's Project Re-Assessed*. New York: Basic Books.

Radzinowicz, L. (1977). *The Growth of Crime*. New York: Basic Books.

Rosenthal, D. and S. Kety (1968). *Transmission of Schizophrenia*. New York: Pergamon.

Rothman, D. J. (1971). *The Discovery of the Asylum*. Boston: Little, Brown.

Stine, G. (1977). *Biosocial Genetics*. New York: Macmillan.

Van Praag, H. M. and J. Bruinvels (1977). *Neurotransmission and Disturbed Behavior*. Utrecht: Bohn, Scheltema, & Holkema.

Williams, R. (1967). *You Are Extraordinary*. New York: Random House.

———— and D. Kalita (1977). *A Physician Handbook on Orthomolecular Medicine*. New York: Pergamon.

25

Crime and Human Nature

James Q. Wilson   Richard J. Herrnstein

Explaining Crime

. . . Our theory—or perspective—is a statement about the forces that control individual behavior. To most people, that is not a very interesting assertion, but to many scholars, it is a most controversial one. Some students of crime are suspicious of the view that explanations of criminality should be based on an analysis of individual psychology. Such a view, they argue, is "psychological reductionism" that neglects the setting in which crime occurs and the broad social forces that determine levels of crime. These suspicions, while understandable, are ill-founded. Whatever factors contribute to crime—the state of the economy, the competence of the police, the nurturance of the family, the availability of drugs, the quality of the schools—they must all affect the behavior of *individuals* if they are to affect crime. If people differ in their tendency to commit crime, we must express those differences in terms of how some array of factors affects their individual decisions. If crime rates differ among nations, it must be because individuals in those nations differ or are exposed to different arrays of factors. If crime rates rise or fall, it must be that changes have occurred in the variables governing individual behavior.

Our theory is eclectic, drawing from different, sometimes opposing, schools of thought. We incorporate both genetic predispositions and social learning and consider the influence of both delayed and immediate factors. An individual act is sometimes best understood as a reaction to immediate circumstances and at other times as an expression of enduring behavioral dispositions; both sorts of explanations have a place in our theory. Though eclectic, the theory is built upon modern behavioral psychology.*

Crime as Choice: The Theory in Brief

. . . Our theory rests on the assumption that people, when faced with a choice, choose the preferred course of action. This assumption is quite weak; it says nothing more than that whatever people choose to do, they choose it because they prefer it. In fact, it is more than weak; without further clarification, it is a tautology. When we say people "choose," we do not necessarily mean that they consciously deliberate about what to do. All we mean is that their behavior is determined by its consequences. A person will do that thing the consequences of which are perceived by him or her to be preferable to the consequences of doing something else. What can save such a statement from being a tautology is how plausibly we describe the gains and losses associated with alternative courses of action and the standards by which a person evaluates those gains and losses.

These assumptions are commonplace in philosophy and social science. Philosophers speak of hedonism or utilitarianism, economists of value or utility, and psychologists of reinforcement or reward. We will use the language of psychology, but it should not be hard to translate our terminology into that of other disciplines. Though social scientists differ as to how much behavior can reasonably be described as the result of a choice, all agree that at least some behavior is guided, or even precisely controlled, by things variously termed pleasure, pain, happiness, sorrow, desirability, or the like. Our object is to show how this simple and widely used idea can be used to explain behavior.

At any given moment, a person can choose between committing a crime and not committing it (all these alternatives to crime we lump together as "noncrime"). The consequences of committing the crime consist of rewards (what psychologists call "reinforcers") and punishments; the consequences of not committing the crime (i.e., engaging in noncrime) also entail gains and losses. The larger the ratio of the net rewards of crime to the net rewards of noncrime, the greater the tendency to commit the crime. The net rewards of crime include, obviously, the likely material gains from the crime, but they also include intangible benefits, such as obtaining emotional or sexual gratification, receiving the approval of peers, satisfying an old score against an enemy, or enhancing one's sense of justice. One must deduct from these rewards of crime any losses that accrue immediately—that are, so to speak, contemporaneous with the crime. They include the pangs of conscience, the disapproval of onlookers, and the retaliation of the victim.

The value of noncrime lies all in the future. It includes the benefits to the individual of avoiding the risk of being caught and punished and, in addition, the benefits of avoiding penalties not controlled by the criminal justice system, such as the loss of reputation or the sense of shame afflicting a person later discovered to have broken the law and the possibility that, being known as a criminal, one cannot get or keep a job.

The value of any reward or punishment associated with either crime or noncrime is, to some degree, uncertain. A would-be burglar can rarely know exactly how much loot he will take away or what its cash value will prove to be. The assaulter or rapist may exaggerate the satisfaction he thinks will follow the assault or the rape. Many people do not know how sharp the bite of conscience will be until they have done something that makes them feel the bite. The anticipated approval of one's buddies may or may not be forthcoming. Similarly, the benefits of noncrime are uncertain. One cannot know with confidence whether one will be caught, convicted, and punished, or whether one's friends will learn about the crime and as a result withhold valued esteem, or whether one will be able to find or hold a job.

Compounding these uncertainties is time. The opportunity to commit a crime may be ready at hand (an open, unattended cash register in a store) or well in the future (a bank that, with planning and preparation, can be robbed). And the rewards associated with noncrime are almost invariably more distant than those connected with crime, perhaps many weeks or months distant. The strength of reinforcers tends to decay over time at rates that differ among individuals. As a result, the extent to which people take into account distant possibilities—a crime that can be committed only tomorrow, or punishment that will be inflicted only in a year—will affect whether they choose crime or noncrime. . . .

Reinforcers

All human behavior is shaped by two kinds of reinforcers: primary and secondary. A primary reinforcer derives its strength from an innate drive, such as hunger or sexual appetite; a secondary reinforcer derives its strength from learning. The line dividing reinforcers that are innate from those that are learned is hard to draw, and people argue, often passionately, over where it ought to be drawn. When we disagree over whether people are innately altruistic, men are innately more aggressive than women, or mankind is innately warlike or competitive, we are disagreeing over whether behavior responds to primary or to secondary reinforcers.

In fact, most reinforcers combine primary and secondary elements. Part of the benefit that comes from eating either bread or spaghetti must derive from the fact that their common ingredient, wheat, satisfies an innate drive—hunger. In this sense, both are primary reinforcers. But bread and spaghetti differ in texture, flavor, and appearance, and the preferences we have for these qualities are in part learned. These qualities constitute secondary reinforcers. The diversity of the world's cuisines shows, to some extent, how extraordinarily varied are the secondary aspects of even a highly biological reinforcer such as food.

The distinction between primary and secondary reinforcers is important in part because it draws attention to the link between innate drives and social conventions. For example, in every society men and women adorn themselves to enhance their sexual appeal. At the same time, styles in clothing and cosmetics vary greatly among societies and throughout history. As we are all immersed in the fashions of our place and time, we may suppose that fashion is purely arbitrary. But we are probably wrong, for these conventions of personal beauty are dependent on primary sexual reinforcers. But what constitutes acceptable adornment changes within broad limits. Once, for a woman to appear nude in a motion picture meant that she was wanton and the film was trash. Today, female nudity, though it is still offensive to some, is not construed by most viewers as an indication of the moral worth of the woman.

Not only do innate primary reinforcers become blended with learned secondary ones, the strength of even primary reinforcers (and of course of secondary reinforcers) will vary. Bread that we eat hungrily at seven o'clock in the morning may have no appeal to us at one o'clock in the afternoon, right after lunch. In fact, many forms of food may appeal to us before breakfast even though none may appeal after lunch. A class of reinforcers whose strengths vary together allows us to speak of a "drive"—in this case, the hunger drive.

Drives vary in strength. The various food drives can be depended on to assert themselves several times a day, but the sexual drive may be felt much less frequently and then in ways powerfully affected by circumstances. The aggressive drive may occur very rarely in some of us and frequently in others, and it may appear suddenly, in response to events, and blow over almost as quickly. We repeat these commonplace observations because we wish to emphasize that though much behavior, including criminal behavior, is affected by innate drives, this does not mean that crime is committed by "born criminals" with uncontrollable, antisocial drives. We can, in short, include innate drives (and thus genetic factors) in our theory without embracing a view of the criminal as an atavistic savage or any other sort of biological anomaly.

Secondary reinforcers change in strength along with the primary reinforcers with which they are associated. Those secondary reinforcers that change the least in strength are those associated with the largest variety of primary reinforcers. Money is an especially powerful reward, not because it is intrinsically valuable (paper currency has almost no intrinsic worth), but because it is associated with so many primary reinforcers that satisfy innate drives. Money can buy food, shelter, relief from pain, and even sexual gratification. (It can also buy status and power, but we will not discuss here the interesting question of whether the desire for these things is innate.) The reinforcing power of money is relatively steady because the many primary rewards with which it is connected make it somewhat impervious to fluctuations in the value of any one drive.

Because of the constant and universal reinforcing power of money, people are inclined to think of crimes for money gain as more natural, and thus more the product of voluntary choice and rational thought, than crimes involving "senseless" violence or sexual deviance. Stealing is an understandable, if not pardonable, crime; bestiality, "unprovoked" murder, and drug addiction seem much less understandable, and therefore, perhaps, less voluntary or deliberate. People sometimes carry this line of thought even further: These "senseless" crimes are the result of overpowering compulsions or irrational beliefs. But this is a false distinction. Certain reinforcers may have a steadier, more predictable effect, but all behavior, even the bizarre, responds to reinforcement. It is sometimes useful to distinguish between crimes that arise out of long-lasting, hard-to-change reinforcers (such as money) from those that stem from short-acting, (possibly) changeable drives (such as sexual deviance), but we must always bear in mind that these are distinctions of degree, not of kind.

Conditioning

Thus far, we have spoken of the "association" between primary and secondary reinforcers. Now we must ask how that association arises. The answer is the process known as conditioning. The simplest form of conditioning is the well-known experiment involving Pavlov's dog. The dog repeatedly heard a buzzer a few moments before receiving some dried meat powder in its mouth. Soon, the dog salivated at the mere sound of the buzzer. Two different stimuli—meat and buzzers—were associated. The meat elicited an innate tendency to salivate; the buzzer came to elicit salivation through learning. Pavlov's successors extended his discovery to much more complex responses than salivation and to many other species, including man. These Pavlovian experiments involved what psychologists now call "classical conditioning," which typically involves the autonomic nervous system (that part of our neural structure controlling reflexive behavior, such as heartbeats, salivation, and perspiration, and internal emotional states, such as fear, anxiety, and relaxation) and in which the behavior of the subject (the dog or the man) does not affect the stimulus being administered.

Classical (or Pavlovian) conditioning can make an arbitrary stimulus reinforce behavior by associating the stimulus with either a primary (i.e., innate) reinforcer or some already-learned secondary reinforcer. As we have seen, money is an arbitrary stimulus (a collection of scraps of paper and bits of metal) that has become one of the most universal and powerful secondary reinforcers. But there are many other examples. If a child is regularly praised for scrubbing his or her hands before dinner, then (provided that the praise is already felt to be rewarding), the child will in time scrub his hands without being told or praised. The satisfaction he feels in having scrubbed hands is now the internal feeling of reinforcement. In the same way, hand-scrubbing can be taught by scolding a child who does not wash up. If the scolding is already felt by the child to be punishing, in time the child will feel uncomfortable whenever he has dirty hands.

Classical conditioning does not produce only secretions or muscle twitches. These external responses may be accompanied by a complex array of internalized dispositions. The child who learns to scrub his hands, because of either parental praise or parental disapproval, will have learned things on which his mind and his subsequent experience will come to work in elaborate ways. In time, the satisfaction he feels from having clean hands may merge with other similar satisfactions and become a general sense of cleanliness, which he may eventually believe is next to godliness. He imputes virtue to cleanliness and regards filth with great distaste, even when he finds it in the world at large rather than simply on his own hands. Of course, all this presupposes growing up in a society in which neighbors, friends, and even the government regularly praise cleanliness and condemn slovenliness. . . .

Many people have a conscience strong enough to prevent them from committing a crime some of the time but not all of the time . . . a reasonably strong conscience is probably sufficient to prevent a person from committing a crime that would have only a modest yield *and* that could not take place for, say, two days. This would be true even if the person was confident he would not be caught. But now suppose the opportunity for committing the offense is immediately at hand—say, your poker-playing friends have left the room after the hand was dealt and you have a chance to peek at their cards, or the jewelry salesman has left the store with a tray of diamond rings open on the counter. Now, if the bite of conscience is not sufficient by itself to prevent the offense, the would-be offender will calculate, however roughly or inarticulately, the chances of being caught. He will know that if the friends suddenly return or the jewelry salesman is watching, he will lose things—in the first instance, reputation, and in the second, his freedom. People differ in how they calculate these risks. Some worry about any chance, however slight, of being caught and would be appalled at any loss of esteem, however small or fleeting; others will peek at the cards or grab a ring if they think they have any chance at all of getting away with it.

When present actions are governed by their consequences, "instrumental" (or operant) conditioning is at work. Unlike classically conditioned responses, instrumental conditioning involves behavior that affects the stimulus (e.g., not peeking at the cards or not taking the ring avoids the costs of the offense). Instrumental behavior affects the stimuli we receive and this, in turn, affects subsequent behavior.

The distinction between classical and instrumental conditioning is by no means as clear as our simple definitions may make it appear. But if we bear in mind that behavior cannot be neatly explained by one or the other process, we can use the distinction to help us understand individual differences in criminality. Persons deficient in conscience may turn out to be persons who for various reasons resist classical conditioning—they do not internalize rules as easily as do others. Persons who, even with a strong conscience, commit crimes anyway may be persons who have difficulty imagining the future consequences of present action or who are so impulsive as to discount very heavily even those consequences they can foresee, and hence will resist the instrumental conditioning that might lead them to choose noncrime over crime.

Delay and Uncertainty

Our argument so far is that behavior is controlled by its consequences. Those consequences—the primary and secondary reinforcers and punishers—may be immediate or postponed, certain or uncertain. Because not everyone has a conscience sufficiently strong to prevent every illegal act, the influence of delay and uncertainty on individual differences in criminality is great. Consequences gradually lose their ability to control behavior in proportion to how delayed or improbable they are. We have just observed that instrumental conditioning works best with persons who can conceive of future consequences and who attach a high value to even distant consequences. It can easily be shown that for many people, improbable or distant effects have very little influence on their behavior. For example, millions of cigarette smokers ignore the (possibly) fatal consequences of smoking because they are distant and uncertain. If smoking one cigarette caused certain death tomorrow, we would anticipate a rather sharp reduction in tobacco consumption.

The theft of $100 with eight chances in ten of getting away with it is worth more to a prospective thief than the theft of $100 with a one-in-two chance of success. A convenient, though somewhat fictitious, way of expressing these differences is with the concept of "expected value," which equals the product of the value of the gain times the probability of obtaining it ($100 × .8 = $80; $100 × .5 = $50). In fact, people may evaluate alternative gambles somewhat differently from what is implied by these objective expected values, but those differences can be ignored here. Other things being equal, a crime more certain of success will be valued more than one less certain; a more certain punishment will be feared more than a less certain one.

The increase in criminality resulting from the decreased probability of punishment occurs as a result of two processes—one involving instrumental conditioning, and the other, classical conditioning. If the threat of being punished oneself is reduced, the rewards for noncrime (i.e., the punishment that is not received) are weakened, making noncrime seem less profitable: This is an example of applying the principles of instrumental conditioning. If the spectacle of others being punished becomes less frequent, the rewards of crime may be strengthened because it now seems less wrong. The tendency for the punishment of others to affect the extent to which we feel guilty when we contemplate committing the same crime is an example of the use of classical conditioning.

Delay affects crime because there is almost always a lapse between when the crime may be committed and when the legal or social consequences, if any, will be felt. Put another way, the rewards of crime usually precede the costs of crime (except for such contemporaneous costs as those of conscience). Because of this, time discounting becomes extremely important in explaining criminal behavior. . . .

Individuals differ in the degree to which they discount the future. These differences are often part of a personality trait that can be measured. . . . They may also differ in their ability to conceive of the future or to plan for it. They may lack the imagination, experience, or intelligence to commit a crime that requires planning or to visualize what state of affairs may exist long in the future when the benefits of noncrime become available. This may help explain why criminals tend to be less intelligent than noncriminals, though there are other possible explanations for this connection.

Individual differences in criminality may also exist because of the different values people assign to crime and noncrime. . . .

Persons who commit "irresistible" crimes, especially ones that involve violence or passion, are sometimes thought by society to be in the grip of a strange compulsion or a deranged mind. What seems rational from the offender's point of view appears irrational from society's. Some people will urge that such an offender be excused or his penalty mitigated because they cannot imagine themselves acting in this way. But if the crime is distinctive at all, it is only because the underlying drive for its reward is uncommon, or uncommonly intense. The crime is no more irresistible than cheating on one's income tax; it could have been suppressed by a greater or more certain penalty. . . .

Equity and Inequity

In assigning a value to the rewards of crime or noncrime, an individual often takes into account not only what he stands to gain but what others stand to gain from what he perceives as comparable efforts. The individual has some notion of what he is entitled to, and that notion is affected by what he sees other people getting.

This interaction between what one person thinks he deserves and what he sees other people getting is expressed by sociologists and social psychologists in terms of an "equity equation."[1] It is based on a much older notion of distributive justice, first elaborated by Aristotle in the *Nichomachean Ethics*. To Aristotle, an equitable allocation of goods or honors is one that gives to each person a share proportional to his or her merit.[2] In other words, the ratio of one person's share to another person's share will be the same as the ratio between one person's worth and the other's. The worth of the two parties will depend on their age, status, wealth, skill, effort, or virtue; which measure of worth is selected is influenced by the prior understandings of the parties or the nature of the political regime. For example, a sixteen-year-old boy lounging on a street corner may decide that what he and others ought to earn should be determined by how hard they work, their level of education, or by their racial or class status. The identity of the other person with whom one compares one's own merit will also vary. The sixteen-year-old boy may compare his income to that of other sixteen-year-old boys, to that of all males in the city, or to that of all persons in the nation as a whole. What standard of comparison he uses and with whom he makes the comparison will obviously determine whether he thinks he has less or more money than he is entitled to have. For a given standard and a given reference group, he will feel he has what he is entitled to if the ratio between his income and his worth is the same as the ratio of the relevant other fellow's income to worth. . . .

During their lives, most people change the way they evaluate a distribution of goods or honors. As infants, they are selfish, wanting everything without regard to the worth or contributions of others. As children, they may feel they are entitled to the same share as everybody else because, though they recognize that others are entitled to something, they do not recognize that others may deserve more than they.[3] As adults, they make finer distinctions regarding whom they should compare themselves with and on what grounds; some may even come to endorse altruistic standards.[4] A similar progression also occurs as people enter into more intimate and enduring relationships with each other, from the selfishness that often governs the relations of strangers to the altruism sometimes tying together husband and wife or parents and children.[5] A distribution that would be intolerably inequitable between strangers or business associates might be quite acceptable among friends or within a family. Changes in the way in which equity is defined, in short, may result from natural mental and moral development, from social learning,[6] from situational factors, or from all three. Moreover, individuals may differ in what they define as equitable because of differences in their level of understanding and, perhaps, their general intelligence.)[7] . . .

The Theory as a Whole

. . . The larger the ratio of the rewards (material and nonmaterial) of noncrime to the rewards (material and nonmaterial) of crime, the weaker the tendency to commit crimes. The bite of conscience, the approval of peers, and any sense of inequity will increase or decrease the total value of crime; the opinions of family, friends, and employers are important benefits of noncrime, as is the desire to avoid the penalties that can be imposed by the criminal justice system. The strength of any reward declines with time, but people differ in the rate at which they discount the future. The strength of a given reward is also affected by the total supply of reinforcers.

Some implications of the theory are obvious: Other things being equal, a reduction in the delay and uncertainty attached to the rewards of noncrime will reduce the probability of crime. But other implications are not so obvious. For instance, increasing the value of the rewards of noncrime (by increasing the severity of punishment) may not reduce a given individual's tendency to commit crime if he believes that these rewards are not commensurate with what he deserves. In this case, punishing him for preferring crime to noncrime may trigger hostility toward society in retaliation for the shortfall. The increased rewards for noncrime may be offset by an increased sense of inequity and hence an increased incentive for committing a crime. Or again: It may be easier to reduce crime by making penalties swifter or more certain, rather than more severe, if the persons committing crime are highly present-oriented (so that they discount even large rewards very sharply) or if they are likely to have their sense of inequity heightened by increases in the severity of punishment. Or yet again: An individual with an extroverted personality is more likely than one with an introverted one to externalize his feelings of inequity and act directly to correct them. . . .

The connection between crime and impulsiveness has been demonstrated, as has the link between (low) intelligence and crime. Those features of family life that produce stronger or weaker internalized inhibitions will be seen to have a connection to the presence or absence of aggressiveness and criminality. Certain subcultures, such as street-corner gangs, appear to affect the value members attach to both crime and noncrime. The mass media, and in particular television, may affect both aggressiveness directly and a viewer's sense of inequity that can affect crime indirectly. Schooling may affect crime rates by bringing certain persons together into groups that reinforce either crime or noncrime and by determining the extent to which children believe that their skills will give them access to legitimate rewards. The condition of the economy will have a complex effect on crime depending on whether the (possibly) restraint-weakening impact of affluence dominates the restraint-strengthening influence of employment opportunities.

. . . [T]he theory is quite consistent with the more bizarre and unusual forms of crime. Psychopathic personalities lack to an unusual degree internalized inhibitions on crime. Persons possessed by some obsessive interest—for example, pyromania—attach an inordinately high value to the rewards of certain crimes. If everyone loved fire too much, society would try hard to teach the moral evil of fire, as well as its practical danger. As it is, what society does teach is sufficient to overcome whatever slight tendency toward pyromania every average person may have, but it is insufficient to inhibit the rare pyromaniac. One reason society punishes arsonists is not only to make it more costly for persons to use fire for material gain but also to provide extra moral education to the occasional person who loves fire for its own sake.

In addition to pathological drives, there are ordinary ones that can, under certain conditions, become so strong as to lead to crime. History and literature abound with normal men and women in the grip of a too powerful reinforcement. Many people have broken the law for love, honor, family, and country, as well as for money, sex, vengeance, or delusion. Such criminals may be psychologically unremarkable; they transgressed because as they perceived the situation the reward for crime exceeded that for noncrime, and an opportunity presented itself.

Notes

*The specialist will recognize the debt we owe to, and the liberties we have taken with, the work of Edward L. Thorndike, Albert Bandura, B. F. Skinner, R. B. Cattell, H. J. Eysenck, I. P. Pavlov, and E. C. Tolman, among others.

1. Adams, J. S., 1965; Blau, P. M., 1964; Greenberg, J., and Cohen, R. L., 1982; Homans, 1961.
2. Aristotle, *Nichomachean Ethics*, v, iii, 1131b.
3. Hook, J. G., and Cook, T. D., 1979.
4. Damon, W., 1975.
5. Greenberg, J., and Cohen, R. L., 1982.
6. Blau, P. M., 1964; Sampson, E. E., 1975.
7. Krebs, 1982.

References

Adams, J. S. 1965. Inequity in social exchange. In L. Berkowitz (ed.), *Advances in Experimental Social Psychology*, Vol. 2. New York: Academic Press.

Aristotle. 1941. *Nichomachean Ethics*. In Richard McKeon (ed.), *The Basic Works of Aristotle*. New York: Random House.

Blau, P. M. 1964. *Exchange and Power in Social Life*. New York: John Wiley.

Damon, W. 1975. Early conception of positive justice as related to the development of logical operations. *Child Development* 46:301–312.

Greenberg, J., and Cohen, R. L. 1982. Why justice? Normative and instrumental interpretations. In Greenberg and Cohen (eds.), *Equity and Justice in Social Behavior*. New York: Academic Press.

Homans, G. C. 1961. *Social Behavior: Its Elementary Forms*. New York: Harcourt, Brace & World.

Hook, J. G., and Cook, T. D. 1979. Equity theory and the cognitive ability of children. *Psychological Bulletin* 86:429–445.

Krebs, D. 1982. Prosocial behavior, equity, and justice. In J. Greenberg and R. L. Cohen (eds.), *Equity and Justice in Social Behavior*. New York: Academic Press.

Sampson, E. E. 1975. On justice as equality. *Journal of Social Issues* 31:45–64.

26

Suicide
Émile Durkheim

. . . No living being can be happy or even exist unless his needs are sufficiently proportioned to his means. In other words, if his needs require more than can be granted, or even merely something of a different sort, they will be under continual friction and can only function painfully. Movements incapable of production without pain tend not to be reproduced. Unsatisfied tendencies atrophy, and as the impulse to live is merely the result of all the rest, it is bound to weaken as the others relax.

In the animal, at least in a normal condition, this equilibrium is established with automatic spontaneity because the animal depends on purely material conditions. All the organism needs is that the supplies of substance and energy constantly employed in the vital process should be periodically renewed by equivalent quantities; that replacement be equivalent to use. When the void created by existence in its own resources is filled, the animal, satisfied, asks nothing further. Its power of reflection is not sufficiently developed to imagine other ends than those implicit in its physical nature. On the other hand, as the work demanded of each organ itself depends on the general state of vital energy and the needs of organic equilibrium, use is regulated in turn by replacement and the balance is automatic. The limits of one are those of the other; both are fundamental to the constitution of the existence in question, which cannot exceed them.

This is not the case with man, because most of his needs are not dependent on his body or not to the same degree. Strictly speaking, we may consider that the quantity of material supplies necessary to the physical maintenance of a human life is subject to computation, though this be less exact than in the preceding case and a wider margin left for the free combinations of the will; for beyond the indispensable minimum which satisfies nature when instinctive, a more awakened reflection suggests better conditions, seemingly desirable ends craving fulfillment. Such appetites, however, admittedly sooner or later reach a limit which they cannot pass. But how determine the quantity of well-being, comfort or luxury legitimately to be craved by a human being? Nothing appears in a man's organic nor in his psychological constitution which sets a limit to such tendencies. The functioning of individual life does not require them to cease at one point rather than at another; the proof being that they have constantly increased since the beginnings of history, receiving more

Source: Reprinted with the permission of The Free Press, a Division of Simon & Schuster Adult Publishing Group, from *Suicide: A Study in Sociology* by Émile Durkheim, translated by John A. Spaulding and George Simpson. Edited by George Simpson. Copyright ©1951 by The Free Press. Copyright © renewed 1979 by The Free Press.

and more complete satisfaction, yet with no weakening of average health. Above all, how establish their proper variation with different conditions of life, occupations, relative importance of services, etc.? In no society are they equally satisfied in the different stages of the social hierarchy. Yet human nature is substantially the same among all men, in its essential qualities. It is not human nature which can assign the variable limits necessary to our needs. They are thus unlimited so far as they depend on the individual alone. Irrespective of any external regulatory force, our capacity for feeling is in itself an insatiable and bottomless abyss.

But if nothing external can restrain this capacity, it can only be a source of torment to itself. Unlimited desires are insatiable by definition and insatiability is rightly considered a sign of morbidity. Being unlimited, they constantly and infinitely surpass the means at their command; they cannot be quenched. Inextinguishable thirst is constantly renewed torture. It has been claimed, indeed, that human activity naturally aspires beyond assignable limits and sets itself unattainable goals. But how can such an undetermined state be any more reconciled with the conditions of mental life than with the demands of physical life? All man's pleasure in acting, moving and exerting himself implies the sense that his efforts are not in vain and that by walking he has advanced. However, one does not advance when one walks toward no goal, or—which is the same thing—when his goal is infinity. Since the distance between us and it is always the same, whatever road we take, we might as well have made the motions without progress from the spot. Even our glances behind and our feeling of pride at the distance covered can cause only deceptive satisfaction, since the remaining distance is not proportionately reduced. To pursue a goal which is by definition unattainable is to condemn oneself to a state of perpetual unhappiness. Of course, man may hope contrary to all reason, and hope has its pleasures even when unreasonable. It may sustain him for a time; but it cannot survive the repeated disappointments of experience indefinitely. What more can the future offer him than the past, since he can never reach a tenable condition nor even approach the glimpsed ideal? Thus, the more one has, the more one wants, since satisfactions received only stimulate instead of filling needs. Shall action as such be considered agreeable? First, only on condition of blindness to its uselessness. Secondly, for this pleasure to be felt and to temper and half veil the accompanying painful unrest, such unending motion must at least always be easy and unhampered. If it is interfered with only restlessness is left, with the lack of ease which it, itself, entails. But it would be a miracle if no insurmountable obstacle were never encountered. Our thread of life on these conditions is pretty thin, breakable at any instant.

To achieve any other result, the passions first must be limited. Only then can they be harmonized with the faculties and satisfied. But since the individual has no way of limiting them, this must be done by some force exterior to him. A regulative force must play the same role for moral needs which the organism plays for physical needs. This means that the force can only be moral. The awakening of conscience interrupted the state of equilibrium of the animal's dormant existence; only conscience, therefore, can furnish the means to re-establish it. Physical restraint would be ineffective; hearts cannot be touched by physiochemical forces. So far as the appetites are not automatically restrained by physiological mechanisms, they can be halted only by a limit that they recognize as just. Men would never consent to restrict their desires if they felt justified in passing the assigned limit. But, for reasons given above, they cannot assign themselves this law of justice. So they must receive it from an authority which they respect, to which they yield spontaneously. Either directly and as a whole, or through the agency of one of its organs, society alone can play this moderating role; for it is the only moral power superior to the individual, the authority of which he accepts. It alone has the power necessary to stipulate law and to set the point beyond which the passions must not go. Finally, it alone can estimate the reward to be prospectively offered to every class of human functionary, in the name of the common interest.

As a matter of fact, at every moment of history there is a dim perception, in the moral consciousness of societies, of the respective value of different social services, the relative reward due to each, and the consequent degree of comfort appropriate on the average to workers in each occupation. The different functions are graded in public opinion and a certain coefficient of well-being assigned to each, according to its place in the hierarchy. According to accepted ideas, for example, a certain way of living is considered the upper limit to which a workman may aspire in his efforts to improve his existence, and there is another limit below which he is not willingly permitted to fall unless he has seriously demeaned himself. Both differ for city and country workers, for the domestic servant and the day-laborer, for the business clerk and the official, etc. Likewise the man of wealth is reproved if he lives the life of a poor man, but also if he seeks the refinements of luxury overmuch. Economists may protest in vain; public feeling will always be scandalized if an individual spends too much wealth for wholly superfluous use, and it even seems that this severity relaxes only in time of moral disturbance.[1] A genuine regimen exists, therefore, although not always legally formulated, which fixes with relative precision the maximum degree of ease of living to which each social class may legitimately aspire. However, there is nothing immutable about such a scale. It changes with the increase or decrease of collective revenue and the changes occurring in the moral ideas of society. Thus what appears luxury to one period no longer does so to another; and the well-being which for long periods was granted to a class only by exception and supererogation, finally appears strictly necessary and equitable.

Under this pressure, each in his sphere vaguely realizes the extreme limit set to his ambitions and aspires to nothing beyond. At least if he respects regulations and is docile to collective authority, that is, has a wholesome moral constitution, he feels that it is not well to ask more. Thus, an end and goal are set to the passions. Truly, there is nothing rigid nor absolute about such determination. The economic ideal assigned each class of citizens is itself confined to certain limits, within which the desires have free range. But it is not infinite. This relative limitation and the moderation it involves, make men contented with their lot while stimulating them moderately to improve it; and this average contentment causes the feeling of calm, active happiness, the pleasure in existing and living which characterizes health for societies as well as for individuals. Each person is then at least, generally speaking, in harmony with his condition, and desires only what he may legitimately hope for as the normal reward of his activity. Besides, this does not condemn man to a sort of immobility. He may seek to give beauty to his life; but his attempts in this direction may fail without causing him to despair. For, loving what he has and not fixing his desire solely on what he lacks, his wishes and hopes may fail of what he has happened to aspire to, without his being wholly destitute. He has the essentials. The equilibrium of his happiness is secure because it is defined, and a few mishaps cannot disconcert him.

But it would be of little use for everyone to recognize the justice of the hierarchy of functions established by public opinion, if he did not also consider the distribution of these functions just. The workman is not in harmony with his social position if he is not convinced that he has his desserts. If he feels justified in occupying another, what he has would not satisfy him. So it is not enough for the average level of needs for each social condition to be regulated by public opinion, but another, more precise rule, must fix the way in which these conditions are open to individuals. There is no society in which such regulation does not exist. It varies with times and places. Once it regarded birth as the almost exclusive principle of social classification; today it recognizes no other inherent inequality than hereditary fortune and merit. But in all these various forms its object is unchanged. It is also only possible, everywhere, as a restriction upon individuals imposed by superior authority, that is, by collective authority. For it can be established only by requiring of one or another group of men, usually of all, sacrifices and concessions in the name of the public interest.

Some, to be sure, have thought that this moral pressure would become unnecessary if men's economic circumstances were only no longer determined by heredity. If inheritance were abolished, the argument runs, if everyone began life with equal resources and if the competitive struggle were fought out on a basis of perfect equality, no one could think its results unjust. Each would instinctively feel that things are as they should be.

Truly, the nearer this ideal equality were approached, the less social restraint will be necessary. But it is only a matter of degree. One sort of heredity will always exist, that of natural talent. Intelligence, taste, scientific, artistic, literary or industrial ability, courage and manual dexterity are gifts received by each of us at birth, as the heir to wealth receives his capital or as the nobleman formerly received his title and function. A moral discipline will therefore still be required to make those less favored by nature accept the lesser advantages which they owe to the chance of birth. Shall it be demanded that all have an equal share and that no advantage be given those more useful and deserving? But then there would have to be a discipline far stronger to make these accept a treatment merely equal to that of the mediocre and incapable.

But like the one first mentioned, this discipline can be useful only if considered just by the peoples subject to it. When it is maintained only by custom and force, peace and harmony are illusory; the spirit of unrest and discontent are latent; appetites superficially restrained are ready to revolt. This happened in Rome and Greece when the faiths underlying the old organization of the patricians and plebeians were shaken, and in our modern societies when aristocratic prejudices began to lose their old ascendancy. But this state of upheaval is exceptional; it occurs only when society is passing through some abnormal crisis. In normal conditions the collective order is regarded as just by the great majority of persons. Therefore, when we say that an authority is necessary to impose this order on individuals, we certainly do not mean that violence is the only means of establishing it. Since this regulation is meant to restrain individual passions, it must come from a power which dominates individuals; but this power must also be obeyed through respect, not fear.

It is not true, then, that human activity can be released from all restraint. Nothing in the world can enjoy such a privilege. All existence being a part of the universe is relative to the remainder; its nature and method of manifestation accordingly depend not only on itself but on other beings, who consequently restrain and regulate it. Here there are only differences of degree and form between the mineral realm and the thinking person. Man's characteristic privilege is that the bond he accepts is not physical but moral; that is, social. He is governed not by a material environment brutally imposed on him, but by a conscience superior to his own, the superiority of which he feels. Because the greater, better part of his existence transcends the body, he escapes the body's yoke, but is subject to that of society.

But when society is disturbed by some painful crisis or by beneficent but abrupt transitions, it is momentarily incapable of exercising this influence; thence comes the sudden rises in the curve of suicides which we have pointed out above.

In the case of economic disasters, indeed, something like a declassification occurs which suddenly casts certain individuals into a lower state than their previous one. Then they must reduce their requirements, restrain their needs, learn greater self-control. All the advantages of social influence are lost so far as they are concerned; their moral education has to be recommenced. But society cannot adjust them instantaneously to this new life and teach them to practice the increased self-repression to which they are unaccustomed. So they are not adjusted to the condition forced on them, and its very prospect is intolerable; hence the suffering which detaches them from a reduced existence even before they have made trial of it.

It is the same if the source of the crisis is an abrupt growth of power and wealth. Then, truly, as the conditions of life are changed, the standard according to which needs were regulated can no longer remain the same; for it varies with social resources, since it largely determines the share of each class of producers. The scale is upset; but a new scale cannot be immediately improvised. Time is required for the public conscience to reclassify men and things. So long as the social forces thus freed have not regained equilibrium, their respective values are unknown and so all regulation is lacking for a time. The limits are unknown between the possible and the impossible, what is just and what is unjust, legitimate claims and hopes and those which are immoderate. Consequently, there is no restraint upon aspirations. If the disturbance is profound, it affects even the principles controlling the distribution of men among various occupations. Since the relations between various parts of society are necessarily modified, the ideas expressing these relations must change. Some particular class especially favored by the crisis is no longer resigned to its former lot, and, on the other hand, the example of its greater good fortune arouses all sorts of jealousy below and about it. Appetites, not being controlled by a public opinion become disoriented, no longer recognize the limits proper to them. Besides, they are at the same time seized by a sort of natural erethism simply by the greater intensity of public life. With increased prosperity desires increase. At the very moment when traditional rules have lost their authority, the richer prize offered these appetites stimulates them and makes them more exigent and impatient of control. The state of de-regulation or anomy is thus further heightened by passions being less disciplined, precisely when they need more disciplining.

But then their very demands make fulfillment impossible. Overweening ambition always exceeds the results obtained, great as they may be, since there is no warning to pause here. Nothing gives satisfaction and all this agitation is uninterruptedly maintained without appeasement. Above all, since this race for an unattainable goal can give no other pleasure but that of the race itself, if it is one, once it is interrupted the participants are left empty-handed. At the same time the struggle grows more violent and painful, both from being less controlled and because competition is greater. All classes contend among themselves because no established classification any longer exists. Effort grows, just when it becomes less productive. How could the desire to live not be weakened under such conditions?

This explanation is confirmed by the remarkable immunity of poor countries.

Poverty protects against suicide because it is a restraint in itself. No matter how one acts, desires have to depend upon resources to some extent; actual possessions are partly the criterion of those aspired to. So the less one has the less he is tempted to extend the range of his needs indefinitely. Lack of power, compelling moderation, accustoms men to it, while nothing excites envy if no one has superfluity. Wealth, on the other hand, by the power it bestows, deceives us into believing that we depend on ourselves only. Reducing the resistance we encounter from objects, it suggests the possibility of unlimited success against them. The less limited one feels, the more intolerable all limitation appears. Not without reason, therefore, have so many religions dwelt on the advantages and moral value of poverty. It is actually the best school for teaching self-restraint. Forcing us to constant self-discipline, it prepares us to accept collective discipline with equanimity, while wealth, exalting the individual, may always arouse the spirit of rebellion which is the very source of immorality. This, of course, is no reason why humanity should not improve its material condition. But though the moral danger involved in every growth of prosperity is not irremediable, it should not be forgotten. . . .

Note

1. Actually, this is a purely moral reprobation and can hardly be judicially implemented. We do not consider any reestablishment of sumptuary laws desirable or even possible.

27

Social Structure and Anomie

Robert K. Merton

There persists a notable tendency in sociological theory to attribute the malfunctioning of social structure primarily to those of man's imperious biological drives which are not adequately restrained by social control. In this view, the social order is solely a device for "impulse management" and the "social processing" of tensions. These impulses which break through social control, be it noted, are held to be biologically derived. Nonconformity is assumed to be rooted in original nature.[1] Conformity is by implication the result of an utilitarian calculus or unreasoned conditioning. This point of view, whatever its other deficiencies, clearly begs one question. It provides no basis for determining the nonbiological conditions which induce deviations from prescribed patterns of conduct. In this paper, it will be suggested that certain phases of social structure generate the circumstances in which infringement of social codes constitutes a "normal" response.[2]

The conceptual scheme to be outlined is designed to provide a coherent, systematic approach to the study of socio-cultural sources of deviate behavior. Our primary aim lies in discovering how some social structures *exert a definite pressure* upon certain persons in the society to engage in nonconformist rather than conformist conduct. The many ramifications of the scheme cannot all be discussed; the problems mentioned outnumber those explicitly treated.

Among the elements of social and cultural structure, two are important for our purposes. These are analytically separable although they merge imperceptibly in concrete situations. The first consists of culturally defined goals, purposes, and interests. It comprises a frame of aspirational reference. These goals are more or less integrated and involve varying degrees of prestige and sentiment. They constitute a basic, but not the exclusive, component of what Linton aptly has called "designs for group living." Some of these cultural aspirations are related to the original drives of man, but they are not determined by them. The second phase of the social structure defines, regulates, and controls the acceptable modes of achieving these goals. Every social group invariably couples its scale of desired ends with moral or institutional regulation of permissible and required procedures for attaining these ends. These regulatory norms and moral imperatives do not necessarily coincide with technical or efficiency norms. Many procedures which from the standpoint of *particular*

Source: Robert K. Merton, "Social Structure and Anomie," *American Sociological Review*, Vol. 3 (October 1938), pp. 672–682, Copyright © 1938 American Sociological Association.

individuals would be most efficient in securing desired values, *e.g.*, illicit oil-stock schemes, theft, fraud, are ruled out of the institutional area of permitted conduct. The choice of expedients is limited by the institutional norms.

To say that these two elements, culture goals and institutional norms, operate jointly is not to say that the ranges of alternative behaviors and aims bear some constant relation to one another. The emphasis upon certain goals may vary independently of the degree of emphasis upon institutional means. There may develop a disproportionate, at times, a virtually exclusive, stress upon the value of specific goals, involving relatively slight concern with the institutionally appropriate modes of attaining these goals. The limiting case in this direction is reached when the range of alternative procedures is limited only by technical rather than institutional considerations. Any and all devices which promise attainment of the all important goal would be permitted in this hypothetical polar case.[3] This constitutes one type of cultural malintegration. A second polar type is found in groups where activities originally conceived as instrumental are transmuted into ends in themselves. The original purposes are forgotten and ritualistic adherence to institutionally prescribed conduct becomes virtually obsessive.[4] Stability is largely ensured while change is flouted. The range of alternative behaviors is severely limited. There develops a tradition-bound, sacred society characterized by neophobia. The occupational psychosis of the bureaucrat may be cited as a case in point. Finally, there are the intermediate types of groups where a balance between culture goals and institutional means is maintained. These are the significantly integrated and relatively stable, though changing, groups.

An effective equilibrium between the two phases of the social structure is maintained as long as satisfactions accrue to individuals who conform to both constraints, viz., satisfactions from the achievement of the goals and satisfactions emerging directly from the institutionally canalized modes of striving to attain these ends. Success, in such equilibrated cases, is twofold. Success is reckoned in terms of the product and in terms of the process, in terms of the outcome and in terms of activities. Continuing satisfactions must derive from sheer *participation* in a competitive order as well as from eclipsing one's competitors if the order itself is to be sustained. The occasional sacrifices involved in institutionalized conduct must be compensated by socialized rewards. The distribution of statuses and roles through competition must be so organized that positive incentives for conformity to roles and adherence to status obligations are provided *for every position* within the distributive order. Aberrant conduct, therefore, may be viewed as a symptom of dissociation between culturally defined aspirations and socially structured means.

Of the types of groups which result from the independent variation of the two phases of the social structure, we shall be primarily concerned with the first, namely, that involving a disproportionate accent on goals. This statement must be recast in a proper perspective. In no group is there an absence of regulatory codes governing conduct, yet groups do vary in the degree to which these folkways, mores, and institutional controls are effectively integrated with the more diffuse goals which are part of the culture matrix. Emotional convictions may cluster about the complex of socially acclaimed ends, meanwhile shifting their support from the culturally defined implementation of these ends. As we shall see, certain aspects of the social structure may generate countermores and antisocial behavior precisely because of differential emphases on goals and regulations. In the extreme case, the latter may be so vitiated by the goal-emphasis that the range of behavior is limited only by considerations of technical expediency. The sole significant question then becomes, which available means is most efficient in netting the socially approved value?[5] The technically most feasible procedure, whether legitimate or not, is preferred to the institutionally prescribed conduct. As this process continues, the integration of the society becomes tenuous and anomie ensues.

Thus, in competitive athletics, when the aim of victory is shorn of its institutional trappings and success in contests becomes construed as "winning the game" rather than "winning through circumscribed modes of activity," a premium is implicitly set upon the use of illegitimate but technically efficient means. The star of the opposing football team is surreptitiously slugged; the wrestler furtively incapacitates his opponent through ingenious but illicit techniques; university alumni covertly subsidize "students" whose talents are largely confined to the athletic field. The emphasis on the goal has so attenuated the satisfactions deriving from sheer participation in the competitive activity that these satisfactions are virtually confined to a successful outcome. Through the same process, tension generated by the desire to win in a poker game is relieved by successfully dealing oneself four aces, or, when the cult of success has become completely dominant, by sagaciously shuffling the cards in a game of solitaire. The faint twinge of uneasiness in the last instance and the surreptious nature of public delicts indicate clearly that the institutional rules of the game *are known* to those who evade them, but that the emotional supports of these rules are largely vitiated by cultural exaggeration of the success-goal.[6] They are microcosmic images of the social macrocosm.

Of course, this process is not restricted to the realm of sport. The process whereby exaltation of the end generates a *literal demoralization, i.e.,* a deinstitutionalization, of the means is one which characterizes many[7] groups in which the two phases of the social structure are not highly integrated. The extreme emphasis upon the accumulation of wealth as a symbol of success[8] in our own society militates against the completely effective control of institutionally regulated modes of acquiring a fortune.[9] Fraud, corruption, vice, crime, in short, the entire catalogue of proscribed behavior, becomes increasingly common when the emphasis on the *culturally induced* success-goal becomes divorced from a coordinated institutional emphasis. This observation is of crucial theoretical importance in examining the doctrine that antisocial behavior most frequently derives from biological drives breaking through the restraints imposed by society. The difference is one between a strictly utilitarian interpretation which conceives man's ends as random and an analysis which finds these ends deriving from the basic values of the culture.[10]

Our analysis can scarcely stop at this juncture. We must turn to other aspects of the social structure if we are to deal with the social genesis of the varying rates and types of deviate behavior characteristic of different societies. Thus far, we have sketched three ideal types of social orders constituted by distinctive patterns of relations between culture ends and means. Turning from these types of *culture patterning*, we find five logically possible, alternative modes of adjustment or adaptation *by individuals* within the culture-bearing society or group.[11] These are schematically presented in the following table, where (+) signifies "acceptance," (–) signifies "elimination" and (±) signifies "rejection and substitution of new goals and standards."

	Culture Goals	Institutionalized Means
I. Conformity	+	+
II. Innovation	+	−
III. Ritualism	−	+
IV. Retreatism	−	−
V. Rebellion[12]	±	±

Our discussion of the relation between these alternative responses and other phases of the social structure must be prefaced by the observation that persons may shift from one alternative to another as they engage in different social activities. These categories refer to role adjustments in specific situations, not to personality *in toto*. To treat the development of this process in various spheres of conduct would introduce a complexity unmanageable within the confines of this paper. For this reason, we shall be concerned primarily with economic activity in the broad sense, "the production, exchange, distribution and consumption of goods and services" in our competitive society, wherein wealth has taken on a highly symbolic cast. Our task is to search out some of the factors which exert pressure upon individuals to engage in certain of these logically possible alternative responses. This choice, as we shall see, is far from random.

In every society, Adaptation I (conformity to both culture goals and means) is the most common and widely diffused. Were this not so, the stability and continuity of the society could not be maintained. The mesh of expectancies which constitutes every social order is sustained by the modal behavior of its members falling within the first category. Conventional role behavior oriented toward the basic values of the group is the rule rather than the exception. It is this fact alone which permits us to speak of a human aggregate as comprising a group or society.

Conversely, Adaptation IV (rejection of goals and means) is the least common. Persons who "adjust" (or maladjust) in this fashion are, strictly speaking, *in* the society but not *of* it. Sociologically, these constitute the true "aliens." Not sharing the common frame of orientation, they can be included within the societal population merely in a fictional sense. In this category are *some* of the activities of psychotics, psychoneurotics, chronic autists, pariahs, outcasts, vagrants, vagabonds, tramps, chronic drunkards and drug addicts.[13] These have relinquished, in certain spheres of activity, the culturally defined goals, involving complete aim-inhibition in the polar case, and their adjustments are not in accord with institutional norms. This is not to say that in some cases the source of their behavioral adjustments is not in part the very social structure which they have in effect repudiated nor that their very existence within a social area does not constitute a problem for the socialized population.

This mode of "adjustment" occurs, as far as structural sources are concerned, when both the culture goals and institutionalized procedures have been assimilated thoroughly by the individual and imbued with affect and high positive value, but where those institutionalized procedures which promise a measure of successful attainment of the goals are not available to the individual. In such instances, there results a twofold mental conflict insofar as the moral obligation for adopting institutional means conflicts with the pressure to resort to illegitimate means (which may attain the goal) and inasmuch as the individual is shut off from means which are both legitimate *and* effective. The competitive order is maintained, but the frustrated and handicapped individual who cannot cope with this order drops out. Defeatism, quietism and resignation are manifested in escape mechanisms which ultimately lead the individual to "escape" from the requirements of the society. It is an expedient which arises from continued failure to attain the goal by legitimate measures and from an inability to adopt the illegitimate route because of internalized prohibitions and institutionalized compulsives, *during which process the supreme value of the success-goal has as yet not been renounced.* The conflict is resolved by eliminating *both* precipitating elements, the goals and means. The escape is complete, the conflict is eliminated and the individual is asocialized.

Be it noted that where frustration derives from the inaccessibility of effective institutional means for attaining economic or any other type of highly valued "success," that Adaptations Il, III and V (innovation, ritualism and rebellion) are also possible. The result will be determined by the particular personality, and thus, the *particular* cultural background, involved. Inadequate socialization will result in the innovation response whereby the conflict and frustration are eliminated by relinquishing the institutional means and retaining the success-aspiration; an extreme assimilation of institutional demands will lead to ritualism wherein the goal is dropped as beyond one's reach but conformity to the mores persists; and rebellion occurs when emancipation from the reigning standards, due to frustration or to marginalist perspectives, leads to the attempt to introduce a "new social order."

Our major concern is with the illegitimacy adjustment. This involves the use of conventionally proscribed but frequently effective means of attaining at least the simulacrum of culturally defined success—wealth, power, and the like. As we have seen, this adjustment occurs when the individual has assimilated the cultural emphasis on success without equally internalizing the morally prescribed norms governing means for its attainment. The question arises, Which phases of our social structure predispose toward this mode of adjustment? We may examine a concrete instance, effectively analyzed by Lohman,[14] which provides a clue to the answer. Lohman has shown that specialized areas of vice in the near north side of Chicago constitute a "normal" response to a situation where the cultural emphasis upon pecuniary success has been absorbed, but where there is little access to conventional and legitimate means for attaining such success. The conventional occupational opportunities of persons in this area are almost completely limited to manual labor. Given our cultural stigmatization of manual labor, and its correlate, the prestige of white collar work, it is clear that the result is a strain toward innovational practices. The limitation of opportunity to unskilled labor and the resultant low income cannot compete *in terms of conventional standards of achievement* with the high income from organized vice.

For our purposes, this situation involves two important features. First, such antisocial behavior is in a sense "called forth" by certain conventional values of the culture *and* by the class structure involving differential access to the approved opportunities for legitimate, prestige-bearing pursuit of the culture goals. The lack of high integration between the means-and-end elements of the cultural pattern and the particular class structure combine to favor a heightened frequency of antisocial conduct in such groups. The second consideration is of equal significance. Recourse to the first of the alternative responses, legitimate effort, is limited by the fact that actual advance toward desired success-symbols through conventional channels is, despite our persisting open-class ideology,[15] relatively rare and difficult for those handicapped by little formal education and few economic resources. The dominant pressure of group standards of success is, therefore, on the gradual attenuation of legitimate, but by and large ineffective, strivings and the increasing use of illegitimate, but more or less effective, expedients of vice and crime. The cultural demands made on persons in this situation are incompatible. On the one hand, they are asked to orient their conduct toward the prospect of accumulating wealth and on the other, they are largely denied effective opportunities to do so institutionally. The consequences of such structural inconsistency are psychopathological personality, and/or antisocial conduct, and/or revolutionary activities. The equilibrium between culturally designated means and ends becomes highly unstable with the progressive emphasis on attaining the prestige-laden ends by any means whatsoever. Within this context, Capone represents the triumph of amoral intelligence over morally prescribed "failure," when the channels of vertical mobility are closed or narrowed[16] *in a society which places a high premium on economic affluence and social ascent for all its members.*[17]

This last qualification is of primary importance. It suggests that other phases of the social structure besides the extreme emphasis on pecuniary success, must be considered if we are to understand the social sources of antisocial behavior. A high frequency of deviate behavior is not generated simply by "lack of opportunity" or by this exaggerated pecuniary emphasis. A comparatively rigidified class structure, a feudalistic or caste order, may limit such opportunities far beyond the point which obtains in our society today. It is only when a system of cultural values extols, virtually above all else, certain *common* symbols of success *for the population at large* while its social structure rigorously restricts or completely eliminates access to approved modes of acquiring these symbols *for a considerable part of the same population*, that antisocial behavior ensues on a considerable scale. In other words, our egalitarian ideology denies by implication the existence of noncompeting groups and individuals in the pursuit of pecuniary success. The same body of success-symbols is held to be desirable for all. These goals are held to *transcend class lines*, not to be bounded by them, yet the actual social organization is such that there exist class differentials in the accessibility of these *common* success-symbols. Frustration and thwarted aspiration lead to the search for avenues of escape from a culturally induced intolerable situation; or unrelieved ambition may eventuate in illicit attempts to acquire the dominant values.[18] The American stress on pecuniary success and ambitiousness for all thus invites exaggerated anxieties, hostilities, neuroses and antisocial behavior.

This theoretical analysis may go far toward explaining the varying correlations between crime and poverty.[19] Poverty is not an isolated variable. It is one in a complex of interdependent social and cultural variables. When viewed in such a context, it represents quite different states of affairs. Poverty as such, and consequent limitation of opportunity, are not sufficient to induce a conspicuously high rate of criminal behavior. Even the often mentioned "poverty in the midst of plenty" will not necessarily lead to this result. Only insofar as poverty and associated disadvantages in competition for the culture values approved for *all* members of the society is linked with the assimilation of a cultural emphasis on monetary accumulation as a symbol of success is antisocial conduct a "normal" outcome. Thus, poverty is less highly correlated with crime in southeastern Europe than in the United States. The possibilities of vertical mobility in these European areas would seem to be fewer than in this country, so that neither poverty *per se* nor its association with limited opportunity is sufficient to account for the varying correlations. It is only when the full configuration is considered, poverty, limited opportunity and a commonly shared system of success symbols, that we can explain the higher association between poverty and crime in our society than in others where rigidified class structure is coupled with *differential class symbols of achievement*.

In societies such as our own, then, the pressure of prestige-bearing success tends to eliminate the effective social constraint over means employed to this end. "The-end-justifies-the-means" doctrine becomes a guiding tenet for action when the cultural structure unduly exalts the end and the social organization unduly limits possible recourse to approved means. Otherwise put, this notion and associated behavior reflect a lack of cultural coordination. In international relations, the effects of this lack of integration are notoriously apparent. An emphasis upon national power is not readily coordinated with an inept organization of legitimate, *i.e.*, internationally defined and accepted, means for attaining this goal. The result is a tendency toward the abrogation of international law, treaties become scraps of paper, "undeclared warfare" serves as a technical evasion, the bombing of civilian populations is rationalized,[20] just as the same societal situation induces the same sway of illegitimacy among individuals.

The social order we have described necessarily produces this "strain toward dissolution." The pressure of such an order is upon outdoing one's competitors. The choice of means within the ambit of institutional control will persist as long as the sentiments supporting a competitive system, *i.e.*, deriving from the possibility of outranking competitors and hence enjoying the favorable response of others, are distributed throughout the entire system of activities and are not confined merely to the final result. A stable social structure demands a balanced distribution of affect among its various segments. When there occurs a shift of emphasis from the satisfactions deriving from competition itself to almost exclusive concern with successful competition, the resultant stress leads to the breakdown of the regulatory structure.[21] With the resulting attenuation of the institutional imperatives, there occurs an approximation of the situation erroneously held by utilitarians to be typical of society generally wherein calculations of advantage and fear of punishment are the sole regulating agencies. In such situations, as Hobbes observed, force and fraud come to constitute the sole virtues in view of their relative efficiency in attaining goals,—which were for him, of course, not culturally derived.

It should be apparent that the foregoing discussion is not pitched on a moralistic plane. Whatever the sentiments of the writer or reader concerning the ethical desirability of coordinating the means-and-goals phases of the social structure, one must agree that lack of such coordination leads to anomie. Insofar as one of the most general functions of social organization is to provide a basis for calculability and regularity of behavior, it is increasingly limited in effectiveness as these elements of the structure become dissociated. At the extreme, predictability virtually disappears and what may be properly termed cultural chaos or anomie intervenes.

This statement, being brief, is also incomplete. It has not included an exhaustive treatment of the various structural elements which predispose toward one rather than another of the alternative responses open to individuals; it has neglected, but not denied the relevance of, the factors determining the specific incidence of these responses; it has not enumerated the various concrete responses which are constituted by combinations of specific values of the analytical variables; it has omitted, or included only by implication, any consideration of the social functions performed by illicit responses; it has not tested the full explanatory power of the analytical scheme by examining a large number of group variations in the frequency of deviate and conformist behavior; it has not adequately dealt with rebellious conduct which seeks to refashion the social framework radically; it has not examined the relevance of cultural conflict for an analysis of culture-goal and institutional-means malintegration. It is suggested that these and related problems may be profitably analyzed by this scheme.

Notes

1. *E.g.*, Ernest Jones, *Social Aspects of Psychoanalysis*, 28, London, 1924. If the Freudian notion is a variety of the "original sin" dogma, then the interpretation advanced in this paper may be called the doctrine of "socially derived sin."

2. "Normal" in the sense of a culturally oriented, if not approved, response. This statement does not deny the relevance of biological and personality differences which may be significantly involved in the *incidence* of deviate conduct. Our focus of interest is the social and cultural matrix; hence we abstract from other factors. It is in this sense, I take it, that James S. Plant speaks of the "normal reaction of normal people to abnormal conditions." See his *Personality and the Cultural Pattern*, 248, New York, 1937.

3. Contemporary American culture has been said to tend in this direction. See André Siegfried, *America Comes of Age*, 26–37, New York, 1927. The alleged extreme(?) emphasis on the goals of monetary success and material prosperity leads to dominant concern with technological and social instruments designed to produce the desired result, inasmuch as institutional controls become of secondary importance. In such a situation, innovation flourishes as the *range of means* employed is broadened. In a sense, then, there occurs the paradoxical emergence of "materialists" from an "idealistic" orientation. Cf. Durkheim's analysis of the cultural conditions which predispose toward crime and innovation, both of which are aimed toward efficiency, not moral norms. Durkheim was one of the first to see that "contrairement aux idées courantes le criminel n'apparait plus comme un être radicalement insociable, comme une sorte d'elément parasitaire, de corps étranger et inassimilable, introduit au sein de la société; c'est un agent régulier de la vie sociale." See *Les Règles de la Méthode Sociologique*, 86–89, Paris, 1927.

4. Such ritualism may be associated with a mythology which rationalizes these actions so that they appear to retain their status as means, but the dominant pressure is in the direction of strict ritualistic conformity, irrespective of such rationalizations. In this sense, ritual has proceeded farthest when such rationalizations are not even called forth.

5. In this connection, one may see the relevance of Elton Mayo's paraphrase of the title of Tawney's well known book. "Actually the problem *is not that of the sickness of an acquisitive society; it is that of the acquisitiveness of a sick society*," *Human Problems of an Industrial Civilization*, 153, New York, 1933. Mayo deals with the process through which wealth comes to be a symbol of social achievement. He sees this as arising from a state of anomie. We are considering the unintegrated monetary-success goal as an element in producing anomie. A complete analysis would involve both phases of this system of interdependent variables.

6. It is unlikely that interiorized norms are completely eliminated. Whatever residuum persists will induce personality tensions and conflict. The process involves a certain degree of ambivalence. A manifest rejection of the institutional norms is coupled with some latent retention of their emotional correlates. "Guilt feelings," "sense of sin," "pangs of conscience" are obvious manifestations of this unrelieved tension; symbolic adherence to the nominally repudiated values or rationalizations constitute a more subtle variety of tensional release.

7. "Many," and not all, unintegrated groups, for the reason already mentioned. In groups

where the primary emphasis shifts to institutional means, *i.e.*, when the range of alternatives is very limited, the outcome is a type of ritualism rather than anomie.

8. Money has several peculiarities which render it particularly apt to become a symbol of prestige divorced from institutional controls. As Simmel emphasized, money is highly abstract and impersonal. However acquired, through fraud or institutionally, it can be used to purchase the same goods and services. The anonymity of metropolitan culture, in conjunction with this peculiarity of money, permits wealth, the sources of which may be unknown to the community in which the plutocrat lives, to serve as a symbol of status.

9. The emphasis upon wealth as a success-symbol is possibly reflected in the use of the term "fortune" to refer to a stock of accumulated wealth. This meaning becomes common in the late sixteenth century (Spenser and Shakespeare). A similar usage of the Latin *fortuna* comes into prominence during the first century B.C. Both these periods are marked by the rise to prestige and power of the "bourgeoisie."

10. See Kingsley Davis, "Mental Hygiene and the Class Structure," *Psychiatry*, 1928, I, esp.62–63; Talcott Parsons, *The Structure of Social Action*, 59–60, New York, 1937.

11. This is a level intermediate between the two planes distinguished by Edward Sapir; namely, culture patterns and personal habit systems. See his "Contribution of Psychiatry to an Understanding of Behavior in Society," *Amer. J. Sociol.*, 1937, 42:862–70.

12. This fifth alternative is on a plane clearly different from that of the others. It represents a *transitional* response which seeks to *institutionalize* new procedures oriented toward revamped cultural goals shared by the members of the society. It thus involves efforts to *change* the existing structure rather than to perform accommodative actions *within* this structure, and introduces additional problems with which we are not at the moment concerned.

13. Obviously, this is an elliptical statement. These individuals may maintain some orientation to the values of their particular differentiated groupings within the larger society or, in part, of the conventional society itself. Insofar as they do so, their conduct cannot be classified in the "passive rejection" category (IV). Nels Anderson's description of the behavior and attitudes of the bum, for example, can readily be recast in terms of our analytical scheme. See *The Hobo*, 93–98, *et passim*, Chicago, 1923.

14. Joseph D. Lohman, "The Participant Observer in Community Studies," *Amer. Sociol. Rev.*, 1937, 2:890–98.

15. The shifting historical role of this ideology is a profitable subject for exploration. The "office-boy-to-president" stereotype was once in approximate accord with the facts. Such vertical mobility was probably more common then than now, when the class structure is more rigid. (See the following note.) The ideology largely persists, however, possibly because it still performs a useful function for maintaining the *status quo*. For insofar as it is accepted by the "masses," it constitutes a useful sop for those who might rebel against the entire structure, were this consoling hope removed. This ideology now serves to lessen the probability of Adaptation V. In short, the role of this notion has changed from that of an approximately valid empirical theorem to that of an ideology, in Mannheim's sense.

16. There is a growing body of evidence, though none of it is clearly conclusive, to the effect that our class structure is becoming rigidified and that vertical mobility is declining. Taussig and Joslyn found that American business leaders are being *increasingly* recruited from the upper ranks of our society. The Lynds have also found a "diminished chance to get ahead" for the working classes in Middletown. Manifestly, these objective changes are not alone significant; the individual's subjective evaluation of the situation is a major determinant of the response. The extent to which this change is opportunity for social mobility has been recognized by the least advantaged classes is still conjectural, although the Lynds present some suggestive materials. The writer suggests that a case in point is the increasing frequency of cartoons which observe in a tragi-comic vein that "my old man says everybody can't be President. He says if ya can get three days a week steady

on W.P.A. work ya ain't doin' so bad either.'' See F. W. Taussig and C. S. Joslyn, *American Business Leaders*, New York, 1932; R. S. and H. M. Lynd, *Middletown in Transition*, 67 ff., chap. 12, New York, 1937.

17. The role of the Negro in this respect is of considerable theoretical interest. Certain elements of the Negro population have assimilated the dominant caste's value of pecuniary success and social advancement, but they also recognize that social ascent is at present restricted to their own caste almost exclusively. The pressures upon the Negro which would otherwise derive from the structural inconsistencies we have noticed are hence not identical with those upon lower class whites. See Kingsley Davis, *op. cit.*, 63; John Dollard, *Caste and Class in a Southern Town*, 66 ff., New Haven, 1936; Donald Young, *American Minority Peoples*, 581, New York, 1932.

18. The psychical coordinates of these processes have been partly established by the experimental evidence concerning *Anspruchsniveaus* and levels of performance. See Kurt Lewin, *Vorsatz, Willie und Bedurfnis*, Berlin, 1926; N. F. Hoppe, ''Erfolg und Missenolg,'' *Psychol. Forschung*. 1930, 14:1–63; Jerome D. Frank, ''Individual Differences in Certain Aspects of the Level of Aspiration,'' *Amer. J. Psychol.*, 1935, 47:119–28.

19. Standard criminology texts summarize the data in this field. Our scheme of analysis may serve to resolve some of the theoretical contradictions which P. A. Sorokin indicates. For example, ''not everywhere nor always do the poor show a greater proportion of crime . . . many poorer countries have had less crime than the richer countries . . . The [economic] improvement in the second half of the nineteenth century, and the beginning of the twentieth, has not been followed by a decrease of crime.'' See his *Contemporary Sociological Theories*, 560-61, New York, 1928. The crucial point is, however, that poverty has varying social significance in different social structures, as we shall see. Hence, one would not expect a linear correlation between crime and poverty.

20. See M. W. Royse, *Aerial Bombardment and the International Regulation of War*, New York, 1928.

21. Since our primary concern is with the sociocultural aspects of this problem, the psychological correlates have been only implicitly considered. See Karen Horney, *The Neurotic Personality of Our Time*, New York, 1937, for a psychological discussion of this process.

28

Foundation for a General Strain Theory of Crime and Delinquency
Robert Agnew

... This paper argues that strain theory has a central role to play in explanations of crime/delinquency, but that the theory has to be substantially revised to play this role. Most empirical studies of strain theory continue to rely on the strain models developed by Merton (1938), A. Cohen (1955), and Cloward and Ohlin (1960). In recent years, however, a wealth of research in several fields has questioned certain of the assumptions underlying those theories and pointed to new directions for the development of strain theory. . . .

The theory is written at the social-psychological level: It focuses on the individual and his or her immediate social environment—although the macroimplications of the theory are explored at various points. The theory is also written with the empirical researcher in mind, and guidelines for testing the theory in adolescent populations are provided. The focus is on adolescents because most currently available data sets capable of testing the theory involve surveys of adolescents. This general theory, it will be argued, is capable of overcoming the theoretical and empirical criticisms of previous strain theories and of complementing the crime/delinquency theories that currently dominate the field. . . .

Strain Theory as Distinguished from Control and Differential Association/Social Learning Theory

Strain, social control, and differential association theory are all sociological theories: They explain delinquency in terms of the individual's social relationships. Strain theory is distinguished from social control and social learning theory in its specification of (1) the type of social relationship that leads to delinquency and (2) the motivation for delinquency. First, strain theory focuses explicitly on *negative relationships with others*: relationships in which the individual is not treated as he or she wants to be treated. Strain theory has typically focused on relationships in which others prevent the individual from achieving positively valued goals. Agnew (1985a), however, broadened the focus of strain theory to include relationships in which others present the individual with noxious or negative stimuli. Social control theory, by contrast, focuses on the *absence of significant relationships with conventional others and institutions. . . .*

Second, strain theory argues that adolescents are *pressured into delinquency by the negative affective states—most notably anger and related emotions—that often result from negative relationships* (see Kemper, 1978, and Morgan and Heise, 1988, for typologies of negative affective states). This negative affect creates pressure for corrective action and *may* lead adolescents to (1) make use of illegitimate channels of goal achievement, (2) attack or escape from the source of their adversity, and/or (3) manage their negative affect through the use of illicit drugs. Control theory, by contrast, denies that outside forces pressure the adolescent into delinquency. . . .

Phrased in the above manner, it is easy to see that strain theory complements the other major theories of delinquency in a fundamental way. While these other theories focus on the absence of relationships or on positive relationships, strain theory is the only theory to focus explicitly on negative relationships. And while these other theories view delinquency as the result of drift or of desire, strain theory views it as the result of pressure.

The Major Types of Strain

Strain as the Failure to Achieve Positively Valued Goals

Strain as the Disjunction between Aspirations and Expectations/Actual Achievements.   The classic strain theories of Merton, A. Cohen, and Cloward and Ohlin argue that the cultural system encourages everyone to pursue the ideal goals of monetary success and/or middle-class status. Lower-class individuals, however, are often prevented from achieving such goals through legitimate channels. In line with such theories, adolescent strain is typically measured in terms of the disjunction between *aspirations* (or ideal goals) and *expectations* (or expected levels of goal achievement). . . .

The most popular revision argues that there is a youth subculture that emphasizes a variety of immediate goals. The achievement of these goals is further said to depend on a variety of factors besides social class: factors such as intelligence, physical attractiveness, personality, and athletic ability. As a result, many middle-class individuals find that they lack the traits or skills necessary to achieve their goals through legitimate channels. This version of strain theory, however, continues to argue that strain stems from the inability to achieve certain ideal goals emphasized by the (sub)cultural system. As a consequence, strain continues to be measured in terms of the disjunction between aspirations and actual achievements (since we are dealing with immediate rather than future goals, actual achievements rather than expected achievements may be examined).

It should be noted that empirical support for this revised version of strain theory is also weak (see Agnew, 1991b, for a summary). . . .

Strain as the Disjunction between Expectations and Actual Achievements.
As indicated above, strain theories in criminology focus on the inability to achieve *ideal* goals derived from the cultural system. This approach stands in contrast to cer-

tain of the research on justice in social psychology. Here the focus is on the disjunction between *expectations* and *actual achievements* (rewards), and it is commonly argued that such expectations are existentially based. In particular, it has been argued that such expectations derive from the individual's past experience and/or from comparisons with referential (or generalized) others who are similar to the individual (see Berger et al., 1972, 1983; Blau, 1964; Homans, 1961; Jasso and Rossi, 1977; Mickelson, 1990; Ross et al., 1971; Thibaut and Kelley, 1959). Much of the research in this area has focused on income expectations, although the above theories apply to expectations regarding all manner of positive stimuli. The justice literature argues that the failure to achieve such expectations may lead to such emotions as anger, resentment, rage, dissatisfaction, disappointment, and unhappiness—that is, all the emotions customarily associated with strain in criminology. Further, it is argued that individuals will be strongly motivated to reduce the gap between expectations and achievements—with deviance being commonly mentioned as one possible option. . . .

Strain as the Disjunction between Just/Fair Outcomes and Actual Outcomes. The above models of strain assume that individual goals focus on the achievement of specific outcomes. Individual goals, for example, focus on the achievement of a certain amount of money or a certain grade-point average. A third conception of strain, also derived from the justice/equity literature, makes a rather different argument. It claims that individuals do not necessarily enter interactions with specific outcomes in mind. Rather, they enter interactions expecting that certain distributive justice rules will be followed, rules specifying how resources should be allocated. The rule that has received the most attention in the literature is that of equity. An equitable relationship is one in which the outcome/input ratios of the actors involved in an exchange/allocation relationship are equivalent (see Adams, 1963, 1965; Cook and Hegtvedt, 1983; Walster et al., 1978). Outcomes encompass a broad range of positive and negative consequences, while inputs encompass the individual's positive and negative contributions to the exchange. Individuals in a relationship will compare the ratio of their outcomes and inputs to the ratio(s) of specific others in the relationship. If the ratios are equal to one another, they feel that the outcomes are fair or just. This is true, according to equity theorists, even if the outcomes are low. If outcome/input ratios are not equal, actors will feel that the outcomes are unjust and they will experience distress as a result. Such distress is especially likely when individuals feel they have been underrewarded rather than overrewarded (Hegtvedt, 1990). . . .

The literature on equity builds on the strain theory literature in criminology in several ways. First, all of the strain literature assumes that individuals are pursuing some specific outcome, such as a certain amount of money or prestige. The equity literature points out that individuals do not necessarily enter into interactions with specific outcomes in mind, but rather with the expectation that a particular distributive justice rule will be followed. Their goal is that the interaction conform to the justice principle. This perspective, then, points to a new source of strain not considered in the criminology literature. Second, the strain literature in criminology focuses largely on the individual's outcomes. Individuals are assumed to be pursuing a specific goal, and strain is judged in terms of the disjunction between the goal and the actual outcome. The equity literature suggests that this may be an oversimplified conception and that the individual's *inputs* may also have to be considered. In particular, an equity theorist would argue that inputs will condition the individual's evaluation of outcomes. That is, individuals who view their inputs as limited will be more likely to accept limited outcomes as fair. Third, the equity literature also highlights the importance of the social comparison process. In particular, the equity literature stresses that one's evaluation of outcomes is at least partly a function of the outcomes (and inputs) of those with whom one is involved in exchange/allocation relations. A given outcome, then, may be evaluated as fair or unfair depending on the outcomes (and inputs) of others in the exchange/allocation relation. . . .

Summary: Strain as the Failure to Achieve Positively Valued Goals. Three types of strain in this category have been listed: strain as the disjunction between (1) aspirations and expectations/actual achievements, (2) expectations and actual achievements, and (3) just/fair outcomes. . . .

Given these multiple sources of strain, one might ask which is the most relevant to the explanation of delinquency. This is a difficult question to answer given current research. The most fruitful strategy at the present time may be to assume that all of the above sources are relevant—that there are several sources of frustration. . . .

Strain as the Removal of Positively Valued Stimuli from the Individual

The psychological literature on aggression and the stress literature suggest that strain may involve more than the pursuit of positively valued goals. . . .

Drawing on the stress literature, then, one may state that a second type of strain or negative relationship involves the actual or anticipated removal (loss) of positively valued stimuli from the individual. The actual or anticipated loss of positively valued stimuli may lead to delinquency as the individual tries to prevent the loss of the positive stimuli, retrieve the lost stimuli or obtain substitute stimuli, seek revenge against those responsible for the loss, or manage the negative affect caused by the loss by taking illicit drugs. . . .

Strain as the Presentation of Negative Stimuli

The literature on stress and the recent psychological literature on aggression also focus on the actual or anticipated presentation of negative or noxious stimuli.[1] Except for the work of Agnew (1985a), however, this category of strain has been neglected in criminology. . . .

In one of the few studies in criminology to focus specifically on the presentation of negative stimuli, Agnew (1985a) found that delinquency was related to three scales measuring negative relations at home and school. The effect of the scales on delinquency was partially mediated through a measure of anger, and the effect held when measures of social control and deviant beliefs were controlled. And in a recent study employing longitudinal data, Agnew (1989) found evidence suggesting that the relationship between negative stimuli and delinquency was due to the causal effect of the negative stimuli on delinquency (rather than the effect of delinquency on the negative stimuli). Much evidence, then, suggests that the presentation of negative or noxious stimuli constitutes a third major source of strain. . . .

The Links between Strain and Delinquency

Three sources of strain have been presented: strain as the actual or anticipated failure to achieve positively valued goals, strain as the actual or anticipated removal of positively valued stimuli, and strain as the actual or anticipated presentation of negative stimuli. . . .

Each type of strain increases the likelihood that individuals will experience one or more of a range of negative emotions. Those emotions include disappointment, depression, and fear. Anger, however, is the most critical emotional reaction for the purposes of the general strain theory. Anger results when individuals blame their adversity on others, and anger is a key emotion because it increases the individual's level of felt injury, creates a desire for retaliation/revenge, energizes the individual for action, and lowers inhibitions, in part because individuals believe that others will feel their aggression is justified (see Averill, 1982; Berkowitz, 1982; Kemper, 1978; Kluegel and Smith, 1986: Ch. 10; Zillman, 1979). Anger, then, affects the individual in several ways that are conducive to delinquency. . . .

Each type of strain may create a *predisposition* for delinquency or function as a *situational event* that instigates a particular delinquent act. In the words of Hirschi and Gottfredson (1986), then, the strain theory presented in this paper is a theory of both "criminality" and "crime" (or to use the words of Clarke and Cornish [1985], it is a theory of both "criminal involvement" and "criminal events"). Strain creates a predisposition for delinquency in those cases in which it is chronic or repetitive. . . .

Adolescents subject to such strain are predisposed to delinquency because (1) nondelinquent strategies for coping with strain are likely to be taxed; (2) the threshold for adversity may be lowered by chronic strains (see Averill, 1982:289); (3) repeated or chronic strain may lead to a hostile attitude—a general dislike and suspicion of others and an associated tendency to respond in an aggressive manner (see Edmunds and Kendrick, 1980:21); and (4) chronic strains increase the likelihood that individuals will be high in negative affect/arousal at any given time (see Bandura, 1983; Bernard, 1990). . . .

Adaptations to (Coping Strategies for) Strain

The discussion thus far has focused on the types of strain that might promote delinquency. Virtually all strain theories, however, acknowledge that only *some* strained individuals turn to delinquency. Some effort has been made to identify those factors that determine whether one adapts to strain through delinquency. . . .

Adaptations to Strain

Cognitive Coping Strategies.   Several literatures suggest that individuals sometimes cognitively reinterpret objective stressors in ways that minimize their subjective adversity. Three general strategies of cognitive coping are described below; each strategy has several forms. These strategies for coping with adversity may be summarized in the following phrases: "It's not important," "It's not that bad," and "I deserve it." This typology represents a synthesis of the coping strategies described in the stress, equity, stratification, and victimization literatures (Adams, 1963, 1965; Agnew, 1985b; Agnew and Jones, 1988; Averill, 1982; Della Fave, 1980; Donnerstein and Hatfield, 1982; Pearlin and Schooler, 1978; Walster et al., 1973, 1978). . . .

Ignore/Minimize the Importance of Adversity. The subjective impact of objective strain depends on the extent to which the strain is related to the central goals, values, and/or identities of the individual. As Pearlin and Schooler (1978:7) state, individuals may avoid subjective strain "to the extent that they are able to keep the most strainful experiences within the least valued areas of their life." Individuals, therefore, may minimize the strain they experience by reducing the absolute and/or relative importance assigned to goals/values and identities (see Agnew, 1983; Thoits, 1991a). . . .

Maximize Positive Outcomes/Minimize Negative Outcomes. . . . In a second adaptation, individuals attempt to deny the existence of adversity by maximizing their positive outcomes and/or minimizing their negative outcomes. This may be done in two ways: lowering the standards used to evaluate outcomes or distorting one's estimate of current and/or expected outcomes.

Lowering one's standards basically involves lowering one's goals or raising one's threshold for negative stimuli (see Suls, 1977). Such action, of course, makes one's current situation seem less adverse than it otherwise would be. Individuals may, for example, lower the amount of money they desire (which is distinct from lowering the importance attached to money). . . .

Accept Responsibility for Adversity. Third, individuals may *minimize* the subjective adversity of objective strain by convincing themselves, that they *deserve* the adversity they have experienced. . . .

Drawing on equity theory, one may argue that there are two basic strategies for convincing oneself that strain is deserved. First, individuals may cognitively minimize their positive inputs or maximize their negative inputs to a relationship. Inputs are conceived as contributions to the relationship and/or status characteristics believed to be relevant to the relationship (see Cook and Yamagishi, 1983). Second, individuals may maximize the positive inputs or minimize the negative inputs of others. . . .

Behavioral Coping Strategies.   There are two major types of behavioral coping: those that seek to minimize or eliminate the source of strain and those that seek to satisfy the need for revenge.

Maximizing Positive Outcomes/Minimizing Negative Outcomes. Behavioral coping may assume several forms, paralleling each of the major types of strain. Individuals, then, may seek to achieve positively valued goals, protect or retrieve positively valued stimuli, or terminate or escape from negative stimuli. Their actions in these areas may involve conventional or delinquent behavior. . . .

Vengeful Behavior. Data indicate that when adversity is blamed on others it creates a desire for revenge that is distinct from the desire to end the adversity. A second method of behavioral coping, then, involves the taking of revenge. Vengeful behavior may also assume conventional or delinquent forms, although the potential for delinquency is obviously high. Such behavior may involve efforts to minimize the positive outcomes, increase the negative outcomes, and/or increase the inputs of others (as when adolescents cause teachers and parents to work harder through their incorrigible behavior).

Emotional Coping Strategies.   Finally, individuals may cope by acting directly on the negative emotions that result from adversity. Rosenberg (1990), Thoits (1984, 1989, 1990, 1991b), and others list several strategies of emotional coping. They include the use of drugs such as stimulants and depressants, physical exercise and deep-breathing techniques, meditation, biofeedback and progressive relaxation, and the behavioral manipulation of expressive gestures through playacting or "expression work." In all of these examples, the focus is on alleviating negative emotions rather than cognitively reinterpreting or behaviorally altering the situation that produced those emotions. . . .

Predicting the Use of Delinquent versus Nondelinquent Adaptations

The above typology suggests that there are many ways to cope with strain—only some of which involve delinquency. And data from the stress literature suggest that individuals vary in the extent to which they use the different strategies (Compas et al., 1988; Menaghan, 1983; Pearlin and Schooler, 1978). These facts go a long way toward explaining the weak support for strain theory. With certain limited exceptions, the strategies are not taken into account in tests of strain theory.

The existence of the above coping strategies poses a serious problem for strain theory. If strain theory is to have any value, it must be able to explain the selection of delinquent versus nondelinquent adaptations. This issue has, of course, been raised before. Critics contend that Merton and other strain theorists fail to explain adequately why only *some* strained individuals turn to delinquency. This issue, however, is all the more pressing when one considers the full range of nondelinquent adaptations to strain listed above. It is therefore important to specify those factors that influence the choice of delinquent versus nondelinquent coping strategies. . . .

Constraints to Nondelinquent and Delinquent Coping.   While there are many adaptations to objective strain, those adaptations are not equally available to everyone. Individuals are constrained in their choice of adaptation(s) by a variety of internal and external factors. The following is a partial list of such factors.

Initial Goals/Values/Identities of the Individual. If the objective strain affects goals/values/identities that are high in absolute and relative importance, and if the individual has few alternative goals/values/identities in which to seek refuge, it will be more difficult to relegate strain to an unimportant area of one's life (see Agnew, 1986; Thoits, 1991a). This is especially the case if the goals/values/identities receive strong social and cultural support (see below). As a result, strain will be more likely to lead to delinquency in such cases.

Individual Coping Resources. A wide range of traits can be listed in this area, including temperament, intelligence, creativity, problem-solving skills, interpersonal skills, self-efficacy, and self-esteem. These traits affect the selection of coping strategies by influencing the individual's sensitivity to objective strains and ability to engage in cognitive, emotional, and behavioral coping (Agnew, 1991; Averill, 1982; Bernard, 1990; Compas, 1987; Edmunds and Kendrick, 1980; Slaby and Guerra, 1988; Tavris, 1984). . . .

Conventional Social Support. . . . The major types of social support, in fact, correspond to the major types of coping listed above. Thus, there is informational support, instrumental support, and emotional support (House, 1981). Adolescents with conventional social supports, then, should be better able to respond to objective strains in a nondelinquent manner.

Constraints to Delinquent Coping. The crime/delinquency literature has focused on certain variables that constrain delinquent coping. They include (1) the costs and benefits of engaging in delinquency in a particular situation (Clarke and Cornish, 1985), (2) the individual's level of social control (see Hirschi 1969), and (3) the possession of those "illegitimate means" necessary for many delinquent acts (see Agnew, 1991a, for a full discussion).

Macro-Level Variables. The larger social environment may affect the probability of delinquent versus nondelinquent coping by affecting all of the above factors. First, the social environment may affect coping by influencing the importance attached to selected goals/values/identities. For example, certain ethnographic accounts suggest that there is a strong social and cultural emphasis on the goals of money/status among certain segments of the urban poor. Many poor individuals, in particular, are in a situation in which (1) they face strong economic/status demands, (2) people around them stress the importance of money/status on a regular basis, and (3) few alternative goals are given cultural support (Anderson, 1978; MacLeod, 1987; Sullivan, 1989). As such, these individuals should face more difficulty in cognitively minimizing the importance of money and status.

Second, the larger social environment may affect the individual's sensitivity to particular strains by influencing the individual's beliefs regarding what is and is not adverse. The subculture of violence thesis, for example, is predicated on the assumption that young black males in urban slums are taught that a wide range of provocations and insults are highly adverse. Third, the social environment may influence the individual's ability to minimize cognitively the severity of objective strain. Individuals in some environments are regularly provided with external information about their accomplishments and failings (see Faunce, 1989), and their attempts at cognitively distorting such information are quickly challenged. . . .

Fourth, certain social environments may make it difficult to engage in behavioral coping of a nondelinquent nature. Agnew (1985a) has argued that adolescents often find it difficult to escape legally from negative stimuli, especially negative stimuli encountered in the school, family, and neighborhood. Also, adolescents often lack the resources to negotiate successfully with adults, such as parents and teachers (although see Agnew, 1991a). Similar arguments might be made for the urban underclass. They often lack the resources to negotiate successfully with many others, and they often find it difficult to escape legally from adverse environments—by, for example, quitting their job (if they have a job) or moving to another neighborhood.

The larger social environment, then, may affect individual coping in a variety of ways. And certain groups, such as adolescents and the urban underclass, may face special constraints that make nondelinquent coping more difficult. This may explain the higher rate of deviance among these groups.

Factors Affecting the Disposition to Delinquency.   The selection of delinquent versus nondelinquent coping strategies is not only dependent on the constraints to coping, but also on the adolescent's disposition to engage in delinquent versus nondelinquent coping. This disposition is a function of (1) certain temperamental variables (see Tonry et al., 1991), (2) the prior learning history of the adolescent, particularly the extent to which delinquency was reinforced in the past (Bandura, 1973; Berkowitz, 1982), (3) the adolescent's beliefs, particularly the rules defining the appropriate response to provocations (Bernard's, 1990, "regulative rules"), and (4) the adolescent's attributions regarding the causes of his or her adversity. Adolescents who attribute their adversity to others are much more likely to become angry, and as argued earlier, that anger creates a strong predisposition to delinquency. . . .

A key variable affecting several of the above factors is association with delinquent peers. It has been argued that adolescents who associate with delinquent peers are more likely to be exposed to delinquent models and beliefs and to receive reinforcement for delinquency (see especially, Akers, 1985). It may also be the case that delinquent peers increase the likelihood that adolescents will attribute their adversity to others. . . .

Conclusion

Much of the recent theoretical work in criminology has focused on the integration of different delinquency theories. This paper has taken an alternative track and, following Hirschi's (1979) advice, has focused on the refinement of a single theory. The general strain theory builds upon traditional strain theory in criminology in several ways. First, the general strain theory points to several new sources of strain. In particular, it focuses on three categories of strain or negative relationships with others: (1) the actual or anticipated failure to achieve positively valued goals, (2) the actual or anticipated removal of positively valued stimuli, and (3) the actual or anticipated presentation of negative stimuli. Most current strain theories in criminology only focus on strain as the failure to achieve positively valued goals, and even then the focus is only on the disjunction between aspirations and expectations/actual achievements. The disjunctions between expectations and achievements and just/fair outcomes and achievements are ignored. The general strain theory, then, significantly expands the focus of strain theory to include all types of negative relations between the individual and others.

Second, the general strain theory more precisely specifies the relationship between strain and delinquency, pointing out that strain is likely to have a cumulative effect on delinquency after a certain threshold level is reached. The theory also points to certain relevant dimensions of strain that should be considered in empirical research, including the magnitude, recency, duration, and clustering of strainful events.

Third, the general strain theory provides a more comprehensive account of the cognitive, behavioral, and emotional adaptations to strain. This account sheds additional light on the reasons why many strained individuals do *not* turn to delinquency, and it may prove useful in devising strategies to prevent and control delinquency. Individuals, in particular, may be taught those nondelinquent coping strategies found to be most effective in preventing delinquency.

Fourth, the general strain theory more fully describes those factors affecting the choice of delinquent versus nondelinquent adaptations. The failure to consider such factors is a fundamental reason for the weak empirical support for strain theory. . . .

Strain theory is the only major theory to focus explicitly on negative relations with others and to argue that delinquency results from the negative affect caused by such relations. As such, it complements social control and differential association/social learning theory in a fundamental way. It is hoped that the general strain theory will revive interest in negative relations and cause criminologists to "bring the bad back in."

Note

1. Some researchers have argued that it is often difficult to distinguish the presentation of negative stimuli from the removal of positive stimuli (Michael, 1973; Van Houten, 1983; Zillman, 1979). Suppose, for example, that an adolescent argues with parents. Does this represent the presentation of negative stimuli (the arguing) or the removal of positive stimuli (harmonious relations with one's parents)? The point is a valid one, yet the distinction between the two types of strain still seems useful since it helps ensure that all major types of strain are considered by researchers.

References

Adams, J. Stacy. 1963. "Toward an understanding of inequity." *Journal of Abnormal and Social Psychology* 67:422–436.

————.1965. "Inequity in social exchange." In Leonard Berkowitz (ed.), *Advances in Experimental Social Psychology*. New York: Academic Press.

Agnew, Robert. 1985a. "A revised strain theory of delinquency." *Social Forces* 64:151–167.

————.1985b. "Neutralizing the impact of crime." *Criminal Justice and Behavior* 12:221–239.

————.1989. "A longitudinal test of the revised strain theory." *Journal of Quantitative Criminology* 5:373–387.

————.1991. "Adolescent resources and delinquency." *Criminology* 28:535–566.

Agnew, Robert and Diane Jones. 1988. "Adapting to deprivation: An examination of inflated educational expectations." *Sociological Quarterly* 29:315–337.

Anderson, Elijah. 1978. *A Place on the Corner*. Chicago: University of Chicago Press.

Averill, James R. 1982. *Anger and Aggression*. New York: Springer-Verlag.

Bandura, Albert. 1973. *Aggression: A Social Leaning Analysis*. Englewood Cliffs, NJ: Prentice-Hall.

Berger, Joseph, Morris Zelditch, Jr., Bo Anderson, and Bernard Cohen. 1972. "Structural aspects of distributive justice: A status-value formulation." In Joseph Berger, Morris Zelditch, Jr., and Bo Anderson (eds.), *Sociological Theories in Progress*. New York: Houghton Mifflin.

Berkowitz, Leonard. 1978. "Whatever happened to the frustration-aggression hypothesis?" *American Behavioral Scientist* 21:691–708.

————.1982. "Aversive conditions as stimuli to aggression." In Leonard Berkowitz (ed.), *Advances in Experimental Social Psychology*. Vol. 15. New York: Academic Press.

Bernard, Thomas J. 1990. "Angry aggression among the truly disadvantaged." *Criminology* 28:73–96.

Blau, Peter. 1964. *Exchange and Power in Social Life*. New York: John Wiley & Sons.

Clarke, Ronald V. and Derek B. Cornish. 1985. "Modeling offenders' decisions: A framework for research and policy." In Michael Tonry and Norval Morris (eds.), *Crime and Justice: An Annual Review of Research*. Vol. 6. Chicago: University of Chicago Press.

Cloward, Richard A. and Lloyd E. Ohlin. 1960. *Delinquency and Opportunity*. New York: Free Press.

Cohen, Albert K. 1955. *Delinquent Boys*. New York: Free Press.

Compas, Bruce E. 1987. "Coping with stress during childhood and adolescence." *Psychological Bulletin* 101:393–403.

Compas, Bruce E., Vanessa L. Malcarne, and Karen M. Fondacaro. 1988. "Coping with stressful events in older children and young adolescents." *Journal of Consulting and Clinical Psychology* 56:405–411.

Cook, Karen S., and Karen A. Hegtvedt. 1983. "Distributive justice, equity, and equality." *Annual Review of Sociology* 9:217–241.

Cook, Karen S. and Toshio Yamagishi. 1983. "Social determinants of equity judgments: The problem of multidimensional input." In David M. Messick and Karen S. Cook (eds.), *Equity Theory: Psychological and Sociological Perspectives*. New York: Praeger.

Della Fave, L. Richard. 1980. "The meek shall not inherit the earth: Self-evaluations and the legitimacy of stratification." *American Sociological Review* 45:955–971.

Donnerstein, Edward and Elaine Hatfield. 1982. "Aggression and equity." In Jerald Greenberg and Ronald L. Cohen (eds.), *Equity and Justice in Social Behavior*. New York: Academic Press.

Edmunds, G. and D. C. Kendrick. 1980. *The Measurement of Human Aggressiveness*. New York: John Wiley & Sons.

Hirschi, Travis. 1969. *Causes of Delinquency*. Berkeley: University of California Press.

————.1979. "Separate and unequal is better." *Journal of Research in Crime and Delinquency* 16:34–38.

Hirschi, Travis, and Michael Gottfredson. 1986. "The distinction between crime and criminality." In Timothy F. Hartnagel and Robert A. Silverman (eds.), *Critique and Explanation*. New Brunswick, NJ: Transaction Books.

Homans, George C. 1961. *Social Behavior: Its Elementary Forms*. New York: Harcourt, Brace and World.

Jasso, Guillermina and Peter H. Rossi. 1977. "Distributive justice and earned income." *American Sociological Review* 42:639–651.

Kemper, Theodore D. 1978. *A Social Interactional Theory of Emotions*. New York: John Wiley & Sons.

Kluegel, James R. and Eliot R. Smith. 1986. *Beliefs about Inequality*. New York: Aldine De Gruyter.

MacLeod, Jay. 1987. *Ain't No Makin' It*. Boulder, CO: Westview Press.

Menaghan, Elizabeth. 1983. "Individual coping efforts: Moderators of the relationship between life stress and mental health outcomes." In Howard B. Kaplan (ed.), *Psychosocial Stress: Trends in Theory and Research*. New York: Academic Press.

Merton, Robert. 1938. "Social structure and anomie." *American Sociological Review* 3:672–682.

Michael, Jack. 1973. "Positive and negative reinforcement, a distinction that is no longer necessary; or a better way: to talk about bad things." In Eugene Ramp and George Semb (eds.), *Behavior Analysis: Areas of Research and Application.* Englewood Cliffs NJ: Prentice-Hall.

Mickelson, Roslyn Arlin. 1990. "The attitude-achievement paradox among black adolescents." *Sociology of Education* 63:44–61.

Morgan, Rick L. and David Heise. 1988. "Structure of emotions." *Social Psychology Quarterly* 51:19–31.

Pearlin, Leonard I. and Carmi Schooler. 1978. "The structure of coping." *Journal of Health and Social Behavior* 19:2–21.

Rosenberg, Morris. 1990. "Reflexivity and emotions." *Social Psychology Quarterly* 53:3–12.

Ross, Michael, John Thibaut, and Scott Evenback. 1971. "Some determinants of the intensity of social protest." *Journal of Experimental Social Psychology* 7:401–418.

Slaby, Ronald G. and Nancy G. Guerra. 1988. "Cognitive mediators of aggression in adolescent offenders: 1." *Developmental Psychology* 24:580–588.

Sullivan, Mercer L. 1989. *Getting Paid.* Ithaca, NY: Cornell University Press.

Suls, Jerry M. 1977. "Social comparison theory and research: An overview from 1954." In Jerry M. Suls and Richard L. Miller (eds.), *Social Comparison Processes.* New York: Hemisphere.

Tavris, Carol. 1984. "On the wisdom of counting to ten." In Philip Shaver (ed.), *Review of Personality and Social Psychology:* 5. Beverly Hills, CA: Sage.

Thibaut, John W. and Harold H. Kelley. 1959. *The Social Psychology of Groups.* New York: John Wiley & Sons.

Thoits, Peggy. 1984. "Coping, social support, and psychological outcomes: The central role of emotion." In Philip Shaver (ed.), *Review of Personality and Social Psychology:* 5. Beverly Hills, CA: Sage.

———.1989. "The sociology of emotions." In W. Richard Scott and Judith Blake (eds.), *Annual Review of Sociology.* Vol. 15. Palo Alto, CA: Annual Reviews.

———.1990. "Emotional deviance research." In Theodore D. Kemper (ed.), *Research Agendas in the Sociology of Emotions.* Albany: State University of New York Press.

———.1991a. "On merging identity theory and stress research." *Social Psychology Quarterly* 54:101–112.

———.1991b. "Patterns of coping with controllable and uncontrollable events." In E. Mark Cummings, Anita L. Greene, and Katherine H. Karraker (eds.), *Life-Span Developmental Psychology: Perspectives on Stress and Coping.* Hillsdale, NJ: Lawrence Erlbaum.

Tonry, Michael, Lloyd E. Ohlin, and David P. Farrington. 1991. *Human Development and Criminal Behavior.* New York: Springer-Verlag.

Van Houten, Ron. 1983. "Punishment: From the animal laboratory to the applied setting." In Saul Axelrod and Jack Apsche (eds.), *The Effects of Punishment on Human Behavior.* New York: Academic Press.

Walster, Elaine, Ellen Berscheid, and G. William Walster. 1973. "New directions in equity research." *Journal of Personality and Social Psychology* 25:151–176.

Walster, Elaine, G. William Walster, and Ellen Berscheid. 1978. *Equity: Theory and Research.* Boston: Allyn & Bacon.

Zillman, Dolf. 1979. *Hostility and Aggression.* Hillsdale, NJ: Lawrence Erlbaum.

29

Culture Conflict and Crime

Thorsten Sellin

Culture Conflicts as Conflicts of Cultural Codes

Conflicts of conduct norms may arise in a different manner from that just described. There are social groups on the surface of the earth which possess complexes of conduct norms which, due to differences in the mode of life and the social values evolved by these groups, appear to set them apart from other groups in many or most respects. We may expect conflicts of norms when the rural dweller moves to the city, but we assume that he has absorbed the basic norms of the culture which comprises both town and country. How much greater is not the conflict likely to be when Orient and Occident meet, or when the Corsican mountaineer is transplanted to the lower East Side of New York. Conflicts of cultures are inevitable when the norms of one cultural or subcultural area migrate to or come in contact with those of another, and it is interesting to note that most of the specific researches on culture conflict and delinquency have been concerned with this aspect of conflict rather than the one mentioned earlier.

Conflicts between the norms of divergent cultural codes may arise

1. when these codes clash on the border of contiguous culture areas;
2. when, as may be the case with legal norms, the law of one cultural group is extended to cover the territory of another; or
3. when members of one cultural group migrate to another.[1]

Speck, for instance, notes that "where the bands popularly known as Montagnais have come more and more into contact with Whites, their reputation has fallen lower among the traders who have known them through commercial relationships within that period. The accusation is made that they have become less honest in connection with their debts, less trustworthy with property, less truthful, and more inclined to alcoholism and sexual freedom as contacts with the frontier towns have become easier for them. Richard White reports in 1933 unusual instances of Naskapi breaking into traders' storehouses."[2]

Source: Thorsten Sellin, *Culture Conflict and Crime,* Bulletin No. 41 (New York: Social Science Research Council, 1938), pp. 63–70. Footnotes renumbered.

Similar illustrations abound in the works of the cultural anthropologists. We need only to recall the effect on the American Indian of the culture conflicts induced by our policy of acculturation by guile and force. In this instance, it was not merely contact with the white man's culture, his religion, his business methods, and his liquor, which weakened the tribal mores. In addition, the Indian became subject to the white man's law and this brought conflicts as well, as has always been the case when legal norms have been imposed upon a group previously ignorant of them. Maunier,[3] in discussing the diffusion of French law in Algeria, recently stated:

> In introducing the *Code Pénal* in our colonies, as we do, we transform into offenses the ancient usages of the inhabitants which their customs permitted or imposed. Thus, among the Khabyles of Algeria, the killing of adulterous wives is ritual murder committed by the father or brother of the wife and not by her husband, as elsewhere. The woman having been sold by her family to her husband's family, the honor of her relatives is soiled by her infidelity. Her father or brother has the right and the duty to kill her in order to cleanse by her blood the honor of her relatives. Murder in revenge is also a duty, from family to family, in case of murder of or even in case of insults to a relative: the vendetta, called the *rekba* in Khabylian, is imposed by the law of honor. But these are crimes in French law! Murder for revenge, being premeditated and planned, is assassination, punishable by death! . . . What happens, then, often when our authorities pursue the criminal, guilty of an offense against public safety as well as against morality: public enemy of the French order, but who has acted in accord with a respected custom? The witnesses of the assassination, who are his relatives, or neighbors, fail to lay charges against the assassin; when they are questioned, they pretend to know nothing; and the pursuit is therefore useless. A French magistrate has been able to speak of the 'conspiracy of silence among the Algerians'; a conspiracy aiming to preserve traditions, always followed and obeyed, against their violation by our power. This is the tragic aspect of the conflict of laws. A recent decree forbids the husband among the Khabyles to profit arbitrarily by the power given him according to this law to repudiate his wife, demanding that her new husband pay an exorbitant price for her-this is the custom of the *lefdi*. Earlier, one who married a repudiated wife paid nothing to the former husband. It appears that the first who tried to avail himself of the new law was killed for violating the old custom. The abolition of the ancient law does not always occur without protest or opposition. That which is a crime was a duty; and the order which we cause to reign is sometimes established to the detriment of "superstition;" it is the gods and the spirits, it is believed, that would punish any one who fails to revenge his honor.

When Soviet law was extended to Siberia, similar effects were observed. Anossow[4] and Wirschubski[5] both relate that women among the Siberian tribes, who in obedience to the law, laid aside their veils were killed by their relatives for violating one of the most sacred norms of their tribes.

The relations between delinquency and the migration of the members of one cultural group to the area of another will be discussed later in this chapter.

We have noted that culture conflicts are the natural outgrowth of processes of social differentiation, which produce an infinity of social groupings, each with its own definitions of life situations, its own interpretations of social relationships, its own ignorance or misunderstanding of the social values of other groups. The transformation of a culture from a homogeneous and well-integrated type to a heterogeneous and disintegrated type is therefore accompanied by an increase of conflict situations. Conversely, the operation of integrating processes will reduce the number of conflict situations. Such conflicts within a changing culture may be distinguished from those created when different cultural systems come in contact with one another, regardless of the character or stage of development of these systems. In either case, the conduct of members of a group involved in the conflict of codes will in some respects be judged abnormal by the other group.

The Study of Culture Conflicts

In the study of culture conflicts, some scholars have been concerned with the effect of such conflicts on the conduct of specific persons, an approach which is naturally preferred by psychologists and psychiatrists and by sociologists who have used the life history technique. These scholars view the conflict as internal. Wirth[6] states categorically that a culture "conflict can be said to be a factor in delinquency only if the individual feels it or acts as if it were present." Culture conflict is mental conflict, but the character of this conflict is viewed differently by the various disciplines which use this term. Freudian psychiatrists[7] regard it as a struggle between deeply rooted biological urges which demand expression and the culturally created rules which give rise to inhibitive mechanisms which thwart this expression and drive them below the conscious level of the mind, whence they rise either by ruse in some socially acceptable disguise, as abnormal conduct when the inhibiting mechanism breaks down, or as neuroses when it works too well. The sociologist, on the other hand, thinks of mental conflict as being primarily the clash between antagonistic conduct norms incorporated in personality. "Mental conflict in the person," says Burgess in discussing the case presented by Shaw in the *The Jack-Roller*, "may always be explained in terms of the conflict of divergent cultures."[8]

If this view is accepted, sociological research on culture conflict and its relationships to abnormal conduct would have to be strictly limited to a study of the personality of cultural hybrids. Significant studies could be conducted only by the life-history case technique applied to persons in whom the conflict is internalized, appropriate control groups being utilized, of course. . . .

The absence of mental conflict, in the sociological sense, may, however, be well studied in terms of culture conflict. An example may make this clear. A few years ago a Sicilian father in New Jersey killed the sixteen-year-old seducer of his daughter, expressing surprise at his arrest since he had merely defended his family honor in a traditional way. In this case a mental conflict in the sociological sense did not exist. The conflict was external and occurred between cultural codes or norms. We may assume that where such conflicts occur violations of norms will arise merely because persons who have absorbed the norms of one cultural group or area migrate to another and that such conflict will continue so long as the acculturation process has not been completed. . . . Only then may the violations be regarded in terms of mental conflict.

If culture conflict may be regarded as sometimes personalized, or mental, and sometimes as occurring entirely in an impersonal way solely as a conflict of group codes, it is obvious that research should not be confined to the investigation of mental conflicts and that contrary to Wirth's categorical statement that it is impossible to demonstrate the existence of a culture conflict "objectively . . . by a comparison between two cultural codes"[9] this procedure has not only a definite function, but may be carried out by researches employing techniques which are familiar to the sociologist.

The emphasis on the life history technique has grown out of the assumption that "the experiences of one person at the same time reveals the life activities of his group" and that "habit in the individual is an expression of custom in society."[10] This is undoubtedly one valid approach. Through it we may hope to discover generalizations of a scientific nature by studying persons who (1) have drawn their norms of conduct from a variety of groups with conflicting norms, or (2) who possess norms drawn from a group whose code is in conflict with that of the group which judges the conduct. In the former case alone can we speak of mental or internal culture conflict; in the latter, the conflict is external.

If the conduct norms of a group are, with reference to a given life situation, inconsistent, or if two groups possess inconsistent norms, we may assume that the members of these various groups will individually reflect such group attitudes. Paraphrasing Burgess, the experiences of a group will reveal the life activities of its members. While these norms can, no doubt, be best established by a study of a sufficient number of representative group members, they may for some groups at least be fixed with sufficient certainty to serve research purposes by a study of the social institutions, the administration of justice, the novel, the drama, the press, and other expressions of group attitudes. The identification of the groups in question having been made, it might be possible to determine to what extent such conflicts are reflected in the conduct of their members. Comparative studies based on the violation rates of the members of such groups, the trends of such rates, etc., would dominate this approach to the problem.

In conclusion, then, culture conflict may be studied either as mental conflict or as a conflict of cultural codes. The criminologist will naturally tend to concentrate on such conflicts between legal and nonlegal conduct norms. The concept of conflict fails to give him more than a general framework of reference for research. In practice, it has, however, become nearly synonymous with conflicts between the norms of cultural systems or areas. Most researches which have employed it have been done on immigrant or race groups in the United States, perhaps due to the ease with which such groups may be identified, the existence of more statistical data recognizing such groupings, and the conspicuous differences between some immigrant norms and our norms. . . .

Notes

1. This is unfortunately not the whole story, for with the rapid growth of impersonal communication, the written (press, literature) and the spoken word (radio, talkie), knowledge concerning divergent conduct norms no longer grows solely out of direct personal contact with their carriers. And out of such conflicts grow some violations of custom and of law which would not have occurred without them.
2. Speck, Frank G., *op. cit.*, p. 589.
3. Maunier, René. "La diffusion du droit français en Algérie." Harvard Tercentenary Publications, *Independence, Convergence, and Borrowing in Institutions, Thought, and Art* (Cambridge: Harvard University Press, 1937), pp. 84–85.
4. Anossow, J. J. "Die volkstümlichen Verbrechen im Strafkodex der USSR." *Monatsschrift für Kriminalpsychologie und Strafrechtsreform.* 24:534–37 (September 1933).
5. Wirschubski, Gregor. "Der Schutz der Sittlichkeit im Sowjetstrafrecht." *Zeitschrift für*

die gesamte Strafrechtswissenschaft. 51:317–28 (1931).

6. Wirth, Louis, "Culture Conflict and Misconduct." *Social Forces*. 9:484–92. (June 1931), p. 490. *Cf.* Allport, Floyd H. "Culture Conflict versus the Individual as Factors in Delinquency." *Ibid.*, pp. 493–97.

7. White, William A. *Crimes and Criminals* (New York: Farrar & Rinehart, 1933). Healy, William. *Mental Conflict and Misconduct* (Boston: Little, Brown & Co. 1917). Alexander, Franz and Healy, William. *Roots of Crime* (New York: Alfred A. Knopf, 1935).

8. Burgess, Ernest W. in Clifford R. Shaw's *The Jack-Roller* (Chicago: University of Chicago Press, 1930), pp. 184–197, p. 186.

9. Wirth, Louis, *op. cit.*, p. 490. It should be noted that Wirth also states that culture should be studied "on the objective side" and that "the sociologist is not primarily interested in personality but in culture."

10. Burgess. Ernest W., *op. cit.*, p. 186.

30

Differential Systems of Values

Clifford R. Shaw   Henry D. McKay

In general, the more subtle differences between types of communities in Chicago may be encompassed within the general proposition that in the areas of low rates of delinquents there is more or less uniformity, consistency, and universality of conventional values and attitudes with respect to child care, conformity to law, and related matters; whereas in the high-rate areas systems of competing and conflicting moral values have developed. Even though in the latter situation conventional traditions and institutions are dominant, delinquency has developed as a powerful competing way of life. It derives its impelling force in the boy's life from the fact that it provides a means of securing economic gain, prestige, and other human satisfactions and is embodied in delinquent groups and criminal organizations, many of which have great influence, power, and prestige.

In the areas of high economic status where the rates of delinquents are low there is, in general, a similarity in the attitudes of the residents with reference to conventional values, as has been said, especially those related to the welfare of children. This is illustrated by the practical unanimity of opinion as to the desirability of education and constructive leisure-time activities and of the need for a general health program. It is shown, too, in the subtle, yet easily recognizable, pressure exerted upon children to keep them engaged in conventional activities, and in the resistance offered by the community to behavior which threatens the conventional values. It does not follow that all the activities participated in by members of the community are lawful; but, since any unlawful pursuits are likely to be carried out in other parts of the city, children living in the low-rate communities are, on the whole, insulated from direct contact with these deviant forms of adult behavior.

In the middle-class areas and the areas of high economic status, moreover, the similarity of attitudes and values as to social control is expressed in institutions and voluntary associations designed to perpetuate and protect these values. Among these may be included such organizations as the parent-teachers associations, women's clubs, service clubs, churches, neighborhood centers, and the like. Where these institutions represent dominant values, the child is exposed to, and participates in a significant way in one mode of life only. While he may have knowledge of alternatives, they are not integral parts of the system in which he participates.

Source: Reprinted with permission from Clifford R. Shaw and Henry D. McKay, *Juvenile Delinquency in Urban Areas*, pp. 164–170, 435–441. Copyright © 1942 The University of Chicago Press. Footnotes renumbered. Selection title taken from a subheading at beginning of excerpt.

In contrast, the areas of low economic status, where the rates of delinquents are high, are characterized by wide diversity in norms and standards of behavior. The moral values range from those that are strictly conventional to those in direct opposition to conventionality as symbolized by the family, the church, and other institutions common to our general society. The deviant values are symbolized by groups and institutions ranging from adult criminal gangs engaged in theft and the marketing of stolen goods, on the one hand, to quasi-legitimate businesses and the rackets through which partial or complete control of legitimate business is sometimes exercised, on the other. Thus, within the same community, theft may be defined as right and proper in some groups and as immoral, improper, and undesirable in others. In some groups wealth and prestige are secured through acts of skill and courage in the delinquent or criminal world, while in neighboring groups any attempt to achieve distinction in this manner would result in extreme disapprobation. Two conflicting systems of economic activity here present roughly equivalent opportunities for employment and for promotion. Evidence of success in the criminal world is indicated by the presence of adult criminals whose clothes and automobiles indicate unmistakably that they have prospered in their chosen fields. The values missed and the greater risks incurred are not so clearly apparent to the young.

Children living in such communities are exposed to a variety of contradictory standards and forms of behavior rather than to a relatively consistent and conventional pattern.[1] More than one type of moral institution and education are available to them. A boy may be familiar with, or exposed to, either the system of conventional activities or the system of criminal activities, or both. Similarly, he may participate in the activities of groups which engage mainly in delinquent activities, those concerned with conventional pursuits, or those which alternate between the two worlds. His attitudes and habits will be formed largely in accordance with the extent to which he participates in and becomes identified with one or the other of these several types of groups.

Conflicts of values necessarily arise when boys are brought in contact with so many forms of conduct not reconcilable with conventional morality as expressed in church and school. A boy may be found guilty of delinquency in the court, which represents the values of the larger society, for an act which has had at least tacit approval in the community in which he lives. It is perhaps common knowledge in the neighborhood that public funds are embezzled and that favors and special consideration can be received from some public officials through the payment of stipulated sums; the boys assume that all officials can be influenced in this way. They are familiar with the location of illegal institutions in the community and with the procedures through which such institutions are opened and kept in operation; they know where stolen goods can be sold and the kinds of merchandise for which there is a ready market; they know what the rackets are; and they see in fine clothes, expensive cars, and other lavish expenditures the evidences of wealth among those who openly engage in illegal activities. All boys in the city have some knowledge of these activities; but in the inner-city areas they are known intimately, in terms of personal relationships, while in other sections they enter the child's experience through more impersonal forms of communication, such as motion pictures, the newspaper, and the radio.

Other types of evidence tending to support the existence of diverse systems of values in various areas are to be found in the data on delinquency and crime. In the previous chapter, variations by local areas in the number and rates of adult offenders were presented. When translated into its significance for children, the presence of a large number of adult criminals in certain areas means that children there are in contact with crime as a career and with the criminal way of life, symbolized by organized crime. In this type of organization can be seen the delegation of authority, the division of labor, the specialization of function, and all the other characteristics common to well-organized business institutions wherever found.

Similarly, the delinquency data presented graphically on spot maps and rate maps in the preceding pages give plausibility to the existence of a coherent system of values supporting delinquent acts. In making these interpretations it should be remembered that delinquency is essentially group behavior. A study of boys brought into the Juvenile Court of Cook County during the year 1928[2] revealed that 81.8 percent of these boys committed the offenses for which they were brought to court as members of groups. And when the offenses were limited to stealing, it was found that 89 percent of all offenders were taken to court as group or gang members. In many additional cases where the boy actually committed his offense alone, the influence of companions was, nevertheless, apparent. This point is illustrated in certain cases of boys charged with stealing from members of their own families, where the theft clearly reflects the influence and instigation of companions, and in instances where the problems of the boy charged with incorrigibility reveal conflicting values, those of the family competing with those of the delinquent group for his allegiance.

The heavy concentration of delinquency in certain areas means, therefore, that boys living in these areas are in contact not only with individuals who engage in proscribed activity but also with groups which sanction such behavior and exert pressure upon their members to conform to group standards. Examination of the distribution map reveals that, in contrast with the areas of concentration of delinquents, there are many other communities where the cases are so widely dispersed that the chances of a boy's having intimate contact with other delinquents or with delinquent groups are comparatively slight.

The importance of the concentration of delinquents is seen most clearly when the effect is viewed in a temporal perspective. The maps representing distribution of delinquents at successive periods indicate that, year after year, decade after decade, the same areas have been characterized by these concentrations. This means that delinquent boys in these areas have contact not only with other delinquents who are their contemporaries but also with older offenders, who in turn had contact with delinquents preceding them, and so on back to the earliest history of the neighborhood. This contact means that the traditions of delinquency can be and are transmitted down through successive generations of boys, in much the same way that language and other social forms are transmitted.

The cumulative effect of this transmission of tradition is seen in two kinds of data, which will be presented here only very briefly. The first is a study of offenses, which reveals that certain types of delinquency have tended to characterize certain city areas. The execution of each type involves techniques which must be learned from others who have participated in the same activity. Each involves specialization of function, and each has its own terminology and standards of behavior. Jack-rolling, shoplifting, stealing from junkmen, and stealing automobiles are examples of offenses with well-developed techniques, passed on by one generation to the next.

The second body of evidence on the effects of the continuity of tradition within delinquent groups comprises the results of a study of the contacts between delinquents, made through the use of official records.[3] The names of boys who appeared together in court were taken, and the range of their association with other boys whose names appeared in the same records was then analyzed and charted. It was found that some members of each delinquent group had participated in offenses in the company of other older boys, and so on, backward in time in an unbroken continuity as far as the records were available. The continuity thus traced is roughly comparable to that which might be established among baseball players through their appearance in official lineups or regularly scheduled games. In baseball it is known that the techniques are transmitted through practice in back yards, playgrounds, sand lots, and in other places where boys congregate. Similarly in the case of delinquency traditions, if an unbroken continuity can be traced through formal institutions such as the Juvenile Court, the actual contacts among delinquents in the community must be numerous, continuous, and vital.

The way in which boys are inducted into unconventional behavior has been revealed by large numbers of case studies of youths living in areas where the rates of delinquents are high. Through the boy's own life-story the wide range of contacts with other boys has been revealed. These stories indicate how at early ages the boys took part with older boys in delinquent activities, and how, as they themselves acquired experience, they initiated others into the same pursuits. These cases reveal also the steps through which members are incorporated into the delinquent group organization. Often at early ages boys engage in malicious mischief and simple acts of stealing. As their careers develop, they become involved in more serious offenses, and finally become skilled workmen or specialists in some particular field of criminal activity. In each of these phases the boy is supported by the sanction and the approbation of the delinquent group to which he belongs. . . .

Summary and Interpretation

It is clear from the data included in this volume that there is a direct relationship between conditions existing in local communities of American cities and differential rates of delinquents and criminals. Communities with high rates have social and economic characteristics which differentiate them from communities with low rates. Delinquency—particularly group delinquency, which constitutes a preponderance of all officially recorded offenses committed by boys and young men—has its roots in the dynamic life of the community.

It is recognized that the data included in this volume may be interpreted from many different points of view. However, the high degree of consistency in the association between delinquency and other characteristics of the community not only sustains the conclusion that delinquent behavior is related dynamically to the community but also appears to establish that all community characteristics, including delinquency, are products of the operation of general processes more or less common to American cities. Moreover, the fact that in Chicago the rates of delinquents for many years have remained relatively constant in the areas adjacent to centers of commerce and heavy industry, despite successive changes in the nativity and nationality composition of the population, supports emphatically the conclusion that the delinquency-producing factors are inherent in the community.

From the data available it appears that local variations in the conduct of children, as revealed in differential rates of delinquents, reflect the differences in social values, norms, and attitudes to which the children are exposed. In some parts of the city attitudes which support and sanction delinquency are, it seems, sufficiently extensive and dynamic to become the controlling forces in the development of delinquent careers among a relatively large number of boys and young men. These are the low-income areas, where delinquency has developed in the form of a social tradition, inseparable from the life of the local community.

This tradition is manifested in many different ways. It becomes meaningful to the child through the conduct, speech, gestures, and attitudes of persons with whom he has contact. Of particular importance is the child's intimate association with predatory gangs or other forms of delinquent and criminal organization. Through his contacts with these groups and by virtue of his participation in their activities he learns the techniques of stealing, becomes involved in binding relationships with his companions in delinquency, and acquires the attitudes appropriate to his position as a member of such groups. To use the words of Frank Tannenbaum:

> It is the group that sets the pattern, provides the stimulus, gives the rewards in glory and companionship, offers the protection and loyalty, and, most of all, gives the criminal life its ethical content without which it cannot persist.[4]

In these communities many children encounter competing systems of values. Their community, which provides most of the social forms in terms of which their life will be organized, presents conflicting possibilities. A career in delinquency and crime is one alternative, which often becomes real and enticing to the boy because it offers the promise of economic gain, prestige, and companionship and because he becomes acquainted with it through relationships with persons whose esteem and approbation are vital to his security and to the achievement of satisfactory status. In this situation the delinquent group may become both the incentive and the mechanism for initiating the boy into a career of delinquency and crime and for sustaining him in such a career, once he has embarked upon it.

In cases of group delinquency it may be said, therefore, that from the point of view of the delinquent's immediate social world, he is not necessarily disorganized, maladjusted, or antisocial. Within the limits of his social world and in terms of its norms and expectations, he may be a highly organized and well-adjusted person.

The residential communities of higher economic status, where the proportion of persons dealt with as delinquents and criminals is relatively low, stand in sharp contrast to the situation described above. Here the norms and values of the child's social world are more or less uniformly and consistently conventional. Generally speaking, the boy who grows up in this situation is not faced with the problem of making a choice between conflicting systems of moral values. Throughout the range of his contacts in the community he encounters similar attitudes of approval or disapproval. Cases of delinquency are relatively few and sporadic. The system of conventional values in the community is sufficiently pervasive and powerful to control and organize effectively, with few exceptions, the lives of most children and young people.

In both these types of communities the dominant system of values is conventional. In the first, however, a powerful competing system of of delinquency values exists; whereas in the second, such a system, if it exists at all, is not sufficiently extensive and powerful to exercise a strong influence in the lives of many children. Most of the communities of the city fall between these two extremes and represent gradations in the extent to which delinquency has become an established way of life.

It is important to ask what the forces are which give rise to these significant differences in the organized values in different communities. Under what conditions do the conventional forces in the community become so weakened as to tolerate the development of a conflicting system of criminal values? Under what conditions is the conventional community capable of maintaining its integrity and exercising such control over the lives of its members as to check the development of the competing system? Obviously, any discussion of this question at present must be tentative. The data presented in this volume, however, afford a basis for consideration of certain points which may be significant.

It may be observed, in the first instance, that the variations in rates of officially recorded delinquents in communities of the city correspond very closely with variations in economic status. The communities with the highest rates of delinquents are occupied by those segments of the population whose position is most disadvantageous in relation to the distribution of economic, social, and cultural values. Of all the communities in the city, these have the fewest facilities for acquiring the economic goods indicative of status and success in our conventional culture. Residence in the community is in itself an indication of inferior status, from the standpoint of persons residing in the more prosperous areas. It is a handicap in securing employment and in making satisfactory advancement in industry and the professions. Fewer opportunities are provided for securing the training, education, and contacts which facilitate advancement in the fields of business, industry, and the professions.

The communities with the lowest rates of delinquents, on the other hand, occupy a relatively high position in relation to the economic and social hierarchy of the city. Here the residents are relatively much more secure; and adequate provision is offered to young people for securing the material possessions symbolic of success and the education, training, and personal contacts which facilitate their advancement in the conventional careers they may pursue.

Despite these marked differences in the relative position of people in different communities, children and young people in all areas, both rich and poor, are exposed to the luxury values and success patterns of our culture. In school and elsewhere they are also exposed to ideas of equality, freedom, and individual enterprise. Among children and young people residing in low-income areas, interests in acquiring material goods and enhancing personal status are developed which are often difficult to realize by legitimate means because of limited access to the necessary facilities and opportunities.

This disparity in the facilities available to people in different communities for achieving a satisfactory position of social security and prestige is particularly important in relation to delinquency and crime in the urban world. In the city, relationships are largely impersonal. Because of the anonymity in urban life. the individual is freed from much of the scrutiny and control which characterize life in primary-group situations in small towns and rural communities. Personal status and the status of one's community are, to a very great extent, determined by economic achievement. Superior status depends not so much on character as on the possession of those goods and values which symbolize success. Hence, the kind of clothes one wears, the automobile one drives, the type of building in which one lives, and the physical character of one's community become of great importance to the person. To a large degree these are the symbols of his position-the external evidences of the extent to which he has succeeded in the struggle for a living. The urban world, with its anonymity, its greater freedom, the more impersonal character of its relationships, and the varied assortment of economic, social, and cultural backgrounds in its communities, provides a general setting particularly conducive to the development of deviations in moral norms and behavior practices.

In the low-income areas, where there is the greatest deprivation and frustration, where, in the history of the city, immigrant and migrant groups have brought together the widest variety of divergent cultural traditions and institutions, and where there exists the greatest disparity between the social values to which the people aspire and the availability of facilities for acquiring these values in conventional ways, the development of crime as an organized way of life is most marked. Crime, in this situation, may be regarded as one of the means employed by people to acquire, or to attempt to acquire, the economic and social values generally idealized in our culture, which persons in other circumstances acquire by conventional means. While the origin of this tradition of crime is obscure, it can be said that its development in the history of the community has been facilitated by the fact that many persons have, as a result of their criminal activities, greatly improved their economic and social status. Their clothes, cars, and other possessions are unmistakable evidence of this fact. That many of these persons also acquire influence and power in politics and elsewhere is so well known that it does not need elaboration at this point. The power and affluence achieved, at least temporarily, by many persons involved in crime and illegal rackets are well known to the children and youth of the community and are important in determining the character of their ideals.

It may be said, therefore, that the existence of a powerful system of criminal values and relationships in low-income urban areas is the product of a cumulative process extending back into the history of the community and of the city. It is related both to the general character of the urban world and to the fact that the population in these communities has long occupied a disadvantageous position. It has developed in somewhat the same way as have all social traditions, that is, as a means of satisfying certain felt needs within the limits of a particular social and economic framework.

It should be observed that, while the tradition of delinquency and crime is thus a powerful force in certain communities, it is only a part of the community's system of values. As was pointed out previously, the dominant tradition in every community is conventional, even in those having the highest rates of delinquents. The traditionally conventional values are embodied in the family, the church, the school, and many other such institutions and organizations. Since the dominant tradition in the community is conventional, more persons pursue law-abiding careers than careers of delinquency and crime, as might be expected.

In communities occupied by Orientals, even those communities located in the most deteriorated sections of our large cities, the solidarity of Old World cultures and institutions has been preserved to such a marked extent that control of the child is still sufficiently effective to keep at a minimum delinquency and other forms of deviant behavior. As Professor Hayner has pointed out in his chapter on five cities of the Pacific Northwest, the close integration of the Oriental family, the feeling of group responsibility for the behavior of the child, and the desire of these groups to maintain a good reputation in American communities have all been important elements in preserving this cultural solidarity.

It is the assumption of this volume that many factors are important in determining whether a particular child will become involved in delinquency, even in those communities in which a system of delinquent and criminal values exists. Individual and personality differences, as well as differences in family relationships and in contacts with other institutions and groups, no doubt influence greatly his acceptance or rejection of opportunities to engage in delinquent activities. It may be said, however, that if the delinquency tradition were not present and the boys were not thus exposed to it, a preponderance of those who become delinquent in low-income areas would find their satisfactions in activities other than delinquency.

In conclusion, it is not assumed that this theoretical proposition applies to all cases of officially proscribed behavior. It applies primarily to those delinquent activities which become embodied in groups and social organizations. For the most part, these are offenses against property, which comprise a very large proportion of all the cases of boys coming to the attention of the courts.

Implications for Prevention and Treatment

The theoretical formulation set forth in the preceding pages has certain definite implications with regard to the task of dealing with the problem of delinquency in large American cities. Some of the more important may be stated as follows:

1. Any great reduction in the volume of delinquency in large cities probably will not occur except as general changes take place which effect improvements in the economic and social conditions surrounding children in those areas in which the delinquency rates are relatively high.

2. Individualized methods of treatment probably will not be successful in a sufficiently large number of cases to result in any substantial diminution of the volume of delinquency and crime.

3. Treatment and preventive efforts, if they are to achieve general success, should increasingly take the form of broad programs which seek to utilize more effectively the constructive institutional and human resources available in every local community in the city. Tannenbaum states this point vividly: "The criminal is a product of the community, and his own criminal gang is part of the whole community, natural and logical to it; but it is only part of it. In that lies the hope that the rest of the community can do something with the gang as such."[5]

Notes

1. Edwin H. Sutherland has called this process "differential association." See E. H. Sutherland, *Principles of Criminology* (Chicago: J.B. Lippincott Co., 1939), chap. i.
2. Clifford R. Shaw and Henry D. McKay, *Social Factors in Juvenile Delinquency*, Vol. II of *Report on the Causes of Crime*, National Commission on Law Observance and Enforcement, Report No. 13 (Washington, DC: U.S. Government Printing Office, 1931), pp. 191–99.
3. "Contacts between Successive Generations of Delinquent Boys in a Low-Income Area in Chicago" (unpublished study by the Department of Sociology, Illinois Institute for Juvenile Research, 1940).
4. *Crime and the Community* (New York: Ginn & Co., 1938), p. 475.
5. *Op. cit.*, p. 474.

31

The Content of the Delinquent Subculture

Albert K. Cohen

. . . What we see when we look at the delinquent subculture (and we must not even assume that this describes *all juvenile crime*) is that it is *nonutilitarian, malicious* and *negativistic*.

We usually assume that when people steal things, they steal because they want them. They may want them because they can eat them, wear them or otherwise use them; or because they can sell them; or even—if we are given to a psychoanalytic turn of mind—because on some deep symbolic level they substitute or stand for something unconsciously desired but forbidden. All of these explanations have this in common, that they assume that the stealing is a means to an end, namely, the possession of some object of value, and that it is, in this sense, rational and "utilitarian." However, the fact cannot be blinked—and this fact is of crucial importance in defining our problem—that much gang stealing has no such motivation at all. Even where the value of the object stolen is itself a motivating consideration, the stolen sweets are often sweeter than those acquired by more legitimate and prosaic means. In homelier language, stealing "for the hell of it" and apart from considerations of gain and profit is a valued activity to which attaches glory, prowess and profound satisfaction. There is no accounting in rational and utilitarian terms for the effort expended and the danger run in stealing things which are often discarded, destroyed or casually given away. A group of boys enters a store where each takes a hat, a ball or a light bulb. They then move on to another store where these things are covertly exchanged for like articles. Then they move on to other stores to continue the game indefinitely. They steal a basket of peaches, desultorily munch on a few of them and leave the rest to spoil. They steal clothes they cannot wear and toys they will not use. Unquestionably, most delinquents are from the more "needy" and "under-privileged" classes, and unquestionably many things are stolen because they are intrinsically valued. However, a humane and compassionate regard for their economic disabilities should not blind us to the fact that stealing is not merely an alternative means to the acquisition of objects otherwise difficult of attainment.[1]

Can we then account for this stealing by simply describing it as another form of recreation, play or sport? Surely it is that, but why is this form of play so attractive to some and so unappealing to others? Mountain climbing, chess, pinball, number

Source: Reprinted with the permission of The Free Press, a Division of Simon & Schuster Adult Publishing Group, from *Delinquent Boys: The Culture of the Gang* by Albert K. Cohen. Copyright © 1955 by The Free Press. Copyright © renewed 1983 by Albert K. Cohen.

pools and bingo are also different kinds of recreation. Each of us, child or adult, can choose from a host of alternative means for satisfying our common "need" for recreation. But every choice expresses a preference, and every preference reflects something about the chooser or his circumstances that endows the object of his choice with some special quality or virtue. The choice is not self-explanatory nor is it arbitrary or random. Each form of recreation is distributed in a characteristic way among the age, sex and social class sectors of our population. The explanation of these distributions and of the way they change is often puzzling, sometimes fascinating and rarely platitudinous.

By the same logic, it is an imperfect answer to our problem to say: "Stealing is but another way of satisfying the universal desire for status." Nothing is more obvious from numberless case histories of subcultural delinquents that they steal to achieve recognition and to avoid isolation or opprobrium. This is an important insight and part of the foundation on which we shall build. But the question still haunts us: "Why is stealing a claim to status in one group and a degrading blot in another"?

If stealing itself is not motivated by rational, utilitarian considerations, still less are the manifold other activities which constitute the delinquent's repertoire. Throughout there is a kind of *malice* apparent, an enjoyment in the discomfiture of others, a delight in the defiance of taboos itself. Thrasher quotes one gang delinquent:

> We did all kinds of dirty tricks for fun. We'd see a sign, "Please keep the streets clean," but we'd tear it down and say, "We don't feel like keeping it clean." One day we put a can of glue in the engine of a man's car. We would always tear things down. That would make us laugh and feel good, to have so many jokes.[2]

The gang exhibits this gratuitous hostility toward non-gang peers as well as adults. Apart from its more dramatic manifestations in the form of gang wars, there is keen delight in terrorizing "good" children, in driving them from playgrounds and gyms for which the gang itself may have little use, and in general in making themselves obnoxious to the virtuous. The same spirit is evident in playing hookey and in misbehavior in school. The teacher and her rules are not merely something onerous to be evaded. They are to be *flouted*. There is an element of active spite and malice, contempt and ridicule, challenge and defiance, exquisitely symbolized, in an incident described to the writer by Mr. Henry D. McKay, of defecating on the teacher's desk.[3]

All this suggests also the intention of our term "negativistic." The delinquent subculture is not only a set of rules, a design for living which is different from or indifferent to or even in conflict with the norms of the "respectable" adult society. It would appear at least plausible that it is defined by its "negative polarity" to those norms. That is, the delinquent subculture takes its norms from the larger culture but turns them upside down. The delinquent's conduct is right, by the standards of his subculture, precisely *because* it is wrong by the norms of the larger culture.[4] "Malicious" and "negativistic" are foreign to the delinquent's vocabulary but he will often assure us, sometimes ruefully, sometimes with a touch of glee or even pride, that he is "just plain mean."

In describing what might be called the "spirit" of the delinquent culture, we have suggested also its *versatility*. Of the "antisocial" activities of the delinquent gangs, stealing, of course, looms largest. Stealing itself can be, and for the gang usually is, a diversified occupation. It may steal milk bottles, candy, fruit, pencils, sports equipment and cars; it may steal from drunks, homes, stores, schools and filling stations. No gang runs the whole gamut but neither is it likely to "specialize" as do many adult criminal gangs and "solitary" delinquents. More to our point, however, is the fact that stealing tends to go hand-in-hand with "other property offenses," "malicious mischief," "vandalism," "trespass," and truancy. This quality of versatility and the fusion of versatility and malice are manifest in the following quotation:

> We would get some milk bottles in front of the grocery store and break them in somebody's hallway. Then we would break windows or get some garbage cans and throw them down someone's front stairs. After doing all this dirty work and running through alleys and yards, we'd go over to a grocery store. There, some of the boys would hide in a hallway while I would get a basket of grapes. When the man came after me, why the boys would jump out of their places and each grab a basket of grapes.[5]

Dozens of young offenders, after relating to the writer this delinquent episode and that, have summarized: "I guess we was just ornery." A generalized, diversified, protean "orneriness," not this or that specialized delinquent pursuit seems best to describe the vocation of the delinquent gang.[6]

Another characteristic of the subculture of the delinquent gang is *short-run hedonism*. There is little interest in long-run goals, in planning activities and budgeting time, or in activities involving knowledge and skills to be acquired only through practice, deliberation and study. The members of the gang typically congregate, with no specific activity in mind, at some street corner, candy store or other regular rendezvous. They "hang around," "rough-housing," "chewing the fat," and "waiting for something to turn up." They may respond impulsively to somebody's suggestion to play ball, go swimming, engage in some sort of mischief, or do something else that offers excitement. They do not take kindly to organized and supervised recreation, which subjects them to a regime of schedules and impersonal rules. They are impatient, impetuous and out for "fun," with little heed to the remoter gains and costs. It is to be noted that this short-run hedonism is not inherently delinquent and indeed it would be a serious error to think of the delinquent gang as dedicated solely to the cultivation of juvenile crime. Even in the most seriously delinquent gang only a small fraction of the "fun" is specifically and intrinsically delinquent. Furthermore, short-run hedonism is not characteristic of delinquent groups alone. On the contrary, it is common throughout the social class from which delinquents characteristically come. However, in the delinquent gang it reaches its finest flower. It is the fabric, as it were, of which delinquency is the most brilliant and spectacular thread.[7]

Another characteristic not peculiar to the delinquent gang but a conspicuous ingredient of its culture is an emphasis on *group autonomy*, or intolerance of restraint except from the informal pressures within the group itself. Relations with gang members tend to be intensely solidary and imperious. Relations with other groups tend to be indifferent, hostile or rebellious. Gang members are unusually resistant to the efforts of home, school and other agencies to regulate, not only their delinquent activities, but any activities carried on within the group, and to efforts to compete with the gang for the time and other resources of its members. It may be argued that the resistance of gang members to the authority of the home may not be a result of their membership in gangs but that membership in gangs, on the contrary, is a result of ineffective family supervision, the breakdown of parental authority and the hostility of the child toward the parents; in short, that the delinquent gang recruits members who have already achieved autonomy. Certainly a previous breakdown in family controls facilitates recruitment into delinquent gangs. But we are not speaking of the autonomy, the emancipation of *individuals*. It is not the individual delinquent but the gang that is autonomous. For many of our subcultural delinquents the claims of the home are very real and very compelling. The point is that the gang is a separate, distinct and often irresistible focus of attraction, loyalty and solidarity. The claims of the home versus the claims of the gang may present a real dilemma, and in such cases the breakdown of family controls is as much a casualty as a cause of gang membership.[8]

Notes

1. See H. M. Tiebout and M. E. Kirkpatrick, "Psychiatric Factors in Stealing," *American Journal of Orthopsychiatry*, II (April, 1932), 114–123, which discusses, in an exceptionally lucid manner, the distinction between motivating factors which center around the acquisition of the object and those which center around the commission of the act itself.

    The non-utilitarian nature of juvenile delinquency has been noted by many students. ". . . while older offenders may have definitely crystallized beliefs about profitable returns from anti-social conduct, it is very clear that in childhood and in earlier youth delinquency is certainly not entered into as a paying proposition in any ordinary sense." William Healy and Augusta F. Bronner, *op. cit.*, p. 22. "The juvenile property offender's thefts, at least at the start, are usually 'for fun' and not for gain." Paul Tappan, *Juvenile Delinquency* (New York: McGraw Hill Book Company, 1949), p. 143. "Stealing, the leading predatory activity of the adolescent gang, is as much a result of the sport motive as of a desire for revenue." Frederic M. Thrasher, *The Gang* (Chicago: University of Chicago Press, 1936), p. 143. "In its early stages, delinquency is clearly a form of play." Henry D. McKay, "The Neighborhood and Child Conduct," *Annals of the American Academy of Political and Social Science*, CCLXI (January, 1949), 37. See also Barbara Bellow, Milton L. Blum, Kenneth B. Clark, et al., "Prejudice in Seaside," *Human Relations*, I (1947), 15–16 and Sophia M. Robison, Nathan Cohen and Murray Sachs, "An Unsolved Problem in Group Relations," *Journal of Educational Psychology*, XX (November, 1946), 154–162. The last cited paper is an excellent description of the nonutilitarian, malicious and negativistic quality of the delinquent subculture and is the clearest statement in the literature that a satisfactory theory of delinquency must make sense of these facts.
2. Frederic M. Thrasher, *The Gang* (Chicago: University of Chicago Press, 1936), pp. 94–95.
3. To justify the characterization of the delinquent subculture as "malicious" by multiplying citations from authorities would be empty pedantry. The malice is evident in any detailed description of juvenile gang life. We commend in particular, however, the cited works of Thrasher, Shaw and McKay and Robison *et al.* One aspect of this "gratuitous hostility" deserves special mention, however, for the benefit of those who see in the provision of facilities for "wholesome recreation" some magical therapeutic virtue. "On entering a playground or a gym the first activity of gang members is to disrupt and interrupt whatever activities are going on. Nongang members flee, and when the coast is clear the gang plays desultorily on the apparatus or carries on horseplay." Sophia Robison *et al.*, *op. cit.*, p. 159. See, to the same effect, the excellent little book by Kenneth H. Rogers, *Street Gangs in Toronto* (Toronto: The Ryerson Press, 1945), pp. 18–19.
4. Shaw and McKay, in their *Social Factors in Juvenile Delinquency*, p. 241, come very close to making this point quite explicitly: "In fact the standards of these groups may represent a complete reversal of the standards and norms of conventional society. Types of conduct which result in personal degradation and dishonor in a conventional group, serve to enhance and elevate the personal prestige and status of a member of the delinquent group."
5. Clifford R. Shaw and Henry D. McKay, *Social Factors in Juvenile Delinquency*, Vol. II of National Commission on Law Observance and Enforcement, *Report on the Causes of Crime* (Washington: U.S. Government Printing Office, 1931), p. 18.

6. *Federal Probation*, XVIII (March, 1954), 3–16 contains an extremely valuable symposium on vandalism, which highlights all of the characteristics we have imputed to the delinquent subculture. In the belief that no generalization can convey the flavor and scope of this subculture as well as a simple but massive enumeration, we quote at length from Joseph E. Murphy's contribution, pp. 8–9:

> Studies of the complaints made by citizens and public officials reveal that hardly any property is safe from this form of aggression. Schools are often the object of attack by vandals. Windows are broken; records, books, desks, typewriters, supplies, and other equipment are stolen or destroyed. Public property of all types appears to offer peculiar allurement to children bent on destructton. Parks, playgrounds, highway signs, and markers are frequently defaced or destroyed. Trees, shrubs, flowers, benches, and other equipment suffer in like manner. Autoists are constantly reporting the slashing or releasing of air from tires, broken windows, stolen accessories. Golf clubs complain that benches, markers, flags, even expensive and difficult-to-replace putting greens are defaced, broken or uprooted. Libraries report the theft and destruction of books and other equipment. Railroads complain of and demand protection from the destruction of freight car seals, theft of property, willful and deliberate throwing of stones at passenger car windows, tampering with rails and switches. Vacant houses are always the particular delight of children seeking outlets for destructive instincts; windows are broken, plumbing and hardware stolen, destroyed, or rendered unusable: Gasoline operators report pumps and other service equipment stolen, broken, or destroyed. Theatre managers, frequently in the "better" neighborhoods, complain of the slashing of seats, willful damaging of toilet facilities, even the burning of rugs, carpets, etc.
>
> Recently the Newark *Evening News*, commenting editorially on the problem of vandalism in New York City housing projects, stated "housing authorities complain of the tearing out of steel banisters, incinerator openings, and mail boxes, damaging of elevators, defacing walls, smashing windows and light bulbs, stealing nozzles of fire hoses, destroying trees and benches on the project's grounds and occasionally plundering and setting fire to parked cars. Moreover, gangs have terrorized not only tenants but also the three hundred unarmed watchmen hired to protect the property."

This quotation places "stealing" in the context of a host of other manifestations of the protean "orneriness" of which we have spoken. The implication is strong that the fact that an object is "stolen" rather than destroyed or damaged is, from the standpoint of motivation, almost incidental. J. P. Shalloo, *ibid.*, pp. 6–7, states in a forceful way the problem which this creates for criminological theory: "Delinquency and crime are, and have been regarded as, purposeful behavior. But wanton and vicious destruction of property both public and private by teen-age hoodlums reveals no purpose, no rhyme, no reason. . . . These are not the actions of thoughtless youth. These are actions based upon a calculated contempt for the rights of others . . . ."

It is widely believed that vandalism, on the scale we know it today, is a relatively recent phenomenon. Douglas H. MacNeil, *ibid.*, p. 16, observes that, although vandalism is a form of delinquency which has been neglected by social scientists, there is little reason to believe that it has increased spectacularly, if at all, in recent years. Apparently it is and it has been for many years part and parcel, indeed the very spirit, of the delinquent subculture.

In connection with the versatility of the delinquent subculture, it should be noted that truancy is also institutionalized in the delinquent gang. In Lester E. Hewitt and Richard L. Jenkins, *op. cit.*, p. 94, habitual truancy is found to have a tetrachoric coefficient of correlation of .10 with the "unsocialized aggressive" syndrome, −.08 with the "overinhibited behavior" syndrome and .75 with the "socialized delinquent" syndrome. These findings are of special interest because the latter syndrome corresponds closely to what we have called the delinquent subculture. For summaries of studies on the relationship between truancy and other forms of delinquency see Norman Fenton, *The Delinquent Boy and the Correctional*

School (Claremont, California: Claremont Colleges Guidance Center, 1935), pp. 66–69 and William Kvaraceus, *Juvenile Delinquency and the School* (Yonkers-on-Hudson: World Book Company, 1945), pp. 144–146.

7. See the splendid report on "Working with a Street Gang" in Sylvan S. Furman (ed.), *Reaching the Unreached* (New York: New York City Youth Board, 1952), pp. 112–121. On this quality of short-run hedonism we quote, p. 13:

> One boy once told me, "Now, for example, you take an average day. What happens? We come down to the restaurant and we sit in the restaurant, and sit and sit. All right, say, er . . . after a couple of hours in the restaurant, maybe we'll go to a poolroom, shoot a little pool, that's if somebody's got the money. 0. K., a little pool, come back. By this time the restaurant is closed. We go in the candy store, sit around the candy store for a while, and that's it, that's all we do, man."

See also Barbara Bellow *et al.*, *op. cit.*, pp. 4–15, and Ruth Topping, *op. cit.*, p. 353.

8. The solidarity of the gang and the dependence of its members upon one another are especially well described in Barbara Bellow *et al., op. cit.*, p. 16 and Sophia Robison *et al., op. cit.*, p. 158.

32

Lower Class Culture as a Generating Milieu of Gang Delinquency

Walter B. Miller

The etiology of delinquency has long been a controversial issue, and is particularly so at present. As new frames of reference for explaining human behavior have been added to traditional theories, some authors have adopted the practice of citing the major postulates of each school of thought as they pertain to delinquency, and going on to state that causality must be conceived in terms of the dynamic interaction of a complex combination of variables on many levels. The major sets of etiological factors currently adduced to explain delinquency are, in simplified terms, the physiological (delinquency results from organic pathology), the psychodynamic (delinquency is a "behavioral disorder" resulting primarily from emotional disturbance generated by a defective mother-child relationship), and the environmental (delinquency is the product of disruptive forces, "disorganization," in the actor's physical or social environment).

This paper selects one particular kind of "delinquency"[1]—law-violating acts committed by members of adolescent street corner groups in lower class communities—and attempts to show that the dominant component of motivation underlying these acts consists in a directed attempt by the actor to adhere to forms of behavior, and to achieve standards of value as they are defined within that community. It takes as a premise that the motivation of behavior in this situation can be approached most productively by attempting to understand the nature of cultural forces impinging on the acting individual as they are perceived *by the actor himself*—although by no means only that segment of these forces of which the actor is consciously aware—rather than as they are perceived and evaluated from the reference position of another cultural system. In the case of "gang" delinquency, the cultural system which exerts the most direct influence on behavior is that of the lower class community itself—a long-established, distinctively patterned tradition with an integrity of its own—rather than a so-called "delinquent subculture" which has arisen through conflict with middle class culture and is oriented to the deliberate violation of middle class norms.

The bulk of the substantive data on which the following material is based was collected in connection with a service-research project in the control of gang

Source: Walter B. Miller, "Lower Class Culture as a Generating Milieu of Gang Delinquency," *Journal of Social Issues,* Vol. 14, No. 3 (1958), pp. 5–19. Permission granted by Blackwell Publishing, Ltd.

delinquency. During the service aspect of the project, which lasted for three years, seven trained social workers maintained contact with twenty-one corner group units in a "slum" district of a large eastern city for periods of time ranging from ten to thirty months. Groups were Negro and white, male and female, and in early, middle, and late adolescence. Over eight thousand pages of direct observational data on behavior patterns of group members and other community residents were collected; almost daily contact was maintained for a total time period of about thirteen worker years. Data include workers' contact reports, participant observation reports by the writer—a cultural anthropologist—and direct tape recordings of group activities and discussions.[2]

Focal Concerns of Lower Class Culture

There is a substantial segment of present-day American society whose way of life, values, and characteristic patterns of behavior are the product of a distinctive cultural system which may be termed "lower class." Evidence indicates that this cultural system is becoming increasingly distinctive, and that the size of the group which shares this tradition is increasing.[3] The lower class way of life, in common with that of all distinctive cultural groups, is characterized by a set of focal concerns—areas or issues which command widespread and persistent attention and a high degree of emotional involvement. The specific concerns cited here, while by no means confined to the American lower classes, constitute a distinctive *patterning* of concerns which differs significantly, both in rank order and weighting from that of American middle class culture. The following chart presents a highly schematic and simplified listing of six of the major concerns of lower class culture. Each is conceived as a

Chart 1

FOCAL CONCERNS OF LOWER CLASS CULTURE

Area	Perceived Alternatives (state, quality, condition)	
1. *Trouble:*	law-abiding behavior	law-violating behavior
2. *Toughness:*	physical prowess, skill; "masculinity"; fearlessness, bravery, daring	weakness, ineptitude; effeminacy; timidity, cowardice, caution
3. *Smartness:*	ability to outsmart, dupe, "con"; gaining money by "wits"; shrewdness, adroitness in repartee	gullibility, "con-ability"; gaining money by hard work; slowness, dull-wittedness, verbal maladroitness
4. *Excitement:*	thrill; risk, danger; change, activity	boredom; "deadness," safeness; sameness, passivity
5. *Fate:*	favored by fortune, being "lucky"	ill-omened, being "unlucky"
6. *Autonomy:*	freedom from external constraint; freedom from superordinate authority; independence	presence of external constraint; presence of strong authority; dependency, being "cared for"

"dimension" within which a fairly wide and varied range of alternative behavior patterns may be followed by different individuals under different situations. They are listed roughly in order of the degree of *explicit* attention accorded each, and, in this sense represent a weighted ranking of concerns. The "perceived alternatives" represent polar positions which define certain parameters within each dimension. As will be explained in more detail, it is necessary in relating the influence of these "concerns" to the motivation of delinquent behavior to specify *which* of its aspects is oriented to, whether orientation is *overt* or *covert, positive* (conforming to or seeking the aspect), or *negative* (rejecting or seeking to avoid the aspect).

The concept "focal concern" is used here in preference to the concept "value" for several interrelated reasons: (1) It is more readily derivable from direct field observation. (2) It is descriptively neutral—permitting independent consideration of positive and negative valences as varying under different conditions, whereas "value" carries a built-in positive valence. (3) It makes possible more refined analysis of subcultural differences, since it reflects actual behavior, whereas "value" tends to wash out intracultural differences since it is colored by notions of the "official" ideal.

Trouble

Concern over "trouble" is a dominant feature of lower class culture. The concept has various shades of meaning; "trouble" in one of its aspects represents a situation or a kind of behavior which results in unwelcome or complicating involvement with official authorities or agencies of middle class society. "Getting into trouble" and "staying out of trouble" represent major issues for male and female, adults and children. For men, "trouble" frequently involves fighting or sexual adventures while drinking; for women, sexual involvement with disadvantageous consequences. Expressed desire to avoid behavior which violates moral or legal norms is often based less on an explicit commitment to "official" moral or legal standards than on a desire to avoid "getting into trouble," *e.g.*, the complicating consequences of the action.

The dominant concern over "trouble" involves a distinction of critical importance for the lower class community—that between "law-abiding" and "non-law-abiding" behavior. There is a high degree of sensitivity as to where each person stands in relation to these two classes of activity. Whereas in the middle class community a major dimension for evaluating a person's status is "achievement" and its external symbols, in the lower class, personal status is very frequently gauged along the law-abiding-non-law-abiding dimension. A mother will evaluate the suitability of her daughter's boyfriend less on the basis of his achievement potential than on the basis of his innate "trouble" potential. This sensitive awareness of the opposition of "trouble-producing" and "non-trouble-producing" behavior represents both a major basis for deriving status distinctions, and an internalized conflict potential for the individual.

As in the case of other focal concerns, which of two perceived alternatives—"law-abiding" or "non-law-abiding"—is valued varies according to the individual and the circumstances; in many instances there is an overt commitment to the "law-abiding" alternative, but a covert commitment to the "non-law-abiding." In certain situations, "getting into trouble" is overtly recognized as prestige-conferring; for example, membership in certain adult and adolescent primary groupings ("gangs") is contingent on having demonstrated an explicit commitment to the law-violating alternative. It is most important to note that the choice between "law-abiding" and "non-law-abiding" behavior is still a choice *within* lower class culture; the distinction between the policeman and the criminal, the outlaw and the sheriff, involves primarily this one dimension; in other respects they have a high community of interests. Not infrequently brothers raised in an identical cultural milieu will become police and criminals respectively.

For a substantial segment of the lower class population "getting into trouble" is not in itself overtly defined as prestige-conferring, but is implicitly recognized as a means to other valued ends, *e.g.*, the covertly valued desire to be "cared for" and subject to external constraint, or the overtly valued state of excitement or risk. Very frequently "getting into trouble" is multi-functional, and achieves several sets of valued ends.

Toughness

The concept of "toughness" in lower class culture represents a compound combination of qualities or states. Among its most important components are physical prowess, evidenced both by demonstrated possession of strength and endurance and athletic skill; "masculinity," symbolized by a distinctive complex of acts and avoidances (bodily tattooing; absence of sentimentality; non-concern with "art," "literature," conceptualization of women as conquest objects, etc.); and bravery in the face of physical threat. The model for the "tough guy"—hard, fearless, undemonstrative, skilled in physical combat—is represented by the movie gangster of the thirties, the "private eye," and the movie cowboy.

The genesis of the intense concern over "toughness" in lower class culture is probably related to the fact that a significant proportion of lower class males are reared in a predominantly female household, and lack a consistently present male figure with whom to identify and from whom to learn essential components of a "male" role. Since women serve as a primary object of identification during pre-adolescent years, the almost obsessive lower class concern with "masculinity" probably resembles a type of compulsive reaction-formation. A concern over homosexuality runs like a persistent thread through lower class culture. This is manifested by the institutionalized practice of baiting "queers," often accompanied by violent physical attacks, an expressed contempt for "softness" or frills, and the use of the local term for "homosexual" as a generalized pejorative epithet (*e.g.*, higher class individuals or upwardly mobile peers are frequently characterized as "fags" or "queers"). The distinction between "overt" and "covert" orientation to aspects of an area of concern is especially important in regard to "toughness." A positive overt evaluation of behavior defined as "effeminate" would be out of the question for a lower class male; however, built into lower class culture is a range of devices which permit men to adopt behaviors and concerns which in other cultural milieux fall within the province of women, and at the same time to be defined as "tough" and manly. For example, lower class men can be professional short-order cooks in a diner and still be regarded as "tough." The highly intimate circumstances of the street corner gang involve the recurrent expression of strongly affectionate feelings towards other men. Such expressions, however, are disguised as their opposite, taking the form of ostensibly aggressive verbal and physical interaction (kidding, "ranking," roughhousing, etc.).

Smartness

"Smartness," as conceptualized in lower class culture, involves the capacity to outsmart, outfox, outwit, dupe, "take," "con" another or others, and the concomitant capacity to avoid being outwitted, "taken," or duped oneself. In its essence, smartness involves the capacity to achieve a valued entity—material goods, personal status—through a maximum use of mental agility and a minimum use of physical effort. This capacity has an extremely long tradition in lower class culture, and is highly valued. Lower class culture can be characterized as "non-intellectual" only if intellectualism is defined specifically in terms of control over a particular body of formally learned knowledge involving "culture" (art, literature, "good" music, etc.), a generalized perspective on the past and present conditions of our own and other societies, and other areas of knowledge imparted by formal educational institutions. This particular type of mental attainment is, in general, overtly disvalued and frequently associated with effeminacy; "smartness" in the lower class sense, however, is highly valued.

The lower class child learns and practices the use of this skill in the street corner situation. Individuals continually practice duping and outwitting one another through recurrent card games and other forms of gambling, mutual exchanges of insults, and "testing" for mutual "conability." Those who demonstrate competence in this skill are accorded considerable prestige. Leadership roles in the corner group are frequently allocated according to demonstrated capacity in the two areas of "smartness" and "toughness"; the ideal leader combines both, but the "smart" leader is often accorded more prestige than the "tough" one—reflecting a general lower class respect for "brains" in the "smartness" sense.[4]

The model of the "smart" person is represented in popular media by the card shark, the professional gambler, the "con" artist, the promoter. A conceptual distinction is made between two kinds of people: "suckers," easy marks, "lushes," dupes, who work for their money and are legitimate targets of exploitation; and sharp operators, the "brainy" ones, who live by their wits and "getting" from the suckers by mental adroitness.

Involved in the syndrome of capacities related to "smartness" is a dominant emphasis in lower class culture on ingenious aggressive repartee. This skill, learned and practiced in the context of the corner group, ranges in form from the widely prevalent semi-ritualized teasing, kidding, razzing, "ranking," so characteristic of male peer group interaction, to the highly ritualized type of mutual insult interchange known as "the dirty dozens," "the dozens," "playing house," and other terms. This highly patterned cultural form is practiced on its most advanced level in adult male Negro society, but less polished variants are found throughout lower class culture—practiced, for example, by white children, male and female, as young as four or five. In essence, "doin' the dozens" involves two antagonists who vie with each other in the exchange of increasingly inflammatory insults, with incestuous and perverted sexual relations with the mother a dominant theme. In this form of insult interchange, as well as on other less ritualized occasions for joking, semi-serious, and serious mutual invective, a very high premium is placed on ingenuity, hair-trigger responsiveness, inventiveness, and the acute exercise of mental faculties.

Excitement

For many lower class individuals the rhythm of life fluctuates between periods of relatively routine or repetitive activity and sought situations of great emotional stimulation. Many of the most characteristic features of lower class life are related to the search for excitement or "thrill." Involved here are the highly prevalent use of alcohol by both sexes and the widespread use of gambling of all kinds—playing the numbers, betting on horse races, dice, cards. The quest for excitement finds what is perhaps its most vivid expression in the highly patterned practice of the recurrent "night on the town." This practice, designated by various terms in different areas ("honky-tonkin'"; "goin' out on the town"; "bar hoppin'"), involves a patterned set of activities in which alcohol, music, and sexual adventuring are major components. A group or individual sets out to "make the rounds" of various bars or night clubs. Drinking continues progressively throughout the evening. Men seek to "pick up" women, and women play the risky game of entertaining sexual advances. Fights between men involving women, gambling, and claims of physical prowess, in various combinations, are frequent consequences of a night of making the rounds. The explosive potential of this type of adventuring with sex and aggression, frequently leading to "trouble," is semi-explicitly sought by the individual. Since there is always a good likelihood that being out on the town will eventuate in fights, etc., the practice involves elements of sought risk and desired danger.

Counterbalancing the "flirting with danger" aspect of the "excitement" concern is the prevalence in lower class culture of other well established patterns of activity which involve long periods of relative inaction, or passivity. The term "hanging out" in lower class culture refers to extended periods of standing around, often with peer mates, doing what is defined as "nothing," "shooting the breeze," etc. A definite periodicity exists in the pattern of activity relating to the two aspects of the "excitement" dimension. For many lower class individuals the venture into the high risk world of alcohol, sex, and fighting occurs regularly once a week, with interim periods devoted to accommodating to possible consequences of these periods, along with recurrent resolves not to become so involved again.

Fate

Related to the quest for excitement is the concern with fate, fortune, or luck. Here also a distinction is made between two states—being "lucky" or "in luck," and being unlucky or jinxed. Many lower class individuals feel that their lives are subject to a set of forces over which they have relatively little control. These are not directly equated with the supernatural forces of formally organized religion, but relate more to a concept of "destiny," or man as a pawn of magical powers. Not infrequently this often implicit world view is associated with a conception of the ultimate futility of directed effort towards a goal: if the cards are right, or the dice good to you, or if your lucky number comes up, things will go your way; if luck is against you, it's not worth trying. The concept of performing semi-magical rituals so that one's "luck will change" is prevalent; one hopes that as a result he will move from the state of being "unlucky" to that of being "lucky." The element of fantasy plays an important part in this area. Related to and complementing the notion that "only suckers work" (Smartness) is the idea that once things start going your way, relatively independent of your own effort, all good things will come to you. Achieving great material rewards (big cars, big houses, a roll of cash to flash in a fancy night club), valued in lower class as well as in other parts of American culture, is a recurrent theme in lower class fantasy and folk lore; the cocaine dreams of Willie the Weeper or Minnie the Moocher present the components of this fantasy in vivid detail.

The prevalence in the lower class community of many forms of gambling, mentioned in connection with the "excitement" dimension, is also relevant here. Through cards and pool which involve skill, and thus both "toughness" and "smartness"; or through race horse betting, involving "smartness"; or through playing the numbers, involving predominantly "luck," one may make a big killing with a minimum of directed and persistent effort within conventional occupational channels. Gambling in its many forms illustrates the fact that many of the persistent features of lower class culture are multi-functional—serving a range of desired ends at the same time. Describing some of the incentives behind gambling has involved mention of all of the focal concerns cited so far—Toughness, Smartness, and Excitement, in addition to Fate.

Autonomy

The extent and nature of control over the behavior of the individual—an important concern in most cultures—has a special significance and is distinctively patterned in lower class culture. The discrepancy between what is overtly valued and what is covertly sought is particularly striking in this area. On the overt level there is a strong and frequently expressed resentment of the idea of external controls, restrictions on behavior, and unjust or coercive authority. "No one's gonna push *me* around," or "I'm gonna tell him he can take the job and shove it. . . ." are commonly expressed sentiments. Similar explicit attitudes are maintained to systems of behavior-restricting rules, insofar as these are perceived as representing the injunctions, and bearing the sanctions of superordinate authority. In addition, in lower class culture a close conceptual connection is made between "authority" and "nurturance." To be restrictively or firmly controlled is to be cared for. Thus the overtly negative evaluation of superordinate authority frequently extends as well to nurturance, care, or protection. The desire for personal independence is often expressed in such terms as "I don't need *nobody* to take care of me. I can take care of myself!" Actual patterns of behavior, however, reveal a marked discrepancy between expressed sentiment and what is covertly valued. Many lower class people appear to seek out highly restrictive social environments wherein stringent external controls are maintained over their behavior. Such institutions as the armed forces, the mental hospital, the disciplinary school, the prison or correctional institution, provide environments which incorporate a strict and detailed set of rules defining and limiting behavior, and enforced by an authority system which controls and applies coercive sanctions for deviance from these rules. While under the jurisdiction of such systems, the lower class person generally expresses to his peers continual resentment of the coercive, unjust, and arbitrary exercise of authority. Having been released, or having escaped from these milieux, however, he will often act in such a way as to insure recommitment, or choose recommitment voluntarily after a temporary period of "freedom."

Lower class patients in mental hospitals will exercise considerable ingenuity to insure continued commitment while voicing the desire to get out; delinquent boys will frequently "run" from a correctional institution to activate efforts to return them; to be caught and returned means that one is cared for. Since "being controlled" is equated with "being cared for," attempts are frequently made to "test" the severity or strictness of superordinate authority to see if it remains firm. If intended or executed rebellion produces swift and firm punitive sanctions, the individual is reassured, at the same time that he is complaining bitterly at the injustice of being caught and punished. Some environmental milieux, having been tested in this fashion for the "firmness" of their coercive sanctions, are rejected, ostensibly for being too strict, actually for not being strict enough. This is frequently so in the case of "problematic" behavior by lower class youngsters in the public schools, which generally cannot command the coercive controls implicitly sought by the individual.

A similar discrepancy between what is overtly and covertly desired is found in the area of dependence-independence. The pose of tough rebellious independence often assumed by the lower class person frequently conceals powerful dependency cravings. These are manifested primarily by obliquely expressed resentment when "care" is not forthcoming rather than by expressed satisfaction when it is. The concern over autonomy-dependency is related both to "trouble" and "fate." Insofar as the lower class individual feels that his behavior is controlled by forces which often propel him into "trouble" in the face of an explicit determination to avoid it, there is an implied appeal to "save me from myself." A solution appears to lie in arranging things so that his behavior will be coercively restricted by an externally imposed set of controls strong enough to forcibly restrain his inexplicable inclination to get in trouble. The periodicity observed in connection with the "excitement" dimension is also relevant here; after involvement in trouble-producing behavior (assault, sexual adventure, a "drunk"), the individual will actively seek a locus of imposed control (his wife, prison, a restrictive job); after a given period of subjection to this control, resentment against it mounts, leading to a "break away" and a search for involvement in further "trouble."

Focal Concerns of the Lower Class Adolescent Street Corner Group

The one-sex peer group is a highly prevalent and significant structural form in the lower class community. There is a strong probability that the prevalence and stability of this type of unit is directly related to the prevalence of a stabilized type of lower class childrearing unit—the "female-based" household. This is a nuclear kin unit in which a male parent is either absent from the household, present only sporadically, or, when present, only minimally or inconsistently involved in the support and rearing of children. This unit usually consists of one or more females of child-bearing age and their offspring. The females are frequently related to one another by blood or marriage ties, and the unit often includes two or more generations of women, *e.g.*, the mother and/or aunt of the principal child-bearing female.

The nature of social groupings in the lower class community may be clarified if we make the assumption that it is the *one-sex peer unit* rather than the two-parent family unit which represents the most significant relational unit for both sexes in lower class communities. Lower class society may be pictured as comprising a set of age-graded one-sex groups which constitute the major psychic focus and reference group for those over twelve or thirteen. Men and women of mating age leave these groups periodically to form temporary marital alliances, but these lack stability, and after varying periods of "trying out" the two-sex family arrangement, gravitate back to the more "comfortable" one-sex grouping, whose members exert strong pressure on the individual *not* to disrupt the group by adopting a two-sex household pattern of life.[5] Membership in a stable and solidary peer unit is vital to the lower class individual precisely to the extent to which a range of essential functions—psychological, educational, and others, are not provided by the "family" unit.

The adolescent street corner group represents the adolescent variant of this lower class structural form. What has been called the "delinquent gang" is one subtype of this form, defined on the basis of frequency of participation in law-violating activity; this subtype should not be considered a legitimate unit of study *per se*, but rather as one particular variant of the adolescent street corner group. The "hanging" peer group is a unit of particular importance for the adolescent male. In many cases it is the most stable and solidary primary group he has ever belonged to; for boys reared in female-based households the corner group provides the first real opportunity to learn essential aspects of the male role in the context of peers facing similar problems of sex-role identification.

The form and functions of the adolescent corner group operate as a selective mechanism in recruiting members. The activity patterns of the group require a high level of intra-group solidarity; individual members must possess a good capacity for subordinating individual desires to general group interests as well as the capacity for intimate and persisting interaction. Thus highly "disturbed" individuals, or those who cannot tolerate consistently imposed sanctions on "deviant" behavior cannot remain accepted members; the group itself will extrude those whose behavior exceeds limits defined as "normal." This selective process produces a type of group whose members possess to an unusually high degree both the *capacity* and *motivation* to conform to perceived cultural norms, so that the nature of the system of norms and values oriented to is a particularly influential component of motivation.

Focal concerns of the male adolescent corner group are those of the general cultural milieu in which it functions. As would be expected, the relative weighting and importance of these concerns pattern somewhat differently for adolescents than for adults. The nature of this patterning centers around two additional "concerns" of particular importance to this group—concern with "belonging," and with "status." These may be conceptualized as being on a higher level of abstraction than concerns previously cited, since "status" and "belonging" are achieved *via* cited concern areas of Toughness, etc.

Belonging

Since the corner group fulfills essential functions for the individual, being a member in good standing of the group is of vital importance for its members. A continuing concern over who is "in" and who is not involves the citation and detailed discussion of highly refined criteria for "in-group" membership. The phrase "he hangs with us" means "he is accepted as a member in good standing by current consensus;" conversely, "he don't hang with us" means he is not so accepted. One achieves "belonging" primarily by demonstrating knowledge of and a determination to adhere to the system of standards and valued qualities defined by the group. One maintains membership by acting in conformity with valued aspects of Toughness, Smartness, Autonomy, etc. In those instances where conforming to norms of this reference group at the same time violates norms of other reference groups (*e.g.*, middle class adults, institutional "officials"), immediate reference group norms are much more compelling since violation risks invoking the group's most powerful sanction: exclusion.

Status

In common with most adolescents in American society, the lower class corner group manifests a dominant concern with "status." What differentiates this type of group from others, however, is the particular set of criteria and weighting thereof by which "status" is defined. In general, status is achieved and maintained by demonstrated possession of the valued qualities of lower class culture—Toughness, Smartness, expressed resistance to authority, daring, etc. It is important to stress once more that the individual orients to these concerns *as they are defined within lower class society*; *e.g.*, the status-conferring potential of "smartness" in the sense of scholastic achievement generally ranges from negligible to negative.

The concern with "status" is manifested in a variety of ways. Intra-group status is a continued concern, and is derived and tested constantly by means of a set of status-ranking activities; the intra-group "pecking order" is constantly at issue. One gains status within the group by demonstrated superiority in Toughness (physical prowess, bravery, skill in athletics and games such as pool and cards), Smartness (skill in repartee, capacity to "dupe" fellow group members), and the like. The term "ranking," used to refer to the pattern of intra-group aggressive repartee, indicates awareness of the fact that this is one device for establishing the intra-group status hierarchy.

The concern over status in the adolescent corner group involves in particular the component of "adultness," the intense desire to be seen as "grown up," and a corresponding aversion to "kid stuff." "Adult" status is defined less in terms of the assumption of "adult" responsibility than in terms of certain external symbols of adult status—a car, ready cash, and, in particular, a perceived "freedom" to drink, smoke, and gamble as one wishes and to come and go without external restrictions. The desire to be seen as "adult" is often a more significant component of much involvement in illegal drinking, gambling, and automobile driving than the explicit enjoyment of these acts as such.

The intensity of the corner group member's desire to be seen as "adult" is sufficiently great that he feels called upon to demonstrate qualities associated with adultness (Toughness, Smartness, Autonomy) to a much greater degree than a lower class adult. This means that he will seek out and utilize those avenues to these qualities which he perceives as available with greater intensity than an adult and less regard for their "legitimacy." In this sense the adolescent variant of lower class culture represents a maximization or an intensified manifestation of many of its most characteristic features.

Concern over status is also manifested in reference to other street corner groups. The term "rep" used in this regard is especially significant, and has broad connotations. In its most frequent and explicit connotation, "rep" refers to the "toughness" of the corner group as a whole relative to that of other groups; a "pecking order" also exists among the several corner groups in a given interactional area, and there is a common perception that the safety or security of the group and all its members depends on maintaining a solid "rep" for toughness vis-á-vis other groups. This motive is most frequently advanced as a reason for involvement in gang fights: "We *can't* chicken out on this fight; our rep would be shot!"; this implies that the group would be relegated to the bottom of the status ladder and become a helpless and recurrent target of external attack.

On the other hand, there is implicit in the concept of "rep" the recognition that "rep" has or may have a dual basis—corresponding to the two aspects of the "trouble" dimension. It is recognized that group as well as individual status can be based on both "law-abiding" and "law-violating" behavior. The situational resolution of the persisting conflict between the "law-abiding" and "law-violating" bases of status comprises a vital set of dynamics in determining whether a "delinquent" mode of behavior will be adopted by a group, under what circumstances, and how persistently. The determinants of this choice are evidently highly complex and fluid, and rest on a range of factors including the presence and perceptual immediacy of different community reference-group loci (*e.g.*, professional criminals, police, clergy, teachers, settlement house workers), the personality structures and "needs" of group members, the presence in the community of social work, recreation, or educational programs which can facilitate utilization of the "law-abiding" basis of status, and so on.

What remains constant is the critical importance of "status" both for the members of the group as individuals and for the group as a whole insofar as members perceive their individual destinies as linked to the destiny of the group, and the fact that action geared to attain status is much more acutely oriented to the fact of status itself than to the legality or illegality, morality or immorality of the means used to achieve it.

Lower Class Culture and the Motivation of Delinquent Behavior

The customary set of activities of the adolescent street corner group includes activities which are in violation of laws and ordinances of the legal code. Most of these center around assault and theft of various types (the gang fight; auto theft; assault on an individual; petty pilfering and shoplifting; "mugging"; pocketbook theft). Members of street corner gangs are well aware of the law-violating nature of these acts; they are not psychopaths, nor physically or mentally "defective"; in fact, since the corner group supports and enforces a rigorous set of standards which demand a high degree of fitness and personal competence, it tends to recruit from the most "able" members of the community.

Why, then, is the commission of crimes a customary feature of gang activity? The most general answer is that the commission of crimes by members of adolescent street corner groups is motivated primarily by the attempt to achieve ends, states, or conditions which are valued, and to avoid those that are disvalued within their most meaningful cultural milieu, through those culturally available avenues which appear as the most feasible means of attaining those ends.

The operation of these influences is well illustrated by the gang fight—a prevalent and characteristic type of corner group delinquency. This type of activity comprises a highly stylized and culturally patterned set of sequences. Although details vary under different circumstances, the following events are generally included. A member or several members of group A "trespass" on the claimed territory of group B. While there they commit an act or acts which group B defines as a violation of its rightful privileges, an affront to their honor, or a challenge to their "rep."

Frequently this act involves advances to a girl associated with group B; it may occur at a dance or party; sometimes the mere act of "trespass" is seen as deliberate provocation. Members of group B then assault members of group A, if they are caught while still in B's territory. Assaulted members of group A return to their "home" territory and recount to members of their group details of the incident, stressing the insufficient nature of the provocation ("I just *looked* at her! Hardly even said anything!"), and the unfair circumstances of the assault ("About *twenty* guys jumped just the *two* of us!"). The highly colored account is acutely inflammatory; group A, perceiving its honor violated and its "rep" threatened, feels obligated to retaliate in force. Sessions of detailed planning now occur; allies are recruited if the size of group A and its potential allies appears to necessitate larger numbers; strategy is plotted, and messengers dispatched. Since the prospect of a gang fight is frightening to even the "toughest" group members, a constant rehearsal of the provocative incident or incidents and the essentially evil nature of the opponents accompanies the planning process to bolster possibly weakening motivation to fight. The excursion into "enemy" territory sometimes results in a full scale fight; more often group B cannot be found, or the police appear and stop the fight, "tipped off" by an anonymous informant. When this occurs, group members express disgust and disappointment; secretly there is much relief; their honor has been avenged without incurring injury; often the anonymous tipster is a member of one of the involved groups.

The basic elements of this type of delinquency are sufficiently stabilized and recurrent as to constitute an essentially ritualized pattern, resembling both in structure and expressed motives for action classic forms such as the European "duel," the American Indian tribal war, and the Celtic clan feud. Although the arousing and "acting out" of individual aggressive emotions are inevitably involved in the gang fight, neither its form nor motivational dynamics can be adequately handled within a predominantly personality-focused frame of reference.

It would be possible to develop in considerable detail the processes by which the commission of a range of illegal acts is either explicitly supported by, implicitly demanded by, or not materially inhibited by factors relating to the focal concerns of lower class culture. In place of such a development, the following three statements condense in general terms the operation of these processes:

1. Following cultural practices which comprise essential elements of the total life pattern of lower class culture automatically violates certain legal norms.
2. In instances where alternate avenues to similar objectives are available, the non-law-abiding avenue frequently provides a relatively greater and more immediate return for a relatively smaller investment of energy.
3. The "demanded" response to certain situations recurrently engendered within lower class culture involves the commission of illegal acts.

The primary thesis of this paper is that the dominant component of the motivation of "delinquent" behavior engaged in by members of lower class corner groups involves a positive effort to achieve states, conditions, or qualities valued within the actor's most significant cultural milieu. If "conformity to immediate reference group values" is the major component of motivation of "delinquent" behavior by gang members, why is such behavior frequently referred to as negativistic, malicious, or rebellious? Albert Cohen, for example, in *Delinquent Boys*

(Glencoe: Free Press, 1955) describes behavior which violates school rules as comprising elements of "active spite and malice, contempt and ridicule, challenge and defiance." He ascribes to the gang "keen delight in terrorizing 'good' children, and in general making themselves obnoxious to the virtuous." A recent national conference on social work with "hard-to-reach" groups characterized lower class corner groups as "youth groups in conflict with the culture of their (*sic*) communities." Such characterizations are obviously the result of taking the middle class community and its institutions as an implicit point of reference.

A large body of systematically interrelated attitudes, practices, behaviors, and values characteristic of lower class culture are designed to support and maintain the basic features of the lower class way of life. In areas where these differ from features of middle class culture, action oriented to the achievement and maintenance of the lower class system may violate norms of middle class culture and be perceived as deliberately non-conforming or malicious by an observer strongly cathected to middle class norms. This does not mean, however, that violation of the middle class norm is the dominant component of motivation; it is a by-product of action primarily oriented to the lower class system. The standards of lower class culture cannot be seen merely as a reverse function of middle class culture—as middle class standards "turned upside down"; lower class culture is a distinctive tradition many centuries old with an integrity of its own.

From the viewpoint of the acting individual, functioning within a field of well-structured cultural forces, the relative impact of "conforming" and "rejective" elements in the motivation of gang delinquency is weighted preponderantly on the conforming side. Rejective or rebellious elements are inevitably involved, but their influence during the actual commission of delinquent acts is relatively small compared to the influence of pressures to achieve what is valued by the actor's most immediate reference groups. Expressed awareness by the actor of the element of rebellion often represents only that aspect of motivation of which he is explicitly conscious; the deepest and most compelling components of motivation—adherence to highly meaningful group standards of Toughness, Smartness, Excitement, etc.—are often unconsciously patterned. No cultural pattern as well-established as the practice of illegal acts by members of lower class corner groups could persist if buttressed primarily by negative, hostile, or rejective motives; its principal motivational support, as in the case of any persisting cultural tradition, derives from a positive effort to achieve what is valued within that tradition, and to conform to its explicit and implicit norms.

Notes

1. The complex issues involved in deriving a definition of "delinquency" cannot be discussed here. The term "delinquent" is used in this paper to characterize behavior or acts committed by individuals within specified age limits which if known to official authorities could result in legal action. The concept of a "delinquent" individual has little or no utility in the approach used here; rather, specified types of *acts* which may be committed rarely or frequently by few or many individuals are characterized as "delinquent."

2. A three year research project is being financed under National Institutes of Health Grant M—1414, and administered through the Boston University School of Social Work. The primary research effort has subjected all collected material to a uniform data-coding process. All information bearing on some seventy areas of behavior (behavior in reference

to school, police, theft, assault, sex, collective athletics, etc.) is extracted from the records, recorded on coded data cards, and filed under relevant categories. Analysis of these data aims to ascertain the actual nature of customary behavior in these areas, and the extent to which the social work effort was able to effect behavioral changes.

3. Between 40 and 60 percent of all Americans are directly influenced by lower class culture, with about 15 percent, or twenty-five million, comprising the "hard core" lower class group—defined primarily by its use of the "female-based" household as the basic form of child-rearing unit and of the "serial monogamy" mating pattern as the primary form of marriage. The term "lower class culture" as used here refers most specifically to the way of life of the "hard core" group; systematic research in this area would probably reveal at least four to six major subtypes of lower class culture, for some of which the "concerns" presented here would be differently weighted, especially for those subtypes in which "law-abiding" behavior has a high overt valuation. It is impossible within the compass of this short paper to make the finer intracultural distinctions which a more accurate presentation would require.

4. The "brains-brawn" set of capacities are often paired in lower class folk lore or accounts of lower class life, *e.g.*, "Brer Fox" and "Brer Bear" in the Uncle Remus stories, or George and Lennie in "Of Mice and Men."

5. Further data on the female-based household unit (estimated as comprising about 15 percent of all American "families") and the role of one-sex groupings in lower class culture are contained in Walter B. Miller, Implications of Urban Lower Class Culture for Social Work. *Social Service Review*, 1959, *33*, No. 3.

33

Techniques of Neutralization

Gresham M. Sykes   David Matza

. . . It is our argument that much delinquency is based on what is essentially an unrecognized extension of defenses to crimes, in the form of justifications for deviance that are seen as valid by the delinquent but not by the legal system or society at large.
These justifications are commonly described as rationalizations. They are viewed as following deviant behavior and as protecting the individual from self-blame and the blame of others after the act. But there is also reason to believe that they precede deviant behavior and make deviant behavior possible. . . . Disapproval flowing from internalized norms and conforming others in the social environment is neutralized, turned back, or deflected in advance. Social controls that serve to check or inhibit deviant motivational patterns are rendered inoperative, and the individual is freed to engage in delinquency without serious damage to his self image. In this sense, the delinquent both has his cake and eats it too, for he remains committed to the dominant normative system and yet so qualifies its imperatives that violations are "acceptable" if not "right." Thus the delinquent represents not a radical opposition to law-abiding society but something more like an apologetic failure, often more sinned against than sinning in his own eyes. We call these justifications of deviant behavior techniques of neutralization; and we believe these techniques make up a crucial component of Sutherland's "definitions favorable to the violation of law." It is by learning these techniques that the juvenile becomes delinquent, rather than by learning moral imperatives, values or attitudes standing in direct contradiction to those of the dominant society. In analyzing these techniques, we have found it convenient to divide them into five major types.

The Denial of Responsibility

In so far as the delinquent can define himself as lacking responsibility for his deviant actions, the disapproval of self or others is sharply reduced in effectiveness as a restraining influence. . . . As a technique of neutralization, the denial of responsibility extends much further than the claim that deviant acts are an "accident" or some similar negation of personal accountability. It may also be asserted that

Source: Gresham M. Sykes and David Matza, "Techniques of Neutralization: A Theory of Delinquency," *American Sociological Review*, Vol. 22 (December), pp. 664–670, copyright © 1957 by the American Sociological Association. Reprinted with permission. Footnotes renumbered.

delinquent acts are due to forces outside of the individual and beyond his control such as unloving parents, bad companions, or a slum neighborhood. In effect, the delinquent approaches a "billiard ball" conception of himself in which he sees himself as helplessly propelled into new situations. From a psychodynamic viewpoint, this orientation toward one's own actions may represent a profound alienation from self, but it is important to stress the fact that interpretations of responsibility are cultural constructs and not merely idiosyncratic beliefs. The similarity between this mode of justifying illegal behavior assumed by the delinquent and the implications of a "sociological" frame of reference or a "humane" jurisprudence is readily apparent.[1] It is not the validity of this orientation that concerns us here, but its function of deflecting blame attached to violations of social norms and its relative independence of a particular personality structure.[2] By learning to view himself as more acted upon than acting, the delinquent prepares the way for deviance from the dominant normative system without the necessity of a frontal assault on the norms themselves.

The Denial of Injury

A second major technique of neutralization centers on the injury or harm involved in the delinquent act. The criminal law has long made a distinction between crimes which are *mala in se* and *mala prohibita*—that is between acts that are wrong in themselves and acts that are illegal but not immoral—and the delinquent can make the same kind of distinction in evaluating the wrongfulness of his behavior. For the delinquent, however, wrongfulness may turn on the question of whether or not anyone has clearly been hurt by his deviance, and this matter is open to a variety of interpretations. Vandalism, for example, may be defined by the delinquent simply as "mischief"—after all, it may be claimed, the persons whose property has been destroyed can well afford it. Similarly, auto theft may be viewed as "borrowing," and gang fighting may be seen as a private quarrel, an agreed upon duel between two willing parties, and thus of no concern to the community at large. We are not suggesting that this technique of neutralization, labelled the denial of injury, involves an explicit dialectic, rather, we are arguing that the delinquent frequently, and in a hazy fashion, feels that his behavior does not really cause any great harm despite the fact that it runs counter to law. Just as the link between the individual and his acts may be broken by the denial of responsibility, so may the link between acts and their consequences be broken by the denial of injury. Since society sometimes agrees with the delinquent, e.g., in matters such as truancy, "pranks," and so on, it merely reaffirms the idea that the delinquent's neutralization of social controls by means of qualifying the norms is an extension of common practice rather than a gesture of complete opposition.

The Denial of the Victim

Even if the delinquent accepts the responsibility for his deviant actions and is willing to admit that his deviant actions involve an injury or hurt, the moral indignation of self and others may be neutralized by an insistence that the injury is not wrong in light of the circumstances. The injury, it may be claimed, is not really an injury; rather, it is a form of rightful retaliation or punishment. By a subtle alchemy the delinquent moves himself into the position of an avenger and the victim is transformed into a wrong-doer. Assaults on homosexuals or suspected homosexuals, attacks on members of minority groups who are said to have gotten "out of place," vandalism as revenge on an unfair teacher or school official, thefts from a "crooked" store owner—all may be hurts inflicted on a transgressor, in the eyes of the delinquent. . . . Robin Hood, and his latter day derivatives such as the tough detective seeking justice outside the law, still capture the popular imagination, and the delinquent may view his acts as part of a similar role.

To deny the existence of the victim, then, by transforming him into a person deserving injury is an extreme form of a phenomenon we have mentioned before, namely, the delinquent's recognition of appropriate and inappropriate targets for his delinquent acts. In addition, however, the existence of the victim may be denied for the delinquent, in a somewhat different sense, by the circumstances of the delinquent act itself. Insofar as the victim is physically absent, unknown, or a vague abstraction (as is often the case in delinquent acts committed against property), the awareness of the victim's existence is weakened. Internalized norms and anticipations of the reactions of others must somehow be activated, if they are to serve as guides for behavior; and it is possible that a diminished awareness of the victim plays an important part in determining whether or not this process is set in motion.

The Condemnation of the Condemners

A fourth technique of neutralization would appear to involve a condemnation of the condemners or, as McCorkle and Korn have phrased it, a rejection of the rejectors.[3] The delinquent shifts the focus of attention from his own deviant acts to the motives and behavior of those who disapprove of his violations. His condemners, he may claim, are hypocrites, deviants in disguise, or impelled by personal spite. This orientation toward the conforming world may be of particular importance when it hardens into a bitter cynicism directed against those assigned the task of enforcing or expressing the norms of the dominant society. Police, it may be said, are corrupt, stupid, and brutal. Teachers always show favoritism and parents always "take it out" on their children. By a slight extension, the rewards of conformity—such as material success—become a matter of pull or luck, thus decreasing still further the stature of those who stand on the side of the law-abiding. The validity of this jaundiced viewpoint is not so important as its function in turning back or deflecting the negative sanctions attached to violations of the norms. The delinquent, in effect, has changed the subject of the conversation in the dialogue between his own deviant impulses and the reactions of others; and by attacking others, the wrongfulness of his own behavior is more easily repressed or lost to view.

The Appeal to Higher Loyalties

Fifth, and last, internal and external social controls may be neutralized by sacrificing the demands of the larger society for the demands of the smaller social groups to which the delinquent belongs such as the sibling pair, the gang, or the friendship clique. It is important to note that the delinquent does not necessarily repudiate the imperatives of the dominant normative system, despite his failure to follow them. Rather, the delinquent may see himself as caught up in a dilemma that must be resolved, unfortunately, at the cost of violating the law. One aspect of this situation has been studied by Stouffer and Toby in their research on the conflict between particularistic and universalistic demands, between the claims of friendship and general social obligations, and their results suggest that "it is possible to classify people according to a predisposition to select one or the other horn of a dilemma in role conflict.''[4] For our purposes, however, the most important point is that deviation from certain norms may occur not because the norms are rejected but because other norms, held to be more pressing or involving a higher loyalty, are accorded precedence. Indeed, it is the fact that both sets of norms are believed in that gives meaning to our concepts of dilemma and role conflict.

The conflict between the claims of friendship and the claims of law, or a similar dilemma, has of course long been recognized by the social scientist (and the novelist) as a common human problem. If the juvenile delinquent frequently resolves his dilemma by insisting that he must "always help a buddy" or "never squeal on a friend," even when it throws him into serious difficulties with the dominant social order, his choice remains familiar to the supposedly law-abiding. The delinquent is unusual, perhaps, in the extent to which he is able to see the fact that he acts in behalf of the smaller social groups to which he belongs as a justification for violations of society's norms, but it is a matter of degree rather than of kind.

"I didn't mean it." "I didn't really hurt anybody." "They had it coming to them." "Everybody's picking on me." "I didn't do it for myself." These slogans or their variants, we hypothesize, prepare the juvenile for delinquent acts. These "definitions of the situation" represent tangential or glancing blows at the dominant normative system rather than the creation of an opposing ideology; and they are extensions of patterns of thought prevalent in society rather than something created *de novo.*

Techniques of neutralization may not be powerful enough to fully shield the individual from the force of his own internalized values and the reactions of conforming others, for as we have pointed out, juvenile delinquents often appear to suffer from feelings of guilt and shame when called into account for their deviant behavior. And some delinquents may be so isolated from the world of conformity that techniques of neutralization need not be called into play. Nonetheless, we would argue that techniques of neutralization are critical in lessening the effectiveness of social controls and that they lie behind a large share of delinquent behavior. . . .

Notes

1. A number of observers have wryly noted that many delinquents seem to show a surprising awareness of sociological and psychological explanations for their behavior and are quick to point out the causal role of their poor environment.
2. It is possible, of course, that certain personality structures can accept some techniques of neutralization more readily than others, but this question remains largely unexplored.
3. Lloyd W. McCorkle and Richard Korn, "Resocialization Within Walls," *The Annals of the American Academy of Political and Social Science*, 293, (May, 1954), pp. 88–98.
4. See Samuel A. Stouffer and Jackson Toby, "Role Conflict and Personality," in *Toward a General Theory of Action*, edited by Talcott Parsons and Edward A. Shils, Cambridge, MA: Harvard University Press, 1951, p. 494.

34

Differential Association

Edwin H. Sutherland

The scientific explanation of a phenomenon may be stated either in terms of the factors which are operating at the moment of the occurrence of a phenomenon or in terms of the processes operating in the earlier history of that phenomenon. In the first case the explanation is mechanistic, in the second historical or genetic; both are usable. The physical and biological scientists favor the first of these methods, and it would probably be superior as an explanation of criminal behavior. Efforts at explanations of the mechanistic type have been notably unsuccessful, perhaps largely because they have been concentrated on the attempt to isolate personal and social pathologies. Work from this point of view has, at least, resulted in the conclusion that the immediate factors in criminal behavior lie in the person-situation complex. Person and situation are not factors exclusive of each other, for the situation which is important is the situation as defined by the person who is involved. The tendencies and inhibitions at the moment of the criminal behavior are, to be sure, largely a product of the earlier history of the person, but the expression of these tendencies and inhibitions is a reaction to the immediate situation as defined by the person. The situation operates in many ways, of which perhaps the least important is the provision of an opportunity for a criminal act. A thief may steal from a fruit stand when the owner is not in sight but refrain when the owner is in sight; a bank burglar may attack a bank which is poorly protected but refrain from attacking a bank protected by watchmen and burglar alarms. A corporation which manufactures automobiles seldom or never violates the Pure Food and Drug Law, but a meatpacking corporation violates this law with great frequency.

The second type of explanation of criminal behavior is made in terms of the life experience of a person and is a historical or genetic explanation of criminal behavior. This, to be sure, assumes a situation to be defined by the person in terms of the inclinations and abilities which the person has acquired up to that date. The following paragraphs state such a genetic theory [*i.e.*, the theory of differential association] of criminal behavior on the assumption that a criminal act occurs when a situation appropriate for it, as defined by a person, is present.

1. Criminal behavior is learned. Negatively, this means that criminal behavior is not inherited, as such; also, the person who is not already trained in crime does not invent criminal behavior, just as a person does not make mechanical inventions unless he has had training in mechanics.

2. Criminal behavior is learned in interaction with other persons in a process of communication. This communication is verbal in many respects but includes also "the communication of gestures."

3. The principal part of the learning of criminal behavior occurs within intimate personal groups. Negatively, this means that the impersonal agencies of communication, such as picture shows and newspapers, play a relatively unimportant part in the genesis of criminal behavior.

4. When criminal behavior is learned, the learning includes (a) techniques of committing the crime, which are sometimes very complicated, sometimes very simple; *(b) the specific direction of motives, drives, rationalizations, and attitudes.*

5. The specific direction of motives and drives is learned from definitions of legal codes as favorable and unfavorable. In some societies an individual is surrounded by persons who invariably define the legal codes as rules to be observed, whereas in others he is surrounded by persons whose definitions are favorable to the violation of the legal codes. In our American society these definitions are almost always mixed, and consequently we have culture conflict in relation to the legal codes.

6. A person becomes delinquent because of an excess of definitions favorable to violation of law over definitions unfavorable to violation of law. This is the principle of differential association. It refers to both criminal and anti-criminal associations and has to do with counteracting forces. When persons become criminals, they do so because of contacts with criminal patterns and also because of isolation from anti-criminal patterns. Any person inevitably assimilates the surrounding culture unless other patterns are in conflict; a Southerner does not pronounce "r" because other Southerners do not pronounce "r." Negatively, this proposition of differential association means that associations which are neutral so far as crime is concerned have little or no effect on the genesis of criminal behavior. Much of the experience of a person is neutral in this sense, *e.g.*, learning to brush one's teeth. This behavior has no negative or positive effect on criminal behavior except as it may be related to associations which are concerned with the legal codes. This neutral behavior is important especially as an occupier of the time of a child so that he is not in contact with criminal behavior during the time he is engaged in neutral behavior.

7. Differential associations may vary in frequency, duration, priority, and intensity. This means that associations with criminal behavior and also associations with anti-criminal behavior vary in those respects. "Frequency" and "duration" as modalities of associations are obvious and need no explanation. "Priority" is assumed to be important in the sense that lawful behavior developed in early childhood may persist throughout life, and also that delinquent behavior developed in early childhood may persist throughout life. This tendency, however, has not been adequately demonstrated, and priority seems to be important principally through its selective influence. "Intensity" is not precisely defined, but it has to do with such things as the prestige of the source of a criminal or anti-criminal pattern and with emotional reactions related to the associations. In a precise description of the criminal behavior of a person these modalities would be stated in quantitative form and a mathematical ratio be reached. A formula in this sense has not been developed, and the development of such a formula would be extremely difficult.

8. The process of learning criminal behavior by association with criminal and anti-criminal patterns involves all of the mechanisms that are involved in any other learning. Negatively, this means that the learning of criminal behavior is not restricted to the process of imitation. A person who is seduced, for instance, learns criminal behavior by association, but this process would not ordinarily be described as imitation.

9. *Though criminal behavior is an expression of general needs and values, it is not explained by those general needs and values since non-criminal behavior is an expression of the same needs and values.* Thieves generally steal in order to secure money, but likewise honest laborers work in order to secure money. The attempts by many scholars to explain criminal behavior by general drives and values, such as the happiness principle, striving for social status, the money motive, or frustration, have been and must continue to be futile since they explain lawful behavior as completely as they explain criminal behavior. They are similar to respiration, which is necessary for any behavior but which does not differentiate criminal from non-criminal behavior.

It is not necessary, on this level of discussion, to explain why a person has the associations which he has; this certainly involves a complex of many things. In an area where the delinquency rate is high a boy who is sociable, gregarious, active, and athletic is very likely to come in contact with the other boys in the neighborhood, learn delinquent behavior from them, and become a gangster; in the same neighborhood the psychopathic boy who is isolated, introvert, and inert may remain at home, not become acquainted with the other boys in the neighborhood, and not become delinquent. In another situation, the sociable, athletic, aggressive boy may become a member of a scout troop and not become involved in delinquent behavior. The person's associations are determined in a general context of social organization. A child is ordinarily reared in a family; the place of residence of the family is determined largely by family income; and the delinquency rate is in many respects related to the rental value of the houses. Many other factors enter into this social organization, including many personal group relationships.

The preceding explanation of criminal behavior was stated from the point of view of the person who engages in criminal behavior. It is also possible to state theories of criminal behavior from the point of view of the community, nation, or other group. The problem, when thus stated, is generally concerned with crime rates and involves a comparison of the crime rates of various groups or the crime rates of a particular group at different times. One of the best explanations of crime rates from this point of view is that a high crime rate is due to social disorganization. The term "social disorganization" is not entirely satisfactory, and it seems preferable to substitute for it the term "differential social organization." The postulate on which this theory is based, regardless of the name, is that crime is rooted in the social organization and is an expression of that social organization. A group may be organized for criminal behavior or organized against criminal behavior. Most communities are organized both for criminal and anti-criminal behavior, and in that sense the crime rate is an expression of the differential group organization. Differential group organization as an explanation of a crime rate must be consistent with the explanation of the criminal behavior of the person, since the crime rate is a summary statement of the number of persons in the group who commit crimes and the frequency with which they commit crimes.

35

A Differential Association-Reinforcement Theory of Criminal Behavior

Robert L. Burgess   *Ronald L. Akers*

. . . In this [article] the nine formal propositions in which [Edwin H.] Sutherland expressed his theory will be analyzed in terms of behavior theory and research and will be reformulated as seven new propositions.

I. "Criminal behavior is learned." VIII. "The process of learning criminal behavior by association with criminal and anti-criminal patterns involves all of the mechanisms that are involved in any other learning."

Since both the first and eighth sentence in the theory obviously form a unitary idea, it seems best to state them together. . . . Modern behavior theory as a general theory provides us with a good idea of what the mechanisms are that are involved in the process of acquiring behavior.[1]

According to this theory, there are two major categories of behavior. On the one hand, there is reflexive or *respondent* behavior which is behavior that is governed by the stimuli that elicit it. Such behaviors are largely associated with the autonomic system. The work of Pavlov is of special significance here. On the other hand, there is *operant* behavior: behavior which involves the central nervous system. Examples of operant behavior include verbal behavior, playing ball, driving a car, and buying a new suit. It has been found that this class of behavior is a function of its past and present environmental consequences. Thus, when a particular operant is followed by certain kinds of stimuli, that behavior's frequency of occurrence will increase in the future. These stimuli are called reinforcing stimuli or reinforcers and include food, money, clothes, objects of various sorts, social attention, approval, affection and social status. This entire process is called positive reinforcement. One distinguishing characteristic of operant behavior as opposed to respondent behavior, then, is that the latter is a function of its antecedent stimuli, whereas the former is a function of its antecedent environmental consequences. . . .

In everyday life, different consequences are usually contingent upon different classes of behavior. This relationship between behavior and its consequences functions to alter the rate and form of behavior as well as its relationship to many features of the environment. The process of operant reinforcement is the most important

Source: From *Social Problems*, Vol. 14, No. 2 (Fall, 1966), pp. 128–147. Copyright © 1966 The Society for the Study of Social Problems. Reprinted by permission.

process by which behavior is generated and maintained. . . .

The increase in the frequency of occurrence of a behavior that is reinforced is the very property of reinforcement that permits the fascinating variety and subtlety that occur in operant as opposed to respondent behavior. Another process producing the variety we see in behavior is that of *conditioning*. When a primary or unconditioned reinforcing stimulus such as food is repeatedly paired with a neutral stimulus, the latter will eventually function as a reinforcing stimulus as well. An illustration of this would be as follows. The milk a mother feeds to her infant is an unconditioned reinforcer. If the food is repeatedly paired with social attention, affection, and approval, these latter will eventually become reinforcing as will the mother herself as a stimulus object. Later these *conditioned reinforcers* can be used to strengthen other behaviors by making these reinforcers contingent upon those new behaviors.

Differential reinforcement may also alter the form of a response. This process is called *shaping* or *response differentiation*. It can be exemplified by a child learning to speak. At first, the parent will reinforce any vocalization, but as time wears on, and as the child grows older, the parent will differentially reinforce only those responses which successfully approximate certain criteria. The child will be seen to proceed from mere grunts to "baby-talk" to articulate speech.

Of course, organisms, whether pigeons, monkeys or people, do not usually go around behaving in all possible ways at all possible times. In short, behavior does not occur in a vacuum; a given behavior is appropriate to a given situation. By appropriate we mean that reinforcement has been forthcoming only under certain conditions and it is under these conditions that the behavior will occur. In other words, differential reinforcement not only increases the probability of a response, it also makes that response more probable upon the recurrence of conditions the same as or similar to those that were present during previous reinforcements. Such a process is called *stimulus control* or *stimulus discrimination*. For example, a child when he is first taught to say "daddy" may repeat it when any male is present, or even, in the very beginning, when any adult is present. But through differential reinforcement, the child will eventually only speak the word "daddy" when his father is present or in other "appropriate" conditions. We may say that the father, as a stimulus object, functions as a discriminative stimulus (S^D) setting the occasion for the operant verbal response "daddy" because in the past such behavior has been reinforced under such conditions.

It has also been discovered that the pattern or schedule of reinforcement is as important as the amount of reinforcement. For example, a *fixed-interval* schedule of reinforcement, where a response is reinforced only after a certain amount of time has passed, produces a lower rate of response than that obtained with reinforcement based on a *fixed-ratio* schedule where a response is reinforced only after a certain number of responses have already been emitted. Similarly a response rate obtained with a fixed-ratio schedule is lower than that obtained with a *variable-ratio* schedule, where reinforcement occurs for a certain proportion of responses randomly varied about some central value. A schedule of reinforcement, then, refers to the response *contingencies* upon which reinforcement depends. All of the various schedules of reinforcement, besides producing lawful response characteristics, produce lawful extinction rates, once reinforcement is discontinued. Briefly, behavior reinforced on an intermittent schedule takes longer to extinguish than behavior reinforced on a continuous schedule.

This concept, schedules of reinforcement, is one of the implications of which are little understood by many behavioral scientists, so a few additional words are in order. First of all, social reinforcements are for the most part intermittent. One obvious result of this fact is the resistance to extinction and satiation of much social behavior, desirable as well as undesirable. This is not peculiar to human social behavior, for even lower organisms seldom are faced with a continuous reinforcement schedule. Nevertheless, reinforcements mediated by another organism are probably much less reliable than those produced by the physical environment. This is the case because social reinforcement depends upon behavioral processes in the reinforcer which are not under good control by the reinforcee. A more subtle, though essentially methodological, implication of this is that because most social behaviors are maintained by complex intermittent schedules which have been shaped over a long period of time, a social observer newly entering a situation may have extreme difficulty in immediately determining exactly what is maintaining a particular behavior or set of behaviors. Nor can the individual himself be expected to be able to identify his own contingencies of reinforcement. . . .

The most general behavioral principle is the Law of Operant Behavior which says that behavior is a function of its past and current environmental consequences. . . .

Another of the behavioral principles we mentioned was that of stimulus discrimination. A discriminative stimulus is a stimulus in the presence of which a particular operant response is reinforced. Much of our behavior has come under the control of certain environmental, including social stimuli because in the past it has been reinforced in the presence of those stimuli. . . .

. . . Many forms of deviant behavior are shaped and maintained by various contingencies of reinforcement. Given this experimental evidence we would amend Sutherland's first and eighth propositions to read: *1. Criminal behavior is learned according to the principles of operant conditioning.*

II. "Criminal behavior is learned in interaction with other persons in the process of communication."

As DeFleur and Quinney have noted, the major implication of this proposition is that symbolic interaction is a necessary condition for the learning of criminal behavior.[2] Of direct relevance to this is an experiment designed to test the relative significance of verbal instructions and reinforcement contingencies in generating and maintaining a certain class of behaviors.[3] In brief, the results indicated that behavior could not be maintained solely through verbal instructions. . . . Symbolic interaction is, then, not enough, contingencies of reinforcement must also be present.

From the perspective of modern behavior theory, two aspects of socialization are usually considered to distinguish it from other processes of behavioral change: (1) Only those behavioral changes occurring through learning are considered relevant; (2) only the changes in behavior having their origins in interaction with other persons are considered products of socialization.[4] Sutherland's theory may, then, be seen to be a theory of differential socialization since he, too, restricted himself to learning having its origin in interaction with other persons. While social learning is, indeed, important and even predominant, it certainly does not exhaust the learning process. In short, we may learn (and, thus, our behavior would be modified) without any direct contact with another person. As such, Sutherland's theory may be seen to suffer from a significant lacuna in that it neglected the possibility of deviant behavior being learned in nonsocial situations. Consequently, to be an adequate theory of deviant behavior, the theory must be amended further to include those forms of deviant behavior that are learned in the absence of social reinforcement. Other people are not the only source of reinforcement although they are the most important. As Jeffery[5] has aptly noted, stealing is reinforcing in and by itself whether other people know about it and reinforce it socially or not. The same may be said to apply to many forms of aggressive behaviors. . . .

. . . The parent, who controls more of his child's reinforcers, will exercise more power than an older sibling or the temporary "baby sitter." As the child becomes older and less dependent upon the parent for many of his reinforcers, other individuals or groups such as his peers may exercise more power. Carrying the analysis one step further, the person who has access to a large range of aversive stimuli will exert more power than one who has not. Thus a peer group may come to exercise more power over a child's behavior than the parent even though the parent may still control a large share of the child's positive reinforcers.

In addition to the reinforcing function of an individual or group, there is . . . the discriminative stimulus function of a group. For example, specific individuals as physical stimuli may acquire discriminative control over an individual's behavior. The child in our example above is reinforced for certain kinds of behaviors in the presence of his parent, thus the parent's presence may come to control this type of behavior. He is reinforced for different behaviors in the presence of his peers, who then come to set the occasion for this type of behavior. Consequently this proposition must be amended to read: *2. Criminal behavior is learned both in nonsocial situations that are reinforcing or discriminative, and through that social interaction in which the behavior of other persons is reinforcing or discriminative for criminal behavior.*

III. "The principal part of the learning of criminal behavior occurs within intimate personal groups."

In terms of our analysis, the primary group would be seen to be the major source of an individual's social reinforcements. The bulk of behavioral training which the child receives occurs at a time when the trainers, usually the parents, possess a very powerful system of reinforcers. In fact, we might characterize a primary group as a generalized reinforcer (one associated with many reinforcers, conditioned as well as unconditioned). And, as we suggested above, as the child grows older, groups other than the family may come to control a majority of an individual's reinforcers, e.g., the adolescent peer group.

To say that the primary group is the principal molder of an individual's behavioral repertoire is not to ignore social learning which may occur in other contexts. As we noted above, learning from social models can be adequately explained in terms of these behavioral principles. The analysis we employed there can also be extended to learning from the mass media and from "reference" groups. In any case, we may alter this proposition to read: *3. The principal part of the learning of criminal behavior occurs in those groups which comprise the individual's major source of reinforcements.*

IV. "When criminal behavior is learned, the learning includes (a) techniques of committing the crime, which are sometimes very complicated, sometimes very simple; (b) the specific direction of motives, drives, rationalizations, and attitudes.''

A study by Klaus and Glaser[6] as well as many other studies[7] indicate that reinforcement contingencies are of prime importance in learning various behavioral techniques. And, of course, many techniques, both simple and complicated, are specific to a particular deviant act such as jimmying, picking locks of buildings and cars, picking pockets, short- and big-con techniques, counterfeiting and safe-cracking. Other techniques in criminal behavior may be learned in conforming or neutral contexts, e.g., driving a car, signing checks, shooting a gun, etc. In any event, we need not alter the first part of this proposition.

The second part of this proposition does, however, deserve some additional comments. Sutherland's major focus here seems to be motivation. Much of what we have already discussed in this paper often goes under the general heading of motivation. The topic of motivation is as important as it is complex. This complexity is related to the fact that the same stimulus may have two functions: it may be both a reinforcing stimulus and a discriminative stimulus controlling the behavior which is followed by reinforcement.[8] Thus, motivation may be seen to be a function of the processes by which stimuli acquire conditioned reinforcing value and become discriminative stimuli. Reinforcers and discriminative stimuli here would become the dependent variables; the independent variables would be the conditioning procedures previously mentioned and the level of deprivation. For example, when a prisoner is deprived of contact with members of the opposite sex, such sex reinforcers will become much more powerful. Thus, those sexual reinforcers that are available, such as homosexual contact, would come to exert a great deal of influence and would shape behaviors that would be unlikely to occur without such deprivation. And, without going any further into this topic, some stimuli may be more reinforcing, under similar conditions of deprivation, for certain individuals or groups than for others. Furthermore, the satiation of one or more of these reinforcers would allow for an increase in the relative strength of others. . . .

. . . We may, therefore, rewrite this proposition to read: *4. The learning of criminal behavior, including specific techniques, attitudes, and avoidance procedures, is a function of the effective and available reinforcers, and the existing reinforcement contingencies.*

V. ''The specific direction of motives and drives is learned from definitions of the legal codes as favorable or unfavorable.''. . .

Behavior theory specifies the place of normative statements and sanctions in the dynamics of acquiring ''conforming'' or ''normative'' behavior. Just as the behavior and even the physical characteristics of the individual may serve discriminative functions, verbal behavior, and this includes normative statements, can be analyzed as S^D's. A normative statement can be analyzed as an S^D indicating that the members of a group ought to behave in a certain way in certain circumstances. Such ''normative'' behavior would be developed and maintained by social reinforcement . . . We may now say that we can learn a great deal about an individual's or a group's behavior when we are able to specify, not only what the effective reinforcers are, but also what the rules or norms are by which these reinforcers are applied.[9] For these two types of knowledge will tell us much about the types of behavior that the individual will develop or the types of behaviors that are dominant in a group.

. . . Thus we may formulate this proposition to read: *5. The specific class of behaviors which are learned and their frequency of occurrence are a function of the reinforcers which are effective and available, and the rules or norms by which these reinforcers are applied.*

VI. "A person becomes delinquent because of an excess of definitions favorable to violation of law over definitions unfavorable to violation of law."

This proposition is generally considered the heart of Sutherland's theory; it is the principle of differential association. It follows directly from proposition V, and we must now refer back to that proposition. In proposition V, the use of the preposition "from" in the phrase, "learned from definitions of the legal codes as favorable or unfavorable," is somewhat misleading. The meaning here is not so much that learning results *from* these definitions as it is that they form part of the *content* of one's learning, determining which direction one's behavior will go in relation to the law, i.e., law-abiding or lawbreaking.

These definitions of the law make lawbreaking seem either appropriate or inappropriate. Those definitions which place lawbreaking in a favorable light in a sense can be seen as essentially norms of evasion and/or norms directly conflicting with conventional norms. They are, as Sykes and Matza and Cressey note, "techniques of neutralization," "rationalizations," or "verbalizations" which make criminal behavior seem "all right" or justified, or which provide defenses against self-reproach and disapproval from others.[10] The principle of negative reinforcement would be of major significance in the acquisition and maintenance of such behaviors.

This analysis suggests that it may not be an "excess" of one kind of definition over another in the sense of a cumulative ratio, but rather in the sense of the relative amount of discriminative stimulus value of one set of verbalizations or normative statements over another. . . .

In other terms, a person will become delinquent if the official norms or laws do not perform a discriminative function and thereby control "normative" or conforming behavior. . . .

The concept "excess" in the statement, "excess of definitions favorable to violation of law," has been particularly resistant to operationalization. A translation of this concept in terms of modern behavior theory would involve the "balance" of reinforcement consequences, positive and negative. The Law of Differential Reinforcement is crucial here. That is, a person would engage in those behaviors for which he had been reinforced most highly in the past. . . . Criminal behavior would, then, occur under those conditions where an individual has been most highly reinforced for such behavior, and the aversive consequences contingent upon the behavior have been of such a nature that they do not perform a "punishment function." This leads us to a discussion of proposition VII. But, first, let us reformulate the sixth proposition to read: *6. Criminal behavior is a function of norms which are discriminative for criminal behavior, the learning of which takes place when such behavior is more highly reinforced than noncriminal behavior.*

VII. "Differential associations may vary in frequency, duration, priority, and intensity."

In terms of our analysis, the concepts frequency, duration, and priority are straightforward enough. The concept *intensity* could be operationalized to designate the number of the individual's positive and negative reinforcers another individual or group controls, as well as the reinforcement value of that individual or group. As previously suggested the group which can mediate the most positive reinforcers and which has the most reinforcement value, as well as access to a larger range of aversive stimuli, will exert the most control over an individual's behavior.

There is a good reason to suspect, however, that Sutherland was not so much referring to differential associations with other persons, as differential associations with criminal *patterns*. If this supposition is correct, then this proposition can be clarified by relating it to differential contingencies of reinforcement rather than differential social associations. From this perspective, the experimental evidence with regard to the various schedules of reinforcement is of major importance. There are three aspects of the schedules of reinforcement which are of particular importance here: (1) the *amount* of reinforcement: the greater the amount of reinforcement, the higher the response rate; (2) the *frequency* of reinforcement which refers to the number of reinforcements per given time period: the shorter the time period between reinforcements, the higher the response rate; and (3) the *probability* of reinforcement which is the reciprocal of responses per reinforcement: the lower the ratio of responses per reinforcement, the higher the rate of response.[11]

Priority, frequency, duration, and intensity of association with criminal persons and groups are important to the extent that they insure that deviant behavior will receive greater amounts of reinforcement at more frequent intervals or with a higher probability than conforming behavior. But the frequency, probability, and amount of reinforcement are the crucial elements. This means that it is the coming under the control of contingencies of reinforcement that selectively produces the criminal definitions and behavior. Consequently, let us rewrite this proposition to read: *7. The strength of criminal behavior is a direct function of the amount, frequency, and probability of its reinforcement.*

IX. "While criminal behavior is an expression of general needs and values, it is not explained by those general needs and values since noncriminal behavior is an expression of the same needs and values."

In this proposition, Sutherland may have been reacting, at least in part, to the controversy regarding the concept "need." This controversy is now essentially resolved. For, we have finally come to the realization that "needs" are unobservable, hypothetical, fictional inner-causal agents which were usually invented on the spot to provide spurious explanations of some observable behavior. Furthermore, they were inferred from precisely the same behavior they were supposed to explain.

While we can ignore the reference to needs, we must discuss values. Values may be seen as reinforcers which have salience for a number of the members of a group or society. We agree with Sutherland to the extent that he means that the nature of these general reinforcers do not necessarily determine which behavior they will strengthen. Money, or something else of general value in society, will reinforce any behavior that produces it. This reinforcement may depend upon noncriminal behavior, but it also may become contingent upon a set of behaviors that are labelled as criminal. Thus, if Sutherland can be interpreted as meaning that criminal and noncriminal behavior cannot be maintained by the same set of reinforcers, we must disagree. However, it may be that there are certain reinforcing consequences which only criminal behavior will produce, for the behavior finally shaped will depend upon the reinforcer that is effective for the individual. Nevertheless, it is the reinforcement, not the specific nature of the reinforcer, which explains the rate and form of behavior. But since this issue revolves around contingencies of reinforcement which are handled elsewhere, we will eliminate this last proposition. . . .

Notes

1. It should be mentioned at the outset that there is more than one learning theory. The one we will employ is called Behavior Theory. More specifically, it is that variety of behavior theory largely associated with the name of B. F. Skinner. (*Science and Human Behavior*, New York: Macmillan, 1953.) It differs from other learning theories in that it restricts itself to the relations between observable, measurable behavior and observable, measurable conditions. There is nothing in this theory that denies the existence, or importance, or even the inherent interest of the nervous system or brain. However, most behavioral scientists in this area are extremely careful in hypothesizing intervening variables or constructs, whether they are egos, personalities, response sets, or some sort of internal computers. Generally they adopt the position that the only real value of a construct is its ability to improve one's predictions. If it does not, then it must be excluded in accordance with the rule of parsimony.
2. DeFleur and Quinney, *op. cit.*, p. 3.
3. T. Ayllon and N. Azrin, "Reinforcement and Instructions with Mental Patients," *Journal of the Experimental Analysis of Behavior*, 7, 1964, pp. 327–331.
4. Paul E. Secord and Carl W. Backman, *Social Psychology*, New York: McGraw-Hill, 1964.
5. Jeffery, *op. cit.*
6. D. J. Klaus and R. Glaser, "Increasing Team Proficiency Through Training," Pittsburgh: American Institute of Research, 1960.
7. See Robert L. Burgess, "Communication Networks and Behavioral Consequences," forthcoming.
8. A central principle underlying this analysis is that reinforcing stimuli, both positive and negative, elicit certain respondents. Unconditioned reinforcers elicit these responses without training, conditioned reinforcers elicit such responses through respondent conditioning. Staats and Staats (*Complex Human Behavior*, New York: Holt, Rinehart and Winston, 1964) have characterized such respondents as "attitude" responses. Thus, a positive reinforcer elicits a positive attitude. Furthermore, these respondents have stimulus characteristics which may become discriminative stimuli setting the occasion for a certain class of operants called "striving" responses for positive reinforcers and escape and/or avoidance behaviors for negative reinforcers. These respondents and their attendant stimuli may be generalized to other reinforcing stimuli. Thus, striving responses can be seen to generalize to new positive reinforcers since these also will elicit the respondent responses and their characteristic stimuli which have become S^D's for such behavior.
9. Staats and Staats, *op. cit.*
10. Sykes and Matza, *op. cit.*, Cressey, *Other People's Money, op. cit*, pp. 93–138; Donald R. Cressey, "The Differential Association Theory and Compulsive Crimes," *Journal of Criminal Law, Criminology and Police Science*, 45 (May-June, 1954), pp. 29–40; Donald R. Cressey, "Social Psychological Foundations for Using Criminals in the Rehabilitation of Criminals," *Journal of Research in Crime and Delinquency*, 2 (July, 1965), pp. 45–59. See revised proposition IV.
11. R. T. Kelleher and L. R. Gollub, "A Review of Positive Conditioned Reinforcement," *Journal of the Experimental Analysis of Behavior* (October, 1962), pp. 543–597. Because the emission of a fixed ratio or variable ratio of responses requires a period of time, the rate of responding will indirectly determine the frequency of reinforcement.

36

Delinquency and Opportunity

Richard A. Cloward   Lloyd E. Ohlin

. . . Social norms are two-sided. A prescription implies the existence of a prohibition, and *vice versa*. To advocate honesty is to demarcate and condemn a set of actions which are dishonest. In other words, norms that define legitimate practices also implicitly define illegitimate practices. One purpose of norms, in fact, is to delineate the boundary between legitimate and illegitimate practices. In setting this boundary in segregating and classifying various types of behavior, they make us aware not only of behavior that is regarded as right and proper but also of behavior that is said to be wrong and improper. Thus the criminal who engages in theft or fraud does not invent a new way of life; the possibility of employing alternative means is acknowledged, tacitly at least, by the norms of the culture.

This tendency for proscribed alternatives to be implicit in every prescription, and *vice versa*, although widely recognized, is nevertheless a reef upon which many a theory of delinquency has foundered. Much of the criminological literature assumes, for example, that one may explain a criminal act simply by accounting for the individual's readiness to employ illegal alternatives of which his culture, through its norms, has already made him generally aware. Such explanations are quite unsatisfactory, however, for they ignore a host of questions regarding the *relative availability* of illegal alternatives to various potential criminals. The aspiration to be a physician is hardly enough to explain the fact of becoming a physician; there is much that transpires between the aspiration and the achievement. This is no less true of the person who wants to be a successful criminal. Having decided that he "can't make it legitimately," he cannot simply choose among an array of illegitimate means, all equally available to him. As we have noted earlier, it is assumed in the theory of anomie that access to conventional means is differentially distributed, that some individuals, because of their social class, enjoy certain advantages that are denied to those elsewhere in the class structure. For example, there are variations in the degree to which members of various classes are fully exposed to and thus acquire the values, knowledge, and skills that facilitate upward mobility. It should not be startling, therefore, to suggest that there are socially structured variations in the availability of illegitimate means as well. In connection with delinquent subcultures, we shall be concerned principally with differentials in access to illegitimate means

Source: Reprinted with permission of The Free Press, a Division of Simon & Schuster Adult Publishing Group, from Richard A. Cloward and Lloyd C. Ohlin, *Delinquency and Opportunity: A Theory of Delinquent Gangs.* Copyright © 1960 by The Free Press. Copyright © renewed 1988 by Lloyd C. Ohlin.

within the lower class.

Many sociologists have alluded to differentials in access to illegitimate means without explicitly incorporating this variable into a theory of deviant behavior. This is particularly true of scholars in the "Chicago tradition" of criminology. Two closely related theoretical perspectives emerged from this school. The theory of "cultural transmission," advanced by Clifford R. Shaw and Henry D. McKay, focuses on the development in some urban neighborhoods of a criminal tradition that persists from one generation to another despite constant changes in population.[1] In the theory of "differential association," Edwin H. Sutherland described the processes by which criminal values are taken over by the individual.[2] He asserted that criminal behavior is learned, and that it is learned in interaction with others who have already incorporated criminal values. Thus the first theory stresses the value systems of different areas; the second, the systems of social relationships that facilitate or impede the acquisition of these values.

Scholars in the Chicago tradition, who emphasized the processes involved in learning to be criminal, were actually pointing to differentials in the availability of illegal means—although they did not explicitly recognize this variable in their analysis. This can perhaps best be seen by examining Sutherland's classic work, *The Professional Thief*. "An inclination to steal," according to Sutherland, "is not a sufficient explanation of the genesis of the professional thief."[3] The "self-made" thief, lacking knowledge of the ways of securing immunity from prosecution and similar techniques of defense, "would quickly land in prison; . . . a person can be a professional thief only if he is recognized and received as such by other professional thieves." But recognition is not freely accorded: "Selection and tutelage are the two necessary elements in the process of acquiring recognition as a professional thief. . . . A person cannot acquire recognition as a professional thief until he has had tutelage in professional theft, *and tutelage is given only to a few persons selected from the total population*." For one thing, "the person must be appreciated by the professional thieves. He must be appraised as having an adequate equipment of wits, front, talking-ability, honesty, reliability, nerve and determination." Furthermore, the aspirant is judged by high standards of performance, for only "a very small percentage of those who start on this process ever reach the stage of professional thief. . . ." Thus motivation and pressures toward deviance do not fully account for deviant behavior any more than motivation and pressures toward conformity account for conforming behavior. The individual must have access to a learning environment and, once having been trained, must be allowed to perform his role. Roles, whether conforming or deviant in content, are not necessarily freely available; access to them depends upon a variety of factors, such as one's socioeconomic position, age, sex, ethnic affiliation, personality characteristics, and the like. The potential thief, like the potential physician, finds that access to his goal is governed by many criteria other than merit and motivation.

What we are asserting is that access to illegitimate roles is not freely available to all, as is commonly assumed. Only those neighborhoods in which crime flourishes as a stable, indigenous institution are fertile criminal learning environments for the young. Because these environments afford integration of different age-levels of offender, selected young people are exposed to "differential association" through which tutelage is provided and criminal values and skills are acquired. To be prepared for the role may not, however, ensure that the individual will ever discharge it. One important limitation is that more youngsters are recruited into these patterns of differential associations than the adult criminal structure can possibly absorb. Since there is a surplus of contenders for these elite positions, criteria and mechanisms of selection must be evolved. Hence a certain proportion of those who aspire may not be permitted to engage in the behavior for which they have prepared themselves.

Thus we conclude that access to illegitimate roles, no less than access to legitimate roles, is limited by both social and psychological factors. We shall here be concerned primarily with socially structured differentials in illegitimate opportunities. Such differentials, we contend, have much to do with the type of delinquent subculture that develops.

Learning and Performance Structures

Our use of the term "opportunities," legitimate or illegitimate, implies access to both learning and performance structures. That is, the individual must have access to appropriate environments for the acquisition of the values and skills associated with the performance of a particular role, and he must be supported in the performance of the role once he has learned it.

Tannenbaum, several decades ago, vividly expressed the point that criminal role performance, no less than conventional role performance, presupposes a patterned set of relationships through which the requisite values and skills are transmitted by established practitioners to aspiring youth:

> It takes a long time to make a good criminal, many years of specialized training and much preparation. But training is something that is given to people. People learn in a community where the materials and the knowledge are to be had. A craft needs an atmosphere saturated with purpose and promise. The community provides the attitudes, the point of view, the philosophy of life, the example, the motive, the contacts, the friendships, the incentives. No child brings those into the world. He finds them here and available for use and elaboration. The community gives the criminal his materials and habits, just as it gives the doctor, the lawyer, the teacher, and the candlestick-maker theirs.[4]

Sutherland systematized this general point of view, asserting that opportunity consists, at least in part, of learning structures. Thus "criminal behavior is learned" and, furthermore, it is learned "in interaction with other persons in a process of communication." However, he conceded that the differential-association theory does not constitute a full explanation of criminal behavior. In a paper circulated in 1944, he noted that "criminal behavior is partially a function of opportunities to commit [*i.e.*, to perform] specific classes of crime, such as embezzlement, bank burglary, or illicit heterosexual intercourse." Therefore, "while opportunity may be partially a function of association with criminal patterns and of the specialized techniques thus acquired, it is not determined entirely in that manner, and consequently differential association is not the sufficient cause of criminal behavior."[5]

To Sutherland, then, illegitimate opportunity included conditions favorable to the performance of a criminal role as well as conditions favorable to the learning of such a role (differential associations). These conditions, we suggest, depend upon certain features of the social structure of the community in which delinquency arises.

Differential Opportunity: A Hypothesis

We believe that each individual occupies a position in both legitimate and illegitimate opportunity structures. This is a new way of defining the situation. The theory of anomie views the individual primarily in terms of the legitimate opportunity structure. It poses questions regarding differentials in access to legitimate routes to success-goals; at the same time it assumes either that illegitimate avenues to success-goals are freely available or that differentials in their availability are of little significance. This tendency may be seen in the following statement by Merton:

> Several researches have shown that specialized areas of vice and crime constitute a "normal" response to a situation where the cultural emphasis upon pecuniary success has been absorbed, but where there is little access to conventional and legitimate means for becoming successful. The occupational opportunities of people in these areas are largely confined to manual labor and the lesser white-collar jobs. Given the American stigmatization of manual labor *which has been found to hold rather uniformly for all social classes*, and the absence of realistic opportunities for advancement beyond this level, the result is a marked tendency toward deviant behavior. The status of unskilled labor and the consequent low income cannot readily compete *in terms of established standards of worth* with the promises of power and high income from organized vice, rackets and crime. . . . [Such a situation] leads toward the gradual attenuation of legitimate, but by and large ineffectual, strivings and the increasing use of illegitimate, but more or less effective, expedients.[6]

The cultural-transmission and differential-association tradition, on the other hand, assumes that access to illegitimate means is variable, but it does not recognize the significance of comparable differentials in access to legitimate means. Sutherland's "ninth proposition" in the theory of differential association states:

> *Though criminal behavior is an expression of general needs and values, it is not explained by those general needs and values since non-criminal behavior is an expression of the same needs and values.* Thieves generally steal in order to secure money, but likewise honest laborers work in order to secure money. The attempts by many scholars to explain criminal behavior by general drives and values, such as the happiness principle, striving for social status, the money motive, or frustration, have been and must continue to be futile since they explain lawful behavior as completely as they explain criminal behavior.[7]

In this statement, Sutherland appears to assume that people have equal and free access to legitimate means regardless of their social position. At the very least, he does not treat access to legitimate means as variable. It is, of course, perfectly true that "striving for social status," "the money motive," and other socially approved drives do not fully account for either deviant or conforming behavior. But if goal-oriented behavior occurs under conditions in which there are socially structured obstacles to the satisfaction of these drives by legitimate means, the resulting pressures, we contend, might lead to deviance.

The concept of differential opportunity structures permits us to unite the theory of anomie, which recognizes the concept of differentials in access to legitimate means, and the "Chicago tradition," in which the concept of differentials in access to illegitimate means is implicit. We can now look at the individual, not simply in relation to one or the other system of means, but in relation to both legitimate and illegitimate systems. This approach permits us to ask, for example, how the relative availability of illegitimate opportunities affects the resolution of adjustment problems leading to deviant behavior. We believe that the way in which these problems are resolved may depend upon the kind of support for one or another type of illegitimate activity that is given at different points in the social structure. If, in a given social location, illegal or criminal means are not readily available, then we should not expect a criminal subculture to develop among adolescents. By the same logic, we should expect the manipulation of violence to become a primary avenue to higher status only in areas where the means of violence are not denied to the young. To give a third example, drug addiction and participation in subcultures organized around the consumption of drugs presuppose that persons can secure access to drugs and knowledge about how to use them. In some parts of the social structure, this would be very difficult; in others, very easy. In short, there are marked differences from one part of the social structure to another in the types of illegitimate adaptation that are available to persons in search of solutions to problems of adjustment arising from the restricted availability of legitimate means.[8] In this sense, then, we can think of individuals as being located in two opportunity structures—one legitimate, the other illegitimate. Given limited access to success-goals by legitimate means, the nature of the delinquent response that may result will vary according to the availability of various illegitimate means. . . .[9]

Notes

1. See esp. C. R. Shaw, *The Jack-Roller* (Chicago: University of Chicago Press, 1930); Shaw, *The Natural History of a Delinquent Career* (Chicago: University of Chicago Press, 1931); Shaw et al., *Delinquency Areas* (Chicago: University of Chicago Press, 1940); and Shaw and H. D. McKay, *Juvenile Delinquency and Urban Areas* (Chicago: University of Chicago Press, 1942).
2. E. H. Sutherland, ed., *The Professional Thief* (Chicago: University of Chicago Press, 1937); and Sutherland, *Principles of Criminology*, 4th Ed. (Philadelphia: Lippincott, 1947).
3. All quotations on this page are from *The Professional Thief*, pp. 211–13. Emphasis added.
4. Frank Tannenbaum, "The Professional Criminal," *The Century*, Vol. 110 (May–Oct. 1925), p. 577.
5. See A. K. Cohen, Alfred Lindesmith, and Karl Schuessler, eds., *The Sutherland Papers* (Bloomington, IN: Indiana University Press, 1956), pp. 31–35.
6. R. K. Merton, *Social Theory and Social Structure*, Rev. and Enl. Ed. (Glencoe, IL: Free Press, 1957), pp. 145–46.
7. *Principles of Criminology*, *op. cit.*, pp. 7–8.
8. For an example of restrictions on access to illegitimate roles, note the impact of racial definitions in the following case: "I was greeted by two prisoners who were to be my cell buddies. Ernest was a first offender, charged with being a "hold-up" man. Bill, the other buddy, was an old offender, going through the machinery of becoming a habitual criminal, in and out of jail. . . . The first thing they asked me was, 'What are you in for?' I said, 'Jack-rolling.' The hardened one (Bill) looked at me with a superior air and said, 'A hoodlum eh? An ordinary sneak thief. Not willing to leave jack-rolling to the niggers, eh? That's all they're good for. Kid, jack-rolling's not a white man's job.' I could see that he was disgusted with me, and I was too scared to say anything" (Shaw, *The Jack-Roller*, *op. cit.*, p. 101).
9. For a discussion of the way in which the availability of illegitimate means influences the adaptations of inmates to prison life, see R. A. Cloward, "Social Control in the Prison," *Theoretical Studies of the Social Organization of the Prison*, Bulletin No. 15 (New York: Social Science Research Council, March 1960), pp. 20–48.

37

Unraveling Juvenile Delinquency

Sheldon Glueck   *Eleanor Glueck*

. . . By and large, examination of existing researches in juvenile delinquency discloses a tendency to emphasize a particular approach or explanation. Proponents of various theories of causation still too often insist that the truth is to be found only in their own special fields of study, and that, *ex hypothesi*, researches made by those working in other disciplines can contribute very little to the understanding and management of the crime problem. Like the blind men and the elephant of the fable, each builds the entire subject in the image of that piece of it which he happens to have touched.

Yet it stands to reason that since so little is as yet known about the intricacies of normal human behavior, it is the better part of wisdom not to be overawed by any branch of science or methodology to the neglect of other promising leads in the study of aberrant behavior. When, therefore, research into the causes of delinquency emphasizes the sociologic, or ecologic, or cultural, or psychiatric, or psychoanalytic, or anthropologic approach, relegating the others to a remote position, if not totally ignoring them, we must immediately be on guard. The problems of human motivation and behavior involve the study of man as well as society, of nature as well as nurture, of segments or mechanisms of human nature as well as the total personality, of patterns of intimate social activity as well as larger areas of social process or masses of culture. They involve, therefore, the participation of several disciplines. Without recognition of such factors, bias must weaken the validity of both method and interpretation. . . .

Need for Eclectic Approach to Study of Crime Causation

At the present stage of knowledge an eclectic approach to the study of the causal process in human motivation and behavior is obviously necessary. It is clear that such an inquiry should be designed to reveal meaningful integrations of diverse data from several levels of inquiry. There is need for a systematic approach that will not ignore any promising leads to crime causation, covering as many fields and utilizing as many of the most reliable and relevant techniques of investigation and measurement as are necessary for a fair sampling of the various aspects of a complex biosocial problem. Ideally, the focus in such a study should be upon the selectivity

Source: Reprinted by permission of the publisher from Sheldon and Eleanor Glueck, *Unraveling Juvenile Delinquency,* pp. 4, 5, 7, 14, 15, 20, 41, 54, 272, 281–282, Cambridge, MA: Harvard University Press. Copyright © 1950 by the President and Fellows of Harvard College. Permission granted by the Commonwealth Fund.

that occurs when environment and organism interact. The searchlight should be played upon the point of contact between specific social and biologic processes as they coalesce, accommodate, or conflict in individuals.

But while the most promising areas of research in human conduct and misconduct are to be found in the nexus of physical and mental functions and in the interplay of person and milieu, the complexities of motivation and varieties of behavior compel a division of the field into areas or levels. These must be interpreted serially before arriving at a meaningful pattern. . . .

Control of the Inquiry

In order to arrive at the clearest differentiation of disease and health, comparison must be made between the unquestionably pathologic and the normal. (This metaphor does not carry with it any implication that we view delinquency as a disease.) Therefore nondelinquents as well as delinquents become the subjects of our inquiry. Comparison is a fundamental method of science; and the true value of any phenomenon disclosed by exploration of human behavior cannot be reliably determined without comparing its incidence in an experimental group with that in a control group. This method in the present research should result not only in isolating the factors which most markedly differentiate delinquents from nondelinquents, but in casting light on the causal efficacy of a number of factors generally accepted as criminogenic.

The control group must of course be truly nondelinquent. But this one factor, although basic, is not enough. Some factors must be held constant as a prerequisite to the comparison of delinquents and nondelinquents in respect to still other factors.

In deciding which factors to use in matching delinquents with nondelinquents, we were guided by several aims. First, since the ultimate comparison should cover subtle processes of personality and environment, the more general or cruder factors should be controlled in the matching; second, those traits that typically affect a whole range of factors ought to be held constant; third, those general characteristics that have already been explored sufficiently by other investigators and about which there is much agreement ought to be equalized in the two groups. Overriding all these aims, however, is the practical difficulty of matching two series of hundreds of human beings, while holding several factors constant.

We therefore decided to match 500 delinquent boys with 500 nondelinquent boys in four respects:

1. *Age*, because it is often asserted that tendencies to maladjustment and misbehavior vary with age (especially puberty and adolescence); also because morphologic and psychologic factors are more or less affected by age.

2. *General intelligence*, because there is considerable claim that intelligence, as measured by standard tests, bears an intimate relationship to varieties of behavior-tendency. From the point of view of the clinical psychologist concerned with determining the extent and quality of intelligence of the individual before him, the intelligence quotient—standing alone—is nowadays regarded as somewhat naive and not always helpful. However, it still forms an important part of the protocol covering the diagnosis of

intellectual make-up, and for our purpose of matching delinquents with nondelinquents it is adequate.

3. *National (ethnico-racial) origin*, because there is a school of thought which stresses ethnic derivation and associated culture patterns in accounting for variations in behavior tendencies. Since we are interested, also, in determining whether meaningful differences exist between delinquents and nondelinquents in respect to bodily morphology (somatotypes and bodily disproportions), such differences or similarities as may emerge from the anthropologic analysis should gain in significance by the fact that ethnico-racial derivation has been controlled in the matching process.

4. *Residence in underprivileged neighborhoods*, because, as noted in Chapter 1, the conception is widespread that delinquency is largely bred by the conditions in such areas. In selecting both delinquents and nondelinquents from unwholesome neighborhoods, we were attempting to control a complex of socioeconomic and cultural factors whose similarity would permit us to find out why it is that even in regions of most adverse social conditions, most children do not commit legally prohibited acts of theft, burglary, assault, sexual aggression, and the like. . . .

Levels of the Inquiry

Though we look at the problem of delinquency from the point of view of the integration of the total personality, it is revealing to study discord or conflict and accord or harmony at various levels: (1) the socio-cultural level, where conflict is shown by delinquency, crime, or other forms of maladjustment of the individual to the taboos, demands, conventions, and laws of society; (2) the somatic level, where disharmony is indicated by dysplasias or disproportions between the structure of two or more segments of the physique and by ill health; (3) the intellectual level, where discord may be revealed by contrasts between capacities of abstract intelligence and those of concrete intelligence, or between special abilities and special disabilities, or by excessive variability in types of intellectual capacity; (4) the emotional-temperamental level, where disharmony is shown by mental conflict and by the tensions between repressed and forgotten emotional experiences and more recent experiences or between divergent instinctual energy propulsions typically reflected in the phenomenon of ambivalence.

In gathering and interpreting data on each of these four levels separately, we are not overlooking the fact that we are dealing with the motivations and behavior of the total organism in its milieu. . . .

. . . Always remembering our main objective—to compare boys reared in underprivileged areas of a large city who become serious and persistent delinquents with boys bred in similar neighborhoods who are not antisocial—we finally arrived at what seemed to be as nearly an ideal plan as could be devised; it promised to produce the necessary data by the most direct means and with the least possible inconvenience to the boys, their families, and the many institutional authorities and social workers who would be involved. This plan called for the examination of delinquent boys preponderantly from the Boston area who at the time of selection were inmates of a state correctional school, the Lyman School for Boys in Westboro, Massachusetts, and the examination of a comparable number of proven nondelinquents from public schools in the city of Boston. (Later it proved necessary to include some boys from the Industrial School for Boys in Shirley, Massachusetts.) . . .

Delimiting the Social Inquiry

In deciding which factors to include, we had to keep in mind the limitations of data gathered so many years after the original event, not only regarding purely objective facts but especially regarding qualitative information about the home environment in which the boy had been reared, his early behavioral difficulties, and the like. Long experience in gathering social histories had taught us the dangers and pitfalls in reconstructing the past because of limitations in recorded data and in the memories of those from whom the information must necessarily be derived. It is also difficult to secure any valid qualitative data, such as the emotional atmosphere surrounding past and even current situations, without the most intensive investigations.

The factors which we had sought in connection with our other studies had all been subjected to rigid testing; and as we were interested, among other things, to secure data that would be comparable to those already compiled on the two thousand case histories of our earlier studies, we incorporated all these factors and added others of special pertinence to the current research. The result was a total of 149 social factors.

In general, we set ourselves to gather vital statistics on the boy and the members of his immediate family, as well as his paternal and maternal grandparents and paternal and maternal aunts and uncles. We were concerned also with reconstructing the history of delinquency and securing evidences of excessive drinking, mental deficiency, emotional disturbance, and certain physical ailments, not only among the members of the boy's immediate family but also among grandparents on both sides and paternal and maternal aunts and uncles, in order to determine the differences in the burden of familial defects among the delinquents and nondelinquents. We were interested, further, as part of the exploration of the family history, to determine the education and economic condition of the boy's parents and of his paternal and maternal grandparents.

With respect to the boy himself, one of our major quests was to achieve a chronological picture of his whereabouts from birth until the time we selected him for study and to describe the physical aspects of his present home and environment.

Another major concern in the social investigation was with the kind of cultural, intellectual, and emotional atmosphere in which the boy had been reared. Still another area of exploration dealt with the boy's habits and his use of leisure, our attention being specifically directed to an inquiry concerning his age at the onset of aberrant behavior and the nature of the earliest manifestations of his antisociality. Of special interest to us was a determination of the parents' knowledge of the boy's habits and use of leisure time, as contrasted with the actual facts in the case, and the parents' explanation of the boy's behavior.

A history of the boy's schooling was also to be secured, as well as an estimate of his behavior in school. . . .

Testing and Examining Delinquents and Nondelinquents

As a preliminary to determining the content of the somatic, intellectual, and emotional-temperamental levels of the research project, various tests and examinations were explored. The clinicians on our staff as well as other specialists were consulted, the main focus always being on what a particular test or examination might contribute to answering the basic question of the study: What are the differences between juvenile delinquents and nondelinquents that might throw light on crime causation?

The sum total of our explorations resulted in a plan to photograph each boy for ultimate classification into a somatotype and to make a twenty-to thirty-minute medical examination (somatic level); to administer a Wechsler-Bellevue Test and Stanford Achievement Tests in Reading and Arithmetic (intellectual level); and to administer a Rorschach Test and hold a psychiatric interview (emotional-temperamental level). . . .

Dynamic Pattern of Delinquency

The finding of marked differences between the persistently delinquent group and the nondelinquent group in the incidence of many biologic, sociologic, and biosocial factors reveals the operation of cause and effect by establishing the probability of a functional relationship between the factors taken as a whole and a tendency to antisocial behavior. This does not mean that a boy possessing one or more of the differentiating traits must inevitably become delinquent. A group of differentiative factors derived from any single level of the inquiry is not, standing alone, too likely to bring about delinquency. But when to that cluster of distinguishing traits are added those from one or more of the other levels, the possibilities of delinquent behavior are greatly enhanced. In a case in which many differentiative factors from all levels are present the impulsion to delinquency is virtually unavoidable.

Three points ought to be borne in mind: (1) The selection and matching of the two groups of boys with respect to ethnic-racial derivation, age, intelligence quotient, and residence in underprivileged areas has, of course, meant the exclusion of these controlled variables from the comparison. (2) In planning the research, we took into account the fact that statistical correlation in itself may not necessarily mean actual functional relationship. Therefore, in choosing factors for comparison, we selected only those which, from our own experience and from the writings of those who have made inquiries into various branches of the behavior disciplines, seemed to us to have a possible functional connection with delinquent or nondelinquent behavior tendencies. (3) Although we included a great many factors, and although, as has been shown in the preceding chapter, we have been able to construct efficient predictive instrumentalities based on the more differentiative among them, further investigations may well disclose still other causal factors. . . .

The Causal Complex

It will be observed that in drawing together the more significant threads of each area explored, we have not resorted to a theoretical explanation from the standpoint, exclusively, of any one discipline. It has seemed to us, at least at the present stage of our reflections upon the materials, that it is premature and misleading to give exclusive or even primary significance to any one of the avenues of interpretation. On the contrary, the evidence seems to point to the participation of forces from several areas and levels in channeling the persistent tendency to socially unacceptable behavior. The foregoing summation of the major resemblances and dissimilarities between the two groups included in the present inquiry indicates that the separate findings, independently gathered, integrate into a dynamic pattern which is neither exclusively biologic nor exclusively socio-cultural, but which derives from an interplay of somatic, temperamental, intellectual, and socio-cultural forces.

We are impelled to such a multidimensional interpretation because, without it, serious gaps appear. If we resort to an explanation exclusively in terms of somatic constitution, we leave unexplained why most persons of mesomorphic tendency do *not* commit crimes; and we further leave unexplained how bodily structure affects behavior. If we limit ourselves to a socio-cultural explanation, we cannot ignore the fact that socio-cultural forces are selective; even in underprivileged areas most boys do *not* become delinquent and many boys from such areas do not develop into persistent offenders. And, finally, if we limit our explanation to psychoanalytic theory, we fail to account for the fact that the great majority of nondelinquents, as well as of delinquents, show traits usually deemed unfavorable to sound character development, such as vague feelings of insecurity and feelings of not being wanted; the fact that many boys who live under conditions in which there is a dearth of parental warmth and understanding nevertheless remain nondelinquent; and the fact that some boys, under conditions unfavorable to the development of a wholesome superego, do not become delinquents, but do become neurotics.

If, however, we take into account the dynamic interplay of these various levels and channels of influence, a tentative causal formula or law emerges, which tends to accommodate these puzzling divergences so far as the great mass of delinquents is concerned:

> The delinquents as a group are distinguishable from the nondelinquents: (1) *physically*, in being essentially mesomorphic in constitution (solid, closely knit, muscular); (2) *temperamentally*, in being restlessly energetic, impulsive, extroverted, aggressive, destructive (often sadistic)—traits which may be related more or less to the erratic growth pattern and its physiologic correlates or consequences; (3) *in attitude*, by being hostile, defiant, resentful, suspicious, stubborn, socially assertive, adventurous, unconventional, nonsubmissive to authority; (4) *psychologically*, in tending to direct and concrete, rather than symbolic, intellectual expression, and in being less methodical in their approach to problems; (5) *socio-culturally*, in having been reared to a far greater extent than the control group in homes of little understanding, affection, stability, or moral fibre by parents usually unfit to be effective guides and protectors or, according to psychoanalytic theory, desirable sources for emulation and the construction of a consistent, well-balanced, and socially normal superego during the early stages of character development. While in individual cases the stresses contributed by any one of the above pressure-areas of dissocial-behavior tendency may adequately account for persistence in delinquency, in general the high probability of delinquency is dependent upon the interplay of the conditions and forces from all these areas.
>
> In the exciting, stimulating, but little-controlled and culturally inconsistent environment of the underprivileged area, such boys readily give expression to their untamed impulses and their self-centered desires by means of various forms of delinquent behavior. Their tendencies toward uninhibited energy-expression are deeply anchored in soma and psyche and in the malformations of character during the first few years of life. . . .

38

A Control Theory of Delinquency

Travis Hirschi

> The more weakened the groups to which [the individual] belongs, the less he
> depends on them, the more he consequently depends only on himself and recognizes
> no other rules of conduct than what are founded on his private interests.[1]

Control theories assume that delinquent acts result when an individual's bond to
society is weak or broken. Since these theories embrace two highly complex concepts,
the *bond* of the individual to *society*, it is not surprising that they have at one time
or another formed the basis of explanations of most forms of aberrant or unusual
behavior. It is also not surprising that control theories have described the elements
of the bond to society in many ways, and that they have focused on a variety of
units as the point of control.

I begin with a classification and description of the elements of the bond to
conventional society. I try to show how each of these elements is related to delinquent
behavior and how they are related to each other. I then turn to the question of
specifying the unit to which the person is presumably more or less tied, and to the
question of the adequacy of the motivational force built into the explanation of
delinquent behavior.

Elements of the Bond

Attachment

In explaining conforming behavior, sociologists justly emphasize sensitivity
to the opinion of others.[2] Unfortunately, as suggested in the preceding chapter, they
tend to suggest that man *is* sensitive to the opinion of others and thus exclude
sensitivity from their explanations of deviant behavior. In explaining deviant behavior,
psychologists, in contrast, emphasize insensitivity to the opinion of others.[3]
Unfortunately, they too tend to ignore variation, and, in addition, they tend to tie
sensitivity inextricably to other variables, to make it part of a syndrome or "type,"
and thus seriously to reduce its value as an explanatory concept. The psychopath
is characterized only in part by "deficient attachment to or affection for others, a
failure to respond to the ordinary motivations founded in respect or regard for one's
fellows";[4] he is also characterized by such things as "excessive aggressiveness,"

Source: From Travis Hirschi, *Causes of Delinquency*, pp. 16–26. Copyright © 1969 by Transaction Publishers. Reprinted by permission of the publisher.

"lack of superego control," and "an infantile level of response."[5] Unfortunately, too, the behavior that psychopathy is used to explain often becomes part of the *definition* of psychopathy. As a result, in Barbara Wootton's words:

> [The psychopath] is . . . *par excellence*, and without shame or qualification, the model of the circular process by which mental abnormality is inferred from anti-social behavior while anti-social behavior is explained by mental abnormality.[6]

The problems of diagnosis, tautology, and name-calling are avoided if the dimensions of psychopathy are treated as causally and therefore problematically interrelated, rather than as logically and therefore necessarily bound to each other. In fact, it can be argued that all of the characteristics attributed to the psychopath follow from, are effects of, his lack of attachment to others. To say that to lack attachment to others is to be free from moral restraints is to use lack of attachment to explain the guiltlessness of the psychopath, the fact that he apparently has no conscience or superego. In this view, lack of attachment to others is not merely a symptom of psychopathy, it *is* psychopathy; lack of conscience is just another way of saying the same thing; and the violation of norms is (or may be) a consequence.

For that matter, given that man is an animal, "impulsivity" and "aggressive-ness" can also be seen as natural consequences of freedom from moral restraints. However, since the view of man as endowed with natural propensities and capacities like other animals is peculiarly unpalatable to sociologists, we need not fall back on such a view to explain the amoral man's aggressiveness.[7] The process of becoming alienated from others often involves or is based on active interpersonal conflict. Such conflict could easily supply a reservoir of *socially derived* hostility sufficient to account for the aggressiveness of those whose attachments to others have been weakened.

Durkheim said it many years ago: "We are moral beings to the extent that we are social beings."[8] This may be interpreted to mean that we are moral beings to the extent that we have "internalized the norms" of society. But what does it mean to say that a person has internalized the norms of society? The norms of society are by definition shared by the members of society. To violate a norm is, therefore, to act contrary to the wishes and expectations of other people. If a person does not care about the wishes and expectations of other people—that is, if he is insensitive to the opinion of others—then he is to that extent not bound by the norms. He is free to deviate.

The essence of internalization of norms, conscience, or superego thus lies in the attachment of the individual to others.[9] This view has several advantages over the concept of internalization. For one, explanations of deviant behavior based on attachment do not beg the question, since the extent to which a person is attached to others can be measured independently of his deviant behavior. Furthermore, change or variation in behavior is explainable in a way that it is not when notions of internalization or superego are used. For example, the divorced man is more likely after divorce to commit a number of deviant acts, such as suicide or forgery. If we explain these acts by reference to the superego (or internal control), we are forced to say that the man "lost his conscience" when he got a divorce; and, of course, if he remarries, we have to conclude that he gets his conscience back.

This dimension of the bond to conventional society is encountered in most social control-oriented research and theory. F. Ivan Nye's "internal control" and "indirect control" refer to the same element, although we avoid the problem of explaining changes over time by locating the "conscience" in the bond to others rather than making it part of the personality.[10] Attachment to others is just one aspect of Albert J. Reiss's "personal controls"; we avoid his problems of tautological empirical *observations* by making the relationship between attachment and delinquency problematic rather than definitional.[11] Finally, Scott Briar and Irving Piliavin's "commitment" or "stake in conformity" subsumes attachment, as their discussion illustrates, although the terms they use are more closely associated with the next element to be discussed.[12]

Commitment

> Of all passions, that which inclineth men least to break the laws, is fear. Nay, excepting some generous natures, it is the only thing, when there is the appearance of profit or pleasure by breaking the laws, that makes men keep them.[13]

Few would deny that men on occasion obey the rules simply from fear of the consequences. This rational component in conformity we label commitment. What does it mean to say that a person is committed to conformity? In Howard S. Becker's formulation it means the following:

> First, the individual is in a position in which his decision with regard to some particular line of action has consequences for other interests and activities not necessarily [directly] related to it. Second, he has placed himself in that position by his own prior actions. A third element is present though so obvious as not to be apparent: the committed person must be aware [of these other interests] and must recognize that his decision in this case will have ramifications beyond it.[14]

The idea, then, is that the person invests time, energy, himself, in a certain line of activity—say, getting an education, building up a business, acquiring a reputation for virtue. When or whenever he considers deviant behavior, he must consider the costs of this deviant behavior, the risk he runs of losing the investment he has made in conventional behavior.

If attachment to others is the sociological counterpart of the superego or conscience, commitment is the counterpart of the ego or common sense. To the person committed to conventional lines of action, risking one to ten years in prison for a ten-dollar holdup is stupidity, because to the committed person the costs and risks obviously exceed ten dollars in value. (To the psychoanalyst, such an act exhibits failure to be governed by the "reality-principle.") In the sociological control theory, it can be and is generally assumed that the decision to commit a criminal act may well be rationally determined—that the actor's decision was not irrational given the risks and costs he faces. Of course, as Becker points out, if the actor is capable of in some sense calculating the costs of a line of action, he is also capable of calculational errors: ignorance and error return, in the control theory, as possible explanations of deviant behavior.

The concept of commitment assumes that the organization of society is such that the interests of most persons would be endangered if they were to engage in criminal acts. Most people, simply by the process of living in an organized society, acquire goods, reputations, prospects that they do not want to risk losing. These accumulations are society's insurance that they will abide by the rules. Many hypotheses about the antecedents of delinquent behavior are based on this premise. For example, Arthur L. Stinchcombe's hypothesis that "high school rebellion . . . .

occurs when future status is not clearly related to present performance''[15] suggests that one is committed to conformity not only by what one has but also by what one hopes to obtain. Thus ''ambition'' and/or ''aspiration'' play an important role in producing conformity. The person becomes committed to a conventional line of action, and he is therefore committed to conformity.

Most lines of action in a society are of course conventional. The clearest examples are educational and occupational careers. Actions thought to jeopardize one's chances in these areas are presumably avoided. Interestingly enough, even nonconventional commitments may operate to produce conventional conformity. We are told, at least, that boys aspiring to careers in the rackets or professional thievery are judged by their ''honesty'' and ''reliability''—traits traditionally in demand among seekers of office boys.[16]

Involvement

Many persons undoubtedly owe a life of virtue to a lack of opportunity to do otherwise. Time and energy are inherently limited: ''Not that I would not, if I could, be both handsome and fat and well dressed, and a great athlete, and make a million a year, be a wit, a bon vivant, and a lady killer, as well as a philosopher, a philanthropist, a statesman, warrior, and African explorer, as well as a ''tone-poet'' and saint. But the thing is simply impossible.''[17] The things that William James here says he would like to be or do are all, I suppose, within the realm of conventionality, but if he were to include illicit actions he would still have to eliminate some of them as simply impossible.

Involvement or engrossment in conventional activities is thus often part of a control theory. The assumption, widely shared, is that a person may be simply too busy doing conventional things to find time to engage in deviant behavior. The person involved in conventional activities is tied to appointments, deadlines, working hours, plans, and the like, so the opportunity to commit deviant acts rarely arises. To the extent that he is engrossed in conventional activities, he cannot even think about deviant acts, let alone act out his inclinations.[18]

This line of reasoning is responsible for the stress placed on recreational facilities in many programs to reduce delinquency, for much of the concern with the high school dropout, and for the idea that boys should be drafted into the Army to keep them out of trouble. So obvious and persuasive is the idea that involvement in conventional activities is a major deterrent to delinquency that it was accepted even by Sutherland: ''In the general area of juvenile delinquency it is probable that the most significant difference between juveniles who engage in delinquency and those who do not is that the latter are provided abundant opportunities of a conventional type for satisfying their recreational interests, while the former lack those opportunities or facilities.''[19]

The view that ''idle hands are the devil's workshop'' has received more sophisticated treatment in recent sociological writings on delinquency. David Matza and Gresham M. Sykes, for example, suggest that delinquents have the values of a leisure class, the same values ascribed by Veblen to *the* leisure class: a search for kicks, disdain of work, a desire for the big score, and acceptance of aggressive toughness as proof of masculinity.[20] Matza and Sykes explain delinquency by reference to this system of values, but they note that adolescents at all class levels are ''to some extent'' members of a leisure class, that they ''move in a limbo between earlier parental domination and future integration with the social structure through the bonds of work and marriage.''[21] In the end, then, the leisure of the adolescent produces a set of values, which, in turn, leads to delinquency.

Belief

Unlike the cultural deviance theory, the control theory assumes the existence of a common value system within the society or group whose norms are being violated. If the deviant is committed to a value system different from that of conventional society, there is, within the context of the theory, nothing to explain. The question is, "Why does a man violate the rules in which he believes?" It is not, "Why do men differ in their beliefs about what constitutes good and desirable conduct?" The person is assumed to have been socialized (perhaps imperfectly) into the group whose rules he is violating; deviance is not a question of one group imposing its rules on the members of another group. In other words, we not only assume the deviant *has* believed the rules, we assume he believes the rules even as he violates them.

How can a person believe it is wrong to steal at the same time he is stealing? In the strain theory, this is not a difficult problem. (In fact, as suggested in the previous chapter, the strain theory was devised specifically to deal with this question.) The motivation to deviance adduced by the strain theorist is so strong that we can well understand the deviant act even assuming the deviator believes strongly that it is wrong.[22] However, given the control theory's assumptions about motivation, if both the deviant and the nondeviant believe the deviant act is wrong, how do we account for the fact that one commits it and the other does not?

Control theories have taken two approaches to this problem. In one approach, beliefs are treated as mere words that mean little or nothing if the other forms of control are missing. "Semantic dementia," the dissociation between rational faculties and emotional control which is said to be characteristic of the psychopath, illustrates this way of handling the problem.[23] In short, beliefs, at least insofar as they are expressed in words, drop out of the picture; since they do not differentiate between deviants and nondeviants, they are in the same class as "language" or any other characteristic common to all members of the group. Since they represent no real obstacle to the commission of delinquent acts, nothing need be said about how they are handled by those committing such acts. The control theories that do not mention beliefs (or values), and many do not, may be assumed to take this approach to the problem.

The second approach argues that the deviant rationalizes his behavior so that he can at once violate the rule and maintain his belief in it. Donald R. Cressey has advanced this argument with respect to embezzlement,[24] and Sykes and Matza have advanced it with respect to delinquency.[25] In both Cressey's and Sykes and Matza's treatments, these rationalizations (Cressey calls them "verbalizations," Sykes and Matza term them "techniques of neutralization") occur prior to the commission of the deviant act. If the neutralization is successful, the person is free to commit the act(s) in question. Both in Cressey and in Sykes and Matza, the strain that prompts the effort at neutralization also provides the motive force that results in the subsequent deviant act. Their theories are thus, in this sense, strain theories. Neutralization is difficult to handle within the context of a theory that adheres closely to control theory assumptions, because in the control theory there is no special motivational force to account for the neutralization. This difficulty is especially noticeable in Matza's later treatment of this topic, where the motivational component, the "will to delinquency" appears *after* the moral vacuum has been created by the techniques of neutralization.[26] The question thus becomes: Why neutralize?

In attempting to solve a strain theory problem with control theory tools, the control theorist is thus led into a trap. He cannot answer the crucial question. The concept of neutralization assumes the existence of moral obstacles to the commission of deviant acts. In order plausibly to account for a deviant act, it is necessary to generate motivation to deviance that is at least equivalent in force to the resistance provided by these moral obstacles. However, if the moral obstacles are removed, neutralization and special motivation are no longer required. We therefore follow the implicit logic of control theory and remove these moral obstacles by hypothesis. Many persons do not have an attitude of respect toward the rules of society; many persons feel no moral obligation to conform regardless of personal advantage. Insofar as the values and beliefs of these persons are consistent with their feelings, and there should be a tendency toward consistency, neutralization is unnecessary; it has already occurred.

Does this merely push the question back a step and at the same time produce conflict with the assumption of a common value system? I think not. In the first place, we do not assume, as does Cressey, that neutralization occurs in order to make a specific criminal act possible.[27] We do not assume, as do Sykes and Matza, that neutralization occurs to make many delinquent acts possible. We do not assume, in other words, that the person constructs a system of rationalizations in order to justify commission of acts he *wants* to commit. We assume, in contrast, that the beliefs that free a man to commit deviant acts are *unmotivated* in the sense that he does not construct or adopt them in order to facilitate the attainment of illicit ends. In the second place, we do not assume, as does Matza, that "delinquents concur in the conventional assessment of delinquency."[28] We assume, in contrast, that there is *variation* in the extent to which people believe they should obey the rules of society, and, furthermore, that the less a person believes he should obey the rules, the more likely he is to violate them.[29]

In chronological order, then, a person's beliefs in the moral validity of norms are, for no teleological reason, weakened. The probability that he will commit delinquent acts is therefore increased. When and if he commits a delinquent act, we may justifiably use the weakness of his beliefs in explaining it, but no special motivation is required to explain either the weakness of his beliefs or, perhaps, his delinquent act.

The keystone of this argument is of course the assumption that there is variation in belief in the moral validity of social rules. This assumption is amenable to direct empirical test and can thus survive at least until its first confrontation with data. For the present, we must return to the idea of a common value system with which this section was begun.

The idea of a common (or, perhaps better, a single) value system is consistent with the fact, or presumption, of variation in the strength of moral beliefs. We have not suggested that delinquency is based on beliefs counter to conventional morality; we have not suggested that delinquents do not believe delinquent acts are wrong. They may well believe these acts are wrong, but the meaning and efficacy of such beliefs are contingent upon other beliefs and, indeed, on the strength of other ties to the conventional order. . . .[30]

Notes

1. Emile Durkheim, *Suicide*, trans. John A. Spaulding and George Simpson (New York: The Free Press, 1951), p. 209.
2. Books have been written on the increasing importance of interpersonal sensitivity in modern life. According to this view, controls from within have become less important than controls from without in *producing* conformity. Whether or not this observation is true as a description of historical trends, it is true that interpersonal sensitivity has become more important in *explaining* conformity. Although logically it should also have become more important in explaining nonconformity, the opposite has been the case, once again showing that Cohen's observation that an explanation of conformity should be an explanation of deviance cannot be translated as "an explanation of conformity has to be an explanation of deviance." For the view that interpersonal sensitivity currently plays a greater role than formerly in producing conformity, see William J. Goode, "Norm Commitment and Conformity to Role-Status Obligations," *American Journal of Sociology*, LXVI (1960), 246–258. And, of course, also see David Riesman, Nathan Glazer, and Reuel Denney, *The Lonely Crowd* (Garden City, NY: Doubleday, 1950), especially Part 1.
3. The literature on psychopathy is voluminous. See William McCord and Joan McCord, *The Psychopath* (Princeton: D. Van Nostrand, 1964).
4. John M. Martin and Joseph P. Fitzpatrick, *Delinquent Behavior* (New York: Random House, 1964), p. 130.
5. *Ibid*. For additional properties of the psychopath, see McCord and McCord, *The Psychopath*, pp. 1–22.
6. Barbara Wootton, *Social Science and Social Pathology* New York: Macmillan, 1959), p. 250.
7. "The logical untenability [of the position that there are forces in man 'resistant to socialization'] was ably demonstrated by Parsons over 30 years ago, and it is widely recognized that the position is empirically unsound because it assumes [!] some universal biological drive system distinctly separate from socialization and social context—a basic and intransigent human nature" (Judith Blake and Kingsley Davis, "Norms, Values, and Sanctions," *Handbook of Modern Sociology*, ed. Robert E. L. Faris [Chicago: Rand McNally, 1964], p. 471).
8. Emile Durkheim, *Moral Education*, trans. Everett K. Wilson and Herman Schnurer (New York: The Free Press, 1961), p.64.
9. Although attachment alone does not exhaust the meaning of internalization, attachments and beliefs combined would appear to leave only a small residue of "internal control" not susceptible in principle to direct measurement.
10. F. Ivan Nye, *Family Relationships and Delinquent Behavior* (New York: Wiley, 1958), pp. 5–7.
11. Albert J. Reiss, Jr., "Delinquency as the Failure of Personal and Social Controls," *American Sociological Review*, XVI (1951), 196–207. For example, "Our observations show . . . that delinquent recidivists are less often persons with mature ego ideals or nondelinquent social roles" (p. 204).
12. Scott Briar and Irving Piliavin, "Delinquency, Situational Inducements, and Commitment to Conformity," *Social Problems*, XIII (1965), 41–42. The concept "stake in conformity" was introduced by Jackson Toby in his "Social Disorganization and Stake in Conformity: Complementary Factors in the Predatory Behavior of Hoodlums," *Journal of Criminal Law, Criminology and Police Science*, XLVIII (1957), 12–17. See also his "Hoodlum or Business Man: An American Dilemma," *The Jews*, ed. Marshall Sklare (New York: The Free Press, 1958), pp. 542–550. Throughout the text, I occasionally use "stake in conformity" in speaking in general of the strength of the bond to conventional society. So used, the concept is somewhat broader than is true for either Toby or Briar and Piliavin, where the concept is roughly equivalent to what is here called "commitment."

13. Thomas Hobbes, *Leviathan* (Oxford: Basil Blackwell, 1957), p. 195.
14. Howard S. Becker, "Notes on the Concept of Commitment," *American Journal of Sociology,* LXVI (1960), 35–36.
15. Arthur L. Stinchcombe, *Rebellion in a High School* (Chicago: Quadrangle, 1964), p.5.
16. Richard A. Cloward and Lloyd E. Ohlin, *Delinquency and Opportunity* (New York: The Free Press, 1960), p. 147, quoting Edwin H. Sutherland, ed. *The Professional Thief* (Chicago: University of Chicago Press, 1937), pp. 211–213.
17. William James, *Psychology* (Cleveland: World Publishing Co., 1948), p. 186.
18. Few activities appear to be so engrossing that they rule out contemplation of alternative lines of behavior, at least if estimates of the amount of time men spend plotting sexual deviations have any validity.
19. *The Sutherland Papers,* ed. Albert K. Cohen et al. (Bloomington: Indiana University Press, 1956), p. 37.
20. David Matza and Gresham M. Sykes, "Juvenile Delinquency and Subterranean Values," *American Sociological Review,* XXVI (1961), 712–719.
21. *Ibid.,* p. 718.
22. The starving man stealing the loaf of bread is the image evoked by most strain theories. In this image, the starving man's belief in the wrongness of his act is clearly not something that must be explained away. It can be assumed to be present without causing embarrassment to the explanation.
23. McCord and McCord, *The Psychopath,* pp. 12–15.
24. Donald R. Cressey, *Other People's Money* (New York: The Free Press, 1953).
25. Gresham M. Sykes and David Matza, "Techniques of Neutralization: A Theory of Delinquency," *American Sociological Review,* XXII (1957), 664–670.
26. David Matza, *Delinquency and Drift* (New York: Wiley, 1964), pp. 181–191.
27. In asserting that Cressey's assumption is invalid with respect to delinquency, I do not wish to suggest that it is invalid for the question of embezzlement, where the problem faced by the deviator is fairly specific and he can reasonably be assumed to be an upstanding citizen. (Although even here the fact that the embezzler's nonshareable financial problem often results from some sort of hanky-panky suggests that "verbalizations" may be less necessary than might otherwise be assumed.)
28. *Delinquency and Drift,* p. 43.
29. This assumption is not, I think, contradicted by the evidence presented by Matza against the existence of a delinquent subculture. In comparing the attitudes and actions of delinquents with the picture painted by delinquent subculture theorists, Matza emphasizes—and perhaps exaggerates—the extent to which delinquents are tied to the conventional order. In implicitly comparing delinquents with a supermoral man, I emphasize—and perhaps exaggerate—the extent to which they are not tied to the conventional order.
30. The position taken here is therefore somewhere between the "semantic dementia" and the "neutralization" positions. Assuming variation, the delinquent is, at the extremes, freer than the neutralization argument assumes. Although the possibility of wide discrepancy between what the delinquent professes and what he practices still exists, it is presumably much rarer than is suggested by studies of articulate "psychopaths."

39

A General Theory of Crime

Michael R. Gottfredson   Travis Hirschi

A Modern Version of the Classical Conception of Crime

Force and fraud are ever-present possibilities in human affairs. Denial of this fact promotes the development of theories of crime that are misleading as guides to policy. Awareness of this fact allows the development of a theory of crime consistent with research and the needs of sound public policy. It has implications for how crime itself is construed, how it should be measured, the kind of people who are likely to engage in it, the institutional context within which it is controlled, and the most useful ways of studying it. One purpose of [the book from which this reading is taken] is to promote this view of crime.

People vary in their propensity to use force and fraud (criminality). This fact has implications for the way crime is measured, for the kinds of crimes that occur, for understanding the relation between crimes and social problems such as accidents and disease, for the proper design of research, and for the creation of useful public policies. Another purpose of [the aforementioned] book is to promote explicit consideration of the propensity to crime as distinct from the commission of criminal acts.

These ideas about crime and criminality have been around a long time, surfacing again and again in academic criminology. Today, however, they are contrary to the views dominant in the field, where "crime" is seen as aberrant behavior and "criminality" as a distasteful relic of earlier modes of thought. In our view, the reason these views of crime and criminality come and go is that they have never been fully and systematically developed and defended. . . .

A conception of crime presupposes a conception of human nature. In the classical tradition, represented by Thomas Hobbes, Jeremy Bentham, and Cesare Beccaria, human nature was easily described: "Nature has laced mankind under the governance of two sovereign masters, *pain* and *pleasure*" Bentham 1970 [1789]: 11). In this view, all human conduct can be understood as the self-interested pursuit of pleasure or the avoidance of pain. By definition, therefore, crimes too are merely acts designed to satisfy some combination of these basic tendencies. The idea that criminal acts are an expression of fundamental human tendencies has straightfor-

Source: Excerpted from Michael R. Gottfredson and Travis Hirschi, *A General Theory of Crime.* Copyright © 1990 by the Board of Trustees of the Leland Stanford Jr. University. Used with permission of Stanford University Press, *www.sup.org.*

ward and profound implications. It tells us that crime is not unique with respect to the motives or desires it is intended to satisfy. It tells us that crime presupposes no particular skills or abilities, that it is within the reach of everyone without specialized learning. It tells us that all crimes are alike in that they satisfy ordinary and universal desires. It tells us that people behave rationally when they commit crimes and when they do not. It tells us that people are free to choose their course of conduct, whether it be legal or illegal. And it tells us that people think of and act first for themselves, that they are not naturally inclined to subordinate their interests to the interests of others.

Sanction Systems

. . . Crime was eventually distinguished from other forms of behavior by introducing the notion of political sanctions: pleasures and pains manipulated by the state. By introducing and then focusing on state sanctions, the early classicists identified the behavior that eventually became the subject matter of the discipline of criminology.

Deviant behavior was distinguished from other forms of behavior by introducing the notion of group sanctions or social control: pleasures and pains manipulated by public opinion. By introducing group sanctions, the early classicists identified the behavior that eventually became the subject matter of the discipline of sociology.

Sinful behavior was distinguished from other forms of behavior by introducing the notion of religious sanctions: pleasures and pains controlled by supernatural forces. Because the supernatural by definition does not exist in positivistic thought, sinful behavior did not become the focus of a positivistic discipline.

Reckless or imprudent behavior was distinguished from other forms of behavior by introducing the notion of natural harm or physical sanctions. This large class of behavior is not systematically incorporated into any modern discipline but is partitioned among problem-oriented researchers in a variety of disciplines. For example, work on the causes of accidents, injuries, and illnesses and on the physical consequences of certain foods, drugs, and activity patterns is carried out by a multitude of researchers without any notion of the common element in these phenomena.

In our view, the common element in crime, deviant behavior, sin, and accident is so overriding that the tendency to treat them as distinct phenomena subject to distinct causes is one of the major intellectual errors of positive thought and is a major cost of the tendency to divide intellectual problems among academic disciplines. . . . Had it remained true to classical logic, sociology would have developed broad theories of *deviant behavior* (theories to include crime, sin, and recklessness) using the general principles of "hedonic calculus," where the important sanctioning bodies are the social groups to which the individual belongs. In other words, following classical logic would have led sociology to theories of social control, theories in which crimes differ from other norms of deviant behavior only because in their case the state is interested in adding sanctions to those operating at the group level. But sociology has tended to reject hedonic calculus in favor of the positivistic view that people are naturally social and must therefore be compelled to commit deviant or criminal acts by forces over which they have no control. . . .

In the classical tradition, the qualities of acts are implicated in their own causation. Thus acts are fun, worthwhile, enjoyable, easy, and exciting, or they are painful, boring, and difficult. The classical theory of causation combines its explanation of an act with its conception of the nature of the act. . . .

Thus, other things being equal, acts that have immediate consequences will tend to be more pleasurable than those whose consequences are delayed. For example, smoking marijuana after school, which provides immediate benefit, is more pleasurable than doing one's homework, the benefit of which is delayed. Similarly, acts that are mentally and physically easy are more pleasurable than acts that require physical exertion. For example, walking into an unlocked house and taking the coins from the dresser is more pleasurable than earning the same amount of money by selling newspapers. Swindling a government bureaucracy by submitting excessive Medicaid claims is more pleasurable than earning the same amount of money by treating recalcitrant patients. And finally, risky or exciting acts are more pleasurable than routine or dull acts. Driving fast is more pleasurable than driving within the speed limit.

Note that all qualities of criminal acts may be found in acts that are not crimes; note too that noncriminal acts vary among themselves in their "proximity" to crime. For example, riding a motorcycle is more exciting than driving a car; the benefits from smoking a cigarette are more immediate than the benefits from homework; sexual activity is more pleasurable than abstinence; and cursing the boss is more fun than suffering in silence. In addition, the use of force or fraud is often easier, simpler, faster, more exciting, and more certain than other means of securing one's ends. In this sense, then, the use of force or fraud (crime) enhances the pleasure of self-interested pursuit.

Given these properties, the nature of criminal acts is fully predicted: they will tend, on the whole, to require little foresight, planning, or effort. Between the thought and the deed, little time will elapse. Thus the carefully planned and executed crime will be extremely rare. The tendency of crime to take place at little remove from the present also implies that crimes will tend to take place at little remove from the offender's usual location. The time and space boundaries of criminal acts will be highly circumscribed. The preference for simplicity over complexity implies that potential targets will be selected based on the ease with which they can be victimized. The same considerations lead to the conclusion that targets that provide immediate benefits will be selected over targets that occasion delay. The spontaneity of criminal acts further implies that they will, on the whole, produce little in the way of profit. Targets that pose little risk of detection and little risk of resistance will be chosen over those with greater risks. . . .

The Characteristics of Ordinary Crime

It is easy to be misled about the nature of crime in American society. All one has to do is read the newspaper, where the unusual, bizarre, or uncharacteristic crime is routinely portrayed. The fact of the matter is that the vast majority of criminal acts are trivial and mundane affairs that result in little loss and less gain. These are events whose temporal and spatial distributions are highly predictable, that require little preparation, leave few lasting consequences and often do not produce the result intended by the offender. . . .

[The] characteristics of crime have significance for etiological questions. They show a pattern of crime consistent with the recreational patterns of youth and inconsistent with the vocational patterns of adults; they show a disinclination to expend effort in pursuit of crime; they show that accessibility increases the risk of potential victims; and they show that avoiding detection is part of the calculation of the offender.

The Requirements of a Criminal Act

Available data are consistent with the view that ordinary crime requires little in the way of effort, planning, or skill. Most crime in fact occurs in close proximity to the offender's residence (Suttles 1968; Turner 1969; Reiss 1976): the burglar typically walks to the scene of the crime; the robber victimizes available targets on the street; the embezzler steals from his own cash register; and the car thief drives away cars with keys left in the ignition.

What planning does take place in burglary, for example, seems designed to minimize the momentary probability of detection and to minimize the effort required to complete the crime. Thus the burglar searches for an unlocked door or an open window in an unoccupied, single-story house. Once inside, he concentrates on easily portable goods of interest to himself without concern for potential value in a larger market.

The robber prefers to avoid direct confrontation with the victim and, when confrontation cannot be avoided, tends to select targets incapable of, or unlikely to offer, resistance. The occasional use of weapons is designed to minimize the likelihood of resistance. Commercial targets, too, are selected largely on the basis of accessibility. It is no accident that "convenience" stores and gas stations are common targets or that businesses located along major thoroughfares and at freeway offramps are especially attractive.

The skill required to complete the general run of crime is minimal. Consider crimes of personal violence, assault, rape, and homicide. The major requirement for successful completion of these crimes is the appearance of superior strength or the command of instruments of force. A gun, a club, or a knife is often sufficient. Property crimes may require physical strength or dexterity, but in most cases no more than is necessary for the ordinary activities of life.

The Benefits of Crime to the Offender

Many crimes do not produce the results intended by those committing them. One reason for this high rate of failure is that crimes are, by definition, opposed by their would-be victims. Potential victims seek to protect themselves from the inclinations of others. They therefore lock doors, hide valuables, watch strangers, move in groups, carry weapons, travel during the day, avoid provocation, and resist assaults. As a result, the intention to commit a crime does not in itself assure a successful result. Indeed, according to victim surveys, most crimes are attempts to commit crime (Hindelang, Gottfredson, and Garofalo 1978; Hough 1987). Because these reported crimes are by definition known to the potential victims, we must assume that many more attempted crimes are known only to the would-be offender. For example, would-be burglars may try many doors before finding one that is unlocked.

Among crimes completed, the average loss is remarkably small. For example, according to victim reports, the median loss for robbery is less than $50, whereas the median loss for burglary is something like $100 (McGarrell and Flanagan 1985: 312). Trustworthy figures are not available, but the average shoplifting appears to involve items of trivial value, items whose loss must be discounted by the items often purchased to cover the crime. Even fraud does not typically involve large sums, and embezzlements rarely make the offender wealthy (it is hard to get rich stealing from the till of a fast-food restaurant or service station). Auto theft would appear to be an exception, but most stolen automobiles are soon abandoned, and the ratio of attempted to completed auto thefts is very large indeed.

Of course the ramifications of crime must include not only the money and goods for the offender but also the personal suffering and physical injury of the victim. Here too, however, it is easy to be misled by popular accounts about the true level of loss. According to the National Crime Survey—a large, nationally representative sample of adults—many victims elect not to inform the police of criminal events because they consider those events to be too trivial or to be an inappropriate concern of the criminal justice system. And this is true even for offenses that bear such labels as rape, aggravated assault, robbery, and burglary. Indeed, in 1982 (National Crime Survey results are remarkably consistent from one year to the next), 39 percent of aggravated assaults, 42 percent of robberies, 45 percent of rapes, and 49 percent of burglaries were not reported to the police (McGarrell and Flanagan 1985: 273).

Most assaults result in little if any physical injury to the victim. Many assaults and homicides involve disputes between people previously known to each other where it is difficult to distinguish victim from offender in terms of provocation or responsibility. (Although the consequences of such ambiguous events may be serious, it remains true that the benefits to the offender from such acts have little or no connection to their "seriousness" and are in any event typically difficult to ascertain.) . . .

Even crimes producing relatively large sums of cash turn out to provide the offender only short-term benefits as compared to alternative sources of cash income. Consider, for example, the benefit of what by any estimate would be a "successful" robbery ($500) as compared with the gains from a minimum-wage job. The robbery cannot be repeated for any period of time with reasonable expectation of success, whereas the minimum-wage job can be a continuous source of income. Seen in this context, even the extremely rare big scores of criminal activity are at best only supplemental sources of income and must therefore be interpreted as sources of short-term gratification only.

The white-collar offender is not exempt from this problem. Embezzlement and fraud are difficult to carry out successfully over a long period. The larger the embezzlement or fraud, the more remote the likelihood of long-term success. As a result, white-collar crime too tends to provide relatively small or short-term benefit as compared to stable and honest employment. . . .

Although it may be more glamorous and profitable for law enforcement to portray an image of crime as a highly profitable alternative to legal work, a valid theory of crime must see it as it is: largely petty, typically not completed, and usually of little lasting or substantial benefit to the offender.

Connections among Crimes

Recall the classical definition of crime as an event involving force or fraud that satisfies self-interest. This tradition evinces little interest in connections among crimes. Whatever connections exist are merely definitional. However, the classical view would certainly assume that acts promoting self-interest in some meaningful or substantial way would tend to be repeated. And this, of course, is the basic, straightforward, and eminently reasonable assumption of modern learning theories of crime. Nevertheless, the evidence shows that specific crimes, regardless of their outcome, do not tend to be repeated. That is, burglary, even "successful" burglary, does not tend to be followed by burglary, *even in the short run.* Robbery is not followed by robbery with any more likelihood than by some other short-term pleasure, a pleasure that may well be inconsistent with another robbery (such as rape, drug use, or assault).

The reason for all of this interchangeability among crimes must be that these diverse events provide benefits with similar qualities, such qualities as immediacy, brevity of obligation, and effortlessness. . . .

Events Theoretically Equivalent to Crime

Crimes result from the pursuit of immediate, certain, easy benefits. Some noncriminal events appear to result from pursuit of the same kinds of benefits. As a result, these noncriminal events are correlated with crime, and examination of them can help elucidate the nature of crime and criminality.

One class of events analogous to crimes is accidents. Accidents are not ordinarily seen as producing benefits. On the contrary, they are by definition costly, and their long-term costs may be substantial. However, examination of the correlates of accidents and the circumstances under which they occur suggests that they have much in common with crimes. For example, motor vehicle accidents tend to be associated with speed, drinking, tailgating, inattention, risk-taking, defective equipment, and young males. House fires tend to be associated with smoking, drinking, number of children, and defective equipment.

Distinctions among Crimes

There is nothing more deeply ingrained in the common sense of criminology than the idea that not all crimes are alike. This commonsense criminology distinguishes between trivial and serious crimes (e.g., Elliott, Huizinga, and Ageton 1985; Wilson and Herrnstein 1985), between instrumental and expressive crimes (Chambliss 1969), between status offenses and delinquency, between victim and victimless crimes (Morris and Hawkins 1970), between crimes *mala in se* and crimes *mala prohibita*, and, most important, between person and property crimes. As should be clear by now, our theory regards all of these distinctions as irrelevant or misleading. . . .

The Nature of Criminality: Low Self-Control

. . . If individual differences in the tendency to commit criminal acts (within an overall tendency for crime to decline with age) are at least potentially explicable within classical theory by reference to the social location of individuals and their comprehension of how the world works, the fact remains that classical theory cannot shed much light on the positivistic finding that these differences *remain reasonably stable with change in the social location of individuals and change in their knowledge of the operation of sanction systems.* This is the problem of self-control, the differential tendency of people to avoid criminal acts whatever the circumstances in which they find themselves. Since this difference among people has attracted a variety of names, we begin by arguing the merits of the concept of self-control. . . .

[C]lassical theory is a theory of social of external control, a theory based on the idea that the costs of crime depend on the individual's current location in or bond to society. What classical theory lacks is an explicit idea of self-control, the idea that people also differ in the extent to which they are vulnerable to the temptations of the moment. Combining the two ideas thus merely recognizes the simultaneous existence of social and individual restraints on behavior. . . .

We are now in position to describe the nature of self-control, the individual characteristic relevant to the commission of criminal acts. We assume that the nature of this characteristic can be derived directly from the nature of criminal acts. We thus infer from the nature of crime what people who refrain from criminal acts are like before they reach the age at which crime becomes a logical possibility. We then work back further to the factors producing their restraint, back to the causes of self-control. In our view, lack of self-control does not require crime and can be counteracted by situational conditions or other properties of the individual. At the same time, we suggest that high self-control effectively reduces the possibility of crime— that is, those possessing it will be substantially less likely at all periods of life to engage in criminal acts.

The Elements of Self-Control

Criminal acts provide *immediate* gratification of desires. A major characteristic of people with low self-control is therefore a tendency to respond to tangible stimuli in the immediate environment, to have a concrete "here and now" orientation. People with high self-control, in contrast, tend to defer gratification.

Criminal acts provide *easy or simple* gratification of desires. They provide money without work, sex without courtship, revenge without court delays. People lacking self-control also tend to lack diligence, tenacity, or persistence in a course of action.

Criminal acts are *exciting, risky,* or *thrilling.* They involve stealth, danger, speed, agility, deception, or power. People lacking self-control therefore tend to be adventuresome, active, and physical. Those with high levels of self-control tend to be cautious, cognitive, and verbal.

Crimes provide *few or meager long-term benefits.* They are not equivalent to a job or a career. On the contrary, crimes interfere with long-term commitments to jobs, marriages, family, or friends. People with low self-control thus tend to have unstable marriages, friendships, and job profiles. They tend to be little interested in and unprepared for long-term occupational pursuits.

Crimes require *little skill or planning.* The cognitive requirements for most crimes are minimal. It follows that people lacking self-control need not possess or value cognitive or academic skills. The manual skills required for most crimes are minimal. It follows that people lacking self-control need not possess manual skills that require training or apprenticeship.

Crimes often result in *pain or discomfort for the victim.* Property is lost, bodies are injured, privacy is violated, trust is broken. It follows that people with low self-control tend to be self-centered, indifferent, or insensitive to the suffering and needs of others. It does not follow, however, that people with low self-control are routinely unkind or antisocial. On the contrary, they may discover the immediate and easy rewards of charm and generosity.

Recall that crime involves the pursuit of immediate pleasure. It follows that people lacking self-control will also tend to pursue immediate pleasures that are *not* criminal: they will tend to smoke, drink, use drugs, gamble, have children out of wedlock, and engage in illicit sex.

Crimes require the interaction of an offender with people or their property. It does not follow that people lacking self-control will tend to be gregarious or social. However, it does follow that, other things being equal, gregarious or social people are more likely to be involved in criminal acts.

The major benefit of many crimes is not pleasure but relief from momentary irritation. The irritation caused by a crying child is often the stimulus for physical abuse. That caused by a taunting stranger in a bar is often the stimulus for aggravated assault. It follows that people with low self-control tend to have minimal tolerance for frustration and little ability to respond to conflict through verbal rather than physical means.

Crimes involve the risk of violence and physical injury, of pain and suffering on the part of the offender. It does not follow that people with low self-control will tend to be tolerant of physical pain or to be indifferent to physical discomfort. It does follow that people tolerant of physical pain or indifferent to physical discomfort will be more likely to engage in criminal acts whatever their level of self-control.

The risk of criminal penalty for any given criminal act is small, but this depends in part on the circumstances of the offense. Thus, for example, not all joyrides by teenagers are equally likely to result in arrest. A car stolen from a neighbor and returned unharmed before he notices its absence is less likely to result in official notice than is a car stolen from a shopping center parking lot and abandoned at the convenience of the offender. Drinking alcohol stolen from parents and consumed in the family garage is less likely to receive official notice than drinking in the parking lot outside a concert hall. It follows that offenses differ in their validity as measures of self-control: those offenses with large risk of public awareness are better measures than those with little risk.

In sum, people who lack self-control will tend to be impulsive, insensitive, physical (as opposed to mental), risk-taking, shortsighted, and nonverbal, and they will tend therefore to engage in criminal and analogous acts. Since these traits can be identified prior to the age of responsibility for crime, since there is considerable tendency for these traits to come together in the same people, and since the traits tend to persist through life, it seems reasonable to consider them as comprising a stable construct useful in the explanation of crime.

The Many Manifestations of Low Self-Control

Our image of the "offender" suggests that crime is not an automatic or necessary consequence of low self-control. It suggests that many noncriminal acts analogous to crime (such as accidents, smoking, and alcohol use) are also manifestations of low self-control. Our image therefore implies that no specific act, type of crime, or form of deviance is uniquely required by the absence of self-control.

Because both crime and analogous behaviors stem from low self-control (that is, both are manifestations of low self-control), they will all be engaged in at a relatively high rate by people with low self-control. Within the domain of crime, then, there will be much versatility among offenders in the criminal acts in which they engage.

Research on the versatility of deviant acts supports these predictions in the strongest possible way. The variety of manifestations of low self-control is immense. In spite of years of tireless research motivated by a belief in specialization, no credible evidence of specialization has been reported. . . .

The Causes of Self-Control

We know better what deficiencies in self-control lead to than where they come from. One thing is, however, clear: low self-control is not produced by training, tutelage, or socialization. As a matter of fact, all of the characteristics associated with low self-control tend to show themselves in the absence of nurturance, discipline, or training. Given the classical appreciation of the causes of human behavior, the implications of this fact are straightforward: the causes of low self-control are negative rather than positive; self-control is unlikely in the absence of effort, intended or unintended, to create it. . . .

Child-Rearing and Self-Control: The Family

The major "cause" of low self-control thus appears to be ineffective child-rearing. Put in positive terms, several conditions appear necessary to produce a socialized child. Perhaps the place to begin looking for these conditions is the research literature on the relation between family conditions and delinquency. This research (e.g., Glueck and Glueck 1950; McCord and McCord 1959) has examined the connection between many family factors and delinquency. It reports that discipline, supervision, and affection tend to be missing in the homes of delinquents, that the behavior of the parents is often "poor" (e.g., excessive drinking and poor supervision [Glueck and Glueck 1950: 110–11]); and that the parents of delinquents are unusually likely to have criminal records themselves. Indeed, according to Michael Rutter and Henri Giller, "of the parental characteristics associated with delinquency, criminality is the most striking and most consistent" 1984: 182).

Such information undermines the many explanations of crime that ignore the family, but in this form it does not represent much of an advance over the belief of the general public (and those who deal with offenders in the criminal justice system) that "defective upbringing" or "neglect" in the home is the primary cause of crime.

To put these standard research findings in perspective, we think it necessary to define the conditions necessary for adequate child-rearing to occur. The minimum conditions seem to be these: in order to teach the child self-control, someone must (1) monitor the child's behavior; (2) recognize deviant behavior when it occurs; and (3) punish such behavior. . . .

References

Bentham, Jeremy. 1970 [1789]. *An Introduction to the Principles of Morals and Legislation.* London: The Athlone Press.

Chambliss, William. 1969. *Crime and Legal Process.* New York: McGraw-Hill

Elliott, Delbert, David Huizinga, and Suzanne Ageton. 1985. *Explaining Delinquency and Drug Use.* Beverly Hills, CA: Sage.

Glueck, Sheldon, and Eleanor Glueck. 1950. *Unraveling Juvenile Delinquency.* Cambridge, MA: Harvard University Press.

Hindelang, Michael, Michael R. Gottfredson, and James Garofalo. 1978. *Victims of Personal Crime.* Cambridge, MA: Ballinger.

Morris, Norval, and Gordon Hawkins. 1970. *The Honest Politician's Guide to Crime Control.* Chicago: University of Chicago Press.

Reiss, Albert J., Jr. 1976. "Settling the Frontiers of a Pioneer in American Criminology: Henry McKay." In *Delinquency, Crime, and Society,* edited by J. F. Short (pp. 64–88). Chicago: University of Chicago Press.

Rutter, Michael, and Henri Giller. 1984. *Juvenile Delinquency: Trends and Perspectives*. New York: Guilford.

Suttles, Gerald D. 1968. *The Social Order of the Slum*. Chicago: University of Chicago Press.

Turner, Stanley. 1969. "Delinquency and Distance." In *Delinquency: Selected Studies*, edited by T. Selling and M. Wolfgang (pp. 11–27). New York: Wiley.

Wilson, James Q., and Richard Herrnstein. 1985. *Crime and Human Nature*. New York: Simon and Schuster.

40

The Dramatization of Evil

Frank Tannenbaum

The first dramatization of the "evil" which separates the child out of his group for specialized treatment plays a greater role in making the criminal than perhaps any other experience. It cannot be too often emphasized that for the child the whole situation has become different. He now lives in a different world. He has been tagged. A new and hitherto non-existent environment has been precipitated out for him.

The process of making the criminal, therefore, is a process of tagging, defining, identifying, segregating, describing, emphasizing, making conscious and self-conscious; it becomes a way of stimulating, suggesting, emphasizing, and evoking the very traits that are complained of. If the theory of relation of response to stimulus has any meaning, the entire process of dealing with the young delinquent is mischievous in so far as it identifies him to himself or to the environment as a delinquent person.

The person becomes the thing he is described as being. Nor does it seem to matter whether the valuation is made by those who would punish or by those who would reform. In either case the emphasis is upon the conduct that is disapproved of. The parents or the policeman, the older brother or the court, the probation officer or the juvenile institution, in so far as they rest upon the thing complained of, rest upon a false ground. Their very enthusiasm defeats their aim. The harder they work to reform the evil, the greater the evil grows under their hands. The persistent suggestion, with whatever good intentions, works mischief, because it leads to bringing out the bad behavior that it would suppress. The way out is through a refusal to dramatize the evil. The less said about it the better. The more said about something else, still better.

> The hard-drinker who keeps thinking of not drinking is doing what he can to initiate the acts which lead to drinking. He is starting with the stimulus to his habit. To succeed he must find some positive interest or line of action which will inhibit the drinking series and which by instituting another course of action will bring him to his desired end.[1]

The dramatization of the evil therefore tends to precipitate the conflict situation which was first created through some innocent maladjustment. The child's isolation forces him into companionship with other children similarly defined, and the gang

Source: Frank Tannenbaum, *Crime and the Community* (New York: Ginn, 1938), pp, 18–20. Reprinted by permission of Columbia University Press.

becomes his means of escape, his security. The life of the gang gives it special mores, and the attack by the community upon these mores merely overemphasizes the conflict already in existence, and makes it the source of a new series of experiences that lead directly to a criminal career.

In dealing with the delinquent, the criminal, therefore, the important thing to remember is that we are dealing with a human being who is responding normally to the demands, stimuli, approval, expectancy, of the group with whom he is associated. We are dealing not with an individual but with a group.

Note

1. John Dewey, *Human Nature and Conduct*, p. 35. New York, 1922.

41

Primary and Secondary Deviation
Edwin Lemert

There has been an embarrassingly large number of theories, often without any relationship to a general theory, advanced to account for various specific pathologies in human behavior. For certain types of pathology, such as alcoholism, crime, or stuttering, there are almost as many theories as there are writers on these subjects. This has been occasioned in no small way by the preoccupation with the origins of pathological behavior and by the fallacy of confusing *original* causes with *effective* causes. All such theories have elements of truth, and the divergent viewpoints they contain can be reconciled with the general theory here if it is granted that original causes or antecedents of deviant behaviors are many and diversified. This holds especially for the psychological processes leading to similar pathological behavior, but it also holds for the situational concomitants of the initial aberrant conduct. A person may come to use excessive alcohol not only for a wide variety of subjective reasons but also because of diversified situational influences, such as the death of a loved one, business failure, or participating in some sort of organized group activity calling for heavy drinking of liquor. Whatever the original reasons for violating the norms of the community, they are important only for certain research purposes, such as assessing the extent of the "social problem" at a given time or determining the requirements for a rational program of social control. From a narrower sociological viewpoint the deviations are not significant until they are organized subjectively and transformed into active roles and become the social criteria for assigning status. The deviant individuals must react symbolically to their own behavior aberrations and fix them in their sociopsychological patterns. The deviations remain primary deviations or symptomatic and situational as long as they are rationalized or otherwise dealt with as functions of a socially acceptable role. Under such conditions normal and pathological behaviors remain strange and somewhat tensional bedfellows in the same person. Undeniably a vast amount of such segmental and partially integrated pathological behavior exists in our society and has impressed many writers in the field of social pathology.

Just how far and for how long a person may go in dissociating his sociopathic tendencies so that they are merely troublesome adjuncts of normally conceived roles is not known. Perhaps it depends upon the number of alternative definitions of the same overt behavior that he can develop; perhaps certain physiological factors (limits) are also involved. However, if the deviant acts are repetitive and have a high visibility, and if there is a severe societal reaction, which, through a process of identification is incorporated as part of the "me" of the individual, the probability is greatly increased that the integration of existing roles will be disrupted and that reorganization based upon a new role or roles will occur. (The "me" in this context is simply the subjective aspect of the societal reaction.) Reorganization may be the adoption of another normal role in which the tendencies previously defined as "pathological" are given a more acceptable social expression. The other general possibility is the assumption of a deviant role, if such exists; or, more rarely, the person may organize an aberrant sect or group in which he creates a special role of his own. *When a person begins to employ his deviant behavior or a role based upon it as a means of defense, attack, or adjustment to the overt and covert problems created by the consequent societal reaction to him, his deviation is secondary.* Objective evidences of this change will be found in the symbolic appurtenances of the new role, in clothes, speech, posture, and mannerisms, which in some cases heighten social visibility, and which in some cases serve as symbolic cues to professionalization.

Role Conceptions of the Individual Must Be Reinforced by Reactions of Others

It is seldom that one deviant act will provoke a sufficiently strong societal reaction to bring about secondary deviation, unless in the process of introjection the individual imputes or projects meanings into the social situation which are not present. In this case anticipatory fears are involved. For example, in a culture where a child is taught sharp distinctions between "good" and "bad" women, a single act of questionable morality might conceivably have a profound meaning for the girl so indulging. However, in the absence of reactions by the person's family, neighbors, or the larger community, reinforcing the tentative "bad-girl" self-definition, it is questionable whether a transition to secondary deviation would take place. It is also doubtful whether a temporary exposure to a severe punitive reaction by the community will lead a person to identify himself with a pathological role, unless, as we have said, the experience is highly traumatic. Most frequently there is a progressive reciprocal relationship between the deviation of the individual and the societal reaction, with a compounding of the societal reaction out of the minute accretions in the deviant behavior, until a point is reached where ingrouping and outgrouping between society and the deviant is manifest.[1] At this point a stigmatizing of the deviant occurs in the form of name calling, labeling, or stereotyping.

The sequence of interaction leading to secondary deviation is roughly as follows:

1. primary deviation;
2. social penalties;
3. further primary deviation;
4. stronger penalties and rejections;
5. further deviation, perhaps with hostilities and resentment beginning to focus upon those doing the penalizing;
6. crisis reached in the tolerance quotient, expressed in formal action by the community stigmatizing of the deviant;

7. strengthening of the deviant conduct as a reaction to the stigmatizing and penalties;

8. ultimate acceptance of deviant social status and efforts at adjustment on the basis of the associated role.

As an illustration of this sequence the behavior of an errant schoolboy can be cited. For one reason or another, let us say excessive energy, the schoolboy engages in a classroom prank. He is penalized for it by the teacher. Later, due to clumsiness, he creates another disturbance and again he is reprimanded. Then, as sometimes happens, the boy is blamed for something he did not do. When the teacher uses the tag "bad boy" or "mischief maker" or other invidious terms, hostility and resentment are excited in the boy, and he may feel that he is blocked in playing the role expected of him. Thereafter, there may be a strong temptation to assume his role in the class as defined by the teacher, particularly when he discovers that there are rewards as well as penalties deriving from such a role. There is, of course, no implication here that such boys go on to become delinquents or criminals, for the mischief-maker role may later become integrated with or retrospectively rationalized as part of a role more acceptable to school authorities.[2] If such a boy continues this unacceptable role and becomes delinquent, the process must be accounted for in the light of the general theory of this volume. There must be a spreading corroboration of a sociopathic self-conception and societal reinforcement at each step in the process.

The most significant personality changes are manifest when societal definitions and their subjective counterpart become generalized. When this happens, the range of major role choices becomes narrowed to one general class.[3] This was very obvious in the case of a young girl who was the daughter of a paroled convict and who was attending a small Middle Western college. She continually argued with herself and with the author, in whom she had confided, that in reality she belonged on the "other side of the railroad tracks" and that her life could be enormously simplified by acquiescing in this verdict and living accordingly. While in her case there was a tendency to dramatize her conflicts, nevertheless there was enough societal reinforcement of her self-conception by the treatment she received in her relationship with her father and on dates with college boys to lend it a painful reality. Once these boys took her home to the shoddy dwelling in a slum area where she lived with her father, who was often in a drunken condition, they abruptly stopped seeing her again or else became sexually presumptive. . . .

Notes

1. Mead, G., "The Psychology of Punitive Justice," *American Journal of Sociology*, 23 (March 1918), pp. 577–602.
2. Evidence for fixed or inevitable sequences from predelinquency to crime is absent. Sutherland, E. H., *Principles of Criminology*, 1939, 4th ed., p. 202.
3. Sutherland seems to say something of this sort in connection with the development of criminal behavior. *Ibid.*, p. 86.

42

Outsiders

Howard S. Becker

. . . [One] sociological view . . . defines deviance as the infraction of some agreed-upon rule. It then goes on to ask who breaks rules, and to search for the factors in their personalities and life situations that might account for the infractions. This assumes that those who have broken a rule constitute a homogeneous category, because they have committed the same deviant act.

Such an assumption seems to me to ignore the central fact about deviance: it is created by society. I do not mean this in the way it is ordinarily understood, in which the causes of deviance are located in the social situation of the deviant or in "social factors" which prompt his action. I mean, rather, that *social groups create deviance by making the rules whose infraction constitutes deviance*, and by applying those rules to particular people and labeling them as outsiders. From this point of view, deviance is *not* a quality of the act the person commits, but rather a consequence of the application by others of rules and sanctions to an "offender." The deviant is one to whom that label has successfully been applied; deviant behavior is behavior that people so label.[1]

Since deviance is, among other things, a consequence of the responses of others to a person's act, students of deviance cannot assume that they are dealing with a homogeneous category when they study people who have been labeled deviant. That is, they cannot assume that these people have actually committed a deviant act or broken some rule, because the process of labeling may not be infallible; some people may be labeled deviant who in fact have not broken a rule. Furthermore, they cannot assume that the category of those labeled deviant will contain all those who actually have broken a rule, for many offenders may escape apprehension and thus fail to be included in the population of "deviants" they study. Insofar as the category lacks homogeneity and fails to include all the cases that belong in it, one cannot reasonably expect to find common factors of personality or life situation that will account for the supposed deviance.

What, then, do people who have been labeled deviant have in common? At the least, they share the label and the experience of being labeled as outsiders. I will begin my analysis with this basic similarity and view deviance as the product of a transaction that takes place between some social group and one who is viewed

Source: Reprinted with permission of The Free Press, a Division of Simon & Schuster Adult Publishing Group, from *Outsiders: Studies in the Sociology of Deviance* by Howard S. Becker. Copyright © 1963 by The Free Press. Copyright © renewed 1991 by Howard S. Becker.

by that group as a rule-breaker. . . .

Whether an act is deviant, then, depends on how other people react to it. You can commit clan incest and suffer from no more than gossip as long as no one makes a public accusation; but you will be driven to your death if the accusation is made. The point is that the response of other people has to be regarded as problematic. Just because one has committed an infraction of a rule does not mean that others will respond as though this had happened. (Conversely, just because one has not violated a rule does not mean that he may not be treated, in some circumstances, as though he had.)

The degree to which other people will respond to a given act as deviant varies greatly. Several kinds of variation seem worth noting. First of all, there is variation over time. A person believed to have committed a given "deviant" act may at one time be responded to much more leniently than he would be at some other time. . . .

The degree to which an act will be treated as deviant depends also on who commits the act and who feels he has been harmed by it. Rules tend to be applied more to some persons than others. Studies of juvenile delinquency make the point clearly. Boys from middle-class areas do not get as far in the legal process when they are apprehended as do boys from slum areas. The middle-class boy is less likely, when picked up by the police, to be taken to the station; less likely when taken to the station to be booked; and it is extremely unlikely that he will be convicted and sentenced.[2] This variation occurs even though the original infraction of the rule is the same in the two cases. Similarly, the law is differentially applied to Negroes and whites. It is well known that a Negro believed to have attacked a white woman is much more likely to be punished than a white man who commits the same offense; it is only slightly less well known that a Negro who murders another Negro is much less likely to be punished than a white man who commits murder.[3] This, of course, is one of the main points of Sutherland's analysis of white-collar crime: crimes committed by corporations are almost always prosecuted as civil cases, but the same crime committed by an individual is ordinarily treated as a criminal offense.[4]

Some rules are enforced only when they result in certain consequences. The unmarried mother furnishes a clear example. Vincent[5] points out that illicit sexual relations seldom result in severe punishment or social censure for the offenders. If, however, a girl becomes pregnant as a result of such activities the reaction of others is likely to be severe. (The illicit pregnancy is also an interesting example of the differential enforcement of rules on different categories of people. Vincent notes that unmarried fathers escape the severe censure visited on the mother.)

Why repeat these commonplace observations? Because, taken together, they support the proposition that deviance is not a simple quality, present in some kinds of behavior and absent in others. Rather, it is the product of a process which involves responses of other people to the behavior. The same behavior may be an infraction of the rules at one time and not at another; may be an infraction when committed by one person, but not when committed by another; some rules are broken with impunity, others are not. In short, whether a given act is deviant or not depends in part on the nature of the act (that is, whether or not it violates some rule) and in part on what other people do about it.

Some people may object that this is merely a terminological quibble, that one can, after all, define terms any way he wants to and that if some people want to speak of rule-breaking behavior as deviant without reference to the reactions of others they are free to do so. This, of course, is true. Yet it might be worthwhile to refer to such behavior as *rule-breaking behavior* and reserve the term *deviant* for those labeled as deviant by some segment of society. I do not insist that this usage be followed. But it should be clear that insofar as a scientist uses "deviant" to refer to any rule-breaking behavior and takes as his subject of study only those who have been *labeled* deviant, he will be hampered by the disparities between the two categories.

If we take as the object of our attention behavior which comes to be labeled as deviant, we must recognize that we cannot know whether a given act will be categorized as deviant until the response of others has occurred. Deviance is not a quality that lies in behavior itself, but in the interaction between the person who commits an act and those who respond to it.

Rules and Their Enforcement

The question here is simply: when are rules made and enforced? I noted earlier that the existence of a rule does not automatically guarantee that it will be enforced. There are many variations in rule enforcement. We cannot account for rule enforcement by invoking some abstract group that is ever vigilant; we cannot say that "society" is harmed by every infraction and acts to restore the balance. We might posit, as one extreme, a group in which this was the case, in which all rules were absolutely and automatically enforced. But imagining such an extreme case only serves to make more clear the fact that social groups are ordinarily not like this. It is more typical for rules to be enforced only when something provokes enforcement. Enforcement, then, requires explanation.

The explanation rests on several premises. First, enforcement of a rule is an enterprising act. Someone—an entrepreneur—must take the initiative in punishing the culprit. Second, enforcement occurs when those who want the rule enforced publicly bring the infraction to the attention of others; an infraction cannot be ignored once it is made public. Put another way, enforcement occurs when someone blows the whistle. Third, people blow the whistle, making enforcement necessary, when they see some advantage in doing so. Personal interest prods them to take the initiative. Finally, the kind of personal interest that prompts enforcement varies with the complexity of the situation in which enforcement takes place. . . .

Moral Entrepreneurs

Rules are the products of someone's initiative and we can think of the people who exhibit such enterprise as *moral entrepreneurs*. Two related species—rule creators and rule enforcers—will occupy our attention.

Rule Creators

The prototype of the rule creator, but not the only variety as we shall see, is the crusading reformer. He is interested in the content of rules. The existing rules do not satisfy him because there is some evil which profoundly disturbs him. He feels that nothing can be right in the world until rules are made to correct it. He operates with an absolute ethic; what he sees is truly and totally evil with no qualification. Any means is justified to do away with it. The crusader is fervent and righteous, often self-righteous.

It is appropriate to think of reformers as crusaders because they typically believe that their mission is a holy one. The prohibitionist serves as an excellent example, as does the person who wants to suppress vice and sexual delinquency or the person who wants to do away with gambling. . . .

Moral crusaders typically want to help those beneath them to achieve a better status. That those beneath them do not always like the means proposed for their salvation is another matter. But this fact—that moral crusades are typically dominated by those in the upper levels of the social structure—means that they add to the power they derive from the legitimacy of their moral position, the power they derive from their superior position in society. . . .

The moral crusader, however, is more concerned with ends than with means. When it comes to drawing up specific rules (typically in the form of legislation to be proposed to a state legislature or the federal Congress), he frequently relies on the advice of experts. Lawyers, expert in the drawing of acceptable legislation, often play this role. Government bureaus in whose jurisdiction the problem falls may also have the necessary expertise, as did the Federal Bureau of Narcotics in the case of the marihuana problem.

As psychiatric ideology, however, becomes increasingly acceptable, a new expert has appeared—the psychiatrist. . . .

The influence of psychiatrists in other realms of the criminal law has increased in recent years.

In any case, what is important about this example is not that psychiatrists are becoming increasingly influential, but that the moral crusader, at some point in the development of his crusade, often requires the services of a professional who can draw up the appropriate rules in an appropriate form. The crusader himself is often not concerned with such details. Enough for him that the main point has been won; he leaves its implementation to others.

By leaving the drafting of the specific rule in the hands of others, the crusader opens the door for many unforeseen influences. For those who draft legislation for crusaders have their own interests, which may affect the legislation they prepare. It is likely that the sexual psychopath laws drawn by psychiatrists contain many features never intended by the citizens who spearheaded the drives to ''do something about sex crimes,'' features which do however reflect the professional interests of organized psychiatry.

The Fate of Moral Crusades

A crusade may achieve striking success, as did the Prohibition movement with the passage of the Eighteenth Amendment. It may fail completely, as has the drive to do away with the use of tobacco or the anti-vivisection movement. It may achieve great success, only to find its gains whittled away by shifts in public morality and increasing restrictions imposed on it by judicial interpretations; such has been the case with the crusade against obscene literature.

One major consequence of a successful crusade, of course, is the establishment of a new rule or set of rules, usually with the appropriate enforcement machinery being provided at the same time. . . .

Only some crusaders, then, are successful in their mission and create, by creating a new rule, a new group of outsiders. Of the successful, some find they have a taste for crusades and seek new problems to attack. Other crusaders fail in their attempt and either support the organization they have created by dropping their distinctive mission and focusing on the problem of organizational maintenance itself or become outsiders themselves, continuing to espouse and preach a doctrine which sounds increasingly queer as time goes on.

Rule Enforcers

The most obvious consequence of a successful crusade is the creation of a new set of rules. With the creation of a new set of rules we often find that a new set of enforcement agencies and officials is established. Sometimes, of course, existing agencies take over the administration of the new rule, but more frequently a new set of rule enforcers is created. The passage of the Harrison Act presaged the creation of the Federal Narcotics Bureau, just as the passage of the Eighteenth Amendment led to the creation of police agencies charged with enforcing the Prohibition Laws.

With the establishment of organizations of rule enforcers, the crusade becomes institutionalized. What started out as a drive to convince the world of the moral necessity of a new rule finally becomes an organization devoted to the enforcement of the rule. Just as radical political movements turn into organized political parties and lusty evangelical sects become staid religious denominations, the final outcome of the moral crusade is a police force. To understand, therefore, how the rules creating a new class of outsiders are applied to particular people we must understand the motives and interests of police, the rule enforcers.

Although some policemen undoubtedly have a kind of crusading interest in stamping out evil, it is probably much more typical for the policeman to have a certain detached and objective view of his job. He is not so much concerned with the content of any particular rule as he is with the fact that it is his job to enforce the rule. When the rules are changed, he punishes what was once acceptable behavior just as he ceases to punish behavior that has been made legitimate by a change in the rules. The enforcer, then, may not be interested in the content of the rule as such, but only in the fact that the existence of the rule provides him with a job, a profession, and a *raison d'être*.

Since the enforcement of certain rules provides justification for his way of life, the enforcer has two interests which condition his enforcement activity: first, he must justify the existence of his position and, second, he must win the respect of those he deals with.

These interests are not peculiar to rule enforcers. Members of all occupations feel the need to justify their work and win the respect of others. Musicians, as we have seen, would like to do this but have difficulty finding ways of successfully impressing their worth on customers. Janitors fail to win their tenants' respect, but develop an ideology which stresses the quasi-professional responsibility they have to keep confidential the intimate knowledge of tenants they acquire in the course of their work.[6] Physicians, lawyers, and other professionals, more successful in winning the respect of clients, develop elaborate mechanisms for maintaining a properly respectful relationship.

In justifying the existence of his position, the rule enforcer faces a double problem. On the one hand, he must demonstrate to others that the problem still exists: the rules he is supposed to enforce have some point, because infractions occur. On the other hand, he must show that his attempts at enforcement are effective and worthwhile, that the evil he is supposed to deal with is in fact being dealt with adequately. Therefore, enforcement organizations, particularly when they are seeking funds, typically oscillate between two kinds of claims. First, they say that by reason of their efforts the problem they deal with is approaching solution. But, in the same breath, they say the problem is perhaps worse than ever (though through no fault of their own) and requires renewed and increased effort to keep it under control. Enforcement officials can be more vehement than anyone else in their insistence that the problem they are supposed to deal with is still with us, in fact is more with us than ever before. In making these claims, enforcement officials provide good reason for continuing the existence of the position they occupy. . . .

In the same way, a rule enforcer is likely to believe that it is necessary for the people he deals with to respect him. If they do not, it will be very difficult to do his job; his feeling of security in his work will be lost. Therefore, a good deal of enforcement activity is devoted not to the actual enforcement of rules, but to coercing respect from the people the enforcer deals with. This means that one may be labeled as deviant not because he has actually broken a rule, but because he has shown disrespect to the enforcer of the rule. . . .

Ordinarily, the rule enforcer has a great deal of discretion in many areas, if only because his resources are not sufficient to cope with the volume of rule breaking he is supposed to deal with. This means that he cannot tackle everything at once and to this extent must temporize with evil. He cannot do the whole job and knows it. He takes his time, on the assumption that the problems he deals with will be around for a long while. He establishes priorities, dealing with things in their turn, handling the most pressing problems immediately and leaving others for later. His attitude toward his work, in short, is professional. He lacks the naïve moral fervor characteristic of the rule creator. . . .

Enforcers of rules, since they have no stake in the content of particular rules themselves, often develop their own private evaluation of the importance of various kinds of rules and infractions of them. This set of priorities may differ considerably from those held by the general public. For instance, drug users typically believe (and a few policemen have personally confirmed it to me) that police do not consider the use of marihuana to be as important a problem or as dangerous a practice as the use of opiate drugs. Police base this conclusion on the fact that, in their experience, opiate users commit other crimes (such as theft or prostitution) in order to get drugs, while marihuana users do not.

Enforcers, then, responding to the pressures of their own work situation, enforce rules and create outsiders in a selective way. Whether a person who commits a deviant act is in fact labeled a deviant depends on many things extraneous to his actual behavior: whether the enforcement official feels that at this time he must make some show of doing his job in order to justify his position, whether the misbehaver shows proper deference to the enforcer, whether the "fix" has been put in, and where the kind of act he has committed stands on the enforcer's list of priorities.

The professional enforcer's lack of fervor and routine approach to dealing with evil may get him into trouble with the rule creator. The rule creator, as we have said, is concerned with the content of the rules that interest him. He sees them as the means by which evil can be stamped out. He does not understand the enforcer's long-range approach to the same problems and cannot see why all the evil that is apparent cannot be stamped out at once.

When the person interested in the content of a rule realizes or has called to his attention the fact that enforcers are dealing selectively with the evil that concerns him, his righteous wrath may be aroused. The professional is denounced for viewing the evil too lightly, for failing to do his duty. The moral entrepreneur, at whose instance the rule was made, arises again to say that the outcome of the last crusade has not been satisfactory or that the gains once made have been whittled away and lost.

Deviance and Enterprise: A Summary

Deviance—in the sense I have been using it, of publicly labeled wrongdoing—is always the result of enterprise. Before any act can be viewed as deviant, and before any class of people can be labeled and treated as outsiders for committing the act, someone must have made the rule which defines the act as deviant. Rules are not made automatically. Even though a practice may be harmful in an objective sense to the group in which it occurs, the harm needs to be discovered and pointed out. People must be made to feel that something ought to be done about it. Someone must call the public's attention to these matters, supply the push necessary to get things done, and direct such energies as are aroused in the proper direction to get a rule created. Deviance is the product of enterprise in the largest sense; without the enterprise required to get rules made, the deviance which consists of breaking the rule could not exist.

Deviance is the product of enterprise in the smaller and more particular sense as well. Once a rule has come into existence, it must be applied to particular people before the abstract class of outsiders created by the rule can be peopled. Offenders must be discovered, identified, apprehended and convicted (or noted as "different" and stigmatized for their nonconformity, as in the case of legal deviant groups such as dance musicians). This job ordinarily falls to the lot of professional enforcers who, by enforcing already existing rules, create the particular deviants society views as outsiders.

It is an interesting fact that most scientific research and speculation on deviance concerns itself with the people who break rules rather than those who make and enforce them. If we are to achieve a full understanding of deviant behavior, we must get these two possible foci of inquiry into balance. We must see deviance, and the outsiders who personify the abstract conception, as a consequence of a process of interaction between people, some of whom in the service of their own interests make and enforce rules which catch others who, in the service of their own interests, have committed acts which are labeled deviant.

Notes

1. The most important earlier statements of this view can be found in Frank Tannenbaum, *Crime and the Community* (New York: McGraw-Hill Book Co., Inc., 1951), and E. M. Lemert, *Social Pathology* (New York: McGraw-Hill Book Co., Inc., 1951). A recent article stating a position very similar to mine is John Kitsuse, "Societal Reaction to Deviance: Problems of Theory and Method," *Social Problems*, 9 (Winter 1962), 247–256.
2. See Albert K. Cohen and James F. Short, Jr., "Juvenile Delinquency," in [Robert K. Merton and Robert A. Nisbet (eds.), *Contemporary Social Problems* (New York: Harcourt, Brace and World, Inc., 1961)], p. 87.
3. See Harold Garfinkel, "Research Notes on Inter- and Intra-Racial Homicides," *Social Forces*, 27 (May 1949), 369–381.

4. Edwin H. Sutherland, "White Collar Criminality," *American Sociological Review*, V (February 1940), 1–12.
5. Clark Vincent, *Unmarried Mothers* (New York: The Free Press of Glencoe, 1961), pp. 3–5.
6. See Ray Gold, "Janitors Versus Tenants: A Status-Income Dilemma," *American Journal of Sociology*, LVII (March 1952), 486–493.

43

The Etiology of Female Crime: A Review of the Literature

Dorie Klein

I. Introduction

The criminality of women has long been a neglected subject area of criminology. Many explanations have been advanced for this, such as women's low official rate of crime and delinquency and the preponderance of male theorists in the field. Female criminality has often ended up as a footnote to works on men that purport to be works on criminality in general.

There has been, however, a small group of writings specifically concerned with women and crime. This paper will explore those works concerned with the etiology of female crime and delinquency, beginning with the turn-of-the-century writing of Lombroso and extending to the present. Writers selected to be included have been chosen either for their influence on the field, such as Lombroso, Thomas, Freud, Davis and Pollak, or because they are representative of the kinds of work being published, such as Konopka, Vedder and Somerville, and Cowie, Cowie and Slater. The emphasis is on the continuity between these works, because it is clear that, despite recognizable differences in analytical approaches and specific theories, the authors represent a tradition to a great extent. It is important to understand, therefore, the shared assumptions made by the writers that are used in laying the groundwork for their theories.

The writers see criminality as the result of *individual* characteristics that are only peripherally affected by economic, social and political forces. These characteristics are of a *physiological* or *psychological* nature and are uniformly based on implicit or explicit assumptions about the *inherent nature of women*. This nature is *universal*, rather than existing within a specific historical framework.

Since criminality is seen as an individual activity, rather than as a condition built into existing structures, the focus is on biological, psychological and social factors that would turn a woman toward criminal activity. To do this, the writers create two distinct classes of women: good women who are "normal" noncriminals, and bad women who are criminals, thus taking a moral position that often masquerades as a scientific distinction. The writers, although they may be biological or social deter-

Source: Klein, Dorie, "The Etiology of Female Crime," *Issues in Criminology*, 8 (1973):3–30. Permission granted by the author.

nists to varying degrees, assume that individuals have *choices* between criminal and noncriminal activity. They see persons as atomistically moving about in a social and political vacuum; many writers use marketplace models for human interaction.

Although the theorists may differ on specific remedies for individual criminality, ranging from sterilization to psychoanalysis (but always stopping far short of social change), the basic thrust is toward *individual adjustment*, whether it be physical or mental, and the frequent model is rehabilitative therapy. Widespread environmental alterations are usually included as casual footnotes to specific plans for individual therapy. Most of the writers are concerned with *social harmony* and the welfare of the existing social structure rather than with the women involved or with women's position in general. None of the writers come from anything near a "feminist" or "radical" perspective. . . .

The specific characteristics ascribed to women's nature and those critical to theories of female criminality are uniformly *sexual* in their nature. Sexuality is seen as the root of female behavior and the problem of crime. Women are defined as sexual beings, as sexual capital in many cases, physiologically, psychologically and socially. This definition *reflects* and *reinforces* the economic position of women as reproductive and domestic workers. It is mirrored in the laws themselves and in their enforcement, which penalize sexual deviations for women and may be more lenient with economic offenses committed by them, in contrast to the treatment given men. The theorists accept the sexual double standard inherent in the law, often noting that "chivalry" protects women, and many of them build notions of the universality of *sex repression* into their explanations of women's position. Women are thus the sexual backbone of civilization.

In setting hegemonic standards of conduct for all women, the theorists define *femininity*, which they equate with healthy femaleness, in classist, racist and sexist terms, using their assumptions of women's nature, specifically their sexuality, to justify what is often in reality merely a defense of the existing order. Lombroso, Thomas and Freud consider the upper-class white woman to be the highest expression of femininity, although she is inferior to the upper-class white man. These standards are adopted by later writers in discussing femininity. To most theorists, women are inherently inferior to men at masculine tasks such as thought and production, and therefore it is logical that their sphere should be reproductive. . . .

The writers ignore the problems of poor and Third World women, concentrating on affluent white standards of femininity. The experiences of these overlooked women, who *in fact* constitute a good percentage of women caught up in the criminal justice system, negate the notions of sexually motivated crime. These women have real economic needs which are not being met, and in many cases engage in illegal activities as a viable economic alternative. Furthermore, chivalry has never been extended to them.

The writers largely ignore the problems of sexism, racism and class, thus their work is sexist, racist and classist in its implications. Their concern is adjustment of the woman to society, not social change. Hence, they represent a tradition in criminology and carry along a host of assumptions about women and humanity in general. It is important to explore these assumptions and traditions in depth in order to understand what kinds of myths have been propagated around women and crime. The discussions of each writer or writers will focus on these assumptions and their relevance to criminological theories. These assumptions of universal, biological/psychological characteristics, of individual responsibility for crime, of the necessity for maintaining social harmony, and of the benevolence of the state link different theories along a continuum, transcending political labels and minor divergences. The road from Lombroso to the present is surprisingly straight.

II. Lombroso: "There Must Be Some Anomaly . . ."

Lombroso's work on female criminality (1920) is important to consider today despite the fact that his methodology and conclusions have long been successfully discredited. Later writings on female crime by Thomas, Davis, Pollak and others use more sophisticated methodologies and may proffer more palatable liberal theories. However, to varying degrees they rely on those sexual ideologies based on *implicit* assumptions about the physiological and psychological nature of women that are *explicit* in Lombroso's work. Reading the work helps to achieve a better understanding of what kinds of myths have been developed for women in general and for female crime and deviance in particular.

One specific notion of women offered by Lombroso is women's physiological immobility and psychological passivity, later elaborated by Thomas, Freud and other writers. Another ascribed characteristic is the Lombrosian notion of women's adaptability to surroundings and their capacity for survival as being superior to that of men. A third idea discussed by Lombroso is women's amorality: they are cold and calculating. This is developed by Thomas (1923), who describes women's manipulation of the male sex urge for ulterior purposes; by Freud (1933), who sees women as avenging their lack of a penis on men; and by Pollak (1950), who depicts women as inherently deceitful. . . .

They are seen as rational (although they are irrational, too!), atomistic individuals making choices in a vacuum, prompted only by personal, physiological/psychological factors. These choices relate only to the *sexual* sphere. Women have no place in any other sphere. Men, on the other hand, are not held sexually accountable, although, as Thomas notes (1907), they are held responsible in *economic* matters. Men's sexual freedom is justified by the myth of masculine, irresistible sex urges. This myth, still worshipped today, is frequently offered as a rationalization for the existence of prostitution and the double standard. As Davis maintains, this necessitates the parallel existence of classes of "good" and "bad" women.

These dual moralities for the sexes are outgrowths of the economic, political and social *realities* for men and women. Women are primarily workers within the family, a critical institution of reproduction and socialization that services such basic needs as food and shelter. Laws and codes of behavior for women thus attempt to maintain the smooth functioning of women in that role, which requires that women act as a conservative force in the continuation of the nuclear family. Women's main tasks are sexual, and the law embodies sexual limitations for women, which do not exist for men, such as the prohibition of promiscuity for girls. This explains why theorists of female criminality are not only concerned with sexual violations by female offenders, but attempt to account for even *nonsexual* offenses, such as prostitution, in sexual terms, *e.g.*, women enter prostitution for sex rather than for money. Such women are not only economic offenders but are sexual deviants, falling neatly into the category of "bad" women.

The works of Lombroso, particularly *The Female Offender* (1920), are a foremost example of the biological explanation of crime. Lombroso deals with crime as an atavism, or survival of "primitive" traits in individuals, particularly those of the female and nonwhite races. He theorizes that individuals develop differentially within sexual and racial limitations which differ hierarchically from the most highly developed, the white men, to the most primitive, the nonwhite women. . . .

Although women lack the higher sensibilities of men, they are thus restrained from criminal activity in most cases by lack of intelligence and passion, qualities which *criminal* women possess as well as all *men*. Within this framework of biological limits of women's nature, the female offender is characterized as *masculine* whereas the normal woman is *feminine*. . . .

III. Thomas: "The Stimulation She Craves"

The works of W. I. Thomas are critical in that they mark a transition from purely physiological explanations such as Lombroso's to more sophisticated theories that embrace physiological, psychological and social-structural factors. However, even the most sophisticated explanations of female crime rely on implicit assumptions about the *biological* nature of women. In Thomas' *Sex and Society* (1907) and *The Unadjusted Girl* (1923), there are important contradictions in the two approaches that are representative of the movements during that period between publication dates: a departure from biological Social-Darwinian theories to complex analyses of the interaction between society and the individual, *i.e.*, societal repression and manipulation of the "natural" wishes of persons.

In *Sex and Society* (1907), Thomas poses basic biological differences between the sexes as his starting point. Maleness is "katabolic," the animal force which is destructive of energy and allows men the possibility of creative work through this outward flow. Femaleness is "anabolic," analogous to a plant which stores energy, and is motionless and conservative. . . . This statement ignores the hard physical work done by poor *white* women at home and in the factories and offices in "civilized" countries, and accepts a *ruling-class* definition of femininity. . . .

In *The Unadjusted Girl* (1923), Thomas deals with female delinquency as a "normal" response under certain social conditions, using assumptions about the nature of women which he leaves unarticulated in this work. Driven by basic "wishes," an individual is controlled by society in her activities through institutional transmission of codes and mores. Depending on how they are manipulated, wishes can be made to serve social or antisocial ends. Thomas stresses the institutions that socialize, such as the family, giving people certain "definitions of the situation.". . .

This is an important shift in perspective, from the traditional libertarian view of protecting society by punishing transgressors, to the *rehabilitative* and *preventive* perspective of crime control that seeks to control *minds* through socialization rather than to merely control behavior through punishment. The autonomy of the individual to choose is seen as the product of his environment which the state can alter. This is an important refutation of the Lombrosian biological perspective, which maintains that there are crime-prone individuals who must be locked up, sterilized or otherwise incapacitated. Today, one can see an amalgamation of the two perspectives in new theories of "behavior control" that use tactics such as conditioning and brain surgery, combining biological and environmental viewpoints.[1]

Thomas proposes the manipulation of individuals through institutions to prevent antisocial attitudes, and maintains that there is no such person as the "crime prone" individual. A hegemonic system of belief can be imposed by sublimating natural urges and by correcting the poor socialization of slum families. In this perspective, the *definition* of the situation rather than the situation *itself* is what should be changed; a situation is what someone *thinks* it is. The response to a criminal woman who is dissatisfied with her conventional sexual roles is to change not the roles, which would mean widespread social transformations, but to change her attitudes. This concept of civilization as repressive and the need to adjust is later refined by Freud.

Middle-class women, according to Thomas, commit little crime because they are socialized to sublimate their natural desires and to behave well, treasuring their chastity as an investment. The poor woman, however, "is not immoral, because this implies a loss of morality, but amoral" (*Ibid.*:98). Poor women are not objectively driven to crime; they long for it. Delinquent girls are motivated by the desire for excitement or "new experience," and forget the repressive urge of "security." However, these desires are well within Thomas's conception of *femininity*: delinquents are not rebelling against womanhood, as Lombroso suggests, but merely acting it out illegally. Davis and Pollak agree with this notion that delinquent women are not "different" from nondelinquent women.

Thomas maintains that it is not sexual desire that motivates delinquent girls, for they are no more passionate than other women, but they are *manipulating* male desires for sex to achieve their own ulterior ends. . . .

Here Thomas is expanding on the myth of the manipulative woman, who is cold and scheming and vain. To him, good female sexual behavior is a protective measure—"instinctive, of course" (1907:241), whereas male behavior is uncontrollable as men are caught by helpless desires. This is the common Victorian notion of the woman as seductress which in turn perpetuates the myth of a lack of real sexuality to justify her responsibility for upholding sexual mores. Thomas uses a market analogy to female virtue: good women *keep* their bodies as capital to sell in matrimony for marriage and security, whereas bad women *trade* their bodies for excitement. One notes, of course, the familiar dichotomy. It is difficult, in this framework, to see how Thomas can make *any* moral distinctions, since morality seems to be merely good business sense. In fact, Thomas's yardstick is social harmony, necessitating *control*.

Thomas shows an insensitivity to real human relationships and needs. He also shows ignorance of economic hardships in his denial of economic factors in delinquency. . . .

IV. Freud: "Beauty, Charm and Sweetness"

The Freudian theory of the position of women is grounded in explicit biological assumptions about their nature, expressed by the famous "Anatomy is Destiny." Built upon this foundation is a construction incorporating psychological and social-structural factors.

Freud himself sees women as anatomically inferior; they are destined to be wives and mothers, and this is admittedly an inferior destiny as befits the inferior sex. The root of this inferiority is that women's *sex organs* are inferior to those of men, a fact *universally* recognized by children in the Freudian scheme. The girl assumes that she has lost a penis as punishment, is traumatized, and grows up envious and revengeful. The boy also sees the girl as having lost a penis, fears a similar punishment himself, and dreads the girl's envy and vengeance. Feminine traits can be traced to the inferior genitals themselves, or to women's inferiority complex arising from their response to them: women are exhibitionistic, narcissistic, and attempt to compensate for their lack of a penis by being well dressed and physically beautiful. Women become mothers trying to replace the lost penis with a baby. Women are also masochistic, as Lombroso and Thomas have noted, because their *sexual* role is one of receptor, and their sexual pleasure consists of pain. This woman, Freud notes, is the *healthy* woman. In the familiar dichotomy, the men are aggressive and pain inflicting. . . . Freud, like Lombroso and Thomas, takes the notion of men's activity and women's inactivity and *reduces* it to the sexual level, seeing the sexual union itself through Victorian eyes: ladies don't move.

Women are also inferior in the sense that they are concerned with personal matters and have little social sense. Freud sees civilization as based on repression of the sex drive, where it is the duty of men to repress their strong instincts in order to get on with the worldly business of civilization. Women, on the other hand,

> have little sense of justice, and this is no doubt connected with the preponderance of envy in their mental life; for the demands of justice are a modification of envy; they lay down the conditions under which one is willing to part with it. We also say of women that their social interests are weaker than those of men and that their capacity for the sublimation of their instincts is less. (1933:183)

In this framework, the deviant woman is one who is attempting to be a *man*. She is aggressively rebellious, and her drive to accomplishment is the expression of her longing for a penis; this is a hopeless pursuit, of course, and she will only end up "neurotic." Thus the deviant woman should be treated and helped to *adjust* to her sex role. . . .

In speaking of femininity, Freud, like his forebearers, is speaking along racist and classist lines. Only upper- and middle-class women could possibly enjoy lives as sheltered darlings. Freud sets hegemonic standards of femininity for poor and Third World women.

It is important to understand Freudianism because it reduces categories of sexual ideology to explicit sexuality and makes these categories scientific. For the last fifty years, Freudianism has been a mainstay of sexist social theory. . . .

Freudian notions of the repression of sexual instincts, the sexual passivity of women, and the sanctity of the nuclear family are conservative not only in their contemporary context, but in the context of their own time. . . .

V. Davis: "The Most Convenient Sexual Outlet for Armies . . ."

Kingsley Davis's work on prostitution (1961) is still considered a classical analysis on the subject with a structural-functionalist perspective. It employs assumptions about "the organic nature of man" and woman, many of which can be traced to ideas proffered by Thomas and Freud.

Davis sees prostitution as a structural necessity whose roots lie in the sexual nature of men and women; for example, female humans, unlike primates, are sexually available year-round. He asserts that prostitution is *universal* in time and place, eliminating the possibilities of historical change and ignoring critical differences in the quality and quantity of prostitution in different societies. He maintains that there will always be a class of women who will be prostitutes, the familiar class of "bad" women. The reason for the universality of prostitution is that sexual *repression*, a concept stressed by Thomas and Freud, is essential to the functioning of society.

Once again there is the notion of sublimating "natural" sex urges to the overall needs of society, namely social order. Davis notes that in our society sexuality is permitted only within the structure of the nuclear family, which is an institution of stability. He does not, however, analyze in depth the economic and social functions of the family, other than to say it is a bulwark of morality. . . .

Davis is linking the concept of prostitution to promiscuity, defining it as a *sexual* crime, and calling prostitutes sexual transgressors. Its origins, he claims, lie not in economic hardship, but in the marital restraints on sexuality. As long as men seek women, prostitutes will be in demand. One wonders why sex-seeking women have not created a class of male prostitutes.

Davis sees the only possibility of eliminating prostitution in the liberalization of sexual mores, although he is pessimistic about the likelihood of total elimination. In light of the contemporary American "sexual revolution" of commercial sex, which has surely created more prostitutes and semi-prostitutes rather than eliminating the phenomenon, and in considering the revolution in China where, despite a "puritanical" outlook on sexuality, prostitution has largely been eliminated through major economic and social change, the superficiality of Davis's approach becomes evident. Without dealing with root economic, social and political, factors, one cannot analyze prostitution. . . .

Prostitution "functions," therefore it must be good. Davis, like Thomas, is motivated by concerns of social order rather than by concerns of what the needs and desires of the women involved might be. He denies that the women involved are economically oppressed; they are on the streets through autonomous, *individual* choice. . . . It is important to understand that, given a *sexual* interpretation of what is an *economic* crime, and given a refusal to consider widespread change (even equalization of wages, hardly a revolutionary act), Davis's conclusion is the logical technocratic solution.

In this framework, the deviant women are merely adjusting to their feminine role in an illegitimate fashion, as Thomas has theorized. They are *not* attempting to be rebels or to be "men," as Lombroso's and Freud's positions suggest. Although Davis sees the main difference between wives and prostitutes in a macrosocial sense as the difference merely between legal and illegal roles, in a personal sense he sees the women who *choose* prostitution as maladjusted and neurotic. However, given the universal necessity for prostitution, this analysis implies the necessity of having a perpetually ill and maladjusted class of women. Thus oppression is *built into* the system, and a healthy *system* makes for a sick *individual*. Here Davis is integrating Thomas's notions of social integration with Freudian perspectives on neurosis and maladjustment.

VI. Pollak: "A Different Attitude Toward Veracity"

Otto Pollak's *The Criminality of Women* (1950) has had an outstanding influence on the field of women and crime, being the major work on the subject in the postwar years. Pollak advances the theory of "hidden" female crime to account for what he considers unreasonably low official rates for women.

A major reason for the existence of hidden crime, as he sees it, lies in the *nature* of women themselves. They are instigators rather than perpetrators of criminal activity. While Pollak admits that this role is partly a socially enforced one, he insists that women are inherently deceitful for *physiological* reasons. . . . Pollak *reduces* women's nature to the *sex act*, as Freud has done, and finds women inherently more capable of manipulation, accustomed to being sly, passive and passionless. As Thomas suggests, women can use sex for ulterior purposes. . . . Women's abilities at concealment thus allow them to successfully commit crimes in stealth.

Women are also vengeful. Menstruation, in the classic Freudian sense, seals their doomed hopes to become men and arouses women's desire for vengeance, especially during that time of the month. Thus Pollak offers new rationalizations to bolster old myths.

A second factor in hidden crime is the roles played by women which furnish them with opportunities as domestics, nurses, teachers and housewives to commit undetectable crimes. The *kinds* of crimes women commit reflect their nature: false accusation, for example, is an outgrowth of women's treachery, spite or fear and is a sign of neurosis; shoplifting can be traced in many cases to a special mental disease—kleptomania. Economic factors play a minor role; *sexual-psychological* factors account for female criminality. Crime in women is *personalized* and often accounted for by mental illness. . . . Pollak is defining crimes with economic motives that employ overt action as *masculine*, and defining as *feminine* those crimes for *sexual* activity, such as luring men as baits. Thus he is using circular reasoning by saying that feminine crime is feminine. To fit women into the scheme and justify the statistics, he must invent the notion of hidden crime.

It is important to recognize that, to some extent, women *do* adapt to their enforced sexual roles and may be more likely to instigate, to use sexual traps, and to conform to all the other feminine role expectations. However, it is not accidental that theorists label women as conforming even when they are *not*; for example, by inventing sexual motives for what are clearly crimes of economic necessity, or by invoking "mental illness" such as kleptomania for shoplifting. It is difficult to separate the *theory* from the *reality*, since the reality of female crime is largely unknown. But it is not difficult to see that Pollak is using sexist terms and making sexist assumptions to advance theories of hidden female crime. . . .

The final factor that Pollak advances as a root cause of hidden crime is that of "chivalry" in the criminal justice system. Pollak uses Thomas's observation that women are differentially treated by the law, and carries it to a sweeping conclusion based on *cultural* analyses of men's feelings toward women. . . .

Pollak rejects the possibility of an actual discrepancy between crime rates for men and women; therefore, he must look for factors to expand the scope of female crime. He assumes that there is chivalry in the criminal justice system that is extended to the women who come in contact with it. Yet the women involved are likely to be poor and Third World women or white middle-class women who have stepped *outside* the definitions of femininity to become hippies or political rebels, and chivalry is *not* likely to be extended to them. Chivalry is a racist and classist concept founded on the notion of women as "ladies" which applies only to wealthy white women and ignores the double sexual standard. These "ladies," however, are the least likely women to ever come in contact with the criminal justice system in the first place.[2]

VII. The Legacy of Sexism

A major purpose in tracing the development and interaction of ideas pertaining to sexual ideology based on implicit assumptions of the inherent nature of women throughout the works of Lombroso, Thomas, Freud, Davis and Pollak, is to clarify their positions in relation to writers in the field today. One can see the influence their ideas still have by looking at a number of contemporary theorists on female criminality. Illuminating examples can be found in Gisela Konopka's *Adolescent Girl in Conflict* (1966), Vedder and Somerville's *The Delinquent Girl* (1970) and Cowie, Cowie and Slater's *Delinquency in Girls* (1968). The ideas in these minor works have direct roots in those already traced in this paper.

Konopka justifies her decision to study delinquency in girls rather than in boys by noting girls' *influence* on boys in gang fights and on future generations as mothers. This is the notion of women as instigators of men and influencers on children.

Konopka's main point is that delinquency in girls can be traced to a specific emotional response: loneliness. . . . In this perspective, girls are driven to delinquency by an emotional problem—loneliness and dependency. There are *inherent* emotional differences between the sexes. . . .

Coming from a Freudian perspective, Konopka's emphasis on female emotions as cause for delinquency, which ignores economic and social factors, is questionable. She employs assumptions about the *physiological* and *psychological* nature of women that very well may have led her to see only those feelings in the first place. For example, she cites menstruation as a significant event in a girl's development. Thus Konopka is rooted firmly in the tradition of Freud and, apart from sympathy, contributes little that is new to the field.[3]

Vedder and Somerville (1970) account for female delinquency in a manner similar to that of Konopka. They also feel the need to justify their attention to girls by remarking that (while female delinquency may not pose as much of a problem as that of boys) because women raise families and are critical agents of socialization, it is worth taking the time to study and control them. Vedder and Somerville also stress the dependence of girls on boys and the instigatory role girls play in boys' activities.

Like Freud and Konopka, the authors view delinquency as blocked access or maladjustment to the normal feminine role. In a blatant statement that ignores the economic and social factors that result from racism and poverty, they attribute the high rates of delinquency among black girls to their lack of "healthy" feminine narcissism, *reducing* racism to a psychological problem in totally sexist and racist terms. . . .

The resurgence of biological or physiological explanations of criminality in general has been noteworthy in the last several years, exemplified by the XYY chromosome controversy and the interest in brainwaves in "violent" individuals.[4] In the case of women, biological explanations have *always* been prevalent; every writer has made assumptions about anatomy as destiny. Women are prey, in the literature, to cycles of reproduction, including menstruation, pregnancy, maternity and menopause; they experience emotional responses to these cycles that make them inclined to irrationality and potentially violent activity.

Cowie, Cowie and Slater (1968) propose a *chromosomal* explanation of female delinquency that hearkens back to the works of Lombroso and others such as Healy (1926), Edith Spaulding (1923) and the Gluecks (1934). . . . The authors equate *masculinity* and *femininity* with maleness and femaleness, although contemporary feminists point out that the first categories are *social* and the latter ones *physical*.[5] What relationship exists between the two—how femaleness determines femininity—is dependent on the larger social structure. There is no question that a wide range of possibilities exist historically, and in a non-sexist society it is possible that "masculinity" and "femininity" would disappear, and that the sexes would differ only biologically, specifically by their sex organs. The authors, however, lack this understanding and assume an ahistorical sexist view of women, stressing the universality of femininity in the Freudian tradition, and of women's inferior role in the nuclear family.[6]

In this perspective, the female offender is *different* physiologically and psychologically from the "normal" girl. . . .

Crime defined as masculine seems to mean violent, overt crime, whereas "ladylike" crime usually refers to sexual violations and shoplifting. Women are neatly categorized no matter *which* kind of crime they commit: if they are violent, they are "masculine" and suffering from chromosomal deficiencies, penis envy, or atavisms. If they conform, they are manipulative, sexually maladjusted and promiscuous. The *economic* and *social* realities of crime—the fact that poor women commit crimes, and that most crimes for women are property offenses—are overlooked. Women's behavior must be *sexually* defined before it will be considered, for women count only in the sexual sphere. The theme of sexuality is a unifying thread in the various, often contradictory theories.

VIII. Conclusion

A good deal of the writing on women and crime being done at the present time is squarely in the tradition of the writers that have been discussed. The basic assumptions and technocratic concerns of these writers have produced work that is sexist, racist and classist; assumptions that have served to maintain a repressive ideology with its extensive apparatus of control. To do a new kind of research on women and crime—one that has feminist roots and a radical orientation—it is necessary to understand the assumptions made by the traditional writers and to break away from them. Work that focuses on human needs, rather than those of the state, will require new definitions of criminality, women, the individual and her/his relation to the state. It is beyond the scope of this paper to develop possible areas of study, but it is nonetheless imperative that this work be made a priority by women *and* men in the future.

Notes

1. For a discussion of the possibilities of psychosurgery in behavior modification for "violence-prone" individuals, see Frank Ervin and Vernon Mark, *Violence and the Brain* (1970). For an eclectic view of this perspective on crime, see the 1973 proposal for the Center for the Study and Reduction of Violence prepared by Dr. Louis J. West, Director, Neuropsychiatric Institute, UCLA.
2. The concept of hidden crime is reiterated in Reckless and Kay's report to the President's Commission on Law Enforcement and the Administration of Justice. They note:
   > A large part of the infrequent officially acted upon involvement of women in crime can be traced to the masking effect of women's roles, effective practice on the part of women of deceit and indirection, their instigation of men to commit their crimes (the Lady Macbeth factor), and the unwillingness on the part of the public and law enforcement officials to hold women accountable for their deeds (the chivalry factor) (1967:13).
3. Bertha Payak in "Understanding the Female Offender" (1963) stresses that women offenders have poor self-concepts, feelings of insecurity and dependency, are emotionally selfish, and prey to irrationality during menstruation, pregnancy, and menopause (a good deal of their life!).
4. See Theodore R. Sarbin and Jeffrey E. Miller, "Demonism Revisited: The XYY Chromosomal Anomaly." *Issues in Criminology* 5(2)(Summer 1970).

5. Kate Millett (1970) notes that "sex is biological, gender psychological and therefore cultural . . . if the proper terms for sex are male and female, the corresponding terms for gender are masculine and feminine; these latter may be quite independent of biological sex" (*Ibid*: 30).
6. Zelditch (1960), a structural-functionalist, writes that the nuclear family is an inevitability and that within it, women, the "expressive" sex, will inevitably be the domestics.

References

Bishop, Cecil. 1931. *Women and Crime*. London: Chatto and Windus.

Cowie, John, Valerie Cowie and Eliot Slater. 1968. *Delinquency in Girls*. London: Heinemann.

Davis, Kingsley. 1961. "Prostitution." *Contemporary Social Problems*, edited by Robert K. Merton and Robert A. Nisbet. New York: Harcourt Brace and Jovanovich. Originally published as "The Sociology of Prostitution," *American Sociological Review* 2(5)(October 1937).

Ervin, Frank and Vernon Mark. 1970. *Violence and the Brain*. New York: Harper and Row.

Fernald, Mabel, Mary Hayes and Almena Dawley. 1920. *A Study of Women Delinquents in New York State*. New York: Century Company.

Freud, Sigmund. 1933. *New Introductory Lectures on Psychoanalysis*. New York: W. W. Norton.

Glueck, Eleanor and Sheldon. 1934. *Four Hundred Delinquent Women*. New York: Alfred A. Knopf.

Healy, William and Augusta Bronner. 1926. *Delinquents and Criminals: Their Making and Unmaking*. New York: Macmillan and Company.

Hemming, James. 1960. *Problems of Adolescent Girls*. London: Heinemann.

Jones, Ernest. 1961. *The Life and Works of Sigmund Freud*. New York: Basic Books.

Konopka, Gisela. 1966. *The Adolescent Girl in Conflict*. Englewood Cliffs, NJ: Prentice-Hall.

Lombroso, Cesare. 1920. *The Female Offender* (translation). New York: Appleton. Originally published in 1903.

Millet, Kate. 1970. *Sexual Politics*. New York: Doubleday and Company.

Monahan, Florence. 1941. *Women in Crime*. New York: I. Washburn.

Parsons, Talcott. 1942. "Age and Sex in the Social Structure." *American Sociological Review* 7 (October).

Parsons, Talcott and Renee Fox. 1960. "Illness, Therapy and the Modern 'Urban' American Family." *The Family*, edited by Norman Bell and Ezra Vogel. Glencoe, IL: The Free Press.

Payak, Bertha. 1963. "Understanding the Female Offender." *Federal Probation* XXVII.

Pollak, Otto. 1950. *The Criminality of Women*. Philadelphia: University of Pennsylvania Press.

Reckless, Walter and Barbara Kay. 1967. *The Female Offender. Report to the President's Commission on Law Enforcement and the Administration of Justice*. Washington, D.C.: U.S. Government Printing Office.

Sarbin, Theodore R. and Jeffrey E. Miller. 1970. "Demonism Revisited: The XYY Chromosomal Anomaly." *Issues in Criminology* 5(2) (Summer).

Schwendinger, Herman and Julia. 1973. "The Founding Fathers: Sexists to a Man." *Sociologists of the Chair*. New York: Basic Books.

Spaulding, Edith. 1923. *An Experimental Study of Psychopathic Delinquent Women*. New York: Rand McNally.

Thomas, W. I. 1907. *Sex and Society*. Boston: Little, Brown and Company.

———. 1923. *The Unadjusted Girl*. New York: Harper and Row.

Vedder, Clyde and Dora Somerville. 1970. *The Delinquent Girl*. Springfield, IL: Charles C. Thomas.

West, Dr. Louis J. 1973. *Proposal for the Center for the Study and Reduction of Violence*. Neuropsychiatric Institute, UCLA (April 10).

Zelditch, Morris, Jr. 1960. "Role Differentiation in the Nuclear Family: A Comparative Study." *The Family*, edited by Norman Bell and Ezra Vogel. Glencoe, IL: The Free Press.

44

Girls' Crime and Woman's Place: Toward a Feminist Model of Female Delinquency

Meda Chesney-Lind

. . . Who is the typical female delinquent? What causes her to get into trouble? What happens to her if she is caught? These are questions that few members of the general public could answer quickly. By contrast, almost every citizen can talk about "delinquency," by which they generally mean male delinquency, and can even generate some fairly specific complaints about, for example, the failure of the juvenile justice system to deal with such problems as "the alarming increase in the rate of serious juvenile crime" and the fact that the juvenile courts are too lenient on juveniles found guilty of these offenses (Opinion Research Corporation, 1982).

This situation should come as no surprise since even the academic study of delinquent behavior has, for all intents and purposes, been the study of male delinquency. "The delinquent is a rogue male" declared Albert Cohen (1955, p. 140) in his influential book on gang delinquency. More than a decade later, Travis Hirschi, in his equally important book entitled *The Causes of Delinquency*, relegated women to a footnote that suggested, somewhat apologetically, that "in the analysis that follows, the 'non-Negro' becomes 'white,' and the girls disappear."

This pattern of neglect is not all that unusual. All areas of social inquiry have been notoriously gender blind. What is perhaps less well understood is that theories developed to describe the misbehavior of working- or lower-class male youth fail to capture the full nature of delinquency in America; and, more to the point, are woefully inadequate when it comes to explaining female misbehavior and official reactions to girls' deviance.

To be specific, delinquent behavior involves a range of activities far broader than those committed by the stereotypical street gang. Moreover, many more young people than the small visible group of "troublemakers" that exist on every intermediate and high school campus commit some sort of juvenile offense, and many of these youth have brushes with the law. One study revealed, for example, that 33% of

Source: Meda Chesney-Lind, "Girls' Crime and Woman's Place: Toward a Feminist Model of Female Delinquency," *Crime and Delinquency*, Vol. 35, No. 1, pp. 5–29. Copyright © 1989 by Sage Publications, Inc. Reprinted by permission of Sage Publications, Inc.

all the boys and 14% of the girls born in 1958 had at least one contact with the police before reaching their eighteenth birthday (Tracy, Wolfgang, and Figlio, 1985, p. 5). Indeed, some forms of serious delinquent behavior, such as drug and alcohol abuse, are far more frequent than the stereotypical delinquent behavior of gang fighting and vandalism and appear to cut across class and gender lines.

Studies that solicit from youth themselves the volume of their delinquent behavior consistently confirm that large numbers of adolescents engage in at least some form of misbehavior that could result in their arrest. As a consequence, it is largely trivial misconduct, rather than the commission of serious crime, that shapes the actual nature of juvenile delinquency. . . .

[W]hile trivial offenses dominate both male and female delinquency, trivial offenses, particularly status offenses, are more significant in the case of girls' arrests; . . . [such offenses] account for nearly three-quarters of female offenses and only slightly more than half of male offenses. More to the point, it is clear that, though routinely neglected in most delinquency research, status offenses play a significant role in girls' official delinquency. Status offenses accounted for about 25.2% of all girls' arrests in 1986 (as compared to 26.9% in 1977) and only about 8.3% of boys' arrests (compared to 8.8% in 1977). . . .

Looking at girls who find their way into juvenile court populations, it is apparent that status offenses continue to play an important role in the character of girls' official delinquency. In total, 34% of the girls, but only 12% of the boys, were referred to court in 1983 for these offenses (Snyder and Finnegan, 1987, pp. 6–20). Stating these figures differently, they mean that while males constituted about 81% of all delinquency referrals, females constituted 46% of all status offenders in courts (Snyder and Finnegan, 1987, p. 20). Similar figures were reported for 1977 by Black and Smith (1981). Fifteen years earlier, about half of the girls and about 20% of the boys were referred to court for these offenses (Children's Bureau, 1965). These data do seem to signal a drop in female status offense referrals, though not as dramatic a decline as might have been expected.

For many years statistics showing large numbers of girls arrested and referred for status offenses were taken to be representative of the different types of male and female delinquency. However, self-report studies of male and female delinquency do not reflect the dramatic differences in misbehavior found in official statistics. Specifically, it appears that girls charged with these noncriminal status offenses have been and continue to be significantly overrepresented in court populations.

Teilmann and Landry (1981) compared girls' contribution to arrests for runaway and incorrigibility with girls' self-reports of these two activities, and found a 10.4% overrepresentation of females among those arrested for runaway and a 30.9% overrepresentation in arrests for incorrigibility. From these data they concluded that girls are "arrested for status offenses at a higher rate than boys, when contrasted to their self-reported delinquency rates" (Teilmann and Landry, 1981, pp. 74–75). These findings were confirmed in another recent self-report study. Figueira-McDonough (1985, p. 277) analyzed the delinquent conduct of 2,000 youths and found "no evidence of greater involvement of females in status offenses." Similarly, Canter (1982) found in the National Youth Survey that there was no evidence of greater female involvement, compared to males, in any category of delinquent behavior. Indeed, in this sample, males were significantly more likely than females to report status offenses.

Utilizing Canter's national data on the extensiveness of girls' self-reported delinquency and comparing these figures to official arrests of girls reveals that girls are underrepresented in every arrest category with the exception of status offenses and larceny theft. These figures strongly suggest that official practices tend to exaggerate the role played by status offenses in girls' delinquency.

Delinquency theory, because it has virtually ignored female delinquency, failed to pursue anomalies such as these found in the few early studies examining gender differences in delinquent behavior. Indeed, most delinquency theories have ignored status offenses. As a consequence, there is considerable question as to whether existing theories that were admittedly developed to explain male delinquency can adequately explain female delinquency. Clearly, these theories were much influenced by the notion that class and protest masculinity were at the core of delinquency. Will the "add women and stir approach" be sufficient? Are these really theories of delinquent behavior as some (Simons, Miller, and Aigner, 1980) have argued?

This article will suggest that they are not. The extensive focus on male delinquency and the inattention to the role played by patriarchal arrangements in the generation of adolescent delinquency and conformity has rendered the major delinquency theories fundamentally inadequate to the task of explaining female behavior. There is, in short, an urgent need to rethink current models in light of girls' situation in patriarchal society. . . .

The Romance of the Gang or the *West Side Story* Syndrome

From the start, the field of delinquency research focused on visible lower-class male delinquency, often justifying the neglect of girls in the most cavalier of terms. Take, for example, the extremely important and influential work of Clifford R. Shaw and Henry D. McKay who, beginning in 1929, utilized an ecological approach to the study of juvenile delinquency. . . . [H]owever, Shaw and McKay analyzed only the official arrest data on male delinquents in Chicago and repeatedly referred to these rates as "delinquency rates" (though they occasionally made parenthetical reference to data on female delinquency) (see Shaw and McKay, 1942, p. 356). Similarly, their biographical work traced only male experiences with the law; in *Brothers in Crime*, for example, the delinquent and criminal careers of five brothers were followed for fifteen years. In none of these works was any justification given for the equation of male delinquency with delinquency.

Early fieldwork on delinquent gangs in Chicago set the stage for another style of delinquency research. Yet here too researchers were interested only in talking to and following the boys. Thrasher studied over a thousand juvenile gangs in Chicago during roughly the same period as Shaw and McKay's more quantitative work was being done. He spent approximately one page out of 600 on the five of six female gangs he encountered in his field observation of juvenile gangs. . . .

Another major theoretical approach to delinquency focuses on the subculture of lower-class communities as a generating milieu for delinquent behavior. Here again, noted delinquency researchers concentrated either exclusively or nearly exclusively on male lower-class culture. For example, Cohen's work on the subculture of delinquent gangs, which was written nearly twenty years after Thrasher's, deliberately considers only boys' delinquency. . . .

Emphasis on blocked opportunities (sometimes the "strain" theories) emerged out of the work of Robert K. Merton (1938), who stressed the need to consider how some social structures exert a definite pressure upon certain persons in the society to engage in nonconformist rather than conformist conduct. His work influenced research largely through the efforts of Cloward and Ohlin, who discussed access to "legitimate" and "illegitimate" opportunities for male youth. No mention of female delinquency can be found in their *Delinquency and Opportunity* except that women are blamed for male delinquency. . . .

The work of Edwin Sutherland emphasized the fact that criminal behavior was learned in intimate personal groups. His work, particularly the [nature] of differential association, which also influenced Cloward and Ohlin's work, was similarly male oriented as much of his work was affected by case studies he conducted of male criminals. Indeed, in describing his notion of how differential association works, he utilized male examples (e.g., "In an area where the delinquency rate is high a boy who is sociable, gregarious, active, and athletic is very likely to come in contact with the other boys, in the neighborhood, learn delinquent behavior from them, and become a gangster" [Sutherland, 1978, p. 131]). Finally, the work of Travis Hirschi on the social bonds that control delinquency ("social control theory") was, as was stated earlier, derived out of research on male delinquents (though he, at least, studied delinquent behavior as reported by youth themselves rather than studying only those who were arrested).

Such a persistent focus on social class and such an absence of interest in gender in delinquency is ironic for two reasons. As even the work of Hirschi demonstrated, and as later studies would validate, a clear relationship between social class position and delinquency is problematic, while it is clear that gender has a dramatic and consistent effect on delinquency causation (Hagan, Gillis, and Simpson, 1985). The second irony, and one that consistently eludes even contemporary delinquency theorists, is the fact that while the academics had little interest in female delinquents, the same could not be said for the juvenile justice system. Indeed, work on the early history of the separate system for youth reveals that concerns about girls' immoral conduct were really at the center of what some have called the "childsaving movement" (Platt, 1969) that set up the juvenile justice system.

"The Best Place to Conquer Girls"

The movement to establish separate institutions for youthful offenders was part of the larger Progressive movement, which among other things was keenly concerned about prostitution and other "social evils" (white slavery and the like) (Schlossman and Wallach, 1978; Rafter, 1985, p. 54). Childsaving was also a celebration of women's domesticity, though ironically women were influential in the movement (Platt, 1969; Rafter, 1985). In a sense, privileged women found, in the moral purity crusades and the establishment of family courts, a safe outlet for their energies. As the legitimate guardians of the moral sphere, women were seen as uniquely suited to patrol the normative boundaries of the social order. Embracing rather than challenging these stereotypes, women carved out for themselves a role in the policing of women and girls (Feinman, 1980; Freedman, 1981; Messerschmidt, 1987). Ultimately, many of the early childsavers' activities revolved around the monitoring of young girls', particularly immigrant girls', behavior to prevent their straying from the path.

This state of affairs was the direct consequence of a disturbing coalition between some feminists and the more conservative social purity movement. Concerned about female victimization and distrustful of male (and to some degree female) sexuality, notable women leaders, including Susan B. Anthony, found common cause with the social purists around such issues as opposing the regulation of prostitution and raising the age of consent (see Messerschmidt, 1987). The consequences of such a partnership are an important lesson for contemporary feminist movements that are, to some extent, faced with the same possible coalitions.

Girls were the clear losers in this reform effort. Studies of early family court activity reveal that virtually all the girls who appeared in these courts were charged for immorality or waywardness (Chesney-Lind, 1971; Schlossman and Wallach, 1978; Shelden, 1981). More to the point, the sanctions for such misbehavior were extremely severe. For example, in Chicago (where the first family court was founded), one-half of the girl delinquents, but only one-fifth of the boy delinquents, were sent to reformatories between 1899–1909. In Milwaukee, twice as many girls as boys were committed to training schools (Schlossman and Wallach, 1978, p. 72); and in Memphis females were twice as likely as males to be committed to training schools (Shelden, 1981, p. 70).

In Honolulu, during the period 1929–1930, over half of the girls referred to court were charged with "immorality," which meant evidence of sexual intercourse. In addition, another 30% were charged with "waywardness." Evidence of immorality was vigorously pursued by both arresting officers and social workers through lengthy questioning of the girl and, if possible, males with whom she was suspected of having sex. Other evidence of "exposure" was provided by gynecological examinations that were routinely ordered in virtually all girls' cases. Doctors, who understood the purpose of such examinations, would routinely note the condition of the hymen: "admits intercourse hymen rupture," "no laceration," "hymen ruptured" are typical of the notations on the forms. Girls during this period were also twice as likely as males to be detained, where they spent five times as long on the average as their male counterparts. They were also nearly three times more likely to be sentenced to the training school (Chesney-Lind, 1971). Indeed, girls were half of those committed to training schools in Honolulu well into the 1950s (Chesney-Lind, 1973).

Not surprisingly, large numbers of girls' reformatories and training schools were established during this period as well as places of "rescue and reform." For example, Schlossman and Wallach note that 23 facilities for girls were opened during the 1910–1920 decade (in contrast to the 1850–1910 period where the average was 5 reformatories per decade [Schlossman and Wallach, 1978, p. 70]), and these institutions did much to set the tone of official response to female delinquency. Obsessed with precocious female sexuality, the institutions set about to isolate the females from all contact with males while housing them in bucolic settings. The intention was to hold the girls until marriageable age and to occupy them in domestic pursuits during their sometimes lengthy incarceration. . . .

In their historic obsession about precocious female sexuality, juvenile justice workers rarely reflected on the broader nature of female misbehavior or on the sources of this misbehavior. It was enough for them that girls' parents reported them out of control. Indeed, court personnel tended to "sexualize" virtually all female defiance that lent itself to that construction and ignore other misbehavior (Chesney-Lind, 1973, 1971; Smith, 1978). For their part, academic students of delinquency were so entranced with the notion of the delinquent as a romantic rogue male challenging a rigid and unequal class structure, that they spent little time on middle-class delinquency, trivial offenders, or status offenders. Yet it is clear that the vast bulk of delinquent behavior is of this type. . . .

More to the point, police and court personnel are, it turns out, far more interested in youth they charge with trivial or status offenses than anyone imagined.

Efforts to deinstitutionalize "status offenders," for example, ran afoul of juvenile justice personnel who had little interest in releasing youth guilty of noncriminal offenses (Chesney-Lind, 1988). As has been established, much of this is a product of the system's history that encouraged court officers to involve themselves in the noncriminal behavior of youth in order to "save" them from a variety of social ills.

Indeed, parallels can be found between the earlier Progressive period and current national efforts to challenge the deinstitutionalization components of the Juvenile Justice and Delinquency Prevention Act of 1974. These come complete with their celebration of family values and concerns about youthful independence. One of the arguments against the act has been that it allegedly gave children the "freedom to run away" (Office of Juvenile Justice and Delinquency Prevention, 1985) and that it has hampered "reunions" of "missing" children with their parents (Office of Juvenile Justice, 1986). Suspicions about teen sexuality are reflected in excessive concern about the control of teen prostitution and child pornography.

Opponents have also attempted to justify continued intervention into the lives of status offenders by suggesting that without such intervention, the youth would "escalate" to criminal behavior. Yet there is little evidence that status offenders escalate to criminal offenses, and the evidence is particularly weak when considering female delinquents (particularly white female delinquents) (Datesman and Aickin, 1984). Finally, if escalation is occurring, it is likely the product of the justice system's insistence on enforcing status offense laws, thereby forcing youth in crisis to live lives of escaped criminals.

The most influential delinquency theories, however, have largely ducked the issue of status and trivial offenses and, as a consequence, neglected the role played by the agencies of official control (police, probation officers, juvenile court judges, detention home workers, and training school personnel) in the shaping of the "delinquency problem." When confronting the less than distinct picture that emerges from the actual distribution of delinquent behavior, however, the conclusion that agents of social control have considerable discretion in labeling or choosing not to label particular behavior as "delinquent" is inescapable. This symbiotic relationship between delinquent behavior and the official response to that behavior is particularly critical when the question of female delinquency is considered.

Toward a Feminist Theory of Delinquency

To sketch out completely a feminist theory of delinquency is a task beyond the scope of this article. It may be sufficient, at this point, simply to identify a few of the most obvious problems with attempts to adapt male-oriented theory to explain female conformity and deviance. Most significant of these is the fact that all existing theories were developed with no concern about gender stratification.

Note that this is not simply an observation about the power of gender roles (though this power is undeniable). It is increasingly clear that gender stratification in patriarchal society is as powerful a system as is class. A feminist approach to delinquency means construction of explanations of female behavior that are sensitive to its patriarchal context. Feminist analysis of delinquency would also examine ways in which agencies of social control—the police, the courts, and the prisons—act in ways to reinforce woman's place in male society (Harris, 1977; Chesney-Lind, 1986). Efforts to construct a feminist model of delinquency must first and foremost be sensitive to the situations of girls. Failure to consider the existing empirical evidence on girls' lives and behavior can quickly lead to stereotypical thinking and theoretical dead ends.

An example of this sort of flawed theory building was the early fascination with the notion that the women's movement was causing an increase in women's crime; a notion that is now more or less discredited (Steffensmeier, 1980; Gora, 1982). A more recent example of the same sort of thinking can be found in recent work on the "power-control" model of delinquency (Hagan, Simpson, and Gillis, 1987). Here, the authors speculate that girls commit less delinquency in part because their behavior is more closely controlled by the patriarchal family. The authors' promising beginning quickly gets bogged down in a very limited definition of patriarchal control (focusing on parental supervision and variations in power within the family). Ultimately, the authors' narrow formulation of patriarchal control results in their arguing that mother's workforce participation (particularly in high-status occupations) leads to increases in daughters' delinquency since these girls find themselves in more "egalitarian families."

This is essentially a not-too-subtle variation on the earlier "liberation" hypothesis. Now, mother's liberation causes daughter's crime. Aside from the methodological problems with the study (e.g., the authors argue that female-headed households are equivalent to upper-status "egalitarian" families where both parents work, and they measure delinquency using a six-item scale that contains no status offense items), there is a more fundamental problem with the hypothesis. There is no evidence to suggest that as women's labor force participation has increased, girls' delinquency has increased. Indeed, during the last decade when both women's labor force participation accelerated and the number of female-headed households soared, aggregate female delinquency measured both by self-report and official statistics either declined or remained stable (Ageton, 1983; Chilton and Datesman, 1987; Federal Bureau of Investigation, 1987).

By contrast, a feminist model of delinquency would focus more extensively on the few pieces of information about girls' actual lives and the role played by girls' problems, including those caused by racism and poverty, in their delinquency behavior. Fortunately, a considerable literature is now developing on girls' lives and much of it bears directly on girls' crime.

Criminalizing Girls' Survival

It has long been understood that a major reason for girls' presence in juvenile courts was the fact that their parents insisted on their arrest. In the early years, conflicts with parents were by far the most significant referral source; in Honolulu 44% of the girls who appeared in court in 1929 through 1930 were referred by parents.

Recent national data, while slightly less explicit, also show that girls are more likely to be referred to court by "sources other than law enforcement agencies" (which would include parents). In 1983, nearly a quarter (23%) of all girls but only 16% of boys charged with delinquent offenses were referred to court by non-law-enforcement agencies. The pattern among youth referred for status offenses (for which girls are overrepresented) was even more pronounced. Well over half (56%) of the girls charged with these offenses and 45% of the boys were referred by sources other than law enforcement (Snyder and Finnegan, 1987, p. 21; see also Pope and Feyerherm, 1982).

The fact that parents are often committed to two standards of adolescent behavior is one explanation for such a disparity—and one that should not be discounted as a major source of tension even in modern families. Despite expectations to the contrary, gender-specific socialization patterns have not changed very much and this is especially true for parents' relationships with their daughters (Katz, 1979). It appears that even parents who oppose sexism in general feel "uncomfortable tampering with existing traditions" and "do not want to risk their children becoming misfits" (Katz, 1979, p. 24). Clearly, parental attempts to adhere to and enforce these traditional notions will continue to be a source of conflict between girls and their elders. Another important explanation for girls' problems with their parents, which has received attention only in more recent years, is the problem of physical and sexual abuse. Looking specifically at the problem of childhood sexual abuse, it is increasingly clear that this form of abuse is a particular problem for girls.

Girls are, for example, much more likely to be the victims of child sexual abuse than are boys. Finkelhor and Baron estimate from a review of community studies that roughly 70% of the victims of sexual abuse are female (Finkelhor and Baron, 1986, p. 45). . . .

Many young women, then, are running away from profound sexual victimization at home, and once on the streets they are forced further into crime in order to survive. Interviews with girls who have run away from home show, very clearly, that they do not have a lot of attachment to their delinquent activities. In fact, they are angry about being labeled as delinquent, yet all engaged in illegal acts (Koroki and Chesney-Lind, 1985). The Wisconsin study found that 54% of the girls who ran away found it necessary to steal money, food, and clothing in order to survive. A few exchanged sexual contact for money, food, and/or shelter (Phelps et al., 1982, p. 67). In their study of runaway youth, McCormack, Janus, and Burgess (1986, pp. 392–393) found that sexually abused female runaways were significantly more likely than their nonabused counterparts to engage in delinquent or criminal activities such as substance abuse, petty theft, and prostitution. No such pattern was found among male runaways.

Research (Chesney-Lind and Rodriguez, 1983) on the backgrounds of adult women in prison underscores the important links between women's childhood victimizations and their later criminal careers. The interviews revealed that virtually all of this sample were the victims of physical and/or sexual abuse as youngsters; over 60% had been sexually abused and about half had been raped as young women. This situation prompted these women to run away from home (three-quarters had been arrested for status offenses) where once on the streets they began engaging in prostitution and other forms of petty property crime. They also begin what becomes a lifetime problem with drugs. As adults, the women continue in these activities since they possess truncated educational backgrounds and virtually no marketable occupational skills (see also Miller, 1986). . . .

Given this information, a brief example of how a feminist perspective on the causes of female delinquency might look seems appropriate. First, like young men, girls are frequently the recipients of violence and sexual abuse. But unlike boys, girls' victimization and their response to that victimization is specifically shaped by their status as young women. Perhaps because of the gender and sexual scripts found in patriarchal families, girls are much more likely than boys to be victims of family-related sexual abuse. Men, particularly men with traditional attitudes toward women, are likely to define their daughters or stepdaughters as their sexual property (Finkelhor, 1982). In a society that idealizes inequality in male/female relationships and venerates youth in women, girls are easily defined as sexually attractive by older men (Bell, 1984). In addition, girls' vulnerability to both physical and sexual abuse is heightened by norms that require that they stay at home where their victimizers have access to them.

Moreover, their victimizers (usually males) have the ability to invoke official agencies of social control in their efforts to keep young women at home and vulnerable. That is to say, abusers have traditionally been able to utilize the uncritical commitment of the juvenile justice system toward parental authority to force girls to obey them. Girls' complaints about abuse were, until recently, routinely ignored. For this reason, statutes that were originally placed in law to "protect" young people have, in the case of girls' delinquency, criminalized their survival strategies. As they run away from abusive homes, parents have been able to employ agencies to enforce their return. If they persisted in their refusal to stay in that home, however intolerable, they were incarcerated.

Young women, a large number of whom are on the run from homes characterized by sexual abuse and parental neglect, are forced by the very statutes designed to protect them into the lives of escaped convicts. Unable to enroll in school or take a job to support themselves because they fear detection, young female runaways are forced into the streets. Here they engage in panhandling, petty theft, and occasional prostitution in order to survive. Young women in conflict with their parents (often for very legitimate reasons) may actually be forced by present laws into petty criminal activity, prostitution, and drug use.

In addition, the fact that young girls (but not necessarily young boys) are defined as sexually desirable and, in fact, more desirable then their older sisters due to the double standard of aging means that their lives on the streets (and their survival strategies) take on unique shape—one again shaped by patriarchal values. It is no accident that girls on the run from abusive homes, or on the streets because of profound poverty, get involved in criminal activities that exploit their sexual object status. American society has defined as desirable youthful, physically perfect women. This means that girls on the streets, who have little else of value to trade, are encouraged to utilize this "resource" (Campagna and Poffenberger, 1988). It also means that the criminal subculture views them from this perspective (Miller, 1986).

Female Delinquency, Patriarchal Authority, and Family Courts

. . . It is clear that throughout most of the court's history, virtually all female delinquency has been placed within the larger context of girls' sexual behavior. One explanation for this pattern is that familial control over girls' sexual capital has historically been central to the maintenance of patriarchy (Lerner,1986). The fact that young women have relatively more of this capital has been one reason for the excessive concern that both families and official agencies of social control have expressed about youthful female defiance (otherwise much of the behavior of criminal justice personnel makes virtually no sense). Only if one considers the role of women's control over their sexuality at the point in their lives that their value to patriarchal society is so pronounced, does the historic pattern of jailing of huge numbers of girls guilty of minor misconduct make sense.

This framework also explains the enormous resistance that the movement to curb the juvenile justice system's authority over status offenders encountered. Supporters of the change were not really prepared for the political significance of giving youth the freedom to run. Horror stories told by the opponents of deinstitutionalization about victimized youth, youthful prostitution, and youthful involvement in pornography (Office of Juvenile Justice and Delinquency Prevention, 1985) all neglect the unpleasant reality that most of these behaviors were often in direct response to earlier victimization, frequently by parents, that officials had, for years, routinely ignored. What may be at stake in efforts to roll back deinstitutionalization efforts is not so much "protection" of youth as it is curbing the right of young women to defy patriarchy.

In sum, research in both the dynamics of girls' delinquency and official reactions to that behavior is essential to the development of theories of delinquency that are sensitive to its patriarchal as well as class and racial context.

References

Ageton, Suzanne S. 1983. "The Dynamics of Female Delinquency, 1976–1980." *Criminology* 21:555–584.

Bell, Inge Powell. 1984. "The Double Standard: Age." In *Women: A Feminist Perspective*, edited by Jo Freeman. Palo Alto, CA: Mayfield.

Black, T. Edwin and Charles P. Smith. 1981. *A Preliminary National Assessment of the Number and Characteristics of Juveniles Processed in the Juvenile Justice System*. Washington, DC: Government Printing Office.

Campagna, Daniel S. and Donald L. Poffenberger. 1988. *The Sexual Trafficking in Children*. Dover, DE: Auburn House.

Canter, Rachelle J. 1982. "Sex Differences in Self-Report Delinquency." *Criminology* 20:373–393.

Chesney-Lind, Meda. 1971. *Female Juvenile Delinquency in Hawaii*. Master's thesis, University of Hawaii.

———. 1973. "Judicial Enforcement of the Female Sex Role." *Issues in Criminology* 3:51–71.

———. 1978. "Young Women in the Arms of the Law." In *Women, Crime and the Criminal Justice System*, edited by Lee H. Bowker. Boston: Lexington.

———. 1986. "Women and Crime: The Female Offender." *Signs* 12:78–96.

———. 1988. "Girls and Deinstitutionalization: Is Juvenile Justice Still Sexist?" *Journal of Criminal Justice Abstracts* 20:144–165.

——— and Noelie Rodriguez. 1983. "Women Under Lock and Key." *Prison Journal* 63:47–65.

Children's Bureau, Department of Health, Education and Welfare. 1965. *1964 Statistics on Public Institutions for Delinquent Children*. Washington, DC: Government Printing Office.

Chilton, Roland and Susan K. Datesman. 1987. "Gender, Race and Crime: An Analysis of Urban Arrest Trends, 1960–1980." *Gender and Society* 1:152–171.

Cloward, Richard A. and Lloyd E. Ohlin. 1960. *Delinquency and Opportunity*. New York: Free Press.

Cohen, Albert K. 1955. *Delinquent Boys: The Culture of the Gang*. New York: Free Press.

Datesman, Susan and Mikel Aickin. 1984. "Offense Specialization and Escalation Among Status Offenders." *Journal of Criminal Law and Criminology* 75:1246–1275.

Federal Bureau of Investigation. 1987. *Crime in the United States 1986*. Washington, DC: Government Printing Office.

Feinman, Clarice. 1980. *Women in the Criminal Justice System*. New York: Praeger.

Figueira-McDonough, Josefina. 1985. "Are Girls Different? Gender Discrepancies between Delinquent Behavior and Control," *Child Welfare* 64:273–289.

Finkelhor, David. 1982. "Sexual Abuse: A Sociological Perspective." *Child Abuse and Neglect* 6:95–102.

——— and Larry Baron. 1986. "Risk Factors for Child Sexual Abuse." *Journal of Interpersonal Violence* 1:43–71.

Freedman, Estelle. 1981. *Their Sisters' Keepers*. Ann Arbor: University of Michigan Press.

Gora, JoAnn. 1982. *The New Female Criminal: Empirical Reality or Social Myth*. New York: Praeger.

Hagan, John, A. R. Gillis, and John Simpson. 1985. "The Class Structure of Gender and Delinquency: Toward a Power-Control Theory of Common Delinquent Behavior." *American Journal of Sociology* 90:1151–1178.

Hagan, John, John Simpson, and A. R. Gillis. 1987. "Class in the Household: A Power-Control Theory of Gender and Delinquency." *American Journal of Sociology* 92:788–816.

Harris, Anthony. 1977. "Sex and Theories of Deviance." *American Sociological Review* 42:3–16.

Katz, Phyllis A. 1979. "The Development of Female Identity." In *Becoming Female: Perspectives on Development*, edited by Claire B. Kopp. New York: Plenum.

Koroki, Jan and Meda Chesney-Lind. 1985. *Everything Just Going Down the Drain.* Hawaii: Youth Development and Research Center.

Lerner, Gerda. 1986. *The Creation of Patriarchy.* New York: Oxford.

McCormack, Arlene, Mark-David Janus, and Ann Wolbert Burgess. 1986. "Runaway Youths and Sexual Victimization: Gender Differences in an Adolescent Runaway Population." *Child Abuse and Neglect* 10:387–395.

Merton, Robert K. 1938. "Social Structure and Anomie." *American Sociological Review* 3 (October): 672–682.

Messerschmidt, James. 1986. *Capitalism, Patriarchy, and Crime: Toward a Socialist Feminist Criminology.* Totowa, NJ: Rowman & Littlefield.

———. 1987. "Feminism, Criminology, and the Rise of the Female Sex Delinquent, 1880–1930." *Contemporary Crises* 11:243–263.

Miller, Eleanor. 1986. *Street Woman.* Philadelphia: Temple University Press.

Office of Juvenile Justice and Delinquency Prevention. 1985. *Runaway Children and the Juvenile Justice and Delinquency Prevention Act: What is the Impact?* Washington, DC: Government Printing Office.

———. 1986. *America's Missing and Exploited Children. Report and Recommendations of the U.S. Attorney General's Advisory Board on Missing Children.* Washington, DC: Government Printing Office.

Opinion Research Corporation. 1982. "Public Attitudes Toward Youth Crime: National Public Opinion Poll." Mimeographed. Minnesota: Hubert Humphrey Institute of Public Affairs, University of Minnesota.

Phelps, R. J. et al. 1982. *Wisconsin Female Juvenile Offender Study Project Summary Report.* Wisconsin: Youth Policy and Law Center, Wisconsin Council on Juvenile Justice.

Platt, Anthony M. 1969. *The Childsavers.* Chicago: University of Chicago Press.

Pope, Carl and William H. Feyerherm. 1982. "Gender Bias in Juvenile Court Dispositions." *Social Service Review* 6:1–17.

Rafter, Nicole Hahn. 1985. *Partial Justice.* Boston: Northeastern University

Schlossman, Steven and Stephanie Wallach. 1978. "The Crime of Precocious Sexuality: Female Juvenile Delinquency in the Progressive Era." *Harvard Educational Review* 48:65–94.

Shaw, Clifford R. and Henry D. McKay. 1942. *Juvenile Delinquency in Urban Areas.* Chicago: University of Chicago Press.

Shelden, Randall. 1981. "Sex Discrimination in the Juvenile Justice System: Memphis, Tennessee, 1900–1917." In *Comparing Female and Male Offenders*, edited by Marguerite Q. Warren. Beverly Hills, CA: Sage.

Simons, Ronald L., Martin G. Miller, and Stephen M. Aigner. 1980. "Contemporary Theories of Deviance and Female Delinquency: An Empirical Test." *Journal of Research in Crime and Delinquency* 17:42–57.

Smith, Lesley Shacklady. 1978. "Sexist Assumptions and Female Delinquency." In *Women, Sexuality and Social Control*, edited by Carol Smart and Barry Smart. London: Routledge & Kegan Paul.

Snyder, Howard N. and Terrence A. Finnegan. 1987. *Delinquency in the United States.* Washington, DC: Department of Justice.

Steffensmeier, Darrell J. 1980. "Sex Differences in Patterns of Adult Crime, 1965–1977." *Social Forces* 58:1080–1109.

Sutherland, Edwin. 1978. "Differential Association." In *Children of Ishmael: Critical Perspectives on Juvenile Justice*, edited by Barry Krisberg and James Austin. Palo Alto, CA: Mayfield.

Teilmann, Katherine S. and Pierre H. Landry, Jr. 1981. "Gender Bias in Juvenile Justice." *Journal of Research in Crime and Delinquency* 18:47–80.

Tracy, Paul E., Marvin E. Wolfgang, and Robert M. Figlio. 1985. *Delinquency in Two Birth Cohorts: Executive Summary.* Washington, DC: Department of Justice.

Section III

The Social Response to Crime

Writings on the social response to crime come from a variety of disciplines—law, philosophy, social psychology, and sociology. Like the descriptions of crime in the first section, they are founded on the dominant philosophies and available methods of the periods when they were written. Here, then, is a selection of the classic writings on punishment, the police, prisons, and crime prevention.

Cesare Beccaria's *On Crimes and Punishments* is a fitting introduction to this section, symbolizing the enormous impact of this small treatise by a previously obscure, young, Italian philosopher on the entire field of criminal justice. This work, first published in 1764, summarized the best of rationalist thinking about crime, its causes, and appropriate punishments. Perhaps its greatest contribution was the idea that the punishment should fit the crime, but here also were arguments against torture to gain evidence, arguments against capital punishment, and a clear statement that, to achieve deterrence, the certainty of punishment was much more important than its severity.

The federal government has organized several national commissions to study the issue of crime in the United States. The first of these, the National Commission on Law Observance and Enforcement (the Wickersham Commission), issued a series of reports in 1931 describing the inefficiency and corruption of much of the criminal justice system. The second national effort, The President's Commission on Law Enforcement and the Administration of Justice, issued its final report in 1967. This report, entitled *The Challenge of Crime in a Free Society*, provided a guide for change for all criminal justice agencies. The recommendations of the commission echo an important theme introduced by Cesare Beccaria 200 years before: imposing unfair and excessively harsh punishments is not an effective method of controlling crime.

In the early 1970s a group of prominent Americans, calling themselves the Committee for the Study of Incarceration, studied the contemporary system of choosing penalties and punishing incarcerated offenders. At that time sentences were indeterminate, a rehabilitative philosophy guided both sentencing and prison programming, and parole release was granted at the discretion of parole boards. In their report, authored by Andrew von Hirsch and entitled *Doing Justice: The Choice of Punishments*, the committee concluded that the existing system of punishment was both unjust and ineffective. They advocated that sentences should be short and determinate, and should be dictated by a sentencing grid that included only the current offense and the offender's prior convictions. Their proposals were widely adopted, beginning in the mid-1970s, with the exception of sentence length—prison sentences, particularly for violent and drug offenses, became much longer under the new determinate sentencing laws.

Few general theories exist that explain why and how societies punish criminal offenders. The earliest of these, by Georg Rusche and Otto Kirchheimer, was published in 1939. It is based on a historical economic analysis and argues that the forms of punishment chosen in each society and period, and the degree to which incapacitating punishments are applied, are both determined by the supply of, and demand for, human labor.

William Chambliss, writing in the conflict tradition, provided an especially clear historical account of the criminalization of previously tolerated behavior. As Chambliss shows, the crime of vagrancy was created, and the legal prohibition subsequently has been used to serve a variety of economic interests.

In his presentation of two models of the operation of criminal justice—due process and crime control—Herbert Packer illuminates, perhaps better than anyone, the irreconcilable tension that exists in democratic society between the effort to reduce crime and at the same time leave alone the citizen whose guilt has not been proven in a court of law.

Seven empirical studies of the police are presented here. William Westley conducted the first sociological study of police behavior, which was actually completed in 1950 although not published until 1970. In *Violence and the Police*, Westley describes the internal norms of the police occupation and how those norms regulate, and at times permit, the use of excessive force.

Jerome Skolnick conducted the best of the "ride along" studies. In *Justice Without Trial*, he developed the concept of "working personality" as it determines the behavior of police officers who work various types of assignments. In another observational study of police behavior, Donald Black and Albert Reiss documented the relative importance of such factors as the type of offense and the suspect's race and demeanor in the decision by police to arrest juvenile suspects or dispose of their cases informally.

Truly scientific experiments are rare in police work, largely because random assignment of subjects to experimental and control conditions would violate conventional standards of justice and might place the police and the public at risk. The paucity of such experiments makes the article by George Kelling and his colleagues all the more remarkable. They conducted the first large-scale, experimental evaluation of police resource allocation in *The Kansas City Preventive Patrol Experiment*, and described how they determined the impact of different levels of police patrol on crime in a city.

Policing involves a blend of law enforcement and social service. Egon Bittner provides a clear analysis of the reasons why so much police work involves activities that seem to be unrelated to crime and the law. Often the police are the only people with the authority, means, and availability to respond to emergencies by providing assistance and restoring order.

In the early 1980s several large U.S. cities adopted a new strategy to reduce crime—they cited and arrested people for minor, public infractions of the law, like littering, and worked with community groups to improve the physical appearance of neighborhoods. The theory underlying this strategy, called "Broken Windows Policing," is described by James Q. Wilson and George L. Kelling. When the appearance of an urban area deteriorates, people involved in crime infer that conventional rules and laws are not enforced in the area, so they are free to engage in crime. Crime is prevented, therefore, by cleaning up deteriorating neighborhoods. This strategy produced both apparent reductions in crime and public criticism, when police arrested or harassed unconventional or poor people in their overzealous attempts at "street cleaning."

Lawrence Sherman and Richard Berk compared the consequences of two common police intervention strategies (counsel-and-release versus arrest) in response to domestic assault cases.

Seven selections on the prison are presented next. The idea of the penitentiary was formulated first by the Pennsylvania Quakers as a logical outgrowth of the philosophy of the rationalists, who saw in humanity the possibility of correction and rejected the previous belief in predestined damnation or salvation. In the penitentiary the offenders would work, pray, and contemplate their errors rather than being physically mutilated or killed, as was then the practice throughout the world.

The philosophy of the penitentiary underwent a major change with the introduction of the concept of the reformatory around 1870. Zebulon Brockway, creator and warden of New York's Elmira Reformatory, described the principles of the reformatory system, stressing the importance of the indeterminate sentence, education, work, and military drill in the reformation of the offender. In this formulation are the origins of the "medical model" of correctional treatment, which requires that criminal sentences be tailored to fit the problems of each individual offender rather than be a simple reflection of the heinousness of the offense.

Michel Foucault, who wrote about many modern institutions, including prisons, offered a general and distinctive theory of imprisonment. Foucault argued that prisons were created as part of a general strategy to control not just criminal offenders, but society generally. Some poor people are labeled criminals or delinquents and imprisoned to deter other poor people. Prison inmates are tested, classified, and subjected to highly structured routines. The consequence of this system of discipline, argued Foucault, is the governmental domination of the whole population with the use of little overt violence.

Donald Clemmer introduced the concept of socialization into the prison, which he called "prisonization," taking on the culture of the current inmates. Recognizing that the belief system of inmates was antagonistic to the ideals of the administration, Clemmer sought factors likely to facilitate or impede the process of prisonization. Gresham Sykes' *Society of Captives* is an especially clearly written sociological study of a maximum-security prison as it existed in the 1950s. In the selection presented here he describes in detail the "pains of imprisonment." Many of these pains may not be evident to the casual observer, who, upon seeing little physical pain being inflicted, may erroneously conclude that imprisonment is not a sufficiently painful experience.

Gresham Sykes and Sheldon Messinger describe *The Inmate Social System*, which includes informal behavior norms that exert considerable control over prison inmates and discourage inmates from accepting the rehabilitative goals of the prison. Sykes and Messinger explain that the inmate code encourages inmate solidarity, which serves to reduce the pains of imprisonment.

The earliest scholarly studies of women's prisons were conducted in the 1960s. Rose Giallombardo studied the informal social structure of a federal prison for women and found an elaborate pseudo-family system modeled after conventional, working class, male-female relationships and family structures outside prison. Female inmates engaged in elaborate courtship rituals, took roles of both male and female family members, and developed complex norms governing their behavior within these families. Giallombardo explains that involvement in pseudo-families provides inmates with emotional outlets and practical assistance that the prison does not offer.

Phillip Zimbardo conducted the "Stanford Prison Experiment," probably the most controversial experiment in corrections since the early nineteenth-century experiment with solitary confinement at Auburn Prison. Zimbardo and his colleagues built a small, prison-like environment in a university building at Stanford University. They populated the prison with male, college-age volunteers, whom they randomly assigned to "guard" and "inmate" roles. Within a few days the behavior of some "guards" became very harmful, and some "inmates" apparently developed serious psychological problems, so the experiment was stopped. A lively debate followed publication of reports about the Stanford Prison Experiment. Opponents of imprisonment argued that the experiment proved that prison environments are inherently destructive. Defenders of imprisonment argued that the experiment did not simulate prisons realistically, so the results did not prove that real prisons were destructive to staff and inmates.

In the early 1970s, Douglas Lipton, Robert Martinson, and Judith Wilks conducted a review of previously conducted evaluations of correctional treatment programs. Their complete review filled a large book (*The Effectiveness of Correctional Treatment: A Survey of Treatment Evaluation Studies*, 1975), which provides many examples of correctional treatment programs that reduce recidivism among some categories of offenders. It reports *no* interventions, however, that consistently reduce recidivism for all offenders. Martinson summarized the major conclusions in an article entitled *What Works? Questions and Answers about Prison Reform*. This article became a key source of evidence for detractors of correctional rehabilitation, who overlooked treatments that did "work" and misquoted Martinson's conclusion. The emphatic, rhetorical answer to the question, "What works in correctional treatment?" became "Nothing works!" This refrain was used to justify eliminating correctional treatment programs and research on correctional treatment.

The work of Martinson and his colleagues helped to undermine scholarly and liberal support for rehabilitation. The ideas contained in *Doing Justice* appealed to both liberals who criticized injustices arising from indeterminate sentencing and conservatives who decried examples of offenders' being punished too leniently. Determinate sentencing under a retributive model of punishment, therefore, replaced indeterminate sentencing and discretionary parole release, beginning in the 1970s.

The selections in the last section of this book highlight the enormous philosophical tensions and practical problems that must be resolved for the social response to crime to be both effective and just. These selections also reflect the contributors' creativity and commitment to understanding the social response to crime and securing justice while reducing crime.

45

Of Crimes and Punishments

Cesare Beccaria

... If we look into history we shall find that laws, which are, or ought to be, conventions between men in a state of freedom have been, for the most part the work of the passions of a few, or the consequences of a fortuitous or temporary necessity; not dictated by a cool examiner of human nature, who knew how to collect in one point the actions of a multitude, and had this only end in view, the greatest happiness of the greatest number. Happy are those few nations who have not waited till the slow succession of human vicissitudes should, from the extremity of evil, produce a transition to good; but by prudent laws have facilitated the progress from one to the other! And how great are the obligations due from mankind to that philosopher, who, from the obscurity of his closet, had the courage to scatter among the multitude the seeds of useful truths, so long unfruitful! . . .

Of the Right to Punish.

Every punishment which does not arise from absolute necessity, says the great Montesquieu, is tyrannical. A proposition which may be made more general thus: every act of authority of one man over another, for which there is not an absolute necessity, is tyrannical. It is upon this then that the sovereign's right to punish crimes is founded; that is, upon the necessity of defending the public liberty, entrusted to his care, from the usurpation of individuals; and punishments are just in proportion, as the liberty, preserved by the sovereign, is sacred and valuable.

Let us consult the human heart, and there we shall find the foundation of the sovereign's right to punish; for no advantage in moral policy can be lasting which is not founded on the indelible sentiments of the heart of man. Whatever law deviates from this principle will always meet with a resistance which will destroy it in the end; for the smallest force continually applied will overcome the most violent motion communicated to bodies.

No man ever gave up his liberty merely for the good of the public. Such a chimera exists only in romances. Every individual wishes, if possible, to be exempt from the compacts that bind the rest of mankind.

Excerpted from the second American edition (Philip H. Nicklin, 1819). Translated from the French by Edward D. Ingraham. Available: http://www.constitution.org/cb/crim_pun.htm

The multiplication of mankind, though slow, being too great, for the means which the earth, in its natural state, offered to satisfy necessities which every day became more numerous, obliged men to separate again, and form new societies. These naturally opposed the first, and a state of war was transferred from individuals to nations.

Thus it was necessity that forced men to give up a part of their liberty. It is certain, then, that every individual would choose to put into the public stock the smallest portion possible, as much only as was sufficient to engage others to defend it. The aggregate of these, the smallest portions possible, forms the right of punishing; all that extends beyond this, is abuse, not justice.

Observe that by justice I understand nothing more than that bond which is necessary to keep the interest of individuals united, without which men would return to their original state of barbarity. All punishments which exceed the necessity of preserving this bond are in their nature unjust. We should be cautious how we associate with the word justice an idea of any thing real, such as a physical power, or a being that actually exists. I do not, by any means, speak of the justice of God, which is of another kind, and refers immediately to rewards and punishments in a life to come.

Consequences of the Foregoing Principles.

. . . If every individual be bound to society, society is equally bound to him, by a contract which from its nature equally binds both parties. This obligation, which descends from the throne to the cottage, and equally binds the highest and lowest of mankind, signifies nothing more than that it is the interest of all, that conventions, which are useful to the greatest number, should be punctually observed. The violation of this compact by any individual is an introduction to anarchy. . . .

If it can only be proved, that the severity of punishments, though not immediately contrary to the public good, or to the end for which they were intended, viz. to prevent crimes, be useless, then such severity would be contrary to those beneficent virtues, which are the consequence of enlightened reason, which instructs the sovereign to wish rather to govern men in a state of freedom and happiness than of slavery. It would also be contrary to justice and the social compact. . . .

Of the Proportion between Crimes and Punishments.

It is not only the common interest of mankind that crimes should not be committed, but that crimes of every kind should be less frequent, in proportion to the evil they produce to society. Therefore the means made use of by the legislature to prevent crimes should be more powerful in proportion as they are destructive of the public safety and happiness, and as the inducements to commit them are stronger. Therefore there ought to be a fixed proportion between crimes and punishments.

It is impossible to prevent entirely all the disorders which the passions of mankind cause in society. These disorders increase in proportion to the number of people and the opposition of private interests. If we consult history, we shall find them increasing, in every state, with the extent of dominion. In political arithmetic, it is necessary to substitute a calculation of probabilities to mathematical exactness. That force which continually impels us to our own private interest, like gravity, acts incessantly, unless it meets with an obstacle to oppose it. The effects of this force are the confused series of human actions. Punishments, which I would call political obstacles, prevent the fatal effects of private interest, without destroying the impelling cause, which is that sensibility inseparable from man. The legislator acts, in this case, like a skilful architect, who endeavours to counteract the force of gravity by combining the circumstances which may contribute to the strength of his edifice.

The necessity of uniting in society being granted, together with the conventions which the opposite interests of individuals must necessarily require, a scale of crimes may be formed, of which the first degree should consist of those which immediately tend to the dissolution of society, and the last of the smallest possible injustice done to a private member of that society. Between these extremes will be comprehended all actions contrary to the public good which are called criminal, and which descend by insensible degrees, decreasing from the highest to the lowest. If mathematical calculation could be applied to the obscure and infinite combinations of human actions, there might be a corresponding scale of punishments, descending from the greatest to the least; but it will be sufficient that the wise legislator mark the principal divisions, without disturbing the order, left to crimes of the first degree be assigned punishments of the last. If there were an exact and universal scale of crimes and punishments, we should there have a common measure of the degree of liberty and slavery, humanity and cruelty of different nations. . . .

Of the Intent of Punishments.

. . . The intent of punishments is not to torment a sensible being, nor to undo a crime already committed. Is it possible that torments and useless cruelty, the instrument of furious fanaticism or the impotency of tyrants, can be authorized by a political body, which, so far from being influenced by passion, should be the cool moderator of the passions of individuals? Can the groans of a tortured wretch recall the time past, or reverse the crime he has committed?

The end of punishment, therefore, is no other than to prevent the criminal from doing further injury to society, and to prevent others from committing the like offence. Such punishments, therefore, and such a mode of inflicting them, ought to be chosen, as will make the strongest and most lasting impressions on the minds of others, with the least torment to the body of the criminal. . . .

Of Torture.

The torture of a criminal during the course of his trial is a cruelty consecrated by custom in most nations. It is used with an intent either to make him confess his crime, or to explain some contradictions into which he had been led during his examination, or discover his accomplices, or for some kind of metaphysical and incomprehensible purgation of infamy, or, finally, in order to discover other crimes of which he is not accused, but of which he may be guilty.

No man can be judged a criminal until he be found guilty; nor can society take from him the public protection until it have been proved that he has violated the conditions on which it was granted. What right, then, but that of power, can authorize the punishment of a citizen so long as there remains any doubt of his guilt? This dilemma is frequent. Either he is guilty, or not guilty. If guilty, he should only suffer the punishment ordained by the laws, and torture becomes useless, as his confession is unnecessary. If he be not guilty, you torture the innocent; for, in the eye of the law, every man is innocent whose crime has not been proved. Besides, it is confounding all relations to expect that a man should be both the accuser and accused; and that pain should be the test of truth, as if truth resided in the muscles and fibers of a wretch in torture. By this method the robust will escape, and the feeble be condemned. These are the inconveniences of this pretended test of truth, worthy only of a cannibal, and which the Romans, in many respects barbarous, and whose savage virtue has been too much admired, reserved for the slaves alone.

What is the political intention of punishments? To terrify and be an example to others. Is this intention answered by thus privately torturing the guilty and the innocent? It is doubtless of importance that no crime should remain unpunished; but it is useless to make a public example of the author of a crime hid in darkness. A crime already committed, and for which there can be no remedy, can only be punished by a political society with an intention that no hopes of impunity should induce others to commit the same. If it be true, that the number of those who from fear or virtue respect the laws is greater than of those by whom they are violated, the risk of torturing an innocent person is greater, as there is a greater probability that, cæteris paribus, an individual hath observed, than that he hath infringed the laws. . . .

Another intention of torture is to oblige the supposed criminal to reconcile the contradictions into which he may have fallen during his examination; as if the dread of punishment, the uncertainty of his fate, the solemnity of the court, the majesty of the judge, and the ignorance of the accused, were not abundantly sufficient to account for contradictions, which are so common to men even in a state of tranquility, and which must necessarily be multiplied by the perturbation of the mind of a man entirely engaged in the thoughts of saving himself from imminent danger.

This infamous test of truth is a remaining monument of that ancient and savage legislation, in which trials by fire, by boiling water, or the uncertainty of combats, were called judgments of God; as if the links of that eternal chain, whose beginning is in the breast of the first cause of all things, could ever be disunited by the institutions of men. The only difference between torture and trials by fire and boiling water is, that the event of the first depends on the will of the accused, and of the second on a fact entirely physical and external: but this difference is apparent only, not real. A man on the rack, in the convulsions of torture, has it as little in his power to declare the truth, as, in former times, to prevent without fraud the effects of fire or boiling water.

Every act of the will is invariably in proportion to the force of the impression on our senses. The impression of pain, then, may increase to such a degree, that, occupying the mind entirely, it will compel the sufferer to use the shortest method of freeing himself from torment. His answer, therefore, will be an effect as necessary as that of fire or boiling water, and he will accuse himself of crimes of which he is innocent: so that the very means employed to distinguish the innocent from the guilty will most effectually destroy all difference between them.

It would be superfluous to confirm these reflections by examples of innocent persons who, from the agony of torture, have confessed themselves guilty: innumerable instances may be found in all nations, and in every age. How amazing that mankind have always neglected to draw the natural conclusion! Lives there a man who, if he has carried his thoughts ever so little beyond the necessities of life, when he reflects on such cruelty, is not tempted to fly from society, and return to his natural state of independence?

The result of torture, then, is a matter of calculation, and depends on the constitution, which differs in every individual, and it is in proportion to his strength and sensibility; so that to discover truth by this method, is a problem which may be better solved by a mathematician than by a judge, and may be thus stated: The force of the muscles and the sensibility of the nerves of an innocent person being given, it is required to find the degree of pain necessary to make him confess himself guilty of a given crime.

The examination of the accused is intended to find out the truth; but if this be discovered with so much difficulty in the air, gesture, and countenance of a man at ease, how can it appear in a countenance distorted by the convulsions of torture? Every violent action destroys those small alterations in the features which sometimes disclose the sentiments of the heart. . . .

It appears also that these truths were known, though imperfectly, even to those by whom torture has been most frequently practised; for a confession made during torture, is null, if it be not afterwards confirmed by an oath, which if the criminal refuses, he is tortured again. Some civilians and some nations permit this infamous *petitio principii* to be only three times repeated, and others leave it to the discretion of the judge; therefore, of two men equally innocent, or equally guilty, the most robust and resolute will be acquitted, and the weakest and most pusillanimous will be condemned, in consequence of the following excellent mode of reasoning. I, the judge, must find some one guilty. Thou, who art a strong fellow, hast been able to resist the force of torment; therefore I acquit thee. Thou, being weaker, hast yielded to it; I therefore condemn thee. I am sensible, that the confession which was extorted from thee has no weight; but if thou dost not confirm by oath what thou hast already confessed, I will have thee tormented again.

A very strange but necessary consequence of the use of torture is, that the case of the innocent is worse than that of the guilty. With regard to the first, either he confesses the crime which he has not committed, and is condemned, or he is acquitted, and has suffered a punishment he did not deserve. On the contrary, the person who is really guilty has the most favourable side of the question; for, if he supports the torture with firmness and resolution, he is acquitted, and has gained, having exchanged a greater punishment for a less. . . .

Of the Advantage of Immediate Punishment.

The more immediately after the commission of a crime a punishment is inflicted, the more just and useful it will be. It will be more just, because it spares the criminal the cruel and superfluous torment of uncertainty, which increases in proportion to the strength of his imagination and the sense of his weakness; and because the privation of liberty, being a punishment, ought to be inflicted before condemnation but for as short a time as possible. Imprisonment, I say, being only the means of securing the person of the accused until he be tried, condemned, or acquitted, ought not only to be of as short duration, but attended with as little severity as possible. The time should be determined by the necessary preparation for the trial, and the right of priority in the oldest prisoners. The confinement ought not to be closer than is requisite to prevent his flight, or his concealing the proofs of the crime; and the trial should be conducted with all possible expedition. Can there be a more cruel contrast than that between the indolence of a judge and the painful anxiety of the accused; the comforts and pleasures of an insensible magistrate, and the filth and misery of the prisoner? In general, as I have before observed, the degree of the punishment, and the consequences of a crime, ought to be so contrived as to have the greatest possible effect on others, with the least possible pain to the delinquent. If there be any society in which this is not a fundamental principle, it is an unlawful society; for mankind, by their union, originally intended to subject themselves to the least evils possible.

An immediate punishment is more useful; because the smaller the interval of time between the punishment and the crime, the stronger and more lasting will be the association of the two ideas of crime and punishment; so that they may be considered, one as the cause, and the other as the unavoidable and necessary effect. It is demonstrated, that the association of ideas is the cement which unites the fabric of the human intellect, without which pleasure and pain would be simple and ineffectual sensations. The vulgar, that is, all men who have no general ideas or universal principles, act in consequence of the most immediate and familiar associations; but the more remote and complex only present themselves to the minds of those who are passionately attached to a single object, or to those of greater understanding, who have acquired an habit of rapidly comparing together a number of objects, and of forming a conclusion; and the result, that is, the action in consequence, by these means becomes less dangerous and uncertain.

It is, then, of the greatest importance that the punishment should succeed the crime as immediately as possible, if we intend that, in the rude minds of the multitude, the seducing picture of the advantage arising from the crime should instantly awake the attendant idea of punishment. Delaying the punishment serves only to separate these two ideas, and thus affects the minds of the spectators rather as being a terrible sight than the necessary consequence of a crime, the horror of which should contribute to heighten the idea of the punishment. . . .

Of the Mildness of Punishments.

The course of my ideas has carried me away from my subject, to the elucidation of which I now return. Crimes are more effectually prevented by the certainty than the severity of punishment. Hence in a magistrate the necessity of vigilance, and in a judge of implacability, which, that it may become an useful virtue, should be joined to a mild legislation. The certainty of a small punishment will make a stronger impression than the fear of one more severe, if attended with the hopes of escaping; for it is the nature of mankind to be terrified at the approach of the smallest inevitable evil, whilst hope, the best gift of Heaven hath the power of dispelling the apprehension of a greater, especially if supported by examples of impunity, which weakness or avarice too frequently afford.

If punishments be very severe, men are naturally led to the perpetration of other crimes, to avoid the punishment due to the first. The countries and times most notorious for severity of punishments were always those in which the most bloody and inhuman actions and the most atrocious crimes were committed; for the hand of the legislator and the assassin were directed by the same spirit of ferocity, which on the throne dictated laws of iron to slaves and savages, and in private instigated the subject to sacrifice one tyrant to make room for another.

In proportion as punishments become more cruel, the minds of men, as a fluid rises to the same height with that which surrounds it, grow hardened and insensible; and the force of the passions still continuing, in the space of an hundred years the wheel terrifies no more than formerly the prison. That a punishment may produce the effect required, it is sufficient that the evil it occasions should exceed the good expected from the crime, including in the calculation the certainty of the punishment, and the privation of the expected advantage. All severity beyond this is superfluous, and therefore tyrannical.

Men regulate their conduct by the repeated impression of evils they know, and not by those with which they are unacquainted. Let us, for example, suppose two nations, in one of which the greatest punishment is perpetual slavery, and in the other the wheel: I say, that both will inspire the same degree of terror, and that their can be no reasons for increasing the punishments of the first, which are not equally valid for augmenting those of the second to more lasting and more ingenious modes of tormenting, and so on to the most exquisite refinements of a science too well known to tyrants.

There are yet two other consequences of cruel punishments, which counteract the purpose of their institution, which was, to prevent crimes. The first arises from the impossibility of establishing an exact proportion between the crime and punishment; for though ingenious cruelty hath greatly multiplied the variety of torments, yet the human frame can suffer only to a certain degree, beyond which it is impossible to proceed, be the enormity of the crime ever so great. The second consequence is impunity. Human nature is limited no less in evil than in good. Excessive barbarity can never be more than temporary, it being impossible that it should be supported by a permanent system of legislation; for if the laws be too cruel, they must be altered, or anarchy and impunity will succeed. . . .

Of the Punishment of Death.

The useless profusion of punishments, which has never made men better induces me to inquire, whether the punishment of death be really just or useful in a well governed state? What right, I ask, have men to cut the throats of their fellow-creatures? Certainly not that on which the sovereignty and laws are founded. The laws, as I have said before, are only the sum of the smallest portions of the private liberty of each individual, and represent the general will, which is the aggregate of that of each individual. Did any one ever give to others the right of taking away his life? Is it possible that, in the smallest portions of the liberty of each, sacrificed to the good of the public, can be contained the greatest of all good, life? If it were so, how shall it be reconciled to the maxim which tells us, that a man has no right to kill himself, which he certainly must have, if he could give it away to another?

But the punishment of death is not authorized by any right; for I have demonstrated that no such right exists. It is therefore a war of a whole nation against a citizen whose destruction they consider as necessary or useful to the general good. But if I can further demonstrate that it is neither necessary nor useful, I shall have gained the cause of humanity.

The death of a citizen cannot be necessary but in one case: when, though deprived of his liberty, he has such power and connections as may endanger the security of the nation; when his existence may produce a dangerous revolution in the established form of government. But, even in this case, it can only be necessary when a nation is on the verge of recovering or losing its liberty, or in times of absolute anarchy, when the disorders themselves hold the place of laws: but in a reign of tranquility, in a form of government approved by the united wishes of the nation, in a state well fortified from enemies without and supported by strength within, and opinion, perhaps more efficacious, where all power is lodged in the hands of a true sovereign, where riches can purchase pleasures and not authority, there can be no necessity for taking away the life of a subject.

If the experience of all ages be not sufficient to prove, that the punishment of death has never prevented determined men from injuring society, if the example of the Romans, if twenty years' reign of Elizabeth, empress of Russia, in which she gave the fathers of their country an example more illustrious than many conquests bought with blood; if, I say, all this be not sufficient to persuade mankind, who always suspect the voice of reason, and who choose rather to be led by authority, let us consult human nature in proof of my assertion.

It is not the intenseness of the pain that has the greatest effect on the mind, but its continuance; for our sensibility is more easily and more powerfully affected by weak but repeated impressions, than by a violent but momentary impulse. The power of habit is universal over every sensible being. As it is by that we learn to speak, to walk, and to satisfy our necessities, so the ideas of morality are stamped on our minds by repeated impression. The death of a criminal is a terrible but momentary spectacle, and therefore a less efficacious method of deterring others than the continued example of a man deprived of his liberty, condemned, as a beast of burden, to repair, by his labour, the injury he has done to society, If I commit such a crime, says the spectator to himself, I shall be reduced to that miserable condition for the rest of my life. A much more powerful preventive than the fear of death which men always behold in distant obscurity. . . .

The execution of a criminal is to the multitude a spectacle which in some excites compassion mixed with indignation. These sentiments occupy the mind much more than that salutary terror which the laws endeavor to inspire; but, in the contemplation of continued suffering, terror is the only, or at least predominant sensation. The severity of a punishment should be just sufficient to excite compassion in the spectators, as it is intended more for them than for the criminal.

A punishment, to be just, should have only that degree of severity which is sufficient to deter others. Now there is no man who upon the least reflection, would put in competition the total and perpetual loss of his liberty, with the greatest advantages he could possibly obtain in consequence of a crime. Perpetual slavery, then, has in it all that is necessary to deter the most hardened and determined, as much as the punishment of death. I say it has more. There are many who can look upon death with intrepidity and firmness, some through fanaticism, and others through vanity, which attends us even to the grave; others from a desperate resolution, either to get rid of their misery, or cease to live: but fanaticism and vanity forsake the criminal in slavery, in chains and fetters, in an iron cage, and despair seems rather the beginning than the end of their misery. The mind, by collecting itself and uniting all its force, can, for a moment, repel assailing grief; but its most vigorous efforts are insufficient to resist perpetual wretchedness.

In all nations, where death is used as a punishment, every example supposes a new crime committed; whereas, in perpetual slavery, every criminal affords a frequent and lasting example; and if it be necessary that men should often be witnesses of the power of the laws, criminals should often be put to death: but this supposes a frequency of crimes; and from hence this punishment will cease to have its effect, so that it must be useful and useless at the same time.

I shall be told that perpetual slavery is as painful a punishment as death, and therefore as cruel. I answer, that if all the miserable moments in the life of a slave were collected into one point, it would be a more cruel punishment than any other;

but these are scattered through his whole life, whilst the pain of death exerts all its force in a moment. There is also another advantage in the punishment of slavery, which is, that it is more terrible to the spectator than to the sufferer himself; for the spectator considers the sum of all his wretched moments whilst the sufferer, by the misery of the present, is prevented from thinking of the future. All evils are increased by the imagination, and the sufferer finds resources and consolations of which the spectators are ignorant, who judge by their own sensibility of what passes in a mind by habit grown callous to misfortune. . . .

The punishment of death is pernicious to society, from the example of barbarity it affords. If the passions, or the necessity of war, have taught men to shed the blood of their fellow creatures, the laws, which are intended to moderate the ferocity of mankind, should not increase it by examples of barbarity, the more horrible as this punishment is usually attended with formal pageantry. Is it not absurd, that the laws, which detest and punish homicide, should, in order to prevent murder, publicly commit murder themselves? . . .

Conclusion.

I conclude with this reflection, that the severity of punishments ought to be in proportion to the state of the nation. Among a people hardly yet emerged from barbarity, they should be most severe, as strong impressions are required; but, in proportion as the minds of men become softened by their intercourse in society, the severity of punishments should be diminished, if it be intended that the necessary relation between the object and the sensation should be maintained.

From what I have written results the following general theorem, of considerable utility, though not conformable to custom, the common legislator of nations: That a punishment may not be an act of violence, of one, or of many, against a private member of society, it should be public, immediate, and necessary, the least possible in the case given, proportioned to the crime, and determined by the laws.

46

The Challenge of Crime in a Free Society

*President's Commission on Law Enforcement
and the Administration of Justice*

This report is about crime in America—about those who commit it, about those who are its victims, and about what can be done to reduce it.

The report is the work of 19 commissioners, 63 staff members, 175 consultants, and hundreds of advisers. The commissioners, staff, consultants, and advisers come from every part of America and represent a broad range of opinion and profession.

In the process of developing the findings and recommendations of the report the Commission called three national conferences, conducted five national surveys, held hundreds of meetings, and interviewed tens of thousands of persons.

The report makes more than 200 specific recommendations—concrete steps the Commission believes can lead to a safer and more just society. These recommendations call for a greatly increased effort on the part of the Federal Government, the States, the counties, the cities, civic organizations, religious institutions, business groups, and individual citizens. They call for basic changes in the operations of police, schools, prosecutors, employment agencies, defenders, social workers, prisons, housing authorities, and probation and parole officers.

But the recommendations are more than just a list of new procedures, new tactics, and new techniques. They are a call for a revolution in the way America thinks about crime.

Many Americans take comfort in the view that crime is the vice of a handful of people. This view is inaccurate. In the United States today, one boy in six is referred to the juvenile court. A Commission survey shows that in 1965 more than two million Americans were received in prisons or juvenile training schools, or placed on probation. Another Commission study suggests that about 40 percent of all male children now living in the United States will be arrested for a nontraffic offense during their lives. An independent survey of 1,700 persons found that 91 percent of the sample admitted they had committed acts for which they might have received jail or prison sentences.

Many Americans also think of crime as a very narrow range of behavior. It is not. An enormous variety of acts make up the "crime problem." Crime is not just a tough teenager snatching a lady's purse. It is a professional thief stealing cars "on order." It is a well-heeled loan shark taking over a previously legitimate business

Source: From *The Challenge of Crime in a Free Society*, A Report by the President's Commission on Law Enforcement and the Administration of Justice. (Washington: U.S. Government Printing Office, 1967), pp. v–xi.

for organized crime. It is a polite young man who suddenly and inexplicably murders his family. It is a corporation executive conspiring with competitors to keep prices high. No single formula, no single theory, no single generalization can explain the vast range of behavior called crime.

Many Americans think controlling crime is solely the task of the police, the courts, and correction agencies. In fact, as the Commission's report makes clear, crime cannot be controlled without the interest and participation of schools, businesses, social agencies, private groups, and individual citizens.

What, then, is America's experience with crime and how has this experience shaped the Nation's way of living? A new insight into these two questions is furnished by the Commission's National Survey of Criminal Victims. In this survey, the first of its kind conducted on such a scope, 10,000 representative American households were asked about their experiences with crime, whether they reported those experiences to the police, and how those experiences affected their lives.

An important finding of the survey is that for the Nation as a whole there is far more crime than ever is reported. Burglaries occur about three times more often than they are reported to police. Aggravated assaults and larcenies over $50 occur twice as often as they are reported. There are 50 percent more robberies than are reported. In some areas, only one-tenth of the total number of certain kinds of crimes are reported to the police. Seventy-four percent of the neighborhood commercial establishments surveyed do not report to police the thefts committed by their employees.

The existence of crime, the talk about crime, the reports of crime, and the fear of crime have eroded the basic quality of life of many Americans. A Commission study conducted in high crime areas of two large cities found that:

- 43 percent of the respondents say they stay off the streets at night because of their fear of crime.
- 35 percent say they do not speak to strangers any more because of their fear of crime.
- 21 percent say they use cars and cabs at night because of their fear of crime.
- 20 percent say they would like to move to another neighborhood because of their fear of crime.

The findings of the Commission's national survey generally support those of the local surveys. One-third of a representative sample of all Americans say it is unsafe to walk alone at night in their neighborhoods. Slightly more than one-third say they keep firearms in the house for protection against criminals. Twenty-eight percent say they keep watchdogs for the same reason.

Under any circumstance, developing an effective response to the problem of crime in America is exceedingly difficult. And because of the changes expected in the population in the next decade, in years to come it will be more difficult. Young people commit a disproportionate share of crime and the number of young people in our society is growing at a much faster rate than the total population. Although the 15- to 17-year-old age group represents only 5.4 percent of the population, it accounts for 12.8 percent of all arrests. Fifteen and sixteen year olds have the highest arrest rate in the United States. The problem in the years ahead is dramatically foretold by the fact that 23 percent of the population is 10 or under.

Despite the seriousness of the problem today and the increasing challenge in the years ahead, the central conclusion of the Commission is that a significant reduction in crime is possible if the following objectives are vigorously pursued:

First, society must seek to prevent crime before it happens by assuring all Americans a stake in the benefits and responsibilities of American life, by strengthening law enforcement, and by reducing criminal opportunities.

Second, society's aim of reducing crime would be better served if the system of criminal justice developed a far broader range of techniques with which to deal with individual offenders.

Third, the system of criminal justice must eliminate existing injustices if it is to achieve its ideals and win the respect and cooperation of all citizens.

Fourth, the system of criminal justice must attract more people and better people—police, prosecutors, judges, defense attorneys, probation and parole officers, and corrections officials with more knowledge, expertise, initiative, and integrity.

Fifth, there must be much more operational and basic research into the problems of crime and criminal administration, by those both within and without the system of criminal justice.

Sixth, the police, courts, and correctional agencies must be given substantially greater amounts of money if they are to improve their ability to control crime.

Seventh, individual citizens, civic and business organizations, religious institutions, and all levels of government must take responsibility for planning and implementing the changes that must be made in the criminal justice system if crime is to be reduced.

In terms of specific recommendations, what do these seven objectives mean?

1. Preventing Crime

The prevention of crime covers a wide range of activities: Eliminating social conditions closely associated with crime; improving the ability of the criminal justice system to detect, apprehend, judge, and reintegrate into their communities those who commit crimes; and reducing the situations in which crimes are most likely to be committed.

Every effort must be made to strengthen the family, now often shattered by the grinding pressures of urban slums.

Slum schools must be given enough resources to make them as good as schools elsewhere and to enable them to compensate for the various handicaps suffered by the slum child—to rescue him from his environment.

Present efforts to combat school segregation, and the housing segregation that underlies it, must be continued and expanded.

Employment opportunities must be enlarged and young people provided with more effective vocational training and individual job counseling. Programs to create new kinds of jobs—such as probation aides, medical assistants, and teacher helpers—seem particularly promising and should be expanded.

The problem of increasing the ability of the police to detect and apprehend criminals is complicated. In one effort to find out how this objective could be achieved, the Commission conducted an analysis of 1,905 crimes reported to the Los Angeles Police Department during a recent month. The study showed the importance of identifying the perpetrator at the scene of the crime. Eighty-six percent of the crimes with named suspects were solved, but only 12 percent of the unnamed suspect crimes were solved. Another finding of the study was that there is a relationship between the speed of response and certainty of apprehension. On the average, response to emergency calls resulting in arrests was 50 percent faster than response to emergency calls not resulting in arrest. On the basis of this finding, and a cost effectiveness study to discover the best means to reduce response time, the Commission recommends an experimental program to develop computer-aided command-and-control systems for large police departments.

To insure the maximum use of such a system, headquarters must have a direct link with every onduty police officer. Because large scale production would result in a substantial reduction of the cost of miniature two-way radios, the Commission recommends that the Federal Government assume leadership in initiating a development program for such equipment and that it consider guaranteeing the sale of the first production lot of perhaps 20,000 units.

Two other steps to reduce police response time are recommended:

- Police callboxes, which are locked and inconspicuous in most cities, should be left open, brightly marked, and designated "public emergency callboxes."
- The telephone company should develop a single police number for each metropolitan area, and eventually for the entire United States.

Improving the effectiveness of law enforcement, however, is much more than just improving police response time. For example a study in Washington, D.C., found that courtroom time for a felony defendant who pleads guilty probably totals less than 1 hour, while the median time from his initial appearance to his disposition is 4 months.

In an effort to discover how courts can best speed the process of criminal justice, the known facts about felony cases in Washington were placed in a computer and the operation of the system was simulated. After a number of possible solutions to the problem of delay were tested, it appeared that the addition of a second grand jury—which, with supporting personnel, would cost less than $50,000 a year—would result in a 25-percent reduction in the time required for the typical felony case to move from initial appearance to trial.

The application of such analysis—when combined with the Commission's recommended timetable laying out timespans for each step in the criminal process—should help court systems to ascertain their procedural bottlenecks and develop ways to eliminate them.

Another way to prevent crime is to reduce the opportunity to commit it. Many crimes would not be committed, indeed many criminal careers would not begin, if there were fewer opportunities for crime.

Auto theft is a good example. According to FBI statistics, the key had been left in the ignition or the ignition had been left unlocked in 42 percent of all stolen cars. Even in those cars taken when the ignition was locked, at least 20 percent were stolen simply by shorting the ignition with such simple devices as paper clips or tinfoil. In one city, the elimination of the unlocked "off" position on the 1965 Chevrolet, resulted in 50 percent fewer of those models being stolen in 1965 than were stolen in 1964.

On the basis of these findings, it appears that an important reduction in auto theft could be achieved simply by installing an ignition system that automatically ejects the key when the engine is turned off.

A major reason that it is important to reduce auto theft is that stealing a car is very often the criminal act that starts a boy on a course of lawbreaking.

Stricter gun controls also would reduce some kinds of crime. Here, the Commission recommends a strengthening of the Federal law governing the interstate shipment of firearms and enactment of State laws requiring the registration of all handguns, rifles, and shotguns, and prohibiting the sale or ownership of firearms by certain categories of persons—dangerous criminals, habitual drunkards, and drug addicts. After 5 years, the Commission recommends that Congress pass a Federal registration law applying to those States that have not passed their own registration laws.

2. New Ways of Dealing With Offenders

The Commission's second objective—the development of a far broader range of alternatives for dealing with offenders—is based on the belief that, while there are some who must be completely segregated from society, there are many instances in which segregation does more harm than good. Furthermore, by concentrating the resources of the police, the courts, and correctional agencies on the smaller number of offenders who really need them, it should be possible to give all offenders more effective treatment.

A specific and important example of this principle is the Commission's recommendation that every community consider establishing a Youth Services Bureau, a community-based center to which juveniles could be referred by the police, the courts, parents, schools, and social agencies for counseling, education, work, or recreation programs and job placement.

The Youth Services Bureau—an agency to handle many troubled and troublesome young people outside the criminal system—is needed in part because society has failed to give the juvenile court the resources that would allow it to function as its founders hoped it would. In a recent survey of juvenile court judges, for example, 83 percent said no psychologist or psychiatrist was available to their courts on a regular basis and one-third said they did not have probation officers or social workers. Even where there are probation officers, the Commission found, the average officer supervises 76 probationers, more than double the recommended caseload.

The California Youth Authority for the last 5 years has been conducting a controlled experiment to determine the effectiveness of another kind of alternative treatment program for juveniles. There, after initial screening, convicted juvenile delinquents are assigned on a random basis to either an experimental group or a control group. Those in the experimental group are returned to the community and receive intensive individual counseling, group counseling, group therapy, and family counseling. Those in the control group are assigned to California's regular institutional treatment program. The findings so far: 28 percent of the experimental group have had their paroles revoked, compared with 52 percent in the control group. Furthermore, the community treatment program is less expensive than institutional treatment.

To make community-based treatment possible for both adults and juveniles, the Commission recommends the development of an entirely new kind of correctional institution: located close to population centers; maintaining close relations with schools, employers, and universities; housing as few as 50 inmates; serving as a classification center, as the center for various kinds of community programs and as a port of reentry to the community for those difficult and dangerous offenders who have required treatment in facilities with tighter custody.

Such institutions would be useful in the operation of programs—strongly recommended by the Commission—that permit selected inmates to work or study in the community during the day and return to control at night, and programs that permit long-term inmates to become adjusted to society gradually rather than being discharged directly from maximum security institutions to the streets.

Another aspect of the Commission's conviction that different offenders with different problems should be treated in different ways, is its recommendation about the handling of public drunkenness, which, in 1965, accounted for one out of every three arrests in America. The great number of these arrests—some 2 million—burdens the police, clogs the lower courts and crowds the penal institutions. The Commission therefore recommends that communities develop civil detoxification units and comprehensive aftercare programs, and that with the development of such programs, drunkenness, not accompanied by other unlawful conduct, should not be a criminal offense.

Similarly, the Commission recommends the expanded use of civil commitment for drug addicts.

3. Eliminating Unfairness

The third objective is to eliminate injustices so that the system of criminal justice can win the respect and cooperation of all citizens. Our society must give the police, the courts, and correctional agencies the resources and the mandate to provide fair and dignified treatment for all.

The Commission found overwhelming evidence of institutional shortcomings in almost every part of the United States.

A survey of the lower court operations in a number of large American cities found cramped and noisy courtrooms, undignified and perfunctory procedures, badly trained personnel overwhelmed by enormous caseloads. In short, the Commission found assembly line justice.

The Commission found that in at least three States, justices of the peace are paid only if they convict and collect a fee from the defendant, a practice held unconstitutional by the Supreme Court 40 years ago.

The Commission found that approximately one-fourth of the 400,000 children detained in 1965—for a variety of causes but including truancy, smoking, and running away from home—were held in adult jails and lockups, often with hardened criminals.

In addition to the creation of new kinds of institutions—such as the Youth Services Bureau and the small, community-based correctional centers—the Commission recommends several important procedural changes. It recommends counsel at various points in the criminal process.

For juveniles, the Commission recommends providing counsel whenever coercive action is a possibility.

For adults, the Commission recommends providing counsel to any criminal defendant who faces a significant penalty—excluding traffic and similar petty charges—if he cannot afford to provide counsel for himself.

In connection with this recommendation, the Commission asks each State to finance regular, statewide assigned counsel and defender systems for the indigent.

Counsel also should be provided in parole and probation revocation hearings.

Another kind of broad procedural change that the Commission recommends is that every State, county, and local jurisdiction provide judicial officers with sufficient information about individual defendants to permit the release without money bail of those who can be safely released.

In addition to eliminating the injustice of holding persons charged with a crime merely because they cannot afford bail, this recommendation also would save a good deal of money. New York City alone, for example, spends approximately $10 million a year holding persons who have not yet been found guilty of any crime.

Besides institutional injustices, the Commission found that while the great majority of criminal justice and law enforcement personnel perform their duties with fairness and understanding, even under the most trying circumstances, some take advantage of their official positions and act in a callous, corrupt, or brutal manner.

Injustice will not yield to simple solutions. Overcoming it requires a wide variety of remedies including improved methods of selecting personnel, the massive infusion of additional funds, the revamping of existing procedures and the adoption of more effective internal and external controls.

The relations between the police and urban poor deserve special mention. Here the Commission recommends that every large department—especially in communities with substantial minority populations—should have community-relations machinery consisting of a headquarters planning and supervising unit and precinct units to carry out recommended programs. Effective citizen advisory committees should be established in minority group neighborhoods. All departments with substantial minority populations should make special efforts to recruit minority group officers and to deploy and promote them fairly. They should have rigorous internal investigation units to examine complaints of misconduct. The Commission believes it is of the utmost importance to insure that complaints of unfair treatment are fairly dealt with.

Fair treatment of every individual—fair in fact and also perceived to be fair by those affected—is an essential element of justice and a principal objective of the American criminal justice system.

4. Personnel

The fourth objective is that higher levels of knowledge, expertise, initiative, and integrity be achieved by police, judges, prosecutors, defense attorneys, and correctional authorities so that the system of criminal justice can improve its ability to control crime.

The Commission found one obstacle to recruiting better police officers was the standard requirement that all candidates—regardless of qualifications—begin their careers at the lowest level and normally remain at this level from 2 to 5 years before being eligible for promotion. Thus, a college graduate must enter a department at the same rank and pay and perform the same tasks as a person who enters with only a high school diploma or less.

The Commission recommends that police departments give up single entry and establish three levels at which candidates may begin their police careers. The Commission calls these three levels the "community service officer," the "police officer," and the "police agent."

This division, in addition to providing an entry place for the better educated, also would permit police departments to tap the special knowledge, skills, and understanding of those brought up in the slums.

The community service officer would be a uniformed but unarmed member of the police department. Two of his major responsibilities would be to maintain close relations with juveniles in the area where he works and to be especially alert to crime-breeding conditions that other city agencies had not dealt with. Typically, the CSO might be under 21, might not be required to meet conventional education requirements, and might work out of a store-front office. Serving as an apprentice policeman—a substitute for the police cadet—the CSO would work as a member of a team with the police officer and police agent.

The police officer would respond to calls for service, perform routine patrol, render emergency services, make preliminary investigations, and enforce traffic regulations. In order to qualify as a police officer at the present time, a candidate should possess a high school diploma and should demonstrate a capacity for college work.

The police agent would do whatever police jobs were most complicated, most sensitive, and most demanding. He might be a specialist in police community-relations or juvenile delinquency. He might be in uniform patrolling a high-crime neighborhood. He might have staff duties. To become a police agent would require at least 2 years of college work and preferably a baccalaureate degree in the liberal arts or social sciences.

As an ultimate goal, the Commission recommends that all police personnel with general enforcement powers have baccalaureate degrees.

While candidates could enter the police service at any one of the three levels, they also could work their way up through the different categories as they met the basic education and other requirements.

In many jurisdictions there is a critical need for additional police personnel. Studies by the Commission indicate a recruiting need of 50,000 policemen in 1967 just to fill positions already authorized. In order to increase police effectiveness, additional staff specialists will be required, and when the community service officers are added manpower needs will be even greater.

The Commission also recommends that every State establish a commission on police standards to set minimum recruiting and training standards and to provide financial and technical assistance for local police departments.

In order to improve the quality of judges, prosecutors, and defense attorneys, the Commission recommends a variety of steps: Taking the selection of judges out of partisan politics; the more regular use of seminars, conferences, and institutes to train sitting judges; the establishment of judicial commissions to excuse physically or mentally incapacitated judges from their duties without public humiliation; the general abolition of part-time district attorneys and assistant district attorneys; and a broad range of measures to develop a greatly enlarged and better trained pool of defense attorneys.

In the correctional system there is a critical shortage of probation and parole officers, teachers, caseworkers, vocational instructors, and group workers. The need for major manpower increases in this area was made clear by the findings from the Commission's national corrections survey:

- Less than 3 percent of all personnel working in local jails and institutions devote their time to treatment and training.
- Eleven States do not offer any kind of probation services for adult misdemeanants,

six offer only the barest fragments of such services, and most States offer them on a spotty basis.

• Two-thirds of all State adult felony probationers are in caseloads of over 100 persons.

To meet the requirements of both the correctional agencies and the courts, the Commission has found an immediate need to double the Nation's pool of juvenile probation officers, triple the number of probation officers working with adult felons, and increase sevenfold the number of officers working with misdemeanants.

Another area with a critical need for large numbers of expert criminal justice officers is the complex one of controlling organized crime. Here, the Commission recommends that prosecutors and police in every State and city where organized crime is known to, or may, exist develop special organized crime units.

5. Research

The fifth objective is that every segment of the system of criminal justice devote a significant part of its resources for research to insure the development of new and effective methods of controlling crime.

The Commission found that little research is being conducted into such matters as the economic impact of crime; the effects on crime of increasing or decreasing criminal sanctions; possible methods for improving the effectiveness of various procedures of the police, courts, and correctional agencies.

Organized crime is another area in which almost no research has been conducted. The Commission found that the only group with any significant knowledge about this problem was law enforcement officials. Those in other disciplines—social scientists, economists and lawyers, for example—have not until recently considered the possibility of research projects on organized crime.

A small fraction of 1 percent of the criminal justice system's total budget is spent on research. This figure could be multiplied many times without approaching the 3 percent industry spends on research, much less the 15 percent the Defense Department spends. The Commission believes it should be multiplied many times.

That research is a powerful force for change in the field of criminal justice perhaps can best be documented by the history of the Vera Institute in New York City. Here the research of a small, nongovernment agency has in a very short time led to major changes in the bail procedures of approximately 100 cities, several States, and the Federal Government.

Because of the importance of research, the Commission recommends that major criminal justice agencies—such as State court and correctional systems and big-city police departments—organize operational research units as integral parts of their structures.

In addition, the criminal justice agencies should welcome the efforts of scholars and other independent experts to understand their problems and operations. These agencies cannot undertake needed research on their own; they urgently need the help of outsiders.

The Commission also recommends the establishment of several regional research institutes designed to concentrate a number of different disciplines on the problem of crime. It further recommends the establishment of an independent National Criminal Research Foundation to stimulate and coordinate research and disseminate its results.

One essential requirement for research is more complete information about the operation of the criminal process. To meet this requirement, the Commission recommends the creation of a National Criminal Justice Statistics Center. The Center's first responsibility would be to work with the FBI, the Children's Bureau, the Federal Bureau of Prisons, and other agencies to develop an integrated picture of the number of crimes reported to police, the number of persons arrested, the number of accused persons prosecuted, the number of offenders placed on probation, in prison, and subsequently on parole.

Another major responsibility of the Center would be to continue the Commission's initial effort to develop a new yardstick to measure the extent of crime in our society as a supplement to the FBI's Uniform Crime Reports. The Commission believes that the Government should be able to plot the levels of different kinds of crime in a city or a State as precisely as the Labor Department and the Census Bureau now plot the rate of unemployment. Just as unemployment information is essential to sound economic planning, so some day may criminal information help official planning in the system of criminal justice.

6. Money

Sixth, the police, the courts, and correctional agencies will require substantially more money if they are to control crime better.

Almost all of the specific recommendations made by the Commission will involve increased budgets. Substantially higher salaries must be offered to attract topflight candidates to the system of criminal justice. For example, the median annual salary for a patrolman in a large city today is $5,300. Typically, the maximum salary is something less than $1,000 above the starting salary. The Commission believes the most important change that can be made in police salary scales is to increase maximums sharply. An FBI agent, for example, starts at $8,421 a year and if he serves long and well enough can reach $16,905 a year without being promoted to a supervisory position. The Commission is aware that reaching such figures immediately is not possible in many cities, but it believes that there should be a large range from minimum to maximum everywhere.

The Commission also recommends new kinds of programs that will require additional funds: Youth Services Bureaus, greatly enlarged misdemeanant probation services and increased levels of research, for example.

The Commission believes some of the additional resources—especially those devoted to innovative programs and to training, education, and research—should be contributed by the Federal Government.

The Federal Government already is conducting a broad range of programs—aid to elementary and secondary schools, the Neighborhood Youth Corps, Project Head Start, and others—designed to attack directly the social problems often associated with crime.

Through such agencies as the Federal Bureau of Investigation, the Office of Law Enforcement Assistance, the Bureau of Prisons, and the Office of Manpower Development and Training, the Federal Government also offers comparatively limited financial and technical assistance to the police, the courts, and corrections authorities.

While the Commission is convinced State and local governments must continue to carry the major burden of criminal administration, it recommends a vastly enlarged program of Federal assistance to strengthen law enforcement, crime prevention, and the administration of justice.

The program of Federal support recommended by the Commission would be directed to eight major needs:

(1) State and local planning.

(2) Education and training of criminal justice personnel.

(3) Surveys and advisory services concerning the organization and operation of police departments, courts, prosecuting offices, and corrections agencies.

(4) Development of a coordinated national information system for operational and research purposes.

(5) Funding of limited numbers of demonstration programs in agencies of justice.

(6) Scientific and technological research and development.

(7) Development of national and regional research centers.

(8) Grants-in-aid for operational innovations.

The Commission is not in a position to recommend the exact amount of money that will be needed to carry out its proposed program. It believes, however, that a Federal program totaling hundreds of millions of dollars a year during the next decade could be effectively utilized. The Commission also believes the major responsibility for administering this program should lie within the Department of Justice.

The States, the cities, and the counties also will have to make substantial increases in their contributions to the system of criminal justice.

7. Responsibility for Change

Seventh, individual citizens, social-service agencies, universities, religious institutions, civic and business groups, and all kinds of governmental agencies at all levels must become involved in planning and executing changes in the criminal justice system.

The Commission is convinced that the financial and technical assistance program it proposes can and should be only a small part of the national effort to develop a more effective and fair response to crime.

In March of 1966, President Johnson asked the Attorney General to invite each Governor to form a State committee on criminal administration. The response to this request has been encouraging; more than two-thirds of the States already have such committees or have indicated they intend to form them.

The Commission recommends that in every State and city there should be an agency, or one or more officials, with specific responsibility for planning improvements in criminal administration and encouraging their implementation.

Planning agencies, among other functions, play a key role in helping State legislatures and city councils decide where additional funds and manpower are most needed, what new programs should be adopted, and where and how existing agencies might pool their resources on either a metropolitan or regional basis.

The planning agencies should include both officials from the system of criminal justice and citizens from other professions. Plans to improve criminal administration will be impossible to put into effect unless those responsible for criminal administration help make them. On the other hand, crime prevention must be the task of the community as a whole.

While this report has concentrated on recommendations for action by governments, the Commission is convinced that governmental actions will not be enough. Crime is a social problem that is interwoven with almost every aspect of American life. Controlling it involves improving the quality of family life, the way schools are run, the way cities are planned, the way workers are hired. Controlling crime is the business of every American institution. Controlling crime is the business of every American.

Universities should increase their research on the problems of crime; private social welfare organizations and religious institutions should continue to experiment with advanced techniques of helping slum children overcome their environment; labor unions and business can enlarge their programs to provide prisoners with vocational training; professional and community organizations can help probation and parole workers with their work.

The responsibility of the individual citizen runs far deeper than cooperating with the police or accepting jury duty or insuring the safety of his family by installing adequate locks—important as they are. He must respect the law, refuse to cut corners, reject the cynical argument that "anything goes as long as you don't get caught."

Most important of all, he must, on his own and through the organizations he belongs to, interest himself in the problems of crime and criminal justice, seek information, express his views, use his vote wisely, get involved.

In sum, the Commission is sure that the Nation can control crime if it will.

47

Doing Justice:
The Choice of Punishments

Andrew von Hirsch

Preface

In early 1971, the Field Foundation asked me to chair this study. There was growing disenchantment with prisons, and with the disparities and irrationalities of the sentencing process. Yet reformers lacked a rationale to guide them in their quest for alternatives, save for the more-than-century-old notion of rehabilitation that had nurtured the rise of the penitentiary. The purpose of our study was to consider afresh the fundamental concepts concerning what is to be done with the offender after conviction. The members of the Committee were chosen from a wide variety of disciplines, extending well beyond traditional correctional specialties. The project was staffed and organized during the spring and summer of 1971, and began its deliberations that fall.

This book is the product of the Committee's work over a four-year period, during which more than twenty working sessions were held. The conclusions herein represent the thinking of the group as it emerged in these discussions. All the members of the Committee subscribe to the report: that is, they support, on balance, its contentions (although not all of them necessarily agree with every conclusion, recommendation, or emphasis). A few of the members have furnished individual statements in the Appendix, noting additional thoughts or reservations.

We were aware that, in committee writings, coherence of argument can too easily be lost in the effort to accommodate divergent viewpoints. To avoid that pitfall, we charged one person with the task of weaving together into a single argument the different thoughts emerging in our discussions. We chose for that task our Executive Director, Andrew von Hirsch—who had already played a crucial role in our deliberations, both in innovating ideas for us to consider and in pressing us to refine our own thinking. In the writing task, he continued his dual function—as he both incorporated the themes of our discussions into the book and put his own philosophical stamp on the product in synthesizing them into a unified framework of ideas.

What emerges from our study is a conceptual model that differs considerably from the dominant thinking about punishment during this century. The conventional wisdom has been that the sentence should be fashioned so as to rehabilitate the offender and isolate him from society if he is dangerous. To accomplish that, the sentencer was to be given the widest discretion to suit the disposition to the particular criminal. For reasons which this book explains, we reject these notions as unworkable and unjust. We conclude that the severity of the sentence should depend on the seriousness of the defendant's crime or crimes—on what he *did* rather than on what the sentencer expects he will do if treated in a certain fashion.

From our conceptual model, there follow a number of important reforms which I might note briefly:

- Stringent limitation on incarceration as punishment. Only offenders convicted of serious offenses would be confined. Even for such offenders, the duration of confinement would be strictly rationed: instead of the ten-, fifteen-, and twenty-year sentences now imposed, we would allow very few sentences exceeding three years.

- Alternatives to incarceration for the bulk of criminal offenses—namely, for those which do not qualify as serious. These alternatives would not be rehabilitative measures but, simply and explicitly, less severe punishments. Warnings, limited deprivations of leisure time, and, perhaps, fines would be used in lieu of imprisonment.

- Sharply scaled-down penalties for first offenders. The sentence would depend not only on the seriousness of the crime of which the defendant now stands convicted but also on his record of prior offenses. Where there were no prior convictions, the sentence would be diminished substantially (except for the very serious crimes).

- Reduction in sentencing disparity. Offenders with similar criminal histories would receive similar punishments.

- Narrowing of sentencing discretion. The wide, uncharted discretionary leeway which sentencing judges now enjoy—and which contributes so much to disparity of sentence—would be discontinued. Instead, sentencing guidelines would be established that prescribe standardized penalties for offenses of different degrees of seriousness (with a limited amount of variation permitted for aggravating and mitigating circumstances).

- Elimination of indeterminacy of sentence. Now, when a defendant is sentenced to prison, he has no idea how long he will stay. That is decided at an indefinite future date by a parole board, which is supposedly expert in telling how well he is "adjusting." The uncertainty of the release date has been one of the worst agonies of prison life—with prisoners kept for years in suspense as to when they may finally leave. In our theory, there is no need for indeterminacy, as the sentence is to be based on the seriousness of the defendant's past offense or offenses—and that is knowable at the time of conviction. In the instances when an offender is to be confined, he will at least know for how long.

To this book's arguments and conclusions—which, I think, speak for themselves—I might add one observation of my own. It is possible, I believe, to create a fairer and less brutal penal system. Disparity can be reduced, intelligible standards for sentencing can be formulated, and severe punishments can be strictly limited.

What I do not think is a feasible goal, however, is to "solve the crime problem" by tinkering with penal methods. It is a strength of this report, I believe, that it offers its suggested reforms as a means of making the system fairer.

It does not offer illusory promises of eradicating crime, as reformers too often have done in the past.

It is surely an understatement that there is too much crime in this society and that crime causes terrible suffering. The criminal sanction, however, is a quite limited tool, and we should do well to remember its limitations. Judging from my own observations and from what I have learned in the course of this project, I doubt that changes in the sentencing and correctional system can work a dramatic reduction in crime rates. However enlightened or ingenious our penal methods become, this country probably will long be condemned to suffer the high crime rates now in evidence—given our history of domestic violence and the extent of disparities in wealth and social status. Certainly, the evidence does not suggest that further increases in the already inflated penalty levels will make a dent in today's crime rates. In increasing penalties—in order to appease our frustrations that previous increases didn't "solve the problem"—we long ago reached the point of diminishing returns. There are, as this book points out, important moral objections to any further inflation of penalties; in fact, a substantial deflation is essential as a matter of justice.

Today we have not only rampant crime but a gruesome system of punishment: harsh, arbitrary, and lacking in coherent rationale. The latter, at least, we can try to change. We can mitigate severities of punishment to levels more consistent with our pretenses of being a civilized society, and we can have some intelligible conception of why we are punishing. We can, I am convinced, mitigate the harshness and caprice of the penal system without losing whatever usefulness in crime prevention it now has. If we could accomplish this much, it would be no mean achievement.

From *Discretion and Sentencing Standards*

Wide discretion in sentencing has been sustained by the traditional assumptions about rehabilitation and predictive restraint. Once these assumptions are abandoned, the basis for such broad discretion crumbles. On our theory, the sentence is not a means of altering the offender's behavior that has to be especially suited to his "needs"; it is a deserved penalty based on the seriousness of his past criminal conduct. In order for the principle of commensurate deserts to govern, there *must* be standards specifying how much offenders receive for different crimes. Were questions of offenders' deserts left mainly to the discretion of individual judges, no consistent scale of penalties would emerge: one judge could treat certain offenses as serious and punish accordingly; another judge, having a different set of values, could deal with the same infractions as minor ones.

Without sentencing standards, moreover, there would be little to prevent the individual judge from making decisions on grounds other than commensurate deserts (e.g., basing his sentences on predictions of dangerousness if that was the sentencing theory he preferred).

General guidelines are suited for defining the comparative gravity of different categories of crimes and specifying the punishments which ordinarily apply to them. Some degree of flexibility is needed, however, to deal with the atypical cases— where the harmfulness of the particular offender's conduct or the extent of his culpability is substantially greater or less than is characteristic for that kind of offense.

We therefore suggest that each crime category be assigned a "presumptive sentence"—that is, a specific penalty based on the crime's characteristic seriousness. This would be the disposition for most offenders convicted of that crime. However, the judge should be authorized—within specified limits—to depart from the presumptive sentence if he finds aggravating or mitigating circumstances. Uniform treatment is thus provided for the unexceptional cases that make up the bulk of judges' caseloads, while still allowing variation in out-of-the-ordinary cases. (This would be a significant departure from the pattern of current sentencing statutes, where no specific penalty is fixed as the presumptive sentence and only outside limits—usually maxima, occasionally maxima and minima—are set.)

Using this approach, the sentencing system should have the following structure:

- Graded levels of seriousness would be established, and the guidelines would specify which offense categories belong on which seriousness levels.

- For each level of seriousness, a specific penalty—the presumptive sentence—would be prescribed. An offender convicted of a crime of that gradation of seriousness would ordinarily receive this sentence.

- For those offenders who had been convicted before, there would be a prescribed increase in the presumptive sentence, depending on the number and seriousness of the prior crimes.

- The judge would have authority to raise the penalty above or reduce it below the presumptive sentence, in cases where he finds there were special circumstances affecting the gravity of the violation[1] and where he specifies what these circumstances of aggravation or mitigation were. But such variations could not depart from the presumptive sentence by more than a prescribed amount. The limits on the permitted variations should be designed to preserve the basic ranking of penalties—and restrict overlaps in the severity of punishments for offenses of characteristically distinct seriousness. Intentional homicides, even under mitigating circumstances, should preserve their rank above, say, burglaries.

- General principles governing aggravation and mitigation should be set forth in the standards.[2] In our theory, only those special circumstances that affect the seriousness of the offender's crime could qualify.

To illustrate: Suppose a defendant were convicted of armed robbery for the second time. Were no special circumstances of aggravation or mitigation shown, he would receive the disposition which the guidelines specify as the presumptive sentence for a second armed robbery. Were there several participants in the robbery and his role in the crime a peripheral one, however, this could be a mitigating circumstance permitting a limited reduction below the presumptive sentence.

This scheme could be altered with experience. The number of gradations of seriousness could be increased or decreased, or the range of permitted variation widened or narrowed.

Any scheme—with more discretion or less—will lead to some inequities. Standards will operate arbitrarily in some instances, just as discretion risks disparities and bias. The most one can do is find a reasonable mix—to allow some degree of discretion structured by standards. Because our proposal would limit the permitted variation from the presumptive sentence, there will be some cases that fit badly—where the maximum permissible punishment seems too low, or the minimum permissible too high. We recognize this as a disadvantage, but we feel that the alternative of not having such limits would have worse consequences still.

Indeterminacy of sentence has been another outgrowth of the conventional assumptions: the timing of the offender's release, it was thought, should depend on his progress toward cure and the degree of continuing risk he represents. Our theory undercuts the need for indeterminacy. The commensurate-deserts principle looks to the past—to the seriousness of the defendant's crimes. Seriousness—the extent of the harm done or risked and the degree of the actor's culpability—can just as well be ascertained at the time of conviction as at an indefinite later date: for this purpose, as Marvin Frankel states, "whatever complexities and imponderables there are—and there are plenty . . . there is none that is not knowable on the day of sentencing."[3, 4]

The elimination of indeterminacy should he a welcome change to convicted offenders—who now suffer the agonies of not knowing how long their punishments will continue. When indeterminacy is eliminated, however, sentences will have to be scaled down. Many judges now impose long sentences in the expectation (not always fulfilled) that a parole board will permit earlier release. Under our approach, the initially imposed sentence would be the one actually served.

From *Arraying Penalties on a Scale*

How should penalties be arrayed on a scale, and what should the overall dimensions of the scale be? Our rationale calls for the construction of a scale of modest dimensions. Penalties, like currency, can become inflated; and in this country, inflation has reached runaway proportions. A substantial deflation must be undertaken.

The internal structure of the scale—that is, the ranking of penalties relative to each other—should be governed by the principle of commensurate deserts. A presumptive sentence should be prescribed for each gradation of seriousness—with limited discretionary authority to raise or lower it for aggravating or mitigating circumstances.[5] The scale should thus consist of an array of presumptive sentences, ranked in severity to correspond to the relative gravity of the offenses involved.

The weight given to prior offenses should expressly be built into the scale, with separate presumptive penalties set for first infractions and for repeated violations. Penalties for first offenses can then be scaled down substantially, for the reasons explained.

The scale should be two-dimensional. The dimensions should be: (1) the seriousness of the crime for which the offender currently stands convicted, and (2) the seriousness of his prior record. (The second factor is, in turn, composed of two variables: the number of his prior convictions and the seriousness of each. But a "seriousness of prior record" rating can readily be developed that combines both of these: the best "prior record" rating would be given someone never previously convicted, and the worst would be given someone with a record of more than one serious offense prior to the current conviction.)

There need be only a few gradations of seriousness, if refined discriminations in relative gravity are not practicable. (Conceivably, there could be as few as five categories—minor, lower intermediate, upper intermediate, lower-range serious, and upper-range serious.) An important advantage of a scale having two dimensions is that it has ample power to differentiate penalties, even if the number of gradations of seriousness is kept small. With five degrees of seriousness and four "prior record" gradations, for example, the scale would have room for twenty different penalty levels.[6]

A scale constructed in this fashion has the further advantage of simplicity. It would not be necessary to devise a lengthy sentencing code specifying a distinct presumptive penalty for each offense. The guidelines could simply list the few gradations of seriousness, and state which categories of crimes fall into which gradations. Knowing the offender's crime and his prior record, one could then consult these guidelines to obtain the applicable seriousness rating and seriousness-of-prior-record rating—and, having these, look up the indicated presumptive sentence on the two-dimensional scale.

The magnitude of the scale is the next concern. Should the scale, for example, run up to a highest penalty of five years' confinement? or fifteen? or fifty?

While regulating the scale's internal composition in detail, the principle of commensurate deserts sets only certain outer bounds on the scale's magnitude. The upper limit, as we have seen is: the scale may not be inflated to the point that the severe sanction of incarceration is visited on non-serious offenses. The lower limit is: the scale may not be deflated so much that the *most* serious offenses receive less-than-severe punishments. Within these limits, there remains considerable choice as to the scale's magnitude—where its overall deterrent effect may be taken into account. The difficulty is the absence of data: the deterrent impact of an untried scale of penalties is not known. It will be necessary to choose the scale's magnitude on the basis of surmise—on a best guess of what its deterrent effect is likely to be. Once a scale has been implemented, with its magnitude chosen in somewhat arbitrary fashion, it can then be altered with experience. If the magnitude selected leads to a substantial rise in overall crime rates,[7] an upward adjustment can be made (within the upper bounds of commensurate deserts). If no such rise results, it would then be appropriate to experiment with further reductions—diminishing the scale's magnitude in stages and observing whether any significant loss of deterrent effect occurs. (Such a step-by-step approach to reducing penalty levels should limit the risk of a large, unexpected jump in the crime rate.)

How, then, should one go about selecting a particular magnitude if the initial choice contains so much guesswork? We would suggest taking into account two factors touched upon earlier. One is our principle of "parsimony," that less intervention is preferred unless a strong case for a greater degree of intervention can be made. The other is the hypothesis of diminishing returns: once penalties reach modest levels of severity, further increases are unlikely to have much added deterrent usefulness.

With these two factors in mind, we recommend adoption of a scale whose highest penalty (save, perhaps, for the offense of murder) is five years[8]—with sparing use made of sentences of imprisonment for more than three years. If the hypothesis of diminishing returns is correct, the elimination of very long sentences could be undertaken without significant diminution of the overall deterrent usefulness of the system.[9, 10] (Moreover, the sentences, while shorter, would be more certain—and greater certainty could have some additional deterrent benefits. *All* persons convicted of sufficiently serious offenses would face a period of imprisonment—rather than the situation with today's discretionary system, where a few such persons receive lengthy sentences but many other serious offenders only get probation.)[11] Bearing in mind our principle of parsimony and the fact that any initial choice of magnitude is somewhat arbitrary, we think that keeping most prison sentences well below three years is a risk worth taking. If events proved us wrong and such a scale led to a substantial increase in the crime rate, the magnitude of scale could still be adjusted upward, subject to the desert-imposed limit that incarceration could be used only for offenses that were serious.

Notes

1. That is, if he found that either the harmfulness of the particular offender's conduct or the degree of his culpability was greater or less than usual for that kind of crime. In an assault, for example, it could be an aggravating factor that the physical injury was more than usually severe (increased harm); and a mitigating factor that the act was done in response to provocation by the victim (reduced culpability).
2. A statement of principles governing aggravation and mitigation would be preferable, we think, to a mere listing of aggravating and mitigating factors such as some European codes contain. (For a description of some such European codes, see G. O. W. Mueller and Fré Le Poole, "Appellate Review of Legal But Excessive Sentence: A Comparative Study," 21 *Vanderbilt L. Rev.* 411 [1988].)
3. An alternative, suggested by Norval Morris, is to have the final decision as to the amount of punishment (for serious offenses, it least) set a few weeks after the initial sentence. "The judge," Morris states, "imposes sentence at a time of high emotional response to the facts of the crime. Even within our grossly dilatory system of justice, the sentence follows closely upon the public narration of the criminal events, if not upon the commission of the crime." The delay would enable the decision to be made "in what one hopes will be a less punitive social atmosphere." However, this would not require indeterminacy. The decision still could be made at a determinate time knowable in advance and set fairly soon after conviction.
4. Marvin E. Frankel, *Criminal Sentences* (New York: Hill & Wang, 1972), p. 109.
5. See previous section on Discretion and Sentencing Standards.
6. With five seriousness gradations and four "poor record" gradations, the penalty scale would look something like this—with the *P*s representing the presumptive sentences.

Hypothetical Penalty Scale

	5	$P_{5,1}$	$P_{5,2}$	$P_{5,3}$	$P_{5,4}$ (most severe)
Seriousness level of most recent offense	4	$P_{4,1}$	$P_{4,2}$	$P_{4,3}$	$P_{4,4}$
	3	$P_{3,1}$	$P_{3,2}$	$P_{3,3}$	$P_{3,4}$
	2	$P_{2,2}$	$P_{2,2}$	$P_{2,3}$	$P_{2,4}$
	1	$P_{1,1}$ (least severe)	$P_{1,2}$	$P_{1,3}$	$P_{1,4}$
		1	2	3	4

Rating for seriousness of prior record
(based on number and seriousness of prior offenses)

The penalty in the lower left-hand corner ($P_{1,1}$) is that prescribed for someone convicted of a minor offense who had no prior record. It would be the least severe penalty on the scale. That in the lower right-hand corner ($P_{1,4}$) is for the person whose current offense is minor but who had a record of serious prior offenses. (This penalty would be somewhat severer, but not very much so, since the offense of which the defendant now stands convicted is still a minor one.) The penalty in the upper right-hand corner ($P_{5,4}$) is that prescribed for someone convicted of a very serious offense who already had a record of major crimes. It would be the severest on the scale. That in the upper left ($P_{5,1}$) would be for someone convicted of a serious crime who had no prior record. Thus the penalties would increase in severity as one goes from left to right and from bottom to top.

7. This measure—the impact on the crime rate—will reflect not only the scale's deterrent effect but (to the extent incarceration is utilized) its incapacitative effects as well.

   In determining the effect of the scales magnitude on the crime rate, it will be necessary to try to control for other variables that could have influenced the rates.

8. A five-year limit has been suggested before, on the basis of more traditional theories of sentencing. See, e.g., American Bar Association, Project on Minimum Standards for Criminal Justice, *Sentencing Alternatives and Procedures* (New York: American Bar Association, 1968), §2.1(d); NACCJSG, *Corrections*, Standard 5.2; *Model Sentencing Act*, §9.

9. Even if there is a diminishing *deterrent* effect of increasing severity, a larger magnitude will mean longer prison sentences—and hence some added *incapacitative* effect. But we are assuming that this added incapacitative effect will not be very large—at least if the use of incarceration is kept within the bounds of commensurate deserts.

   It has been recently claimed—by James Q. Wilson and Reuel Shinnar, among others—that dramatic reductions in crime can be achieved through isolating a lager proportion of offenders for longer periods. The evidence to support these claims remains in dispute, however.

10. James Q. Wilson, *Thinking about Crime* (New York: Basic Books, 1975), ch. 10; Shlomo and Reuel Shinnar, "A Simplified Model for Estimating the Effects of the Criminal Justice System on the Control of Crime," School of Engineering, City College of New York, 1974 (unpublished), cited in Wilson, *Thinking about Crime.*

    For a different view of incapacitative effects, see David F. Greenberg, "The Incapacitative Effect of Imprisonment: Some Estimates," Department of Sociology, New York University, 1975 (unpublished).

11. For statistics on the relatively low percentage of serious offenders now sent to prison, see e.g., Adrienne Weir, "The Robbery Offender," in *The Prevention and Control of Robbery*, ed. by Floyd Feeney and Adrienne Weir (Davis, CA: U. Cal. at Davis, Center for Administration of Criminal Justice, 1973) (percentage of convicted robbery offenders sent to prison).

48

Punishment and Social Structure
Georg Rusche   *Otto Kirchheimer*

In order to provide a more fruitful approach to the sociology of penal systems, it is necessary to strip from the social institution of punishment its ideological veils and juristic appearance and to describe it in its real relationships. The bond, transparent or not, that is supposed to exist between crime and punishment prevents any insight into the independent significance of the history of penal systems. It must be broken. Punishment is neither a simple consequence of crime, nor the reverse side of crime, nor a mere means which is determined by the end to be achieved. Punishment must be understood as a social phenomenon freed from both its juristic concept and its social ends. We do not deny that punishment has specific ends, but we do deny that it can be understood from its ends alone. By way of analogy, it might be noted that no one would dream of developing the history of military institutions or of a specific army out of the immutable purpose of such institutions.

Punishment as such does not exist; only concrete systems of punishment and specific criminal practices exist. The object of our investigation, therefore, is punishment in its specific manifestations, the causes of its changes and developments, the grounds for the choice or rejection of specific penal methods in specific historical periods. The transformation in penal systems cannot be explained only from changing needs of the war against crime, although this struggle does play a part. Every system of production tends to discover punishments which correspond to its productive relationships. It is thus necessary to investigate the origin and fate of penal systems, the use or avoidance of specific punishments, and the intensity of penal practices as they are determined by social forces, above all by economic and then fiscal forces.

Such an interpretation does not mean that the goals of punishment should be ignored, but rather that they constitute a negative conditioning factor. So long as society believes that the prospect and infliction of punishment can frighten people away from crime, methods are selected which shall have a frightening effect on the potential criminal. If one accepts that premise, furthermore, there is validity in the doctrine that deterrent penalties are a necessary evil, a tax on a socially protected good. If we consider the actual structure of modern society with all its differentiations, however, this principle means that to combat crime among the underprivileged social strata, the penalties must be of such a nature that the latter will fear a further decline in their mode of existence. It is obvious that this negative condition, this teleological

Source: Georg Rusche and Otto Kirchheimer, *Punishment and Social Structure*, copyright © 1939 Columbia University Press, New York. Reprinted with the permission of the publisher. Footnotes omitted.

side of the selection of penalties, will also find its concrete pattern in the transformations of the social structure.

When we return to the positive conditioning factors, we see that the mere statement that specific forms of punishment correspond to a given stage of economic development is a truism. It is self-evident that enslavement as a form of punishment is impossible without a slave economy, that prison labor is impossible without manufacture or industry, that monetary fines for all classes of society are impossible without a money economy. On the other hand, the disappearance of a given system of production makes its corresponding punishments inapplicable. Only a specific development of the productive forces permits the introduction or rejection of corresponding penalties. But before these potential methods can be introduced, society must be in a position to incorporate them as integrated parts of the whole social and economic system. Thus, if a slave economy finds the supply of slaves meager and the demand pressing, it cannot neglect penal slavery. In feudalism, on the other hand, not only could this form of punishment no longer be used but no other method was discovered for the proper use of the labor power of the convict. A return to the old methods, capital and corporal punishment, was therefore necessary, since the introduction of monetary fines for all classes was impossible on economic grounds. The house of correction reached a peak under mercantilism and gave great impetus to the development of the new mode of production. The economic importance of the house of correction then disappeared with the rise of the factory system. These problems form part of the subject matter of the present work. A particular aim is to show that the transition to modern industrial society, which demands the freedom of labor as a necessary condition for the productive employment of labor power, reduced the economic role of convict labor to a minimum.

Insofar as the basic economic needs of a commodity-producing society do not directly determine the creation and shaping of punishments, that is to say, insofar as convicts are not used to fill out the gaps in the labor market, the choice of methods is largely influenced by fiscal interests. Society struggles to keep to a minimum the *faux frais* which are tied up with the existence of crime and the need for criminal procedure. This is very clear in the penal practice of the feudal lords, which served them as a good source of income and involved punishments which cost nothing. That is not possible in modern society for obvious reasons. The fiscal approach has not disappeared, however, despite the fact that the rise of a state bureaucracy and the ''budgeting of crime'' have militated against it. We shall see that fiscal motives have shaped the typical punishment of modern society, the fine, both in its rise and in its form. With the decline of convict labor as an essential element in production and with the disappearance of the crudest forms of fiscalism in the nineteenth century, the social consciousness acquired a wider field of activity in developing punishments. Just how broad the field is, and what determines its limits, constitute a further problem of the present study.

Social Conditions and Penal Administration in the Later Middle Ages

In the history of penal administration several epochs can be distinguished during which entirely different systems of punishment were prevalent. Penance and fines were the preferred methods of punishment in the early Middle Ages. They were gradually replaced during the later Middle Ages by a harsh system of corporal and capital punishment which, in its turn, gave way to imprisonment about the seventeenth century.

1. Penance and Fines

The different penal systems and their variations are closely related to the phases of economic development. In the early Middle Ages there was not much room for a system of state punishment. The law of feud and penance was essentially a law regulating relations between equals in status and wealth. It assumed the existence of sufficient land to meet the requirements of a continually increasing population without lowering their standard of living. Although the population of western and central Europe increased rapidly after 1200, the social conditions of the lower classes remained relatively favorable, particularly on the land. The colonization of eastern European territories by the Germans, with its constant demand for man power, enabled the agricultural population of other provinces to escape the pressure to which the landlords sometimes subjected them. The possibility of migrating to the new towns provided a similar opportunity of escape through the attainment of personal freedom. These developments induced the landlords to treat their serfs with more care. The relations between the warrior-landlords and their serfs were of a traditional character, tantamount to a precisely determined legal relationship. These conditions tended to prevent social tension and to provide that cohesion which was characteristic of the period. Criminal law played an unimportant role as a means of preserving the social hierarchy. Tradition, a well-balanced system of social dependence, and the religious acknowledgment of the established order of things were sufficient and efficient safeguards. The main emphasis of criminal law lay on the maintenance of public order between equals in status and wealth. If, in the heat of the moment or in a state of intoxication, someone committed an offense against decency, accepted morality, or religion, or severely injured or killed his neighbor—violation of property rights did not count much in this society of landowners—a solemn gathering of free men would be held to pronounce judgment and make the culprit pay *Wergeld* or do penance so that the vengeance of the injured parties should not develop into blood feud and anarchy. An English proverb says: "Buy off the spear or bear it." The chief deterrent to crime was fear of the private vengeance of the injured party. Crime was looked upon as an act of war. In the absence of a strong central power the public peace was endangered by the smallest quarrel between neighbors, as these quarrels automatically involved relatives and servants. The preservation of peace was, therefore, the primary preoccupation of criminal law. As a result of its method of private arbitration, it performed this task almost entirely by the imposition of fines.

Class distinctions were manifested by differences in the extent of penance. Penance was carefully graded according to the social status of the evildoer and of the wronged party. Although this class differentiation affected only the degree of penance at first, it was at the same time one of the principal factors in the evolution of systems of corporal punishment. The inability of lower-class evildoers to pay fines in money led to the substitution of corporal punishment in their case. The penal system thus came to be more and more restricted to a minority of the population. This development can be traced in every European country. A Sion statute of 1338 provided a fine of twenty livres in assault cases; if the offender could not pay he was to receive corporal punishment by being thrown into prison and fed on bread and water until the citizens interceded or the bishop pardoned him. This statute not only illustrates the automatic character of the transformation of penance into corporal punishment, but it also shows that imprisonment was regarded as a form of corporal punishment at this time.

There were three main forces which militated against the private character of early medieval criminal law and which transformed it into an instrument of domination. One lay in the increasing prominence of the disciplinary function of the feudal lords against those who were in a state of economic subjection. The only limit to the exercise of this disciplinary power was a jurisdictional claim by another lord. The second factor was the struggle of the central authorities to strengthen their influence by extending their judicial rights. It is immaterial for the decline of private criminal law whether the tendency toward centralization was fostered by royalty, as in England and France, or by the princes, as in Germany. The third and most significant factor was the fiscal interest, common to authorities of every type. The administration of criminal law, as we shall see later, proved to be a fruitful source of income rather than a financial burden until comparatively recent times. The payment of those who administered the law or empowered others to do so in their name was financed by the legal costs imposed upon those under trial. Far from involving expenditures, the administration of justice brought in a considerable revenue in the form of confiscations and fines imposed in addition to, or instead of, the penance due the damaged party. The remark of Holdsworth, that the king's rights to escheats and forfeitures and to the chattels of felons sometimes seemed to interest the judges almost as much as the due maintenance of law and order, reveals the main consideration of the administrators of justice at the time. In Tuscany and upper Germany, in England and France, the attempt to extract revenue from the administration of criminal justice was one of the principal factors in transforming criminal law from a mere arbitration between private interests, with the representative of public authority simply in the position of arbitrator, to a decisive part of the public law.

2. Social Developments in the Middle Ages

The conditions of the lower classes began to become less favorable in Italy in the fifteenth century, and then in Germany, Flanders, and France. The decline in population caused by the Black Death all over Europe in the middle of the fourteenth century, with the possible exception of France, had been overcome. The urban population, which was steadily being replenished from the land, increased with particular rapidity. The number of downtrodden, unemployed, and propertyless people rose everywhere. Several concomitant causes were responsible for this change. One important factor seems to have been the exhaustion of the soil and decreasing yield. In earlier days, with a smaller population, it had frequently been possible to open up tracts of virgin land by draining marshes or burning down forests, so that previously cultivated lands could be left fallow for a very long period in order to give them an opportunity to regain their fertility. As the population increased, however, the newly won land became permanently occupied and the three-field system had to be introduced, whereby only a third of the land was allowed to lie fallow. The yield of the soil then began to decrease steadily in spite of the temporary rise in fertility from improved methods of cultivation.

At this stage, part of western Germany was turned into meadow land, while large estates in the east were devoted to the cultivation of grain which was then exported to the west by way of Danzig. This became possible when agriculture in the west could no longer meet the needs of the growing urban population and a demand arose for cheap imported grain. Originally, land in the east had little value. Because of the impossibility of marketing their products locally, landowners were glad to find small farmers who paid them a nominal rent for the right to till the soil. Now that markets were assured, however, agriculture became a paying proposition. Land became valuable and was closed to the newcomers.

Mercantilism and the Rise of Imprisonment

1. The Labor Market and the State

Methods of punishment began to undergo a gradual but profound change toward the end of the sixteenth century. The possibility of exploiting the labor of prisoners now received increasing attention. Galley slavery, deportation, and penal servitude at hard labor were introduced, the first two only for a time, the third as the hesitant precursor of an institution which has lasted into the present. Sometimes they appeared together with the traditional system of fines and capital and corporal punishment; at other times they tended to displace the latter. These changes were not the result of humanitarian considerations, but of certain economic developments which revealed the potential value of a mass of human material completely at the disposal of the administration.

The rise of larger and wealthier town populations created an increased demand for certain consumer's goods. The steadiness of the demand and the growth of the financial system led to a constant extension of markets; the possibility that the entrepreneur would not be able to dispose of his products became almost negligible. Merchants from the countries which had been least affected by the new treasure were able to sell at a great profit to those which had been more strongly affected. Countries which had established trade relations with the Levant and Asia were able to export the treasure on extraordinarily profitable terms. The conquest of colonies not only led to greater importation of precious metals, with all its economic consequences, but also to an extension of markets for mass-consumption goods.

The population, after the middle of the sixteenth century, failed to keep pace with this increase in the possibility of employment. In England and in France population growth was checked by the wars of religion and other internal disturbances, and it remained very small. The most extreme case was that of Germany. As a result of the Thirty Years' War, population declined in the middle of the seventeenth century at a rate comparable only to certain local drops during the Black Death. An estimated fall from eighteen million to seven million, given by some authors, may be exaggerated, but the more conservative estimates are impressive enough. Inama-Sternegg estimates 17.64 million in 1475, 20.95 in 1600–1620 and 13.29 in the middle of the seventeenth century. A slow increase did not set in again until the second half of the seventeenth century, and in many cases a century or more was needed to make up the loss. In the period before the Thirty Years' War real wages fell while population increased, but from 1620 to 1670 real wages rose. As Elsas has recently formulated the relationship, real wages throughout the sixteenth and seventeenth centuries followed a course contrary to the movement of prices and population; in other words, real wages corresponded to the supply of labor.

Spinoza's friend, De la Court, drew a vivid picture of Holland, where there was such a shortage of foreign labor that farmers were obliged to pay their hands at so high a rate that their own standard of living was very low in comparison with the laborer's. He describes similar conditions in the towns, where the apprentices and servants were less tractable and more highly paid than in any other country. We hear similar complaints from Germany because of the destructiveness of the Thirty Years' War. There was often so great a lack of the least skilled manual workers that some enterprises were forced to close down altogether. In Germany, as in Holland, there was a distinct improvement in the standard of living of both town and agricultural laborers. Various factors aggravated the situation still more. Labor was quite immobile in France and England, and even more so in Germany, divided as it was into innumerable sovereign states. Scarcity of labor and high wages in one region could coexist with low living standards in others, without any interaction resulting. This is in contrast to the situation in our present society, in which, as Hauser says, markets tend to act like vessels communicating with one another. Under the *ancien régime*, both the shortage of roads and the legislation prohibiting the circulation of grain blocked the tendency of prices to become interregionally uniform. A shortage which appears to be general may nevertheless spare some small local market cut off from the lines of communication. The fact that extensive local poverty could coincide with scarcity of labor was due in part to the existing poor laws, which forced paupers back to their native towns and villages even when there was not the slightest possibility of their finding work at home. These laws thus hindered the rational distribution of labor. Deterioration of local conditions, famine, war, and pestilence also drove newly trained hands back home almost automatically.

This lack of constancy in the labor supply and the low productivity of labor meant a tremendous change in the position of the owning classes. At the very time when the extension of markets and the increasing requirements of technical equipment called for more invested capital, labor became a relatively scarce commodity. Capitalists of the mercantilist period could obtain labor on the open market only by paying high wages and granting favorable working conditions. When one considers the diametrically opposed conditions of the previous century, one realizes what the change must have meant to the propertied classes. The beginning of the disappearance of the labor reserve was a severe blow to those who owned the means of production. Workers had the power to insist on radical improvements in their working conditions. Accumulation of capital was necessary for the expansion of trade and manufacture, and it was being severely hampered by the new wage and labor conditions. The capitalist was obliged to turn to the state for working capital and for the restriction of wages.

The ruling classes left no means unexplored in order to overcome the condition of the labor market. A series of rigorous measures restricting the liberty of the individual was introduced. These measures are mentioned in all the writings about the period, and they have been more or less thoroughly discussed. But they are often evaluated merely as curious historical anomalies, paradoxical and absurd aberrations of the *Polizeigeist* of the time which were wiped out by a subsequent evolution. Such a viewpoint fails to see their historical importance as measures aimed at the serious lack of labor that was threatening the very existence of the social order. . . .

The shortage of men eventually became so serious that the army had to be reinforced with criminals. In the great wars which England waged with France and Spain during the latter half of the eighteenth century it was difficult to find enough soldiers and sailors by any process of enlistment, impressment, or importation. Judges and gaolers were consulted about the fitness of convicts for military service, and the qualification was physical, not moral. The army came to be considered a kind of penal organization suited only for ne'er-do-wells, spendthrifts, black sheep, and ex-convicts. Countries even went so far as to take criminals over from other governments which did not know what to do with them. Avé-Lallemant writes that the record of almost every criminal of the eighteenth century contained instances of recruiting and subsequent desertion. This was a very practical means of avoiding prosecution until time and circumstances became more favorable.

Not only could the criminal cheat the gallows by enlistment, but he often received special treatment if he committed a crime while serving in the army. Special offenses of a military character were provided for in the statute books and very severe punishments were in law imposed upon soldiers guilty of any sort of crime, but in practice soldiers were frequently treated quite leniently. It was considered both unjust and inexpedient to execute a trained soldier or sailor. In 1626, for example, four soldiers were condemned to death in Breslau for breach of military discipline; then they were pardoned with the understanding that they would be placed in particularly dangerous positions in case of war. Such leniency naturally had a significant influence upon army morality and upon the general security of life and property. . . .

3. The Evolution of the Prison System

Carcer enim ad continendos homines non ad puniendos haberi debet (Prisons exist only in order to keep men, not to punish them). This was the dominant principle all through the Middle Ages and in the early modern period. Until the eighteenth century, jails were primarily places of detention before trial, where the defendants often spent several months or years until the case came to an end. The conditions defy description. The authorities usually made no provision for the inmate's upkeep, and the office of warden was a business proposition until the end of the eighteenth century. The wealthier prisoners were able to purchase more or less tolerable conditions at a high price. Most of the poor prisoners supported themselves by begging and by alms supplied by church fraternities founded for the purpose.

Sentences to imprisonment do occur, but only exceptionally. The largest group of prisoners not awaiting trial probably consisted of members of the lowest classes who were jailed for their inability to pay a fine. That led to a vicious circle. Men were imprisoned because they could not pay fines, and they could not leave the prison because they were unable to repay the jailer for maintenance. The first task of a liberated prisoner was frequently the repayment of his debt to the jailer, which explains why the conception of the sturdy beggar in the English Vagrancy Act of 1597 includes ex-convicts who beg for their fees. What created this appalling state of affairs was not so much intentional cruelty as the universally accepted administrative method of operating prisons on a commercial basis.

The idea of exploiting the labor powers of prisoners, as against the jailer's way of deriving income from them, already existed in the *opus publicum* of antiquity, a punishment for the lower classes which persisted through medieval times. The smaller states and towns saw in this institution a method comparable to the galleys for disposing of prisoners. They transferred their convicts as cheaply as possible to other public bodies who employed them in forced labor or military service. But the modern prison system as a method of exploiting labor and, equally important in the mercantilist period, as a way of training new labor reserves was really the outgrowth of the houses of correction.

A theoretical distinction can be drawn between a house of correction (*Zuchthaus*), a prison for duly sentenced thieves, pickpockets, and other serious offenders, and a workhouse (*Arbeitshaus*), an institution for the detention of beggars and similar people who had run foul of the police, until they mended their ways. In practice, however, the recognition of this distinction took a slow and uneven course.

The minutes of the Amsterdam town council of July 15, 1589, read:

> Whereas numerous wrongdoers, for the most part young persons, are arrested in the streets of this town daily, and whereas the attitude of the citizens is such that the juries hesitate to condemn such young persons to corporal punishment of life imprisonment, the mayors have asked whether it would not be advisable to set up a house and decree where vagabonds, wrongdoers, rogues, and the like, may be shut up and made to work for their correction.

No differentiation is proposed for the various categories of offenders. An administrative order sent to the managers of the *Tuchthuis* on March 27, 1598, ruled that persons not handed over by court sentence could be accepted only upon approval of the mayors. This was a mere matter of form, however, for the same order proceeded to instruct the regents to arrest all able-bodied persons found begging without the permission of the authorities. Real differentiation was hardly to be expected, for a respectable Amsterdam merchant would find little distinction between an idler arrested by the regents' officers and a thief duly tried and sentenced. Both were guilty of violating the principles of Calvinist ethics. When the council decided on November 12, 1600, to enlarge the establishment and to subdivide it according to new principles, the division was not made between condemned criminals and persons arrested for administrative reasons. The new establishment erected in 1603 housed the children whom their parents, respectable citizens, interned for correction. Elsewhere we find the same failure to divide condemned persons from other inmates. The rules of the Bremen house of correction of January 26, 1609, did draw a line between various categories, but there is no indication that they were actually handled separately.

The regulations of the Lübeck house drew no distinction, but it is worth noting that the administrators constantly refused to accept prisoners who had been condemned by the courts. Was this due to pedagogical considerations and practical objections or simply to a bureaucratic conflict between the administration of the houses and the council, as the correspondence of the council leads one to suspect? In opposition to the latter's policy of sending more and more criminals to the house, the administration wished to uphold its honorable character. The same situation developed in Hamburg, where the necessity of wider application of prison sentences led to the establishment of a spinning house for dishonorable persons in 1669. In Danzig, beggars, idlers, and persons interned by their relatives were separated from convicts as early as 1636 when the house of correction was instituted. In 1690, the courts proposed the erection of a special house for the incarceration and employment of serious offenders against whom the death sentence could hardly be applied and who could not be reformed by other punishments. These instances show that the practice of sending criminals to the houses of correction did occasionally lead to a separation. Since the exploitation of labor power was the decisive consideration, however, local conditions, and particularly population problems, usually determined whether the separation indicated for pedagogical reasons would be carried out in practice.

As late as the end of the eighteenth century it was common to combine the most widely different purposes in the same institution. The Pforzheim house, supported with such affection and care by the princes of Baden, was an orphanage, an institution for the blind, deaf, and dumb, a lunatic asylum, an infant welfare center, and a penal colony, all in one. The Leipzig house bore the following inscription: *Et improbis coercendis et quos deseruit sanae mentis usura custodiendis* (In order to correct the dishonest and to guard the lunatic). In 1780, only 148 of the 283 inmates of the Ludwigsburg institution were convicts; the rest were orphans, paupers, or lunatics. The same variety was to be found in the *Hôpitaux généraux*, although only minor criminals were included at first, because of the harsh sentences under the *ancien régime*. They, too, gradually took on the character of prisons, but without abandoning the practice of admitting the aged, the insane, and children.

The early form of the modern prison was thus bound up with the manufacturing houses of correction. Since the principal objective was not the reformation of the inmates but the rational exploitation of labor power, the manner of recruiting the inmates was not a central problem for the administration. Nor was it an important consideration in the matter of liberation. We have already seen how the period of detention in the case of young or newly trained inmates was determined solely by reference to the needs of the institution or its lessees. Valuable workers whose maintenance and training involved considerable expense must be retained as long as possible. The length of confinement was, therefore, arbitrarily fixed by the administrators in all cases except those voluntarily committed by their relatives. We hear of houses in Brandenburg where, in the absence of determinate sentences laid down in the judgment, some inmates were set free after a fortnight while other minor offenders were retained for years.

The gradual rise of imprisonment was implemented by the necessity for special treatment of women and for differentiation in the treatment of the various social strata. The majority of the women in the *Hôpitaux généraux*, for example, were guilty of crimes punished by galley slavery in the case of male offenders. Incarceration in a *Hôpital* or house of correction was often employed in order to spare members of the privileged classes the humiliation of corporal punishment or galley slavery. Thus, a son of a wealthy citizen of Bremen was tried for housebreaking in 1693 and sentenced to the house of correction for life at the request of his father. He was released on August 20, 1694, on condition that he go to India and not return. The *poena extraordinaria*, which allowed the judge arbitrarily to increase or decrease punishments, everywhere paved the way for a broad extension of the practice of incarceration in the houses of correction.

An especially interesting privilege is found in the decisions of the Tübingen faculty of law and in Württemberg decrees of the seventeenth and eighteenth centuries. The practice had developed of replacing capital or corporal punishment and banishment in the case of craftsmen by public works or confinement in houses of correction. Confirmed by several ducal decrees, this practice had two grounds. One grew out of considerations of social policy, as shown by an edict of 1620—a dishonorable judgment would have condemned the craftsman and his family to ruin by depriving him of the right to exercise his trade. The second motive was the desire to use trained craftsmen in the service of the state, and one decision explicitly justifies a sentence to public works by reference to the shortage of labor power. The same motive was responsible for the replacement of banishment by the houses of correction.

The legislator who exiles evil-doers is not a good householder, people argued, for every subject is a treasure and no sane man would throw a treasure away. Furthermore, it was becoming clear that banishment was the least effective method of suppressing crime. It merely led criminals to shift their fields of activity and had no more utility than present-day expulsion of aliens.

The tendency became rather general to replace even physical punishment by forced labor, and to retain only those forms which "gave old Adam as much pain as possible without doing the slightest damage to a single limb of his body." The necessity of keeping the state supplied with labor power was complicated by the desire not to withdraw labor power from the employers. As a result, economic considerations occasionally led to the opposite of the prevailing tendency, that is, to the retention of corporal punishment, especially in agricultural regions. An additional argument in the case of farm servants arose from the fact that imprisonment was no deterrent when their conditions were so bad. Knapp relates that in Upper Silesia as late as the end of the eighteenth century many punishments administered to farm laborers and gardeners failed to stop their stealing. When the master threatened them with hard labor, they would tell him to his face that they preferred ten years of that to one year on his lordship's estate. The landowners drew the conclusion that some form of punishment should be chosen for serfs which did not entail a loss to the landowners themselves. It must be emphasized that these were exceptional cases created by the social and political situation of the eastern farm laborer, which temporarily increased the value of corporal punishment.

The increasing proportion of sentences to houses of correction was brought about by judicial practice and by the sovereign's prerogative of confirmation and mercy, not by general rules. It was commonly, but mistakenly, assumed that the reduction and attenuation of statutory punishments would be very dangerous from the point of view of deterring prospective criminals. All laws carefully avoided too precise statements of the punishment in order not to weaken their efficacy. Thus, in as late a code as the *Allgemeine preussische Landrecht*, the Prussian government played hide and seek with the people, as Dilthey says. . . .

49

The Law of Vagrancy

William J. Chambliss

Legal Innovation: The Emergence of the Law of Vagrancy in England

There is general agreement among legal scholars that the first full fledged vagrancy statute was passed in England in 1349. . . . .

> Because that many valiant beggars, as long as they may live of begging, do refuse to labor, giving themselves to idleness and vice, and sometimes to theft and other abominations; it is ordained, that none, upon pain of imprisonment shall, under the colour of pity or alms, give anything to such which may labour, or presume to favour them towards their desires; so that thereby they may be compelled to labour for their necessary living.

It was further provided by this statute that:

> . . . every man and woman, of what condition he be, free or bond, able in body, and within the age of threescore years, not living in merchandize nor exercising any craft, nor having of his own whereon to live, nor proper land whereon to occupy himself, and not serving any other, if he in convenient service (his estate considered) be required to serve, shall be bounded to serve him which shall him require . . . And if any refuse, he shall on conviction by two true men, . . . be commited to gaol till he find surety to serve.

> And if any workman or servant, of what estate or condition he be, retained in any man's service, do depart from the said service without reasonable cause or license, before the term agreed on, he shall have pain of imprisonment.[1]

There was also in this statute the stipulation that the workers should receive a standard wage. In 1351 this statute was strengthened by the stipulation:

> An none shall go out of the town where he dwelled in winter, to serve the summer, if he may serve in the same town.[2]

Source: Social Problems, Vol. 12 (Summer, 1964), pp. 67–77. Copyright © 1964 by the Society for the Study of Social Problems. Reprinted by permission. Footnotes renumbered. The introductory paragraph which appears in the original article has been omitted.

NOTE: For a more complete listing of most of the statutes dealt with in this report the reader is referred to Burn, *The History of the Poor Laws.* Citations of English statutes should be read as follows: 3 Ed. 1. c. 1. refers to the third act of Edward the first, chapter one, etc.

By 34 Ed 3 (1360) the punishment for these acts became imprisonment for fifteen days and if they "do not justify themselves by the end of that time, to be sent to gaol till they do."

A change in official policy so drastic as this did not, of course, occur simply as a matter of whim. The vagrancy statutes emerged as a result of changes in other parts of the social structure. The prime-mover for this legislative innovation was the Black Death which struck England about 1348. Among the many disastrous consequences this had upon the social structure was the fact that it decimated the labor force. It is estimated that by the time the pestilence had run its course at least fifty per cent of the population of England had died from the plague. This decimation of the labor force would necessitate rather drastic innovations in any society but its impact was heightened in England where, at this time, the economy was highly dependent upon a ready supply of cheap labor.

Even before the pestilence, however, the availability of an adequate supply of cheap labor was becoming a problem for the landowners. The crusades and various wars had made money necessary to the lords and, as a result, the lord frequently agreed to sell the serfs their freedom in order to obtain the needed funds. The serfs, for their part, were desirous of obtaining their freedom (by "fair means" or "foul") because the larger towns which were becoming more industrialized during this period could offer the serf greater personal freedom as well as a higher standard of living. . . . The immediate result of these events was of course no surprise: Wages for the "free" man rose considerably and this increased, on the one hand, the landowners problems and, on the other hand, the plight of the unfree tenant. For although wages increased for the personally free laborers, it of course did not necessarily add to the standard of living of the serf; if anything it made his position worse because the landowner would be hard pressed to pay for the personally free labor which he needed and would thus find it more and more difficult to maintain the standard of living for the serf which he had heretofore supplied. Thus the serf had no alternative but flight if he chose to better his position. Furthermore, flight generally meant both freedom and better conditions since the possibility of work in the new weaving industry was great and the chance of being caught was small.[3]

It was under these conditions that we find the first vagrancy statutes emerging. There is little question but that these statutes were designed for one express purpose: to force laborers (whether personally free or unfree) to accept employment at a low wage in order to insure the landowner an adequate supply of labor at a price he could afford to pay. . . . This same conclusion is equally apparent from the wording of the statute where it is stated:

> Because great part of the people, and especially of workmen and servants, late died in pestilence; many seeing the necessity of masters, and great scarcity of servants, will not serve without excessive wages, and some rather willing to beg in idleness than by labour to get their living: it is ordained, that every man and woman, of what condition he be, free or bond, able in body and within the age of threescore years, not living in merchandize, (etc.) be required to serve. . . .

The vagrancy laws were designed to alleviate a condition defined by the lawmakers as undesirable. The solution was to attempt to force a reversal, as it were, of a social process which was well underway; that is, to curtail mobility of laborers in such a way that labor would not become a commodity for which the landowners would have to compete.

Statutory Dormancy: A Legal Vestige

In time, of course, the curtailment of the geographical mobility of laborers was no longer requisite. One might well expect that when the function served by the statute was no longer an important one for the society, the statutes would be eliminated from the law. In fact, this has not occurred. The vagrancy statutes have remained in effect since 1349. . . .

The next alteration in the statutes occurs in 1495 and is restricted to an increase in punishment. Here it is provided that vagrants shall be "set in stocks, there to remain by the space of three days and three nights, and there to have none other sustenance but bread and water; and after the said three days and nights, to be had out and set at large, and then to be commanded to avoid the town."[4]

The tendency to increase the severity of punishment during this period seems to be the result of a general tendency to make finer distinctions in the criminal law. During this period the vagrancy statutes appear to have been fairly inconsequential in either their effect as a control mechanism or as a generally enforced statute.[5] The processes of social change in the culture generally and the trend away from serfdom and into a "free" economy obviated the utility of these statutes. The result was not unexpected. The judiciary did not apply the law and the legislators did not take it upon themselves to change the law. In short, we have here a period of dormancy in which the statute is neither applied nor altered significantly.

A Shift in Focal Concern

Following the squelching of the Peasant's Revolt in 1381, the services of the serfs to the lord ". . . tended to become less and less exacted, although in certain forms they lingered on till the seventeenth century . . . By the sixteenth century few knew that there were any bondmen in England . . . and in 1575 Queen Elizabeth listened to the prayers of almost the last serfs in England . . . and granted them manumission."[6]

In view of this change we would expect corresponding changes in the vagrancy laws. Beginning with the lessening of punishment in the statute of 1503 we find these changes. However, instead of remaining dormant (or becoming more so) or being negated altogether, the vagrancy statutes experienced a shift in focal concern. With this shift the statutes served a new and equally important function for the social order of England. The first statute which indicates this change was in 1530. In this statute (22 H. 8. c. 12 1530) it was stated:

> If any person, being whole and mighty in body, and able to labour, be taken in begging, or be vagrant and can give no reckoning how he lawfully gets his living; . . . and all other idle persons going about, some of them using divers and subtle crafty and unlawful games and plays, and some of them feigning themselves to have knowledge of . . . crafty sciences . . . shall be punished as provided.

What is most significant about this statute is the shift from an earlier concern with laborers to a concern with *criminal* activities. . . . This is the first statute which specifically focuses upon these kinds of criteria for adjudging someone as a vagrant.

It is significant that in this statute the severity of punishment is increased so as to be greater not only than provided by the 1503 statute but the punishment is more severe than that which had been provided by *any* of the pre-1503 statutes as well.

For someone who is merely idle and gives no reckoning of how he makes his living the offender shall be:

> . . . had to the next market town, or other place where they [the constables] shall think most convenient, and there to be tied to the end of a cart naked, and to be beaten with whips throughout the same market town or other place, till his body be bloody by reason of such whipping[7]

But for those who use "divers and subtil crafty and unlawful games and plays," etc. the punishment is ". . . whipping at two days together in manner aforesaid."[8] For the second offense, such persons are:

> . . . scourged two days, and the third day to be put upon the pillory from nine of the clock till eleven before noon of the same day and to have one of his ears cut off.[9]

And if he offend the third time ". . . to have like punishment with whipping, standing on the pillory and to have his other ear cut off."

This statute (1) makes a distinction between types of offenders and applies the more severe punishment to those who are clearly engaged in "criminal" activities, (2) mentions a specific concern with categories of "unlawful" behavior, and (3) applies a type of punishment (cutting off the ear) which is generally reserved for offenders who are defined as likely to be a fairly serious criminal.

Only five years later we find for the first time that the punishment of death is applied to the crime of vagrancy. We also note a change in terminology in the statute:

> and if any ruffians . . . after having been once apprehended . . . shall wander, loiter, or idle use themselves and play the vagabonds . . . shall be eftfoons not only whipped again, but shall have the gristle of his right ear clean cut off. And if he shall again offend, he shall be committed to gaol till the next sessions; and being there convicted upon indictment, he shall have judgment to suffer pains and execution of death, as a felon, as an enemy of the commonwealth.[10]

It is significant that the statute now makes persons who repeat the crime of vagrancy a felon. During this period then, the focal concern of the vagrancy statutes becomes a concern for the control of felons and is no longer primarily concerned with the movement of laborers.

These statutory changes were a direct response to changes taking place in England's social structure during this period. We have already pointed out that feudalism was decaying rapidly. Concomitant with the breakup of feudalism was an increased emphasis upon commerce and industry. The commercial emphasis in England at the turn of the sixteenth century is of particular importance in the development of vagrancy laws. With commercialism came considerable traffic bearing valuable items. Where there were 169 important merchants in the middle of the fourteenth century there were 3,000 merchants engaged in foreign trade alone at the beginning of the sixteenth century.[11] England became highly dependent upon commerce for its economic support. Italians conducted a great deal of the commerce of England during this early period and were held in low repute by the populace. As a result, they were subject to attacks by citizens and, more important, were frequently robbed of their goods while transporting them. . . .

Such a situation not only called for the enforcement of existing laws but also called for the creation of new laws which would facilitate the control of persons preying upon merchants transporting goods. The vagrancy statutes were revived in order to fulfill just such a purpose. Persons who had committed no serious felony but who were suspected of being capable of doing so could be apprehended and incapacitated through the application of vagrancy laws once these laws were refocused so as to include ". . . any ruffians . . . [who] shall wander, loiter, or idle use themselves and play the vagabonds . . ."[12]

The new focal concern is continued in 1 Ed. 6. c. 3 (1547) and in fact is made more general so as to include:

> Whoever man or woman, being not lame, impotent, or so aged or diseased that he or she cannot work, not having whereon to live, shall be lurking in any house, or loitering or idle wandering by the highway side, or in streets, cities, towns, or villages, not applying themselves to some honest labour, and so continuing for three days; or running away from their work; every such person shall be taken for vagabond. And . . . upon conviction of two witnesses . . . the same loiterer (shall) be marked with a hot iron in the breast with the letter V, and adjudged him to the person bringing him, to be his slave for two years . . .

Should the vagabond run away, upon conviction, he was to be branded by a hot iron with the letter S on the forehead and to be thenceforth declared a slave forever. And in 1571 there is modification of the punishment to be inflicted, whereby the offender is to be "branded on the chest with the letter V" (for vagabond). And, if he is convicted the second time, the brand is to be made on the forehead. It is worth noting here that this method of punishment, which first appeared in 1530 and is repeated here with somewhat more force, is also an indication of a change in the type of person to whom the law is intended to apply. For it is likely that nothing so permanent as branding would be applied to someone who was wandering but looking for work, or at worst merely idle and not particularly dangerous *per se*. On the other hand, it could well be applied to someone who was likely to be engaged in other criminal activities in connection with being "vagrant."

By 1571 in the statute of 14 El. C. 5 the shift in focal concern is fully developed:

> All rogues, vagabonds, and sturdy beggars shall . . . be committed to the common gaol . . . he shall be grievously whipped, and burnt thro' the gristle of the right ear with a hot iron of the compass of an inch about; . . . And for the second offense, he shall be adjudged a felon, unless some person will take him for two years in to his service. And, for the third offense, he shall be adjudged guilty of a felony without benefit of clergy.

. . .The major significance of this statute is that it includes all the previously defined offenders and adds some more. Significantly, those added are more clearly criminal types, counterfeiters, for example. It is also significant that there is the following qualification of this statute: "Provided also, that this act shall not extend to cookers, or harvest folks, that travel for harvest work, corn or hay."

That the changes in this statute were seen as significant is indicated by the following statement which appears in the statute:

> And whereas by reason of this act, the common gaols of every shire are like to be greatly pestered with more number of prisoners than heretofore hath been, for that the said vagabonds an other lewd persons before recited shall upon their apprehension be committed to the said gaols; it is enacted . . .[13]

And a provision is made for giving more money for maintaining the gaols. This seems to add credence to the notion that this statute was seen as being significantly more general than those previously.

It is also of importance to note that this is the first time the term *rogue* has been used to refer to persons included in the vagrancy statutes. It seems, *a priori*, that a "rogue" is a different social type than is a "vagrant" or a "vagabond"; the latter terms implying something more equivalent to the idea of a "tramp" whereas the former (rogue) seems to imply a more disorderly and potentially dangerous person.

The emphasis upon the criminalistic aspect of vagrants continue in Chapter 17 of the same statute:

> Whereas divers *licentious* persons wander up and down in all parts of the realm, to countenance their *wicked behavior*; and do continually assemble themselves armed in the highways, and elsewhere in troops, *to the great terror* of her majesty's true subjects, *the impeachment of her laws*, and the disturbance of the peace and tranquility of the realm; and whereas many outrages are daily committed by these dissolute persons, and more are likely to ensue if speedy remedy be not provided. (Italics added)

With minor variations (*e.g.*, offering a reward for the capture of a vagrant) the statutes remain essentially of this nature until 1743. In 1743 there was once more an expansion of the types of persons included such that "all persons going about as patent gatherers, or gatherers of alms, under pretense of loss by fire or other casualty; or going about as collectors for prisons, gaols, or hospitals; all persons playing of betting at any unlawful games; and all persons who run away and leave their wives or children . . . all persons wandering abroad, and lodging in alehouses, barns, outhouses, or in the open air, not giving good account of themselves," were types of offenders added to those already included.

By 1743 the vagrancy statutes had apparently been sufficiently reconstructed by the shifts of concern to as to be once more a useful instrument in the creation of social solidarity. This function has apparently continued down to the present day England and changes from 1743 to the present have been all in the direction of clarifying or expanding the categories covered but little has been introduced to change either the meaning or the impact of this branch of the law. . . .

Vagrancy Laws in the United States

In general, the vagrancy laws of England, as they stood in the middle eighteenth century, were simply adopted by the states. . . . The control of criminals and undesirables was the *raison d'être* of the vagrancy laws in the U.S. This is as true today as it was in 1750. . . . Thus it appears that in America the trend begun in England in the sixteenth, seventeenth and eighteenth centuries has been carried to its logical extreme and the laws are now used principally as a mechanism for "clearing the streets" of the derelicts who inhabit the "skid roads" and "Bowerys" of our large urban areas. . . .

This analysis of the vagrancy statutes (and Hall's analysis of theft as well) has demonstrated the importance of "vested interest" groups in the emergence and/or alteration of laws. The vagrancy laws emerged in order to provide the powerful landowners with a ready supply of cheap labor. When this was no longer seen as necessary and particularly when the landowners were no longer dependent upon cheap labor nor were they a powerful interest group in the society the laws became dormant. Finally a new interest group emerged and was seen as being of great importance to the society and the laws were then altered so as to afford some protection to this group. These findings are thus in agreement with Weber's contention that "status groups" determine the content of the law.[14] The findings are inconsistent, on the other hand, with the perception of the law as simply a reflection of "public opinion" as is sometimes found in the literature. . . .[15]

Notes

1. 23 Ed. 3.
2. 25 Ed. 3 (1351).
3. Bradshaw, F., *A Social History of England*, p. 57.
4. 11 H. & C. 2 (1495).
5. As evidenced for this note the expectation that ". . . the common gaols of every shire are likely to be greatly pestered with more numbers of prisoners than heretofore . . ." when the statutes were changed by the statute of 14 Ed. c. 5 (1571).
6. Bradshaw, *op. cit.*, p. 61.
7. 22 H. 8. c. 12 (1530).
8. *Ibid.*
9. *Ibid.*
10. 27 H. 8. c. 25 (1535).
11. Hall, *op. cit.*, p. 21.
12. 2 H. 8. c. 25 (1535).
13. 14 Ed. c. 5. (1571).
14. M. Rheinstein, *Max Weber on Law in Economy and Society*, Harvard University Press, 1954.
15. Friedman, N., *Law in a Changing Society*, Berkeley and Los Angeles: University of California Press, 1959.

50

Two Models of the Criminal Process

Herbert L. Packer

. . . The kind of model we need is one that permits us to recognize explicitly the value choices that underlie the details of the criminal process. In a word, what we need is a *normative* model or models. It will take more than one model, but it will not take more than two.

Two models of the criminal process will let us perceive the normative antinomy at the heart of the criminal law. These models are not labeled Is and Ought, nor are they to be taken in that sense. Rather, they represent an attempt to abstract two separate value systems that compete for priority in the operation of the criminal process. Neither is presented as either corresponding to reality or representing the ideal to the exclusion of the other. The two models merely afford a convenient way to talk about the operation of a process whose day-to-day functioning involves a constant series of minute adjustments between the competing demands of two value systems and whose normative future likewise involves a series of resolutions of the tensions between competing claims.

I call these two models the Due Process Model and the Crime Control Model. In the rest of this chapter I shall sketch their animating presuppositions, and in succeeding chapters I shall show how the two models apply to a selection of representative problems that arise at successive stages of the criminal process. . . .

Values Underlying the Models

Each of the two models we are about to examine is an attempt to give operational content to a complex of values underlying the criminal law. As I have suggested earlier, it is possible to identify two competing systems of values, the tension between which accounts for the intense activity now observable in the development of the criminal process. The actors in this development—lawmakers, judges, police, prosecutors, defense lawyers—do not often pause to articulate the values that underlie the positions that they take on any given issue. Indeed, it would be a gross oversimplification to ascribe a coherent and consistent set of values to any of these actors. Each of the two competing schemes of values we will be developing in this section contains components that are demonstrably present some of the time in some of the

Source: From Herbert L. Packer, *The Limits of the Criminal Sanction.* Copyright © 1968 by Herbert L. Packer. Used with the permission of Stanford University Press, *www.sup.org*.

actors' preferences regarding the criminal process. No one person has ever identified himself as holding all of the values that underlie these two models. The models are polarities, and so are the schemes of value that underlie them. A person who subscribed to all of the values underlying one model to the exclusion of all of the values underlying the other would be rightly viewed as a fanatic. The values are presented here as an aid to analysis, not as a program for action.

Some Common Ground

However, the polarity of the two models is not absolute. Although it would be possible to construct models that exist in an institutional vacuum, it would not serve our purposes to do so. We are postulating, not a criminal process that operates in any kind of society at all, but rather one that operates within the framework of contemporary American society. This leaves plenty of room for polarization, but it does require the observance of some limits. A model of the criminal process that left out of account relatively stable and enduring features of the American legal system would not have much relevance to our central inquiry. For convenience, these elements of stability and continuity can be roughly equated with minimal agreed limits expressed in the Constitution of the United States and, more importantly, with unarticulated assumptions that can be perceived to underlie those limits. Of course, it is true that the Constitution is constantly appealed to by proponents and opponents of many measures that affect the criminal process. And only the naive would deny that there are few conclusive positions that can be reached by appeal to the Constitution. Yet there are assumptions about the criminal process that are widely shared and that may be viewed as common ground for the operation of any model of the criminal process. Our first task is to clarify these assumptions.

First, there is the assumption, implicit in the ex post facto clause of the Constitution, that the function of defining conduct that may be treated as criminal is separate from and prior to the process of identifying and dealing with persons as criminals. How wide or narrow the definition of criminal conduct must be is an important question of policy that yields highly variable results depending on the values held by those making the relevant decisions. But that there must be a means of definition that is in some sense separate from and prior to the operation of the process is clear. If this were not so, our efforts to deal with the phenomenon of organized crime would appear ludicrous indeed (which is not to say that we have by any means exhausted the possibilities for dealing with that problem within the limits of this basic assumption).

A related assumption that limits the area of controversy is that the criminal process ordinarily ought to be invoked by those charged with the responsibility for doing so when it appears that a crime has been committed and that there is a reasonable prospect of apprehending and convicting its perpetrator. Although police and prosecutors are allowed broad discretion for deciding not to invoke the criminal process, it is commonly agreed that these officials have no general dispensing power. If the legislature has decided that certain conduct is to be treated as criminal, the decision-makers at every level of the criminal process are expected to accept that basic decision as a premise for action. The controversial nature of the occasional case in which the relevant decision-makers appear not to have played their appointed role only serves to highlight the strength with which the premise holds. This assumption may be viewed as the other side of the ex post facto coin. Just as conduct that is not proscribed as criminal may not be dealt with in the criminal process, so conduct that has been denominated as criminal must be treated as such by the participants in the criminal process acting within their respective competences.

Next, there is the assumption that there are limits to the powers of government to investigate and apprehend persons suspected of committing crimes. I do not refer to the controversy (settled recently, at least in broad outline) as to whether the Fourth Amendment's prohibition against unreasonable searches and seizures applies to the states with the same force with which it applies to the federal government.[1] Rather, I am talking about the general assumption that a degree of scrutiny and control must be exercised with respect to the activities of law enforcement officers, that the security and privacy of the individual may not be invaded at will. It is possible to imagine a society in which even lip service is not paid to this assumption. Nazi Germany approached but never quite reached this position. But no one in our society would maintain that any individual may be taken into custody at any time and held without any limitation of time during the process of investigating his possible commission of crimes, or would argue that there should be no form of redress for violation of at least some standards for official investigative conduct. Although this assumption may not appear to have much in the way of positive content, its absence would render moot some of our most hotly controverted problems. If there were not general agreement that there must be some limits on police power to detain and investigate, the highly controversial provisions of the Uniform Arrest Act, permitting the police to detain a person for questioning for a short period even though they do not have grounds for making an arrest, would be a magnanimous concession by the all-powerful state rather than, as it is now perceived, a substantial expansion of police power.

Finally, there is a complex of assumptions embraced by terms such as "the adversary system," "procedural due process," "notice and an opportunity to be heard," and "day in court." Common to them all is the notion that the alleged criminal is not merely an object to be acted upon but an independent entity in the process who may, if he so desires, force the operators of the process to demonstrate to an independent authority (judge and jury) that he is guilty of the charges against him. It is a minimal assumption. It speaks in terms of "may" rather than "must." It permits but does not require the accused, acting by himself or through his own agent, to play an active role in the process. By virtue of that fact the process becomes or has the capacity to become a contest between, if not equals, at least independent actors. As we shall see, much of the space between the two models is occupied by stronger or weaker notions of how this contest is to be arranged, in what cases it is to be played, and by what rules. The Crime Control Model tends to de-emphasize this adversary aspect of the process; the Due Process Model tends to make it central. The common ground, and it is important, is the agreement that the process has, for everyone subjected to it, at least the potentiality of becoming to some extent an adversary struggle.

So much for common ground. There is a good deal of it, even in the narrowest view. Its existence should not be overlooked, because it is, by definition, what permits partial resolutions of the tension between the two models to take place. The rhetoric of the criminal process consists largely of claims that disputed territory is "really" common ground: that, for example, the premise of an adversary system "necessarily" embraces the appointment of counsel for everyone accused of crime, or conversely, that the obligation to pursue persons suspected of committing crimes "necessarily" embraces interrogation of suspects without the intervention of counsel. We may smile indulgently at such claims; they are rhetoric, and no more. But the form in which they are made suggests an important truth: that there *is* a common ground of value assumption about the criminal process that makes continued discourse about its problems possible.

Crime Control Values

The value system that underlies the Crime Control Model is based on the proposition that the repression of criminal conduct is by far the most important function to be performed by the criminal process. The failure of law enforcement to bring criminal conduct under tight control is viewed as leading to the breakdown of public order and thence to the disappearance of an important condition of human freedom. If the laws go unenforced—which is to say, if it is perceived that there is a high percentage of failure to apprehend and convict in the criminal process—a general disregard for legal controls tends to develop. The law-abiding citizen then becomes the victim of all sorts of unjustifiable invasions of his interests. His security of person and property is sharply diminished, and, therefore, so is his liberty to function as a member of society. The claim ultimately is that the criminal process is a positive guarantor of social freedom. In order to achieve this high purpose, the Crime Control Model requires that primary attention be paid to the efficiency with which the criminal process operates to screen suspects, determine guilt, and secure appropriate dispositions of persons convicted of crime.

Efficiency of operation is not, of course, a criterion that can be applied in a vacuum. By "efficiency" we mean the system's capacity to apprehend, try, convict, and dispose of a high proportion of criminal offenders whose offenses become known. In a society in which only the grossest forms of antisocial behavior were made criminal and in which the crime rate was exceedingly low, the criminal process might require the devotion of many more man-hours of police, prosecutorial, and judicial time per case than ours does, and still operate with tolerable efficiency. A society that was prepared to increase even further the resources devoted to the suppression of crime might cope with a rising crime rate without sacrifice of efficiency while continuing to maintain an elaborate and time-consuming set of criminal processes. However, neither of these possible characteristics corresponds with social reality in this country. We use the criminal sanction to cover an increasingly wide spectrum of behavior thought to be antisocial, and the amount of crime is very high indeed, although both level and trend are hard to assess.[2] At the same time, although precise measures are not available, it does not appear that we are disposed in the public sector of the economy to increase very drastically the quantity, much less the quality, of the resources devoted to the suppression of criminal activity through the operation of the criminal process. These factors have an important bearing on the criteria of efficiency, and therefore on the nature of the Crime Control Model.

The model, in order to operate successfully, must produce a high rate of apprehension and conviction, and must do so in a context where the magnitudes being dealt with are very large and the resources for dealing with them are very limited. There must then be a premium on speed and finality. Speed, in turn, depends on informality and on uniformity; finality depends on minimizing the occasions for challenge. The process must not be cluttered up with ceremonious rituals that do not advance the progress of a case. Facts can be established more quickly through interrogation in a police station than through the formal process of examination and cross-examination in a court. It follows that extra-judicial processes should be preferred to judicial processes, informal operations to formal ones. But informality is not enough; there must also be uniformity. Routine, stereotyped procedures are essential if large numbers are being handled. The model that will operate successfully on these presuppositions must be an administrative, almost a managerial, model. The image that comes to mind is an assembly-line conveyor belt down which moves an endless stream of cases, never stopping, carrying the cases to workers who stand at fixed stations and who perform on each case as it comes by the same small but essential operation that brings it one step closer to being a finished product, or, to exchange the metaphor for the reality, a closed file. The criminal process, in this model, is seen as a screening process in which each successive stage—pre-arrest investigation, arrest, post-arrest investigation, preparation for trial, trial or entry of plea, conviction, disposition—involves a series of routinized operations whose success is gauged primarily by their tendency to pass the case along to a successful conclusion.

What is a successful conclusion? One that throws off at an early stage those cases in which it appears unlikely that the person apprehended is an offender and then secures, as expeditiously as possible, the conviction of the rest, with a minimum of occasions for challenge, let alone post-audit. By the application of administrative expertness, primarily that of the police and prosecutors, an early determination of probable innocence or guilt emerges. Those who are probably innocent are screened out. Those who are probably guilty are passed quickly through the remaining stages of the process. The key to the operation of the model regarding those who are not screened out is what I shall call a presumption of guilt. The concept requires some explanation, since it may appear startling to assert that what appears to be the precise converse of our generally accepted ideology of a presumption of innocence can be an essential element of a model that does correspond in some respects to the actual operation of the criminal process.

The presumption of guilt is what makes it possible for the system to deal efficiently with large numbers, as the Crime Control Model demands. The supposition is that the screening processes operated by police and prosecutors are reliable indicators of probable guilt. Once a man has been arrested and investigated without being found to be probably innocent, or, to put it differently, once a determination has been made that there is enough evidence of guilt to permit holding him for further action, then all subsequent activity directed toward him is based on the view that he is probably guilty. The precise point at which this occurs will vary from case to case; in many cases it will occur as soon as the suspect is arrested, or even before, if the evidence of probable guilt that has come to the attention of the authorities is sufficiently strong. But in any case the presumption of guilt will begin to operate well before the "suspect" becomes a "defendant."

The presumption of guilt is not, of course, a thing. Nor is it even a rule of law in the usual sense. It simply is the consequence of a complex of attitudes, a mood. If there is confidence in the reliability of informal administrative fact-finding activities that take place in the early stages of the criminal process, the remaining stages of the process can be relatively perfunctory without any loss in operating efficiency. The presumption of guilt, as it operates in the Crime Control Model, is the operational expression of that confidence.

It would be a mistake to think of the presumption of guilt as the opposite of the presumption of innocence that we are so used to thinking of as the polestar of the criminal process and that, as we shall see, occupies an important position in the Due Process Model. The presumption of innocence is not its opposite; it is irrelevant to the presumption of guilt; the two concepts are different rather than opposite ideas. The difference can perhaps be epitomized by an example. A murderer, for reasons best known to himself, chooses to shoot his victim in plain view of a large number of people. When the police arrive, he hands them his gun and says, ''I did it and I'm glad.'' His account of what happened is corroborated by several eyewitnesses. He is placed under arrest and led off to jail. Under these circumstances, which may seem extreme but which in fact characterize with rough accuracy the evidentiary situation in a large proportion of criminal cases, it would be plainly absurd to maintain that more probably than not the suspect did not commit the killing. But that is not what the presumption of innocence means. It means that until there has been an adjudication of guilt by an authority legally competent to make such an adjudication, the suspect is to be treated, for reasons that have nothing whatever to do with the probable outcome of the case, as if his guilt is an open question.

The presumption of innocence is a direction to officials about how they are to proceed, not a prediction of outcome. The presumption of guilt, however, is purely and simply a prediction of outcome. The presumption of innocence is, then, a direction to the authorities to ignore the presumption of guilt in their treatment of the suspect. It tells them, in effect, to close their eyes to what will frequently seem to be factual probabilities. The reasons why it tells them this are among the animating presuppositions of the Due Process Model, and we will come to them shortly. It is enough to note at this point that the presumption of guilt is descriptive and factual; the presumption of innocence is normative and legal. The pure Crime Control Model has no truck with the presumption of innocence, although its real-life emanations are, as we shall see, brought into uneasy compromise with the dictates of this dominant ideological position. In the presumption of guilt this model finds a factual predicate for the position that the dominant goal of repressing crime can be achieved through highly summary processes without any great loss of efficiency (as previously defined), because of the probability that, in the run of cases, the preliminary screening processes operated by the police and the prosecuting officials contain adequate guarantees of reliable fact-finding. Indeed, the model takes an even stronger position. It is that subsequent processes, particularly those of a formal adjudicatory nature, are unlikely to produce as reliable fact-finding as the expert administrative process that precedes them is capable of. The criminal process thus must put special weight on the quality of administrative fact-finding. It becomes important, then, to place as few restrictions as possible on the character of the administrative fact-finding processes and to limit restrictions to such as enhance reliability, excluding those designed for other purposes. As we shall see, this view of restrictions on administrative fact-finding is a consistent theme in the development of the Crime Control Model.

In this model, as I have suggested, the center of gravity for the process lies in the early, administrative fact-finding stages. The complementary proposition is that the subsequent stages are relatively unimportant and should be truncated as much as possible. This, too, produces tensions with presently dominant ideology. The pure Crime Control Model has very little use for many conspicuous features of the adjudicative process, and in real life works out a number of ingenious compromises with them. Even in the pure model, however, there have to be devices for dealing with the suspect after the preliminary screening process has resulted in a determination of probable guilt. The focal device, as we shall see, is the plea of guilty; through its use, adjudicative fact-finding is reduced to a minimum. It might be said of the Crime Control Model that, when reduced to its barest essentials and operating at its most successful pitch, it offers two possibilities: an administrative fact-finding process leading (1) to exoneration of the suspect or (2) to the entry of a plea of guilty.

Due Process Values

If the Crime Control Model resembles an assembly line, the Due Process Model looks very much like an obstacle course. Each of its successive stages is designed to present formidable impediments to carrying the accused any further along in the process. Its ideology is not the converse of that underlying the Crime Control Model. It does not rest on the idea that it is not socially desirable to repress crime, although critics of its application have been known to claim so. Its ideology is composed of a complex of ideas, some of them based on judgments about the efficacy of crime control devices, others having to do with quite different considerations. The ideology of due process is far more deeply impressed on the formal structure of the law than is the ideology of crime control; yet an accurate tracing of the strands that make it up is strangely difficult. What follows is only an attempt at an approximation.

The Due Process Model encounters its rival on the Crime Control Model's own ground in respect to the reliability of fact-finding processes. The Crime Control Model, as we have suggested, places heavy reliance on the ability of investigative and prosecutorial officers, acting in an informal setting in which their distinctive skills are given full sway, to elicit and reconstruct a tolerably accurate account of what actually took place in an alleged criminal event. The Due Process Model rejects this premise and substitutes for it a view of informal, nonadjudicative fact-finding that stresses the possibility of error. People are notoriously poor observers of disturbing events—the more emotion-arousing the context, the greater the possibility that recollection will be incorrect; confessions and admissions by persons in police custody may be induced by physical or psychological coercion so that the police end up hearing what the suspect thinks they want to hear rather than the truth; witnesses may be animated by a bias or interest that no one would trouble to discover except one specially charged with protecting the interests of the accused (as the police are not). Considerations of this kind all lead to a rejection of informal fact-finding processes as definitive of factual guilt and to an insistence of formal, adjudicative, adversary fact-finding processes in which the factual case against the accused is publicly heard by an impartial tribunal and is evaluated only after the accused has had a full opportunity to discredit the case against him. Even then, the distrust of fact-finding processes that animates the Due Process Model is not dissipated. The possibilities of human error being what they are, further scrutiny is necessary, or at least must be available, in case facts have been overlooked or suppressed in the heat of battle. How far this subsequent scrutiny must be available is a hotly controverted issue today. In the pure Due Process Model the answer would be: at least as long as there is an allegation of factual error that has not received an adjudicative hearing in a fact-finding context. The demand for finality is thus very low in the Due Process Model.

This strand of due process ideology is not enough to sustain the model. If all that were at issue between the two models was a series of questions about the reliability of fact-finding processes, we would have but one model of the criminal process, the nature of whose constituent elements would pose questions of fact not of value. Even if the discussion is confined, for the moment, to the question of reliability, it is apparent that more is at stake than simply an evaluation of what kinds of fact-finding processes, alone or in combination, are likely to produce the most nearly reliable results. The stumbling block is this: how much reliability is compatible with efficiency? Granted that informal fact-finding will make some mistakes that can be remedied if backed up by adjudicative fact-finding, the desirability of providing this backup is not affirmed or negated by factual demonstrations or predictions that the increase in reliability will be x percent or x plus n percent. It still remains to ask how much weight is to be given to the competing demands of reliability (a high degree of probability in each case that factual guilt has been accurately determined) and efficiency (expeditious handling of the large numbers of cases that the process ingests). The Crime Control Model is more optimistic about the improbability of error in a significant number of cases; but it is also, though only in part therefore, more tolerant about the amount of error that it will put up with. The Due Process Model insists on the prevention and elimination of mistakes to the extent possible; the Crime Control Model accepts the probability of mistakes up to the level at which they interfere with the goal of repressing crime, either because too many guilty people are escaping or, more subtly, because general awareness of the unreliability of the process leads to a decrease in the deterrent efficacy of the criminal law. In this view, reliability and efficiency are not polar opposites but rather complementary characteristics. The system is reliable *because* efficient; reliability becomes a matter of independent concern only when it becomes so attenuated as to impair efficiency. All of this the Due Process Model rejects. If efficiency demands shortcuts around reliability, then absolute efficiency must be rejected. The aim of the process is at least as much to protect the factually innocent as it is to convict the factually guilty. It is a little like quality control in industrial technology: tolerable deviation from standard varies with the importance of conformity to standard in the destined uses of the product. The Due Process Model resembles a factory that has to devote a substantial part of its input to quality control. This necessarily cuts down on quantitative output.

All of this is only the beginning of the ideological difference between the two models. The Due Process Model could disclaim any attempt to provide enhanced reliability for the fact-finding process and still produce a set of institutions and processes that would differ sharply from those demanded by the Crime Control Model. Indeed, it may not be too great an oversimplification to assert that in point of historical development the doctrinal pressures emanating from the demands of the Due Process Model have tended to evolve from an original matrix of concern for the maximization of reliability into values quite different and more far-reaching. These values can be expressed in, although not adequately described by, the concept of the primacy of the individual and the complementary concept of limitation on official power.

The combination of stigma and loss of liberty that is embodied in the end result of the criminal process is viewed as being the heaviest deprivation that government can inflict on the individual. Furthermore, the processes that culminate in these highly afflictive sanctions are seen as in themselves coercive, restricting, and demeaning. Power is always subject to abuse—sometimes subtle, other times, as in the criminal process, open and ugly. Precisely because of its potency in subjecting the individual to the coercive power of the state, the criminal process must, in this model, be subjected to controls that prevent it from operating with maximal efficiency. According to this ideology, maximal efficiency means maximal tyranny. And, although no one would assert that minimal efficiency means minimal tyranny, the proponents of the Due Process Model would accept with considerable equanimity a substantial diminution in the efficiency with which the criminal process operates in the interest of preventing official oppression of the individual.

The most modest-seeming but potentially far-reaching mechanism by which the Due Process Model implements these antiauthoritarian values is the doctrine of legal guilt. According to this doctrine, a person is not to be held guilty of crime merely on a showing that in all probability, based upon reliable evidence, he did factually what he is said to have done. Instead, he is to be held guilty if and only if these factual determinations are made in procedurally regular fashion and by authorities acting within competences duly allocated to them. Furthermore, he is not to be held guilty, even though the factual determination is or might be adverse to him, if various rules designed to protect him and to safeguard the integrity of the process are not given effect: the tribunal that convicts him must have the power to deal with his kind of case ("jurisdiction") and must be geographically appropriate ("venue"); too long a time must not have elapsed since the offense was committed ("statute of limitations"); he must not have been previously convicted or acquitted of the same or a substantially similar offense ("double jeopardy"); he must not fall within a category of persons, such as children or the insane, who are legally immune to conviction ("criminal responsibility"); and so on. None of these requirements has anything to do with the factual question of whether the person did or did not engage in the conduct that is charged as the offense against him; yet favorable answers to any of them will mean that he is legally innocent. Wherever the competence to make adequate factual determinations lies, it is apparent that only a tribunal that is aware of these guilt-defeating doctrines and is willing to apply them can be viewed as competent to make determinations of legal guilt. The police and the prosecutors are ruled out by lack of competence, in the first instance, and by lack of assurance of willingness, in the second. Only an impartial tribunal can be trusted to make determinations of legal as opposed to factual guilt.

In this concept of legal guilt lies the explanation for the apparently quixotic presumption of innocence of which we spoke earlier. A man who, after police investigation, is charged with having committed a crime can hardly be said to be presumptively innocent, if what we mean is factual innocence. But if what we mean is that it has yet to be determined if any of the myriad legal doctrines that serve in one way or another the end of limiting official power through the observance of certain substantive and procedural regularities may be appropriately invoked to exculpate the accused man, it is apparent that as a matter of prediction it cannot be said with confidence that more probably than not he will be found guilty.

Beyond the question of predictability this model posits a functional reason for observing the presumption of innocence: by forcing the state to prove its case against the accused in an adjudicative context, the presumption of innocence serves to force into play all the qualifying and disabling doctrines that limit the use of the criminal sanction against the individual, thereby enhancing his opportunity to secure a favorable outcome. In this sense, the presumption of innocence may be seen to operate as a kind of self-fulfilling prophecy. By opening up a procedural situation that permits the successful assertion of defenses having nothing to do with factual guilt, it vindicates the proposition that the factually guilty may nonetheless be legally innocent and should therefore be given a chance to qualify for that kind of treatment.

The possibility of legal innocence is expanded enormously when the criminal process is viewed as the appropriate forum for correcting its own abuses. This notion may well account for a greater amount of the distance between the two models than any other. In theory the Crime Control Model can tolerate rules that forbid illegal arrests, unreasonable searches, coercive interrogations, and the like. What it cannot tolerate is the vindication of those rules in the criminal process itself through the exclusion of evidence illegally obtained or through the reversal of convictions in cases where the criminal process has breached the rules laid down for its observance. And the Due Process Model, although it may in the first instance be addressed to the maintenance of reliable fact-finding techniques, comes eventually to incorporate prophylactic and deterrent rules that result in the release of the factually guilty even in cases in which blotting out the illegality would still leave an adjudicative fact-finder convinced of the accused person's guilt. Only by penalizing errant police and prosecutors within the criminal process itself can adequate pressure be maintained, so the argument runs, to induce conformity with the Due Process Model.

Another strand in the complex of attitudes underlying the Due Process Model is the idea—itself a shorthand statement for a complex of attitudes—of equality. This notion has only recently emerged as an explicit basis for pressing the demands of the Due Process Model, but it appears to represent, at least in its potential, a most powerful norm for influencing official conduct. Stated most starkly, the ideal of equality holds that "there can be no equal justice where the kind of trial a man gets depends on the amount of money he has."[3] The factual predicate underlying this assertion is that there are gross inequalities in the financial means of criminal defendants as a class, that in an adversary system of criminal justice an effective defense is largely a function of the resources that can be mustered on behalf of the accused, and that the very large proportion of criminal defendants who are, operationally speaking, "indigent" will thus be denied an effective defense. This factual premise has been strongly reinforced by recent studies that in turn have been both a cause and an effect of an increasing emphasis upon norms for the criminal process based on the premise.

The norms derived from the premise do not take the form of an insistence upon governmental responsibility to provide literally equal opportunities for all criminal defendants to challenge the process. Rather, they take as their point of departure the notion that the criminal process, initiated as it is by government and containing as it does the likelihood of severe deprivations at the hands of government, imposes some kind of public obligation to ensure that financial inability does not destroy the capacity of an accused to assert what may be meritorious challenges to the processes being invoked against him. At its most gross, the norm of equality would act to prevent situations in which financial inability forms an absolute barrier to the assertion of a right that is in theory generally available, as where there is a right to appeal that is, however, effectively conditional upon the filing of a trial transcript obtained at the defendant's expense. Beyond this, it may provide the basis for a claim whenever the system theoretically makes some kind of challenge available to an accused who has the means to press it. If, for example, a defendant who is adequately represented has the opportunity to prevent the case against him from coming to the trial stage by forcing the state to its proof in a preliminary hearing, the norm of equality may be invoked to assert that the same kind of opportunity must be available to others as well. In a sense the system as it functions for the small minority whose resources permit them to exploit all its defensive possibilities provides a benchmark by which its functioning in all other cases is to be tested: not, perhaps, to guarantee literal identity but rather to provide a measure of whether the process as a whole is recognizably of the same general order. The demands made by a norm of this kind are likely by their very nature to be quite sweeping. Although the norm's imperatives may be initially limited to determining whether in a particular case the accused was injured or prejudiced by his relative inability to make an appropriate challenge, the norm of equality very quickly moves to another level on which the demand is that the process in general be adapted to minimize discriminations rather than that a mere series of post hoc determinations of discrimination be made or makeable.

It should be observed that the impact of the equality norm will vary greatly depending upon the point in time at which it is introduced into a model of the criminal process. If one were starting from scratch to decide how the process ought to work, the norm of equality would have nothing very important to say on such questions as, for example, whether an accused should have the effective assistance of counsel in deciding whether to enter a plea of guilty. One could decide, on quite independent considerations, that it is or is not a good thing to afford that facility to the generality of persons accused of crime. But the impact of the equality norm becomes far greater when it is brought to bear on a process whose contours have already been shaped. If our model of the criminal process affords defendants who are in a financial position to do so the right to consult a lawyer before entering a plea, then the equality norm exerts powerful pressure to provide such an opportunity to all defendants and to regard the failure to do so as a malfunctioning of the process of whose consequences the accused is entitled to be relieved. In a sense, this has been the role of the equality norm in affecting the real-world criminal process. It has made its appearance on the scene comparatively late, and has therefore encountered a system in which the relative financial inability of most persons accused of crime results in treatment very different from that accorded the small minority of the financially capable. For this reason, its impact has already been substantial and may be expected to be even more so in the future.

There is a final strand of thought in the Due Process Model that is often ignored but that needs to be candidly faced if thought on the subject is not to be obscured. This is a mood of skepticism about the morality and utility of the criminal sanction, taken either as a whole or in some of its applications. The subject is a large and complicated one, comprehending as it does much of the intellectual history of our times. It is properly the subject of another essay altogether. To put the matter briefly, one cannot improve upon the statement by Professor Paul Bator:

> In summary we are told that the criminal law's notion of just condemnation and punishment is a cruel hypocrisy visited by a smug society on the psychologically and economically crippled; that its premise of a morally autonomous will with at least some measure of choice whether to comply with the values expressed in a penal code is unscientific and outmoded; that its reliance on punishment as an educational and deterrent agent is misplaced, particularly in the case of the very members of society most likely to engage in criminal conduct; and that its failure to provide for individualized and humane rehabilitation of offenders is inhuman and wasteful.[4]

This skepticism, which may be fairly said to be widespread among the most influential and articulate contemporary leaders of informed opinion, leads to an attitude toward the processes of the criminal law that, to quote Mr. Bator again, engenders "a peculiar receptivity toward claims of injustice which arise within the traditional structure of the system itself; fundamental disagreement and unease about the very bases of the criminal law has, inevitably, created acute pressure at least to expand and liberalize those of its processes and doctrines which serve to make more tentative its judgments or limit its power." In short, doubts about the ends for which power is being exercised create pressure to limit the discretion with which that power is exercised.

The point need not be pressed to the extreme of doubts about or rejection of the premises upon which the criminal sanction in general rests. Unease may be stirred simply by reflection on the variety of uses to which the criminal sanction is put and by a judgment that an increasingly large proportion of those uses may represent an unwise invocation of so extreme a sanction. It would be an interesting irony if doubts about the propriety of certain uses of the criminal sanction prove to contribute to a restrictive trend in the criminal process that in the end requires a choice among uses and finally an abandonment of some of the very uses that stirred the original doubts, but for a reason quite unrelated to those doubts.

There are two kinds of problems that need to be dealt with in any model of the criminal process. One is what the rules shall be. The other is how the rules shall be implemented. The second is at least as important as the first. As we shall see time and again in our detailed development of the models, the distinctive difference between the two models is not only in the rules of conduct that they lay down but also in the sanctions that are to be invoked when a claim is presented that the rules have been breached and, no less importantly, in the timing that is permitted or required for the invocation of those sanctions.

As I have already suggested, the Due Process Model locates at least some of the sanctions for breach of the operative rules in the criminal process itself. The relation between these two aspects of the process—the rules and the sanctions for their breach—is a purely formal one unless there is some mechanism for bringing them into play with each other. The hinge between them in the Due Process Model is the availability of legal counsel. This has a double aspect. Many of the rules that the model requires are couched in terms of the availability of counsel to do various things at various stages of the process—this is the conventionally recognized aspect; beyond it, there is a pervasive assumption that counsel is necessary in order to invoke sanctions for breach of any of the rules. The more freely available these sanctions are, the more important is the role of counsel in seeing to it that the sanctions are appropriately invoked. If the process is seen as a series of occasions for checking its own operation, the role of counsel is a much more nearly central one than is the case in a process that is seen as primarily concerned with expeditious determination of factual guilt. And if equality of operation is a governing norm, the availability of counsel to some is seen as requiring it for all. Of all the controverted aspects of the criminal process, the right to counsel, including the role of government in its provision, is the most dependent on what one's model of the process looks like, and the least susceptible of resolution unless one has confronted the antinomies of the two models.

I do not mean to suggest that questions about the right to counsel disappear if one adopts a model of the process that conforms more or less closely to the Crime Control Model, but only that such questions become absolutely central if one's model moves very far down the spectrum of possibilities toward the pure Due Process Model. The reason for this centrality is to be found in the assumption underlying both models that the process is an adversary one in which the initiative in invoking relevant rules rests primarily on the parties concerned, the state, and the accused. One could construct models that placed central responsibility on adjudicative agents such as committing magistrates and trial judges. And there are, as we shall see, marginal but nonetheless important adjustments in the role of the adjudicative agents that enter into the models with which we are concerned. For present purposes it is enough to say that these adjustments are marginal, that the animating presuppositions that underlie both models in the context of the American criminal system relegate the adjudicative agents to a relatively passive role, and therefore place central importance on the role of counsel.

One last introductory note before we proceed to a detailed examination of some aspects of the two models in operation. What assumptions do we make about the sources of authority to shape the real-world operations of the criminal process? Recognizing that our models are only models, what agencies of government have the power to pick and choose between their competing demands? Once again, the limiting features of the American context come into play. Ours is not a system of legislative supremacy. The distinctively American institution of judicial review exercises a limiting and ultimately a shaping influence on the criminal process. Because the Crime Control Model is basically an affirmative model, emphasizing at every turn the existence and exercise of official power, its validating authority is ultimately legislative (although proximately administrative). Because the Due Process Model is basically a negative model, asserting limits on the nature of official power and on the modes of its exercise, its validating authority is judicial and requires an appeal to supra-legislative law, to the law of the Constitution. To the extent that tensions between the two models are resolved by deference to the Due Process Model, the authoritative force at work is the judicial power, working in the distinctively judicial mode of invoking the sanction of nullity. That is at once the strength and the weakness of the Due Process Model: its strength because in our system the appeal to the Constitution provides the last and the overriding word; its weakness because saying no in specific cases is an exercise in futility unless there is a general willingness on the part of the officials who operate the process to apply negative prescriptions across the board. It is no accident that statements reinforcing the Due Process Model come from the courts, while at the same time facts denying it are established by the police and prosecutors.

Notes

1. *Mapp v. Ohio*, 367 U.S. 643 (1961); *Ker v. California*, 374 U.S. 23 (1963).
2. See President's Commission on Law Enforcement and Administration of Justice, *The Challenge of Crime in a Free Society* (Washington, D.C., 1967), chap. 2.
3. *Griffin v. Illinois*, 351 U.S. 12, 19 (1956).
4. *Finality in Criminal Law and Federal Habeas Corpus for State Prisoners*, 76 Harv. L. Rev. 441, 442 (1963).

51

Violence and the Police
William A. Westley

The Roots of Morality

The policemen in City X are deeply concerned with the hostility they feel from the public. It is a pressure that they constantly endeavor to alleviate or repudiate. Their job requires that they be in constant interaction with the public—it is an ever-present factor in their experience—and they become extremely sensitive to these public accusations. They lean on one another for moral support; they depend on one another for practical support. Against unpleasant experience they have the bulwark of in-group, interpersonal strength. Even if the public doesn't appreciate them, their fellows do. The public must be repudiated and the group affirmed. "We are only one hundred forty against one hundred forty thousand" is a running commentary on their position, expressing their feelings of affinity against a hostile world. The feeling is a powerful lever projecting the policeman into the group.

Public hostility includes the policeman in his symbolic status. It includes an assessment of collective responsibility or guilt by association, in terms of which every member of the force is made responsible for the actions of the individual officer. The result is that the individual policeman finds that his own interests have been forcibly identified with those of the group. Any action that incriminates or smears a member of the force has the same impact on all the others before the bar of public opinion. In City X the public frame of reference represents the police so negatively that every vice is added to their character and every virtue is forgotten. This is the feeling of the police when they complain so bitterly about the unfair publicity that the city newspaper gives them. It is encompassed in the words of an officer, who said, "You have two strikes against you as soon as you put on the uniform." Almost in spite of themselves the policemen come to protect the actions of their comrades and to see little in them that is bad. Almost any beating becomes just; even graft becomes permissible. The policeman is thus permitted to breach the law, for to apprehend him would only do the apprehender harm. The prejudice and the stereotype find the police together and give them a common front against the community.

Source: From William A. Westley, *Violence and the Police: A Sociological Study of Law, Custom, and Morality,* pp. 110–112, 114–116, 118–123, 150–152. Reprinted by permission of the MIT Press, Cambridge, Massachusetts. Copyright © 1970 The MIT Press. All rights reserved.

Through the hostility and through the stereotype, the police become a close, social group, in which collective action is organized for self-protection and an attack on the outside world. These become expressed in two major rules. The vehicle of self-protection is the rule of silence—secrecy. The vehicle of attack is the emphasis on the maintenance of respect for the police.

Silence, Secrecy, and Solidarity

The stool pigeon, the squealer, the one who tells, is anathema to almost any social group. He is an outcast among the police. To him is applied the most powerful sanction the group has available—the silent treatment. This is powerful because it deprives the unfortunate man of information vital to his continued success and necessary to his happiness, and because he works alone. This is the penalty for a serious abrogation of the rule of silence. It is a penalty for a threat to the secrecy of the group.

Secrecy among the police stands as a shield against the attacks of the outside world; against bad newspaper publicity, which would make the police lose respect; against public criticism, from which they feel they suffer too much; against the criminal, who is eager to know the moves of the police; against the law, which they too frequently abrogate. Secrecy is loyalty, for it represents sticking with the group, and its maintenance carries with it a profound sense of participation. Secrecy is solidarity, for it represents a common front against the outside world and consensus in at least one goal.

Secrecy and silence are among the first rules impressed on the rookie. "Keep your mouth shut, never squeal on a fellow officer, don't be a stool pigeon," is what the rookie has dinned into his ears; it is one of the first things he learns.

Secrecy does not apply to achievements—these should be publicized. It applies to mistakes, to plans, to illegal actions, to character defamation. Among the police it applies to mistakes in arrests, to the abrogation of departmental rules, to criminal suspects, to illegal actions, to personal misdemeanors. These are important insofar as they represent a breach in the protective coating that the policeman tries to present to society. . . .

We would suggest, therefore, that the data are indicative of the strength of two characteristics of the police force: (1) secrecy constitutes one of the most important definitions and is represented in the rule of silence; and (2) law enforcement is subordinate to the ends of the group.

Sanctions for Secrecy

The strength of the rule of silence is again emphasized in the statements of some of the respondents when they tried to indicate what they thought would happen to them if they did report or testify against their partners. . . .

These statements indicate the nature of the sanctions that would be applied, or that the men thought would be applied, should they break the group rules. These include a program in which the culprit would be an outcast, isolated from social relationships so that nobody would talk to him, so that he wouldn't know what was going on, so that the other men would go out of their way to get the man in trouble. Thus, the following specific points are made:

1. The man wouldn't be able to find out what was going on. This would seriously incapacitate him, since the men must have a line to the chief in order to comply with his whims or the current of feelings in the town. There are times when the men can get away with anything, and others when they have to be exceedingly careful. Word of this comes down through the grapevine. The man who is detached from this source of information is likely to do something that will get him in trouble.

2. The man would be deprived of friendly contacts. This would have important personal consequences for him, because it means a deprivation of the only real source of consolation for the hostility of the community.

3. The other men would go out of their way to get him in trouble. This can be interpreted in two ways: (1) that the other men would feel free to stool on him when he did anything wrong, and (2) that they would fail to support him when he got into trouble with the public or with the administration. . . .

The Uses of Violence

The essence of any group norm lies in its permissive or prescriptive regulation of the conduct of the members. Since occupational norms can be considered the product of the problematic areas of social interaction, it is probable that they will control or regulate actions in these areas.

Police Powers

For the police, action in large measure is confined to action toward the people of the community. It involves, on the one hand, the nature of police powers, and on the other, their decisions about using these powers.

Police power has two aspects: the positive, which involves coercion in the power to arrest and to use violence in making arrests; and the negative, which involves the power of withdrawal of protection. Policemen's legal privileges entitle them to the first source of power and forbid them the second. Both are used.

Although the police are legally entitled to certain powers, these powers are utilized for their personal ends as well as in the line of duty.

As a group they tend to use the power that they possess to gain their ends as a group, ends that we have indicated are basically embodied in the maintenance of secrecy, the maintenance of respect for the police, and the apprehension of the felon. In addition to the extension of their legal sources of power, they also tend to draw on certain illegal sources of power which are at their disposal. Principal among these is their power to withdraw their protection. In this sense they come to regard protection as a personal commodity, the extension of which is a reward for compliance and the withdrawal of which is a punishment for noncompliance. This source of power is almost completely reserved for expediting the ends of the police, whatever they may be,[1] and is seldom used to back up their legal function.

Police Action

Police action can be seen as a continuum ranging from letting it pass, or giving a warning, to the arrest and/or a beating. Actions in this range can be legally supported or rationalized. The decision on the part of the individual policeman as to what kind of action to take in a specific situation involves the interrelation of three variables: the enforcement of the law, the maintenance of respect for the police, and the apprehension of the felon, or the making of a ''good pinch.''

The enforcement of the law, ceteris paribus, will be confined to actions utilizing the legal sources of power and will seldom extend beyond the arrest. Persons involved in misdemeanors, who constitute the largest number of offenders, will generally be treated with respect, and will be warned more frequently than arrested. The speeder, the drunk, the public nuisance, and so forth, are seldom taken seriously by the police. It is only as one or both of the other variables come into play that the enforcement of the law involves more stringent types of action. Thus, when a drunk curses or reviles a policeman, in front of an audience, and when the policeman interprets this as demeaning the police, as influencing the public respect for the police, as threatening his dignity, the drunk will be susceptible to the more stringent types of police action— the arrest, and very possibly rough treatment. How far the policeman will go will depend (1) on how threatened he feels, (2) on the current attitude toward the police in the city, and (3) on that portion of the public into which he categorizes the drunk. If the policeman feels seriously threatened, if the public attitude toward the police has been quiet, and if the policeman sees the drunk as a professional criminal, or a Negro, some type of rough treatment will probably be the result.

This does not imply that there are not legitimate bases on which the policeman resorts to violence; there are many situations in which he may have to choose this course of action, such as when the prisoner refuses to accept arrest, when the policeman is attacked, when the policeman has to prevent someone from injuring another person or from committing a serious crime. However, even in these situations, frequently he can refrain from injuring the offender by overpowering him. Police usually work in pairs, and the situation, therefore, is frequently one in which they are two against one.

In addition, there are individual differences in the frequency with which the policeman resorts to force based largely on propensity and strength. Some men seem to work out their fears and aggressions on the job. Some men are so powerful that they seldom experience resistance on the part of the public, and when they do they can easily overpower the offender. Other men, who are smaller, seem to pose a challenge to the offender because of their very size, and they will frequently experience resistance and have to use the club to overcome this resistance. Nevertheless, the amount of force used by the police and the situations in which it is applied cannot be accounted for fully under the categories of necessity in the line of duty and personal propensities and strength; they appear to be a matter of prescription in terms of ends not thus accounted for.

This, then, affords an opportunity to test our hypothesis that the maintenance of respect for the police and the apprehension of the felon represent major occupational norms of the police.

The Identification of Norms in the Legitimation of Action

Although the prevalence of similar attitudes among a large proportion of the men, and their logical integration with the problems of the occupation, would suggest that these attitudes reflect group norms, it does not demonstrate the point. Similar experiences may generate similar attitudes which have no collective basis. However, the legitimation of action offers an index to norms which does not have such a basis. This becomes clear if one considers the subjective meaning of norms for the men involved.

Here one can assume (1) that a norm regulates action not only because of the sanctions it involves, but also because it represents to the actor the morally correct choice; (2) that any important norm should function as a source of moral authority to the actor so that he will justify his actions in terms of it; (3) that the more extreme the action, the more likely it will be applied toward ends (normatively defined) that are of importance; and (4) that the more subject to criticism the action is, the more likely the man will feel called upon to justify it.

On the basis of these assumptions it was possible to identify the major norms of the police by asking them to justify certain forms of extreme action. The use of force or violence is such an action, since it is both extreme and subject to heavy criticism by the people of the community. Therefore, the ways in which the police justify the use of force would indicate their major norms.

Legitimation for Violence

Seventy-four policemen in Department X were asked, "When do you think a policeman is justified in roughing a man up?" Their responses were essentially prescriptive in that they tried to indicate to the interviewer the type of situation in which they would prescribe the use of force. The situations for which force was prescribed represented those in which the policeman felt its use would be justified; therefore, these situations could be considered as sources for its legitimation.

Their answers frequently had elements in common, and thus it was possible to group them into rough categories which are indicative of the norms they represent (see Table 4.3). Since many of the respondents gave more than one basis for the use of force, their responses are first classified in terms of the major orientation, summarized in the column "primary responses." Each response in this column indicates a separate case. Their remaining rationalizations are summarized in the column "secondary response." Each item in this column represents an additional rationalization advanced by a respondent listed in the primary response column.

BASES FOR THE USE OF FORCE

Basis	Primary Response Number	%*	Secondary Response Number	Total Number	%*
1. Disrespect for the police	27	37	2	29	39
2. Only when impossible to avoid	17	23	0	17	23
3. To obtain information	14	19	3	17	23
4. To make an arrest	6	8	3	9	12
5. For the hardened criminal	5	7	3	8	11
6. When you know man is guilty	2	3	1	3	4
7. For sex criminals	2	3	4	6	8
8. For self-protection	0	0	4	4	5
9. When pressure is on you	0	0	1	1	1
Total	74	100	20	94	

*Percentages computed only to the nearest 1%.

Interpretation

1. The evidence of 39 percent of the men giving disrespectful behavior as a basis for the use of force supports the thesis that the maintenance of respect for the police is a major orientation of the police.

2. That 23 percent of the men legitimate the use of force to obtain information that would lead to the solution of a crime or the conviction of the criminal would support the thesis that the apprehension of the felon is also a major orientation of the police.

3. That 66 percent of the men gave as their *primary* rationalization an illegal basis for the use of force (categories 1, 3, 5, and 6) while only 8 percent gave a legal basis (category 4) would indicate that the group-engendered values are relatively more important to the men than their legal function.

4. The fact that 23 percent of the men stated that force should be avoided if possible is indicative of the social situation in which the interview took place rather than the feelings of the men. At the time the interviews were being made the chief of police was carrying on a program to reduce the amount of force being used and was applying penalties to deviants; the interviewer was suspected of being connected with the chief. Under these conditions the safest response was to condemn the use of force. Thus, although some of the men undoubtedly indicated their true feelings, the proportion of 23 percent probably exaggerates the number. On the other hand, these same conditions would indicate that the proportion of the men endorsing the use of force is biased conservatively.

5. The apparent guilt of the man and his identification as a hardened criminal as bases for the use of force in 15 percent of the cases does not indicate that these are motivational factors but rather they represent conditions under which the use of force can take place. They represent the feeling on the part of the men that force must be used with caution because of the possibility of a lawsuit against them. . . .

Summary

The preceding materials would indicate that the police in City X possess the characteristics of a social group in having as collective ends the maintenance of secrecy about public affairs and the maintenance of respect for the police by the people of the community; in having a consensus on these ends, developed through a community of experience and discourse resulting from their occupational experiences; in having a set of norms that guide conduct and sanctions to enforce the norms represented in the rule of silence and the use of the silent treatment for offenders, the rule of maintaining respect for the police and the use of ridicule to punish offenders, and in the rule that the means justify the ends in the apprehension of the felon, a rule maintained by the reward of prestige; and finally, in their possession of organized action bodies as represented by the Fraternal Order of Police and the Police Ex-Servicemen's League, to which 88 percent of the men belong and attend an average of ten meetings a year.

This should have implications for other occupations, since the social group characteristics are in large measure the result of its being an occupational group;

the social definition of work should give many occupations a basis for collective action. Common work experiences and common occupational problems, as a part of this experience, should provide the basis for a community of experience and discourse with which to generate consensus and norms when the members of the occupation come in contact with one another.

The importance of secrecy to the police in City X is evidenced by the fact that of a sample of 13 men, 77 percent indicated that they would prefer to perjure themselves rather than testify against another policeman. They indicated that should they break the secrecy rule, they would be labeled a stool pigeon and have an outcast status; that they would receive the silent treatment, which would cut them off from important sources of information and from social contacts with other men. The existence of these powerful sanctions indicates that secrecy has a normative status among the police. That secrecy is felt to be so important, and the degree of consensus on this point, would indicate that it functions both as a collective end and as a solidarity mechanism for the police as a social group.

Secrecy among the police can be traced to the social definition of their occupation as corrupt and brutal, and may be seen as a protective mechanism against this attack. It functions as a shield for actions that may be criticized but that the police feel are necessary to their ends. As such, it should be true of many occupations to some extent. To the degree that members of an occupation or a social group feel it necessary to engage in actions in conflict with the dominant values of the society, or defined as evil by the society, secrecy should prove a necessary bulwark to criticism. Again, since secrecy functions as a mechanism of solidarity in giving the members a sense of mutual involvement and possibly of importance in the belief that they then have special privileges, it should prove convenient to any group.

The police conceive of violence as an instrument to be used for the support of personal goals, and only incidentally as a restricted source of power given to them to facilitate their legal function. Corollary to this is the indication that law enforcement itself is conceived of as an incidental function, to be pursued when it supports group ends or has no reference to them. Law enforcement is subordinate to the maintenance of secrecy, the maintenance of respect for the police, and the apprehension of the felon. Policemen's position on the use of violence was demonstrated in their willingness to use it illegally to force respect and to elicit information, and the group endorsement of this procedure. The subordinate position of law enforcement appeared in the relatively limited degree to which it was used to legitimate violence in comparison with the maintenance of respect and the apprehension of felons; in the willingness to abrogate it to achieve other ends, as evidenced by the withdrawal of protection for this purpose; and in the willingness of the men to cease enforcing the law if the chief of police indicated such a desire.

The significance of this point lies in the suggestion that the most important goals of an occupation's membership are those that involve the self-conceptions of the members. Thus, it is likely that those aspects of the job that affect the self-conception will receive the greatest attention, to the detriment of others.

The maintenance of respect for the police is demonstrated as an occupational norm of the police in its utilization by a large percentage of the men as a source of moral authority in terms of which they legitimate violence. It is meaningful in terms of the policeman's interaction with the public when he feels that his competence is constantly being threatened and his personal value is in question.

The apprehension of the felon appears as a major value of the police in their indication that it is the major source of satisfaction that they gain in the occupation. The rule that "the end justify the means" in the apprehension of the felon is demonstrated as an occupational norm of the police in its utilization as a basis for legitimating violence. This is supported in the policeman's conception of the criminal as a person who has abrogated his basic rights as a citizen, and as a personal challenge to the policeman.

Policemen consider themselves to be persons without particular worth and to be failures when they state that they don't want their sons to become policemen, that they want them to become successes.

Note

1. Thus, when graft becomes an important end of the police, this source of power is frequently used to force the cooperation of the unwilling gamble, bartender, and the like.

52

A Sketch of the Policeman's "Working Personality"

Jerome H. Skolnick

A recurrent theme of the sociology of occupations is the effect of a man's work on his outlook on the world.[1] Doctors, janitors, lawyers, and industrial workers develop distinctive ways of perceiving and responding to their environment. Here we shall concentrate on analyzing certain outstanding elements in the police milieu, danger, authority, and efficiency, as they combine to generate distinctive cognitive and behavioral responses in police: a "working personality." Such an analysis does not suggest that all police are alike in "working personality," but that there are distinctive cognitive tendencies in police as an occupational grouping. Some of these may be found in other occupations sharing similar problems. So far as exposure to danger is concerned, the policeman may be likened to the soldier. His problems as an authority bear a certain similarity to those of the schoolteacher, and the pressures he feels to prove himself efficient are not unlike those felt by the industrial worker. The combination of these elements, however, is unique to the policeman. Thus, the police, as a result of combined features of their social situation, tend to develop ways of looking at the world distinctive to themselves, cognitive lenses through which to see situations and events. The strength of the lenses may be weaker or stronger depending on certain conditions, but they are ground on a similar axis.

Analysis of the policeman's cognitive propensities is necessary to understand the practical dilemma faced by police required to maintain order under a democratic rule of law. We have discussed earlier how essential a conception of order is to the resolution of this dilemma. It was suggested that the paramilitary character of police organization naturally leads to a high evaluation of similarity, routine, and predictability. Our intention is to emphasize features of the policeman's environment interacting with the paramilitary police organization to generate a "working personality." Such an intervening concept should aid in explaining how the social environment of police affects their capacity to respond to the rule of law.

We also stated earlier that emphasis would be placed on the division of labor in the police department, that "operational law enforcement" could not be understood outside these special work assignments. It is therefore important to explain how the

Source: Reprinted with the permission of Pearson Education, Inc. from *Justice Without Trial: Law Enforcement in Democratic Society, 2nd Ed.*, by Jerome H. Skolnick. Copyright © 1966 by Pearson Education, Inc., Upper Saddle River, NJ. Notes renumbered.

hypothesis emphasizing the generalizability of the policeman's "working personality" is compatible with the idea that police division of labor is an important analytic dimension for understanding "operational law enforcement." Compatibility is evident when one considers the different levels of analysis at which the hypotheses are being developed. Janowitz states, for example, that the military profession is more than an occupation; it is a "style of life" because the occupational claims over one's daily existence extend well beyond official duties. He is quick to point out that any profession performing a crucial "life and death" task, such as medicine, the ministry, or the police, develops such claims.[2] A conception like "working personality" of police should be understood to suggest an analytic breadth similar to that of "style of life." That is, just as the professional behavior of military officers with similar "styles of life" may differ drastically depending upon whether they command an infantry battalion or participate in the work of an intelligence unit, so too does the professional behavior of police officers with similar "working personalities" vary with their assignments.

The policeman's "working personality" is most highly developed in his constabulary role of the man on the beat. For analytical purposes that role is sometimes regarded as an enforcement speciality, but in this general discussion of policemen as they comport themselves while working, the uniformed "cop" is seen as the foundation for the policeman's working personality. There is sound organizational basis for making this assumption. The police, unlike the military, draw no caste distinction in socialization, even though their order of ranked titles approximates the military's. Thus, one cannot join a local police department as, for instance, a lieutenant, as a West Point graduate joins the army. Every officer of rank must serve an apprenticeship as a patrolman. This feature of police organization means that the constabulary role is the primary one for all police officers, and that whatever the special requirements of roles in enforcement specialties, they are carried out with a common background of constabulary experience.

The process by which this "personality" is developed may be summarized: the policeman's role contains two principal variables, danger and authority, which should be interpreted in the light of a "constant" pressure to appear efficient.[3] The element of danger seems to make the policeman especially attentive to signs indicating a potential for violence and lawbreaking. As a result, the policeman is generally a "suspicious" person. Furthermore, the character of the policeman's work makes him less desirable as a friend, since norms of friendship implicate others in his work. Accordingly, the element of danger isolates the policeman socially from that segment of the citizenry which he regards as symbolically dangerous and also from the conventional citizenry with whom he identifies.

The element of authority reinforces the element of danger in isolating the policeman. Typically, the policeman is required to enforce laws representing puritanical morality, such as those prohibiting drunkenness, and also laws regulating the flow of public activity, such as traffic laws. In these situations the policeman directs the citizenry, whose typical response denies recognition of his authority, and stresses his obligation to respond to danger. The kind of man who responds well to danger, however, does not normally subscribe to codes of puritanical morality. As a result, the policeman is unusually liable to the charge of hypocrisy. That the whole civilian world is an audience for the policeman further promotes police isolation and, in consequence, solidarity. Finally, danger undermines the judicious use of authority. Where danger, as in Britain, is relatively less, the judicious application of authority is facilitated. Hence, British police may appear to be somewhat more attached to the rule of law, when, in fact, they may appear so because they face less danger, and they are as a rule better skilled than American police in creating the appearance of conformity to procedural regulations.

The Symbolic Assailant and Police Culture

In attempting to understand the policeman's view of the world, it is useful to raise a more general question: What are the conditions under which police, as authorities, may be threatened?[4] To answer this, we must look to the situation of the policeman in the community. One attribute of many characterizing the policeman's role stands out: the policeman is required to respond to assaults against persons and property. When a radio call reports an armed robbery and gives a description of the man involved, every policeman, regardless of assignment, is responsible for the criminal's apprehension. The *raison d'être* of the policeman and the criminal law, the underlying collectively held moral sentiments which justify penal sanctions, arises ultimately and most clearly from the threat of violence and the possibility of danger to the community. Police who "lobby" for severe narcotics laws, for instance, justify their position on grounds that the addict is a harbinger of danger since, it is maintained, he requires one hundred dollars a day to support his habit, and he must steal to get it. Even though the addict is not typically a violent criminal, criminal penalties for addiction are supported on grounds that he may become one.

The policeman, because his work requires him to be occupied continually with potential violence, develops a perceptual shorthand to identify certain kinds of people as symbolic assailants, that is, as persons who use gesture, language, and attire that the policeman has come to recognize as a prelude to violence. This does not mean that violence by the symbolic assailant is necessarily predictable. On the contrary, the policeman responds to the vague indication of danger suggested by appearance.[5] Like the animals of the experimental psychologist, the policeman finds the threat of random damage more compelling than a predetermined and inevitable punishment.

Nor, to qualify for the status of symbolic assailant, need an individual ever have used violence. A man backing out of a jewelry store with a gun in one hand and jewelry in the other would qualify even if the gun were a toy and he had never in his life fired a real pistol. To the policeman in the situation, the man's personal history is momentarily immaterial. There is only one relevant sign: a gun signifying danger. Similarly, a young man may suggest the threat of violence to the policeman by his manner of walking or "strutting," the insolence in the demeanor being registered by the policeman as a possible preamble to later attack.[6] Signs vary from area to area, but a youth dressed in a black leather jacket and motorcycle boots is sure to draw at least a suspicious glance from a policeman.

Policemen themselves do not necessarily emphasize the peril associated with their work when questioned directly, and may even have well developed strategies of denial. The element of danger is so integral to the policeman's work that explicit recognition might induce emotional barriers to work performance. Thus, one patrol officer observed that more police have been killed and injured in automobile accidents in the past ten years than from gunfire. Although his assertion is true, he neglected to mention that the police are the only peacetime occupational group with a systematic record of death and injury from gunfire and other weaponry. Along these lines, it is interesting that of the two hundred and twenty-four working Westville policemen (not including the sixteen juvenile policemen) responding to a question about which assignment they would like most to have in the police department,[7] 50 percent selected the job of detective, an assignment combining elements of apparent danger and initiative. The next category was adult street work, that is, patrol and traffic (37 percent). Eight percent selected the juvenile squad,[8] and only 4 percent selected administrative work. Not a single policeman chose the job of jail guard. Although these findings do not control for such factors as prestige, they suggest that confining and routine jobs are rated low on the hierarchy of police preferences, even though such jobs are least dangerous. Thus, the policeman may well, as a personality, enjoy the possibility of danger, especially its associated excitement, even though he may at the same time be fearful of it. Such "inconsistency" is easily understood. Freud has by now made it an axiom of personality theory that logical and emotional consistency are by no means the same phenomenon.

However complex the motives aroused by the element of danger, its consequences for sustaining police culture are unambiguous. This element requires him, like the combat soldier, the European Jew, the South African (white or black), to live in a world straining toward duality, and suggesting danger when "they" are perceived. Consequently, it is in the nature of the policeman's situation that his conception of order emphasize regularity and predictability. It is, therefore, a conception shaped by persistent *suspicion.* . . .

Social Isolation

The patrolman in Westville, and probably in most communities, has come to identify the black man with danger. James Baldwin vividly expresses the isolation of the ghetto policeman:

> . . . The only way to police a ghetto is to be oppressive. None of the Police Commissioner's men, even with the best will in the world, have any way of understanding the lives led by the people they swagger about in twos and threes controlling. Their very presence is an insult, and it would be, even if they spent their entire day feeding gumdrops to children. They represent the force of the white world, and that world's criminal profit and ease, to keep the black man corralled up here, in his place. The badge, the gun in the holster, and the swinging club make vivid what will happen should his rebellion become overt . . .

> It is hard, on the other hand, to blame the policeman, blank, good-natured, thoughtless, and insuperably innocent, for being such a perfect representative of the people he serves. He, too, believes in good intentions and is astounded and offended when they are not taken for the deed. He has never, himself, done anything for which to be hated—which of us has? and yet he is facing, daily and nightly, people who would gladly see him dead, and he knows it. There is no way for him not to know it: there are few things under heaven more unnerving than the silent, accumulating contempt and hatred of a people. He moves through Harlem, therefore, like an occupying soldier in a bitterly hostile country; which is precisely what, and where he is, and is the reason he walks in twos and threes.[9]

While Baldwin's observations on police-Negro relations cannot be disputed seriously, there is greater social distance between police and "civilians" in general regardless of their color than Baldwin considers. Thus, Colin MacInnes has his English hero, Mr. Justice, explaining:

> . . . The story is all coppers are just civilians like anyone else, living among them not in barracks like on the Continent, but you and I know that's just a legend for mugs. We *are* cut off: we're *not* like everyone else. Some civilians fear us and play up to us,

some dislike us and keep out of our way but no one—well, very few indeed—accepts us as just ordinary like them. In one sense, dear, we're just like hostile troops occupying an enemy country. And say what you like, at times that makes us lonely.[10]

MacInnes' observation suggests that by not introducing a white control group, Baldwin has failed to see that the policeman may not get on well with anybody regardless (to use the hackneyed phrase) of race, creed, or national origin. Policemen whom one knows well often express their sense of isolation from the public as a whole, not just from those who fail to share their color. Westville police were asked, for example, to rank the most serious problems police have. The category most frequently selected was not racial problems, but some form of public relations: lack of respect for the police, lack of cooperation in enforcement of law, lack of understanding of the requirements of police work. One respondent answered:

> As a policeman my most serious problem is impressing on the general public just how difficult and necessary police service is to all. There seems to be an attitude of "law is important, but it applies to my neighbor—not to me."

. . . Although the policeman serves a people who are, as Baldwin says, the established society, the white society, these people do not make him feel accepted. As a result, he develops resources within his own world to combat social rejection.

Police Solidarity

All occupational groups share a measure of inclusiveness and identification. People are brought together simply by doing the same work and having similar career and salary problems. As several writers have noted, however, police show an unusually high degree of occupational solidarity.[11] It is true that the police have a common employer and wear a uniform at work, but so do doctors, milkmen, and bus drivers. Yet it is doubtful that these workers have so close knit an occupation or so similar an outlook on the world as do police. Set apart from the conventional world, the policeman experiences an exceptionally strong tendency to find his social identity within his occupational milieu.

Compare the police with another skilled craft. In a study of the International Typographical Union, the authors asked printers the first names and jobs of their three closest friends. Of the 1,236 friends named by the 412 men in their sample, 35 percent were printers.[12] Similarly, among the Westville police, of 700 friends listed by 250 respondents, 35 percent were policemen. The policemen, however, were far more active than printers in occupational social activities. Of the printers, more than half (54 percent) had never participated in any union clubs, benefit societies, teams, or organizations composed mostly of printers, or attended any printers' social affairs in the past 5 years. Of the Westville police, only 16 percent had failed to attend a single police banquet or dinner in the past *year* (as contrasted with the printers' *5 years*); and of the 234 men answering this question, 54 percent had attended 3 or more such affairs *during the past year*.

These findings are striking in light of the interpretation made of the data on printers. Lipset, Trow, and Coleman do not, as a result of their findings, see printers as an unintegrated occupational group. On the contrary, they ascribe the democratic character of the union in good part to the active social and political participation of the membership. The point is not to question their interpretation, since it is doubtlessly correct when printers are held up against other manual workers. However, when seen in comparison to police, printers appear a minimally participating group; but positively, police emerge as an exceptionally socially active occupational group.

Police Solidarity and Danger

There is still a question, however, as to the process through which danger and authority influence police solidarity. The effect of danger on police solidarity is revealed when we examine a chief complaint of police: lack of public support and public apathy. The complaint may have several referents including police pay, police prestige, and support from the legislature. But the repeatedly voiced broader meaning of the complaint is resentment at being taken for granted. The policeman does not believe that his status as civil servant should relieve the public of responsibility for law enforcement. He feels, however, that payment out of public coffers somehow obscures his humanity and, therefore, his need for help.[13] As one put it:

> Jerry, a cop, can get into a fight with three or four tough kids, and there will be citizens passing by, and maybe they'll look, but they'll never lend a hand. It's their country too, but you'd never know it the way some of them act. They forget that we're made of flesh and blood too. They don't care what happens to the cop so long as they don't get a little dirty.

Although the policeman sees himself as a specialist in dealing with violence, he does not want to fight alone. He does not believe that his specialization relieves the general public of citizenship duties. Indeed, if possible, he would prefer to be the foreman rather than the workingman in the battle against criminals.

The general public, of course, does withdraw from the workaday world of the policeman. The policeman's responsibility for controlling dangerous and sometimes violent persons alienates the average citizen perhaps as much as does his authority over the average citizen. If the policeman's job is to insure that public order is maintained, the citizen's inclination is to shrink from the dangers of maintaining it. The citizen prefers to see the policeman as an automaton, because once the policeman's humanity is recognized, the citizen necessarily becomes implicated in the policeman's work, which is, after all, sometimes dirty and dangerous. What the policeman typically fails to realize is the extent he becomes tainted by the character of the work he performs. The dangers of their work not only draws policemen together as a group but separates them from the rest of the population. Banton, for instance, comments:

> . . . patrolmen may support their fellows over what they regard as minor infractions in order to demonstrate to them that they will be loyal in situations that make the greatest demands upon their fidelity. . . .

> In the American departments I visited it seems as if the supervisors shared many of the patrolmen's sentiments about solidarity. They too wanted their colleagues to back them up in an emergency, and they shared similar frustrations with the public.[14]

Thus, the element of danger contains seeds of isolation which may grow in two directions. In one, a stereotyping perceptual shorthand is formed through which the police come to see certain signs as symbols of potential violence. The police probably differ in this respect from the general middle-class white population only in degree. This difference, however, may take on enormous significance in practice. Thus, the policeman works at identifying and possibly apprehending the symbolic assailant; the ordinary citizen does not. As a result, the ordinary citizen does not assume the responsibility to implicate himself in the policeman's required response to danger.

The element of danger in the policeman's role alienates him not only from populations with a potential for crime but also from the conventionally respectable (white) citizenry, in short, from that segment of the population from which friends would ordinarily be drawn. As Janowitz has noted in a paragraph suggesting similarities between the police and the military,

> . . . any profession which is continually preoccupied with the threat of danger requires a strong sense of solidarity if it is to operate effectively. Detailed regulation of the military style of life is expected to enhance group cohesion, professional loyalty, and maintain the martial spirit.[15]

Social Isolation and Authority

The element of authority also helps to account for the policeman's social isolation. Policemen themselves are aware of their isolation from the community, and are apt to weight authority heavily as a causal factor. When considering how authority influences rejection, the policeman typically singles out his responsibility for enforcement of traffic violations.[16] Resentment, even hostility, is generated in those receiving citations, in part because such contact is often the only one citizens have with police, and in part because municipal administrations and courts have been known to utilize police authority primarily to meet budgetary requirements, rather than those of public order. Thus, when a municipality engages in "speed trapping" by changing limits so quickly that drivers cannot realistically slow down to the prescribed speed or, while keeping the limits reasonable, charging high fines primarily to generate revenue, the policeman carries the brunt of public resentment.

That the policeman dislikes writing traffic tickets is suggested by the quota system police departments typically employ. In Westville, each traffic policeman has what is euphemistically described as a working "norm." A motorcyclist is supposed to write two tickets an hour for moving violations. It is doubtful that "norms" are needed because policemen are lazy. Rather, employment of quotas most likely springs from the reluctance of policemen to expose themselves to what they know to be public hostility. As a result, as one traffic policeman said:

> You learn to sniff out the places where you can catch violators when you're running behind. Of course, the department gets to know that you hang around one place, and they sometimes try to repair the situation there. But a lot of the time it would be too expensive to fix up the engineering fault, so we keep making our norm.

When meeting "production" pressures, the policeman inadvertently gives a false impression of patrolling ability to the average citizen. The traffic cyclist waits in hiding for moving violators near a tricky intersection, and is reasonably sure that such violations will occur with regularity. The violator believes he has observed a policeman displaying exceptional detection capacities and may have two thoughts, each apt to generate hostility toward the policeman: "I have been trapped," or "They can catch me; why can't they catch crooks as easily?" The answer, of course, lies in the different behavior patterns of motorists and "crooks." The latter do not act with either the frequency or predictability of motorists at poorly engineered intersections.

While traffic patrol plays a major role in separating the policemen from the respectable community, other of his tasks also have this consequence. Traffic patrol is only the most obvious illustration of the policeman's general responsibility for maintaining public order, which also includes keeping order at public accidents, sporting events, and political rallies. These activities share one feature: the policeman is called upon to *direct* ordinary citizens, and therefore to restrain their freedom of action. Resenting the restraint, the average citizen in such a situation typically thinks something along the lines of "He is supposed to catch crooks; why is he bothering me?" Thus, the citizen stresses the "dangerous" portion of the policeman's role while belittling his authority.

Closely related to the policeman's authority-based problems as *director* of the citizenry are difficulties associated with his injunction to *regulate public morality*. For instance, the policeman is obliged to investigate "lovers' lanes," and to enforce laws pertaining to gambling, prostitution, and drunkenness. His responsibility in these matters allows him much administrative discretion since he may not actually enforce the law by making an arrest, but instead merely interfere with continuation of the objectionable activity.[17] Thus, he may put the drunk in a taxi, tell the lovers to remove themselves from the back seat, and advise a man soliciting a prostitute to leave the area.

Such admonitions are in the interest of maintaining the proprieties of public order. At the same time, the policeman invites the hostility of the citizen so directed in two respects: he is likely to encourage the sort of response mentioned earlier (that is, an antagonistic reformulation of the policeman's role) and the policeman is apt to cause resentment because of the suspicion that policemen do not themselves strictly conform to the moral norms they are enforcing. Thus, the policeman, faced with enforcing a law against fornication, drunkenness, or gambling, is easily liable to a charge of hypocrisy. Even when the policeman is called on to enforce the laws relating to overt homosexuality, a form of sexual activity for which police are not especially noted, he may encounter the charge of hypocrisy on grounds that he does not adhere strictly to prescribed heterosexual codes. The policeman's difficulty in this respect is shared by all authorities responsible for maintenance of disciplined activity, including industrial foremen, political leaders, elementary school teachers, and college professors. All are expected to conform rigidly to the entire range of norms they espouse.[18] The policeman, however, as a result of the unique combination of the elements of danger and authority, experiences a special predicament. It is difficult to develop qualities enabling him to stand up to danger, and to conform to standards of puritanical morality. The element of danger demands that the policeman be able to carry out efforts that are in their nature overtly masculine. Police work, like soldiering, requires an exceptional caliber of physical fitness, agility, toughness, and the like. The man who ranks high on these masculine characteristics is, again like the soldier, not usually disposed to be puritanical about sex, drinking, and gambling.

On the basis of observations, policemen do not subscribe to moralistic standards for conduct. For example, the morals squad of the police department, when questioned, was unanimously against the statutory rape age limit, on grounds that as late teen-agers they themselves might not have refused an attractive offer from a seventeen-year-old girl.[19] Neither, from observations, are policemen by any means total abstainers from the use of alcoholic beverages. The policeman who is arresting a drunk has probably been drunk himself; he knows it and the drunk knows it.

More than that, a portion of the social isolation of the policeman can be attributed to the discrepancy between moral regulation and the norms and behavior of policemen in these areas. We have presented data indicating that police engage in a comparatively active occupational social life. One interpretation might attribute this attendance to a basic interest in such affairs; another might explain the policeman's occupational social activity as a measure of restraint in publicly violating norms he enforces. The interest in attending police affairs may grow as much out of security in "letting oneself go" in the presence of police, and corresponding feeling of insecurity with civilians, as an authentic preference for police social affairs. Much alcohol is usually consumed at police banquets with all the melancholy and boisterousness accompanying such occasions. As Horace Cayton reports on his experience as a policeman:

> Deputy sheriffs and policemen don't know much about organized recreation; all they usually do when celebrating is get drunk and pound each other on the back, exchanging loud insults which under ordinary circumstances would result in a fight.[20]

To some degree the reason for the behavior exhibited on these occasions is the company, since the policeman would feel uncomfortable exhibiting insobriety before civilians. The policeman may be likened to other authorities who prefer to violate moralistic norms away from onlookers for whom they are routinely supposed to appear as normative models. College professors, for instance, also get drunk on occasion, but prefer to do so where students are not present. Unfortunately for the policeman, such settings are harder for him to come by than they are for the college professor. The whole civilian world watches the policeman. As a result, he tends to be limited to the company of other policemen for whom his police identity is not a stimulus to carping normative criticism.

Correlates of Social Isolation

The element of authority, like the element of danger, is thus seen to contribute to the solidarity of policemen. To the extent that policemen share the experience of receiving hostility from the public, they are also drawn together and become dependent upon one another. Trends in the degree to which police may exercise authority are also important considerations in understanding the dynamics of the relation between authority and solidarity. It is not simply a question of how much absolute authority police are given, but how much authority they have relative to what they had, or think they had, before. If, as Westley concludes, police violence is frequently a response to a challenge to the policeman's authority, so too may a perceived reduction in authority result in greater solidarity. Whitaker comments on the British police as follows:

> As they feel their authority decline, internal solidarity has become increasingly important to the police. Despite the individual responsibility of each police officer to pursue justice, there is sometimes a tendency to close ranks and to form a square when they themselves are concerned.[21]

These inclinations may have positive consequences for the effectiveness of police work, since notions of professional courtesy or colleagueship seem unusually high among police.[22] When the nature of the policing enterprise requires much joint activity, as in robbery and narcotics enforcement, the impression is received that cooperation is high and genuine. Policemen do not appear to cooperate with one another merely because such is the policy of the chief, but because they sincerely attach a high value to teamwork. For instance, there is a norm among detectives that two who work together will protect each other when a dangerous situation arises. During one investigation, a detective stepped out of a car to question a suspect who became belligerent. The second detective, who had remained overly long in the back seat of the police car, apologized indirectly to his partner by explaining how wrong it had been of him to permit his partner to encounter a suspect alone on the street. He later repeated this explanation privately, in genuine consternation at having committed the breach (and possibly at having been culpable in the presence of an observer). Strong feelings of empathy and cooperation, indeed almost of "clannishness," a term several policemen themselves used to describe the attitude of police toward one another, may be seen in the daily activities of police. Analytically, these feelings can be traced to the elements of danger and shared experiences of hostility in the policeman's role.

Finally, to round out the sketch, policemen are notably conservative, emotionally and politically. If the element of danger in the policeman's role tends to make the policeman suspicious, and therefore emotionally attached to the status quo, a similar consequence may be attributed to the element of authority. The fact that a man is engaged in enforcing a set of rules implies that he also becomes implicated in *affirming* them. Labor disputes provide the commonest example of conditions inclining the policeman to support the status quo. In these situations, the police are necessarily pushed on the side of the defense of property. Their responsibilities thus lead them to see the striking and sometimes angry workers as their enemy and, therefore, to be cool, if not antagonistic, toward the whole conception of labor militancy.[23] If a policeman did not believe in the system of laws he was responsible for enforcing, he would have to go on living in a state of conflicting cognitions, a condition which a number of social psychologists agree is painful.[24]

This hypothetical issue of not believing in the laws they are enforcing simply does not arise for most policemen. In the course of the research, however, there was one example. A Negro civil rights advocate (member of CORE) became a policeman with the conviction that by so doing he would be aiding the cause of impartial administration of law for Negroes. For him, however, this outside rationale was not enough to sustain him in administering a system of laws that depends for its impartiality upon a reasonable measure of social and economic equality among the citizenry. Because this recruit identified so much with the Negro community as to be unable to meet the enforcement requirements of the Westville Police Department, his efficiency was impaired, and he resigned in his rookie year.

Police are understandably reluctant to appear to be anything but impartial politically. The police are forbidden from publicly campaigning for political candidates. The London police are similarly prohibited, and before 1887 were not allowed to vote in parliamentary elections, or in local ones until 1893.[25] It was not surprising that the Westville Chief of Police forbade questions on the questionnaire that would have measured political attitudes.[26] One policeman, however, explained the chief's refusal on grounds that, "A couple of jerks here would probably cut up, and come out looking like Commies."

During the course of administering the questionnaire over a three-day period, I talked with approximately fifteen officers and sergeants in the Westville department, discussing political attitudes of police. In addition, during the course of the research itself, approximately fifty were interviewed for varying periods of time. Of these, at least twenty were interviewed more than once, some over time periods of several weeks. Furthermore, twenty police were interviewed in Eastville, several for periods ranging from several hours to several days. Most of the time was *not* spent on investigating political attitudes, but I made a point of raising the question, if possible making it part of a discussion centered around the contents of a right-wing newsletter to which one of the detectives subscribed. One discussion included a group of eight detectives. From these observations, interviews, and discussions, it was clear that a Goldwater type of conservatism was the dominant political and emotional persuasion of police. I encountered only three policemen who claimed to be politically "liberal," at the same time asserting that they were decidedly exceptional.

Whether or not the policeman is an "authoritarian personality" is a related issue, beyond the scope of this discussion partly because of the many questions raised about this concept. Thus, in the course of discussing the concept of "normality" in mental health, two psychologists make the point that many conventional people were high scorers on the California F scale and similar tests. The great mass of the people, according to these authors, is not much further along the scale of ego development than the typical adolescent who, as they describe him, is "rigid, prone to think in stereotypes, intolerant of deviations, punitive and anti-psychological—in short, what has been called an authoritarian personality.[27] Therefore it is preferable to call the policeman's a conventional personality.

Writing about the New York police force, Thomas R. Brooks suggests a similar interpretation. He writes:

> Cops are conventional people. . . . All a cop can swing in a milieu of marijuana smokers, interracial dates, and homosexuals is the night stick. A policeman who passed a Lower East Side art gallery filled with paintings of what appeared to be female genitalia could think of doing only one thing—step in and make an arrest.[28]

Despite his fundamental identification with conservative conventionality, however, the policeman may be familiar, unlike most conventional people, with the argot of the hipster and the underworld. (The policeman tends to resent the quietly respectable liberal who comes to the defense of such people on principle but who has rarely met them in practice.) Indeed, the policeman will use his knowledge of the argot to advantage in talking to a suspect. In this manner, the policeman *puts on* the suspect by pretending to share his moral conception of the world through the use of "hip" expressions. The suspect may put on a parallel show for the policeman by using only conventional language to indicate his respectability. (In my opinion, neither fools the other.) . . .

Notes

1. For previous contributions in this area, see the following: Ely Chinoy, *Automobile Workers and the American Dream* (Garden City: Doubleday and Company, Inc., 1955); Charles R. Walker and Robert H. Guest, *The Man on the Assembly Line* (Cambridge: Harvard University Press, 1952); Everett C. Hughes, "Work and the Self," in his *Men and Their Work* (Glencoe, IL: The Free Press, 1958), pp. 42–55; Harold L. Wilensky, *Intellectuals in Labor Unions: Organizational Pressures on Professional Roles* (Glencoe, IL: The Free Press, 1956); Wilensky, "Varieties of Work Experience," in Henry Borow (ed.), *Man in a World at Work* (Boston: Houghton Mifflin Company, 1964), pp. 125–154; Louis Kriesberg, "The Retail Furrier: Concepts of Security and Success," *American Journal of Sociology*, 57 (March 1952), 478–485; Waldo Burchard, "Role Conflicts of Military Chaplains," *American Sociological Review*, 19 (October 1954), 528–535; Howard S. Becker and Blanche Geer, "The Fate of Idealism in Medical School," *American Sociological Review*, 23 (1958), 50–56; and Howard S. Becker and Anselm L. Strauss, "Careers, Personality, and Adult Socialization," *American Journal of Sociology*, 62 (November 1956), 253–363.

2. Morris Janowitz, *The Professional Soldier: A Social and Political Portrait* (New York: The Free Press of Glencoe, 1964), p. 175.

3. By no means does such an analysis suggest there are no individual or group differences among police. On the contrary, most of this study emphasizes differences, endeavoring to relate these to occupational specialities in police departments. This chapter, however, explores similarities rather than differences, attempting to account for the policeman's general disposition to perceive and to behave in certain ways.

4. William Westley was the first to raise such questions about the police, when he inquired into the conditions under which police are violent. Whatever merit this analysis has, it owes much to his prior insights, as all subsequent sociological studies of the police must. See his "Violence and the Police," *American Journal of Sociology*, 59 (July 1953), 34–41; also his unpublished Ph.D. dissertation *The Police: A Sociological Study of Law, Custom, and Morality*, University of Chicago, Department of Sociology, 1951.
5. Something of the flavor of the policeman's attitude toward the symbolic assailant comes across in a recent article by a police expert. In discussing the problem of selecting subjects for field interrogation, the author writes:
    A. Be suspicious. This is a healthy police attitude, but it should be controlled and not too obvious.
    B. Look for the unusual.
        1. Persons who do not "belong" where they are observed.
        2. Automobiles which do not "look right."
        3. Businesses opened at odd hours, or not according to routine or custom.
    C. Subjects who should be subjected to field interrogations.
        1. Suspicious persons known to the officer from previous arrests, field interrogations, and observations.
        2. Emaciated appearing alcoholics and narcotics users who invariably turn to crime to pay for cost of habit.
        3. Person who fits description of wanted suspect as described by radio, teletype, daily bulletins.
        4. Any person observed in the immediate vicinity of a crime very recently committed or reported as "in progress."
        5. Known trouble-makers near large gatherings.
        6. Persons who attempt to avoid or evade the officer.
        7. Exaggerated unconcern over contact with the officer.
        8. Visibly "rattled" when near the policeman.
        9. Unescorted women or young girls in public places, particularly at night in such places as cafes, bars, bus and train depots, or street corners.
        10. "Lovers" in an industrial area (make good lookouts).
        11. Persons who loiter about places where children play.
        12. Solicitors or peddlers in a residential neighborhood.
        13. Loiterers around public restrooms.
        14. Lone male sitting in car adjacent to schoolground with newspaper or book in his lap.
        15. Lone male sitting in car near shopping center who pays unusual amount of attention to women, sometimes continuously manipulating rearview mirror to avoid direct eye contact.
        16. Hitchhikers.
        17. Person wearing coat on hot days.
        18. Car with mismatched hub caps, or dirty car with clean license plate (or vice versa).
        19. Uniformed "deliverymen" with no merchandise or truck.
        20. Many others. How about your own personal experiences?
    From Thomas F. Adams, "Field Interrogation," *Police* (March-April 1963), 28.
6. See Irving Piliavin and Scott Briar, "Police Encounters with Juveniles," *American Journal of Sociology*, 70 (September 1964), 206–214.
7. A questionnaire was given to all policemen in operating divisons of the police force: patrol, traffic, vice control, and all detectives. The questionnaire was administered at police line-ups over a period of three days, mainly by the author but also by some of the police personnel themselves. Before the questionnaire was administered, it was circulated to and approved by the policemen's welfare association.
8. Indeed, the journalist Paul Jacobs, who has ridden with the Westville juvenile police as part of his own work on poverty, observed in a personal communication that juvenile police

appear curiously drawn to seek out dangerous situations, as if juvenile work without danger is degrading.

9. James Baldwin, *Nobody Knows My Name* (New York: Dell Publishing Company, 1962), pp. 65–67.

10. McInnes, [*Mr. Love and Justice* (London: New English Library, 1962)], p. 20.

11. In addition to Banton, William Westley and James Q. Wilson have noted this characteristic of police. See Westley, op. cit., p. 294; Wilson, "The Police and Their Problems: A Theory," *Public Policy*, 12 (1963), 189–216.

12. S. M. Lipset, Martin H. Trow, and James S. Coleman, *Union Democracy* (New York: Anchor Books, 1962). p. 123. A complete comparison is as follows:

Closest Friends of Printers and Police, by Occupation

	Printers N = 1236 (%)	Police N = 700 (%)
Same occupation	35	35
Professionals, business executives, and independent business owners	21	30
White-collar or sales employees	20	12
Manual workers	25	22

13. On this issue there was no variation. The statement "the policeman feels" means that there was no instance of a negative opinion expressed by the police studied.

14. Banton, op. cit., p. 114.

15. Janowitz, op. cit.

16. O. W. Wilson, for example, mentions this factor as a primary source of antagonism toward police. See his "Police Authority in a Free Society," *Journal of Criminal Law, Criminology and Police Science*, 54 (June 1964), 175–177. In the current study, in addition to the police themselves, other people interviewed, such as attorneys in the system, also attribute the isolation of police to their authority. Similarly, Arthur L. Stinchcombe, in an as yet unpublished manuscript, "The Control of Citizen Resentment in Police Work," provides a stimulating analysis, to which I am indebted, of the ways police authority generates resentment.

17. See Wayne R. La Fave, "The Police and Nonenforcement of the Law," *Wisconsin Law Review* (1962), 104–137, 179–239.

18. For a theoretical discussion of the problems of leadership, see George Homans, *The Human Group* (New York: Harcourt, Brace and Company, 1950), especially the chapter on "The Job of the Leader," pp. 415–440.

19. The work of the Westville morals squad is analyzed in detail in an unpublished master's thesis by J. Richard Woodworth. *The Administration of Statutory Rape Complaints: A Sociological Study* (Berkeley: University of California, 1964).

20. Horace R. Cayton, *Long Old Road* (New York: Trident Press, 1965), p. 154.

21. Ben Whitaker, *The Police* (Middlesex, England: Penguin Books, 1964), p. 137.

22. It would be difficult to compare this factor across occupations, since the indicators could hardly be controlled. Nevertheless, I felt that the sense of responsibility to policemen in other departments was on the whole quite strong.

23. In light of this, the most carefully drawn lesson plan in the "professionalized" Westville police department, according to the officer in charge of training, is the one dealing with

the policeman's demeanor in labor disputes. A comparable concern is now being evidenced in teaching policemen appropriate demeanor in civil rights demonstrations. See, e.g., Juby E. Towler, *The Police Role In Racial Conflicts* (Springfield: Charles C Thomas, 1964).

24. Indeed, one school of social psychology asserts that there is a basic "drive," a fundamental tendency of human nature, to reduce the degree of discrepancy between conflicting cognitions. For the policeman, this tenet implies that he would have to do something to reduce the discrepancy between his beliefs and his behavior. He would have to modify his behavior, his beliefs, or introduce some outside factor to justify the discrepancy. If he were to modify his behavior, so as not to enforce the law in which he disbelieves, he would not hold his position for long. Practically, then, his alternatives are to introduce some outside factor, or to modify his beliefs. However, the outside factor would have to be compelling in order to reduce the pain resulting from the dissonance between his cognitions. For example, he would have to be able to convince himself that the only way he could possibly make a living was by being a policeman. Or he would have to modify his beliefs. See Leon Festinger, *A Theory of Cognitive Dissonance* (Evanston, IL: Row-Peterson, 1957). A brief explanation of Festinger's theory is reprinted in Edward E. Sampson (ed.), *Approaches, Contexts, and Problems of Social Psychology* (Englewood Cliffs, NJ: Prentice-Hall, 1964), pp. 9–15.

25. Whitaker, op. cit., p. 26.

26. The questions submitted to the chief of police were directly analogous to those asked of printers in the study of the I.T.U. See Lipset et al., op. cit., "Appendix II—Interview Schedule," pp. 493–503.

27. Jane Loevinger and Abel Ossorio, "Evaluation of Therapy by Self Report: A Paradox," *Journal of Abnormal and Social Psychology*, 58 (May, 1959), 392; see also Edward A. Shils, "Authoritarianism: 'Right' and 'Left'," in R. Christie and M. Jahoda (ed.), *Studies in Scope and Method of "The Authoritarian Personality,"* (Glencoe, IL: The Free Press, 1954), pp. 24–49.

28. Thomas R. Brooks. "New York's Finest," *Commentary*, 40 (August 1965), 29–30.

53

Police Control of Juveniles
Donald J. Black   *Albert J. Reiss, Jr.*

. . .This paper presents findings on citizen and police detection of juvenile deviance and on the sanctioning of juveniles through arrest in routine police work. It makes problematic situational conditions that increase the probability of sanction subsequent to the detection of violative behavior. Put another way, it makes problematic conditions (besides rule-violative behavior itself) that give rise to differentials in official sanctioning. It is a study of law-in-action. Since all of the data pertain to police encounters with alleged delinquents, the relationship between undetected and detected delinquency is not treated.

The Method

The findings reported here derive from systematic observation of police-citizen transactions conducted during the summer of 1966. Thirty-six observers—persons with law, law enforcement, and social science backgrounds—recorded observations of routine patrol work in Boston, Chicago, and Washington, D.C. The observer training period comprised one week and was identical across the three cities. The daily supervision system also was similar across the cities. The observers rode in scout cars or, less frequently, walked with patrolmen on all shifts on all days of the week for seven weeks in each city. To assure the inclusion of a large number of police-citizen encounters, we gave added weight to the times when police activity is comparatively high (evening watches, particularly weekend evenings).

No attempt was made to survey police-citizen encounters in all localities within the three cities. Instead, police precincts in each city were chosen as observation sites. The precincts were selected so as to maximize observation in lower-socio-economic, high crime rate, racially homogeneous residential areas. This was accomplished through the selection of two precincts each in Boston and Chicago and four precincts in Washington, D.C. The findings pertain to the behavior of uniformed patrolmen rather than to that of policemen in specialized divisions such as juvenile bureaus or detective units.

The data were recorded by the observers in "incident booklets," forms much like interview schedules. One booklet was filled out for every incident that the police

Source: *American Sociological Review*, Vol. 35 (February), pp. 63–77. Copyright © 1970 by the American Sociological Association. Reprinted with permission.

were requested to handle or that they themselves noticed while on patrol. A total of 5,713 of these incidents were observed and recorded. This paper concerns only those 281 encounters that include one or more juvenile suspects among the participants. . . .

Detection of Juvenile Deviance

Observation of police encounters with citizens netted 281 encounters with suspects under 18 years of age, here treated as juveniles. The great majority of the juveniles were from blue-collar families. Of the 281 police-juvenile encounters, 72% were citizen-initiated (by phone) and 28% were initiated by policemen on patrol. Excluding traffic violations, these proportions become 78% and 22%, respectively. The mobilization of police control of juveniles is then overwhelmingly a reactive rather than a proactive process. Hence it would seem that the moral standards of the citizenry have more to do with the definition of juvenile deviance than do the standards of policemen on patrol.

Moreover, the incidents the police handle in citizen-initiated encounters differ somewhat from those in encounters they bring into being on their own initiative. This does not mean, however, that the standards of citizens and policemen necessarily differ; the differences between incidents in reactive and proactive police work seem to result in large part from differences in detection opportunities, since the police are limited to the surveillance of public places (Stinchcombe, 1963). For example, non-criminal disputes are more likely to occur in private than in public places; they account for 10% of the police-juvenile contacts in citizen-initiated work but for only 3% of the proactive encounters. On the other hand, the "suspicious person" is nearly always a police-initiated encounter. Traffic violations, too, are almost totally in the police-initiated category; it is simply not effective or feasible for a citizen to call the police about a "moving" traffic violation (and nearly all of these cases were "moving" rather than "standing" violations). In short, there are a number of contingencies that affect the detection of juvenile deviance in routine policing.

A broader pattern in the occasions for police-juvenile transactions is the overwhelming predominance of incidents of minor legal significance. Only 5% of the police encounters with juveniles involve alleged felonies; the remainder are less serious from a legal standpoint. Sixty percent involve nothing more serious than juvenile rowdiness or mischievous behavior, the juvenile counterpart of "disorderly conduct" or "breach of the peace" by adults. . . .

Another pattern lies in the differences between Negro and white encounters with policemen. In the aggregate, police encounters with Negro juveniles pertain to legally more serious incidents, owing primarily to the differential in felony encounters. None of the encounters with white juveniles involved the allegation of a felony, though this was true of 10% of the transactions with Negro juveniles in both citizen- and police-initiated encounters. Apart from this difference between the races, however, the occasions for encounters with Negro and white juveniles have many similarities.

It might be noted that the data on the occasions for police-juvenile encounters do not in themselves provide evidence of racial discrimination in the selection of juveniles for police attention. Of course, the citizen-initiated encounters cannot speak to the issue of discriminatory *police* selection. On the other hand, if the police tend to stop a disproportionate number of Negroes on the street in minor incident situations, we might infer the presence of discrimination. But the findings do not provide such evidence. Likewise, we might infer police discrimination if a higher proportion of the total Negro encounters is police-initiated than that of the total white encounters. Again the evidence is lacking: police-initiated encounters account for 28% of the total for both Negro and white juveniles. More data would be needed to assess adequately the issue of police selectivity by race.

Incidents and Arrest

Of the encounters patrol officers have with juvenile suspects, only 15% result in arrest. Hence it is apparent that by a large margin most police-juvenile contacts are concluded in the field settings where they arise. These field contacts, 85% of the total, generally are not included in official police statistics on reported cases of juvenile delinquency, and thus they represent the major invisible portion of the delinquency control process. In other words, if these sample data are reasonably representative, the probability is less than one-in-seven that a policeman confronting a juvenile suspect will exercise his discretion to produce an official case of juvenile delinquency. A high level of selectivity enters into the arrest of juveniles. This and subsequent sections of the paper seek to identify some of the conditions which contribute to that selection process.

A differential in police dispositions that appears at the outset of the analysis is that between Negroes and whites. The overall arrest rate for police-Negro encounters is 21%, while the rate for police-white encounters is only 8%. This difference immediately raises the question of whether or not racial discrimination determines the disposition of juvenile suspects. Moreover, the arrest rate for Negroes is also higher within specific incident categories where comparisons are possible. The race difference, therefore, is not merely a consequence of the larger number of legally serious incidents that occasion police-Negro contacts.

Apart from the race difference, patrol officers make proportionately more arrests when the incident is relatively serious from a legal standpoint. The arrest rate for Negro encounters is twice as high for felonies as it is for the more serious misdemeanors, and for encounters with both races the arrest rate for serious misdemeanors doubles the rate for juvenile rowdiness. On the other hand, policemen rarely make arrests of either race for traffic violations or for suspicious person situations. Arrest appears even less likely when the incident is a noncriminal dispute. The disposition pattern for juvenile suspects clearly follows the hierarchy of offenses found in the criminal law, the law for adults. . . .

Situational Organization and Arrest

Apart from the substance of police encounters—the kinds of incidents they involve—these encounters have a social structure. One element in this structure is the distribution of the situational roles played by the participants in the encounter. Major situational roles that arise in police encounters are those of suspect or offender, complainant, victim, informant, and bystander. . . .

All of the encounters involving a citizen complainant in this sample were citizen-initiated typically by the complainants themselves. Proactive police operations rarely involve complainants . . . The police are particularly likely to arrest a Negro juvenile when a citizen enjoins them to handle the incident and participates as a complainant in the situational action, but this is not characteristic of police encounters with white juveniles. Finally, it is noteworthy that Negro juveniles find themselves in encounters that involve a complainant proportionately more than do white juveniles. Hence, the pattern discussed above has all the more impact on the overall arrest rate for Negro juveniles. Accordingly, the next section examines the role of the complainant in more detail.

The Complainant's Preference and Arrest

If the presence of a citizen complainant increases the production of Negro arrests, then the question arises as to whether this pattern occurs as a function of the complainant's mere presence, his situational behavior, or something else. In part, this issue can be broached by inquiring into the relationship between the complainant's behavioral preference for police action in a particular field situation and the kind of disposition the police in fact make.

Before examining this relationship, however, it should be noted that a rather large proportion of complainants do not express clear preferences for police action such that a field observer can make an accurate classification. Moreover, there is a race differential in this respect. Considering only the misdemeanor situations, the Negro complainant's preference for action is unclear in 48% of the police encounters with Negro juveniles, whereas the comparable proportion drops to 27% for the encounters with white complainants and juveniles. Nevertheless, a slightly larger proportion of the Negro complainants express a preference for arrest of their juvenile adversaries—21%, versus 15% for whites. Finally, the complainant prefers an informal disposition in 31% of the Negro cases and in 58% of the white cases. Thus white complainants more readily express a preference for police leniency toward juvenile suspects than do Negro complainants.

White juveniles benefit from this greater leniency, since the police show a quite dramatic pattern of compliance with the expressed preferences of complainants. This pattern seems clear even though the number of cases necessitates caution in interpretation. In not one instance did the police arrest a juvenile when the complainant lobbied for leniency. When a complainant explicitly expresses a preference for an arrest, however, the tendency of the police to comply is also quite strong. For only the two types of misdemeanor, the Negro arrest rate when the complainant's preference is arrest (60%) climbs toward the rate of arrest for felonies (73%). In no other tabulation does the arrest rate for misdemeanors rise so high. Lastly, it is notable that when the complainant's preference is unclear, the arrest rate falls between the rate for complainants who prefer arrest and those who prefer an informal disposition.

These patterns have several implications. First, it is evident that the higher arrest rate for Negro juveniles in encounters with complainants and suspects is largely a consequence of the tendency of the police to comply with the preferences of complainants. This tendency is costly for Negro juveniles, since Negro complainants are relatively severe in their expressed preferences when they are compared to white complainants vis-á-vis white juveniles. . . .

Situational Evidence and Arrest

In about 50% of the situations a police officer observes the juvenile offense, excluding felonies and traffic violations. Hence, even though citizens initially detect most juvenile deviance, the police often respond in time to witness the behavior in question. In roughly 25% of the situations the policeman arrives too late to see the offense committed but a citizen gives testimonial evidence. The remaining cases, composed primarily of non-criminal disputes and suspicious person situations, bear no evidence of criminal conduct. In a heavy majority of routine police-juvenile encounters, the juvenile suspect finds himself with incriminating evidence of some sort. The low arrest rate should be understood in this context. . . .

In "police witness" situations the arrest rate is no higher but is even slightly, though insignificantly, lower than the rate in "citizen testimony" situations. . . .

The low arrest rate in "police witness" situations is striking in itself. It documents the enormous extent to which patrolmen use their discretion to release juvenile deviants without official sanction and without making an official report of the incident. Official statistics on juvenile delinquency vastly underestimate even the delinquent acts that policemen witness while on patrol. In this sense the police keep down the official delinquency rate. One other implication of the low arrest rate should be noted. Because the vast majority of police-juvenile contacts are concluded in field settings, judicial control of police conduct through the exclusion of evidence in juvenile courts is potentially emasculated. Police control of juveniles— like that of adults (Reiss and Black, 1967)—may be less prosecution-oriented than the law assumes. In other words, much about the policing of juveniles follows an informal-processing or harassment model rather than a formal-processing model of control. From a behavioral standpoint, law enforcement generally is not a legal duty of policemen.

On the other hand, the importance of situational evidence should not be analytically underestimated. The police very rarely arrest juveniles when there is no evidence. In only one case was a juvenile arrested when there was no situational evidence in the observer's judgment; this was a suspicious person situation. In sum, then, even when the police have very persuasive situational evidence, they generally release juveniles in the field; but, when they do arrest juveniles, they almost always have evidence of some kind. When there is strong evidence against a suspect, formal enforcement becomes a privilege of the police officer. This privilege provides an opportunity for discriminatory practices (Davis, 1969: 169–176).

The Suspect's Deference and Arrest

. . . Earlier research on police work suggests a strong association between situational outcomes and the degree of respect extended to policemen by suspects, namely, the less respectful the suspect, the harsher the sanction (Piliavin and Briar, 1964; Westley, 1955). . . .

Before the findings on this relationship are examined, however, it should be noted that the potential impact of the suspect's deference on juvenile dispositions in the aggregate is necessarily limited. Only a small minority of juveniles behave at the extremes of a continuum going from very deferential or very respectful at one end to antagonistic or disrespectful at the other. In most encounters with patrolmen the outward behavior of juvenile suspects falls between these two extremes: the typical juvenile is civil toward police officers, neither strikingly respectful nor disrespectful. The juvenile suspect is civil toward the police in 57% of the encounters, a rather high proportion in view of the fact that the degree of deference was not ascertained in 16% of the 281 cases. The juvenile is very deferential in 11% and antagonistic in 16% of the encounters. Thus if disrespectful juveniles are processed with stronger sanctions, the subpopulation affected is fairly small. The majority of juvenile arrests occur when the suspect is civil toward the police. It remains to be seen, however, how great the differences are in the probability of arrest among juveniles who display varying degrees of deference.

The relationship between a juvenile suspect's deference and his liability to arrest is relatively weak and does not appear to be unidirectional. Considering all of the cases, the arrest rate for encounters where the suspect is civil is 16%. When the suspect behaves antagonistically toward the police, the rate is higher—22%. Although this difference is not wide, it is in the expected direction. What was not anticipated, however, is that the arrest rate for encounters involving very deferential suspects is also 22%. . . .

Overview

I: Most police encounters with juveniles arise in direct response to citizens who take the initiative to mobilize the police to action.

II: The great bulk of police encounters with juveniles pertain to matters of minor legal significance.

III: The probability of sanction by arrest is very low for juveniles who have encounters with the police.

IV: The probability of arrest increases with the legal seriousness of alleged juvenile offenses, as that legal seriousness is defined in the criminal law for adults.

V: Police sanctioning of juveniles strongly reflects the manifest preferences of citizen complainants in field encounters.

VI: The arrest rate for Negro juveniles is higher than that for white juveniles, but evidence that the police behaviorally orient themselves to race as such is absent.

VII: The presence of situational evidence linking a juvenile to a deviant act is an important factor in the probability of arrest.

VIII: The probability of arrest is higher for juveniles who are unusually respectful toward the police and for those who are unusually disrespectful.

References

Davis, Kenneth Culp. 1969. *Discretionary Justice: A Preliminary Inquiry*. Baton Rouge, Louisiana: Louisiana State University Press.

Piliavin, Irving and Scott Briar. 1964. "Police encounters with juveniles." *American Journal of Sociology* 70 (1964): 206–214.

Reiss, Albert J., Jr. and Donald J. Black. 1967. "Interrogation and the criminal process." *The Annals of the American Academy of Political and Social Science* 374 (1967):47–57.

Stinchcombe, Arthur L. 1963. "Institutions of privacy in the determination of police administrative practice." *American Journal of Sociology* 69 (1963): 150–160.

Westley, William A. 1955. "Violence and the police." *American Journal of Sociology* 59 (1955): 34–41.

54

The Kansas City Preventive Patrol Experiment

George L. Kelling   Tony Pate
Duane Dieckman   Charles E. Brown

Police patrol strategies have always been based on two unproven but widely accepted hypotheses: first, that visible police presence prevents crime by deterring potential offenders; second, that the public's fear of crime is diminished by such police presence. Thus, routine preventive police patrol was thought both to prevent crime and reassure the public.

The Kansas City, Missouri, Police Department conducted an experiment from October 1, 1972, through September 30, 1973, designed to measure the impact routine patrol had on the incidence of crime and the public's fear of crime. This experiment, made possible by Police Foundation funding, employed a methodology which accurately determined that traditional routine preventive patrol had no significant impact either on the level of crime or the public's feeling of security.

Three controlled levels of routine preventive patrol were used in the experimental areas. One area, termed "reactive," received no preventive patrol. Officers entered the area only in response to citizen calls for assistance. This in effect substantially reduced police visibility in that area. In the second area, called "proactive," police visibility was increase two to three times its usual level. In the third area, termed "control," the normal level of patrol was maintained. Analysis of the data gathered revealed that the three areas experienced no significant differences in the level of crime, citizen's attitudes toward police services, citizens' fear of crime, police response time, or citizens' satisfaction with police response time.

What do these results mean?

A great deal of caution must be used to avoid the error of believing that the experiment proved more than it actually did. One thing the experiment did not show is that a visible police presence can have no impact on crime in selected circumstances. The experiment did show that routine preventive patrol in marked police cars has little value in preventing crime or making citizens feel safe.

It would be a grave error to assume that this study implies in any way that fewer police officers are needed in any specific jurisdiction. The study shows

Source: Excerpted from George L. Kelling, Tony Pate, Duane Dieckman and Charles E. Brown, *The Kansas City Preventive Patrol Experiment: A Technical Report*, Copyright © 1974 by Police Foundation. Excerpted by permission of the Police Foundation, Washington, DC.

something quite different, with profound implications for police administrators. The experiment revealed that the noncommitted time of the police officers (60 percent in the experiment) can be used for purposes other than routine patrol without any negative impact on public safety. . . .

Introduction

The history of policing is a chronicle of unchallenged assumptions. Many contend that control of crime is a police matter, and are bitterly outspoken when the police fail to "do their job." The police, in turn, respond to such criticism in ways that often create a double-bind: rushing to stem such criticism with increases in the size and visibility of patrol, and watching in frustration as crime continues to increase. There is an unquestioned belief that more and more police will result in less and less crime.

Police technology has progressed tremendously in the past 50 years. Tragically, the expectations and premises underlying the police function in modern society have failed to keep pace. The patrol function to this day remains the single, most important police strategy, with commitments of vast sums of money and manpower annually. Patrol is, as many departments will tell their rookies, "a chance to do something about crime." Yet little is known of the deterrent effects of routine preventive patrol.[1] Little is understood of patrol's importance to the police function. And much is misunderstood concerning what the police can and cannot do as a vital element in the criminal justice system.

Having been fed years of distortion in the media, the American public is a true believer in the police officer's glamorous, action-oriented battle against crime. The public would happily assume that policing is a time consuming, intense skirmish in which police officers, usually detectives, pit their superior skills and deductive abilities against criminals who will always be foiled by the "long arm of the law." In fact, policing is anything but this. Yet the police have been willing perpetrators of this delusion; and the American public, eager devotees. This report is a challenge to these assumptions. . . .

In challenging assumptions and attempting to address issues, the experiment described here has examined the deterrent and service delivery effectiveness of police patrol in both its exaggerated and its diminished postures. It has studied citizen fear and perceptions of the police as related to various levels of preventive patrol. It has probed police attitudes toward patrol, and what police officers actually do while on patrol. In doing this, the experiment collected a tremendous amount of data, often calling upon a wide variety of indicators which point in the same direction. This has been done purposely in order to speak with a high degree of confidence about so important an issue as preventive patrol and its effects on crime and the community.

In some cases the findings directly challenge the basic underpinnings of policing and the public's understanding of the police role. In others the findings point to an acute need for further research. And in others they simply point to what many in the field have long suspected—that the disparity between what we want the police to do and what they can and actually should do is often extensive.

It could be argued that because of its large geographical area and relatively low population density, Kansas City is not representative of the more populous urban areas of the United States. However, many of the critical problems and situations facing Kansas City are common to other large cities. For example, in terms of rates of aggravated assault, Kansas City ranks close to Detroit and San Francisco. The rate of murder and manslaughter per 100,000 persons in Kansas City is similar to that of Los Angeles, Denver and Cincinnati. And in terms of burglary, Kansas City is comparable to Boston and Birmingham. Furthermore, the experimental area itself was diverse socio-economically, and has a population density much higher than Kansas City's average, making the experimental area far more representative and comparative than Kansas City as a whole might be. In these respects, the conclusions and implications of this study can be widely applied.

This report is not intended to imply that the police are not central to the solution of crime. It does not suggest that because the major part of the police officer's time is typically spent on non-crime related matters, the amount spent on crime is less important. Nor does it maintain that the provision of public services and maintenance of order should overshadow police work on crime.

Furthermore, despite speculation to the contrary, the report does not in any way suggest that police patrol is an unnecessary function. Nor should it serve as an automatic justification for reductions in the levels of policing. In addition, it neither supports nor addresses such issues as two-officer cars, team policing, generalist-specialist models, and other programs currently under consideration in many departments.

While one of the three patrol strategies used in this experiment called for a greater than usual reduction of police presence in an area, it did not totally withdraw police availability from that area. Therefore, this report should not be interpreted to suggest that complete withdrawal is an acceptable method of policing. A reduction was merely one of three strategies examined, and any conclusions as to its effectiveness must be handled with care. . . .

Implicit in the strategies underlying preventive patrol are assumptions of causal relationships between police presence on the one hand and criminal behavior, citizen attitudes and criminal apprehension on the other. It is assumed, for instance, that police presence generates increased police visibility which, in turn, results in increased citizen feelings of security. It is also assumed that increases in police visibility result in increased fear of apprehension on the part of criminals, and that this, in turn, deters criminal behavior. A further assumption is that police presence in an area reduced police response time which, in turn, results in increased criminal apprehension.

Since police presence is generally equated with police visibility, two questions arise: (1) to what extent was police visibility manipulated by the experiment, and (2) does the fact that neither citizens nor criminals were made aware of the experiment have any impact on its validity?

In answer to the first question, data presented in the chapters on noncommitted time and maintenance of experimental conditions suggest that in the reactive beats, the amount of time spent on routine preventive patrol was reduced 50 to 60 percent. This conclusion is supported by two findings: (1) no more than 40 percent of the time of even the busiest officers is committed, and therefore available for routine patrol; and (2) while there was some unnecessary penetration of reactive beats by police officers during their noncommitted time, such penetration was minimal; further, the amount of time spent on regular preventive patrol in the proactive (increased) beats was increased 250 to 300 percent, and in the control (normal) beats regular patrol was maintained at its normal level.

The experiment concludes with confidence that police visibility was reduced substantially in the reactive beats and increased substantially in the proactive beats.

As to awareness of the experiment, this question ignores the larger issue of the extent to which visibility is a legitimate part of the causal relationship between police presence, citizen feelings of security and criminal deterrence. To reveal the lack of, or increases in, police presence during the experimental period would have been to inform certain groups of participants of the nature of the experimental stimulus. This, without question, would have biased the experiment.

If police presence does make a difference, it should make that difference regardless of awareness of experimental manipulations.

In sum, the experiment represents a crucial first step, but just one in a series of steps toward defining and clarifying the expectations and premises underlying the police function in modern society.

The Experiment

. . . By March 1972 the South Patrol Task Force had completed a basic outline of the preventive patrol experiment it wished to undertake and had begun sampling daily activity logs in the South Patrol Area to determine how officers actually spent their time on duty. The project would test proactive and reactive patrol conditions, the results of which would hopefully allow the department to develop mixes of strategies for its police work. For purposes of comparison, a third factor—control, or the normal level and method of patrol—would be included. In proactive beats, patrol would be intensified. In control beats, patrol would continue at its normal rate. In reactive beats, preventive patrol would be curtailed, and police would enter the beats only when called (or in reaction to citizen or other calls for service). It is important to note that the reactive concept did not imply a total withdrawal of police protection from the reactive beats. Rather, police would be seen and perceived as "on routine preventive patrol" when physically in those beats answering calls for service.

Considerable controversy surrounded the project, the central question being whether long-range benefits outweighed short-term risks. The principal short-term risk was seen as the possibility that crime would increase dramatically in those beats designated as "reactive." Some felt that the project "would experiment with people's lives and property." The predominant view, however, was that the department had a long-term responsibility to the community, and that this responsibility could be better served by determining the actual value of its dominant patrol strategy. To minimize the risks involved crime rate data for the test area would be monitored on a weekly basis, and should a noticeable increase occur within a reactive beat, the experiment would be halted immediately.

As envisioned by the task force, the project would also attempt to establish the quantitative relationship between speed and type of police response and the crime rate, deterrence of crime, probability of on-scene apprehension and citizen satisfaction.

In its ultimate design the project would be a rigorous and systematic attempt to test the outcomes of different patrol strategies, and ultimately could lead to cost-benefit analyses of varied strategies to determine the most efficient methods of undertaking patrol. It was likewise felt that the preventive patrol experiment would help to maintain a climate of innovation and self-evaluation, not only on the part of the department as a whole but also among individual officers. The task force and the Police Foundation realized that since the effectiveness of routine preventive patrol was not self-evident and because the capacity to deal with crime is a central police function, the preventive patrol experiment would fill a real professional need heretofore not addressed by other police agencies.

After much discussion, the project was submitted to and approved by the coordinating council and, ultimately, the chief of police.

The decision as to the size of the experimental area (15 beats) resulted from prolonged discussions between the evaluation staff assigned to the experiment and the task force. Initially the South Patrol Task Force proposed that three beats be selected for the experimental area, resulting in one reactive, one control and one proactive beat. The problems of an inadequate sample size associated with so limited an experimental area were immediately apparent to the evaluation staff, and an attempt was made to increase the number of beats by as large a factor as possible. The task force was convinced that a larger area was unmanageable and seriously concerned over the consequences of "abandoning" even one beat. A compromise was finally reached, and within the South Patrol Division's 24-beat area, nine beats were eliminated from consideration as unrepresentative of the city's socio-economic composition. The remaining 15 beats were then designated as the experimental area.

The 15 beats were computer matched into five groups of three each on the basis of crime data, number of calls for service, ethnic composition, median income figures and transiency of population. The 32.67-square mile experimental area encompassed a commercial-residential mix, with a residential population of 148,395 and a density of 4,542 persons per square mile. (Kansas City's population density in 1970 was relatively low—1,604 persons per square mile; the city ranked 45th among American cities in terms of density, 26th in terms of total population, but eighth in terms of total land area; the experimental area, however, was more densely populated, and therefore could be compared to other urban centers.). . .

It should be noted that after the five random patterns had been established (to determine the mix of reactive, control and proactive among the 15 beats), an optimal configuration was selected (see Figure 1) to avoid the clustering of reactive beats which could have resulted in unacceptable response time in those beats.

It should also be noted that the deployment modifications related only to regular patrol units. Since only the effectiveness of routine preventive patrol by the patrol unit was being tested, specialized units (i.e., traffic, helicopter, tactical, etc.) operated as usual. (Such units maintained city-wide mobility and continued to react to specific problems.) However, operation of these units was to remain at a level consistent with levels established for the preceding year. At the same time the department's two other patrol divisions (Central and Northeast) were requested to refrain from entering the experimental area.

The major variable selected for manipulation in the experiment was the amount of time patrol cars would spend patrolling their designated beats. Although the areas selected for reduced coverage were termed reactive, that term referred only to the fact that cars were withdrawn except during response to calls. Likewise, proactive beats were distinguished only by the increase of routine preventive patrol. No special instructions or strategies were designated. Officers were instructed to patrol their beats as they normally would and within the experimental guidelines.

Figure 1

SCHEMATIC REPRESENTATION OF
THE 15 BEAT EXPERIMENTAL AREA

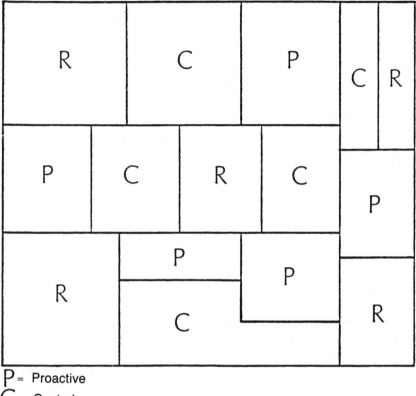

P = Proactive
C = Control
R = Reactive

In designing the project, the following policies were agreed upon:

(1) the design would be as rigorously experimental as possible;

(2) departmental data would be included, but as wide a data base as possible would be generated;

(3) the experiment would be monitored by both the department and the Police Foundation to insure maintenance of experimental conditions; and

(4) The department would commit itself to an eight-month experiment providing reported crime data did not reach "unacceptable" limits. (Unacceptable was defined as a statistically significant variation from predicted crime levels, or as based upon the impressions field commanders received from their daily reports.) If no further major problems developed,

the project would continue an additional four months, totalling a 12-month experiment.

A number of hypotheses were developed for the purpose of measurement. Of them the following were ultimately addressed:

(1) crime, as reflected by victimization surveys and reported crime data, would not vary by type of patrol;

(2) citizen perception of police service would not vary by type of patrol;

(3) citizen fear and behavior as a result of fear would not vary by type of patrol;

(4) traffic accidents would increase in the reactive beats; and

(5) police response time and citizen satisfaction with response time would vary by experimental area.

Variations in incidents of crime by type of patrol area would be measured by a community victimization survey at time 1 (prior to the experiment) and time 2 (after its conclusion); a commercial victimization survey at times 1 and 2; reported crime data compiled throughout the experimental period and, for the purpose of longitudinal perspective, reported crime data from the 1968–1973 time period.

Citizen fear would be measured by a community attitudinal survey (concerning opinions about police service, attitudes toward the police, fear of victimization and actual victimization) of 1,200 households conducted at times 1 and 2; a commercial survey of 150 businesses at times 1 and 2; and a survey of a sample of citizens in the experimental area who had contact with the police during the preventive patrol experiment.

Citizen satisfaction with service in the experimental area would be tested by the three surveys used to measure citizen fear of crime. Citizen attitudes concerning the quality of police service would be tested through the community and encounter surveys. Citizen satisfaction with response time, as well as measurement of response time itself, would be tested by observer measurement of time elapsing between the time an officer received a dispatch call for service and the officer's actual contact with the citizen, and by the encounter survey. Traffic data would be tested through analysis of departmental traffic records.

The use of observers resulted from discussions among task force members and the evaluation consultant assigned to the task force. It was felt that trained observers riding in patrol cars would be useful monitors of unanticipated consequences of the preventive patrol experiment and could help the task force answer questions concerning those duties police officers actually perform on patrol. Observers were also seen as helpful in examining both response time and police-citizen encounters.

At first, many task force members objected to the use of observers, and expressed fears that the observers might arouse hostility among police officers; that officers would alter their normal patterns of behavior; and that because they would feel responsible for the observers, police officers might jeopardize their own safety. These objections were eventually overcome. But the task force did reserve the right to discontinue the use of observers any time they were considered detrimental to the project.

While the preventive patrol experiment began on July 19, 1972, department and foundation monitors recognized by mid-August that despite high aspirations experimental conditions were not being observed. As a result, the experiment was temporarily suspended. Several problems had arisen.

One problem was manpower, which in the South Patrol Area had fallen to a dangerously low level for experimental purposes. To meet this problem additional police officers were assigned to the area and an adequate manpower level restored. A second problem involved violation of the project guidelines. Because of this, additional training sessions were held and administrative emphasis brought to bear to insure adherence to the guidelines. A third problem was boredom among the police officers assigned to reactive beats. To counter this, the guidelines were modified to allow an increased level of activity by reactive officers in proactive beats. These revisions emphasized that an officer could take whatever action was required, regardless of location, should a criminal incident be observed. The revised guidelines also stressed adherence to the spirit of the project rather than to unalterable rules.

On October 1, 1972, the preventive patrol experiment was resumed. It continued successfully over the following 12 months, terminating on September 30, 1973. . . .

Crimes Against Persons

Findings [About Inside and Outside Robberies]

1. Analyses of responses to the Community Survey questionnaire indicated that few citizens were robbed. There were no significant interaction effects, and the number of robberies stayed about the same across years and experimental areas.
   a. The number of robberies per 100 households demonstrated that no trends as related to experimental conditions were revealed.
   b. Generally, the percentage of citizens who said they had reported to the police robberies which occurred to someone in their household increased in all experimental conditions.
2. Police arrest data revealed that the number of robbery arrests in all experimental conditions was greater during the experimental year than during the previous year. There were no significant differences among experimental conditions in the amount of increase.

Conclusion

Inside and outside robberies are crimes of great concern to citizens in general. The prevention of robberies has traditionally been considered an important function of preventive patrol. In this category, those robberies in which no distinction could be made between inside and outside locations were treated. In general, routine preventive patrol had no discernible effect on robberies by any of the measures used. Contrary to the traditional expectations of the police and hopes of the citizens, routine preventive patrol within the range of variation tested by this experiment did not affect undifferentiated robberies. . . .

Findings [About Inside Robberies]

1. Although a few more inside robberies were reported in the victimization survey by persons in business in the reactive beats in 1973 than in 1972, they generally

reported fewer robberies in 1973 than in 1972, indicating a decline in robberies during the experimental year. The interaction effects were not statistically significant.

2. Police department statistics indicate that inside robberies increased in frequency during the experimental year in all experimental beats. However, under the experimental criteria these increases were not significantly different due to experimental conditions.

3. Examining inside robberies as reported to the police by individual beats in the respective experimental areas revealed a great deal of variation between the beats.

Conclusion

Inside robberies are of great concern to the police and to the business community. Such robberies include the typical business holdups. One of the primary purposes of routine patrol is the prevention of inside robberies. Although the number of crimes reported was so small that it limits confidence in the findings of the victimization survey, and although there are problems with reported crime . . . no evidence suggested that the variation of routine patrol tested in this experiment prevented inside robberies. In both the victimization survey and in terms of reported crime, reactive beats experienced the largest increase but never at a statistically significant level. . . .

Findings [About Outside Robberies]

Police department records indicate that outside robbery increased in all experimental areas during the experimental year. However, although the reactive beats experienced the greatest increase, there were no statistically significant differences in the increases due to the experimental conditions.

Conclusion

Records of the Kansas City Police Department have served as the only data source for the findings concerning outside robbery. These findings have all the problems associated with reported crime. If any crime would seem to be highly susceptible to preventive patrol, outside robbery would seem to be one. Nevertheless, routine patrol did not produce results at a statistically significant level. Although some variations do appear between the three experimental conditions, the raw data graphs suggest that in the control and proactive beats one beat seems to account for most of the differences. . . . The raw data itself suggests fairly inconsistent and random changes. In general, routine patrol within the range of variation tested by this experiment seems to have little discernible effect on outside robberies. . . .

Findings [About Common Assault]

1. As measured by community victimization survey data, experimental conditions had no statistically significant effects on the frequency of common assault.

2. The comparison of all three experimental conditions with respect to the frequency of common assault as measured by reported crime during and before the experimental year did not produce a result that met the criteria for significance.

Although there was an increase in the reactive beats and [there were] decreases in proactive and control beats the differences were not significant statistically.

3. For the two beat triplets amenable to statistical analysis (reactive-2, control-2, proactive-2 and reactive-3, control-3, and proactive-3) it was found that the arrests in proactive-3 were significantly lower than the expected frequency during the experiment. Also in proactive-3, control-3 and reactive-3 the arrests were significantly less during the experiment than expected.

Conclusion

Common assault is a relatively minor crime which occurs both inside and outside structures. It is a crime that is considered to be only partially preventable through routine patrol. Although some differences were found in arrest patterns for particular triplets, the fact that they were found in only two of the five triplets limits confidence in the findings. In sum, preventive patrol within the range of variation tested by this experiment seems to have no effect on common assault. . . .

Findings [About Aggravated Assaults]

1. As measured by community victimization data the experimental conditions had no statistically significant interaction effects on aggravated assault.

2. The comparison of all three experimental conditions with respect to the frequency of aggravated assault during and before the experiment as measured by reported crime data produced a result that was not significant according to the established criteria. The experimental conditions apparently had no impact on the reported decrease in reactive and proactive beats and the increase in the control beats.

3. There were no statistically significant experimental effects on the frequency of arrests for aggravated assault.

Conclusion

Aggravated assault is a crime that police have felt is only partially responsive to preventive patrol. Much aggravated assault takes place inside residences, etc., and as such would not be easily viewed from the outside. Aggravated assault is often an impulsive crime without premeditation. Based on the findings presented here, aggravated assault did not appear to respond to experimental changes in the level of preventive patrol. . . .

Findings [About Larceny-Purse Snatch]

1. The number of purse snatches increased in all three experimental areas during the experimental year.

2. The level of change in purse snatch crimes decreased in the proactive beats and increased in the control and reactive beats, but these changes were not statistically significant.

Conclusion

Larceny-purse snatch has been measured through the use of departmental reported crime. Given that purse snatch is a crime committed most often in public streets, police traditionally believe it to be a crime deterrable by preventive patrol. The findings reported above indicate, however, that purse snatch apparently does not respond to the levels of preventive patrol tested by this experiment. . . .

Conclusion [About Rape]

One main concern of those planning the experiment was that crimes of rape would increase, and that should this occur the experiment would be terminated. As the data suggests, however, no great increase in rape occurred, no statistically significant differences were found in the reported number of rapes, and rape remained at relatively low levels throughout the experimental areas. The fears of a catastrophe in this crime category proved to be unfounded. Routine preventive patrol within the range of variation tested by this experiment did not have any significant effect on rape. . . .

Findings [About Other Sex Crimes]

1. Community survey data yielded no significant interaction effects across experimental area and years in terms of "other sex crimes."
2. The number of other sex crimes decreased in the control and reactive beats and increased in the proactive beat during the experimental year.
3. The level of other sex crimes decreased during the experimental year as compared to pre-experimental years in all three areas, but decreased more in the control beats than in the proactive or reactive beats. The overall test for differences was significant. The decrease in level for the control beats was significantly different from that of the reactive beats. The decrease in level for the control beats compared to that of the proactive beats approached the significance criterion but did not meet it. There was no significant difference between the changes in level for proactive and reactive beats.
4. The number of other sex crime arrests decreased during the experimental year in the reactive beats and stayed the same in the other two beats with no significant interaction effects.

Conclusion

Other sex crimes have traditionally not been considered particularly responsive to routine preventive patrol. Many of these crimes take place inside of structures and are therefore not visible. Although some suggestive differences were found between control and proactive and reactive beats, with the decrease favoring the control beats, this seems unattributable to experimental conditions. In sum, preventive patrol seems to have little effect upon other sex crimes as measured by the indicators used in this experiment. . . .

Conclusion [About Homicide]

While homicide is an impulsive crime generally considered by police to be undeterrable by routine preventive patrol, the homicide rate was constantly monitored during the experimental period with a clear understanding that should the rate increase the experiment would be terminated. As the above data suggest, no such increase occurred. No statistically significant differences were found between experimental areas.

Summary

In general, data in this section do not support the contention that routine preventive patrol within the range of variation tested by this experiment is an effective police strategy for dealing with crimes against persons. Although there was great concern at the beginning of the experiment over catastrophic increases in certain crimes against persons in the reactive beats, those increases did not occur.

In retrospect, given the facts that so many crimes against persons are impulsive, take place inside of structures and often take place between people who know each other (especially in cases of homicide, rape and assault), it is not surprising that preventive patrol should have no effect on these crimes. In the case of inside and outside robberies the findings are perhaps more surprising. Routine preventive patrol has long been considered a viable strategy for the prevention of such robberies. These findings suggest, however, that preventive patrol within the range of variation tested has no discernable effect on robberies. Thus, an increase in the level of preventive patrol in response to increasing levels of crimes against persons is seriously questioned in light of these findings. . . .

Crimes Against Property

Findings [About Residence Burglary]

1. Although the proactive beats showed the highest rate of crime, there were no significant differences in non-repeated and repeated samples.

2. In the non-repeated and repeated samples the overall decrease in the rate of reporting is not significant. There were few differences between experimental areas in the community survey.

3. Citizen perceptions of the probability of having their homes burglarized, whether they were home or not, did not vary significantly across year or experimental area in either the non-repeated or repeated samples. In addition, pre-surveying in both samples did not seem to affect responses.

4. In regard to reported crime, there were no statistically significant differences.

5. An analysis of the raw data showed that crime decreased in the proactive beats and increased in the reactive and control beats. Among beats there appeared to be no particular trend and therefore conclusions were difficult to draw.

Conclusion

Residential burglary is one category of crime traditionally considered to be responsive to routine preventive patrol. The patrolling activities of police officers in residential areas are heavily geared toward the prevention of household burglary. The above findings suggest, however, that residential burglaries are not affected by preventive patrol within the range of variation tested by this experiment. In no areas of the findings regarding residential burglary was statistical significance found. . . .

Findings [About Non-Residence Burglary]

1. There were no significant findings in the repeated sample of the business victimization survey.

2. In regard to the rate of reporting of non-residence burglaries, there appeared to be no significant differences as a result of the experiment from the business survey.

3. The findings of the reported crime data showed no significant results in the experimental conditions.

4. The findings of the analysis of the raw data were inconclusive, owing to random changes and general lack of specific trends.

Conclusion

Non-resident burglaries are generally considered by police to be fairly responsive to routine preventive patrol. As a result, police direct a considerable amount of their time toward the prevention of this crime. The findings of this section suggest, however, that non-resident burglaries were not affected by the levels of preventive patrol tested by this experiment. Although reported crime was lowest in the reactive beats, and in fact approached statistical significance, there is no reason to suspect that this difference is anything but random. . . .

Findings [About Larceny—All But Auto Accessory]

1. There were no statistically significant differences in the non-repeated and repeated samples for community victimization.

2. Regarding the estimated number of larcenies—all but auto accessory per 100 households, there was a shift in the repeated sample: in 1972, the proactive beats recorded the greatest estimated number of crimes, while in 1973, the reactive beats recorded the greatest estimated number.

3. There were no significant differences in the rate of reporting larceny—all but auto accessory in the non-repeated sample and repeated sample.

Conclusion

The category larceny—all but auto accessory includes a wide number of crimes, some of which are considered to be responsive to preventive patrol. The above findings indicate that crimes in this category do not respond to the ranges of preventive patrol tested by this experiment. . . .

Summary

Many crimes against property are traditionally considered to be deterrable through routine preventive patrol, but the overall findings of this section indicate that crimes against property are not responsive to preventive patrol. Statistical significance rarely occurred. When it did, it appeared as a random occurrence unrelated to traditional expectations.

One surprising finding in this chapter is that arrests were not affected by the level of routine preventive patrol. Traditionally, arrests have been considered a measure of police productivity and have been used to assess individual officer and departmental performance. The finding suggests that increases or decreases in level of patrol do not significantly affect arrest rates. This area clearly needs more study in light of these findings. . . .

Citizen Fear of Being Victimized

In comparisons of experimental conditions, the majority of the findings concerning fear of crime did not reach statistical significance. When statistical significance was reached, there was no consistent direction to these findings.

The fact that the vast majority of comparisons yielded no statistical significance, coupled with the fact that there was no general direction when significance was achieved, leads to the conclusion that routine preventive patrol within the range of variation tested by this experiment had little effect on citizens' fear of being victimized. . . .

Police and the Community

Findings: Community Attitudes

1. No consistent general trends by experimental area emerged from the data. Overall, citizens believed their chances of being victimized were between "slightly improbable" to "slightly probable."

2. Of the nine scales which measured citizens' perceptions of being victimized in the non-repeated sample, only on one scale—fear of robbery—did perceptions vary significantly by patrol strategy, with proactive being highest. For the repeated sample, in the four scales pertaining to personal crimes—fear of robbery, assault, rape in the streets and rape in the home—perceptions did differ significantly by patrol strategy. There was no consistency in the direction of the findings, however.

3. Citizens' estimations of being victimized did not vary significantly by patrol strategy on the remaining victimization scales.

4. The actions citizens took to protect themselves and their property did not generally vary significantly by experimental condition. In those instances where statistically significant interactions occurred, respondents in the reactive beats took fewer precautions than proactive and control citizens.

5. If taking precautions to defend self and property are viewed as an indication of citizens' fears, it can be concluded that the patrol strategies had little impact on citizens' overall feelings of safety.

6. The survey also indicated that citizens place great emphasis on the need for police patrol. Only on the scale measuring citizens' perceptions of the number of police officers needed in Kansas City as a whole did a statistically significant interaction emerge. Citizens in the reactive beats believed more officers were needed than did proactive and control residents. Nonetheless, proactive and control beat residents indicated that more police patrol was needed and that officers should patrol more aggressively than was perceived as occurring. These findings indicate that the public might not feel completely satisfied with the police until an officer is assigned to each block. Pretesting did not appear to bias citizens'

responses on their estimations of police patrol strategies.

7. The one area in which pretesting appeared to affect responses significantly was on the scales measuring police conduct. Respondents in the repeated sample believed police officers were fairer to citizens and were less harassing than citizens in the non-repeated sample. Moreover, residents in reactive beats thought more police officers pushed people around than did respondents in the control and proactive beats. Citizens in reactive beats also had less positive feelings about the police than did control or proactive beat citizens. Nonetheless, citizens in all beats generally had moderately positive images of police officers.

8. Finally, levels of satisfaction with police service did not vary significantly by experimental condition, although reactive beat residents were somewhat less satisfied than citizens in proactive and control beats.

Conclusion

In terms of community attitudes toward the police, no statistical significance was found in the majority of the comparisons between experimental areas. On those occasions in which statistical significance was achieved, there was no consistent direction in the findings.

In summary, experimental conditions had no effect on community attitudes toward the police. . . .

Findings: Commercial Attitudes

In summary, research into businessmen's attitudes toward the police, police activity, crime and the experiment suggests five general conclusions, none of which was statistically significant:

1. Businessmen's attitudes toward crime in their neighborhoods were not affected by the experiment.

2. Perceptions and feelings of businessmen about police service did not vary by experimental conditions; businessmen in 1973 felt that the number of police officers used was better than in 1972.

3. In all experimental conditions businessmen believed that police officers spent more time questioning and searching in 1972 than they did in 1973; they also felt in 1973 that more time should be spent questioning and searching than they did in 1972.

4. The number of protective devices used by businessmen did not vary significantly across experimental conditions when analyzed on an individual protective measure basis.

5. Statistically significant differences across experimental conditions were found when the various types of protective devices were combined and the resulting data analyzed. Specifically, the increase in the number of protective devices during the experimental year in the proactive and control beats was significantly different from the decrease which occurred in the reactive beats.

Conclusion

Traditionally, patrol has been particularly oriented toward the prevention of crime and the maintenance of feelings of safety and security in business areas. The findings reported here indicate that the changes in routine preventive patrol as tested in this experiment had no effect on businessmen's attitudes towards crime in their neighborhood, their perception of police services or the number of protective devices used. . . .

Findings [About Police-Citizen Encounters]

1. In terms of the experiment, there were no differences between the three conditions.

2. In terms of estimates of job performance, citizens in the reactive beats who called the police for service in many instances assigned police performance a higher satisfaction rating than did citizens in either proactive or control beats. The observers' responses indicated very little difference from condition to condition.

3. In terms of rating police performance in police-initiated encounters, citizens in the reactive beats tended to rate police performance lower than did citizens in either proactive or control. The observers again saw little difference from condition to condition.

4. In neither conclusion 2 or 3 were differences found to be statistically significant.

Conclusion

Since there were no significantly different results from condition to condition, it can be concluded that citizens did not respond differentially to officers assigned to different experimental conditions. . . .

Findings [About Police-Citizen Transactions]

1. The official disposition of the transaction did not vary significantly by officer assignment.

2. Perceived citizen satisfaction with the official disposition of the transaction did not vary significantly by officer assignment.

3. Perceived citizen satisfaction with the officer did not vary significantly by officer assignment.

4. Perceived citizen satisfaction with the disposition of officer-initiated transactions did not vary significantly by officer assignment.

5. Perceived citizen satisfaction with the disposition of citizen-initiated transactions did not vary significantly by officer assignment. . . .

Conclusion

Given the findings summarized above, preventive patrol within the range of variation tested by this experiment had no effect on the outcome of those police-citizen transactions observed. However, it was noted that another variable (type of initiation) did significantly affect the outcome of these transactions. Citizen satisfaction was found higher for citizen-initiated transactions than for officer-initiated transactions. . . .

Findings [About Police Response Time]

Despite originally expressed fears, experiments with patrol strategies can be conducted without interfering with response time or citizen satisfaction with response time.

1. The experiment itself had little effect on response time or citizen satisfaction with response time.
2. Proactive beat officers tended to take more time in arriving at the scene of a call and in contacting the citizen involved than did either reactive or control beat officers, but these differences were not significant.
3. Statistical significance was found in one area, the number of officers at the scene of a call for service. Comparison of reactive and proactive beats showed there were more officers at the scene of an incident in reactive beats than in proactive beats.

Conclusion

One of the unexpected findings of this report is that response time did not vary by experimental condition. It was originally expected that response time to calls in the reactive beats would be greater in both time and distance when compared to proactive or control beats. This expected difference did not occur. The reasons for this lack of difference are unclear. While it may be assumed that officers, whether in reactive, control or proactive beats, would respond more rapidly to calls for service in the reactive beats because they felt some sense of urgency about those calls, the time estimates did not confirm this assumption.

Given the reduction in police presence, an explanation could be that 40 percent of all calls for service were handled by officers assigned to beats other than those in which the calls originated. (There was no attempt to adjust departmental procedures for dispatching calls for service.) Or, it could have been simply a result of the location of the reactive beats relative to the proactive and control areas.

In the final analysis, this finding may have resulted from one or a combination of the above factors. It appears that response time is a complex indicator determined not only by distance and speed, but also by attitude of officer and beat juxtaposition.
. . .

Findings [About Officer Expenditure of Noncommitted Time]

1. Some 60.31 percent of a police officer's time was noncommitted or in-service.
2. Officers assigned to reactive beats spent significantly more time on nonpolice-related activities than did officers assigned to proactive or control beats.
3. There was no significant difference in time expenditures on police-related activities between experimental conditions.

Conclusion

Given these findings, it can be concluded that police officers have significant amounts of time available for preventive patrol or other such activities.

Police officers spent approximately as much time on activities not directly related to police work as they did on police-related mobile patrol. The myth that police officers are continually engaged in "battling" crime, as perpetuated by the media and perhaps even by the police themselves, was not substantiated in the reality of the situation as recorded by the observers. . . .

Findings [About Police Officer Attitudes Toward Routine Preventive Patrol]

1. The traditional concept of routine preventive patrol is not clearly defined nor disseminated to the officer in a standardized manner. This places the individual officer in the position of having to decide the value and effectiveness of routine patrol through personally developed criteria.

2. Two emphases were placed on the value and effectiveness of routine patrol: (1) it enhances citizen's feelings of security; and (2) patrol is somewhat effective in preventing crime.

3. Those officers interviewed were uncertain as to the degree of routine patrol effectiveness as it is now practiced.

4. Although almost all the officers interviewed accepted the traditional value of routine preventive patrol, a majority would make changes in the direction of less visibility. . . .

Note

1. In this report, routine preventive patrol is defined as those patrol activities employed by the Kansas City Police Department during the approximately 35 percent of patrol duty time in which officers are not responding to calls for service, attending court or otherwise unavailable for the self-initiated activities (the 35 percent figure was a pre-experimental estimate developed by the Kansas City Police Department for use in determining officer allocation). Information made available daily to patrol officers includes items such as who in their beats is wanted on a warrant, who is wanted for questioning by detectives, what criminals are active in their beats and types and locations of crimes which have occurred during the previous 24 hours. The officers are expected to be familiar with this information and use it during their noncommitted time. Accordingly, routine preventive patrol includes being guided by this information while observing from police cars, checking on premises and suspicious citizens, serving warrants, checking abandoned vehicles and executing other self-initiated police activities. Thus routine preventive patrol in Kansas City is informed activity based upon information gathered from a wide variety of sources. Whether Kansas City's method of preventive patrol is typical is hard to say with exactness. Clearly, some departments place more emphasis on pedestrian checks, car checks, and field interrogating than does Kansas City (experiments on some of these activities are now taking place elsewhere). Preventive patrol as practiced in Kansas City has some unique characteristics but for the most part is typical of preventive patrol in urban areas.

55

Florence Nightingale in Pursuit of Willie Sutton: A Theory of the Police

Egon Bittner

. . . In this paper I propose to explain the function of the police by drawing attention to what their existence makes available in society that, all things being equal, would not be otherwise available, and by showing how all that policemen are called upon to do falls into place when considered in relationship to it. My thesis is that police are empowered and required to impose or, as the case may be, coerce a provisional solution upon emergent problems without having to brook or defer to opposition of any kind, and that further, their competence to intervene extends to every kind of emergency, without any exceptions whatever. This and this alone is what the existence of the police uniquely provides, and it is on this basis that they may be required to do the work of thief-catchers and of nurses, depending on the occasion. And while the *chances* that a policeman will recognize any problem as properly his business depend on some external regulation, on certain structured social interest, and on historically established patterns of responsiveness and responsibility, every stricture arising out of these factors is defeasible in every *specific case* of police work. This means that the appropriateness of police action is primarily determined with regard to the particular and actual nature of the case at hand, and only secondarily by general norms. The assessment whether the service the police are uniquely competent to provide is on balance desirable or not, in terms of, let us say, the aspirations of a democratic polity, is beyond the scope of the argument. But in reviewing practice and organization I will weigh what is against what ought to be, by certain criteria internal to the enterprise. . . .

The Official Basis of Law Enforcement Mandates

. . . There are scarcely any human activities, any interpersonal relations, any social arrangements left that do not stand under some form of governmental regulation, to the violation of which penalties are attached. To say that modern life is thus controlled does not mean saying that it is more controlled than earlier life. Tribesmen, peasants, or citizens of colonial townships most assuredly did not live in a par-

Source: Herbert Jacob (Ed.), *The Potential for Reform of Criminal Justice*, pp. 17–25, 27–28, 31–44.

adise of freedom. In fact, the most widely accepted explanation of the proliferation of formal control, which associates it with the growth of a market-oriented, industrial, and urban order, implies primarily a shift from reliance on informal mechanisms of traditional authority to reliance on legal rational means (Weber, 1947:324).

Urbanism brought with it the need for explicitly formal regulation because the lives of the people living in cities are replete with opportunities of infringing upon one another and virtually devoid of incentives to avoid it. The former is due to the sheer congestion of very large numbers of people, the latter to the social distance between them. More importantly, perhaps, urban strangers cannot entrust their fate to the hope of somehow muddling through because of the manner in which they attend to the business of making a living, and because of the paramount significance of this interest in their lives.

Two conditions must be met to satisfy the need for formal governmental control that would bind effectively the behavior of individuals to rules of propriety. The first, already recognized in the treatment Blackstone accorded to the matter, is that all controls rest on specific authorization set forth in highly specific legal norms. The second, explicitly acknowledged by Stephen, is that the implementation of the authorizing norm must be entrusted to impersonal enforcement bureaucracies. In sum, "the due regulation and domestic order" in our times is the task of a host of law enforcement bureaucracies, each using procedures legitimized by, and incidental to, the attainment of explicitly formulated legal objectives. . . .

The following considerations appear to justify the presumption that the police are a law enforcement agency whose mandate is basically derivative of the provisions of penal codes. First, the police, together with many others, cultivate and propagate the image of the policeman as the vanguard fighter in the war on crime. Americans from the members of Congress to readers of tabloids are convinced that what the police do about crime is the main part of the struggle against it and that, therefore, doing something about it is the policeman's main care. Second, the formal bureaucratic organization of policework stringently reinforces the view that the police are primarily dedicated to criminal law enforcement. Police training, such as it is, heavily emphasizes criminalistics, criminal law, and related matters; the internal administrative differentiation of departments tends to reflect primarily formal criminal enforcement specializations and units are designated by names of species of offenses; and police record keeping is almost wholly dedicated to the recording of law enforcement activity as a result of which crime control is the only *documentable* output of police work. Most importantly perhaps, career advancement in departments is heavily determined by an officer's show of initiative and ability in criminal law enforcement or, at least, an officer who has some so-called good pinches to his credit can always count that this will weigh more heavily in his favor when it comes to assessing his overall performance than any other factor. Third, the criminal process is virtually always set into motion by the police, and prosecutors, judges, and correctional personnel are heavily dependent on the police to remain occupied. Moreover, the part the police play in the administration of justice is very specific and indispensable. They are charged with the responsibility of conducting investigations leading to the identification of suspects and with securing the evidence required for successful prosecution. And they are obliged to apprehend and detain identified suspects, in the course of which they are empowered to use force if force is necessary. Fourth, the work of a certain number of policemen—the number is probably not very large but large enough to be significant—is in fact quite plainly determined by the provisions of the penal code in more or less the same manner in which the work of building inspectors is determined by building codes. These are officers assigned to various detective bureaus, whose daily routines consist of investigating crimes, arresting offenders, and of otherwise being engaged with matters related to efforts to obtain convictions.

In sum, the exercise of internal, proscriptive control by modern governments has been highly legalized, at least since the end of the eighteenth century. The exercise of this control is assigned to specifically authorized bureaucracies, each of which has a substantively limited field of enforcement competence. Even though it is allowed that officials retain a measure of discretionary freedom, the terms on which substantive decisions can be made are not in dispute. In accordance with this view the police often are viewed as one of several enforcement bureaucracies whose domain of competence is determined by penal codes and certain other statutory delegations.

The Police and Criminal Law Enforcement

With all this admitted as true, why can the police mandate not be conceived as embodying the law enforcement mandate inhering in criminal law enforcement? The answer is quite simple. Regardless of how strenuously criminal law enforcement is emphasized in the image of the policeman and in police administration, and regardless of how important police work might actually be for keeping the administration of criminal justice in business, the activity of criminal law enforcement is not at all characteristic of day-to-day, ordinary occupational practices of the vastly preponderant majority of policemen. In other words, when one looks at what policemen actually do, one finds that criminal law enforcement is something that most of them do with the frequency located somewhere between virtually never and very rarely. . . .

According to a survey of municipal police departments of cities in the 300,000 to 1,000,000 population range which is, alas, neither exhaustive nor complete, 86.5% of all police line personnel—that is, excluding officers occupying supervisory positions from sergeant up—are assigned to uniformed patrol (Kansas City Police Department, 1971; Wilson, 1963:293).[1] Though this figure excludes persons holding the civil service rank of patrolman while assigned to detectives' bureaus, it probably overestimates the relative size of the force of patrolmen actually working on the streets. But it would certainly seem safe to assume that four out of five members of the line personnel do the work of patrolmen, especially since patrol-sergeants, whose work is essentially of the same nature as the work of those they supervise, are not included in the 86.5%. But the importance of the uniformed patrol in the police is not altogether derivative from the preponderance of their number. They represent, in even greater measure than their numbers indicate, the police presence in society. In fact, I will argue that all the other members of the police—in particular, the various special plainclothes details—represent special refinements of police-patrol work that are best understood as derivative of the mandate of the patrol, even though their activities sometimes take on forms that are quite unlike the activities of the patrol. . . .

It is well known that the penal codes the police are presumed to enforce contain thousands of titles. While many of these titles are obscure, unknown, or irrelevant to existing conditions, and the administration of criminal justice is concentrated around a relatively small fraction of all proscribed acts, the police select only some, even from that sample, for enforcement. Relying mainly on my observations, I believe the police tend to avoid involvement with offenses in which it is assumed that the accused or suspected culprits will not try to evade the criminal process by flight. Characteristically, for example, they refer citizens who complain about being defrauded by businesses or landlords directly to the prosecutor. The response is also often given in cases involving other types of allegations of property crimes involving persons, real or fictional, who own substantial property. To be sure, in some of these instances it is possible that the wrong is of a civil rather than a criminal nature, and it also should be taken into account that a principle of economy is at work here, and that the police disavow responsibility for some delicts simply because of lack of resources to deal with them. It is at least reasonable to suggest, however, that police interest in criminal law enforcement is limited to those offenses in which the perpetrator needs to be *caught* and where catching him *may* involve the use of physical force. The point in all this is not that the police are simply ignorant of, and uninterested in, the majority of the provisions of the penal code, but that their selectivity follows a specific principle, namely, that they feel called upon to act only when *their* special competence is required, and that special competence is related to the possibility that force *may* have to be used to secure the appearance of a defendant in court. This restriction is certainly not impermeable, and it happens often enough that policemen are for a variety of circumstantial reasons required to proceed in cases in which the voluntary appearance of a defendant in court is not in doubt. Interestingly, however, in many of these cases the police are likely to put on a symbolic show of force by gratuitously handcuffing the arrested person.

It has become commonplace to say that patrolmen do not invoke the law often. But this is not a very good way of putting things because it could also be said that neurosurgeons do not operate often, at least not when compared with the frequency with which taxi drivers transport their fares. So it might pay to try to be a bit more specific about it. According to estimates issued by the research division of the International Association of Chiefs of Police, "the percentage of the police effort devoted to the traditional criminal law matters probably does not exceed ten per cent" (Niederhoffer, 1969:75). Reiss, who studied the practices of the patrol in a number of American metropolitan centers, in trying to characterize a typical day's work, stated that it defies all efforts of typification "except in the sense that *the modal tour of duty does not involve an arrest of any person*" (Reiss, 1971:19). Observations about arrest frequency are, of course, not a very good source of information about law enforcement concerns. Yet, while they must be viewed skeptically, they deserve mention. According to the Uniform Crime Reports, 97,000 detectives and patrolmen made 2,597,000 arrests, including 548,000 for Index Crimes.[2] This means that the average member of the line staff makes 26 arrests annually, of which slightly more than five involve serious crimes. Though it is admittedly no more than a rough guess, it would seem reasonable to say, allowing for the fact that detectives presumably do nothing else, that patrolmen make about one arrest per man per month, and certainly no more than three Index Crime arrests per man per year. . . .

It could be said, and should be considered, that the mere frequency of arrest does not reflect police work in the area of criminal law enforcement adequately. Two points deserve attention in this regard: first, that clearing crimes and locating suspects takes time; and second, that policemen frequently do not invoke the law where the law could be invoked and thus *are* involved in law enforcement, albeit in an unauthorized way. . . .

In sum, the vastly preponderant number of policemen are assigned to activities in which they have virtually no opportunities for criminal law enforcement, and the available data indicate that they are engaged in it with a frequency that surely casts doubts upon the belief that this is the substance, or even the core, of their mandate. Moreover, criminal law enforcement by the police is limited to those offenses in which it is assumed that force may have to be used to bring the offender to justice. Finally, in the majority of cases in which the law is invoked, the decision to invoke it is not based on considerations of legality. Instead, policemen use the provisions of the law as a resource for handling problems of all sorts, of which *no mention* is made in the formal charge.

The Elements of Routine Police Practice

To explain by what conception of duty policemen feel summoned into action, and what objectives they seek to attain, I should like to use an example of ordinary practice. One of the most common experiences of urban life is the sight of a patrolman directing traffic at a busy street intersection. This service is quite expensive and the assignment is generally disliked among policemen. Nevertheless it is provided on a regular basis. The reason for this is not too difficult to divine. Aside from the private interests of citizens in maintaining safe and otherwise suitable conditions for the use of their automobiles, there is the consideration that the viability of urban life as we know it depends heavily on the mobility of vehicular traffic. No one knows, of course, how helpful police traffic control is in general, much less in the special case of a single patrolman directing traffic at a particular place and time. However uncertain the value of traffic control, the uncertainty is resolved in favor of having it simply because of the anticipated gravity of the consequences its absence might engender. In sum, traffic control is a matter of utmost seriousness. Despite its seriousness and presumed necessity, despite the fact that assignments are planned ahead and specifically funded, no assignment to a traffic control post is ever presumed to be absolutely fixed. The assigned officer is expected to be there, all things being equal, but he is also expected to have an independent grasp of the necessity of his presence. The point is not that this opens the possibility of a somewhat more casual attitude towards traffic control than the police care to admit, but rather that there exists a tacit understanding that no matter how important the post might be, it is always possible for something else to come up that can distract the patrolman's attention from it and cause him to suspend attending to the assigned task.

This understanding is not confined to traffic control assignments, but functions in all prior assigned tasks without any exceptions whatever, regardless whether the assignment involves investigating a heinous crime or feeding ice cream to a lost child, and regardless whether the prior assignment derives from the most solemn dictates of the law or whether it is based on mundane commands of immediate superiors. I am saying more than merely that patrolmen, like everybody else, will suspend the performance of an assigned task to turn to some extraordinary exigency. While everybody might respond to the call of an emergency, the policeman's vocational ear is *permanently and specifically attuned* to such calls, and his work attitude throughout is permeated by preparedness to respond to it, whatever he might happen to be doing. . . .

To make clear what the special and unique competence of the police consists of I should like to characterize the events containing "something-that-ought-not-to-be-happening-and-about-which-somebody-had-better-do-something-now," and the ways the police respond to them. A word of caution: I do not intend to imply that everything policemen attend to can be thus characterized. That is, the special and unique police competence comes into play about as often as practicing medicine, doing engineering, or teaching—in the narrow meanings of these terms—come into play in what physicians, engineers, and teachers do.

First, and foremost, *the need to do something* is assessed with regard for actually existing combinations of circumstances. Even though circumstances of need do become stereotyped, so that some problems appear to importune greater urgency than others, the rule *it depends* takes precedence over typification, and attention is directed to what is singular and particular to the here-and-now. . . . It could be said that while anything at all could become properly the business of the police, the patrolman can only decide whether anything in particular is properly his business after he "gets there" and examines it.

Second, the question whether some situational need justifiably requires police attention is very often answered by persons who solicit the service. Citizen demand is a factor of extraordinary importance for the distribution of police service, and the fact that someone did "call the cops" is, in and of itself, cause for concern. To be sure, there are some false alarms in almost every tour of duty, and one reason why police departments insist on employing seasoned policemen as dispatchers is because they presumably are skilled in detecting calls which lack merit. Generally, however, the determination that some development has reached a critical stage, ripe for police interest, is related to the attitudes of persons involved, and depends on common sense reasoning. . . .

Third, though police departments are highly bureaucratized and patrolmen are enmeshed in a scheme of strict internal regulation, they are, paradoxically, quite alone and independent in their dealings with citizens. Accordingly, the obligation to do something when a patrolman confronts problems—that is, when he does police work—is something he does not share with anyone. He may call for help when there is a risk that he might be overwhelmed, and will receive it; short of such risks, however, he is on his own. He receives very little guidance and almost no supervision; he gets advice when he asks for it, but since policemen do not share information, asking for and giving advice is not built into their relations; his decisions are reviewed only when there are special reasons for review; and records are kept of what he does only when he makes arrests. Thus, in most cases, problems and needs are seen in relationship to the response capacity of an individual patrolman or teams of two patrolmen, and not of the police as an organized enterprise. . . .

Fourth and finally, like everybody else, patrolmen want to succeed in what they undertake. But unlike everybody else, they never retreat. Once a policeman has defined a situation as properly his business and undertakes to do something about it, he will not desist till he prevails. That the policemen are uniquely empowered and required to carry out their decisions in the "then-and-there" of emergent problems is the structurally central feature of police work. There can be no doubt that the decisive and unremitting character of police intervention is uppermost in the minds of people who solicit it, and that persons against whom the police proceed are mindful of this feature and conduct themselves accordingly. . . .

In sum, what policemen do appears to consist of rushing to the scene of any crisis whatever, judging its needs in accordance with canons of common sense reasoning, and imposing solutions upon it without regard to resistance or opposition. In all this they act largely as individual practitioners of a craft.

The Specific Nature of Police Competence

The foregoing considerations suggest the conclusion that what the existence of the police makes available in society is a unique and powerful capacity to cope with all kinds of emergencies: unique, because they are far more than anyone else permanently poised to deal with matters brooking no delay; powerful, because their capacity for dealing with them appears to be wholly unimpeded. But the notion of emergency brings a certain circularity into the definition of the mandate. This is so because, as I have indicated, the discernment of the facts of emergency relies on common sense criteria of judgment, and this makes it altogether too easy to move from saying that the police deal with emergencies, to saying that anything the police deal with is, *ipso facto*, an emergency. And so, while invoking the notion of emergency was useful to bring up certain observations, it now can be dispensed with entirely.

Situations like those involving a criminal on the lam, a person trapped in a burning building, a child in desperate need of medical care, a broken gas line, and so on, made it convenient to show why policemen move decisively in imposing constraints upon them. Having exploited this approach as far as it can take us, I now wish to suggest that the specific competence of the police is wholly contained in their capacity for decisive action. More specifically, that the feature of decisiveness derives from the authority to overpower opposition in the "then-and-there" of the situation of action. *The policeman, and the policeman alone, is equipped, entitled, and required to deal with every exigency in which force may have to be used, to meet it.* Moreover, the authorization to use force is conferred upon the policeman with the mere proviso that force will be used in amounts measured not to exceed the necessary minimum, as determined by an intuitive grasp of the situation. And only the use of deadly force is regulated somewhat more stringently.[3]

Three points must be added in explanation of the foregoing. First, I am *not* saying the police work consists of using force to solve problems, but only that police work consists of coping with problems in which force *may have to be used.* This is a distinction of extraordinary importance. Second, it could not possibly be maintained that everything policemen are actually required to do reflects this feature. For a variety of reasons—especially because of the ways in which police departments are administered—officers are often ordered to do chores that have nothing to do with police work. Interestingly, however, the fact that a policeman is quite at the beck and call of his superior and can be called upon to do menial work does not attenuate his powers vis-à-vis citizens in the least. Third, the proposed definition of police competence *fully embraces* those forms of criminal law enforcement policemen engage in. I have mentioned earlier that the special role the police play in the administration of criminal justice has to do with the circumstance that "criminals"—as distinct from respectable and propertied persons who violate the provisions of penal codes in the course of doing business—can be counted on to try to evade or oppose arrest. Because this is so, and to enable the police to deal effectively with criminals, they are said to be empowered to use force. They also engage in criminal investigations whenever such investigations might be reasonably expected to be instrumental in making arrests. But the conception of the police role in all this is upside down. It is *not* that policemen are entitled to use force because they must deal with nasty criminals. Instead, the duty of handling nasty criminals devolves on them *because* they have the more general authority to use force *as needed* to bring about desired objectives. . . .

Conclusions

. . . Physical force has either vanished or is carefully concealed in the administration of criminal justice, and the use of armed retainers to collect taxes and to recruit into the military is forgotten. Paper, not the sword, is the instrument of coercion of our day. But no matter how faithfully and how methodically the dictates of this civil culture and of the rule of law are followed, and no matter how penetrating and far-reaching the system of peaceful control and regulation might be, there must remain some mechanism for dealing with problems on a catch-as-catch-can basis. In fact, it would seem that the only practical way for banishing the use of force from life generally is to assign its residual exercise—where according to circumstances it appears unavoidable—to a specially deputized corps of officials, that is, to the police as we know it. . . .

The reasons why immense powers over the lives of citizens are assigned to men recruited with a view that they will be engaged in a low-grade occupation are extraordinarily complicated, and I can only touch on some of them briefly. Perhaps the most important factor is that the police were created as a mechanism for coping with the so-called dangerous classes (Silver, 1967:1–24). In the struggle to contain the internal enemy and in the efforts to control violence, depredation, and evil, police work took on some of the features of its targets and became a tainted occupation. Though it may seem perverse, it is not beyond comprehension that in a society which seeks to banish the use of force, those who take it upon themselves to exercise its remaining indispensable residue should be deprecated. Moreover, in the United States the police were used blatantly as in instrument of urban machine-politics, which magnified opportunities for corrupt practices enormously. Thus, the American urban policeman came to be generally perceived as the dumb, brutal, and crooked cop. This image was laced by occasional human interest stories in which effective and humane police work was portrayed as the exception to the rule. The efforts of some reformers to purge the police of brutality and corruption have inadvertently strengthened the view that police work consists of doing what one is told and keeping one's nose clean. To gain the upper hand over sloth, indolence, brutality, and corruption, officials like the late Chief William Parker of Los Angeles militarized the departments under their command. But the development of stringent internal regulation only obscured the true nature of police work. The new image of the policeman as a snappy, low-level, soldier-bureaucrat created no inducement for people who thought they could do better to elect police work as their vocation. Furthermore, the definition of police work remained associated with the least task that could be assigned to an officer. Finally, the most recent attempts to upgrade the selection of policemen have been resisted and produced disappointing results. The resistance is in large measure due to the employee interests of present personnel. It seems quite understandable that the chiefs, captains, and even veteran patrolmen would not be happy with the prospect of having to work with recruits who outrank them educationally. Furthermore, few people who have worked for college degrees would want to elect an occupation that calls only for a high school diploma. And those few will most likely be the least competent among the graduates, thereby showing that higher education is more likely to be harmful than helpful. And it is true, of course, that nothing one learns in college is particularly helpful for police work. In fact, because most college graduates come from middle-class backgrounds, while most of police work is directed towards members of the lower classes, there is a risk of a cultural gap between those who do the policing and the policed.

But if it is correct to say that the police are here to stay, at least for the foreseeable future, and that the mandate of policemen consists of dealing with all those problems in which force may have to be used, and if we further recognize that meeting this task in a socially useful way calls for the most consummate skill, then it would seem reasonable that only the most gifted, the most aspiring, and the most equipoised among us are eligible for it. It takes only three short steps to arrive at this realization. First, when policemen do those things only policemen can do, they invariably deal with matters of absolutely critical importance, at least to the people with whom they deal. True, these are generally not the people whose welfare is carefully considered. But even if democratic ideals cannot be trusted to insure that they will be treated with the same consideration accorded to the powerful, practicality should advise that those who never had a voice in the past now have spoken and succeeded in being heard. In sum, police work, at its core, involves matters of extraordinary seriousness, importance, and necessity. Second, while lawyers, physicians, teachers, social workers, and clergymen also deal with critical problems, they have bodies of technical knowledge or elaborate schemes of norms to guide them in their respective tasks. But in police work there exists little more than an inchoate lore, and most of what a policeman needs to know to do his work he has to learn on his own. Thus, what ultimately gets done depends primarily on the individual officer's perspicacity, judiciousness, and initiative. Third, the mandate to deal with problems in which force may have to be used implies the special trust that force will be used only *in extremis.* The skill involved in police work, therefore, consists of retaining recourse to force while seeking to avoid its use, and using it only in minimal amounts. . . .

Believing that the real ground for his existence is the perennial pursuit of the likes of Willie Sutton—for which he lacks both opportunity and resources—the policeman feels compelled to minimize the significance of those instances of his performance in which he seems to follow the footsteps of Florence Nightingale. Fearing the role of the nurse or, worse yet, the role of the social worker, the policeman combines resentment against what he has to do day-in-day-out with the necessity of doing it. And in the course of it he misses his true vocation.

One more point remains to be touched upon. I began with a statement concerning the exercise of proscriptive control by government, commonly referred to as Law Enforcement. In all instances, except for the police, law enforcement is entrusted to special bureaucracies whose competence is limited by specific substantive authorization. There exists an understandable tendency to interpret the mandate of the police in accordance with this model. The search for a proper authorizing norm for the police led to the assumption that the criminal code provided it. I have argued that this was a mistake. Criminal law enforcement is merely an incidental and derivative part of police work. They do it simply because it falls within the scope of their larger duties—that is, it becomes part of police work exactly to the same extent as anything else in which force may have to be used, and only to that extent. Whether the police should still be considered a law enforcement agency is a purely taxonomic question of slight interest. All I intended to argue is that their mandate cannot be interpreted as resting on the substantive authorizations contained in the penal codes or any other codes. . . .

Notes

1. Kansas City Police Department (1971). The survey contains information on 41 cities of 300,000 to 1,000,000 population. But the percentage cited in the text was computed only for Atlanta, Boston, Buffalo, Dallas, Denver, El Paso, Fort Worth, Honolulu, Kansas City, Memphis, Minneapolis, Oklahoma City, Pittsburgh, Portland, Ore., St. Paul, and San Antonio, because the data for the other cities were not detailed enough. The estimate that detectives make up 13.5 percent of line personnel comports with the estimate of O. W. Wilson (1963:293), who stated that they make up approximately 10 percent of "sworn personnel."

2. Federal Bureau of Investigations, Uniform Crime Reports (1971). The data are for 57 cities of over 250,000 population, to make the figures correspond, at least roughly, to the data about manpower drawn from sources cited in note 1, supra. I might add that the average arrest rate in all the remaining cities is approximately of the same order as the figures I use in the argument. The so-called Index Crimes comprise homicide, forcible rape, robbery, aggravated assault, burglary, larceny, and auto theft. It should also be mentioned that arrests on Index Crime charges are not tantamount to conviction and it is far from unusual for a person to be charged, e.g., with aggravated assault, to induce him to plead guilty to simple assault, quite aside from failure to prosecute, dismissal, or exculpation by trial.

3. "Several modern cases have imposed [a] standard of strict liability . . . upon the officer by conditioning justification of deadly force on the victim's actually having committed a felony, and a number of states have enacted statutes which appear to adopt this strict liability. However, many jurisdictions, such as California, have homicide statutes which permit the police officer to use deadly force for the arrest of a person 'charged' with a felony. It has been suggested that this requirement only indicates the necessity for reasonable belief by the officer that the victim has committed a felony." Note, *Stanford Law Review* (1961:566–609).

References

Kansas City Police Department (1971) *Survey of Municipal Police Departments.* Kansas City, MO.

Niederhoffer, A. (1969) *Behind the Shield: The Police in Urban Society.* Garden City, NY: Anchor Books.

Reiss, A. J., Jr. (1971) *The Police and the Public.* New Haven, CT: Yale University Press.

Silver, A. (1967) "The Demand for Order in Civil Society: A Review of Some Themes in the History of Urban Crime, Police, and Riot," pp. 1–24 in D. J. Bordua (ed.), *The Police: Six Sociological Essays.* New York: John Wiley.

Weber, M. (1947) *The Theory of Social and Economic Organization.* Translation edited by T. Parsons. Glencoe, IL: Free Press.

Wilson, O. W. (1963) *Police Administration*, 2nd ed. New York: McGraw-Hill.

56

Broken Windows:
The Police and Neighborhood Safety

James Q. Wilson   George L. Kelling

. . . Many citizens, of course, are primarily frightened by crime, especially crime involving a sudden, violent attack by a stranger. This risk is very real, in Newark as in many large cities. But we tend to overlook or forget another source of fear—the fear of being bothered by disorderly people. Not violent people, nor, necessarily, criminals, but disreputable or obstreperous or unpredictable people: panhandlers, drunks, addicts, rowdy teenagers, prostitutes, loiterers, the mentally disturbed.

What foot-patrol officers did was to elevate, to the extent they could, the level of public order in these neighborhoods. Though the neighborhoods were predominantly black and the foot patrolmen were mostly white, this "order-maintenance" function of the police was performed to the general satisfaction of both parties.

One of us (Kelling) spent many hours walking with Newark foot-patrol officers to see how they defined "order" and what they did to maintain it. One beat was typical: a busy but dilapidated area in the heart of Newark, with many abandoned buildings, marginal shops (several of which prominently displayed knives and straight-edged razors in their windows), one large department store, and, most important, a train station and several major bus stops. Though the area was run-down, its streets were filled with people, because it was a major transportation center. The good order of this area was important not only to those who lived and worked there but also to many others, who had to move through it on their way home, to supermarkets, or to factories.

The people on the street were primarily black; the officer who walked the street was white. The people were made up of "regulars" and "strangers." Regulars included both "decent folk" and some drunks and derelicts who were always there but who "knew their place." Strangers were, well, strangers, and viewed suspiciously, sometimes apprehensively. The officer—call him Kelly—knew who the regulars were, and they knew him. As he saw his job, he was to keep an eye on strangers, and make certain that the disreputable regulars observed some informal but widely understood rules. Drunks and addicts could sit on the stoops, but could not lie down. People could drink on side streets, but not at the main intersection.

Source: From James Q. Wilson and George Kelling, "Broken Windows," *Atlantic Monthly* (March 1982), pp. 29–38. Permission granted by James Q. Wilson.

Bottles had to be in paper bags. Talking to, bothering, or begging from people waiting at the bus stop was strictly forbidden. If a dispute erupted between a businessman and a customer, the businessman was assumed to be right, especially if the
customer was a stranger. If a stranger loitered, Kelly would ask him if he had any
means of support and what his business was; if he gave unsatisfactory answers, he
was sent on his way. Persons who broke the informal rules, especially those who
bothered people waiting at bus stops, were arrested for vagrancy. Noisy teenagers
were told to keep quiet.

These rules were defined and enforced in collaboration with the "regulars" on
the street. Another neighborhood might have different rules, but these, everybody
understood, were the rules for *this* neighborhood. If someone violated them, the regulars not only turned to Kelly for help but also ridiculed the violator. Sometimes
what Kelly did could be described as "enforcing the law," but just as often it
involved taking informal or extralegal steps to help protect what the neighborhood
had decided was the appropriate level of public order. Some of the things he did
probably would not withstand a legal challenge.

A determined skeptic might acknowledge that a skilled foot-patrol officer can
maintain order but still insist that this sort of "order" has little to do with the real
sources of community fear—that is, with violent crime. To a degree, that is true. But
two things must be borne in mind. First, outside observers should not assume that
they know how much of the anxiety now endemic in many big-city neighborhoods
stems from a fear of "real" crime and how much from a sense that the street is disorderly, a source of distasteful, worrisome encounters. The people of Newark, to judge
from their behavior and their remarks to interviewers, apparently assign a high value
to public order, and feel relieved and reassured when the police help them maintain
that order.

Second, at the community level, disorder and crime are usually inextricably
linked, in a kind of developmental sequence. Social psychologists and police officers
tend to agree that if a window in a building is broken *and is left unrepaired*, all the
rest of the windows will soon be broken. This is as true in nice neighborhoods as in
run-down ones. Window-breaking does not necessarily occur on a large scale because
some areas are inhabited by determined window-breakers whereas others are populated by window-lovers; rather, one unrepaired broken window is a signal that no one
cares, and so breaking more windows costs nothing. (It has always been fun.) . . .

Untended property becomes fair game for people out for fun or plunder, and
even for people who ordinarily would not dream of doing such things and who probably consider themselves law-abiding. Because of the nature of community life in
the Bronx—its anonymity, the frequency with which cars are abandoned and things
are stolen or broken, the past experience of "no one caring"—vandalism begins
much more quickly than it does in staid Palo Alto, where people have come to
believe that private possessions are cared for, and that mischievous behavior is
costly. But vandalism can occur anywhere once communal barriers—the sense of
mutual regard and the obligations of civility—are lowered by actions that seem to
signal that "no one cares."

We suggest that "untended" behavior also leads to the breakdown of community controls. A stable neighborhood of families who care for their homes, mind
each other's children, and confidently frown on unwanted intruders can change, in a
few years or even a few months, to an inhospitable and frightening jungle. A piece
of property is abandoned, weeds grow up, a window is smashed. Adults stop scold-

ing rowdy children; the children, emboldened, become more rowdy. Families move out, unattached adults move in. Teenagers gather in front of the corner store. The merchant asks them to move; they refuse. Fights occur. Litter accumulates. People start drinking in front of the grocery; in time, an inebriate slumps to the sidewalk and is allowed to sleep it off. Pedestrians are approached by panhandlers.

At this point it is not inevitable that serious crime will flourish or violent attacks on strangers will occur. But many residents will think that crime, especially violent crime, is on the rise, and they will modify their behavior accordingly. They will use the streets less often, and when on the streets will stay apart from their fellows, moving with averted eyes, silent lips, and hurried steps. "Don't get involved." For some residents, this growing atomization will matter little, because the neighborhood is not their "home" but "the place where they live." Their interests are elsewhere; they are cosmopolitans. But it will matter greatly to other people, whose lives derive meaning and satisfaction from local attachments rather than worldly involvement; for them, the neighborhood will cease to exist except for a few reliable friends whom they arrange to meet.

Such an area is vulnerable to criminal invasion. Though it is not inevitable, it is more likely that here, rather than in places where people are confident they can regulate public behavior by informal controls, drugs will change hands, prostitutes will solicit, and cars will be stripped. That the drunks will be robbed by boys who do it as a lark, and the prostitutes' customers will be robbed by men who do it purposefully and perhaps violently. That muggings will occur. . . .

In response to fear, people avoid one another, weakening controls. Sometimes they call the police. Patrol cars arrive, an occasional arrest occurs, but crime continues and disorder is not abated. Citizens complain to the police chief, but he explains that his department is low on personnel and that the courts do not punish petty or first-time offenders. To the residents, the police who arrive in squad cars are either ineffective or uncaring; to the police, the residents are animals who deserve each other. The citizens may soon stop calling the police, because "they can't do anything.". . .

In the 1960s, when urban riots were a major problem, social scientists began to explore carefully the order-maintenance function of the police, and to suggest ways of improving it—not to make streets safer (its original function) but to reduce the incidence of mass violence. Order-maintenance became, to a degree, coterminous with "community relations." But, as the crime wave that began in the early 1960s continued without abatement throughout the decade and into the 1970s, attention shifted to the role of the police as crime-fighters. Studies of police behavior ceased, by and large, to be accounts of the order-maintenance function and became, instead, efforts to propose and test ways whereby the police could solve more crimes, make more arrests, and gather better evidence. If these things could be done, social scientists assumed, citizens would be less fearful.

A great deal was accomplished during this transition, as both police chiefs and outside experts emphasized the crime-fighting function in their plans, in the allocation of resources, and in deployment of personnel. The police may well have become better crime-fighters as a result. And doubtless they remained aware of their responsibility for order. But the link between order-maintenance and crime-prevention, so obvious to earlier generations, was forgotten.

That link is similar to the process whereby one broken window becomes many. The citizen who fears the ill-smelling drunk, the rowdy teenager, or the importuning beggar is not merely expressing his distaste for unseemly behavior; he is also giving voice to a bit of folk wisdom that happens to be a correct generalization—namely, that serious street crime flourishes in areas in which disorderly behavior goes unchecked. The unchecked panhandler is, in effect, the first broken window. Muggers and robbers, whether opportunistic or professional, believe they reduce their chances of being caught or even identified if they operate on streets where potential victims are already intimidated by prevailing conditions. If the neighborhood cannot keep a bothersome panhandler from annoying passersby, the thief may reason, it is even less likely to call the police to identify a potential mugger or to interfere if the mugging actually takes place.

Some police administrators concede that this process occurs, but argue that motorized-patrol officers can deal with it as effectively as foot-patrol officers. We are not so sure. In theory, an officer in a squad car can observe as much as an officer on foot; in theory, the former can talk to as many people as the latter. But the reality of police-citizen encounters is powerfully altered by the automobile. An officer on foot cannot separate himself from the street people; if he is approached, only his uniform and his personality can help him manage whatever is about to happen. And he can never be certain what that will be—a request for directions, a plea for help, an angry denunciation, a teasing remark, a confused babble, a threatening gesture. . . .

The essence of the police role in maintaining order is to reinforce the informal control mechanisms of the community itself. The police cannot, without committing extraordinary resources, provide a substitute for that informal control. On the other hand, to reinforce those natural forces the police must accommodate them. And therein lies the problem.

Should police activity on the street be shaped, in important ways, by the standards of the neighborhood rather than by the rules of the state? Over the past two decades, the shift of police from order-maintenance to law-enforcement has brought them increasingly under the influence of legal restrictions, provoked by media complaints and enforced by court decisions and departmental orders. As a consequence, the order-maintenance functions of the police are now governed by rules developed to control police relations with suspected criminals. This is, we think, an entirely new development. For centuries, the role of the police as watchmen was judged primarily not in terms of its compliance with appropriate procedures but rather in terms of its attaining a desired objective. The objective was order, an inherently ambiguous term but a condition that people in a given community recognized when they saw it. The means were the same as those the community itself would employ, if its members were sufficiently determined, courageous, and authoritative. Detecting and apprehending criminals, by contrast, was a means to an end, not an end in itself; a judicial determination of guilt or innocence was the hoped-for result of the law-enforcement mode. From the first, the police were expected to follow rules defining that process, though states differed in how stringent the rules should be. The criminal-apprehension process was always understood to involve individual rights, the violation of which was unacceptable because it meant that the violating officer would be acting as a judge and jury—and that was not his job. Guilt or innocence was to be determined by universal standards under special procedures.

Ordinarily, no judge or jury ever sees the persons caught up in a dispute over the appropriate level of neighborhood order. That is true not only because most cases are handled informally on the street but also because no universal standards are available to settle arguments over disorder, and thus a judge may not be any wiser or more effective than a police officer. Until quite recently in many states, and even today in some places, the police make arrests on such charges as "suspicious person" or "vagrancy" or "public drunkenness"—charges with scarcely any legal meaning. These charges exist not because society wants judges to punish vagrants or drunks but because it wants an officer to have the legal tools to remove undesirable persons from a neighborhood when informal efforts to preserve order in the streets have failed.

Once we begin to think of all aspects of police work as involving the application of universal rules under special procedures, we inevitably ask what constitutes an "undesirable person" and why we should "criminalize" vagrancy or drunkenness. A strong and commendable desire to see that people are treated fairly makes us worry about allowing the police to rout persons who are undesirable by some vague or parochial standard. A growing and not-so-commendable utilitarianism leads us to doubt that any behavior that does not "hurt" another person should be made illegal. And thus many of us who watch over the police are reluctant to allow them to perform, in the only way they can, a function that every neighborhood desperately wants them to perform.

This wish to "decriminalize" disreputable behavior that "harms no one"—and thus remove the ultimate sanction the police can employ to maintain neighborhood order—is, we think, a mistake. Arresting a single drunk or a single vagrant who has harmed no identifiable person seems unjust, and in a sense it is. But failing to do anything about a score of drunks or a hundred vagrants may destroy an entire community. A particular rule that seems to make sense in the individual case makes no sense when it is made a universal rule and applied to all cases. It makes no sense because it fails to take into account the connection between one broken window left untended and a thousand broken windows. Of course, agencies other than the police could attend to the problems posed by drunks or the mentally ill, but in most communities—especially where the "deinstitutionalization" movement has been strong—they do not.

The concern about equity is more serious. We might agree that certain behavior makes one person more undesirable than another, but how do we ensure that age or skin color or national origin or harmless mannerisms will not also become the basis for distinguishing the undesirable from the desirable? How do we ensure, in short, that the police do not become the agents of neighborhood bigotry?

We can offer no wholly satisfactory answer to this important question. We are not confident that there *is* a satisfactory answer, except to hope that by their selection, training, and supervision, the police will be inculcated with a clear sense of the outer limit of their discretionary authority. That limit, roughly, is this—the police exist to help regulate behavior, not to maintain the racial or ethnic purity of a neighborhood.

Consider the case of the Robert Taylor Homes in Chicago, one of the largest public-housing projects in the country. It is home for nearly 20,000 people, all black, and extends over ninety-two acres along South State Street. It was named after a distinguished black who had been, during the 1940s, chairman of the Chicago Housing Authority. Not long after it opened, in 1962, relations between project residents and the police deteriorated badly. The citizens felt that the police were insensitive or brutal; the police, in turn, complained of unprovoked attacks on them. Some Chicago officers tell of times when they were afraid to enter the Homes. Crime rates soared.

Today, the atmosphere has changed. Police–citizen relations have improved—apparently, both sides learned something from the earlier experience. Recently, a boy stole a purse and ran off. Several young persons who saw the theft voluntarily passed along to the police information on the identity and residence of the thief, and they did this publicly, with friends and neighbors looking on. But problems persist, chief among them the presence of youth gangs that terrorize residents and recruit members in the project. The people expect the police to "do something" about this, and the police are determined to do just that.

But do what? Though the police can obviously make arrests whenever a gang member breaks the law, a gang can form, recruit, and congregate without breaking the law. And only a tiny fraction of gang-related crimes can be solved by an arrest; thus, if an arrest is the only recourse for the police, the residents' fears will go unassuaged. The police will soon feel helpless, and the residents will again believe that the police "do nothing." What the police in fact do is to chase known gang members out of the project. In the words of one officer, "We kick ass." Project residents both know and approve of this. The tacit police–citizen alliance in the project is reinforced by the police view that the cops and the gangs are the two rival sources of power in the area, and that the gangs are not going to win.

None of this is easily reconciled with any conception of due process or fair treatment. Since both residents and gang members are black, race is not a factor. But it could be. Suppose a white project confronted a black gang, or vice versa. We would be apprehensive about the police taking sides. But the substantive problem remains the same: how can the police strengthen the informal social-control mechanisms of natural communities in order to minimize fear in public places? Law enforcement, per se, is no answer. A gang can weaken or destroy a community by standing about in a menacing fashion and speaking rudely to passersby without breaking the law.

We have difficulty thinking about such matters, not simply because the ethical and legal issues are so complex but because we have become accustomed to thinking of the law in essentially individualistic terms. The law defines *my* rights, punishes *his* behavior, and is applied by *that* officer because of *this* harm. We assume, in thinking this way, that what is good for the individual will be good for the community, and what doesn't matter when it happens to one person won't matter if it happens to many. Ordinarily, those are plausible assumptions. But in cases where behavior that is tolerable to one person is intolerable to many others, the reactions of the others—fear, withdrawal, flight—may ultimately make matters worse for everyone, including the individual who first professed his indifference.

It may be their greater sensitivity to communal as opposed to individual needs that helps explain why the residents of small communities are more satisfied with their police than are the residents of similar neighborhoods in big cities. . . .

It is possible that the residents and the police of the small towns saw themselves as engaged in a collaborative effort to maintain a certain standard of communal life, whereas those of the big city felt themselves to be simply requesting and supplying particular services on an individual basis.

If this is true, how should a wise police chief deploy his meager forces? The first answer is that nobody knows for certain, and the most prudent course of action would be to try further variations on the Newark experiment, to see more precisely what works in what kinds of neighborhoods. The second answer is also a hedge—many aspects of order-maintenance in neighborhoods can probably best be handled in ways that involve the police minimally, if at all. A busy, bustling shopping center and a quiet, well-tended suburb may need almost no visible police presence. In both cases, the ratio of respectable to disreputable people is ordinarily so high as to make informal social control effective. . . .

Though citizens can do a great deal, the police are plainly the key to order-maintenance. For one thing, many communities, such as the Robert Taylor Homes, cannot do the job by themselves. For another, no citizen in a neighborhood, even an organized one, is likely to feel the sense of responsibility that wearing a badge confers. Psychologists have done many studies on why people fail to go to the aid of persons being attacked or seeking help, and they have learned that the cause is not "apathy" or "selfishness" but the absence of some plausible grounds for feeling that one must personally accept responsibility. Ironically, avoiding responsibility is easier when a lot of people are standing about. On streets and in public places, where order is so important, many people are likely to be "around," a fact that reduces the chance of any one person acting as the agent of the community. The police officer's uniform singles him out as a person who must accept responsibility if asked. In addition, officers, more easily than their fellow citizens, can be expected to distinguish between what is necessary to protect the safety of the street and what merely protects its ethnic purity.

But the police forces of America are losing, not gaining, members. Some cities have suffered substantial cuts in the number of officers available for duty. These cuts are not likely to be reversed in the near future. Therefore, each department must assign its existing officers with great care. Some neighborhoods are so demoralized and crime-ridden as to make foot patrol useless; the best the police can do with limited resources is respond to the enormous number of calls for service. Other neighborhoods are so stable and serene as to make foot patrol unnecessary. The key is to identify neighborhoods at the tipping point—where the public order is deteriorating but not unreclaimable, where the streets are used frequently but by apprehensive people, where a window is likely to be broken at any time, and must quickly be fixed if all are not to be shattered.

Most police departments do not have ways of systematically identifying such areas and assigning officers to them. Officers are assigned on the basis of crime rates (meaning that marginally threatened areas are often stripped so that police can investigate crimes in areas where the situation is hopeless) or on the basis of calls for service (despite the fact that most citizens do not call the police when they are merely frightened or annoyed). To allocate patrol wisely, the department must look at the neighborhoods and decide, from first-hand evidence, where an additional officer will make the greatest difference in promoting a sense of safety.

One way to stretch limited police resources is being tried in some public-housing projects. Tenant organizations hire off-duty police officers for patrol work in their buildings. The costs are not high (at least not per resident), the officer likes the additional income, and the residents feel safer. Such arrangements are probably more successful than hiring private watchmen, and the Newark experiment helps us understand why. A private security guard may deter crime or misconduct by his presence, and he may go to the aid of persons needing help, but he may well not intervene—that is, control or drive away—someone challenging community standards. Being a sworn officer—a "real cop"—seems to give one the confidence, the sense of duty, and the aura of authority necessary to perform this difficult task.

Patrol officers might be encouraged to go to and from duty stations on public transportation and, while on the bus or subway car, enforce rules about smoking, drinking, disorderly conduct, and the like. The enforcement need involve nothing more than ejecting the offender (the offense, after all, is not one with which a booking officer or a judge wishes to be bothered). Perhaps the random but relentless maintenance of standards on buses would lead to conditions on buses that approximate the level of civility we now take for granted on airplanes.

But the most important requirement is to think that to maintain order in precarious situations is a vital job. The police know this is one of their functions, and they also believe, correctly, that it cannot be done to the exclusion of criminal investigation and responding to calls. We may have encouraged them to suppose, however, on the basis of our oft-repeated concerns about serious, violent crime, that they will be judged exclusively on their capacity as crime-fighters. To the extent that this is the case, police administrators will continue to concentrate police personnel in the highest-crime areas (though not necessarily in the areas most vulnerable to criminal invasion), emphasize their training in the law and criminal apprehension (and not their training in managing street life), and join too quickly in campaigns to decriminalize "harmless" behavior (though public drunkenness, street prostitution, and pornographic displays can destroy a community more quickly than any team of professional burglars).

Above all, we must return to our long-abandoned view that the police ought to protect communities as well as individuals. Our crime statistics and victimization surveys measure individual losses, but they do not measure communal losses. Just as physicians now recognize the importance of fostering health rather than simply treating illness, so the police—and the rest of us—ought to recognize the importance of maintaining, intact, communities without broken windows.

57

The Deterrent Effects of Arrest for Domestic Assault

Lawrence W. Sherman   Richard A. Berk

. . . We report here a study of the impact of punishment in a particular setting, for a particular offense, and for particular kinds of individuals. Over an eighteen-month period, police in Minneapolis applied one of three intervention strategies in incidents of misdemeanor domestic assault: arrest; ordering the offender from the premises; or some form of advice which could include mediation. The three interventions were assigned randomly to households, and a critical outcome was the rate of repeat incidents. The relative effect of arrest should hold special interest for the specific deterrence-labeling controversy.

Policing Domestic Assaults

Police have been typically reluctant to make arrests for domestic violence (Berk and Loseke, 1981), as well as for a wide range of other kinds of offenses, unless victims demand an arrest, the suspect insults the officer, or other factors are present (Sherman, 1980). Parnas's (1972) qualitative observations of the Chicago police found four categories of police action in these situations: negotiating or otherwise "talking out" the dispute; threatening the disputants and then leaving; asking one of the parties to leave the premises; or (very rarely) making an arrest. . . .

The best available evidence on the frequency of arrest is the observations from the Black and Reiss study of Boston, Washington and Chicago police in 1966 (Black, 1980:182). Police responding to disputes in those cities made arrests in 27 percent of violent felonies and 17 percent of the violent misdemeanors. Among married couples (Black, 1980:158), they made arrests in 26 percent of the cases, but tried to remove one of the parties in 38 percent of the cases.

An apparent preference of many police for separating the parties rather than arresting the offender has been attacked from two directions over the last fifteen

Source: Lawrence W. Sherman and Richard A. Berk, "The Specific Deterrent Effects of Arrest for Domestic Assault," *American Sociological Review*, Vol. 49 (April), pp. 261–272, Copyright © 1984 by the American Sociological Association. Reprinted with permission.

Written in collaboration with 42 Patrol officers of the Minneapolis Police Department, Nancy Wester, Donileen Loseke, David Rauma, Debra Morrow, Amy Curtis, Kay Gamble, Roy Roberts, Phyllis Newton, and Gayle Gubman.

years. The original critique came from clinical psychologists, who agreed that police should rarely make arrests (Potter, 1978:46; Fagin, 1978:123–24) in domestic assault cases, and argued that police should mediate the disputes responsible for the violence. . . .

By the mid-1970s, police practices were criticized from the opposite direction by feminist groups. Just as psychologists succeeded in having many police agencies respond to domestic violence as "half social work and half police work," feminists began to argue that police put "too much emphasis on the social work aspect and not enough on the criminal.". . .

The feminist critique was bolstered by a study (Police Foundation, 1976) showing that for 85 percent of a sample of spousal homicides, police had intervened at least once in the preceding two years. For 54 percent of the homicides, police had intervened five or more times. But it was impossible to determine from the cross-sectional data whether making more or fewer arrests would have reduced the homicide rate.

In sum, police officers confronting a domestic assault suspect face at least three conflicting options, urged on them by different groups with different theories. The officers' colleagues might recommend forced separation as a means of achieving short-term peace. Alternatively, the officers' trainers might recommend mediation as a means of getting to the underlying cause of the "dispute" (in which both parties are implicitly assumed to be at fault). Finally, the local women's organizations may recommend that the officer protect the victim (whose "fault," if any, is legally irrelevant) and enforce the law to deter such acts in the future.

Research Design

In response to these conflicting recommendations, the Police Foundation and the Minneapolis Police Department agreed to conduct a randomized experiment. The design called for random assignment of arrest, separation, and some form of advice which could include mediation at the officer's discretion. In addition, there was to be a six-month follow-up period to measure the frequency and seriousness of domestic violence after each police intervention. . . .

The design only applied to simple (misdemeanor) domestic assaults, where both the suspect and the victim were present when the police arrived. Thus, the experiment included only those cases in which police were empowered (but not required) to make arrests under a recently liberalized Minnesota state law; the police officer must have probable cause to believe that a cohabitant or spouse had assaulted the victim within the last four hours (but police need not have witnessed the assault). Cases of life-threatening or severe injury, usually labeled as a felony (aggravated assault), were excluded from the design for ethical reasons.

The design called for each officer to carry a pad of report forms, color coded for the three different police actions. Each time the officers encountered a situation that fit the experiment's criteria, they were to take whatever action was indicated by the report form on the top of the pad. We numbered the forms and arranged them in random order for each officer. The integrity of the random assignment was to be monitored by research staff observers riding on patrol for a sample of evenings. . . .

Anticipating something of the victims' background, a predominantly minority, female research staff was employed to contact the victims for a detailed face-to-face interview, to be followed by telephone follow-up interviews every two weeks for 24 weeks. The interviews were designed primarily to measure the frequency and seriousness of victimizations caused by the suspect after the police intervention.[1] The research staff also collected criminal justice reports that mentioned the suspect's name during the six-month follow-up period.

Conduct of the Experiment

. . . Ninety-nine percent of the suspects targeted for arrest actually were arrested, while only 78 percent of those to receive advice did, and only 73 percent of those to be sent out of the residence for eight hours were actually sent. One explanation for this pattern, consistent with the experimental guidelines, is that mediating and sending were more difficult ways for police to control the situation, with a greater likelihood that officers might resort to arrest as a fallback position. When the assigned treatment is arrest, there is no need for a fallback position. For example, some offenders may have refused to comply with an order to leave the premises.

Such differential attrition would potentially bias estimates of the relative effectiveness of arrest by removing uncooperative and difficult offenders from the mediation and separation treatments. Any deterrent effect could be underestimated and, in the extreme, artifactual support for deviance amplification could be found. That is, the arrest group would have too many "bad guys" *relative* to the other treatments. . . .

We also found that five other variables had a statistically significant effect on "upgrading" the separation and advice treatments to arrests: whether police reported the suspect was rude; whether police reported the suspect tried to assault one (or both) of the police officers; whether police reported weapons were involved; whether the victim persistently demanded a citizen's arrest; and whether a restraining order was being violated. We found no evidence that the background or characteristics of the suspect or victim (e.g., race) affected the treatment received. . . .

We were less fortunate with the interviews of the victims; only 205 (of 330, counting the few repeat victims twice) could be located and initial interviews obtained, a 62 percent completion rate. . . .

The response rate to the bi-weekly follow-up interviews was even lower than for the initial interview, as in much research on women crime victims. After the first interview, for which the victims were paid $20, there was a gradual falloff in completed interviews with each successive wave; only 161 victims provided all 12 follow-up interviews over the six months, a completion rate of 49 percent. . . .

There is absolutely no evidence that the experimental treatment assigned to the offender affected the victim's decision to grant initial interviews. . . .

In sum, despite the practical difficulties of controlling an experiment and interviewing crime victims in an emotionally charged and violent social context, the experiment succeeded in producing a promising sample of 314 cases with complete official outcome measures and an apparently unbiased sample of responses from the victims in those cases.

Results

. . . Two kinds of outcome measures will be considered. One is a *police-recorded* "failure" of the offender to survive the six-month follow-up period without having police generate a written report on the suspect for domestic violence, either through an offense or an arrest report written by any officer in the department, or through a subsequent report to the project research staff of a randomized (or other) intervention by officers participating in the experiment. A second kind of measure comes from the *interviews with victims*, in which victims were asked if there had been a repeat incident with the same suspect, broadly defined to include an actual assault, threatened assault, or property damage. . . .

Overall, the police data indicate that the separation treatment produces the highest recidivism, arrest produces the lowest, with the impact of "advise" (from doing nothing to mediation) indistinguishable from the other two effects.

When self-report data are used: A "failure" is defined as a new assault, property destruction or a threatened assault. (Almost identical results follow from a definition including only a new assault.) These results suggest a different ordering of the effects, with arrest still producing the lowest recidivism rate (at 19%), but with advice producing the highest (37%).

Overall, 28.9 percent of the suspects "failed." Still, the results are much the same as found for the official failure measure. . . .

An obvious rival hypothesis to the deterrent effect of arrest is that arrest incapacitates. If the arrested suspects spend a large portion of the next six months in jail, they would be expected to have lower recidivism rates. But the initial interview data show this is not the case: of those arrested, 43 percent were released within one day, 86 percent were released within one week, and only 14 percent were released after one week or had not yet been released at the time of the *initial* victim interview. Clearly, there was very little incapacitation, especially in the context of a six-month follow-up. Indeed, virtually all those arrested were released before the first follow-up interview. Nevertheless, we introduced the length of the initial stay in jail as a control variable. Consistent with expectations, the story was virtually unchanged.

Another perspective on the incapacitation issue can be obtained by looking at repeat violence which occurred shortly after the police intervened. If incapacitation were at work, a dramatic effect should be found in households experiencing arrest, especially compared to the households experiencing advice. . . . It is apparent that *all* of the police interventions effectively stopped the violence for a 24-hour period after the couples were reunited. Even the renewed quarrels were few, at least with our relatively small sample size. Hence, there is again no evidence for an incapacitation effect. There is also no evidence for the reverse: that arrested offenders would take it out on the victim when the offender returned home.

Discussion and Conclusions

. . . We have found no support for the deviance amplification point of view. The arrest intervention certainly did not make things worse and may well have made things better. There are, of course, many rejoinders. In particular, over 80 percent of offenders had assaulted the victims in the previous six months, and in over 60 percent of the households the police had intervened during that interval. Almost 60 percent of the suspects had previously been arrested for something. Thus, the counterproductive consequences of police sanction, if any, may for many offenders have already been felt. In labeling theory terms, secondary deviation may already have been established, producing a ceiling for the amplification effects of formal sanctioning. However, were this the case, the arrest treatment probably should be less effective in households experiencing recent police interventions. No such interaction effects were found. . . .

There are, of course, many versions of labeling theory. For those who theorize that a metamorphosis of self occurs in response to official sanctions over a long period of time, our six-month follow-up is not a relevant test. For those who argue that the development of a criminal self-concept is particularly likely to occur during a lengthy prison stay or extensive contact with criminal justice officials, the dosage of labeling employed in this experiment is not sufficient to falsify that hypothesis. . . . The absolute strength of the dosage is irrelevant to this hypothesis, as long as some variation in dosage is present. While the experiment does not falsify all possible "labeling theory" hypotheses, it does at least seem to falsify this one.

The apparent support for deterrence is perhaps more clear. While we certainly have no evidence that deterrence will work in general, we do have findings that swift imposition of a sanction of temporary incarceration may deter male offenders in domestic assault cases. And we have produced this evidence from an unusually strong research design based on random assignment to treatments. In short, criminal justice sanctions seem to matter for this offense in this setting with this group of experienced offenders.

Notes

1. The protocols were based heavily on instruments designed for an NIMH-funded study of spousal violence conducted by Richard A. Berk, Sarah Fenstermaker Berk, and Ann D. Witte (Center for Studies of Crime and Delinquency, Grant #MH–341616–01). A similar protocol was developed for the suspects, but only twenty-five of them agreed to be interviewed.

References

Berk, Sarah Fenstermaker and Donileen R. Loseke. 1981. "Handling family violence: Situational determinants of police arrest in domestic disturbances." *Law and Society Review* 15:315–46.

Black, Donald. 1980. *The Manners and Customs of the Police*. New York: Academic Press.

Fagin, James A. 1978. "The effects of police interpersonal communications skills on conflict resolution." Ph.D. Dissertation, Southern Illinois University, Ann Arbor: University Microfilms.

Parnas, Raymond I. 1972. "The police response to the domestic disturbance." Pp. 206–36 in Leon Radzinowicz and Marvin E. Wolfgang (eds.), *The Criminal in the Arms of the Law*. New York: Basic Books.

Police Foundation. 1976. *Domestic Violence and the Police: Studies in Detroit and Kansas City*. Washington, D.C.: The Police Foundation.

Potter, Jane. 1978. "The police and the battered wife: The search for understanding." *Police Magazine* 1:40–50.

Sherman, Lawrence W. 1980. "Causes of police behavior: The current state of quantitative research." *Journal of Research in Crime and Delinquency* 17:69–100.

58

The American Reformatory Prison System

Zebulon Reed Brockway

The American reformatory prison system is based on the principle of protection in place of punishment; on the principle of the indeterminate sentence instead of the usual time sentence; and on the purpose of rehabilitation of offenders rather than their restraint by intimidation. This theory works a change of attitude on the part of the state, a change of the relation of the offenders, and involves a different prison procedure. Together with punishments by imprisonment, every other form of punishment for crimes has, doubtless, to some extent, if vaguely, contained a purpose of protection, yet other aims subversive of protection have unduly influenced criminal legislation and the prison practice: a hateful temper bred of gross superstition attached to the punishments in defense of the gods and to gain their favor; punishment inflicted, assumptively, to equalize the world-balance of diffused morality; to the measuring out of pains in order to meet some notion of impossible justice; punishments to mend the fractured laws and vindicate the state; to intimidate offenders and the tempted and thus deter from crimes; and, by the sufferings of punishments, to induce a salutary reforming penitence. This hateful spirit, under the name retribution, but with somewhat softened severity, characterized the penitentiary system of the last century. But during the latter half of that century better biological and moral conceptions, largely due to the investigations and publications of Charles Darwin, enabled the enactment of more rational criminal laws. The New York law (1877) eliminates the punishment theory, and laws patterned after it, since enacted in other states, also exclude the punitive principle. Thus, in theory and gradually in fact the attitude of the state is becoming changed from its former vengefulness to that of dignified serenity, neither vindictive nor lovelorn, but firmly and nobly corrective.

It is not attempted, now, either accurately to estimate or, in any direct way, artfully to influence the unrelated inward moral state of the prisoners. It is not denied that idiosyncrasies influence the individual conduct and that these are subject to changes; nor is it doubted that every human impulse and action is, in some way, related to God and the universe of things. But, since the real relation is inscrutable to any but the individual himself within his own variant range of self-consciousness, that relation cannot be deciphered nor properly directed by the legislature, the courts, or by officers of the law. Of course the majority, at any time, may fix the bounds

Source: Zebulon Reed Brockway, "The American Reformatory Prison System," in Charles R. Henderson (ed.), Prison Reform and Criminal Law (New York: Charities Publication Committee, 1910), pp. 88–95, 98–102, 104–107.

of allowable behavior with due regard to the social welfare, and may erect a standard of social-moral right and wrong; but the morality of motives cannot be so determined. Also this criterion of the social demand may itself be reversed or modified by change of time and place and immediate condition; and the very terms Good and Evil are always of capricious significance. . . .

It is, therefore, a principle of the newer penology that the state shall not judge the heart's intentions, and shall not designedly trespass upon the mystical field of the soul's moral relations; but, instead, shall remain devoted to the rational regulation of the prisoner's conduct with sole regard to the public security.

Having thus relinquished pursuit of mystic morality because it is deemed impossible correctly to estimate intrinsic moral quality, the pursuit of administrative justice is for a similar reason also withdrawn. . . .

Notwithstanding the world-wide similarity in terminology of crimes there is great dissimilarity of the penalties attached; and, within the discretionary margin of the laws, different magistrates and the same magistrate at different times fortuitously change the notion of desert and vary penalties. Casual circumstances and personal peculiarities and moods so affect the judgment of men as to preclude uniformity of rule or practice. And so different is the experience of imprisonment upon different prisoners—one's privation another's privilege—that uniformity itself would subvert the intended equality. The blindfold image of justice is most appropriate, for it not only typifies the intended impartiality but also the impossibility for a correct adjustment of the scales.

It is believed that the nearest possible approach to criminal justice is reached unsought—when it is left to nature; that "according to the natural order of things, the way of the transgressor *is* (already) hard"; and, that nature's truest requital for every phase of morbidity—whether of the body, the mind, or the social status—is found in the necessary accompanying pains of the process of recovery.

Little reliance is placed in the deterrent principle alone for restraint of crimes or regulation of the conduct and character of offenders. No doubt the experience of pain and pleasure possesses a certain educational value, teaching what is profitable and the reverse; but fear is at best but the beginning of wisdom and fear always evidences and usually effects a reduced and inconstant mental condition. Welfare and adversity, antithetically related, supplement each other, but there is a wide difference of the mood and degree of stability when the one or the other is pursued. Avoiding adversity is as voyaging among reefs and breakers in fear of wreck, while pursuit of welfare is like following the charted ocean path voyaging wide at sea. Strong and virtuous characters, well established, do not need and are rarely conscious of amenability to existing penal laws; weak characters easily get themselves enmeshed and stranded; the habitually wayward are unmindful and disregardful of legal penalties; and the small ratio of all the criminals included in the class of deliberate and professional offenders brave penalties and derive zest therefrom.

The bulk of prisoners consists of those who are weak, habitually wayward, and unreflective persons—who do not readily connect, in consciousness, a present infelicitous experience with its remoter cause and consequence. Certainty and celerity of detection and arrest or sudden confrontation with an immediate menacing force may call the halt; but such temporary deterrence cannot effect a permanent change of habitual tendency.

Among the many thousands of this inconsiderate class of prisoners that I have investigated, none is now recalled to memory who, antecedent to his crime, took serious account of the possible consequences. And a habitual criminal, a fair type of his class, on his discharge remarked: "I mean now to quit, *if I get on all right*, but not because I am afraid of prison. I am a man who is never afraid." Such men are no more hindered from crimes by the liability to be imprisoned, than railroad travelers are hindered from traveling because there are occasionally fatal railroad accidents. The professional class feels imprisonment to be accidental rather than naturally consequential. One, worrying over his imprisonment because of its interference with his customary associations and excitements, solemnly said: "This is a judgment on me for leaving my own line. So long as I kept steadily at the sneak line I was prospered, but when I tackled burglary my bad luck began."

Ineffective too, for deterrence, is the supposed disgrace of a criminal conviction and committal to prison. The generality of prisoners do not feel any disgrace. A certain tone of respectability colors the prisoner's conception of crime, which is partly a product of his knowledge of current commercial irregularities, corrupt partisan politics, frauds committed in high places with avoidance of convictions, and jubilant newspaper notices of crimes and criminals. The very notoriety gained compensates and so shields the shallow character from any painful feeling of disgrace. His insensibility and *sangfroid* are further ministered to by the effect of long-delayed trials and the character of the trial; illuminated newspaper detailed accounts of the prisoner's personal appearance and bearing; the gladiatorial show of the legal combat of which the prisoner forms the central figure, the artifice and insincerity of the defense; the excusing and even extolling address of the defending counsel; these together with the chummy attention of jail and court servitors, jail visitors, and salvation seekers, excite the prisoner's self-importance—a new and gratifying consciousness perhaps—displacing the imaginary feeling of disgrace which the inexperienced onlooker himself seems to see. All this show has, too, an evil influence on the common observant crowd. Deterrence is also diminished or destroyed by the previous habitual associations of the average prisoner. In his accustomed haunts, arrests, police-court arraignment, station-house and jail confinement are jokingly mentioned and often considered an interesting personal distinction. Even a color of the heroic tinges the habitué who has actually "done time."

Increased severities either of statutory penalties or conditions of imprisonment cannot evoke and entail a salutary deterrent influence. The history of criminal punishments, the world over, shows that the most crimes accompanied the greatest severity and that they diminished as mitigation took place. Only transitory effects are produced by severities. The public sense as it becomes familiar rises, in due time, to the new conditions—automatically adjusts itself, thus neutralizing the intended effect. And mere severity of the prison régime reacts upon the prisoners with actual, if unconscious, brutalizing effect with diminishing consciousness of apparent discomfort. Beyond the possible temporary stimulation of alternative pain and pleasure experiences, deterrent measures are disused and the deterrent principle itself is disesteemed.

That phase of altruism which, in exercise, holds benevolence to others in subordination to self-interest, is dominantly present in our prison system. This altruistic sentiment exists in the protective purpose of the law which establishes it, pervades the administrative polity in all its details, and gains impulse with its sympathetic reward in individual reclamations achieved. But in its active agency the principle is a rational characteristic, not a mere sentimentalism. It is devoted to prompt enduring welfare rather than passing enjoyments. The paramount object always in view is a collective benefit sought and wrought through the well-being of individuals, and the individual welfare through a better adjustment to ordinary communal relations. . . .

The attitude of the state to our prison system is thus shown to be: negative as to any punitive intention; negative as to administering exact justice for its own sake; negative as to the expectation of deterrence by intimidation; neutral as to regulating the mystical individual moral relations of prisoners; and a qualified attitude as to altruism. The state's affirmative attitude will subsequently casually appear.

This better attitude on the part of the organized state effects also a corresponding change of the relation of offenders toward the state. The change is real, though, for a time, it may not be prized by the prisoners or noticed by the administering authorities. Formerly, the fundamental relation was antagonistic—necessarily so, for under the definite-sentence plan the ever-present desire for release must be opposed by the prison government until expiration of the prescribed period of time. Now, under the new form of prison sentence, the desires of both parties are in accord—the prisoner wants to go and the government wishes the same; but only upon certain conditions. Here contradiction is likely to arise, but it soon of itself disappears, as regards the majority of prisoners, and the remainder of them, when they discern the peaceable fruits of the opposition, change to an accordance, which is often succeeded by a pleasing gratitude. While an outside observer might never note this changed relation by any change in the general appearance, it actually exists. . . .

Affirmative Principles

Under the indeterminate sentence it is intended, either by restraints or reformations, that prisoners once committed to our prisons shall then and thereafter be permanently withdrawn from the ranks of offenders. And the inherent evils of imprisonment are such that only genuine reformations can afford the intended protection.

To accomplish such protective reformations it is necessary, preliminarily, to fix upon the standard of reformatory requirement, to adopt the criterion, to organize and perfect the plan of procedure. The standard fixed is, simply, such habitual behavior, during actual and constructive custody, as fairly comports with the legitimate conduct of the orderly free social class to which the prisoner properly belongs in the community where he should and probably will dwell. The criterion of fitness for release is precisely the same performance subjected to tests while under prison tutelage by the merit and demerit marking system which, somewhat modified in strenuousness and with addition of its monetary valuations, is similar to the marking system of our National Military Academy; and tested, also, by proper supervision during a period of practical freedom while on parole. Both the standard and criterion must be somewhat pliant to meet the variant capacity of communities to absorb incongruous elements and because each prisoner must be fitted for his appropriate industrial and social niche. . . .

So delicate and easily disturbed is the generative reformative process that outsiders—the would-be special philanthropists, professional religious revivalists, advertising salvationists—should generally be excluded; or if at all admitted to any participation, their ministrations should, under the direction of the governor, be made to fit into the established culture course. Even a resident official chaplain may inadvertently interfere with the germination of reformations. I have found the resident chaplain to be less desirable for religious ministrations than an itinerant service. One mind, and that the mind of the resident reformatory governor, must have and hold and wield every operating agency—impel, steady, and direct the whole and every item of the procedure. Such completeness of control requires an exacting and strenuous disciplinary régime which for effectiveness must include the principle and exercise of coercion.

A majority of prisoners instinctively respond to the inherent persuasion of the combined agencies; and of those who do not a majority readily respond to the moral coerciveness of the agencies. Some, only a small ratio, do not respond at first, except to some form of corporal coercion—some bodily inconvenience and discomfort. These, the irresponsive, who for the good of the prison community and for the public safety most need reformation, should not be neglected nor relegated to incorrigibility until every possible effort has unavailingly been made for their recovery. The advantages proffered are, naturally, not appreciated until availed of and enjoyed. Some cannot adopt and carry into execution measures calculated for their own good without the intervention of coercion. Adjustment to environment, even if it is compulsory, leads from the avoidance of bodily risks to the avoidance of social risks and thus to non-criminal habits, which, when duly formed, no longer need the prop of compulsion. "Compulsion first, then the sense of duty, automatic, the connection expanding into knowledge of ethical habit, then the habit creating conviction, then relations, then the capacity for general ideas." Thus coercion is often of initial indispensable educational value. Not infrequently prisoners who were assisted out of a stalled condition by means of an applied physical shock have expressed to the manager their grateful acknowledgments therefor. Many such prisoners who without the physical treatment would have remained long in the ranks of the incorrigible have, after the simple treatment, developed well and ultimately established themselves in the confidence of their community as reliable, useful inhabitants.

There should be within the reformatory course a reserve of penological surgery similar in beneficent design and in scientific use to the minor surgery of the healing art of medicine.

The Procedure

Efficiency of the reformatory procedure depends on completeness of its mechanism composed of means and motives; on the force, balance, and skill with which the means and motives are brought to bear upon the mass, the groups, and the individual prisoners; and not a little on the pervading tone of the reformatory establishment. A mere enumeration of means and motives of the mechanism is, briefly, as follows:

1. The material structural establishment itself. This should be salubriously situated and, preferably, in a suburban locality. The general plan and arrangements should be those of the Auburn Prison System plan, but modified and modernized as at the Elmira Reformatory; and ten percent of the cells might well be constructed like those in the Pennsylvania System structures. The whole should be supplied with suitable modern sanitary appliances and with abundance of natural and artificial light.

2. Clothing for the prisoners, not degradingly distinctive but uniform, yet fitly representing the respective grades or standing of the prisoners. Similarly as to the supply of bedding which, with rare exceptions, should include sheets and pillow slips. For the sake of health, self-respect, and the cultural influence of the general appearance, scrupulous cleanliness should be maintained and the prisoners kept appropriately groomed.

3. A liberal prison dietary designed to promote vigor. Deprivation of food, by a general regulation, for a penal purpose, is deprecated; it is a practice only tolerable in very exceptional instances as a tentative prison disciplinary measure. On the other hand, the giving of food privileges for favor or in return for some special serviceableness rendered to the prison authorities is inadvisable and usually becomes a troublesome precedent. More variety, better quality and service of foods for the higher grades of prisoners is serviceably allowable even to the extent of the *a la carte* method, whenever the prisoners, under the wage system, have the requisite credit balance for such expenditure. Also, for some of the very lowest intractable prisoners, a special, scientifically adjusted dietary, with reference to the constituent nutritive quality, and as to quantities and manner of serving, may be used to lay a foundation for their improvement, otherwise unattainable.

4. All the modern appliances for scientific physical culture: a gymnasium completely equipped with baths and apparatus; and facilities for field athletics. On their first admission to the reformatory all are assigned to the gymnasium to be examined, renovated, and quickened; the more defective of them are longer detained, and the decadents are held under this physical treatment until the intended effect is accomplished. When the population of the Elmira Reformatory was 1,400, the daily attendance at the gymnasium averaged 429.

5. Facilities for special manual training sufficient for about one-third of the resident population. The aim is to aid educational advancement in the trades and school of letters. This special manual training, which at Elmira Reformatory included, at one time, 500 of the prisoners, covered in addition to other exercises in other departments mechanical and freehand drawing; sloyd in wood and metals; cardboard constructive form work; clay modeling; cabinet making; chipping and filing; and iron molding.

6. Trades instruction based on the needs and capacities of individual prisoners, conducted to a standard of perfect work and speed performance that insures the usual wage value to their services. When there are a thousand or more prisoners confined, thirty-six trades and branches of trades may be usefully taught.

7. A regimental military organization of the prisoners with a band of music, swords for officers, and dummy guns for the rank and file of prisoners. The military membership should include all the able bodied prisoners and all available citizens of the employees. The regular army tactics, drill, and daily dress parade should be observed.

8. School of letters with a curriculum that reaches from an adaptation of the kindergarten, and an elementary class in the English language for foreigners unacquainted with it, through various school grades up to the usual high-school course; and, in addition, special classes in college subjects and, limitedly, a

popular lecture course touching biography, history, literature, ethics, with somewhat of science and philosophy.

9. A well-selected library for circulation, consultation, and under proper supervision, for occasional semi-social use. The reading room may be made available for worthy and appreciative prisoners.

10. The weekly institutional newspaper, in lieu of all outside newspapers, edited and printed by the prisoners under due censorship.

11. Recreating and diverting entertainments for the mass of the population, provided in the great auditorium; not any vaudeville nor minstrel shows, but entertainments of such a class as the middle cultured people of a community would enjoy; stereopticon instructive exhibitions and explanations, vocal and instrumental music, and elocution, recitation, and oratory for inspiration and uplift.

12. Religious opportunities, optional, adapted to the hereditary, habitual and preferable denominational predilection of the individual prisoners.

13. Definitely planned, carefully directed, emotional occasions; not summoned, primarily, for either instruction, diversion, nor specifically, for a common religious impression, but, figuratively, for a kind of irrigation. As a descending mountain torrent may irrigate and fertilize an arid plain, scour out the new channels, and change even the physical aspect, so emotional excitation may inundate the human personality with dangerous and deforming effect if misdirected; but when skillfully handled it may work salutary changes in consciousness, in character, and in that which is commonly thought to be the will. Esthetic delight verges on and enkindles the ethical sense, and ethical admiration tends to worthy adoration. The arts, which in essence are the external expression of the idea—the revelation of the reality—have too exclusively remained the heritage of the wealthy and wise; they must ultimately fulfil their God-given design—ennoblement of the common people. "We shall come upon the great canon 'art for man's sake' instead of the little canon 'art for art's sake.'" I have sufficiently experimented with music, pictures, and the drama, in aid of our rational reformatory endeavors, to affirm confidently that art may become an effective means in the scheme for reformation.

In addition to the foregoing items the prisoners are constantly under pressure of intense motives that bear directly upon the mind. The indeterminateness of the sentence breeds discontent, breeds purposefulness, and prompts to new exertion. Captivity, always irksome, is now unceasingly so because of the uncertainty of its duration; because the duty and responsibility of shortening it and of modifying any undesirable present condition of it devolve upon the prisoner himself, and, again, because of the active exactions of the standard and criterion to which he must attain.

Naturally, these circumstances serve to arouse and rivet the attention upon the many matters of the daily conduct which so affect the rate of progress toward the coveted release. Such vigilance, so devoted, supplies a motive equivalent to that of the fixed idea. Then the vicissitudes of the daily experience incite to prudence; and the practice of prudence educates the understanding. Enlightenment thus acquired opens to view the attractive vista where truth and fairness dwell. Habitual careful attention with accompanying expectancy and appropriate exertion and resultant clarified vision constitute a habitus not consistent with criminal tendencies. . . .

Nature—custom—reason; the greatest of these is custom. Criminal behavior may but express a want of regulated channels for the flow of vital force or lack of force. As the stagnant pools of a barren rivulet exhale malaria, and as the freshet serves to spread pollution, so a low rate of vitality may account for vagrant impulses, and, when under even normal pressure, insufficiency or irregularity of ducts of habit may produce pernicious conduct. Habit is formed by practice. By practice new nervous paths are made and connected. Movements of body and mind become more and more under conscious direction of the subject—from mere automatism through various stages until permanent change is wrought. Repeated efforts and movements which tend to produce right habits and, at the same time, disuse of every unsuitable activity, may become so fixed in the constitution that when any spring of action is touched, desirable action will follow and with reasonable certainty of result as a consequence of collaborated forces of mind and body. The degree of perfection of habit may be fairly estimated by the promptness and uniformity of the action responsive to the stimulus.

A signally distinguishing characteristic of the American Reformatory Prison System is the importance attached and the attention given to methodical treatment of the material organism for renovation—mayhap a little of refining effect and adjustment of sense to mind. Such physical training is believed to be a rational basal principle of reformatory procedure.

Another distinguishing feature, still more important because it is the germinal, all-embracing principle from which every progress proceeds, is the use of the economic motive and training to thriftiness. This principle, which is inherent in human nature and in the nature of things, plainly written in history, manifest in current affairs, present in every normal consciousness, the ground principle so long obscured from our educational systems and religious observances by reason of mediaevalism and institutionalism, so blurred in our common life by excess and artifice, so misused in prison labor systems, is now rallied for its appropriate use in the scheme for reforming prisoners.

Successful legitimate industrial performance involves native or acquired capacity and disposition for useful work. This in turn demands such development of physical energy that exertion is pleasurable or not painful; it requires a degree of mechanical and mental integrity which verges on morality and, indeed, is of the same essential quality; there must be sufficient dexterity for competitions, and stability equivalent to reliability that insures a commercial value to the services. It is the observation of experience that such an effect can be produced by industrial training; and, moreover, the possession of means, produced by exercise of the honest qualities made necessary to successful labor, conveys to the workmen a stimulus as of achievement, the ennoblement of proprietorship, and suggests some sense of solidarity of interests which prompts to prudence, thence to proper fraternity of feeling and conduct. After such a course of training and actual achievement, when the prisoner is sent out, on conditional release, to the situation arranged for him, possessed of his self-earned outfit of clothing, tools, and money, having left behind a margin of his savings to be added to from time to time or drawn upon to meet exigencies; after his sustained test on parole under the common circumstances of free inhabitancy; is he not, ordinarily, entitled to reasonable confidence that he will live and remain within the requirements of the laws?

The formation of such a new social habitude is an educational, therefore a gradual, process which requires time as well as practice. Whatever of real value may attend the preaching of disinterested benevolence to the outside general inhabitants, it is, as an independent agency, of little use for a community of common convicts. Such of them as might be moved by such an appeal are, usually, scarcely normal, and their responsive benevolent acts are likely to be injurious. Fellow-feeling for comrades may prompt to crimes, collusions, and public disorder.

The same may, properly, be said of prescriptive moral maxims, generally, and of the possible effects of personal entreaty. Also effort such as is commonly made to induce a habit of moral introspection, is believed to be a mistaken policy. The state standard of practical reformations is not the product of inward moral contrition; more naturally contrition is consequent on reformation. When reformation is accomplished contrition is useless and often harmful. It was deemed not an encouraging indication when, as occasionally happened, a prisoner on his admission to the reformatory, answering interrogatories, flippantly said, "I am going to reform"; not encouraging, because it showed no real purpose or some vague diverting notion of reformation quite aside from the real thing. The most hopeful response was felt to be when a desire was expressed and felt to learn some trade or income-giving occupation.

Moral suasion and religion are recognized as reformative agencies in our prison system, but no particular niche is prescribed for them such as is assigned to other agencies. Moral tone and the religious consciousness are flavoring qualities immediately penetrative. They are attributes inherent in and emanative from the humblest as the noblest effort and exercise intended for any betterment.

Neither punishment nor precept nor both combined constitute the main reliance; but, instead, education by practice—education of the whole man, his capacity, his habits and tastes, by a rational procedure whose central motive and law of development are found in the industrial economies. This is a reversal of the usual contemplated order of effort for reformations—the building of character from the top down; the modern method builds from the bottom upward, and the substratum of the structure rests on work.

This better order of procedure is in accord with the method of human development foreshadowed by the allegorical scriptural Eden episode; and it does not preclude the highest aim and attainment. The far-reaching reformatory possibilities of work are admirably pointed out by Professor Drummond. I quote:

> Work is an incarnation of the unseen. In this loom man's soul is made. There is a subtle machinery behind it all, working while he is working, making or unmaking the unseen in him. Integrity, thoroughness, honesty, accuracy, conscientiousness, faithfulness, patience—these unseen things which complete a soul are woven into the work. Apart from work these things are not. As the conductor leads into our nerves the invisible force, so work conducts into our spirit all high forces of character, all essential qualities of life, truth in the inward parts. Ledgers and lexicons, business letters, domestic duties, striking of bargains, writing of examinations, handling of tools—these are the conductors of the Eternal! So much so that without them there is no Eternal. No man *dreams* integrity, accuracy, and so on. These things require their wire as much as electricity. The spiritual fluids and the electric fluids are under the same law; and messages of grace come along the lines of honest work to the soul, like the invisible message along the telegraph wires.

The principles of the American Reformatory Prison System as here set forth are as yet incompletely practiced; but, more and more, men are learning that the eternal verities are within the acts and incidents of the daily life; that the public safety turns upon a proper adjustment of individual and collective relativeness; and that the fulcrum of leverage is economic efficiency. This better view is fraught with promise for better public protection by means of rational reformation of offenders.

59

Discipline and Punish

Michel Foucault

Translated from the French by Alan Sheridan

. . . This study obeys four general rules:

1. Do not concentrate the study of the punitive mechanisms on their 'repressive' effects alone, on their 'punishment' aspects alone, but situate them in a whole series of their possible positive effects, even if these seem marginal at first sight. As a consequence, regard punishment as a complex social function.

2. Analyze punitive methods not simply as consequences of legislation or as indicators of social structures, but as techniques possessing their own specificity in the more general field of other ways of exercising power. Regard punishment as a political tactic.

3. Instead of treating the history of penal law and the history of the human sciences as two separate series whose overlapping appears to have had on one or the other, or perhaps on both, a disturbing or useful effect, according to one's point of view, see whether there is not some common matrix or whether they do not both derive from a single process of 'epistemologico-juridical' formation; in short, make the technology of power the very principle both of the humanization of the penal system and of the knowledge of man.

4. Try to discover whether this entry of the soul on to the scene of penal justice, and with it the insertion in legal practice of a whole corpus of 'scientific' knowledge, is not the effect of a transformation of the way in which the body itself is invested by power relations.

   In short, try to study the metamorphosis of punitive methods on the basis of a political technology of the body in which might be read a common history of power relations and object relations. Thus, by an analysis of penal leniency as a technique of power, one might understand both how man, the soul, the normal or abnormal individual have come to duplicate crime as objects of penal intervention; and in what way a specific mode of subjection was able to give birth to man as an object of knowledge for a discourse with a 'scientific' status. . . .

Generalized Punishment

. . . Protests against the public executions proliferated in the second half of the eighteenth century: among the philosophers and theoreticians of the law; among lawyers and *parlementaires*; in popular petitions and among the legislators of the assemblies. Another form of punishment was needed: the physical confrontation between the sovereign and the condemned man must end; this hand-to-hand fight between the vengeance of the prince and the contained anger of the people, through the mediation of the victim and the executioner, must be concluded. Very soon the public execution became intolerable. On the side of power, where it betrayed tyranny, excess, the thirst for revenge, and 'the cruel pleasure taken in punishing' (Petion de Villeneuve, 641), it was revolting. On the side of the victim who, though reduced to despair, was still expected to bless 'heaven and its judges who appeared to have abandoned him' (Boucher d'Argis, 1781, 125), it was shameful. It was, in any case, dangerous, in that it provided a support for a confrontation between the violence of the king and the violence of the people. . . .

This need for punishment without torture was first formulated as a cry from the heart or from an outraged nature. In the worst of murderers, there is one thing, at least, to be respected when one punishes: his 'humanity.' The day was to come, in the nineteenth century, when this 'man,' discovered in the criminal, would become the target of penal intervention, the object that it claimed to correct and transform, the domain of a whole series of 'criminological' sciences and strange 'penitentiary' practices. But, at the time of the Enlightenment, it was not as a theme of positive knowledge that man was opposed to the barbarity of the public executions, but as a legal limit: the legitimate frontier of the power to punish. Not that which must be reached in order to alter him, but that which must be left intact in order to respect him. *Noli me tangere*. It marks the end of the sovereign's vengeance. The 'man' that the reformers set up against the despotism of the scaffold has also become a 'man-measure': not of things, but of power.

There is, therefore, a problem here: how was this man-measure opposed to the traditional practice of punishment? How did he become the great moral justification of the reform movement? Why this universal horror of torture and such lyrical insistence that punishment be 'humane'? Or, which amounts to the same thing, how are the two elements, which are everywhere present in demands for a more lenient penal system, 'measure' and 'humanity,' to be articulated upon one another, in a single strategy? These elements are so necessary and yet so uncertain that it is they, as disturbing as ever and still associated in the same dubious relation, that one finds today whenever the problem of an economy of punishment is posed. It is as if the eighteenth century had opened up the crisis of this economy and, in order to resolve it, proposed the fundamental law that punishment must have 'humanity' as its 'measure,' without any definitive meaning being given to this principle, which nevertheless is regarded as insuperable. We must, therefore, recount the birth and early days of this enigmatic 'leniency.'. . .

Beneath the humanization of the penalties, what one finds are all those rules that authorize, or rather demand, 'leniency,' as a calculated economy of the power to punish. But they also provoke a shift in the point of application of this power: it is no longer the body, with the ritual play of excessive pains, spectacular brandings in the ritual of the public execution; it is the mind or rather a play of representations and signs circulating discreetly but necessarily and evidently in the minds of all.

It is no longer the body, but the soul, said Mably. And we see very clearly what he meant by this term: the correlative of a technique of power. Old 'anatomies' of punishment are abandoned. But have we really entered the age of non-corporal punishment?

At the point of departure, then, one may place the political project of rooting out illegalities, generalizing the punitive function and delimiting, in order to control it, the power to punish. From this there emerge two lines of objectification of crime and of the criminal. On the one hand, the criminal designated as the enemy of all, whom it is in the interest of all to track down, falls outside the pact, disqualifies himself as a citizen and emerges, bearing within him as it were, a wild fragment of nature; he appears as a villain, a monster, a madman, perhaps, a sick and, before long, 'abnormal' individual. It is as such that, one day, he will belong to a scientific objectification and to the 'treatment' that is correlative to it. On the other hand, the need to measure, from within, the effects of the punitive power prescribes tactics of intervention over all criminals, actual or potential: the organization of a field of prevention, the calculation of interests, the circulation of representations and signs, the constitution of a horizon of certainty and proof, the adjustment of penalties to ever more subtle variables; all this also leads to an objectification of criminals and crimes. In either case, one sees that the power relation that underlies the exercise of punishment begins to be duplicated by an object relation in which are caught up not only the crime as a fact to be established according to common norms, but the criminal as an individual to be known according to specific criteria. One also sees that this object relation is not superimposed, from the outside, on the punitive practice, as would be a prohibition laid on the fury of the public execution by the limits of the sensibility, or as would be a rational or 'scientific' interrogation as to what this man that one is punishing really is. The processes of objectification originate in the very tactics of power and of the arrangement of its exercise.

However, the two types of objectification that emerge with the project of penal reform are very different from one another: both in their chronology and in their effects. The objectification of the criminal as outside the law, as natural man, is still only a potentiality, a vanishing trace, in which are entangled the themes of political criticism and the figures of the imagination. One will have to wait a long time before *homo criminalis* becomes a definite object in the field of knowledge. The other, on the contrary, has had much more rapid and decisive effects in so far as it was linked more directly to the reorganization of the power to punish: codification, definition of offences, the fixing of a scale of penalties, rules of procedure, definition of the role of magistrates. And also because it made use of the discourse already constituted by the *Idéologues*. This discourse provided, in effect, by means of the theory of interests, representations and signs, by the series and geneses that it reconstituted, a sort of general recipe for the exercise of power over men: the 'mind' as a surface of inscription for power, with semiology as its tool; the submission of bodies through the control of ideas; the analysis of representations as a principle in a politics of bodies that was much more effective than the ritual anatomy of torture and execution. The thought of the *Idéologues* was not only a theory of the individual and society; it developed as a technology of subtle, effective, economic powers, in opposition to the sumptuous expenditure of the power of the sovereign. . . .

It is this semio-technique of punishments, this 'ideological power' which, partly at least, will remain in suspense and will be superseded by a new political anatomy, in which the body, once again, but in a new form, will be the principal character. And this new political anatomy will permit the intersection of the two divergent lines of objectification that are to be seen emerging in the eighteenth century: that which rejects the criminal 'from the other side'—from the side of a nature against nature; and that which seeks to control delinquency by a calculated economy of punishments. A glance at the new art of punishing clearly reveals the supersession of the punitive semio-technique by a new politics of the body.

The Gentle Way in Punishment

The art of punishing, then, must rest on a whole technology of representation. The undertaking can succeed only if it forms part of a natural mechanics. 'Like the gravitation of bodies, a secret force compels us ever towards our well-being. This impulsion is affected only by the obstacles that laws oppose to it. All the diverse actions of man are the effects of this interior tendency.' To find the suitable punishment for a crime is to find the disadvantage whose idea is such that it robs forever the idea of a crime of any attraction. It is an art of conflicting energies, an art of images linked by association, the forging of stable connections that defy time: it is a matter of establishing the representation of pairs of opposing values, of establishing quantitative differences between the opposing forces, of setting up a complex of obstacle-signs that may subject the movement of the forces to a power relation. 'Let the idea of torture and execution be ever present in the heart of the weak man and dominate the feeling that drives him to crime' (Beccaria, 119). These obstacle-signs must constitute the new arsenal of penalties, just as the old public executions were organized around a system of retaliatory marks. But in order to function, they must obey several conditions.

1. They must be as unarbitrary as possible. It is true that it is society that defines, in terms of its own interests, what must be regarded as a crime: it is not therefore natural. But, if punishment is to present itself to the mind as soon as one thinks of committing a crime, as immediate a link as possible must be made between the two: a link of resemblance, analogy, proximity. 'The penalty must be made to conform as closely as possible to the nature of the offence, so that fear of punishment diverts the mind from the road along which the prospect of an advantageous crime was leading it' (Beccaria, 119). The ideal punishment would be transparent to the crime that it punishes; thus, for him who contemplates it, it will be infallibly the sign of the crime that it punishes; and for him who dreams of the crime, the idea of the offence will be enough to arouse the sign of the punishment. This is an advantage for the stability of the link, an advantage for the calculation of the proportions between crime and punishment and the quantitative reading of interests; it also has the advantage that, by assuming the form of a natural sequence, punishment does not appear as the arbitrary effect of a human power: 'To derive the offence from the punishment is the best means of proportioning punishment to crime. If this is the triumph of justice, it is also the triumph of liberty, for then penalties no longer proceed from the will of the legislator, but from the nature of things; one no longer sees man committing violence on man' (Marat, 33). In analogical punishment, the power that punishes is hidden.

The reformers proposed a whole panoply of penalties that were natural by institution and which represented in their form the content of the crime. . . .

Despite cruelties that are strongly reminiscent of the tortures of the Ancien Régime, a quite different mechanism is at work in these analogical penalties. Horror is not opposed to horror in a joust of power; it is no longer the symmetry of vengeance, but the transparency of the sign to that which it signifies; what is required is to establish, in the theatre of punishments, a relation that is immediately intelligible to the senses and on which a simple calculation may be based: a sort of reasonable aesthetic of punishment. . . . The punishment must proceed from the crime; the law must appear to be a necessity of things, and power must act while concealing itself beneath the gentle force of nature.

2. This complex of signs must engage with the mechanics of forces: reduce the desire that makes the crime attractive; increase the interest that makes the penalty be feared; reverse the relation of intensities, so that the representation of the penalty and its disadvantages is more lively than that of the crime and its pleasures. There is a whole mechanics, therefore, of interest, of its movement, of the way that one represents it to oneself and of the liveliness of this representation. . . .

Set the force that drove the criminal to the crime against itself. Divide interest, use it to make the penalty something to be feared. . . .

The penalty that forms stable and easily legible signs must also recompose the economy of interests and the dynamics of passions.

3. Consequently, one must use a temporal modulation. The penalty transforms, modifies, establishes signs, arranges obstacles. What use would it be if it had to be permanent? A penalty that had no end would be contradictory: all the constraints that it imposes on the convict and of which, having become virtuous once more, he would never be able to take advantage, would be little better than torture; and the effort made to reform him would be so much trouble and expense lost by society. If incorrigibles there be, one must be determined to eliminate them. But for all the others, punishment can function only if it comes to an end. . . .

4. For the convict, the penalty is a mechanics of signs, interests and duration. But the guilty person is only one of the targets of punishment. For punishment is directed above all at others, at all the potentially guilty. So these obstacle-signs that are gradually engraved in the representation of the condemned man must therefore circulate rapidly and widely; they must be accepted and redistributed by all; they must shape the discourse that each individual has with others and by which crime is forbidden to all by all—the true coin that is substituted in people's minds for the false profits of crime.

For this, everyone must see punishment not only as natural, but in his own interest; everyone must be able to read in it his own advantage. There must be no more spectacular, but useless penalties. . . .

5. Hence a whole learned economy of publicity. In physical torture, the example was based on terror: physical fear, collective horror, images that must be engraved on the memories of the spectators, like the brand on the cheek or shoulder of the condemned man. The example is now based on the lesson, the

discourse, the decipherable sign, the representation of public morality. It is no longer the terrifying restoration of sovereignty that will sustain the ceremony of punishment, but the reactivation of the code, the collective reinforcements of the link between the idea of crime and the idea of punishment. In the penalty, rather than seeing the presence of the sovereign, one will read the laws themselves. The laws associated a particular crime with a particular punishment. As soon as the crime is committed, the punishment will follow at once, enacting the discourse of the law and showing that the code, which links ideas, also links realities. The junction, immediate in the text, must be immediate in acts. . . .

The publicity of punishment must not have the physical effect of terror; it must open up a book to be read. . . .

This legible lesson, this ritual recoding, must be repeated as often as possible; the punishments must be a school rather than a festival; an ever-open book rather than a ceremony. The duration that makes the punishment effective for the guilty is also useful for the spectators. They must be able to consult at each moment the permanent lexicon of crime and punishment. A secret punishment is a punishment half wasted. . . .

6. This will make possible in society an inversion of the traditional discourse of crime. How can one extinguish the dubious glory of the criminal? This was a matter of grave concern to the law-makers of the eighteenth century. How can one silence the adventures of the great criminals celebrated in the almanacs, broadsheets and popular tales? If the recoding of punishment is well done, if the ceremony of mourning takes place as it should, the crime can no longer appear as anything but a misfortune and the criminal as an enemy who must be re-educated into social life. Instead of those songs of praise that turn the criminal into a hero, only those obstacle-signs that arrest the desire to commit the crime by the calculated fear of punishment will circulate in men's discourse. The positive mechanics will operate to the full in the language of every day, which will constantly reinforce it with new accounts. Discourse will become the vehicle of the law: the constant principle of universal recoding. . . .

This, then, is how one must imagine the punitive city. At the crossroads, in the gardens, at the side of roads being repaired or bridges built, in workshops open to all, in the depths of mines that may be visited, will be hundreds of tiny theatres of punishment. Each crime will have its law; each criminal his punishment. It will be a visible punishment, a punishment that tells all, that explains, justifies itself, convicts: placards, different-colored caps bearing inscriptions, posters, symbols, texts read or printed, tirelessly repeat the code. Scenery, perspectives, optical effects, *trompe-l'œil* sometimes magnify the scene, making it more fearful than it is, but also clearer. From where the public is sitting, it is possible to believe in the existence of certain cruelties which, in fact, do not take place. But the essential point, in all these real or magnified severities, is that they should all, according to a strict economy, teach a lesson: that each punishment should be a fable. And that, in counterpoint with all the direct examples of virtue, one may at each moment encounter, as a living spectacle, the misfortunes of vice. . . .

But no doubt the most important thing was that this control and transformation of behaviour were accompanied—both as a condition and as a consequence—by the development of a knowledge of the individuals. When the new prisoner arrived, the Walnut Street administration received a report concerning his crime, the circumstances in which it was committed, a summary of the examinations of the defendant, notes on his behaviour before and after sentence: indispensable elements if one wished to 'decide what steps will have to be taken to destroy his old habits.'[1] And throughout his detention he would be observed; his conduct would be noted daily and the inspectors—twelve local worthies appointed in 1795—who, two by two, visited the prison each week, would be kept informed of events, follow the conduct of each prisoner and decide which of them deserved a shortening of his term. This ever-growing knowledge of the individuals made it possible to divide them up in the prison not so much according to their crimes as according to the dispositions that they revealed. The prison became a sort of permanent observatory that made it possible to distribute the varieties of vice or weakness. . . . A whole corpus of individualizing knowledge was being organized that took as its field of reference not so much the crime committed (at least in isolation), but the potentiality of danger that lies hidden in an individual and which is manifested in his observed everyday conduct. The prison functions in this as an apparatus of knowledge. . . .

Docile Bodies

The classical age discovered the body as object and target of power. It is easy enough to find signs of the attention then paid to the body—to the body that is manipulated, shaped, trained, which obeys, responds, becomes skilful and increases its forces. The great book of Man-the-Machine was written simultaneously on two registers: the anatomico-metaphysical register, of which Descartes wrote the first pages and which the physicians and philosophers continued, and the technico-political register, which was constituted by a whole set of regulations and by empirical and calculated methods relating to the army, the school and the hospital, for controlling or correcting the operations of the body. These two registers are quite distinct, since it was a question, on the one hand, of submission and use and, on the other, of functioning and explanation: there was a useful body and an intelligible body. And yet there are points of overlap from one to the other. . . .

What was so new in these projects of docility that interested the eighteenth century so much? It was certainly not the first time that the body had become the object of such imperious and pressing investments; in every society, the body was in the grip of very strict powers, which imposed on it constraints, prohibitions or obligations. However, there were several new things in these techniques. To begin with, there was the scale of control: it was a question of not treating the body, *en masse*, 'wholesale,' as if it were an indissociable unity, but of working it 'retail,' individually; of exercising upon it a subtle coercion, of obtaining holds upon it at the level of the mechanism itself—movements, gestures, attitudes, rapidity: an infinitesimal power over the active body. Then there was the object of the control: it was not or was no longer the signifying elements of behaviour or the language of the body, but the economy, the efficiency of movements, their internal organization; constraint bears upon the forces rather than upon the signs; the only truly important ceremony is that of exercise. Lastly, there is the modality: it implies an uninterrupted, constant coercion, supervising the processes of the activity rather than its result and it is exercised according to a codification that partitions as closely as possible time, space, movement. These methods, which made possible the meticulous control of the operations of the body, which assured the constant subjection of its forces and imposed upon them a relation of docility-utility, might be called 'disciplines.'. . . The historical moment of the disciplines was the moment when an art of the human body was born, which was directed not only at the growth of its skills, nor at the intensification of its subjection, but at the formation of a relation that in the mechanism itself makes it more obedient as it becomes more useful, and conversely. What was then being formed was a policy of coercions that act upon the body, a calculated manipulation of its elements, its gestures, its behaviour. The human body was entering a machinery of power that explores it, breaks it down and rearranges it. A 'political anatomy,' which was also a 'mechanics of power,' was being born; it defined how one may have a hold over others' bodies, not only so that they may do what one wishes, but so that they may operate as one wishes, with the techniques, the speed and the efficiency that one determines. Thus discipline produces subjected and practised bodies, 'docile' bodies. Discipline increases the forces of the body (in economic terms of utility) and diminishes these same forces (in political terms of obedience). In short, it dissociates power from the body; on the one hand, it turns into an 'aptitude,' a 'capacity,' which it seeks to increase; on the other hand, it reverses the course of the energy, the power that might result from it, and turns it into a relation of strict subjection. If economic exploitation separates the force and the product of labour, let us say that disciplinary coercion establishes in the body the constricting link between an increased aptitude and an increased domination. . . .

The Means of Correct Training

Normalizing Judgement

1. . . . At the heart of all disciplinary systems functions a small penal mechanism. It enjoys a kind of judicial privilege with its own laws, its specific offences, its particular forms of judgement. The disciplines established an 'infra-penality'; they partitioned an area that the laws had left empty; they defined and repressed a mass of behaviour that the relative indifference of the great systems of punishment had allowed to escape. . . . The workshop, the school, the army were subject to a whole micro-penality of time (latenesses, absences, interruptions of tasks), of activity (inattention, negligence, lack of zeal), of behaviour (impoliteness, disobedience), of speech (idle chatter, insolence), of the body ('incorrect' attitudes, irregular gestures, lack of cleanliness), of sexuality (impurity, indecency). At the same time, by way of punishment, a whole series of subtle procedures was used, from light physical punishment to minor deprivations and petty humiliations. It was a question both of making the slightest departures from correct behaviour subject to punishment, and of giving a punitive function to the apparently indifferent elements of the disciplinary apparatus: so that, if necessary, everything might serve to punish the slightest thing; each subject find himself caught in a punishable, punishing universality. . . .

2. But discipline brought with it a specific way of punishing that was not only a small-scale model of the court. What is specific to the disciplinary penality is non-observance, that which does not measure up to the rule, that departs from it. The whole indefinite domain of the non-conforming is punishable: the soldier

commits an 'offence' whenever he does not reach the level required; a pupil's 'offence' is not only a minor infraction, but also an inability to carry out his tasks. . . .

The order that the disciplinary punishments must enforce is of a mixed nature: it is an 'artificial' order, explicitly laid down by a law, a programme, a set of regulations. But it is also an order defined by natural and observable processes: the duration of an apprenticeship, the time taken to perform an exercise, the level of aptitude refer to a regularity that is also a rule. . . . In a disciplinary régime punishment involves a double juridico-natural reference.

3. Disciplinary punishment has the function of reducing gaps. It must therefore be essentially *corrective*. In addition to punishments borrowed directly from the judicial model (fines, flogging, solitary confinement), the disciplinary systems favour punishments that are exercise—intensified, multiplied forms of training, several times repeated. . . . Disciplinary punishment is, in the main, isomorphic with obligation itself; it is not so much the vengeance of an outraged law as its repetition, its reduplicated insistence. So much so that the corrective effect expected of it involves only incidentally expiation and repentance; it is obtained directly through the mechanics of a training. To punish is to exercise.

4. In discipline, punishment is only one element of a double system: gratification-punishment. And it is this system that operates in the process of training and correction. . . . This mechanism with two elements makes possible a number of operations characteristic of disciplinary penality. First, the definition of behaviour and performance on the basis of the two opposed values of good and evil; instead of the simple division of the prohibition, as practised in penal justice, we have a distribution between a positive pole and a negative pole; all behaviour falls in the field between good and bad marks, good and bad points. Moreover, it is possible to quantify this field and work out an arithmetical economy based on it. A penal accountancy, constantly brought up to date, makes it possible to obtain the punitive balance-sheet of each individual. . . . Through this micro-economy of a perpetual penality operates a differentiation that is not one of acts, but of individuals themselves, of their nature, their potentialities, their level or their value. By assessing acts with precision, discipline judges individuals 'in truth'; the penality that it implements is integrated into the cycle of knowledge of individuals.

5. The distribution according to ranks or grade has a double role: it marks the gaps, hierarchizes qualities, skills and aptitudes; but it also punishes and rewards. It is the penal functioning of setting in order and the ordinal character of judging. Discipline rewards simply by the play of awards, thus making it possible to attain higher ranks and places; it punishes by reversing this process. Rank in itself serves as a reward or punishment. . . .

In short, the art of punishing, in the régime of disciplinary power, is aimed neither at expiation, nor even precisely at repression. It brings five quite distinct operations into play: it refers individual actions to a whole that is at once a field of comparison, a space of differentiation and the principle of a rule to be followed. It differentiates individuals from one another, in terms of the following overall rule: that the rule be made to function as a minimal threshold, as an average to be respected or as an optimum towards which one must move. It measures in quantitative terms and hierarchizes in terms of value the abilities, the level, the 'nature' of individuals. It introduces, through this 'value-giving' measure, the constraint of a conformity that must be achieved. Lastly, it traces the limit that will define difference in relation to all other differences, the external frontier of the abnormal (the 'shameful' class of the École Militaire). The perpetual penality that traverses all points and supervises every instant in the disciplinary institutions compares, differentiates, hierarchizes, homogenizes, excludes. In short, it *normalizes*. . . .

The Examination

The examination combines the techniques of an observing hierarchy and those of a normalizing judgement. It is a normalizing gaze, a surveillance that makes it possible to qualify, to classify and to punish. It establishes over individuals a visibility through which one differentiates them and judges them. That is why, in all the mechanisms of discipline, the examination is highly ritualized. In it are combined the ceremony of power and the form of the experiment, the deployment of force and the establishment of truth. At the heart of the procedures of discipline, it manifests the subjection of those who are perceived as objects and the objectification of those who are subjected. The superimposition of the power relations and knowledge relations assumes in the examination all its visible brilliance. . . .

Complete and Austere Institutions

Baltard called them 'complete and austere institutions' (Baltard, 1829). In several respects, the prison must be an exhaustive disciplinary apparatus: it must assume responsibility for all aspects of the individual, his physical training, his aptitude to work, his everyday conducts, his moral attitude, his state of mind; the prison, much more than the school, the workshop or the army, which always involved a certain specialization, is 'omni-disciplinary.' Moreover, the prison has neither exterior nor gap; it cannot be interrupted, except when its task is totally completed; its action on the individual must be uninterrupted: an unceasing discipline. Lastly, it gives almost total power over the prisoners; it has its internal mechanisms of repression and punishment: a despotic discipline. It carries to their greatest intensity all the procedures to be found in the other disciplinary mechanisms. It must be the most powerful machinery for imposing a new form on the perverted individual; its mode of action is the constraint of a total education. . . . This complete 'reformatory' lays down a recoding of existence very different from the mere juridical deprivation of liberty and very different, too, from the simple mechanism of examplar imagined by the reformers at the time of the *idéologues*. . . .

But the penitentiary Panopticon was also a system of individualizing and permanent documentation. The same year in which variants of the Benthamite schema were recommended for the building of prisons, the system of 'moral accounting' was made compulsory: an individual report of a uniform kind in every prison, on which the governor or head-warder, the chaplain and the instructor had to fill in their observations on each inmate. . . . The overall aim was to make the prison a place for the constitution of a body of knowledge that would regulate the exercise of penitentiary practice. The prison has not only to know the decision of the judges and to apply it in terms of the established regulations: it has to extract unceasingly from the inmate a body of knowledge that will make it possible to transform the penal measure into a penitentiary operation; which will make of the penalty required by the offence a modification of the inmate that will be of use to society. The autonomy of the carceral régime and the knowledge that it creates make it possible to increase the utility of the penalty, which the code had made the very principle of its punitive philosophy. . . . As a highly efficient technology, penitentiary practice produces a return on the capital invested in the penal system and in the building of heavy prisons.

Similarly, the offender becomes an individual to know. This demand for knowledge was not, in the first instance, inserted into the legislation itself, in order to provide substance for the sentence and to determine the true degree of guilt. It is as a convict, as a point of application for punitive mechanisms, that the offender is constituted himself as the object of possible knowledge.

But this implies that the penitentiary apparatus, with the whole technological programme that accompanies it, brings about a curious substitution: from the hands of justice, it certainly receives a convicted person; but what it must apply itself to is not, of course, the offence, nor even exactly the offender, but a rather different object, one defined by variables which at the outset at least were not taken into account in the sentence, for they were relevant only for a corrective technology. This other character, whom the penitentiary apparatus substitutes for the convicted offender, is the *delinquent*.

The delinquent is to be distinguished from the offender by the fact that it is not so much his act as his life that is relevant in characterizing him. The penitentiary operation, if it is to be a genuine re-education, must become the sum total existence of the delinquent, making of the prison a sort of artificial and coercive theatre in which his life will be examined from top to bottom. The legal punishment bears upon an act; the punitive technique on a life; it falls to this punitive technique, therefore, to reconstitute all the sordid detail of a life in the form of knowledge, to fill in the gaps of that knowledge and to act upon it by a practice of compulsion. It is a biographical knowledge and a technique for correcting individual lives. The observation of the delinquent 'should go back not only to the circumstances, but also to the causes of his crime; they must be sought in the story of his life, from the triple point of view of psychology, social position and upbringing, in order to discover the dangerous proclivities of the first, the harmful predispositions of the second and the bad antecedents of the third. This biographical investigation is an essential part of the preliminary investigation for the classification of penalties before it becomes a condition for the classification of moralities in the penitentiary system. . . .

The Carceral

We have seen that, in penal justice, the prison transformed the punitive procedure into a penitentiary technique; the carceral archipelago transported this technique from the penal institution to the entire social body, with several important results.

1. This vast mechanism established a slow, continuous, imperceptible gradation that made it possible to pass naturally from disorder to offence and back from a transgression of the law to a slight departure from a rule, an average, a demand, a norm. In the classical period, despite a certain common reference to offence in general, the order of the crime, the order of sin and the order of bad conduct

remained separate in so far as they related to separate criteria and authorities (court, penitence, confinement). Incarceration with its mechanisms of surveillance and punishment functioned, on the contrary, according to a principle of relative continuity. The continuity of the institutions themselves, which were linked to one another (public assistance with the orphanage, the reformatory, the penitentiary, the disciplinary battalion, the prison; the school with the charitable society, the workshop, the almshouse, the penitentiary convent; the worker's estate with the hospital and the prison). A continuity of the punitive criteria and mechanisms, which on the basis of a mere deviation gradually strengthened the rules and increased the punishment. A continuous gradation of the established, specialized and competent authorities (in the order of knowledge and in the order of power) which, without resort to arbitrariness, but strictly according to the regulations, by means of observation and assessment hierarchized, differentiated, judged, punished and moved gradually from the correction of irregularities to the punishment of crime. The 'carceral' with its many diffuse or compact forms, its institutions of supervision or constraint, of discreet surveillance and insistent coercion, assured the communication of punishments according to quality and quantity; it connected in series or disposed according to subtle divisions the minor and the serious penalties, the mild and the strict forms of treatment, bad marks and light sentences. You will end up in the convict-ship, the slightest indiscipline seems to say; and the harshest of prisons says to the prisoners condemned to life: I shall note the slightest irregularity in your conduct. The generality of the punitive function that the eighteenth century sought in the 'ideological' technique of representations and signs now had as its support the extension, the material framework, complex, dispersed, but coherent, of the various carceral mechanisms. . . . Replacing the adversary of the sovereign, the social enemy was transformed into a deviant, who brought with him the multiple danger of disorder, crime and madness. The carceral network linked, through innumerable relations, the two long, multiple series of the punitive and the abnormal.

2. The carceral, with its far-reaching networks, allows the recruitment of major 'delinquents.' It organizes what might be called 'disciplinary careers' in which, through various exclusions and rejections, a whole process is set in motion. In the classical period, there opened up in the confines or interstices of society the confused, tolerant and dangerous domain of the 'outlaw' or at least of that which eluded the direct hold of power: an uncertain space that was for criminality a training ground and a region of refuge; there poverty, unemployment, pursued innocence, cunning, the struggle against the powerful, the refusal of obligations and laws, and organized crime all came together as chance and fortune would dictate. . . . Through the play of disciplinary differentiations and divisions, the nineteenth century constructed rigorous channels which, within the system, inculcated docility and produced delinquency by the same mechanisms. There was a sort of disciplinary 'training,' continuous and compelling, that had something of the pedagogical curriculum and something of the professional network. Careers emerged from it, as secure, as predictable, as those of public life: assistance associations, residential apprenticeships, penal colonies, disciplinary battalions, prisons, hospitals, almshouses. These networks were already well mapped out at the beginning of the nineteenth century. . . .

The carceral network does not cast the unassimilable into a confused hell; there is no outside. It takes back with one hand what it seems to exclude with the other. It saves everything, including what it punishes. It is unwilling to waste even what it has decided to disqualify. In this panoptic society of which incarceration is the omnipresent armature, the delinquent is not outside the law; he is, from the very outset, in the law, at the very heart of the law, or at least in the midst of those mechanisms that transfer the individual imperceptibly from discipline to the law, from deviation to offence. Although it is true that prison punishes delinquency, delinquency is for the most part produced in and by an incarceration which, ultimately, prison perpetuates in its turn. The prison is merely the natural consequence, no more than a higher degree, of that hierarchy laid down step by step. The delinquent is an institutional product. It is no use being surprised, therefore, that in a considerable proportion of cases the biography of convicts passes through all these mechanisms and establishments, whose purpose, it is widely believed, is to lead away from prison. That one should find in them what one might call the index of an irrepressibly delinquent 'character': the prisoner condemned to hard labour was meticulously produced by a childhood spent in a reformatory, according to the lines of force of the generalized carceral system. . . .

3. But perhaps the most important effect of the carceral system and of its extension well beyond legal imprisonment is that it succeeds in making the power to punish natural and legitimate, in lowering at least the threshold of tolerance to penality. It tends to efface what may be exorbitant in the exercise of punishment. It does this by playing the two registers in which it is deployed—the legal register of justice and the extra-legal register of discipline—against one another. In effect, the great continuity of the carceral system throughout the law and its sentences gives a sort of legal sanction to the disciplinary mechanisms, to the decisions and judgements that they enforce. . . . The carceral, with its long gradation stretching from the convictship or imprisonment with hard labour to diffuse, slight limitations, communicates a type of power that the law validates and that justice uses as its favourite weapon. How could the disciplines and the power that functions in them appear arbitrary, when they merely operate the mechanisms of justice itself, even with a view to mitigating their intensity? When, by generalizing its effects and transmitting it to every level, it makes it possible to avoid its full rigour? Carceral continuity and the fusion of the prison-form make it possible to legalize, or in any case to legitimate disciplinary power, which thus avoids any element of excess or abuse it may entail.

But, conversely, the carceral pyramid gives to the power to inflict legal punishment a context in which it appears to be free of all excess and all violence. In the subtle gradation of the apparatuses of discipline and of the successive 'embeddings' that they involve, the prison does not at all represent the unleashing of a different kind of power, but simply an additional degree in the intensity of a mechanism that has continued to operate since the earliest forms of legal punishment. Between the latest institution of 'rehabilitation,' where one is taken in order to avoid prison, and the prison where one is sent after a definable offence, the difference is (and must be) scarcely perceptible. There is a strict economy that has the effect of rendering as discreet as possible the singular power to punish. There is nothing in it now that recalls the former excess of sovereign power when it revenged its authority on the tortured body of those about to be executed. Prison continues, on those who are entrusted to it, a work begun elsewhere, which the whole of society pursues on each individual through innumerable mechanisms of discipline. By means of a carceral continuum, the authority that sentences infiltrates all those other authorities that supervise, transform, correct, improve. . . . The carceral 'naturalizes' the legal power to punish, as it 'legalizes' the technical power to discipline. In thus homogenizing them, effacing what may be violent in one and arbitrary in the other, attenuating the effects of revolt that they may both arouse, thus depriving excess in either of any purpose, circulating the same calculated, mechanical and discreet methods from one to the other, the carceral makes it possible to carry out that great 'economy' of power whose formula the eighteenth century had sought, when the problem of the accumulation and useful administration of men first emerged.

By operating at every level of the social body and by mingling ceaselessly the art of rectifying and the right to punish, the universality of the carceral lowers the level from which it becomes natural and acceptable to be punished. . . .

4. With this new economy of power, the carceral system, which is its basic instrument, permitted the emergence of a new form of 'law': a mixture of legality and nature, prescription and constitution, the norm. This had a whole series of effects: the internal dislocation of the judicial power or at least of its functioning; an increasing difficulty in judging, as if one were ashamed to pass sentence; a furious desire on the part of the judges to judge, assess, diagnose, recognize the normal and abnormal and claim the honour of curing or rehabilitating. . . . Borne along by the omnipresence of the mechanisms of discipline, basing itself on all the carceral apparatuses, it has become one of the major functions of our society. The judges of normality are present everywhere. We are in the society of the teacher-judge, the doctor-judge, the educator-judge, the 'social worker'-judge; it is on them that the universal reign of the normative is based; and each individual, wherever he may find himself, subjects to it his body, his gestures, his behaviour, his aptitudes, his achievements. The carceral network, in its compact or disseminated forms, with its systems of insertion, distribution, surveillance, observation, has been the greatest support, in modern society, of the normalizing power.

5. The carceral texture of society assures both the real capture of the body and its perpetual observation; it is, by its very nature, the apparatus of punishment that conforms most completely to the new economy of power and the instrument for the formation of knowledge that this very economy needs. Its panoptic functioning enables it to play this double role. By virtue of its methods of fixing, dividing, recording, it has been one of the simplest, crudest, also most concrete, but perhaps most indispensable conditions for the development of this immense activity of examination that has objectified human behaviour. If, after the age of 'inquisitorial' justice, we have entered the age of 'examinatory' justice, if, in an even more general way, the method of examination has been able to spread so widely throughout society, and to give rise in part to the sciences of man, one of the great instruments for this has been the multiplicity and close overlapping of the various mechanisms of incarceration. I am not saying that the human sciences emerged from the prison. But, if they have been able to be formed and to produce so many profound changes in the episteme, it is because

they have been conveyed by a specific and new modality of power: a certain policy of the body, a certain way of rendering the group of men docile and useful. This policy required the involvement of definite relations of knowledge in relations of power; it called for a technique of overlapping subjection and objectification; it brought with it new procedures of individualization. The carceral network constituted one of the armatures of this power-knowledge that has made the human sciences historically possible. Knowable man (soul, individuality, consciousness, conduct, whatever it is called) is the object-effect of this analytical investment, of this domination-observation.

6. This no doubt explains that extreme solidity of the prison, that slight invention that was nevertheless decried from the outset. If it had been no more than an instrument of rejection or repression in the service of a state apparatus, it would have been easier to alter its more overt forms or to find a more acceptable substitute for it. But, rooted as it was in mechanisms and strategies of power, it could meet any attempt to transform it with a great force of inertia. One fact is characteristic: when it is a question of altering the system of imprisonment, opposition does not come from the judicial institutions alone; resistance is to be found not in the prison as penal sanction, but in the prison with all its determinations, links and extra-judicial results; in the prison as the relay in a general network of disciplines and surveillances; in the prison as it functions in a panoptic régime. . . .

Note

1. B. Rush, who was one of the inspectors, notes after a visit to Walnut Street: 'Moral cares: Preaching, reading of good books, cleanliness of clothes and rooms, baths; one does not raise one's voice, little wine, as little tobacco as possible, little obscene or profane conversation. Constant work: The gardens taken care of; it is beautiful: 1,200 head of cabbage' (in Teeters, 1935, 50).

References

Baltard, L., *Architectonographie des prisons*, 1829.
Beccaria, C. de, *Traité des délits et des peines*, 1764, ed. 1856.
Boucher d'Argis, A., *Observations sur les lois criminelles*, 1781.
Marat, J.-P., *Plan de législation criminelle*, 1780.
Petion de Villeneuve, J., 'Discours á la Constituante,' *Arch. parl.* XXVI.

60

Prisonization

Donald Clemmer

. . . When a person or group of ingress penetrates and fuses with another group, assimilation may be said to have taken place. The concept is most profitably applied to immigrant groups and perhaps it is not the best term by which to designate similar processes which occur in prison. Assimilation implies that a process of acculturation occurs in one group whose members originally were quite different from those of the group with whom they mix. It implies that the assimilated come to share the sentiments, memories, and traditions of the static group. It is evident that the men who come to prison are not greatly different from the ones already there so far as broad culture influences are concerned: All speak the same language, all have a similar national heritage, all have been stigmatized, and so on. While the differences of regional conditioning are not to be overlooked, it is doubtful if the interactions which lead the professional offender to have a ''we-feeling'' with the naive offender from Coalville can be referred to as assimilation—although the processes furnishing the development of such an understanding are similar to it. As briefly defined in Chapter IV, the term assimilation describes a slow, gradual, more or less unconscious process during which a person learns enough of the culture of a social unit into which he is placed to make him characteristic of it. While we shall continue to use this general meaning, we recognize that in the strictest sense assimilation is not the correct term. So as we use the term Americanization to describe a greater or less degree of the immigrant's integration into the American scheme of life, we may use the term *prisonization* to indicate the taking on in greater or less degree of the folkways, mores, customs, and general culture of the penitentiary. Prisonization is similar to assimilation, and its meaning will become clearer as we proceed.

Every man who enters the penitentiary undergoes prisonization to some extent. The first and most obvious integrative step concerns his status. He becomes at once an anonymous figure in a subordinate group. A number replaces a name. He wears the clothes of the other members of the subordinate group. He is questioned and admonished. He soon learns that the warden is all-powerful. He soon learns the ranks, titles, and authority of various officials. And whether he uses the prison slang and argot or not, he comes to know its meanings. Even though a new man may hold himself aloof from other inmates and remain a solitary figure, he finds himself within a few months referring to or thinking of keepers as ''screws,'' the physician as the

Source: *The Prison Community* (pp. 298–304) by Donald Clemmer, 1958, Holt, Rinehart and Winston, Inc.

"croaker" and using the local nicknames to designate persons. He follows the examples already set in wearing his cap. He learns to eat in haste and in obtaining food he imitates the tricks of those near him.

After the new arrival recovers from the effects of the swallowing-up process, he assigns a new meaning to conditions he had previously taken for granted. The fact that food, shelter, clothing, and a work activity had been given him originally made no especial impression. It is only after some weeks or months that there comes to him a new interpretation of these necessities of life. This new conception results from mingling with other men and it places emphasis on the fact that the environment *should* administer to him. This point is intangible and difficult to describe in so far as it is only a subtle and minute change in attitude from the taken-for-granted perception. Exhaustive questioning of hundreds of men reveals that this slight change in attitude is a fundamental step in the process we are calling prisonization. Supplemental to it is the almost universal desire on the part of the man, after a period of some months, to get a good job so, as he says, "I can do my time without any trouble and get out of here." A good job usually means a comfortable job of a more or less isolated kind in which conflicts with other men are not likely to develop. The desire for a comfortable job is not peculiar to the prison community, to be sure, but it seems to be a phase of prisonization in the following way. When men have served time before entering the penitentiary they look the situation over and almost immediately express a desire for a certain kind of work. When strictly first offenders come to prison, however, they seldom express a desire for a particular kind of work, but are willing to do anything and frequently say, "I'll do any kind of work they put me at and you won't have any trouble from me." Within a period of a few months, however, these same men, who had no choice of work, develop preferences and make their desires known. They "wise up," as the inmates say, or in other words, by association they become prisonized.

In various other ways men new to prison slip into the existing patterns. They learn to gamble or learn new ways to gamble. Some, for the first time in their lives, take to abnormal sex behavior. Many of them learn to distrust and hate the officers, the parole board, and sometimes each other, and they become acquainted with the dogmas and mores existing in the community. But these changes do not occur in every man. However, every man is subject to certain influences which we may call the *universal factors of prisonization.*

Acceptance of an inferior rôle, accumulation of facts concerning the organization of the prison, the development of somewhat new habits of eating, dressing, working, sleeping, the adoption of local language, the recognition that nothing is owed to the environment for the supplying of needs, and the eventual desire for a good job are aspects of prisonization which are operative for all inmates. It is not these aspects, however, which concern us most but they are important because of their universality, especially among men who have served many years. That is, even if no other factor of the prison culture touches the personality of an inmate of many years residence, the influences of these universal factors are sufficient to make a man characteristic of the penal community and probably so disrupt his personality that a happy adjustment in any community becomes next to impossible. On the other hand, if inmates who are incarcerated for only short periods, such as a year or so, do not become integrated into the culture except in so far as these universal factors of prisonization are concerned, they do not seem to be so characteristic of the penal community and are able when released to take up a new mode of life without much difficulty.

The phases of prisonization which concern us most are the influences which breed or deepen criminality and antisociality and make the inmate characteristic of the criminalistic ideology in the prison community. As has been said, every man feels the influences of what we have called the universal factors, but not every man becomes prisonized in and by other phases of the culture. Whether or not complete prisonization takes place depends first on the man himself, that is, his susceptibility to a culture which depends, we think, primarily on the type of relationships he had before imprisonment, *i.e.*, his personality. A second determinant effecting complete prisonization refers to the kind and extent of relationships which an inmate has with persons outside the walls. A third determinant refers to whether or not a man becomes affiliated in prison primary or semi-primary groups and this is related to the two points already mentioned. Yet a fourth determinant depends simply on chance, a chance placement in work gang, cellhouse, and with cellmate. A fifth determinant pertains to whether or not a man accepts the dogmas or codes of the prison culture. Other determinants depend on age, criminality, nationality, race, regional conditioning, and every determinant is more or less interrelated with every other one.

With knowledge of these determinants we can hypothetically construct schemata of prisonization which may serve to illustrate its extremes. In the least or lowest degree of prisonization the following factors may be enumerated:

1. A short sentence, thus a brief subjection to the universal factors of prisonization.
2. A fairly stable personality made stable by an adequacy of positive and "socialized" relationships during pre-penal life.
3. The continuance of positive relationships with persons outside the walls.
4. Refusal or inability to integrate into a prison primary group or semi-primary group, while yet maintaining a symbiotic balance in relations with other men.
5. Refusal to accept blindly the dogmas and codes of the population, and a willingness, under certain situations, to aid officials, thus making for identification with the free community.
6. A chance placement with a cellmate and workmates who do not possess leadership qualities and who are also not completely integrated into the prison culture.
7. Refraining from abnormal sex behavior, and excessive gambling, and a ready willingness to engage seriously in work and recreative activities.

Other factors no doubt have an influencing force in obstructing the process of prisonization, but the seven points mentioned seem outstanding.

In the highest or greatest degree of prisonization the following factors may be enumerated:

1. A sentence of many years, thus a long subjection to the universal factors of prisonization.
2. A somewhat unstable personality made unstable by an inadequacy of "socialized" relations before commitment, but possessing, none the less, a capacity for strong convictions and a particular kind of loyalty.
3. A dearth of positive relations with persons outside the walls.

4. A readiness and a capacity for integration into a prison-primary group.

5. A blind, or almost blind, acceptance of the dogmas and mores of the primary group and the general penal population.

6. A chance placement with other persons of a similar orientation.

7. A readiness to participate in gambling and abnormal sex behavior.

We can see in these two extremes the degrees with which the prisonization process operates. No suggestion is intended that a high correlation exists between either extreme of prisonization and criminality. It is quite possible that the inmate who fails to integrate in the prison culture may be and may continue to be much more criminalistic than the inmate who becomes completely prisonized. The trends are probably otherwise, however, as our study of group life suggests. To determine prisonization, every case must be appraised for itself. Of the two degrees presented in the schemas it is probable that more men approach the complete degree than the least degree of prisonization, but it is also probable that the majority of inmates become prisonized in some respects and not in others. It is the varying degrees of prisonization among the 2,300 men that contribute to the disassociation which is so common. The culture is made complex, not only by the constantly changing population, but by these differences in the tempo and degree of prisonization.

Assimilation, as the concept is customarily applied, is always a slow, gradual process, but prisonization, as we use the term here is usually slow, but not necessarily so. The speed with which prisonization occurs depends on the personality of the man involved, his crime, age, home neighborhood, intelligence, the situation into which he is placed in prison and other less obvious influences. The process does not necessarily proceed in an orderly or measured fashion but tends to be irregular. In some cases we have found the process working in a cycle. The amount and speed of prisonization can be judged only by the behavior and attitudes of the men, and these vary from man to man and in the same man from time to time. It is the excessive number of changes in orientation which the men undergo which makes generalizations about the process so difficult.

In the free communities where the daily life of the inhabitants is not controlled in every detail, some authors have reported a natural gravitation to social levels. The matter of chance still remains a factor, of course, in open society but not nearly so much so as in the prison. For example, two associates in a particular crime may enter the prison at the same time. Let us say that their criminality, their intelligence, and their background are more or less the same. Each is interviewed by the deputy warden and assigned to a job. It so happens that a certain office is in need of a porter. Of the two associates the man whom the deputy warden happens to see first may be assigned to that job while the one he interviews last is assigned to the quarry. The inmate who becomes the office porter associates with but four or five other men, none of whom, let us suppose, are basically prisonized. The new porter adapts himself to them and takes up their interests. His speed of prisonization will be slow and he may never become completely integrated into the prison culture. His associate, on the other hand, works in the quarry and mingles with a hundred men. The odds are three to five that he will become integrated into a primary or semi-primary group. When he is admitted into the competitive and personal relationships of informal group life we can be sure that, in spite of some disassociation, he is becoming prisonized and will approach the complete degree.

Even if the two associates were assigned to the same work unit, differences in the tempo of prisonization might result if one, for example, worked shoulder to shoulder with a "complete solitary man," or a "hoosier." Whatever else may be said of the tempo of the process, it is always faster when the contacts are primary, providing the persons contacted in a primary way are themselves integrated beyond the minimal into the prison culture. Other factors, of course, influence the speed of integration. The inmate whose wife divorces him may turn for response and recognition to his immediate associates. When the memories of pre-penal experience cease to be satisfying or practically useful, a barrier to prisonization has been removed.

Some men become prisonized to the highest degree, or to a degree approaching it, but then reject their entire orientation and show, neither by behavior nor attitudes, that any sort of integration has taken place. They slip out of group life. They ignore the codes and dogmas and they fall into a reverie or stupor or become "solitary men." After some months or even years of playing this rôle they may again affiliate with a group and behave as other prisonized inmates do.

Determination of the degree of prisonization and the speed with which it occurs can be learned best through the study of specific cases. The innumerable variables and the methodological difficulties which arise in learning what particular stage of prisonization a man has reached, prohibit the use of quantitative methods. It would be a great help to penology and to parole boards in particular, if the student of prisons could say that inmate so-and-so was prisonized to $x^3 + 9y$ degrees, and such a degree was highly correlated with a specific type of criminality. The day will no doubt come when phenomena of this kind can be measured, but it is not yet here. For the present we must bend our efforts to systems of actuarial prediction, and work for refinements in this line. Actuarial procedures do not ignore criteria of attitudes, but they make no effort as yet to conjure with such abstruse phenomena as prisonization. It is the contention of this writer that parole prediction methods which do not give as much study and attention to a man's rôle in the prison community as is given to his adjustment in the free community cannot be of much utility. . . .

61

The Pains of Imprisonment

Gresham M. Sykes

In our discussion of the New Jersey State Prison, the bulk of our remarks has been directed to the custodians—their objectives, their procedures, and their limitations. We have been looking at the prison's system of power from the position of the rulers rather than that of the ruled, and only in passing have we noted the meaning of imprisonment for the prisoners. Now, however, we must examine this society of captives from the viewpoint of the inmates more systematically and in more detail.

It might be argued, of course, that there are certain dangers in speaking of the inmates' perspective of captivity, since it is apt to carry the implication that all prisoners perceive their captivity in precisely the same way. It might be argued that in reality there are as many prisons as there are prisoners—that each man brings to the custodial institution his own needs and his own background and each man takes away from the prison his own interpretation of life within the walls. We do not intend to deny that different men see the conditions of custody somewhat differently and accord these conditions a different emphasis in their personal accounting. Yet when we examine the way the inmates of the New Jersey State Prison perceive the social environment created by the custodians, the dominant fact is the hard core of consensus expressed by the members of the captive population with regard to the nature of their confinement. The inmates are agreed that life in the maximum security prison is depriving or frustrating in the extreme.

In part, the deprivations or frustrations of prison life today might be viewed as punishments which the free community deliberately inflicts on the offender for violating the law; in part, they might be seen as the unplanned (or, as some would argue, the unavoidable) concomitants of confining large groups of criminals for prolonged periods. In either case, the modern pains of imprisonment are often defined by society as a humane alternative to the physical brutality and the neglect which constituted the major meaning of imprisonment in the past. But in examining the pains of imprisonment as they exist today, it is imperative that we go beyond the fact that severe bodily suffering has long since disappeared as a significant aspect of the custodians' regime, leaving behind a residue of apparently less acute hurts such as the loss of liberty, the deprivation of goods and services, the frustration of sexual desire, and so on. These deprivations or frustrations of the modern prison

Source: Gresham M. Sykes, *The Society of Captives: A Study of a Maximum Security Prison.* Copyright © 1958, copyright © renewed 1986 by Princeton University Press. Reprinted by permission of the publisher.

may indeed be the acceptable or unavoidable implications of imprisonment, but we must recognize the fact that they can be just as painful as the physical maltreatment which they have replaced. As Maslow has indicated, there are some frustrating situations which appear as a serious attack on the personality, as a "threat to the life goals of the individual, to his defensive system, to his self-esteem, or to his feelings of security."[1] Such attacks on the psychological level are less easily seen than a sadistic beating, a pair of shackles in the floor, or the caged man on a treadmill, but the destruction of the psyche is no less fearful than bodily affliction and it must play a large role in our discussion. Whatever may be the pains of imprisonment, then, in the custodial institution of today, we must explore the way in which the deprivations and frustrations pose profound threats to the inmate's personality or sense of personal worth.

The Deprivation of Liberty

Of all the painful conditions imposed on the inmates of the New Jersey State Prison, none is more immediately obvious than the loss of liberty. The prisoner must live in a world shrunk to thirteen and a half acres and within this restricted area his freedom of movement is further confined by a strict system of passes, the military formations in moving from one point within the institution to another, and the demand that he remain in his cell until given permission to do otherwise. In short, the prisoner's loss of liberty is a double one—first, by confinement to the institution and second, by confinement within the institution.

The mere fact that the individual's movements are restricted, however, is far less serious than the fact that imprisonment means that the inmate is cut off from family, relatives, and friends, not in the self-isolation of the hermit or the misanthrope, but in the involuntary seclusion of the outlaw. It is true that visiting and mailing privileges partially relieve the prisoner's isolation—if he can find someone to visit him or write to him and who will be approved as a visitor or correspondent by the prison officials. Many inmates, however, have found their links with persons in the free community weakening as the months and years pass by. This may explain in part the fact that an examination of the visiting records of a random sample of the inmate population, covering approximately a one-year period, indicated that 41 percent of the prisoners in the New Jersey State Prison had received no visits from the outside world.

It is not difficult to see this isolation as painfully depriving or frustrating in terms of lost emotional relationships, of loneliness and boredom. But what makes this pain of imprisonment bite most deeply is the fact that the confinement of the criminal represents a deliberate, moral rejection of the criminal by the free community. Indeed, as Reckless has pointed out, it is the moral condemnation of the criminal—however it may be symbolized—that converts hurt into punishment, i.e., the just consequence of committing an offense, and it is this condemnation that confronts the inmate by the fact of his seclusion.

Now it is sometimes claimed that many criminals are so alienated from conforming society and so identified with a criminal subculture that the moral condemnation, rejection, or disapproval of legitimate society does not touch them; they are, it is said, indifferent to the penal sanctions of the free community, at least as far as the moral stigma of being defined as a criminal is concerned. Possibly this is true for a small number of offenders such as the professional thief described by Sutherland[2] or the psychopathic personality delineated by William and Joan McCord.[3] For the great majority of criminals in prison, however, the evidence suggests that neither alienation from the ranks of the law-abiding nor involvement in a system of criminal value is sufficient to eliminate the threat to the prisoner's ego posed by society's rejection.[4] The signs pointing to the prisoner's degradation are many—the anonymity of a uniform and a number rather than a name, the shaven head,[5] the insistence on gestures of respect and subordination when addressing officials, and so on. The prisoner is never allowed to forget that, by committing a crime, he has foregone his claim to the status of a full-fledged, *trusted* member of society. The status lost by the prisoner is, in fact, similar to what Marshall has called the status of citizenship—that basic acceptance of the individual as a functioning member of the society in which he lives.[6] It is true that in the past the imprisoned criminal literally suffered civil death and that although the doctrines of attainder and corruption of blood were largely abandoned in the 18th and 19th Centuries, the inmate is still stripped of many of his civil rights such as the right to vote, to hold office, to sue in court, and so on.[7] But as important as the loss of these civil rights may be, the loss of that more diffuse status which defines the individual as someone to be trusted or as morally acceptable is the loss which hurts most.

In short, the wall which seals off the criminal, the contaminated man, is a constant threat to the prisoner's self-conception and the threat is continually repeated in the many daily reminders that he must be kept apart from "decent" men. Somehow this rejection or degradation by the free community must be warded off, turned aside, rendered harmless. Somehow the imprisoned criminal must find a device for rejecting his rejectors, if he is to endure psychologically.[8]

The Deprivation of Goods and Services

There are admittedly many problems in attempting to compare the standard of living existing in the free community and the standard of living which is supposed to be the lot of the inmate in prison. How, for example, do we interpret the fact that a covering for the floor of a cell usually consists of a scrap from a discarded blanket and that even this possession is forbidden by the prison authorities? What meaning do we attach to the fact that no inmate owns a common piece of furniture, such as a chair, but only a homemade stool? What is the value of a suit of clothing which is also a convict's uniform with a stripe and a stencilled number? The answers are far from simple although there are a number of prison officials who will argue that some inmates are better off in prison, in strictly material terms, than they could ever hope to be in the rough-and-tumble economic life of the free community. Possibly this is so, but at least it has never been claimed by the inmates that the goods and services provided the prisoner are equal to or better than the goods and services which the prisoner could obtain if he were left to his own devices outside the walls. The average inmate finds himself in a harshly Spartan environment which he defines as painfully depriving.

Now it is true that the prisoner's basic material needs are met—in the sense that he does not go hungry, cold, or wet. He receives adequate medical care and he has the opportunity for exercise. But a standard of living constructed in terms of so many calories per day, so many hours of recreation, so many cubic yards of space per individual, and so on, misses the central point when we are discussing the individual's feeling of deprivation, however useful it may be in setting minimum levels of consumption for the maintenance of health. A standard of living can be hopelessly inadequate, from the individual's viewpoint, because it bores him to death or fails to provide those subtle symbolic overtones which we invest in the world of possessions. And this is the core of the prisoner's problem in the area of goods and services. He wants—or needs, if you will—not just the so-called necessities of life but also the amenities: cigarettes and liquor as well as calories, interesting foods as well as sheer bulk, individual clothing as well as adequate clothing, individual furnishings for his living quarters as well as shelter, privacy as well as space. The "rightfulness" of the prisoner's feeling of deprivation can be questioned. And the objective reality of the prisoner's deprivation—in the sense that he has actually suffered a fall from his economic position in the free community—can be viewed with skepticism, as we have indicated above. But these criticisms are irrelevant to the significant issue, namely that legitimately or illegitimately, rationally or irrationally, the inmate population defines its present material impoverishment as a painful loss.

Now in modern Western culture, material possessions are so large a part of the individual's conception of himself that to be stripped of them is to be attacked at the deepest layers of personality. This is particularly true when poverty cannot be excused as a blind stroke of fate or a universal calamity. Poverty due to one's own mistakes or misdeeds represents an indictment against one's basic value or personal worth and there are few men who can philosophically bear the want caused by their own actions. It is true some prisoners in the New Jersey State Prison attempt to interpret their low position in the scale of goods and services as an effort by the State to exploit them economically. Thus, in the eyes of some inmates, the prisoner is poor not because of an offense which he has committed in the past but because the State is a tyrant which uses its captive criminals as slave labor under the hypocritical guise of reformation. Penology, it is said, is a racket. Their poverty, then, is not punishment as we have used the word before, i.e., the just consequence of criminal behavior; rather, it is an unjust hurt or pain inflicted without legitimate cause. This attitude, however, does not appear to be particularly widespread in the inmate population and the great majority of prisoners must face their privation without the aid of the wronged man's sense of injustice. Furthermore, most prisoners are unable to fortify themselves in their low level of material existence by seeing it as a means to some high or worthy end. They are unable to attach any significant meaning to their need to make it more bearable, such as present pleasures foregone for pleasures in the future, self-sacrifice in the interests of the community, or material asceticism for the purpose of spiritual salvation.

The inmate, then, sees himself as having been made poor by reason of his own acts and without the rationale of compensating benefits. The failure is *his* failure in a world where control and possession of the material environment are commonly taken as sure indicators of a man's worth. It is true that our society, as materialistic as it may be, does not rely exclusively on goods and services as a criterion of an individual's value; and, as we shall see shortly, the inmate population defends itself by stressing alternative or supplementary measures of merit. But impoverishment remains as one of the most bitter attacks on the individual's self-image that our society has to offer and the prisoner cannot ignore the implications of his straitened circumstances.[9] Whatever the discomforts and irritations of the prisoner's Spartan existence may be, he must carry the additional burden of social definitions which equate his material deprivation with personal inadequacy.

The Deprivation of Heterosexual Relationships

Unlike the prisoner in many Latin-American countries, the inmate of the maximum security prison in New Jersey does not enjoy the privilege of so-called conjugal visits. And in those brief times when the prisoner is allowed to see his wife, mistress, or "female friend," the woman must sit on one side of a plate glass window and the prisoner on the other, communicating by means of a phone under the scrutiny of a guard. If the inmate, then, is rejected and impoverished by the facts of his imprisonment, he is also figuratively castrated by his involuntary celibacy.

Now a number of writers have suggested that men in prison undergo a reduction of the sexual drive and that the sexual frustrations of prisoners are therefore less than they might appear to be at first glance. The reports of reduced sexual interest have, however, been largely confined to accounts of men imprisoned in concentration camps or similar extreme situations where starvation, torture, and physical exhaustion have reduced life to a simple struggle for survival or left the captive sunk in apathy. But in the American prison these factors are not at work to any significant extent and Linder has noted that the prisoner's access to mass media, pornography circulated among inmates, and similar stimuli serve to keep alive the prisoner's sexual impulses.[10] The same thought is expressed more crudely by the inmates of the New Jersey State Prison in a variety of obscene expressions and it is clear that the lack of heterosexual intercourse is a frustrating experience for the imprisoned criminal and that it is a frustration which weighs heavily and painfully on his mind during his prolonged confinement. There are, of course, some "habitual" homosexuals in the prison—men who were homosexuals before their arrival and who continue their particular form of deviant behavior within the all-male society of the custodial institution. For these inmates, perhaps, the deprivation of heterosexual intercourse cannot be counted as one of the pains of imprisonment. They are few in number, however, and are only too apt to be victimized or raped by aggressive prisoners who have turned to homosexuality as a temporary means of relieving their frustration.

Yet as important as frustration in the sexual sphere may be in physiological terms, the psychological problems created by the lack of heterosexual relationships can be even more serious. A society composed exclusively of men tends to generate anxieties in its members concerning their masculinity regardless of whether or not they are coerced, bribed, or seduced into an overt homosexual liaison. Latent homosexual tendencies may be activated in the individual without being translated into open behavior and yet still arouse strong guilt feelings at either the conscious or unconscious level. In the tense atmosphere of the prison with its known perversions, its importunities of admitted homosexuals, and its constant references to the problems of sexual frustration by guards and inmates alike, there are few prisoners who can escape the fact that an essential component of a man's self conception—his status of male—is called into question. And if an inmate has in fact engaged in homosexual behavior within the walls, not as a continuation of an habitual pattern but as a rare act of sexual deviance under the intolerable pressure of mounting physical desire, the psychological onslaughts on his ego image will be particularly acute.[11]

In addition to these problems stemming from sexual frustration per se, the deprivation of heterosexual relationships carries with it another threat to the prisoner's image of himself—more diffuse, perhaps, and more difficult to state precisely and yet no less disturbing. The inmate is shut off from the world of women which by its very polarity gives the male world much of its meaning. Like most men, the inmate must search for his identity not simply within himself but also in the picture of himself which he finds reflected in the eyes of others; and since a significant half of his audience is denied him, the inmate's self image is in danger of becoming half complete, fractured, a monochrome without the hues of reality. The prisoner's looking-glass self, in short—to use Cooley's fine phrase—is only that portion of the prisoner's personality which is recognized or appreciated by men and this partial identity is made hazy by the lack of contrast.

The Deprivation of Autonomy

We have noted before that the inmate suffers from what we have called a loss of autonomy in that he is subjected to a vast body of rules and commands which are designed to control his behavior in minute detail. To the casual observer, however, it might seem that the many areas of life in which self-determination is withheld, such as the language used in a letter, the hours of sleeping and eating, or the route to work, are relatively unimportant. Perhaps it might be argued, as in the case of material deprivation, that the inmate in prison is not much worse off than the individual in the free community who is regulated in a great many aspects of his life by the iron fist of custom. It could even be argued, as some writers have done, that for a number of imprisoned criminals the extensive control of the custodians provides a welcome escape from freedom and that the prison officials thus supply an external Super-Ego which serves to reduce the anxieties arising from an awareness of deviant impulses. But from the viewpoint of the inmate population, it is precisely the triviality of much of the officials' control which often proves to be most galling. Regulation by a bureaucratic staff is felt far differently than regulation by custom. And even though a few prisoners do welcome the strict regime of the custodians as a means of checking their own aberrant behavior which they would like to curb but cannot, most prisoners look on the matter in a different light. Most prisoners, in fact, express an intense hostility against their far-reaching dependence on the decisions of their captors and the restricted ability to make choices must be included among the pains of imprisonment along with restrictions of physical liberty, the possession of goods and services, and heterosexual relationships.

Now the loss of autonomy experienced by the inmates of the prison does not represent a grant of power freely given by the ruled to the rulers for a limited and specific end. Rather, it is total and it is imposed—and for these reasons it is less endurable. The nominal objectives of the custodians are not, in general, the objectives of the prisoners.[12] Yet regardless of whether or not the inmate population shares some aims with the custodial bureaucracy, the many regulations and orders of the New Jersey State Prison's official regime often arouse the prisoner's hostility because they don't "make sense" from the prisoner's point of view. Indeed, the incomprehensible order or rule is a basic feature of life in prison. Inmates, for example, are forbidden to take food from the mess hall to their cells. Some prisoners see this as a move designed to promote cleanliness; others are convinced that the regulation is for the purpose of preventing inmates from obtaining anything that might be used in the *sub rosa* system of barter. Most, however, simply see the measure as another irritating, pointless gesture of authoritarianism. Similarly, prisoners are denied parole but are left in ignorance of the reasons for the decision. Prisoners are informed that the delivery of mail will be delayed—but they are not told why.

Now some of the inmate population's ignorance might be described as "accidental"; it arises from what we can call the principle of bureaucratic indifference, i.e., events which seem important or vital to those at the bottom of the heap are viewed with an increasing lack of concern with each step upward. The rules, the commands, the decisions which flow down to those who are controlled are not accompanied by explanations on the grounds that it is "impractical" or "too much trouble." Some of the inmate population's ignorance, however, is deliberately fostered by the prison officials in that explanations are often withheld as a matter of calculated policy. Providing explanations carries an implication that those who are ruled have a right to know—and this in turn suggests that if the explanations are not satisfactory, the rule or order will be changed. But this is in direct contradiction to the theoretical power relationship of the inmates and the prison officials. Imprisoned criminals are individuals who are being punished by society and they must be brought to their knees. If the inmate population maintains the right to argue with its captors, it takes on the appearance of an enemy nation with its own sovereignty; and in so doing it raises disturbing questions about the nature of the offender's deviance. The criminal is no longer simply a man who has broken the law; he has become a part of a group with an alternative viewpoint and thus attacks the validity of the law itself. The custodians' refusal to give reasons for many aspects of their regime can be seen in part as an attempt to avoid such an intolerable situation.

The indignation aroused by the "bargaining inmate" or the necessity of justifying the custodial regime is particularly evident during a riot when prisoners have the "impudence" to present a list of demands. In discussing the disturbances at the New Jersey State Prison in the Spring of 1952, for example, a newspaper editorial angrily noted that "the storm, like a nightmarish April Fool's dream, has passed, leaving in its wake a partially wrecked State Prison as a debasing monument to the ignominious rage of desperate men."

The important point, however, is that the frustration of the prisoner's ability to make choices and the frequent refusals to provide an explanation for the regulations and commands descending from the bureaucratic staff involve a profound threat to the prisoner's self image because they reduce the prisoner to the weak, helpless, dependent status of childhood. As Bettelheim has tellingly noted in his comments on the concentration camp, men under guard stand in constant danger of losing their identification with the normal definition of an adult and the imprisoned criminal finds his picture of himself as a self-determining individual being destroyed by the regime of the custodians.[13] It is possible that this psychological attack is particularly painful in American culture because of the deep-lying insecurities produced by the delays, the conditionality and the uneven progress so often observed in the granting of adulthood. It is also possible that the criminal is frequently an individual who has experienced great difficulty in adjusting himself to figures of authority and who finds the many restraints of prison life particularly threatening in so far as earlier struggles over the establishment of self are reactivated in a more virulent form. But without asserting that Americans in general or criminals in particular are notably ill-equipped to deal with the problems posed by the deprivation of autonomy, the helpless or dependent status of the prisoner clearly represents a serious threat to the prisoner's self image as a fully accredited member of adult society. And of the many threats which may confront the individual, either in or out of prison, there are few better calculated to arouse acute anxieties than the attempt to reimpose the subservience of youth. Public humiliation, enforced respect and deference, the finality of authoritarian decisions, the demands for a specified course of conduct because, in the judgment of another, it is in the individual's best interest—all are features of childhood's helplessness in the face of a superior adult world. Such things may be both irksome and disturbing for a child, especially if the child envisions himself as having outgrown such servitude. But for the adult who has escaped such helplessness with the passage of years, to be thrust back into childhood's helplessness is even more painful, and the inmate of the prison must somehow find a means of coping with the issue.

The Deprivation of Security

However strange it may appear that society has chosen to reduce the criminality of the offender by forcing him to associate with more than a thousand other criminals for years on end, there is one meaning of this involuntary union which is obvious— the individual prisoner is thrown into prolonged intimacy with other men who in many cases have a long history of violent, aggressive behavior. It is a situation which can prove to be anxiety-provoking even for the hardened recidivist and it is in this light that we can understand the comment of an inmate of the New Jersey State Prison who said, "The worst thing about prison is you have to live with other prisoners."

The fact that the imprisoned criminal sometimes views his fellow prisoners as "vicious" or "dangerous" may seem a trifle unreasonable. Other inmates, after all, are men like himself, bearing the legal stigma of conviction. But even if the individual prisoner believes that he himself is not the sort of person who is likely to attack or exploit weaker and less resourceful fellow captives, he is apt to view others with more suspicion. And if he himself is prepared to commit crimes while in prison, he is likely to feel that many others will be at least equally ready. In the next chapter, we will examine the solidarity and the exploitation which actually exist among prisoners, but for the moment it is enough to point out that regardless of the patterns of mutual aid and support which may flourish in the inmate population, there are a sufficient number of outlaws within this group of outlaws to deprive the average prisoner of that sense of security which comes from living among men who can be reasonably expected to abide by the rules of society. While it is true that every prisoner does not live in the constant fear of being robbed or beaten, the constant companionship of thieves, rapists, murderers, and aggressive homosexuals is far from reassuring.

An important aspect of this disturbingly problematical world is the fact that the inmate is acutely aware that sooner or later he will be "tested"—that someone will "push" him to see how far they can go and that he must be prepared to fight for the safety of his person and his possessions. If he should fail, he will thereafter be an object of contempt, constantly in danger of being attacked by other inmates who view him as an obvious victim, as a man who cannot or will not defend his rights. And yet if he succeeds, he may well become a target for the prisoner who wishes to prove himself, who seeks to enhance his own prestige by defeating the man with a reputation for toughness. Thus both success and failure in defending one's self against the aggressions of fellow captives may serve to provoke fresh attacks and no man stands assured of the future.[14]

The prisoner's loss of security arouses acute anxiety, in short, not just because violent acts of aggression and exploitation occur but also because such behavior constantly calls into question the individual's ability to cope with it, in terms of his own inner resources, his courage, his "nerve." Can he stand up and take it? Will he prove to be tough enough? These uncertainties constitute an ego threat for the individual forced to live in prolonged intimacy with criminals, regardless of the nature or extent of his own criminality; and we can catch a glimpse of this tense and fearful existence in the comment of one prisoner who said, "It takes a pretty good man to be able to stand on an equal plane with a guy that's in for rape, with a guy that's in for murder, with a man who's well respected in the institution because he's a real tough cookie. . . ." His expectations concerning the conforming behavior of others destroyed, unable and unwilling to rely on the officials for protection, uncertain of whether or not today's joke will be tomorrow's bitter insult, the prison inmate can never feel safe. And at a deeper level lies the anxiety about his reactions to this unstable world, for then his manhood will be evaluated in the public view. . . .

Notes

1. Cf. A. H. Maslow, "Deprivation, Threat, and Frustration," in *Readings in Social Psychology*, edited by T. M. Newcomb and E. L. Hartley (New York: Henry Holt and Company, 1947).
2. Cf. Edwin H. Sutherland, *The Professional Thief* (Chicago: The University of Chicago Press, 1937).
3. Cf. William and Joan McCord, *Psychopathy and Delinquency* (New York: Grune and Stratton, 1956).
4. For an excellent discussion of the symbolic overtones of imprisonment, see Walter C. Reckless, *The Crime Problem* (New York: Appleton-Century-Crofts, Inc., 1955), pp. 428–429.
5. Western culture has long placed a peculiar emphasis on shaving the head as a symbol of degradation, ranging from the enraged treatment of collaborators in occupied Europe to the more measured barbering of recruits in the Armed Forces. In the latter case, as in the prison, the nominal purpose has been cleanliness and neatness, but for the person who is shaved the meaning is somewhat different. In the New Jersey State Prison, the prisoner is clipped to the skull on arrival but not thereafter.
6. See T. H. Marshall, *Citizenship and Social Class* (Cambridge, England: The Cambridge University Press, 1950).
7. Paul W. Tappan, "The Legal Rights of Prisoners," *The Annals of the American Academy of Political and Social Science*. Vol. 293 (May 1954), pp. 99–111.
8. See Lloyd W. McCorkle and Richard R. Korn, "Resocialization Within Walls." Ibid., pp. 88–98.
9. Komarovsky's discussion of the psychological implications of unemployment is particularly apposite here, despite the markedly different context, for she notes that economic failure provokes acute anxiety as humiliation cuts away at the individual's conception of his manhood. He feels useless, undeserving of respect, disorganized, adrift in a society where economic status is a major anchoring point. Cf. Mirra Komarovsky, *The Unemployed Man and His Family* (New York: The Dryden Press, 1940), pp. 74–77.
10. See Robert M. Lindner, "Sex in Prison," *Complex*, Vol. 6 (Fall 1951), pp. 5–20.
11. Estimates of the proportion of inmates who engage in homosexuality during their confinement in the prison are apt to vary. In the New Jersey State Prison, however, Wing

Guards and Shop Guards examined a random sample of inmates who were well known to them from prolonged observation and identified 35 percent of the men as individuals believed to have engaged in homosexual acts. The judgments of these officials were substantially in agreement with the judgments of a prisoner who possessed an apparently well-founded reputation as an aggressive homosexual deeply involved in patterns of sexual deviance within the institution and who had been convicted of sodomy. But the validity of these judgments remains largely unknown and we present the following conclusions, based on a variety of sources, as provisional at best: First, a fairly large proportion of prisoners engage in homosexual behavior during their period of confinement. Second, for many of those prisoners who do engage in homosexual behavior, their sexual deviance is rare or sporadic rather than chronic. And third, as we have indicated before, much of the homosexuality which does occur in prison is not part of a life pattern existing before and after confinement; rather, it is a response to the peculiar rigors of imprisonment. A further discussion of the meaning and range of sexual behavior in the New Jersey State Prison will be presented in the next chapter.

12. We have suggested earlier, in our discussion of the defects of prison as a system of power, that the nominal objectives of the officials tend to be compromised as they are translated into the actual routines of day-to-day life. The modus vivendi reached by guards and their prisoners is oriented toward certain goals which are in fact shared by captors and captives. In this limited sense, the control of the prison officials is partly concurred in by the inmates as well as imposed on them from above. We will explore this issue at greater length in the analysis of crisis and equilibrium in the society of captives, but in discussing the pains of imprisonment our attention is focused on the frustrations or threats posed by confinement rather than the devices which meet these frustrations or threats and render them tolerable. Our interest here is in the vectors of the prison's social system—if we may use an analogy from the physical sciences—rather than the resultant.

13. Cf. Bruno Bettelheim, ''Individual and Mass Behavior in Extreme Situations,'' in *Readings in Social Psychology*, edited by T. M. Newcomb and E. L. Hartley (New York: Henry Holt and Company, 1947).

14. As the Warden of the New Jersey State Prison has pointed out, the arrival of an obviously tough professional hoodlum creates a serious problem for the recognized ''bad man'' in a cellblock who is expected to challenge the newcomer immediately.

62

The Inmate Social System
Gresham M. Sykes   Sheldon L. Messinger

In recent years increased attention has been paid to the custodial institution in terms of general sociological theory rather than in terms of social problems, notably with reference to aspects of prison life commonly identified in the relevant literature as the "inmate culture," the "prisoner community," or the "inmate social system." This system of social relationships—its underlying norms, attitudes, and beliefs—as found in the American prison is examined in this paper. After summarizing the salient features of the society of prisoners as presented in the sociological literature of the last two decades, we comment briefly on the major theoretical approach that has been used in discussing prison life in the past. Then we develop a theory of the structure and functioning of the inmate social system, primarily in terms of inmate values and their related roles, and finally we outline some possibilities for future research.

The Prison Society

Despite the number and diversity of prison populations, observers of such groups have reported only one strikingly pervasive value system. This value system of prisoners commonly takes the form of an explicit code, in which brief normative imperatives are held forth as guides for the behavior of the inmate in his relations with fellow prisoners and custodians. The maxims are usually asserted with great vehemence by the inmate population, and violations call forth a diversity of sanctions ranging from ostracism to physical violence.

Examination of many descriptions of prison life[1] suggests that the chief tenets of the inmate code can be classified roughly into five major groups:

- There are those maxims that caution: *Don't interfere with inmate interests*, which center of course in serving the least possible time and enjoying the greatest possible number of pleasures and privileges while in prison. The most inflexible directive in this category is concerned with betrayal of a fellow captive to the institutional officials: *Never rat on a con*. In general, no qualification or mitigating circumstance is recognized; and no grievance against another inmate—even though it is justified

Source: Gresham M. Sykes and Sheldon L. Messinger, "The Inmate Social System," in *Theoretical Studies in the Social Organization of the Prison* (New York: Social Science Research Council Pamphlet No. 15, 1960), pp. 5-11, 13-19. Footnotes renumbered.

in the eyes of the inmate population—is to be taken to officials for settlement. Other specifics include: *Don't be nosey; don't have a loose lip; keep off a man's back; don't put a guy on the spot.* In brief and positively put: *Be loyal to your class—the cons.* Prisoners must present a unified front against their guards no matter how much this may cost in terms of personal sacrifice.

• There are explicit injunctions to refrain from quarrels or arguments with fellow prisoners: *Don't lose your head.* Emphasis is placed on the curtailment of affect; emotional frictions are to be minimized and the irritants of daily life ignored. Maxims often heard include: *Play it cool* and *do your own time.* As we shall see, there are important distinctions in this category, depending on whether the prisoner has been subjected to legitimate provocation; but in general a definite value is placed on curbing feuds and grudges.

• Prisoners assert that inmates should not take advantage of one another by means of force, fraud, or chicanery: *Don't exploit inmates.* This sums up several directives: *Don't break your word; don't steal from the cons; don't sell favors; don't be a racketeer; don't welsh on debts.* More positively, it is argued that inmates should share scarce goods in a balanced reciprocity of "gifts" or "favors," rather than sell to the highest bidder or selfishly monopolize any amenities: *Be right.*

• There are rules that have as their central theme the maintenance of self: *Don't weaken.* Dignity and the ability to withstand frustration or threatening situations without complaining or resorting to subservence are widely acclaimed. The prisoner should be able to "take it" and to maintain his integrity in the face of privation. When confronted with wrongfully aggressive behavior, whether of inmates or officials, the prisoner should show courage. Although starting a fight runs counter to the inmate code, retreating from a fight started by someone else is equally reprehensible. Some of these maxims are: *Don't whine; don't cop out* (cry guilty); *don't suck around.* Prescriptively put: *Be tough; be a man.*

• Prisoners express a variety of maxims that forbid according prestige or respect to the custodians or the world for which they stand: *Don't be a sucker.* Guards are *hacks* or *screws* and are to be treated with constant suspicion and distrust. In any situation of conflict between officials and prisoners, the former are automatically to be considered in the wrong. Furthermore, inmates should not allow themselves to become committed to the values of hard work and submission to duly constituted authority—values prescribed (if not followed) by *screws*—for thus an inmate would become a *sucker* in a world where the law-abiding are usually hypocrites and the true path to success lies in forming a "connection." The positive maxim is: *Be sharp.*

In the literature on the mores of imprisoned criminals there is no claim that these values are asserted with equal intensity by every member of a prison population; all social systems exhibit disagreements and differing emphases with respect to the values publicly professed by their members. But observers of the prison are largely agreed that the inmate code is outstanding both for the passion with which it is propounded and the almost universal allegiance verbally accorded it.

In the light of this inmate code or system of inmate norms, we can begin to understand the patterns of inmate behavior so frequently reported; for conformity to, or deviation from, the inmate code is the major basis for classifying and describing the social relations of prisoners. As Strong has pointed out, social groups are apt to characterize individuals in terms of crucial "axes of life" (lines of interests, problems, and concerns faced by the groups) and then to attach distinctive names to the resulting roles or types.[2] This process may be discerned in the society of prisoners and its argot for the patterns of behavior or social roles exhibited by inmates; and in these roles the outlines of the prison community as a system of action[3] may be seen.

An inmate who violates the norm proscribing the betrayal of a fellow prisoner is labeled a *rat* or a *squealer* in the vocabulary of the inmate world, and his deviance elicits universal scorn and hatred.[4] Prisoners who exhibit highly aggressive behavior, who quarrel easily and fight without cause, are often referred to as *toughs*. The individual who uses violence deliberately as a means to gain his ends is called a *gorilla* a prisoner so designated is one who has established a satrapy based on coercion in clear contravention of the rule against exploitation by force. The term *merchant*, or *peddler*, is applied to the inmate who exploits his fellow captives not by force but by manipulation and trickery, and who typically sells or trades goods that are in short supply. If a prisoner shows himself unable to withstand the general rigors of existence in the custodial institution, he may be referred to as a *weakling* or a *weak sister*. If, more specifically, an inmate is unable to endure prolonged deprivation of heterosexual relationships and consequently enters into a homosexual liaison, he will be labeled a *wolf* or a *fag*, depending on whether his role is an active or a passive one.[5] If he continues to plead his case, he may soon be sarcastically known as a *rapo* (from "bum rap") or *innocent*. And if an inmate makes the mistake of allying himself with officialdom by taking on and expressing the values of conformity, he may be called a *square John* and ridiculed accordingly.

However, the individual who has received perhaps the greatest attention in the literature is the one who most nearly fulfills the norms of the society of prisoners, who celebrates the inmate code rather than violates it: the *right guy*, the *real con*, the *real man*—the argot varies, but the role is clear-cut. The *right guy* is the hero of the inmate social system, and his existence gives meaning to the villains, the deviants such as the *rat*, the *tough*, the *gorilla*, and the *merchant*. The *right guy* is the base line, however idealized or infrequent in reality, from which the inmate population takes its bearings. It seems worth while, therefore, to sketch his portrait briefly in the language of the inmates.

A *right guy* is always loyal to his fellow prisoners. He never lets you down no matter how rough things get. He keeps his promises; he's dependable and trustworthy. He isn't nosey about your business and doesn't shoot off his mouth about his own. He doesn't act stuck-up, but he doesn't fall all over himself to make friends either—he has a certain dignity. The *right guy* never interferes with other inmates who are conniving against the officials. He doesn't go around looking for a fight, but he never runs away from one when he is in the right. Anybody who starts a fight with a *right guy* has to be ready to go all the way. What he's got or can get of the extras in the prison—like cigarettes, food stolen from the mess hall, and so on—he shares with his friends. He doesn't take advantage of those who don't have much. He doesn't strong-arm other inmates into punking or fagging for him; instead, he acts like a man.

In his dealings with the prison officials, the *right guy* is unmistakably against them, but he doesn't act foolishly. When he talks about the officials with other inmates, he's sure to say that even the hacks with the best intentions are stupid, incompetent, and not to be trusted; that the worst thing a con can do is give the hacks information—they'll only use it against you when the chips are down. A *right* guy sticks up for his rights, but he doesn't ask for pity: he can take all the lousy screws can hand out and more. He doesn't suck around the officials, and the privileges that he's got are his because he deserves them. Even if the *right guy* doesn't look for trouble with the officials, he'll go to the limit if they push him too far. He realizes that there are just two kinds of people in the world, those in the know and the suckers or squares. Those who are in the know skim it off the top; suckers work.[6]

In summary then, from the studies describing the life of men in prison, two major facts emerge: (1) Inmates give strong verbal support to a system of values that has group cohesion or inmate solidarity as its basic theme. Directly or indirectly, prisoners uphold the ideal of a system of social interaction in which individuals are bound together by ties of mutual aid, loyalty, affection, and respect, and are united firmly in their opposition to the enemy out-group. The man who exemplifies this ideal is accorded high prestige. The opposite of a cohesive inmate social system—a state in which each individual seeks his own advantage without reference to the claims of solidarity—is vociferously condemned. (2) The actual behavior of prisoners ranges from full adherence to the norms of the inmate world to deviance of various types. These behavioral patterns, recognized and labeled by prisoners in the pungent argot of the dispossessed, form a collection of social roles which, with their interrelationships, constitute the inmate social system. We turn now to explanation of the inmate social system and its underlying structure of sentiments. . . .

A New Theory

The loss of liberty is but one of the many deprivations or frustrations inflicted on imprisoned criminals, although it is fundamental to all the rest. As Hayner and Ash have pointed out, inmates are deprived of goods and services that are more or less taken for granted even at the lowest socioeconomic levels in the free community.[7] Inmates must live in austerity as a matter of public policy. Barnes and Teeters have discussed the constraints imposed by the mass of institutional regulations under which prisoners are required to live.[8] Clemmer, Fishman, and others have stressed the severe frustrations imposed on prisoners by the denial of heterosexual relationships.[9] Numerous other writers have described the various pains of confinement in conditions of prolonged physical and psychological compression.

Although the inmate population may no longer suffer the brutality and neglect that in the past aroused the anger of John Howard and similar critics of penal institutions, prisoners still must undergo a variety of deprivations and frustrations which flow either by accident or intent from the fact of imprisonment. Furthermore, it is of greatest significance that the rigors imposed on the inmate by the prison officials do not represent relatively minor irritants which he can somehow endure; instead, the conditions of custody involve profound attacks on the prisoner's self-image or sense of personal worth, and these psychological pains may be far more threatening than physical maltreatment.[10] Brief analysis of the nature of these attacks on the inmate's personality is necessary, for it is as a response to them that we can begin to grasp the rationale of the inmate social system.

The isolation of the prisoner from the free community means that he has been rejected by society. His rejection is underscored in some prisons by his shaven head; in almost all, by his uniform and the degradation of no longer having a name but a number. The prisoner is confronted daily with the fact that he has been stripped of his membership in society at large, and now stands condemned as an outcast, an outlaw, a deviant so dangerous that he must be kept behind closely guarded walls and watched both day and night. He has lost the privilege of being *trusted* and his every act is viewed with suspicion by the guards, the surrogates of the conforming social order. Constantly aware of lawful society's disapproval, his picture of himself challenged by frequent reminders of his moral unworthiness, the inmate must find some way to ward off these attacks and avoid their introjection.[11]

In addition, it should be remembered that the offender has been drawn from a society in which personal possessions and material achievement are closely linked with concepts of personal worth by numerous cultural definitions. In the prison, however, the inmate finds himself reduced to a level of living near bare subsistence, and whatever physical discomforts this deprivation may entail, it apparently has deeper psychological significance as a basic attack on the prisoner's conception of his own personal adequacy.

No less important, perhaps, is the ego threat that is created by the deprivation of heterosexual relationships. In the tense atmosphere of the prison, with its perversions and constant references to the problems of sexual frustration, even those inmates who do not engage in overt homosexuality suffer acute attacks of anxiety about their own masculinity. These anxieties may arise from a prisoner's unconscious fear of latent homosexual tendencies in himself, which might be activated by his prolonged heterosexual deprivation and the importunity of others; or at a more conscious level he may feel that his masculinity is threatened because he can see himself as a man—in the full sense—only in a world that also contains women. In either case the inmate is confronted with the fact that the celibacy imposed on him by society means more than simple physiological frustration: an essential component of his self-conception, his status as male, is called into question.

Rejected, impoverished, and figuratively castrated, the prisoner must face still further indignity in the extensive social control exercised by the custodians. The many details of the inmate's life, ranging from the hours of sleeping to the route to work and the job itself, are subject to a vast number of regulations made by prison officials. The inmate is stripped of his autonomy; hence, to the other pains of imprisonment we must add the pressure to define himself as weak, helpless, and dependent. Individuals under guard are exposed to the bitter ego threat of losing their identification with the normal adult role.[12]

The remaining significant feature of the inmate's social environment is the presence of other imprisoned criminals. Murderers, rapists, thieves, confidence men, and sexual deviants are the inmate's constant companions, and this enforced intimacy may prove to be disquieting even for the hardened recidivist. As an inmate has said, "The worst thing about prison is you have to live with other prisoners."[13] Crowded into a small area with men who have long records of physical assaults, thievery, and so on (and who may be expected to continue in the path of deviant social behavior in the future), the inmate is deprived of the sense of security that we more or less take for granted in the free community. Although the anxieties created by such a situation do not necessarily involve an attack on the individual's sense of personal worth—as we are using the concept—the problems of self-protection in a society composed exclusively of criminals constitute one of the inadvertent rigors of confinement.

In short, imprisonment "punishes" the offender in a variety of ways extending far beyond the simple fact of incarceration. However just or necessary such punishments may be, their importance for our present analysis lies in the fact that they form a set of harsh social conditions to which the population of prisoners must respond or *adapt itself*. The inmate feels that the deprivations and frustrations of prison life, with their implications for the destruction of his self-esteem, somehow must be a alleviated. It is, we suggest, as an answer to this need that the functional significance of the inmate code or system of values exhibited so frequently by men in prison can best be understood.

As we have pointed out, the dominant theme of the inmate code is group cohesion, with a "war of all against all"—in which each man seeks his own gain without considering the rights or claims of others—as the theoretical antipode. But if a war of all against all is likely to make life "solitary, poor, nasty, brutish, and short" for men with freedom, as Hobbes suggested, it is doubly so for men in custody. Even those who are most successful in exploiting their fellow prisoners will find it a dangerous and nerve-wracking game, for they cannot escape the company of their victims. No man can assure the safety of either his person or his possessions, and eventually the winner is certain to lose to a more powerful or more skillful exploiter. Furthermore, the victims hold the trump card, since a word to the officials is frequently all that is required to ruin the most dominating figure in the inmate population. A large share of the "extra" goods that enter the inmate social system must do as the result of illicit conniving against the officials, which often requires lengthy and extensive cooperation and trust; in a state of complete conflict the resources of the system will be diminished. Mutual abhorrence or indifference will feed the emotional frictions arising from interaction under compression. And as rejection by others is a fundamental problem, a state of mutual alienation is worse than useless as a solution to the threats created by the inmate's status as an outcast.

As a population of prisoners moves toward a state of mutual antagonism, then, the many problems of prison life become more acute. On the other hand *as a population of prisoners moves in the direction of solidarity, as demanded by the inmate code, the pains of imprisonment become less severe*. They cannot be eliminated, it is true, but their consequences at least can be partially neutralized. A cohesive inmate society provides the prisoner with a meaningful social group with which he can identify himself and which will support him in his struggles against his condemners. Thus it permits him to escape at least in part the fearful isolation of the convicted offender. Inmate solidarity, in the form of toleration of the many irritants of life in confinement, helps to solve the problems of personal security posed by the involuntary intimacy of men noteworthy for their seriously antisocial behavior in the past.

Similarly, group cohesion in the form of a reciprocity of favors undermines one of the most potent sources of aggression among prisoners, the drive for personal aggrandizement through exploitation by force and fraud. Furthermore, although goods in scarce supply will remain scarce even if they are shared rather than monopolized, such goods will be distributed more equitably in the social system marked by solidarity, and this may be of profound significance in enabling the prisoner to endure better the psychological burden of impoverishment. A cohesive population of prisoners has another advantage in that it supports a system of shared beliefs that explicitly deny the traditional link between merit and achievement. Material success, according to this system, is a matter of "connections" rather than skill or hard work, and thus the imprisoned criminal is partially freed from the necessity of defining his material want as a sign of personal inadequacy.

Finally, a cohesive inmate social system institutionalizes the value of "dignity" and the ability to "take it" in a number of norms and reinforces these norms with informal social controls. In effect, the prisoner is called on to endure manfully what he cannot avoid. At first glance this might seem to be simply the counsel of despair; but if the elevation of fortitude into a primary virtue is the last refuge of the powerless, it also serves to shift the criteria of the individual's worth from conditions that cannot be altered to his ability to maintain some degree of personal integration; and the latter, at least, can be partially controlled. By creating an ideal of endurance in the face of harsh social conditions, then, the society of prisoners opens a path to the restoration of self-respect and a sense of independence that can exist despite prior criminality, present subjugation, and the free community's denial of the offender's moral worthiness. Significantly, this path to virtue is recognized by the prison officials as well as the prisoners.

One further point should be noted with regard to the emphasis placed on the maintenance of self as defined by the value system of prisoners. Dignity, composure, courage, the ability to "take it" and "hand it out" when necessary—these are the traits affirmed by the inmate code. They are also traits that are commonly defined as masculine by the inmate population. As a consequence, the prisoner finds himself in a situation where he can recapture his male role, not in terms of its sexual aspects, but in terms of behavior that is accepted as a good indicator of virility.

The effectiveness of the inmate code in mitigating the pains of imprisonment depends of course on the extent to which precepts are translated into action. As we have indicated, the demands of the inmate code for loyalty, generosity, disparagement of officials, and so on are most fully exemplified in the behavior of the *right guy*. On the other hand, much noncohesive behavior occurs on the part of the *rat*, the *tough*, the *gorilla*, the *merchant*, and the *weak sister*. The population of prisoners, then, does not exhibit perfect solidarity in practice, in spite of inmates' vehement assertions of group cohesion as a value; but neither is the population of prisoners a warring aggregate. Rather, the inmate social system typically appears to be balanced in an uneasy compromise somewhere between these two extremes. The problems confronting prisoners in the form of social rejection, material deprivation, sexual frustration, and the loss of autonomy and personal security are not completely eliminated. Indeed, even if the norms of the inmate social system were fully carried out by all, the pains of imprisonment would only be lessened; they would not disappear. But the pains of imprisonment are at least relieved by whatever degree of group cohesion is achieved in fact, and this is crucial in understanding the functional significance of the inmate code for inmates.

One further problem remains. Many of the prisoners who deviate from the maxims of the inmate code are precisely those who are most vociferous in their verbal allegiance to it. How can this discrepancy between words and behavior be explained? Much of the answer seems to lie in the fact that almost all inmates have an interest in maintaining cohesive behavior on the part of others, *regardless of the role they play themselves*, and vehement vocal support of the inmate code is a potent means to this end.

There are, of course, prisoners who "believe" in inmate cohesion both for themselves and others. These hold the unity of the group as a high personal value and are ready to demand cohesive behavior from their fellow prisoners. This collectivistic orientation may be due to a thorough identification with the criminal world in opposition to the forces of lawful society, or to a system of values that transcends such divisions. In any case, for these men the inmate code has much of the quality of a religious faith and they approach its tenets as true believers. In a second category are those prisoners who are relatively indifferent to the cohesion of the inmate population as a personal value, but who are quick to assert it as a guide to behavior because in its absence they would be likely to become chronic victims. They are committed to the ideal of inmate solidarity to the extent that they have little or no desire to take advantage of their fellow captives, but they do not go so far as to subscribe to the ideal of self-sacrifice. Their behavior is best described as passive or neutral; they are believers without passion, demanding adherence from others, but not prepared to let excessive piety interfere with more mundane considerations. Third, there are those who loudly acclaim the inmate code and actively violate its injunctions. These men suffer if their number increases, since they begin to face the difficulties of competition; and they are in particular danger if their depredations are reported to the officials. The prisoners who are thus actively alienated from other inmates and yet give lip service to inmate solidarity resemble a manipulative priesthood, savage in their expression of belief but corrupt in practice. In brief, a variety of motivational patterns underlies allegiance to the inmate code, but few inmates can avoid the need to insist publicly on its observance, whatever the discrepancies in their actions. . . .

Notes

1. The following contain relevant material:

    David Abrahamson, "Evaluation of the Treatment of Criminals," in Paul H. Hoch, ed. *Failures in Psychiatric Treatment* (New York: Grune and Stratton, 1948), pp. 58–77.

    Holley Cantine and Dachine Rainer, eds., *Prison Etiquette* (Bearsville, NY: Retort Press, 1950).

    Donald Clemmer, "Leadership Phenomena in a Prison Community," *Journal of Criminal Law and Criminology*, 28:861–872 (March-April 1938): *The Prison Community* (Boston: Christopher Publishing House, 1940): "Observations on Imprisonment as a Source of Criminality." *Journal of Criminal Law and Criminology*, 41:311–319 September-October 1950).

    R. J. Corsini, "A Study of Certain Attitudes of Prison Inmates," *Journal of Criminal Law and Criminology*, 37:132–140 (July-August 1946); R. J. Corsini and Kenwood Bartleme, "Attitudes of San Quentin Prisoners," *Journal of Correctional Education*, 4:43–46 (October 1952).

    George Devereux and Malcolm C. Moos, "The Social Structure of Prisons, and the Organic Tensions," *Journal of Criminal Psychopathology*, 4:306–324 (October 1942).

    Patrick J. Driscoll, "Factors Related to the Institutional Adjustment of Prison Inmates," *Journal of Abnormal and Social Psychology*, 47:593–596 (July 1952).

    Maurice L. Farber, "Suffering and Time Perspective of the Prisoner," *University of Iowa Studies in Child Welfare*, 20:153–227 (1944).

    Joseph F. Fishman, *Sex Life in American Prisons* (New York: National Library Press, 1934).

    Vernon Fox, "The Effect of Counseling on Adjustment in Prison," *Social Forces*, 32:285–289 (March 1954).

    L. M. Hanks, Jr., "Preliminary for a Study of Problems of Discipline in Prisons," *Journal of Criminal Law and Criminology*, 30:879–887 (March-April 1940).

    James Hargan, "The Psychology of Prison Language," *Journal of Abnormal and Social Psychology*, 30:359–365 (October-December 1935).

Ida Harper, "The Role of the 'Fringer' in a State Prison for Women," *Social Forces*, 31:53–60 (October 1952).

Frank E. Hartung and Maurice Floch, "A Social-Psychological Analysis of Prison Riots: An Hypothesis," *Journal of Criminal Law, Criminology and Police Science*, 47:51–57 (May-June 1956).

Norman S. Hayner, "Washington State Correctional Institutions as Communities," *Social Forces*, 21:316–322 (March 1943); Norman S. Hayner and Ellis Ash, "The Prisoner Community as a Social Group," *American Sociological Review*, 4:362–369 (June 1939), and "The Prison as a Community," *ibid.*, 5:577–583 August 1940).

F. E. Haynes, "The Sociological Study of the Prison Community," *Journal of Criminal Law and Criminology*, 39:432–440 (November-December 1948).

Hans von Hentig, "The Limits of Penal Treatment," *Journal of Criminal Law and Criminology*, 32:401–410 (November-December 1941).

Alfred C. Horsch and Robert A. Davis, "Personality Traits and Conduct of Institutionalized Delinquents," *Journal of Criminal Law and Criminology*, 29:241–244 (July-August 1938).

John James, "The Application of the Small Group Concept to the Study of the Prison Community," *British Journal of Delinquency*. 5:269–280 (April 1955).

Benjamin Karpman, "Sex Life in Prison," *Journal of Criminal Law and Criminology*, 38:475–486 (January-February 1948).

Robert M. Lindner, *Stone Walls and Men* (New York: Odyssey Press, 1946); "Sex in Prison," *Complex*, 6:5–20 (Fall, 1951).

Walter A. Lunden, "Antagonism and Altruism Among Prisoners," in P. A. Sorokin, *Forms and Techniques of Altruistic and Spiritual Growth* (Boston: Beacon Press, 1954), pp. 447–460.

Richard McCleery, *The Strange Journey: A Demonstration Project in Adult Education in Prison*, University of North Carolina Extension Bul., Vol 32 (1953); "Power, Communications and the Social Order: A Study of Prison Government," unpublished doctoral dissertation, University of North Carolina, 1956.

Lloyd W. McCorkle and Richard Korn, "Resocialization Within Walls," *The Annals*, 293:88–98 (May 1954).

Hermann Mannheim, *Group Problems in Crime and Punishment* (London: Routledge and Kegan Paul, 1955).

William R. Morrow, "Criminality and Antidemocratic Trends: A Study of Prison Inmates," in T. W. Adorno and others, *The Authoritarian Personality* (New York: Harper & Brothers, 1950), pp. 817–890.

Victor F. Nelson, *Prison Days and Nights* (Boston: Little, Brown, and Company, 1933).

Paul Nitsche and Karl Wilmanns, *The History of Prison Psychosis*, Nervous and Mental Disease Monograph Series No. 13 (1912).

Norman A. Polansky, "The Prison as an Autocracy," *Journal of Criminal Law and Criminology*, 33:16–22 (May-June 1942).

Harvey Powelson and Reinhard Bendix, "Psychiatry in Prison," *Psychiatry*, 14:73–86 (February 1951).

Donald Rasmussen, "Prisoner Opinions about Parole," *American Sociological Review*, 5:584–595 (August 1940).

Hans Riemer, "Socialization in the Prison Community," *Proceedings of the American Prison Association*, 1937, pp. 151–155.

Clarence Schrag, "Social Types in a Prison Community," unpublished master's thesis, University of Washington, 1944; "Crimeville: A Sociometric Study of a Prison Community," unpublished doctoral dissertation, University of Washington, 1950; "Leadership Among Prison Inmates," *American Sociological Review*, 19:37–42 (February 1954).

Lowell S. Selling, "The Pseudo Family," *American Journal of Sociology*, 37:247–253 (September 1931).

Gresham M. Sykes, "The Corruption of Authority and Rehabilitation," *Social Forces*, 34:257–262 (March 1956); "Men, Merchants, and Toughs: A Study of Reactions to Imprisonment," *Social Problems*, 4:130–138 (October 1956).

Donald R. Taft, "The Group and Community Organization Approach to Prison Administration," *Proceedings of the American Prison Association*, 1942, pp. 275–284.

Ruth Sherman Tolman, "Some Differences in Attitudes Between Groups of Repeating Criminals and of First Offenders," *Journal of Criminal Law and Criminology*, 30:196–203 (July-August 1939).

2. Samuel M. Strong, "Social Types in a Minority Group," *American Journal of Sociology*, 48:563–573 (March 1943). Schrag in "Social Types in a Prison Community" notes the relevance of Strong's discussion for examination of the inmate social system.

3. See Schrag, ibid., and Sykes, "Men, Merchants, and Toughs" for discussion of this approach to the prison as a system of action.

4. The argot applied to a particular role varies somewhat from one prison to another, but it is not difficult to find the synonyms in the prisoners' lexicon.

5. The inmate population, with a keen sense of distinctions, draws a line between the *fag*, who plays a passive role in a homosexual relationship because he "likes" it or "wants" to, and a *punk*, who is coerced or bribed into a passive role.

6. We have not attempted to discuss all the prison roles that have been identified in the literature, although we have mentioned most of the major types. Two exceptions, not discussed because they are not distinctive of the prison, are the *fish*, a novitiate, and the *ding*, an erratic behaver. The homosexual world of the prison, especially, deserves fuller treatment; various role types within it have not yet been described.

7. "The Prisoner Community as a Social Group," op. cit.

8. Harry E. Barnes and Negley K. Teeters, *New Horizons in Criminology* (2nd ed.; New York: Prentice-Hall, 1951), pp. 438–439.

9. Clemmer, *The Prison Community*, pp. 249–273; Fishman, op. cit.

10. A. H. Maslow, "Deprivation, Threat and Frustration," *Psychological Review*, 48:364–366 (July 1941).

11. McCorkle and Korn, op. cit, p. 88.

12. Bruno Bettelheim, "Individual and Mass Behavior in Extreme Situations," *Journal of Abnormal and Social Psychology*, 38:417–452 (October 1943).

13. Gresham M. Sykes, *Crime and Society* (New York: Random House, 1956), p. 109.

63

Society of Women:
A Study of a Women's Prison

Rose Giallombardo

This [article has been abridged from] . . . an exploratory study of an adult prison for women. [Its] purpose is to examine the prison from a sociological perspective, that is, as a system of roles and functions and to make comparisons with the literature on the male prison in order to increase our understanding of the prison structure within its larger societal context.

To analyze a community as a system of roles and functions is by no means an easy task. For the careful observer, the continuity of events is the important aspect. It is necessary, therefore, to examine the structure over a considerable length of time. The data for this study were gathered over a period of one year from July 1962 to July 1963, at the Federal Reformatory for Women, Alderson, West Virginia. . . .

The Nature of the Prison Experience

. . . Like the male prisoner, the female prisoner soon discovers that there are few escape routes in prison—psychological and physical withdrawal are not significant modes of adaptation to mitigate the pains of imprisonment. In contrast to the male prison, however, the evolution of an informal social structure in the female prison to withstand the deleterious effects of physical and social isolation is in many respects an attempt to *resist* the destructive effects of imprisonment by, creating a *substitute universe*—a world in which the inmates may preserve an identity which is relevant to life outside the prison. In this structure, the inmates' orientation is quasi-collectivistic, depending upon where one stands in terms of homosexual or kin relationships; the degree of mutual aid and the expectation of solidarity decrease as one goes from nuclear members or proximal relationships to distal relationships. . . .

The Social Roles

. . . In order to cope with the major problems of institutional living, the Alderson inmates have also labeled the reactions of prisoners according to the mode of

Source: From Rose Giallombardo, *Society of Women: A Study of a Women's Prison,* published by Allyn and Bacon, Boston, MA. Copyright © 1986 by Pearson Education. Reprinted by permission of the publisher.

responses exhibited by the inmate to the prison situation and the quality of the inmate's interaction with inmates and staff. These roles form the basic social structure of the prison community as a system of action. . . .

Snitchers and Inmate Cops or Lieutenants

Communication across caste lines is strictly forbidden in the Alderson prison except for matters of urgent business, and all such interaction is expected to be handled with swift dispatch. Indeed, to violate the ban placed on legitimate communication flowing from inmates and staff is considered to be a very serious matter. The Alderson inmates argue that no inmate should jeopardize the successful execution of activities based upon the common interests of the inmates in illegal functions to relieve the pains of imprisonment; secondly, supplying information to officials may result in the withdrawal of privileges or in other forms of punishment, thereby adding to the pains of imprisonment for the inmate.

In the Alderson prison, the role of the "snitcher" is the female counterpart to the "rat" in the male prison. To accuse an inmate of snitching is the most serious accusation one inmate may hurl at another, for it clearly signifies the division of loyalty between the staff and the inmates. The importance placed upon the "no snitching" norm is apparent; it covers every range of behavior and is put in the imperative to the new inmate or the deviant: "See and see nothing! Hear and hear nothing!"

Although the Alderson prisoners agree that inmates should never snitch or give any information concerning an inmate to the staff, the females' self-orientation and their tendency to see one another as rivals both function to decrease general expectations of rigid allegiance from one another. Consequently, the female inmate rarely expresses any surprise when she suspects another inmate of deviating from the norm prohibiting communication of inmate affairs across caste lines; she feels only a kind of bitterness that the status of inmate is not sufficient to bind and solidify the inmates completely into a cohesive group. The popular culture, then, in connection with the extent to which any female may be trusted, functions to neutralize many deviant acts in the prison. As a result, many deviant acts are overlooked or are not severely punished by the Alderson inmates. . . .

Squares and Jive Bitches

Along with the snitchers and the inmate cops, the "squares" are truly the pariahs of the inmate community. "Square" is a derisive label pinned on inmates who are considered to be accidental criminals. The behavior of the square in the prison community clearly betrays her alien status; she is oriented to the prison administration and tends to possess "anti-criminal" loyalties. Degrees of "squareness" are recognized by the Alderson inmates ranging from the inmate who is thought to be "so square that she's a cube" to the inmate designated as "hip square." The "cube square" is very definitely oriented to societal values and the prison administration, whereas the "hip square" tends to sympathize with the inmate code and adheres to some of its principles, sometimes going so far as to "pin"—act as lookout—for other inmates. The distinguishing characteristic of the hip square, however, is that she does not engage in homosexual activity and is oriented to the administration and societal values. Her sympathy takes the form of stated tolerance for inmate activities. In the Alderson prison, anyone who does not engage in homosexual activities in one form or another is automatically labeled a square. . . .

The deviance of the square is often the consequence of an artless simplicity and presumably leaves open the possibility that induction into the inmate culture may remedy the situation. (Indeed the pressures applied are so great that this frequently does occur.) The deviance of the "jive bitch," on the other hand, is a deliberate, calculated strategy to cause conflict. In short, the jive bitch is a troublemaker. . . .

The jive bitch succeeds in creating unrest among the inmates in several ways. In addition to presenting a deliberate distortion of facts to an injured party, she often tells inmates involved in a "couple" relationship different versions of the same situation in the hope that it will cause conflict between them.

The jive bitch, in short, is an example *par excellence* of the woman-to-woman popular culture translated into role behavior. The fact that she cannot be depended upon weakens even the bonds of calculated solidarity which exist among the Alderson inmates.

Rap Buddies and Homeys

In prison the popular culture on the woman-to-woman level is buttressed by the common criminality which in many ways binds the inmates together, for it is a widespread belief that "There's no honor among thieves." No inmate trusts another inmate completely ("You pick your people, and even then you only go so far"). Within these limitations, an inmate may single out another prisoner in the cottage or on the job as special friend. This individual is one with whom she can converse easily and assume reasonably that the conversation will be mutually binding as secret. Any two people who find one another compatible in this way may become "rap buddies" to one another. This relationship is dissolved if the expectations concerning the relationship are not honored by either of the incumbents of the rap buddy role; or, if the relationship flowers into one of deeper meaning, the inmates become a "couple" and assume the obligations relevant to this relationship.

The "homey" role, on the other hand, is probably as close to "blood" relationship as one finds in the Alderson female prison and holds a special place in the lexicon of the inmates. Technically speaking, even if conflict ensues between homeys, the relationship still holds. The homey is an inmate who is from another inmate's home town or nearby community. Homeys may or may not have known one another before incarceration; but in any case, within the prison these inmates become homeys to one another. . . .

Connects and Boosters

Few legitimate channels are open to the Alderson inmates to improve their economic lot in the prison. . . . Like the male prisoner . . . the Alderson inmate finds it necessary to exploit the environment to improve her material circumstances. She can steal from institutional supplies, and, as we shall see shortly, in the role of the "commissary hustler," she can manipulate other inmates through sexual exploitation. . . . [I]n the Alderson prison the "connect" is any inmate with a "good job" who will cooperate in the procurement of scarce goods and information. A "good job" by inmate standards means placement in the prison organization where information and scarce goods are available. Connects are also those inmates who are in a position to negotiate with other inmates to obtain information or goods, that is, who act both as middleman and distributor. Thus this role includes the procurement of both goods and services.

In this connection, the inmates draw a sharp line between the connect, who often takes a dual role, and the "booster," whose exploitation of the environment consists solely of stealing from official stores and who carries on a successful business enterprise. . . .

Pinners

Since complete elimination of detection is never possible in the performance of many illicit activities, the Alderson inmates find it necessary to minimize the risk of being detected by the prison officials. And for this reason the role of the "pinner" is a very crucial and important one: The pinner in the Alderson prison is a lookout. She is stationed as a sentry to prevent a surprise attack upon inmates engaging in illicit activities from all unauthorized persons, whether they be staff or inmates. With discovery always imminent and punishment certain, the pinner's role cannot be allocated to amateurs or to inmates whose loyalty is in doubt. The pinner must be an inmate who can be trusted, who can stand up under pressure, and who is "in the know.". . .

The Homosexual Cluster: Penitentiary Turnouts, Lesbians, Femmes, Stud Broads, Tricks, Commissary Hustlers, Chippies, Kick Partners, Cherries, Punks and Turnabouts

The problems and concerns of the inmates in adjusting to deprivation of heterosexual relationships are revealed by the number of roles channelized into homosexual behavior. Moreover, the female inmates' *role refinement* of the categories in connection with homosexual activity illustrates its function both as a motivating force in their lives and as an organizing principle of social organization.

The inmates apply a number of labels to homosexual behavior depending upon the specific role assumed, the adeptness with which the assumed role is played, or the motivation for the behavior. Broadly speaking, the inmates differentiate between "penitentiary turnouts" and "lesbians." The "penitentiary turnout" resorts to homosexuality in the prison because hetero-sexual relationships are not available. The "lesbian" by contrast *prefers* homosexual relations in the free community, in this respect resembling the "fags" in the male prison. As with the male prisoner, this stated preference for homosexual relations defines in the eyes of the Alderson inmates the lesbian's behavior as a sexual perversion, as contrasted with the behavior of the penitentiary turnout, which may be viewed as a temporary adjustment to the prison situation. The lesbian, therefore, is labeled as a sick person by the inmates because her preference and selection of homosexual relations in a situation where choice is possible clearly constitutes a *true* perversion. It is only in the penitentiary world where men are unavailable that the values and norms regarding homosexual behavior are redefined by the inmates—and within the limits imposed by this definition—accepted as a temporary substitute for heterosexual relations.

The "femme" or "mommy" plays the female role in a homosexual relationship. The femme role is highly sought-after because most of the inmates want to continue to play the feminine role in a meaningful way in the prison. In the context of a "marital" relationship the femme continues to act out . . . many of the functions assigned to the role of wife in civil society.

The complementary role to the femme is the "stud broad" or "daddy" who assumes the male role. The stud broad is accorded much prestige by other inmates for these reasons: First, the stud provides the prison with the male image; secondly, the role is considered to be a more difficult one for an inmate to assume and sustain over a period of time because it is thought to be "unnatural" for a female to assume the guises of the male. Indeed, an occasional inmate playing a stud role becomes carried away with "his" performance and attempts to transcend psychologically the immutability of anatomy and biological function. . . .

Since one of the important goals in establishing a homosexual alliance is to strive for what is referred to as a "sincere" relationship, which means a stable relationship based upon romantic love, the "trick" is held in low esteem by the inmates because she allows herself to be exploited rather than to develop a relationship that is sincere. And the trick is exploited in a variety of ways—usually economically and as a source of labor. Any individual who allows herself to be exploited in this manner is considered "weak." Moreover, tricks are regarded as "suckers" and "fools" because they may be kept dangling with promises.

Who are the inmates who utilize exploitative tactics? The "commissary hustler" establishes a single homosexual alliance with an inmate living in the same cottage, but also establishes relationships with a number of inmates in other cottages for economic purposes. This is called "mating for commissary reasons," and any femme other than the inmate who lives in the stud's cottage is labeled as a trick in the relationship. . . .

However, when the individual exploits each situation with a partner for its unique possibilities, whether for sexual or material gratification, the inmate is said to occupy a "chippie" role. This role differs from the commissary hustler in a very important way. Although the commissary hustler actually establishes one sincere relationship and exploits other inmates in order to provide for the femme in the relationship, the chippie establishes no single relationship of this type. Chippies are said to be "makin' it," but not to be "in love" with any individual. The chippie is looked upon as the prison prostitute. The inmate who "chippies from one bed to another"— i.e., terminates affairs too quickly—is scorned by the inmates, and her behavior is held to be promiscuous. The ideal cultural pattern in the prison is to establish a permanent relationship: The chippie clearly deviates from the ideal pattern, as her affairs are characterized by their striking temporary quality.

The inmates distinguish clearly between homosexual activity that is of a promiscuous nature and that which is engaged in solely for sexual gratification. Although "kick partners" are also not said to be involved as "lovers," there is, nevertheless, a predictable permanence in their relationships, although the motivation for entering into the partnership is clearly understood to be solely for physical gratification. There is usually no economic exchange in this relationship, and the inmates involved exhibit no jealousy. . . .

In the Alderson prison, the kick partner may be drawn into a permanent tie. And the square may possibly in time "see the light" and enter into the inmate social organization. But one category of inmates in the prison, those labeled "cherries," constitute an uncommitted sizeable reserve for potential mates; they are inmates who have never been "turned out"—initiated into homosexual practices.

Although squares also do not engage in homosexual practices, the cherry is not a square. The difference is that the cherry simply has not been "turned out." Often they are young and first offenders, and they are usually initiated by older women. Cherries in this context are "hep" individuals, i.e., they know what the score is from the point of view of the prisoners, but for one reason or another have not engaged in homosexuality. Sometimes a short sentence may be the reason for her preference not to become emotionally involved; or she may decide that this mode of adjustment may not be desirable.

One who assumes a false part or assumes a character other than the real one is despised for his hypocrisy both within and without the prison gates. Within the Alderson prison, the "punk" is despised for pretense and deceit. In the male prison, the "punk" is an inmate who plays the submissive part because he is coerced into doing so. In this respect, "punks" differ from "fags," who it is said are "born" not "made." In a sense fags resemble the lesbians for the inmates say that they are "born that way," or that "something happened to them in their childhood." In the Alderson prison, the punk is so designated because she acts like a female, that is, takes on the coquettish mannerisms of a woman when the expected behavior is that of the male. The behavior of the punk elicits a combination of anger and ridicule from the inmates. . . .

Whereas the punk is guilty of incomplete role learning, the "turnabout," on the other hand, claims expertise at playing both male and female roles. As a matter of fact, she not only describes herself glowingly in terms of her versatility, that is, "good either way," but stands ready to put her boasted skill to the test. Such protean versatility, however, is viewed with amused contempt by the inmates. . . .

The Alderson inmates prefer a structured situation in their prison world, and inmates playing male roles one day and female roles the next confuse the issue greatly. This is especially true for the inmate who may be planning a strategy of conquest. In addition, anything which tends to decrease the male population in the prison is apt to alarm the inmates. It is not surprising, therefore, that the turnabout is held in low esteem. . . .

These social roles as distinguished and labeled by the Alderson inmates constitute the basic structure of social relationships formed as a response to the problems incidental to a prison commitment. . . . [T]he evolution of an informal social structure in the Alderson prison community represents an attempt to resist the destructive effects of imprisonment by creating a *substitute universe* within which the inmates may preserve an identity relevant to life outside the prison. . . .

The Homosexual Alliance as a Marriage Unit

The fundamental fact recognized by the Alderson inmates is that they must all "do time," or serve a prison sentence. Their culture places stress on the importance of doing "easy time" as the best way to serve a prison sentence. Easy time refers to the process of relating one's thoughts and energies mainly to events within the prison while serving a sentence. Inmates who are overly concerned with events in outside society and with incidents prior to incarceration are said to do "hard time." These inmates fail to adjust to prison life because they tend to maintain strong psychological ties with family and friends in the outside world. The frustration experienced by these inmates sometimes erupts in a violation of prison rules.

A few inmates maintained that hard time was their lot from the beginning of their sentence to the very day of release. Most inmates who claimed to have experienced hard time, however, found that it usually occurred during the early stages of the prison sentence, but at some point in the prison career they began to do easy time. What actually takes place in the transition from hard time to easy time is that the inmate learns with the help of sister inmates to suspend deep emotional involvement in events taking place in outside society and to live completely in the very second of the present—in the prison world of the inmates. . . .

Symbols of Communication

The Alderson inmates are not able to resolve their sense of isolation within the formal organization; therefore they develop relationships and behavior patterns within an informal structure. The vast majority of inmates adjust to the prison world by establishing a homosexual alliance with a compatible partner as a marriage unit. The inmate culture maintains that "to play," that is, to engage in homosexuality as "duplication" of the outside world, "makes time easier" and "go by faster." Furthermore, it is widely held that "no one can do time alone." Inmates engaged in a homosexual alliance are referred to as a couple by other inmates, and the relationship is recognized in the prison as a legitimate marriage. The roles of male and female make up the homosexual alliance. This is the most important structural relationship in the informal prison world of the Alderson inmates, and many other kinship roles . . . pivot about this basic dyad. Our first task, however, must be to examine the anatomy of the marriage relationship from courtship to "fall out," that is, from its inception to the parting of the ways, or divorce.

The sex identities appropriate to the prison marriage alliance are overtly assumed. Inmates assuming male roles are distinguished from those playing female roles by such symbols of communication as dress, hair style, language, and behavior patterns. . . . [I]nmates assuming the female role are referred to as femmes and inmates assuming the male role are referred to as studs. When these roles are incorporated into marriage, however, a femme and stud become husband and wife to one another, and inmates use these terms to refer to each other. . . .

Inmates who assume a female role in a prison marriage dress in feminine attire, wear cosmetics, and play the role in the relationship often expected of the female. Inmates playing the male role, on the other hand, assume many stylized symbols of masculinity. For example, they crop their hair very short to resemble a masculine haircut, and a very few inmates sported sideburns. Their hair is worn straight, as curls are associated with femininity. Cosmetics are not worn by these inmates, nor is jewelry worn with the exception of the rings and religious medals which are sometimes exchanged between inmates at the inception of a marriage as tokens of undying love. Whenever possible, inmates assuming the male role wear slacks styled like men's trousers, that is, with a loosely fitted trouser leg. . . .

Another important way in which Alderson inmates differentiate male and female roles is in terms of the length, shape, and fit of clothing. Femmes, of course, try to make their prison garments resemble whatever is fashionable at the moment in outside society. . . .

Differential dress for studs is intended to disguise externally the curves of the female and to achieve a flattened look; the shape of their skirts can best be described as "baggy." In addition, shirts are worn over the skirt rather than tucked in and are not fitted. Some studs take in the cups of their brassieres to flatten their breasts. Other studs do not wear brassieres, but instead wear the knitted undershirts in khaki color that are issued from the clothing room, and match in color the slacks and shirts issued for many of the work details such as landscaping, farm detail, storehouse, and so on. In addition, men's T-shirts and shorts—which are sometimes laundered at the prison for some of the hospitals in the state—are stolen by the inmates and worn by studs.

Verbal symbols of communication also distinguish the inmates who assume male roles from femmes. When an inmate assumes a male role, a corruption of the individual's feminine name often takes place. For example, Barbara becomes Bob;

Rachel, Ray; Katherine, Kelly; Mary, Marty; Lucille, Lou; and so on. If the inmate's feminine name does not lend itself readily to such corruption, then a masculine name or nickname of one's choice is adopted. In addition, the masculine pronoun is always used to refer to anyone who adopts a male role in the prison, which indicates clearly the highly institutionalized character of this cultural complex. General terms of address such as "man" or "Jack" are acceptable and quite widely used by the inmates. Terms such as "girl" or the use of the stud's feminine name, however, are taboo and inmates taking such liberties with studs are immediately corrected: "Where do you get that girl stuff? Call me ———, or don't call me at all."

Behavioral expectations of the stud's role incorporate in a general way many of the cultural expectations of the male in American society. First, studs are expected to assume a masculine stride; mincing steps and swaying of the hips are associated with females. Secondly, studs are expected to be discreet in their talk and not indulge in wanton gossip. Third, they are expected to incorporate the traits of reliability and emotional control in their character. Injunctions to behavior are: "You should be a square shooter." "Say what you mean and mean what you say." The prerogative often claimed by women, namely, the "right to change her mind," is not part of the male role in the Alderson prison. And, finally—although the association of two women, like that between man and woman, assumes many different forms—in sexual relations the stud is expected by most femmes to assume a relatively aggressive role.

In short, in addition to assuming the external symbols of masculinity in connection with dress, hair length, and nomenclature, the inmate assuming the male role is expected to "put herself in a man's place and act like one." She is to act like a man in a world where there are no men. This point is critical. The stud must attempt to duplicate the behavior patterns of her adopted sex and make "normal" individuals of her anatomic sex feel toward her as though she truly were a male. . . .

Mate Selection, Courtship, and Marriage

. . . The foundation of a lasting marriage is not religious or jural sanction but, rather, a satisfactory relationship between the two individuals involved. It is essentially a personal bond—a mutual adjustment of persons which must be accomplished in very short order, and a mutual satisfactory adjustment of roles. The goal is to enter into a homosexual alliance with a mutually compatible partner, and the sexual bond is of vital importance in this relationship.

Mate selection is based upon romantic love, and marriage is predicated upon the consent of the interested parties. All homosexual relationships are established on a voluntary basis; there was no evidence of any physical coercion such as occurs in the male prison. . . .

With obvious differences, the homosexual alliance is patterned on marriage in civil society. For many inmates the femme role is an important means by which they may preserve in prison an identity which is relevant for civil society. Assumption of this role represents an attempt to seek continued fulfillment of former satisfactory roles in the prison world; it is *substitute role conformity*. For others, the role provides the individual with an opportunity to function in a role which would very likely have been assumed in civil society in a heterosexual relationship in the normal course of events. For this group of inmates, the femme role in prison may be looked upon as *substitute role experience*, as the role incorporates many of the behavioral expectations of the female in heterosexual relationships. . . .

Alderson inmates accord the greatest prestige to couples who are observed to be "sincere." Now this term is not used by the inmates in the ordinary dictionary sense. In the argot of the inmates, "sincere" couples are those that are characterized by a principle of strict equality. These couples are said to have a "better understanding" than other couples, meaning that the relationship is not an exploitative affair, as evidenced by its democratic nature. Everything is shared equally ("fifty-fifty")—washing, ironing, other household chores, as well as commissary buying.

Sincere relationships are an ideal in the prison, but in actuality they are relatively few in number. It must be kept in mind that homosexual gratification (as well as heterosexual gratification) is a service which individuals perform for one another and which, as such, is potentially exploitable. The significance of this fact for the inmate social system is that many prison marriages are fleeting erotic attachments based upon commercial interests. An inmate may engage in a homosexual affair to solve an economic problem in the prison. Although many couples share economic responsibilities in the sense that one week the femme will do the buying and the next week the stud will reciprocate, in the majority of cases the economic function falls to the femme. Moreover, femmes usually do all the housework for both. Regardless of economic arrangements, however, when couples have a "right" or "good" understanding, it is expected that the stud will assume the role of commissary hustler to ease the economic burden when the femme has no money. . . .

The inmate culture prescribes patrilocal residence. As soon as two inmates decide to become a couple, the femme initiates formal arrangements to move into the stud's cottage if she does not already live there. She moves into the cottage at the stud's invitation, and when the marriage is terminated she moves out. Until the formal arrangements for living quarters are processed, these inmates are recognized as married by the inmate community, and prison etiquette regarding social distance is observed. They meet at all functions and sit together, talk on the field, and with the help of pinners occasionally have physical contact during the long weekend. For this purpose the stud goes to the femme's cottage. . . .

The marriage relationship provides the inmates with companionship and a feeling of belonging, meets needs for love and affection, and provides the inmates with an opportunity to express individuality in an adult role. Although the prison marriage performs these positive functions for many of the inmates, it also creates problems for other inmates when a marriage ends in divorce.

Divorce

In most societies ideal patterns of culture hold marriage to be a more or less permanent tie and not one to be dissolved easily at the whim of either partner. Although the ideal of marriage on a permanent basis exists among the Alderson inmates—and indeed a few couples do remain married until one of the partners is released—most couples tend to remain united for only about one to three months and then secure new partners. In short, marriage in the Alderson prison tends to be very unstable.

Although the femme expects fidelity from her mate, she understands clearly that because of the imbalanced "sex" ratio other femmes will be plying her mate with kites [written messages] and verbal proposals in order to break up the marriage. Estimates of the number of inmates who are involved in homosexuality vary. Inmates who are very much involved in this phase of inmate culture place the figure at 90 or 95 percent. The associate warden . . . , on the other hand, estimated that 80 percent of the inmates were involved in homosexual relations. Correctional officers tended to set the figure at 50 or 75 percent, which agrees with the usual estimates I obtained from squares. Some officers and other staff members set the figure at 100 percent. At one point in the study, I made a cottage count of inmates assuming the male role, and the studs totaled 215 inmates. The number of males in the prison tends to vary slightly from day to day depending upon inmate releases and individual role choice. And the same, of course, is true of the inmates playing the femme role. At this time, there were 336 femmes out of a total of 639 inmates. At any rate, it is apparent that femmes are competing for a scarce commodity. In a real sense, the female in the prison marriage experiences great strain, as she can easily be replaced in her husband's affections at any time with other willing femmes. . . .

Community Integration through Kinship

. . . The group structure of the Alderson inmates consists of inmates bound to one another by kinship ties; and the formation of a kinship tie to an inmate in this group structure makes it possible for an inmate to have legitimate close friendly relations with those inmates to whom she is attached in kinship bonds. For this reason, inmates with short sentences or inmates who do not wish to engage in homosexual relations may resort to kinship links in order to become members of groups. Unmarried inmates who are in constant interaction with one another stand the risk of being suspected of homosexual relations, and the culturally defined social distance consistent with homosexual alliances will be respected by other inmates in their interaction with them. As a result, some unmarried inmates may be constrained to form kinship ties. . . .

There is a set of social relationships in the family group that are recognized and are divided into roles and a content of expectations. The formation of kinship ties among the inmates tends to establish an equilibrium point between sexual relations and casual unstable and unregulated contacts. With the exception of the husband-wife relationship cast into the form of a homosexual alliance, the other roles defined in kinship terms are rendered neutralized of sexual content. This makes it possible for an inmate in a homosexual marriage to have a variety of relations with other inmates to whom she is bound up in kinship ties. Such roles as mother, father, daughter, son, brother, sister, aunt, and uncle, for example, may be enjoyed by the inmate within the limitations set by her assumed sex role. . . .

Conclusion

The social spheres into which kinship enters as an articulating principle of social organization in the female prison world are inextricably bound up with the deprivations of imprisonment. The informal system which has evolved among the Alderson female inmates to mitigate the problems of imprisonment, however, is notably absent in the male prison. How can we explain this? Why are kinship and marriage the solution for the female inmates?

We have tried to show throughout that the inmate society and culture exist because they provide a solution to certain problems of adjustment. However, the problems of the female and male inmates arise out of very different circumstances—the differences in the cultural definitions ascribed to their respective roles as male or female. As a result, male and female prisoners seek different solutions in the prison world. They seek solutions that will not endanger their identification as essentially male or female, and that are consistent with their sex role and the distinctive patterns of behavior attached to it.

. . . [C]ultural expectations of male and female roles in American society are seen to differentiate along several crucial axes. The cultural definition of the female role in American society is oriented to that of wife and mother. The male, however, is expected to prepare for an occupational role, and his prestige rank is established by the nature of his life work. From an early age, the male is oriented *outward* to the market place, to the world of affairs rather than to the home. The life goal of the female, however, is achieved through marriage and child-rearing. From an early age, the female is oriented *inward* to the home, and it is in the role of wife and mother that she derives prestige and status. Indeed the status, security, and self-image of the American female depends in large measure upon the kinds of relationships she establishes with the opposite sex.

The family group in the female prison is singularly suited to meet the internalized cultural expectations of the female role. It serves the social, psychological, and physiological needs of the female inmates. These interrelated needs arise mainly from three sources:

1. The individual's dependence and status needs based upon cultural expectations of the female role.

2. The individual's needs which arise from residing within the prison; and the inability of the formal organization to supply the female inmate's need for emotional reciprocity.

3. Needs related to the individual's personality.

The complex series of social relationships formed on the basis of marriage and kinship make it possible for the female inmates to engage in a wide range of satisfying relations. Indeed, the prison world of the Alderson inmates is a functional *substitute* to resolve the female's sense of isolation within the formal organization. The prison homosexual marriage alliance and the larger informal family groupings provide structures wherein the female inmate's needs may find fulfillment and expression during the period of incarceration. Kinship and marriage ties make it possible for the inmates to ascribe and achieve social statuses and personalities in the prison other than that of inmate which are consistent with the cultural expectations of the female role in American society. . . .

The deprivations of imprisonment may provide necessary conditions for the emergence of an inmate system, but our findings clearly indicate that the deprivations of imprisonment in themselves are not sufficient to account for the structural form that the inmate social system assumes in the male and female prison communities.

I suggest, rather, that the culture that forms within the prison by males and females can be understood in these terms: the prison inmate social system is not an intrinsic response to the deprivations of imprisonment, although the deprivations of imprisonment may be important in precipitating inmate culture; nor can inmate culture be viewed as a mere reflection of the values and attitudes inmates bring into the prison world. The evidence presented suggests that the male and female inmate cultures *are* a response to the deprivations of prison life, but the nature of the response in both prison communities is influenced by the differential participation of males and females in the external culture. The culture that emerges within the prison structure may be seen to incorporate and reflect the total external social structure; that is, the way in which roles are defined in the external world influence the definitions made within the prison. General features of American society with respect to the cultural definitions and content of male and female roles are brought into the prison setting and they function to determine the direction and focus of the inmate cultural system. These general features I have suggested are those concerned with the orientation of life goals for males and females; second, cultural definitions with respect to dimensions of passivity and aggression; third, acceptability of public expression of affection displayed toward a member of the same sex; and, finally, perception of the same sex with respect to what I have called the popular culture.

It is the *system* of roles and statuses that is imported into the prison setting, and not merely the values and attitudes of the individuals who enter the prison world. It is in these terms that the importance attached to the female role, marriage ties, and family groups can be understood as salient elements of prison culture in the female prison community, but not in the male prison community. If my analysis is sound, it would seem that there is greater unity between the inner and outer worlds than has heretofore been thought. Greater understanding of the prison communities, then, may best be accomplished by focusing attention on the relationship of the external and internal cultures rather than by trying to understand the prison as an institution isolated from the larger society.

64

Interpersonal Dynamics
in a Simulated Prison

Craig Haney   *Curtis Banks*   *Philip Zimbardo*

Introduction

. . . Attempts to provide an explanation of the deplorable condition of our penal system, and its dehumanising effects upon prisoners and guards, often focus upon what
might be called the *dispositional hypothesis*. While this explanation is rarely
expressed explicitly, it is central to a prevalent non-conscious ideology: that the state
of the social institution of prison is due to the "nature" of the people who administer
it, or the "nature" of the people who populate it, or both. That is, a major contributing cause to despicable conditions, violence, brutality, dehumanisation and degradation existing within any prison can be traced to some innate or acquired
characteristic of the correctional and inmate population. Thus, on the one hand,
there is the contention that violence and brutality exist within prison because guards
are sadistic, uneducated, and insensitive people. It is the "guard mentality," a unique
syndrome of negative traits which they bring into the situation, that engenders the
inhumane treatment of prisoners. Or, from other quarters comes the argument that
violence and brutality in prison are the logical and predictable result of the involuntary confinement of a collective of individuals whose life histories are, by definition,
characterised by disregard for law, order and social convention and a concurrent
propensity for impulsiveness and aggression. Logically, it follows that these individuals, having proved themselves incapable of functioning satisfactorily within the
"normal" structure of society, cannot do so either inside the structure provided by
prisons. To control such men as these, the argument continues, whose basic orientation to any conflict situation is to react with physical power or deception, force must
be met with force, and a certain number of violent encounters must be expected and
tolerated by the public.

The dispositional hypothesis has been embraced by the proponents of the
prison *status quo* (blaming conditions on the evil in the prisoners), as well as by its
critics (attributing the evil to guards and staff with their evil motives and deficient
personality structures). The appealing simplicity of this proposition localises the

Source: Craig Haney, William C. Banks, and Phillip G. Zimbardo, "Interpersonal Dynamics in a Simulated Prison," *International Journal of Sociology of Law*, Vol. II, pp. 71–84, 86–87, 89–90 and 93–97.
Copyright © 1973, reprinted with permission of Elsevier.

source of prison riots, recidivism and corruption in these "bad seeds" and not in the conditions of the "prison soil." Such an analysis directs attention away from the complex matrix of social, economic and political forces which combine to make prisons what they are—and which would require complex, expensive, revolutionary solutions to bring about any meaningful change. Instead, rioting prisoners are identified, punished, transferred to maximum security institutions or shot, outside agitators sought and corrupt officials suspended—while the system itself goes on essentially unchanged, its basic structure unexamined and unchallenged.

However, a critical evaluation of the dispositional hypothesis cannot be made directly through observation in existing prison settings, since such naturalistic observation necessarily confounds the acute effects of the environment with the chronic characteristics of the inmate and guard populations. To separate the effects of the prison environment *per se* from those attributable to *a priori* dispositions of its inhabitants requires a research strategy in which a "new" prison is constructed, comparable in its fundamental social-psychological milieu to existing prison systems, but entirely populated by individuals who are undifferentiated in all essential dimensions from the rest of society.

Such was the approach taken in the present empirical study, namely, to create a prison-like situation in which the guards and inmates were initially comparable and characterised as being "normal-average," and then to observe the patterns of behaviour which resulted, as well as the cognitive, emotional and attitudinal reactions which emerged. Thus, we began our experiment with a sample of individuals who did not deviate from the normal range of the general population on a variety of dimensions we were able to measure. Half were randomly assigned to the role of "prisoner," the others to that of "guard," neither group having any history of crime, emotional disability, physical handicap nor even intellectual or social disadvantage.

The environment created was that of a "mock" prison which physically constrained the prisoners in barred cells and psychologically conveyed the sense of imprisonment to all participants. Our intention was not to create a *literal* simulation of an American prison, but rather a functional representation of one. For ethical, moral and pragmatic reasons we could not detain our subjects for extended or indefinite periods of time, we could not exercise the threat and promise of severe physical punishment, we could not allow homosexual or racist practices to flourish, nor could we duplicate certain other specific aspects of prison life. Nevertheless, we believed that we could create a situation with sufficient mundane realism to allow the role-playing participants to go beyond the superficial demands of their assignment into the deep structure of the characters they represented. To do so, we established functional equivalents for the activities and experiences of actual prison life which were expected to produce qualitatively similar psychological reactions in our subjects— feelings of power and powerlessness, of control and oppression, of satisfaction and frustration, of arbitrary rule and resistance to authority, of status and anonymity, of machismo and emasculation. . . .

Method

Overview

The effects of playing the role of "guard" or "prisoner" were studied in the context of an experimental simulation of a prison environment. The research design was a relatively simple one, involving as it did only a single treatment variable, the random assignment to either a "guard" or "prisoner" condition. These roles were enacted over an extended period of time (nearly one week) within an environment which was physically constructed to resemble a prison. Central to the methodology of creating and maintaining a psychological state of imprisonment was the functional simulation of significant properties of "real prison life" (established through information from former inmates, correctional personnel and texts).

The "guards" were free with certain limits to implement the procedures of induction into the prison setting and maintenance of custodial retention of the "prisoners." These inmates, having voluntarily submitted to the conditions of this total institution in which they now lived, coped in various ways with its stresses and its challenges. The behaviour of both groups of subjects was observed, recorded and analysed. The dependent measures were of two general types: transactions between and within each group of subjects, recorded on video and audio tape as well as directly observed; individual reactions on questionnaires, mood inventories, personality tests, daily guard shift reports, and post-experimental interviews.

Subjects

The 21 subjects who participated in the experiment were selected from an initial pool of 75 respondents, who answered a newspaper advertisement asking for male volunteers to participate in a psychological study of "prison life" in return for payment of $15 per day. Those who responded to the notice completed an extensive questionnaire concerning their family background, physical and mental health history, prior experience and attitudinal propensities with respect to sources of psychopathology (including their involvement in crime). Each respondent who completed the background questionnaire was interviewed by one of two experimenters. Finally, the 24 subjects who were judged to be most stable (physically and mentally), most mature, and least involved in anti-social behaviour were selected to participate in the study. On a random basis, half of the subjects were assigned the role of "guard," half to the role of "prisoner."

The subjects were normal, healthy males attending colleges throughout the United States who were in the Stanford area during the summer. They were largely of middle-class socio-economic status, Caucasians (with the exception of one Oriental subject). . . .

Procedure

Physical aspects of the prison.   The prison was built in a 35-ft section of a basement corridor in the psychology building at Stanford University. It was partitioned by two fabricated walls, one of which was fitted with the only entrance door to the cell block; the other contained a small observation screen. Three small cells (6 × 9 ft) were made from converted laboratory rooms by replacing the usual doors with steel barred, black painted ones, and removing all furniture.

A cot (with mattress, sheet and pillow) for each prisoner was the only furniture in the cells. A small closet across from the cells served as a solitary confinement facility; its dimensions were extremely small (2 × 2 × 7 ft) and it was unlit.

In addition, several rooms in an adjacent wing of the building were used as guards' quarters (to change in and out of uniform or for rest and relaxation), a bedroom for the "warden" and "superintendent," and an interview-testing room. Behind the observation screen at one end of the "yard" was video recording equipment and sufficient space for several observers.

Operational details.   The "prisoner" subjects remained in the mock-prison 24 hours per day for the duration of the study. Three were arbitrarily assigned to each of the three cells; the others were on stand-by call at their homes. The "guard" subjects worked on three-man, eight-hour shifts; remaining in the prison environment only during their work shift, going about their usual lives at other times.

Role instruction.   All subjects had been told that they would be assigned either the guard or the prisoner role on a completely random basis and all had voluntarily agreed to play either role for $15.00 per day for up to two weeks. They signed a contract guaranteeing a minimally adequate diet, clothing, housing and medical care as well as the financial remuneration in return for their stated "intention" of serving in the assigned role for the duration of the study.

It was made explicit in the contract that those assigned to be prisoners should expect to be under surveillance (have little or no privacy) and to have some of their basic civil rights suspended during their imprisonment, excluding physical abuse. They were given no other information about what to expect nor instructions about behaviour appropriate for a prisoner role. Those actually assigned to this treatment were informed by phone to be available at their place of residence on a given Sunday when we would start the experiment.

The subjects assigned to be guards attended an orientation meeting on the day prior to the induction of the prisoners. At this time they were introduced to the principal investigators, the "Superintendent" of the prison (P.G.Z.) and an undergraduate research assistant who assumed the administrative role of "Warden." They were told that we wanted to try to simulate a prison environment within the limits imposed by pragmatic and ethical considerations. Their assigned task was to "maintain the reasonable degree of order within the prison necessary for its effective functioning," although the specifics of how this duty might be implemented were not explicitly detailed. They were made aware of the fact that while many of the contingencies with which they might be confronted were essentially unpredictable (e.g. prisoner escape attempts), part of their task was to be prepared for such eventualities and to be able to deal appropriately with the variety of situations that might arise. The "Warden" instructed the guards in the administrative details, including: the work-shifts, the mandatory daily completion of shift reports concerning the activity of guards and prisoners, the completion of "critical incident" reports which detailed unusual occurrences and the administration of meals, work and recreation programmes for the prisoners. In order to begin to involve these subjects in their roles even before the first prisoner was incarcerated, the guards assisted in the final phases of completing the prison complex—putting the cots in the cells, signs on the walls, setting up the guards' quarters, moving furniture, water coolers, refrigerators, etc.

The guards generally believed that we were primarily interested in studying the behaviour of the prisoners. Of course, we were equally interested in the effect which enacting the role of guard in this environment would have on their behaviour and subjective states.

To optimise the extent to which their behaviour would reflect their genuine reactions to the experimental prison situation and not simply their ability to follow instructions, they were intentionally given only minimal guidelines for what it meant to be a guard. An explicit and categorical prohibition against the use of physical punishment or physical aggression was, however, emphasised by the experimenters. Thus, with this single notable exception, their roles were relatively unstructured initially, requiring each "guard" to carry out activities necessary for interacting with a group of "prisoners" as well as with other "guards" and the "correctional staff."

Uniform.   In order to promote feelings of anonymity in the subjects each group was issued identical uniforms. For the guards, the uniform consisted of: plain khaki shirts and trousers, a whistle, a police nightstick (wooden baton) and reflecting sunglasses which made eye contact impossible. The prisoners' uniform consisted of loosely fitting muslin smocks with an identification number on front and back. No underclothes were worn beneath these "dresses." A chain and lock were placed around one ankle. On their feet they wore rubber sandals and their hair was covered with a nylon stocking made into a cap. Each prisoner was also issued a toothbrush, soap, soapdish, towel and bed linen. No personal belongings were allowed in the cells.

The outfitting of both prisoners and guards in this manner served to enhance group identity and reduce individual uniqueness within the two groups. The khaki uniforms were intended to convey a military attitude, while the whistle and nightstick were carried as symbols of control and power. The prisoners' uniforms were designed not only to deindividuate the prisoners but to be humiliating and serve as symbols of their dependence and subservience. The ankle chain was a constant reminder (even during their sleep when it hit the other ankle) of the oppressiveness of the environment. The stocking cap removed any distinctiveness associated with hair length, colour or style (as does shaving of heads in some "real" prisons and the military). The ill-fitting uniforms made the prisoners feel awkward in their movements, since these dresses were worn without undergarments; the uniforms forced them to assume unfamiliar postures, more like those of a woman than a man— another part of the emasculating process of becoming a prisoner.

Induction procedure.   With the cooperation of Palo Alto City Police Department all of the subjects assigned to the prisoner treatment were unexpectedly "arrested" at their residences. A police officer charged them with suspicion of burglary or armed robbery, advised them of their legal rights, handcuffed them, thoroughly searched them (often as curious neighbours looked on) and carried them off to the police station in the rear of the police car. At the station they went through the standard routines of being fingerprinted, having an identification file prepared and then being placed in a detention cell. Each prisoner was blindfolded and subsequently driven by one of the experimenters and a subject-guard to our mock prison. Throughout the entire arrest procedure, the police officers involved maintained a formal, serious attitude, avoiding answering any questions of clarification as to the relation of this "arrest" to the mock prison study.

Upon arrival at our experimental prison, each prisoner was stripped, sprayed with a delousing preparation (a deodorant spray) and made to stand alone naked for a while in the cell yard. After being given the uniform described previously and having an I.D. picture taken ("mug shot"), the prisoner was put in his cell and ordered to remain silent.

Administrative routine.   When all the cells were occupied, the warden greeted the prisoners and read them the rules of the institution (developed by the guards and the warden). They were to be memorised and to be followed. Prisoners were to be referred to only by the number on their uniforms, also in an effort to depersonalise them.

The prisoners were to be served three bland meals per day, were allowed three supervised toilet visits, and given two hours daily for the privilege of reading or letterwriting. Work assignments were issued for which the prisoners were to receive an hourly wage to constitute their $15 daily payment. Two visiting periods per week were scheduled, as were movie rights and exercise periods. Three times a day all prisoners were lined up for a "count" (one on each guard work-shift). The initial purpose of the "count" was to ascertain that all prisoners were present, and to test them on their knowledge of the rules and their I.D. numbers. The first perfunctory counts lasted only about 10 minutes, but on each successive day (or night) they were spontaneously increased in duration until some lasted several hours. Many of the pre-established features of administrative routine were modified or abandoned by the guards, and some were forgotten by the staff over the course of the study. . . .

Results

Overview

Although it is difficult to anticipate exactly what the influence of incarceration will be upon the individuals who are subjected to it and those charged with its maintenance (especially in a simulated reproduction), the results of the present experiment support many commonly held conceptions of prison life and validate anecdotal evidence supplied by articulate ex-convicts. The environment of arbitrary custody had great impact upon the affective states of both guards and prisoners as well as upon the interpersonal processes taking place between and within those role-groups.

In general, guards and prisoners showed a marked tendency toward increased negativity of affect and their overall outlook became increasingly negative. As the experiment progressed, prisoners expressed intentions to do harm to others more frequently. For both prisoners and guards, self-evaluations were more deprecating as the experience of the prison environment became internalised.

Overt behaviour was generally consistent with the subjective self-reports and affective expressions of the subjects. Despite the fact that guards and prisoners were essentially free to engage in any form of interaction (positive or negative, supportive or affrontive, etc.), the characteristic nature of their encounters tended to be negative, hostile, affrontive and dehumanising. Prisoners immediately adopted a generally passive response mode while guards assumed a very active initiating role in all interactions. Throughout the experiment, commands were the most frequent form of verbal behaviour and, generally, verbal exchanges were strikingly impersonal, with few references to individual identity. Although it was clear to all subjects that the experimenters would not permit physical violence to take place, varieties of less direct aggressive behaviour were observed frequently (especially on the part of guards). In lieu of physical violence, verbal affronts were used as one of the most frequent forms of interpersonal contact between guards and prisoners.

The most dramatic evidence of the impact of this situation upon the participants was seen in the gross reactions of five prisoners who had to be released because of extreme emotional depression, crying, rage and acute anxiety. The pattern of symptoms was quite similar in four of the subjects and began as early as the second day of imprisonment. The fifth subject was released after being treated for a psychosomatic rash which covered portions of his body. Of the remaining prisoners, only two said they were not willing to forfeit the money they had earned in return for being "paroled." When the experiment was terminated prematurely after only six days, all the remaining prisoners were delighted by their unexpected good fortune. In contrast, most of the guards seemed to be distressed by the decision to stop the experiment and it appeared to us that they had become sufficiently involved in their roles so that they now enjoyed the extreme control and power which they exercised and were reluctant to give it up. One guard did report being personally upset at the suffering of the prisoners and claimed to have considered asking to change his role to become one of them—but never did so. None of the guards ever failed to come to work on time for their shift, and indeed, on several occasions guards remained on duty voluntarily and uncomplaining for extra hours—without additional pay.

The extremely pathological reactions which emerged in both groups of subjects testify to the power of the social forces operating, but still there were individual differences seen in styles of coping with this novel experience and in degrees of successful adaptation to it. Half the prisoners did endure the oppressive atmosphere, and not all the guards resorted to hostility. Some guards were tough but fair ("played by the rules"), some went far beyond their roles to engage in creative cruelty and harassment, while a few were passive and rarely instigated any coercive control over the prisoners.

These differential reactions to the experience of imprisonment were not suggested by or predictable from the self-report measures of personality and attitude or the interviews taken before the experiment began. The standardised tests employed indicated that a perfectly normal emotionally stable sample of subjects had been selected. In those few instances where differential test scores do discriminate between subjects, there is an opportunity to, partially at least, discern some of the personality variables which may be critical in the adaptation to and tolerance of prison confinement. . . .

Video Recordings

An analysis of the video recordings indicates a preponderance of genuinely negative interactions, i.e., physical aggression, threats, deprecations, etc. It is also clear that any assertive activity was largely the prerogative of the guards, while prisoners generally assumed a relatively passive demeanour. Guards more often aggressed, more often insulted, more often threatened. Prisoners, when they reacted at all, engaged primarily in resistance to these guard behaviours.

For guards, the most frequent verbal behaviour was the giving of commands and their most frequent form of physical behaviour was aggression. The most frequent form of prisoners' verbal behaviour was question-asking; their most frequent form of physical behaviour was resistance. On the other hand, the most infrequent behaviour engaged in overall throughout the experiment was "helping"—only one such incident was noted from all the video recording collected. That solitary sign of human concern for a fellow occurred between two prisoners. . . .

Audio Recordings

The audio recordings made throughout the prison simulation afforded one opportunity to systematically collect self-report data from prisoners and guards regarding (among other things) their emotional reactions, their outlook, and their interpersonal evaluations and activities within the experimental setting. Recorded interviews with both prisoners and guards offered evidence that: guards tended to express nearly as much negative outlook and negative self-regard as most prisoners (one concerned guard, in fact, expressed more negative self-regard than any prisoner and more general negative affect than all but one of the prisoners); prisoner interviews were marked by negativity in expressions of affect, self-regard and action intentions (including intent to aggress and negative outlook). . . .

Even more remarkable was the discovery that the prisoners had begun to adopt and accept the guards' negative attitude toward them. Half of all reported private interactions between prisoners could be classified as non-supportive and non-cooperative. Moreover, when prisoners made evaluative statements of or expressed regard for, their fellow prisoners, 85% of the time they were uncomplimentary and deprecating. This set of observed frequencies departs significantly from chance expectations based on a conservative binominal probability frequency ($P < 0.01$ for prison $v.$ non-prison topics; $P < 0.05$ for negative $v.$ positive or neutral regard). . . .

Conclusions and Discussion

It should be apparent that the elaborate procedures (and staging) employed by the experimenters to insure a high degree of mundane realism in this mock prison contributed to its effective functional simulation of the psychological dynamics operating in "real" prisons. We observed empirical relationships in the simulated prison environment which were strikingly isomorphic to the internal relations of real prisons, corroborating many of the documented reports of what occurs behind prison walls.

The conferring of differential power on the status of "guard" and "prisoner" constituted, in effect, the institutional validation of those roles. But further, many of the subjects ceased distinguishing between prison role and their prior self-identities. When this occurred, within what was a surprisingly short period of time, we witnessed a sample of normal, healthy American college students fractionate into a group of prison guards who seemed to derive pleasure from insulting, threatening, humiliating and dehumanising their peers—those who by chance selection had been assigned to the "prisoner" role. The typical prisoner syndrome was one of passivity, dependency, depression, helplessness and self-deprecation. Prisoner participation in the social reality which the guards had structured for them lent increasing validity to it and, as the prisoners became resigned to their treatment over time, many acted in ways to justify their fate at the hands of the guards, adopting attitudes and behaviour which helped to sanction their victimisation. Most dramatic and distressing to us was the observation of the ease with which sadistic behaviour could be elicited in individuals who were not "sadistic types" and the frequency with which acute emotional breakdowns could occur in men selected precisely for their emotional stability.

Situational v. Dispositional Attribution

To what can we attribute these deviant behaviour patterns? If these reactions had been observed within the confines of an existing penal institution, it is probable that a dispositional hypothesis would be invoked as an explanation. Some cruel guards might be singled out as sadistic or passive-aggressive personality types who chose to work in a correctional institution because of the outlets provided for sanctioned aggression. Aberrant reactions on the part of the inmate population would likewise be viewed as an extrapolation from the prior social histories of these men as violent, anti-social, psychopathic, unstable character types.

Existing penal institutions may be viewed as *natural experiments* in social control in which any attempts at providing a causal attribution for observed behaviour hopelessly confound dispositional and situational causes. In contrast, the design of our study minimised the utility of trait or prior social history explanations by means of judicious subject selection and random assignment to roles. Considerable effort and care went into determining the composition of the final subject population from which our guards and prisoners were drawn. Through case histories, personal interviews and a battery of personality tests, the subjects chosen to participate manifested no apparent abnormalities, anti-social tendencies or social backgrounds which were other than exemplary. On every one of the scores of the diagnostic tests each subject scored within the normal-average range. Our subjects then, were highly representative of middle-class, Caucasian American society (17 to 30 years in age), although above average in both intelligence and emotional stability.

Nevertheless, in less than one week their *behaviour* in this simulated prison could be characterised as pathological and anti-social. The negative, anti-social reactions observed were not the product of an environment created by combining a collection of deviant, personalities, but rather, the result of an intrinsically pathological situation which could distort and rechannel the behaviour of essentially normal individuals. The abnormality here resided in the psychological nature of the situation and not in those who passed through it. . . .

Pathology of Power

Being a guard carried with it social status within the prison, a group identity (when wearing the uniform), and above all, the freedom to exercise an unprecedented degree of control over the lives of other human beings. This control was invariably expressed in terms of sanctions, punishment, demands and with the threat of manifest physical power. There was no need for the guards to rationally justify a request as they do in their ordinary life, and merely to make a demand was sufficient to have it carried out. Many of the guards showed in their behaviour and revealed in post-experimental statements that this sense of power was exhilarating.

The use of power was self-aggrandising and self-perpetuating. The guard power, derived initially from an arbitrary label, was intensified whenever there was any perceived threat by the prisoners, and this new level subsequently became the baseline from which further hostility and harassment would begin. The most hostile guards on each shift moved spontaneously into the leadership roles of giving orders and deciding on punishments. They became role models whose behaviour was emulated by other members of the shift. Despite minimal contact between the three separate guard shifts and nearly 16 hours a day spent away from the prison, the absolute level of aggression, as well as more subtle and "creative" forms of aggression manifested, increased in a spiralling function. Not to be tough and arrogant was to be seen as a sign of weakness by the guards, and even those "good" guards who did not get as drawn into the power syndrome as the others respected the implicit norm of *never* contradicting or even interfering with an action of a more hostile guard on their shift.

After the first day of the study, practically all prisoner's rights (even such things as the time and conditions of sleeping and eating) came to be redefined by the guards as "privileges" which were to be earned for obedient behaviour. Constructive activities such as watching movies or reading (previously planned and suggested by the experimenters) were arbitrarily cancelled until further notice by the guards—and were subsequently never allowed. "Reward" then became granting approval for prisoners to eat, sleep, go to the toilet, talk, smoke a cigarette, wear glasses or the temporary diminution of harassment. One wonders about the conceptual nature of "positive" reinforcement when subjects are in such conditions of deprivation, and the extent to which even minimally acceptable conditions become rewarding when experienced in the context of such an impoverished environment.

We might also question whether there are meaningful nonviolent alternatives as models for behaviour modification in real prisons. In a world where men are either powerful or powerless, everyone learns to despise the lack of power in others and in oneself. It seems to us, that prisoners learn to admire power for its own sake—power becoming the ultimate reward. Real prisoners soon learn the means to gain power whether through ingratiation, informing, sexual control of other prisoners or development of powerful cliques. When they are released from prison, it is unlikely they will ever want to feel so powerless again and will take action to establish and assert a sense of power.

The Pathological Prisoner Syndrome

Various coping strategies were employed by our prisoners as they began to react to their perceived loss of personal identity and the arbitrary control of their lives. At first they exhibited disbelief at the total invasion of their privacy, constant surveillance and atmosphere of oppression in which they were living. Their next response was rebellion, first by the use of direct force, and later with subtle divisive tactics designed to foster distrust among the prisoners. They then tried to work within the system by setting up an elected grievance committee. When that collective action failed to produce meaningful changes in their existence, individual self-interests emerged. The breakdown in prisoner cohesion was the start of social disintegration which gave rise not only to feelings of isolation but deprecation of other prisoners as well. As noted before, half the prisoners coped with the prison situation by becoming extremely disturbed emotionally—as a passive way of demanding attention and help. Others became excessively obedient in trying to be "good" prisoners. . . .

Let us briefly consider some of the relevant processes involved in bringing about these reactions.

Loss of personal identity.   Identity is, for most people, conferred by social recognition of one's uniqueness, and established through one's name, dress, appearance, behaviour style and history. Living among strangers who do not know your name or history (who refer to you only by number), dressed in a uniform exactly like all other prisoners, not wanting to call attention to one's self because of the unpredictable consequences it might provoke—all led to a weakening of self-identity among the prisoners. As they began to lose initiative and emotional responsivity, while acting ever more compliantly, indeed, the prisoners became deindividuated not only to the guards and the observers, but also to themselves.

Arbitrary control.   On post-experimental questionnaires, the most frequently mentioned aversive aspect of the prison experience was that of being subjugated to the apparently arbitrary, capricious decisions and rules of the guards. A question by a prisoner as often elicited derogation and aggression as it did a rational answer. Smiling at a joke could be punished in the same way that failing to smile might be. An individual acting in defiance of the rules could bring punishment to innocent cell partners (who became, in effect, "mutually yoked controls"), to himself, or to all.

As the environment became more unpredictable, and previously learned assumptions about a just and orderly world were no longer functional, prisoners ceased to initiate any action. They moved about on orders and when in their cells rarely engaged in any purposeful activity. . . .

Dependency and emasculation. The network of dependency relations established by the guards not only promoted helplessness in the prisoners but served to emasculate them as well. The arbitrary control by the guards put the prisoners at their mercy for even the daily, commonplace functions like going to the toilet. To do so, required publicly obtained permission (not always granted) and then a personal escort to the toilet while blindfolded and handcuffed. The same was true for many other activities ordinarily practised spontaneously without thought, such as lighting up a cigarette, reading a novel, writing a letter, drinking a glass of water or brushing one's teeth. These were all privileged activities requiring permission and necessitating a prior show of good behaviour. These low-level dependencies engendered a regressive orientation in the prisoners. Their dependency was defined in terms of the extent of the domain of control over all aspects of their lives which they allowed other individuals (the guards and prison staff) to exercise.

As in real prisons, the assertive, independent, aggressive nature of male prisoners posed a threat which was overcome by a variety of tactics. The prisoner uniforms resembled smocks or dresses, which made them look silly and enabled the guards to refer to them as "sissies" or "girls." Wearing these uniforms without any underclothes forced the prisoners to move and sit in unfamiliar, feminine postures. Any sign of individual rebellion was labelled as indicative of "incorrigibility" and resulted in loss of privileges, solitary confinement, humiliation or punishment of cell mates. Physically smaller guards were able to induce stronger prisoners to act foolishly and obediently. Prisoners were encouraged to belittle each other publicly during the counts. These and other tactics all served to engender in the prisoners a lessened sense of their masculinity (as defined by their external culture). It follows then, that although the prisoners usually outnumbered the guards during line-ups and counts (nine *v.* three) there never was an attempt to directly overpower them. (Interestingly, after the study was terminated, the prisoners expressed the belief that the basis for assignment to guard and prisoner groups was physical size. They perceived the guards were "bigger," when, in fact, there was no difference in average height or weight between these randomly determined groups.)

In conclusion, we believe this demonstration reveals new dimensions in the social psychology of imprisonment worth pursuing in future research. In addition, this research provides a paradigm and information base for studying alternatives to existing guard training, as well as for questioning the basic operating principles on which penal institutions rest. If our mock prison could generate the extent of pathology it did in such a short time, then the punishment of being imprisoned in a real prison does not "fit the crime" for most prisoners—indeed, it far exceeds it! Moreover, since prisoners and guards are locked into a dynamic, symbiotic relationship which is destructive to their human nature, guards are also society's prisoners. . . .

65

What Works?—Questions and Answers about Prison Reform

Robert Martinson

In the past several years, American prisons have gone through one of their recurrent periods of strikes, riots, and other disturbances. Simultaneously, and in consequence, the articulate public has entered another one of its sporadic fits of attentiveness to the condition of our prisons and to the perennial questions they pose about the nature of crime and the uses of punishment. The result has been a widespread call for "prison reform," i.e., for "reformed" prisons which will produce "reformed" convicts. Such calls are a familiar feature of American prison history. American prisons, perhaps more than those of any other country, have stood or fallen in public esteem according to their ability to fulfill their promise of rehabilitation.

One of the problems in the constant debate over "prison reform" is that we have been able to draw very little on any systematic empirical knowledge about the success or failure that we have met when we *have* tried to rehabilitate offenders, with various treatments and in various institutional and noninstitutional settings. The field of penology has produced a voluminous research literature on this subject, but until recently there has been no comprehensive review of this literature and no attempt to bring its findings to bear, in a useful way, on the general question of "What works?". My purpose in this essay is to sketch an answer to that question.

The Travails of a Study

In 1966, the New York State Governor's Special Committee on Criminal Offenders recognized their need for such an answer. The Committee was organized on the premise that prisons could rehabilitate, that the prisons of New York were not in fact making a serious effort at rehabilitation, and that New York's prisons should be converted from their existing custodial basis to a new rehabilitative one. The problem for the Committee was that there was no available guidance on the question of what had been shown to be the most effective means of rehabilitation. My colleagues and I were hired by the committee to remedy this defect in our knowledge; our job was to undertake a comprehensive survey of what was known about rehabilitation. . . .

Source: Reprinted with permission of the author. Copyright © National Affairs, Inc., *The Public Interest*, No. 35, Spring 1974, Washington, DC.

What we set out to do in this study was fairly simple, though it turned into a massive task. First we undertook a six-month search of the literature for any available reports published in the English language on attempts at rehabilitation that had been made in our corrections systems and those of other countries from 1945 through 1967. We then picked from that literature all those studies whose findings were interpretable—that is, whose design and execution met the conventional standards of social science research. Our criteria were rigorous but hardly esoteric: A study had to be an evaluation of a treatment method, it had to employ an independent measure of the improvement secured by that method, and it had to use some control group, some untreated individuals with whom the treated ones could be compared. We excluded studies only for methodological reasons: They presented insufficient data, they were only preliminary, they presented only a summary of findings and did not allow a reader to evaluate those findings, their results were confounded by extraneous factors, they used unreliable measures, one could not understand their descriptions of the treatment in question, they drew spurious conclusions from their data, their samples were undescribed or too small or provided no true comparability between treated and untreated groups, or they had used inappropriate statistical tests and did not provide enough information for the reader to recompute the data. Using these standards, we drew from the total number of studies 231 acceptable ones, which we not only analyzed ourselves but summarized in detail so that a reader of our analysis would be able to compare it with his independent conclusions.

These treatment studies use various measures of offender improvement: recidivism rates (that is, the rates at which offenders return to crime), adjustment to prison life, vocational success, educational achievement, personality and attitude change, and general adjustment to the outside community. We included all of these in our study; but in these pages I will deal only with the effects of rehabilitative treatment on recidivism, the phenomenon which reflects most directly how well our present treatment programs are performing the task of rehabilitation. The use of even this one measure brings with it enough methodological complications to make a clear reporting of the findings most difficult. The groups that are studied, for instance, are exceedingly disparate, so that it is hard to tell whether what "works" for one kind of offender also works for others. In addition, there has been little attempt to replicate studies; therefore one cannot be certain how stable and reliable the various findings are. Just as important, when the various studies use the term "recidivism rate," they may in fact be talking about somewhat different measures of offender behavior—i.e., "failure" measures such as arrest rates or parole violation rates, or "success" measures such as favorable discharge from parole or probation. And not all of these measures correlate very highly with one another. These difficulties will become apparent again and again in the course of this discussion.

With these caveats, it is possible to give a rather bald summary of our findings: *With few and isolated exceptions, the rehabilitative efforts that have been reported so far have had no appreciable effect on recidivism.* Studies that have been done since our survey was completed do not present any major grounds for altering that original conclusion. What follows is an attempt to answer the questions and challenges that might be posed to such an unqualified statement.

Education and Vocational Training

1. *Isn't it true that a correctional facility running a truly rehabilitative program—one that prepares inmates for life on the outside through education and*

vocational training—will turn out more successful individuals than will a prison which merely leaves its inmates to rot?

If this *is* true, the fact remains that there is very little empirical evidence to support it. Skill development and education programs are in fact quite common in correctional facilities, and one might begin by examining their effects on young males, those who might be thought most amenable to such efforts. . . .

In sum, many of these studies of young males are extremely hard to interpret because of flaws in research design. But it can safely be said that they provide us with no clear evidence that education or skill development programs have been successful.

Training Adult Inmates

When one turns to adult male inmates, as opposed to young ones, the results are even more discouraging. There have been six studies of this type; three of them report that their programs, which ranged from academic to prison work experience, produced no significant differences in recidivism rates, and one—by Glaser (1964)—is almost impossible to interpret because of the risk differentials of the prisoners participating in the various programs.

Two studies—by Schnur (1948) and by Saden (1962)—*do* report a positive difference from skill development programs. . . .

Two things should be noted about these studies. One is the difficulty of interpreting them as a whole. The disparity in the programs that were tried, in the populations that were affected and in the institutional settings that surrounded these projects, make it hard to be sure that one is observing the same category of treatment in each case. But the second point is that despite this difficulty, one can be reasonably sure that, so far, educational and vocational programs have not worked. We don't know why they have failed. We don't know whether the programs themselves are flawed, or whether they are incapable of overcoming the effects of prison life in general. The difficulty may be that they lack applicability to the world the inmate will face outside of prison. Or perhaps the type of educational and skill improvement they produce simply doesn't have very much to do with an individual's propensity to commit a crime. What we do know is that, to date, education and skill development have not reduced recidivism by rehabilitating criminals.

The Effects of Individual Counseling

2. *But when we speak of a rehabilitative prison, aren't we referring to more than education and skill development alone? Isn't what's needed some way of counseling inmates, or helping them with the deeper problems that have caused their maladjustment?*

This, too, is a reasonable hypothesis; but when one examines the programs of this type that have been tried, it's hard to find any more grounds for enthusiasm than we found with skill development and education. One method that's been tried—though so far, there have been acceptable reports only of its application to young offenders—has been individual psychotherapy. For young males, we found seven such reported studies. One study, by Guttman (1963) at the Nelles School, found such treatment to be ineffective in reducing recidivism rates; another, by Rudoff (1960), found it unrelated to *institutional* violation rates, which were themselves related to parole success. . . . A third, also by Guttman (1963) but at another institution, found that such treatment was actually related to a slightly *higher* parole viola-tion rate; and a study by Adams (1959b and 1961b) also found a lack of improvement in parole revocation and first suspension rates.

There were two studies at variance with this pattern. One by Persons (1967) said that if a boy was judged to be "successfully" treated—as opposed to simply being sub-jected to the treatment experience—he did tend to do better. And there was one finding both hopeful and cautionary: At the Deuel School (Adams, 1961a), the experimental boys were first divided into two groups, those rated as "amenable" to treatment and those rated "non-amenable." Amenable boys who got the treatment did better than nontreated boys. On the other hand, "non-amenable" boys who were treated actually did *worse* than they would have done if they had received no treatment at all. . . .

There have been two studies of the effects of individual psychotherapy on young incarcerated *female* offenders, and both of them (Adams 1959a, Adams 1961b) report no significant effects from the therapy. But one of the Adams studies (1959a) does contain a suggestive, although not clearly interpretable, finding: If this individual therapy was administered by a psychiatrist or a psychologist, the resulting parole suspension rate was almost two-and-a-half times *higher* than if it was admin-istered by a social worker without this specialized training.

There has also been a much smaller number of studies of two other types of individual therapy: counseling, which is directed towards a prisoner's gaining new insight into his own problems, and casework, which aims at helping a prisoner cope with his more pragmatic immediate needs. These types of therapy both rely heavily on the empathetic relationship that is to be developed between the professional and the client. . . .

The only American study which provides a direct measure of the effects of individual counseling—a study of California's Intensive Treatment Program (Cali-fornia, 1958a), which was "psychodynamically" oriented—found no improvement in recidivism rates.

It was this finding of the failure of the Intensive Treatment Program which contributed to the decision in California to de-emphasize individual counseling in its penal system in favor of group methods. And indeed one might suspect that the pre-ceding reports reveal not the inadequacy of counseling as a whole but only the fail-ure of one *type* of counseling, the individual type. *Group* counseling methods, in which offenders are permitted to aid and compare experiences with one another, might be thought to have a better chance of success. So it is important to ask what results these alternative methods have actually produced.

Group Counseling

Group counseling has indeed been tried in correctional institutions, both with and without a specifically psychotherapeutic orientation. There has been one study of "pragmatic," problem-oriented counseling on *young* institutionalized males, by Seckel (1965). This type of counseling had no significant effect. For adult males, there have been three such studies of the "pragmatic" and "insight" methods. Two (Kassebaum, 1971; Harrison, 1964) report no long-lasting significant effects. (One of these two did report a real but short-term effect that wore off as the program became institutionalized and as offenders were at liberty longer.) . . .

With regard to more professional group *psychotherapy*, the reports are also conflicting. We have two studies of group psychotherapy on young males. One, by

Persons (1966), says that this treatment did in fact reduce recidivism. . . . On the other hand, a study by Craft (1964) of young males designated "psychopaths," comparing "self-government" group psychotherapy with "authoritarian" individual counseling, found that the "group therapy" boys afterwards committed *twice* as many new offenses as the individually treated ones. Perhaps some forms of group psychotherapy work for some types of offenders but not others; a reader must draw his own conclusions, on the basis of sparse evidence.

With regard to young females, the results are just as equivocal. Adams, in his study of females (1959a), found that there was no improvement to be gained from treating girls by group rather than individual methods. A study by Taylor of borstal (reformatory) girls in New Zealand (1967) found a similar lack of any great improvement for group therapy as opposed to individual therapy or even to no therapy at all. . . .

As with the question of skill development, it is hard to summarize these results. The programs administered were various; the groups to which they were administered varied not only by sex but by age as well; there were also variations in the length of time for which the programs were carried on, the frequency of contact during that time, and the period for which the subjects were followed up. Still, one must say that the burden of the evidence is not encouraging. These programs seem to work best when they are new, when their subjects are amenable to treatment in the first place, and when the counselors are not only trained people but "good" people as well. . . .

Transforming the Institutional Environment

3. *But maybe the reason these counseling programs don't seem to work is not that they are ineffective* per se, *but that the institutional environment outside the program is unwholesome enough to undo any good work that the counseling does. Isn't a truly successful rehabilitative institution the one where the inmate's whole environment is directed towards true correction rather than towards custody or punishment?*

. . . One study of such a program, by Robison (1967), found that the therapy did seem to reduce recidivism after one year. After two years, however, this effect disappeared, and the treated convicts did no better than the untreated. Another study by Kassebaum, Ward, and Wilner (1971), dealt with a program which had been able to effect an exceptionally extensive and experimentally rigorous transformation of the institutional environment. This sophisticated study had a follow-up period of 36 months, and it found that the program had no significant effect on parole failure or success rates.

The results of the studies of youth are more equivocal. As for young females, one study by Adams (1966) of such a program found that it had no significant effect on recidivism; another study, by Goldberg and Adams (1964), found that such a program *did* have a positive effect. This effect declined when the program began to deal with girls who were judged beforehand to be worse risks.

As for young males, the studies may conveniently be divided into those dealing with juveniles (under 16) and those dealing with youths. There have been five studies of milieu therapy administered to juveniles. Two of them—by Laulicht (1962) and by Jesness (1965)—report clearly that the program in question either had no significant effect or had a short-term effect that wore off with passing time. Jesness does report that when his experimental juveniles did commit new offenses, the offenses were less serious than those committed by controls. A third study of juveniles, by McCord (1953) at the Wiltwyck School, reports mixed results. Using two measures of performance, a "success" rate and a "failure" rate, McCord found that his experimental group achieved both less failure *and* less success than the controls did.

There have been two positive reports on milieu therapy programs for male juveniles; both of them have come out of the Highfields program, the milieu therapy experiment which has become the most famous and widely quoted example of "success" via this method. A group of boys was confined for a relatively short time to the unrestrictive, supportive environment of Highfields; and at a follow-up of six months, Freeman (1956) found that the group did indeed show a lower recidivism rate (as measured by parole revocation) than a similar group spending a longer time in the regular reformatory. McCorkle (1958) also reported positive findings from Highfields. But in fact, the McCorkle data show, this improvement was not so clear: The Highfields boys had lower recidivism rates at 12 and 36 months in the follow-up period, but not at 24 and 60 months. The length of follow-up, these data remind us, may have large implications for a study's conclusions. But more important were other flaws in the Highfields experiment: The populations were not fully comparable (they differed according to risk level and time of admission); different organizations—the probation agency for the Highfields boys, the parole agency for the others—were making the revocation decisions for each group; more of the Highfields boys were discharged early from supervision, and thus removed from any risk of revocation. In short, not even from the celebrated Highfields case may we take clear assurance that milieu therapy works.

In the case of male youths, as opposed to male juveniles, the findings are just as equivocal, and hardly more encouraging. One such study by Empey (1966) in a residential context did not produce significant results. A study by Seckel (1967) described California's Fremont Program, in which institutionalized youths participated in a combination of therapy, work projects, field trips, and community meetings. Seckel found that the youths subjected to this treatment committed *more* violations of law than did their nontreated counterparts. This difference could have occurred by chance; still, there was certainly no evidence of relative improvement. Another study, by Levinson (1962–1964), also found a lack of improvement in recidivism rates—but Levinson noted the encouraging fact that the treated group spent somewhat more time in the community before recidivating, and committed less serious offenses.

A study by the State of California (1967) also shows a partially positive finding. This was a study of the Marshall Program, similar to California's Fremont Program but different in several ways. The Marshall Program was shorter and more tightly organized than its Fremont counterpart. In the Marshall Program, as opposed to the Fremont Program, a youth could be ejected from the group and sent back to regular institutions before the completion of the program. Also, the Marshall Program offered some additional benefits: the teaching of "social survival skills" (i.e., getting and holding a job), group counseling of parents, and an occasional opportunity for boys to visit home. When youthful offenders were released to the Marshall Program, either directly or after spending some time in a regular institution, they did no better than a comparable regularly institutionalized population, though both Marshall youth and youth in regular institutions did better than those who were directly released by the court and given no special treatment.

So the youth in these milieu therapy programs at least do no worse than their counterparts in regular institutions, and the special programs may cost less. One may therefore be encouraged—not on grounds of rehabilitation but on grounds of cost-effectiveness.

What about Medical Treatment?

4. Isn't there anything you can do in an institutional setting that will reduce recidivism, for instance, through strictly medical treatment?

A number of studies deal with the results of efforts to change the behavior of offenders through drugs and surgery. As for surgery, the one experimental study of a plastic surgery program—by Mandell (1967)—had negative results. For non-addicts who received plastic surgery, Mandell purported to find improvement in performance on parole; but when one reanalyzes his data, it appears that surgery alone did not in fact make a significant difference.

One type of surgery does seem to be highly successful in reducing recidivism. A twenty-year Danish study of sex offenders, by Stuerup (1960), found that while those who had been treated with hormones and therapy continued to commit both sex crimes (29.6 percent of them did so) and non-sex crimes (21.0 percent), those who had been castrated had rates of only 3.5 percent (not, interestingly enough, a rate of zero; where there's a will, apparently there's a way) and 9.2 percent. One hopes that the policy implications of this study will be found to be distinctly limited.

As for drugs, the major report on such a program—involving tranquilization—was made by Adams (1961b). The tranquilizers were administered to male and female institutionalized youths. With boys, there was only a slight improvement in their subsequent behavior; this improvement disappeared within a year. With girls, the tranquilization produced worse results than when the girls were given no treatment at all.

The Effects of Sentencing

5. Well, at least it may be possible to manipulate certain gross features of the existing, conventional prison system—such as length of sentence and degree of security—in order to affect these recidivism rates. Isn't this the case?

At this point, it's still impossible to say that this is the case. As for the degree of security in an institution, Glaser's (1964) work reported that, for both youth and adults, a less restrictive "custody grading" in American federal prisons was related to success on parole; but this is hardly surprising, since those assigned to more restrictive custody are likely to be worse risks in the first place. More to the point, an American study by Fox (1950) discovered that for "older youths" who were deemed to be good risks for the future, a minimum security institution produced better results than a maximum security one. On the other hand, the data we have on youths under 16—from a study by McClintock (1961), done in Great Britain—indicate that so-called Borstals, in which boys are totally confined, are more effective than a less restrictive regime of partial physical custody. In short, we know very little about the recidivism effects of various degrees of security in existing institutions; and our problems in finding out will be compounded by the probability that these effects will vary widely according to the particular *type* of offender that we're dealing with.

The same problems of mixed results and lack of comparable populations have plagued attempts to study the effects of sentence length. A number of studies—by Narloch (1959), by Bernsten (1965), and by the State of California (1956)—suggest that those who are released earlier from institutions than their scheduled parole date, or those who serve short sentences of under three months rather than longer sentences of eight months or more, either do better on parole or at least do no worse.[1] . . .

On the other hand, Glaser's (1964) data show not a consistent linear relationship between the shortness of the sentence and the rate of parole success, but a curvilinear one. Of his subjects, those who served less than a year had a 73 percent success rate, those who served up to two years were only 65 percent successful, and those who served up to three years fell to a rate of 56 percent. But among those who served sentences of *more* than three years, the success rate rose again—to 60 percent. These findings should be viewed with some caution since Glaser did not control for the pre-existing degree of risk associated with each of his categories of offenders. But the data do suggest that the relationship between sentence length and recidivism may not be a simple linear one.

More important, the effect of sentence length seems to vary widely according to type of offender. In a British study (1963), for instance, Hammond found that for a group of "hard-core recidivists," shortening the sentence caused no improvement in the recidivism rate. In Denmark, Bernsten (1965) discovered a similar phenomenon: That the beneficial effect of three-month sentences as against eight-month ones disappeared in the case of these "hard-core recidivists." Garrity found another such distinction in his 1956 study. He divided his offenders into three categories: "pro-social," "anti-social," and "manipulative." "Pro-social" offenders he found to have low recidivism rates regardless of the length of their sentence; "anti-social" offenders did better with short sentences; the "manipulative" did better with long ones. Two studies from Britain made yet another division of the offender population, and found yet other variations. One (Great Britain, 1964) found that previous offenders—but not first offenders—did better with *longer* sentences, while the other (Cambridge, 1952) found the *reverse* to be true with juveniles.

To add to the problem of interpretation, these studies deal not only with different types and categorizations of offenders but with different types of institutions as well. No more than in the case of institution type can we say that length of sentence has a clear relationship to recidivism.

Decarcerating the Convict

6. *All of this seems to suggest that there's not much we know how to do to rehabilitate an offender when he's in an institution. Doesn't this lead to the clear possibility that the way to rehabilitate offenders is to deal with them* outside *an institutional setting?*

This is indeed an important possibility, and it is suggested by other pieces of information as well. For instance, Miner (1967) reported on a milieu therapy program in Massachusetts called Outward Bound. It took youths 15½ and over; it was oriented toward the development of skills in the out-of-doors and conducted in a wilderness atmosphere very different from that of most existing institutions. The culmination of the 26-day program was a final 24 hours in which each youth had to survive alone in the wilderness. And Miner found that the program did indeed work in reducing recidivism rates.

But by and large, when one takes the programs that have been administered in institutions and applies them in a noninstitutional setting, the results do not grow to encouraging proportions. With casework and individual counseling in the community, for instance, there have been three studies; they dealt with counseling methods from psycho-social and vocational counseling to "operant conditioning," in which an offender was rewarded first simply for coming to counseling sessions and then, gradually, for performing other types of approved acts. Two of them report that the community-counseled offenders did no better than their institutional controls, while the third notes that although community counseling produced fewer arrests per person, it did not ultimately reduce the offender's chance of returning to a reformatory. . . .

Psychotherapy in Community Settings

There is some indication that individual psychotherapy may "work" in a community setting. Massimo (1963) reported on one such program, using what might be termed a "pragmatic" psychotherapeutic approach, including "insight" therapy and a focus on vocational problems. The program was marked by its small size and by its use of therapists who were personally enthusiastic about the project; Massimo found that there was indeed a decline in recidivism rates. Adamson (1956), on the other hand, found no significant difference produced by another program of individual therapy (though he did note that arrest rates among the experimental boys declined with what he called "intensity of treatment"). And Schwitzgebel (1963, 1964), studying other, different kinds of therapy programs, found that the programs *did* produce improvements in the attitudes of his boys—but, unfortunately, not in their rates of recidivism.

And with *group* therapy administered in the community, we find yet another set of equivocal results. The results from studies of pragmatic group counseling are only mildly optimistic. Adams (1965) did report that a form of group therapy, "guided group interaction," when administered to juvenile gangs, did somewhat reduce the percentage that were to be found in custody six years later. On the other hand, in a study of juveniles, Adams (1964) found that while such a program did reduce the number of contacts that an experimental youth had with police, it made no ultimate difference in the detention rate. And the attitudes of the counseled youth showed no improvement. Finally, when O'Brien (1961) examined a community-based program of group psychotherapy, he found not only that the program produced no improvement in the recidivism rate, but that the experimental boys actually did worse than their controls on a series of psychological tests. . . .

Intensive Supervision: The Warren Studies

The widely reported Warren studies (1966a, 1966b, 1967) in California constitute an extremely ambitious attempt to answer these questions. In this project, a control group of youths, drawn from a pool of candidates ready for first admission to a California Youth Authority institution, was assigned to regular detention, usually for eight to nine months, and then released to regular supervision. The experimental group received considerably more elaborate treatment. They were released directly to probation status and assigned to 12-man caseloads. To decide what special treatment was appropriate within these caseloads, the youths were divided according to their "interpersonal maturity level classification," by use of a scale developed by Grant and Grant. And each level dictated its own special type of therapy. . . .

Warren reported an encouraging finding: Among all but one of the "subtypes," the experimentals had a significantly lower failure rate than the controls. The experiment did have certain problems: The experimentals might have been performing better because of the enthusiasm of the staff and the attention lavished on them;

none of the controls had been *directly* released to their regular supervision programs instead of being detained first; and it was impossible to separate the effects of the experimentals' small caseloads from their specially designed treatments, since no experimental youths had been assigned to a small caseload with "inappropriate" treatment, or with no treatment at all. Still, none of these problems were serious enough to vitiate the encouraging prospect that this finding presented for successful treatment of probationers.

This encouraging finding was, however, accompanied by a rather more disturbing clue. As has been mentioned before, the experimental subjects, when measured, had a lower *failure* rate than the controls. But the experimentals also had a lower *success* rate. That is, fewer of the experimentals as compared with the controls had been judged to have successfully completed their program of supervision and to be suitable for favorable release. When my colleagues and I undertook a rather laborious reanalysis of the Warren data, it became clear why this discrepancy had appeared. It turned out that fewer experimentals were "successful" because the experimentals were actually committing more offenses than their controls. The reason that the experimentals' relatively large number of offenses was not being reflected in their failure rates was simply that the experimentals' probation officers were using a more lenient revocation policy. In other words, the controls had a higher failure rate because the controls were being revoked for less serious offenses.

So it seems that what Warren was reporting in her "failure" rates was not merely the treatment effect of her small caseloads and special programs. Instead, what Warren was finding was not so much a change in the behavior of the experimental youths as a change in the behavior of the experimental *probation officers*, who knew the "special" status of their charges and who had evidently decided to revoke probation status at a lower than normal rate. The experimentals continued to commit offenses; what was different was that when they committed these offenses, they were permitted to remain on probation. . . .

Intensive Supervision of Adults

The results are similarly ambiguous when one applies this intensive supervision to adult offenders. There have been several studies of the effects of intensive supervision on adult parolees. Some of these are hard to interpret because of problems of comparability between experimental and control groups (general risk ratings, for instance, or distribution of narcotics offenders, or policy changes that took place between various phases of the experiments), but two of them (California, 1966; Stanton, 1964) do not seem to give evidence of the benefits of intensive supervision. By far the most extensive work, though, on the effects of intensive supervision of adult parolees has been a series of studies of California's Special Intensive Parole Unit (SIPU), a 10-year-long experiment designed to test the treatment possibilities of various special parole programs. Three of the four "phases" of this experiment produced "negative results." The first phase tested the effect of a reduced caseload size; no lasting effect was found. The second phase slightly increased the size of the small caseloads and provided for a longer time in treatment; again there was no evidence of a treatment effect. In the fourth phase, caseload sizes and time in treatment were again varied, and treatments were simultaneously varied in a sophisticated way according to personality characteristics of the parolees; once again, significant results did not appear.

The only phase of this experiment for which positive results were reported was Phase Three. Here, it was indeed found that a smaller caseload improved one's chances of parole success. . . .

Does Nothing Work?

7. Do all of these studies lead us irrevocably to the conclusion that nothing works, that we haven't the faintest clue about how to rehabilitate offenders and reduce recidivism? And if so, what shall we do?

We tried to exclude from our survey those studies which were so poorly done that they simply could not be interpreted. But despite our efforts, a pattern has run through much of this discussion—of studies which "found" effects without making any truly rigorous attempt to exclude competing hypotheses, of extraneous factors permitted to intrude upon the measurements, of recidivism measures which are not all measuring the same thing, of "follow-up" periods which vary enormously and rarely extend beyond the period of legal supervision, of experiments never replicated, of "system effects" not taken into account, of categories drawn up without any theory to guide the enterprise. It is just possible that some of our treatment programs *are* working to some extent, but that our research is so bad that it is incapable of telling.

Having entered this very serious caveat, I am bound to say that these data, involving over two hundred studies and hundreds of thousands of individuals as they do, are the best available and give us very little reason to hope that we have in fact found a sure way of reducing recidivism through rehabilitation. This is not to say that we found no instances of success or partial success; it is only to say that these instances have been isolated, producing no clear pattern to indicate the efficacy of any particular method of treatment. And neither is this to say that factors *outside* the realm of rehabilitation may not be working to reduce recidivism—factors such as the tendency for recidivism to be lower in offenders over the age of 30; it is only to say that such factors seem to have little connection with any of the treatment methods now at our disposal.

From this probability, one may draw any of several conclusions. It may be simply that our programs aren't yet good enough—that the education we provide to inmates is still poor education, that the therapy we administer is not administered skillfully enough, that our intensive supervision and counseling do not yet provide enough personal support for the offenders who are subjected to them. If one wishes to believe this, then what our correctional system needs is simply a more full-hearted commitment to the strategy of treatment.

It may be, on the other hand, that there is a more radical flaw in our present strategies—that education at its best, or that psychotherapy at its best, cannot overcome, or even appreciably reduce, the powerful tendency for offenders to continue in criminal behavior. Our present treatment programs are based on a theory of crime as a "disease"—that is to say, as something foreign and abnormal in the individual which can presumably be cured. This theory may well be flawed, in that it overlooks—indeed, denies—both the normality of crime in society and the personal normality of a very large proportion of offenders, criminals who are merely responding to the facts and conditions of our society.

Note

1. A similar phenomenon has been measured indirectly by studies that have dealt with the effect of various parole policies on recidivism rates. Where parole decisions have been liberalized so that an offender could be released with only the "reasonable assurance" of a job rather than with a definite job already developed by a parole officer (Stanton, 1963), this liberal release policy has produced no worsening of recidivism rates.

Bibliography of Studies Referred to by Name

Adams, Stuart. "Effectiveness of the Youth Authority Special Treatment Program: First Interim Report." Research Report No. 5. California Youth Authority, March 6, 1959. (Mimeographed.)

Adams, Stuart. "Assessment of the Psychiatric Treatment Program: Second Interim Report." Research Report No. 15. California Youth Authority, December 13, 1959. (Mimeographed.)

Adams, Stuart. "Assessment of the Psychiatric Treatment Program, Phase I: Third Interim Report." Research Report No. 21. California Youth Authority, January 31, 1961. (Mimeographed.)

Adams, Stuart, Rice, Rogert E., and Olive, Borden. "A Cost Analysis of the Effectiveness of the Group Guidance Program." Research Memorandum 65-3. Los Angeles County Probation Department, January 1965. (Mimeographed.)

Adams, Stuart. "Development of a Program Research Service in Probation." Research Report No. 27 (Final Report, NIMH Project MH007 18.) Los Angeles County Probation Department, January 1966. (Processed.)

Adamson, LeMay, and Dunham, H. Warren. "Clinical Treatment of Male Delinquents. A Case Study in Effort and Result," *American Sociological Review,* XXI, 3 (1956), 312–320.

Bernsten, Karen, and Christiansen, Karl O. "A Resocialization Experiment with Short-term Offenders," *Scandinavian Studies in Criminology,* I (1965), 35–54.

California, Adult Authority, Division of Adult Paroles. "Special Intensive Parole Unit, Phase I: Fifteen Man Caseload Study." Prepared by Walter I. Stone. Sacramento, CA, November 1956. (Mimeographed.)

California, Department of Corrections. "Intensive Treatment Program: Second Annual Report." Prepared by Harold B. Bradley and Jack D. Williams. Sacramento, CA, December 1, 1958. (Mimeographed.)

California, Department of Corrections. "Parole Work Unit Program: An Evaluative Report." A memorandum to the California Joint Legislative Budget Committee, December 30, 1966. (Mimeographed.)

California, Department of the Youth Authority. "James Marshall Treatment Program: Progress Report." January 1967. (Processed.)

Cambridge University, Department of Criminal Science. *Detention in Remard Homes.* London: Macmillan, 1952.

Craft, Michael, Stephenson, Geoffrey, and Granger, Clive. "A Controlled Trial of Authoritarian and Self-Governing Regimes with Adolescent Psychopaths," *American Journal of Orthopsychiatry,* XXXIV, 3 (1964), 543–554.

Empey, LeMar T. "The Provo Experiment: A Brief Review." Los Angeles: Youth Studies Center, University of Southern California. 1966. (Processed.)

Fox, Vernon. "Michigan's Experiment in Minimum Security Penology," *Journal of Criminal Law, Criminology, and Police Science,* XLI, 2 (1950), 150–166.

Freeman, Howard E., and Weeks, H. Ashley. "Analysis of a Program of Treatment of Delinquent Boys," *American Journal of Sociology,* LXII, 1 (1956), 56–61.

Glaser, Daniel. *The Effectiveness of a Prison and Parole System.* New York: Bobbs-Merrill, 1964.

Goldberg, Lisbeth, and Adams, Stuart. "An Experimental Evaluation of the Lathrop Hall Program." Los Angeles County Probation Department, December 1964. (Summarized in: Adams, Stuart. "Development of a Program Research Service in Probation," pp. 19–22.)

Great Britain. Home Office. *The Sentence of the Court: A Handbook for Courts on the Treatment of Offenders.* London: Her Majesty's Stationery Office, 1964.

Guttman, Evelyn S. "Effects of Short-Term Psychiatric Treatment on Boys in Two California Youth Authority Institutions." Research Report No. 36. California Youth Authority, December 1963. (Processed.)

Hammond, W. H., and Chayen, E. *Persistent Criminals: A Home Office Research Unit Report.* London: Her Majesty's Stationery Office, 1963.

Harrison, Robert M., and Mueller, Paul F. C. "Clue Hunting About Group Counseling and Parole Outcome." Research Report No. 11. California Department of Corrections, May 1964. (Mimeographed.)

Jesness, Carl F. The Fricot Ranch Study: Outcomes with Small versus Large Living Groups in the Rehabilitation of Delinquents." Research Report No. 47. California Youth Authority, October 1, 1965. (Processed.)

Johnson, Bertram. "An Analysis of Predictions of Parole Performance and of Judgments of Supervision in the Parole Research Project," Research Report No. 32. California Youth Authority, December 31, 1962. (Mimeographed.)

Kassebaum, Gene, Ward, David, and Wilnet, Daniel. *Prison Treatment and Parole Survival: An Empirical Assessment.* New York; Wiley, 1971.

Lavlicht, Jerome, et al., in *Berkshire Farms Monographs*, I, 1 (1962), 11–48.

Levinson, Robert B., and Kitchenet, Howard L. "Demonstration Counseling Project." 2 vols. Washington, D.C.: National Training School for Boys, 1962–1964. (Mimeographed.)

McClintock, F. H. *Attendance Centres.* London: Macmillan, 1961.

McCord, William and Joan. "Two Approaches to the Cure of Delinquents," *Journal of Criminal Law, Criminology, and Police Science*, XLIV, 4 (1953), 442–467.

McCorkle, Lloyd W., Elias, Albert, and Bixby, F. Lovell. *The Highfields Story: An Experimental Treatment Project for Youthful Offenders.* New York: Holt, 1958.

Mandell, Wallace, et al. "Surgical and Social Rehabilitation of Adult Offenders." Final Report. Montefiore Hospital and Medical Center, With Staten Island Mental Health Society. New York City Department of Correction, 1967. (Processed.)

Massimo, Joseph L., and Shore, Milton F. "The Effectiveness of a Comprehensive Vocationally Oriented Psychotherapeutic Program for Adolescent Delinquent Boys," *American Journal of Orthopsychiatry*, XXXIII, 4 (1963), 634–642.

Miner, Joshua, III, Kelly, Francis J., and Hatch, M. Charles. "Outward Bound Inc.: Juvenile Delinquency Demonstration Project, Year End Report." Massachusetts Division of Youth Service, May 31, 1967.

Narloch, R. P., Adams, Stuart, and Jenkins, Kendall J. "Characteristics and Parole Performance of California Youth Authority Early Releases." Research Report No. 7. California Youth Authority, June 22, 1959. (Mimeographed.)

O'Brien, William J. "Personality Assessment as a Measure of Change Resulting from Group Psychotherapy with Male Juvenile Delinquents." The Institute for the Study of Crime and Delinquency, and the California Youth Authority, December 1961. (Processed.)

Persons, Roy W. "Psychological and Behavioral Change in Delinquents Following Psychotherapy," *Journal of Clinical Psychology*, XXII, 3 (1966), 337–340.

Persons, Roy W. "Relationship Between Psychotherapy with Institutionalized Boys and Subsequent Community Adjustment," *Journal of Consulting Psychology*, XXXI, 2 (1967), 137–141.

Robison, James, and Kevotkian, Marinette. "Intensive Treatment Project: Phase II. Parole Outcome: Interim Report." Research Report No. 27. California Department of Corrections, Youth and Adult Correctional Agency, January 1967. (Mimeographed.)

Rudoff, Alvin. "The Effect of Treatment on Incarcerated Young Adult Delinquents as Measured by Disciplinary History." Unpublished Master's thesis, University of Southern California, 1960.

Saden, S. J. "Correctional Research at Jackson Prison," *Journal of Correctional Education*, XV (October 1962), 22–26.

Schnur, Alfred C. "The Educational Treatment of Prisoners and Recidivism," *American Journal of Sociology*, LIV, 2 (1948), 142–147.

Schwitzgebel, Robert and Ralph. "Therapeutic Research: A Procedure for the Reduction of Adolescent Crime." Paper presented at meetings of the American Psychological Association, Philadelphia, PA, August 1963.

Schwitzgebel, Robert and Kolb, D. A. "Inducing Behavior Change in Adolescent Delinquents," *Behavior Research Therapy*, I (1964), 297–304.

Seckel, Joachim P. "Experiments in Group Counseling at Two Youth Authority Institutions." Research Report No. 46. California Youth Authority, September 1965. (Processed.)

Stanton, John M. "Delinquencies and Types of Parole Programs to Which Inmates are Released." New York State Division of Parole, May 15, 1963. (Mimeographed.)

Stanton, John M. "Board Directed Extensive Supervision." New York State Division of Parole, August 3, 1964. (Mimeographed.)

Stuerup, Georg K. "The Treatment of Sexual Offenders," *Bulletin de la Societe internationale de criminologie* (1960), pp. 320–329.

Sullivan, Clyde E., and Mandell, Wallace. "Restoration of Youth Through Training: A Final Report." Staten Island, New York: Wakoff Research Center, April 1967. (Processed.)

Taylor, A. J. W. "An Evaluation of Group Psychotherapy in a Girls' Borstal," *International Journal of Group Psychotherapy*, XVII, 2 (1967), 168–177.

Warren, Marguerite. "The Community Treatment Project after Five Years." California Youth Authority, 1966. (Processed.)

Warren, Marguerite, et al. "Community Treatment Project, an Evaluation of Community Treatment for Delinquents: A Fifth Progress Report." C.T.P. Research Report No. 7. California Youth Authority, August 1966. (Processed.)

Warren, Marguerite, et al. "Community Treatment Project, an Evaluation of Community Treatment for Delinquents: Sixth Progress Report." C.T.P. Research Report No. 8. California Youth Authority, September 1967. (Processed.)